# A HANDBOOK TO
# Literature

*William Flint Thrall*
*and*
*Addison Hibbard*

# A HANDBOOK TO
# Literature

REVISED and ENLARGED BY

*C. Hugh Holman*

T H E   O D Y S S E Y   P R E S S   ·   *New York*

# PREFACE
## to the Revised and Enlarged Edition

IT HAS been my pleasant duty to act as a remodeler or modernizer of the house that the late Professor William F. Thrall and the late Dean Addison Hibbard built in 1936. The figure of a house being remodeled seems to me an appropriate one to describe this revision, for in modernizing a substantial structure one makes changes in its décor, adds new lighting fixtures, replaces the plumbing, installs the latest kitchen equipment, repaints the walls, and changes the heating system. The result is a house that looks newer than it really is, for if the original building was soundly planned, constructed of excellent materials, and solidly built, the remodeling proves to be a process by which a sound structure is made more useful and comfortable to the present-day user. This is exactly what I have tried to do with the Thrall and Hibbard *Handbook*.

In the process of the revision I have found to my great pleasure that I was working with a basic plan and a fundamental structure so firmly and solidly made that their adaptation to the demands of literary students in our time was a relatively simple task. A host of critical terms and a group of critical attitudes have come into being since the time when Thrall and Hibbard wrote their *Handbook*, with the result that many new terms are now needed; these I have tried to add. Some older terms have undergone modification of meaning since 1936, and it has been necessary to rewrite or to alter these; examples of such terms are *image, ambiguity, myth*. The literary history of the past hundred and fifty years has been undergoing a series of major re-assessments, and it has been necessary to re-adjust historical articles to fit these changes. In the literary history of the older periods, new attitudes and significant new facts have appeared since the writing of the *Handbook*, and some of these needed to be communicated to the inquiring student. Some movements and schools that looked very important in the mid-1930's have lessened greatly in significance, and statements about them needed modification. Teachers using the *Handbook* have noted omissions and have generously communicated them to the publishers and to me; many of these omissions have been remedied, but not all, since the author's ideal for the book is not always the same as that of the individual user. Over the years a great many teachers in various colleges and universities have helped with constructive suggestions. But the ultimate decision to include or exclude a topic has been mine, as all errors of fact and judgment are mine.

In making this revision, I have studied each entry carefully and I have made changes—frequently only slight ones—in practically every article. I have deleted entirely only a handful of the original entries, and I have added almost a fourth again in numbers of articles and in actual length. The result is a thoroughly remodeled house, one comfortable and useful, I hope, for our time, but it is still the house that Thrall and Hibbard built.

My debts are many and beyond even my ability to recall. When I think on my sources I am reminded of Washington Irving's statement: "My brain is filled, therefore, with all kinds of odds and ends. In travelling, these heterogeneous matters have become shaken up in my mind, as the articles are apt to be in an ill-packed travelling trunk; so that when I attempt to draw forth a fact, I cannot determine whether I have read, heard, or dreamt it." And certainly Marcel Proust was speaking the truth when he called a book "a great cemetery in which, for the most part, the names upon the tombs are effaced."

Into the making of such a work as this, all one's study, reading, and conversation go, but I would in this place single out certain persons to whom I am immediately indebted. To my own teachers, both undergraduate and graduate, my debts in this book are immeasurably great. To my students at the University of North Carolina this revision of the Thrall and Hibbard *Handbook* owes perhaps as much as it owes to any single source, for over the years they have shown me what they needed and their critical intelligence has shaped and sharpened my efforts to satisfy those needs. To my colleagues on the English faculty of the University my debts are deep; in the immediate preparation of this revision, I have been appreciably aided by Professors Richmond P. Bond, Robert B. Sharpe, J. O. Bailey, H. K. Russell, and William Wells. For the assistance and encouragement of my wife in this, as in all things, only my debt exceeds my gratitude.

C. Hugh Holman

# Contents

# To the User of this Handbook

THIS HANDBOOK consists of three parts: the Handbook proper, an alphabetical listing of articles discussing terms in current use in English and American literary history and criticism; an essay on "Some Standard Works on English and American Literature," which is intended as a brief bibliographical guide to further study and exploration; and an "Outline of Literary History," which lists in chronological order the major events in English and American literary history from the beginnings to the present.

The authors have attempted to include in the Handbook proper a comparatively brief explanation of the words and phrases peculiar to literary study and which, in their experience, a serious student of literature may wish defined, explained, or illustrated. No effort has been made to be exhaustive in the listings or complete in the comments; those terms likely to cause literary students trouble are listed and those basic things which the student of English and American literature will need to know are given.

A single alphabetical listing is made, with cross references at the proper places in the listing. Whenever it has been possible in the practical limits of the book, the essential information on a given term appears under that term in its alphabetical place in the Handbook. In the body of an article, a term used in a sense which is defined in its proper place in the Handbook is printed in SMALL CAPITAL LETTERS; the term being defined and sometimes its synonyms are printed in *italic letters*. If other articles in the Handbook will enrich the student's understanding of a particular entry, the statement "See AN APPROPRIATE ARTICLE" is made at the end of the entry. For example, the entry on **Complication** uses the terms PLOT, RESOLUTION, DRAMATIC STRUCTURE, RISING ACTION, ACT, and TRAGEDY, all of which are defined in the Handbook; therefore, each of them appears in SMALL CAPITAL LETTERS, a fact indicating that entries on them may be consulted if one of them is not clear to the user of the Handbook. On the other hand, the entry concludes with the statement, "See DRAMATIC STRUCTURE, ACT," which means that these entries contain supplementary material which will enrich the user's understanding of *complication*. The word *complication* is itself italicized since it is the term being defined.

# A HANDBOOK TO
# Literature

# HANDBOOK TO
# Literature

**Abstract Poetry:** Poetry whose meaning results chiefly from its sound qualities. The term is used by Dame Edith Sitwell to describe poetry that is analogous in its use of sounds to abstract painting in its use of colors and shapes. In abstract painting the meaning is conveyed through the arrangement of colors and shapes without the representation of physical objects; in *abstract poetry,* words are chosen not for their customary meanings or connotations but for the effect that can be produced by tonal qualities, RIMES, and RHYTHMS. See ABSTRACT TERMS.

**Abstract Terms:** Terms which represent ideas or generalities as opposed to CONCRETE TERMS, which represent specific and particular objects or entities. *Abstract terms* describes a quality related to but not always the same as that described by GENERAL TERMS, in that *abstract* implies the formulation of an idea by the logical process of abstraction, in which the mind selects characteristics common to the members of a group and builds a conception which describes not one but all things of that same kind or marked by that same quality, whereas *general* broadly means *generic.* For example, "beauty" is an *abstract term,* "girl," a GENERAL TERM, and "Helen of Troy" a concrete, specific term. In another sense, abstract words may be described as words which do not have specific, observable referents to which one may compare their meanings; note, for example, the special use of the term in ABSTRACT POETRY, where this meaning is intended. *Abstract terms* tend to describe ideas, concepts, attitudes, attributes, qualities isolated from their embodiment in a specific object. Their appeal is usually non-sensory. Although they sometimes carry a heavy freight of undefined emotion—for example, "honor," "peace," "patriotism" (see CONNOTATION)—they are more usually lacking in the heightened emotional response evoked by CONCRETE TERMS. *Abstract terms* are, therefore, particularly the language of philosophy and science; whereas the language of literature tends more to the specific and emotional, to

1

that which can express its meanings through IMAGE and METAPHOR. See CONCRETE TERMS.

**Academic Drama:** See SCHOOL PLAYS.

**Academies:** Associations of literary, artistic, or scientific men brought together for the advancement of culture and learning within their special fields of interests. The term is derived from "the olive grove of Academe" where Plato taught at Athens. Though there are thousands of *academies* of one sort or another bringing together men of similar interests, there are in each country a few prominent organizations usually with some sort of official or national responsibility. The Royal Society of London for Improving Natural Knowledge, for example, has agreed to render such service as it can to the British government in the realm of science, and the governmental authorities have often called upon it for the solution of scientific problems. One general purpose of the literary academies has been, to quote the expressed purpose of *l'Académie française* (originated *ca.*1629), "to labor with all care and diligence to give certain rules to our language and to render it pure, eloquent, and capable of treating the arts and sciences." A secondary objective has often been that of immortalizing great writers, though the success with which great writers have been recognized by such organizations is definitely a moot point. In addition to the French Academy and the Royal Society—already mentioned—the following ought to be cited: The Royal Academy of Arts founded in 1768 (England); the *Real Academia Española* founded in 1713 (Spain); and the AMERICAN ACADEMY OF ARTS AND LETTERS founded in 1904 (United States). More like the original academy of Plato was the famous "Platonic Academy" led by Marsilio Ficino, which flourished at Florence, Italy, in the late fifteenth century and from which were disseminated the doctrines of Neo-Platonism (see PLATONISM) which colored much Renaissance English literature.

**Acatalectic:** Metrically complete; applied to a line of poetry that carries out fully the basic metrical pattern of the poem. See CATALEXIS.

**Accent:** In traditional English METRICS, the STRESS given a syllable in pronunciation. Perhaps no aspect of PROSODY has been the subject of greater uncertainty than that dealing with the nature of *accent;* it is considered to be a matter of force, of utterance, of duration, of loudness, of pitch, and of various combinations of these. In common usage, however, it is used to describe some aspect of emphasis, as opposed to duration or QUANTITY. The distinction is sometimes made between *accent* as the emphasis upon a syllable and STRESS as the emphasis upon a word, although the two terms are often used interchangeably.

In versification *accent* usually implies contrast; that is, a patterned succession of opposites, in this case, stressed and unstressed syllables. In traditional terminology ICTUS is the name applied to the STRESS itself, ARSIS the name applied to the stressed syllable, and THESIS the name applied to the unstressed syllable. It should be noted, however, that the earlier Greek usage, predating this Latin usage, reversed these meanings, with THESIS applying to the stressed and ARSIS to the unstressed syllables.

There are three basic types of *accent* in English: WORD ACCENT, or the accepted placement of stress upon the syllable of a word; RHETORICAL ACCENT, in which the placement of stress is determined by the meaning or intention of the sentence; and METRICAL ACCENT, in which the placement of stress is determined by the metrical pattern of the line. If the metrical accent does violence to the word accent, the resulting alteration in pronunciation is called WRENCHED ACCENT, a phenomenon not uncommon in the folk BALLAD. See QUANTITY, METRICS, SCANSION.

**Acrostic:** Usually verse, though sometimes a piece of prose composition, arranged in such a way as to present names or phrases or sentences when certain letters selected according to an orderly sequence are brought together. The form is very old, having been used by early Greek and Latin writers as well as by the monks of the Middle Ages. Though some creditable verse has appeared in this form, *acrostics* are likely to be little more than tricks of versifying. An example of a *true acrostic-telestich* (see below) presented through a conundrum follows: 1. By Apollo was my first made. 2. A shoemaker's tool. 3. An Italian patriot. 4. A tropical fruit. Answer: *Lamb* and *Elia* as shown in the wording:

| | | | |
|---|---|---|---|
| 1. | L | yr | E |
| 2. | A | w | L |
| 3. | M | azzin | I |
| 4. | B | anan | A |

An *acrostic* in which the initial letters form the word is called a *true acrostic;* one in which the final letters form the word is called a *telestich;* one in which the middle letters form the word is called a *mesostich;* one in which the first letter of the first line, the second letter of the second line, the third letter of the third line, etc., form the word is called a *cross acrostic,* of which Poe's "A Valentine" is an example. An *acrostic* in which the initial letters form the alphabet is called an *abecedarius.* Perhaps the best known of all *acrostics* is the word *cabal,* formed from the first letters of the names of the unpopular ministry of Charles II, composed of Clifford, Ashley, Buckingham, Arlington, and Lauderdale.

**Act:** A major division of the action of a DRAMA. The major parts of the Greek plays were distinguished by the appearance of the CHORUS, and they generally fell, as Aristotle implies, into five parts. The Latin tragedies of Seneca were divided into five *acts,* and when, in the ELIZABETHAN AGE, English dramatists began using *act* divisions they followed their Roman models, as did other modern European dramatists. In varying degrees the five-*act* structure corresponded to the five main divisions of dramatic action: EXPOSITION, COMPLICATION, CLIMAX, FALLING ACTION, and CATASTROPHE. Freytag wrote of the "*act* of introduction," the "*act* of the ascent," the "*act* of the climax," the "*act* of the descent," and the "*act* of the catastrophe"; but such a correspondence, especially in Elizabethan plays, is by no means always apparent. The five-*act* structure was followed until the late nineteenth century when, under the influence of Ibsen, the fourth and fifth *acts* were combined. In the twentieth century, the standard form for serious drama has been three *acts,* with MUSICAL COMEDY and COMIC OPERA usually in two; but great variation is used today, with serious plays frequently appearing divided into EPISODES or SCENES, without *act*-division. Late in the nineteenth century a shorter form, the ONE-ACT PLAY, developed and is recognized today as a separate *genre.* See DRAMATIC STRUCTURE.

**Adage:** A proverb or wise saying made familiar by long use. Example: "No bees, no honey" (Erasmus, *Adagia*). See PROVERB.

**Adaptation:** The re-writing of a work from its original form to fit it for another; also the new form of such a re-written work. A novel may be "adapted" for the stage or motion pictures or television; a play may be re-written as a novel or a radio sketch; the new form of any such modifications is called an *"adaptation."* The term is not customarily used when the author of the original work is himself its modifier to a new form. It also implies an attempt to retain the characters, actions, and as much as possible of the language and tone of the original, and thus it differs significantly from the reworking of a SOURCE.

**Adonic Verse:** A verse form associated with Greek and Latin PROSODY and denoting that METER which consists of a DACTYL and a SPONDEE, as __ ⌣ ⌣ | __ __, or TROCHEE, as __ ⌣ ⌣ | __ ⌣, probably so called after the Adonia, the festival of Adonis.

**Aesthetic Distance:** A term applied by critics to describe the effect produced when an emotion or an experience, whether autobiographical or not, is so objectified by the proper use of FORM that it can be understood as being objectively realized and independent of the immediate personal experience of its maker. It is closely related to Keats' NEGATIVE CAPABILITY and T. S. Eliot's OBJECTIVE CORRELATIVE. See OBJECTIVITY.

**Affective Fallacy:** A term used in contemporary criticism to describe the error of judging a work of art in terms of its results, especially its emotional effect. It was introduced by W. K. Wimsatt, Jr., and M. C. Beardsley (see *The Verbal Icon,* by Wimsatt) to describe the "confusion between the poem and its *result* (what it *is* and what it *does*)." It is a converse error to the INTENTIONAL FALLACY. Notable examples of the *affective fallacy* are Aristotle's CATHARSIS and Longinus' "transport."

**Age of Johnson in English Literature:** The interval between 1750 and 1798 was a transitional age in English literature. The NEO-CLASSICISM which dominated the first half of the century was giving way in many different ways to the impulse toward ROMANTICISM, although the period was still predominantly neo-classical. The NOVEL which had come into being in the decade before 1750 continued to flourish, with sentimental attitudes and GOTHIC horrors becoming a significant part of its content. Little was accomplished in DRAMA except for the creation of "laughing" COMEDY by Sheridan and Goldsmith, in reaction against SENTIMENTAL COMEDY. The chief poets were Burns, Gray, Cowper, Johnson, and Crabbe—a list which indicates how thoroughly the pendulum was swinging away from Pope and Dryden. Yet it was Dr. Samuel Johnson, poet, lexicogra-

pher, essayist, novelist, journalist, and neo-classic critic who was
the major literary figure, as his friend Boswell's biography of him
(1791) was the greatest work of the age, challenged for such an
honor, perhaps, only by Gibbon's monumental history, *The Decline
and Fall of the Roman Empire* (1776). An interest in the past,
particularly in the middle ages, in the primitive, and the literature
of the folk was developing and was feeding with increasing strength
the growing tide of ROMANTICISM. See *Outline of Literary History*,
NEO-CLASSIC PERIOD.

**Age of the Romantic Triumph in England, 1798–1832:** Although
a major Romantic poet, Robert Burns, had died in 1796 and adumbrations of ROMANTICISM had been apparent in English writing
throughout much of the eighteenth century, the publication of
*Lyrical Ballads* by Wordsworth and Coleridge in 1798 is generally
recognized as marking the beginning of a period of more than three
decades in which ROMANTICISM triumphed in British letters, a period that is often said to have ended in 1832, with the death of Sir
Walter Scott. During these thirty-four years, the poetic careers of
Wordsworth, Coleridge, Byron, Shelley, and Keats flowered; Scott
created the historical NOVEL and made it a force in international
literature; Wordsworth and Coleridge articulated a revolutionary
theory of Romantic poetry; Jane Austen wrote her NOVELS OF
MANNERS; and Lamb, DeQuincey, and Hazlitt raised the PERSONAL
ESSAY to a high level of accomplishment. ROMANTICISM did not die
with Sir Walter Scott, but the decade of the thirties saw it begin a
process of modification as a result of the varied forces of the Victorian world which played upon it. See ROMANTICISM, ROMANTIC
PERIOD IN ENGLISH LITERATURE, and *Outline of Literary History*.

**Agrarians:** A term applied to a group of Southern American writers
who published in Nashville, Tennessee, between 1922 and 1925,
*The Fugitive*, a LITTLE MAGAZINE of poetry and some criticism
championing agrarian REGIONALISM but attacking "the old high-
caste Brahmins of the Old South." Most of its contributors were associated with Vanderbilt University; among them were John
Crowe Ransom, Allen Tate, Donald Davidson, Robert Penn Warren,
and Merrill Moore. In the 1930's they championed an agrarian
economy as opposed to that of industrial capitalism and issued a
collective manifesto, *I'll Take My Stand*. They were active in the
publication between 1933 and 1937 of *The American Review*, a

socio-economic magazine that also analyzed contemporary literature. They found an effective literary organ in *The Southern Review*
(1935–1942), under the editorship of Cleanth Brooks and Robert
Penn Warren. In addition to their poetry and novels, the *Agrarians*
have been prominent among the founders of the NEW CRITICISM.

**Alba:** A Provençal lament over the parting of lovers at the break
of day, the name coming from the Provençal word for "dawn," with
which the refrain ends. The medieval *albas* were inspired in large
part by Ovid. With the TROUBADOURS the *albas* grew to a distinct
literary form. On occasion they were religious, being addressed to
the Virgin. See AUBADE.

**Alcaics:** Verses written according to the manner of the ODES of Al-
caeus, usually a four-STANZA poem, each STANZA composed of four
lines, each line having four stresses. Since the pattern is a classical one based on quantitative measures, the type can only be
imitated in English; exact English *Alcaics* are practically impossible.
The most notable English attempt is in Tennyson's "Milton," which
begins: "O mighty-mouthed inventor of harmonies."

**Alexandrine:** A verse line with six IAMBIC feet (IAMBIC HEXAM-
ETER). The form, that of HEROIC VERSE in France, received its name
possibly from the fact that it was much used in Old French
romances of the twelfth and thirteenth centuries describing the adventures of Alexander the Great, possibly from the name of
Alexandre Paris, a French poet who used this meter. Its appearance
in English verse has been credited to Wyatt and Surrey. Perhaps
the most conspicuous instance of its successful use in English is by
Spenser, who, in his SPENSERIAN STANZA, after eight PENTAMETER
lines employed a HEXAMETER (*Alexandrine*) in the ninth line. Both
the line and its occasional bad effect are described in Pope's couplet:

> A needless Alexandrine ends the song,
> That, like a wounded snake, drags its slow length along.

**Allegory:** A form of extended METAPHOR in which objects and
persons in a narrative, either in prose or verse, are equated with
meanings that lie outside the narrative itself. Thus it represents one
thing in the guise of another—an abstraction in that of a concrete
IMAGE. The characters are usually PERSONIFICATIONS of abstract
qualities, the action and the setting representative of the relation-

ships among these abstractions. *Allegory* attempts to evoke a dual interest, one in the events, characters, and setting presented, and the other in the ideas they are intended to convey or the significance they bear. The characters, events, and setting may be historical, fictitious, or fabulous; the test is that these materials be so employed in a logical organization or pattern that they represent meanings independent of the action described in the surface story. Such meaning may be religious, moral, political, personal, or satiric. Thus Spenser's *The Faerie Queene* is on one level a chivalric ROMANCE, but it embodies moral, religious, social, and political meanings. Bunyan's *Pilgrim's Progress* describes the efforts of a Christian man to achieve a godly life by triumphing over inner obstacles to his faith, these obstacles being represented by such outward objects as the Slough of Despond and Vanity Fair. In Swift's *Gulliver's Travels* many of man's contemptible attributes are given satiric objective expression through the adventures of a ship's surgeon.

It is important that one distinguish clearly between *allegory* and SYMBOLISM, which attempts to suggest other levels of meaning without making a structure of ideas a formative influence on the work as it is in *allegory*.

Among the kinds of *allegory*, in addition to those suggested above, are PARABLE, FABLE, APOLOGUE, EXEMPLUM, and BEAST EPIC. See also ANAGOGE.

**Alliteration:** The repetition of initial identical consonant sounds or any vowel sounds in successive or closely associated words or syllables. A good example of consonantal *alliteration* is Coleridge's lines:

> The fair breeze blew, the white foam flew,
> The furrow followed free.

Vowel *alliteration* is shown in the sentence: "Apt alliteration's artful aid is often an occasional ornament in prose." *Alliteration* of syllables within words appears in Tennyson's lines:

> The *moan* of doves in *imme*morial el*m*s,
> And *murmur*ing of innu*mer*able bees.

OLD ENGLISH VERSIFICATION rested in large measure on *alliteration*, as did much Middle English poetry. In modern times *alliteration* has usually been a secondary ornament in both verse and prose, although poets as unlike as Whitman, Swinburne, and W. H.

Auden have made extensive and skillful use of it. In our time it has become the stock in trade of the sports writer and the advertising copy writer, in whose hands it often produces the ludicrous effects that Shakespeare mocked in Quince's "Prologue" in *A Midsummer Night's Dream:*

> Whereat, with blade, with bloody blameful blade,
> He bravely broach'd his boiling bloody breast.

**Alliterative Romance:** A METRICAL ROMANCE written in ALLITERATIVE VERSE, especially one produced during the revival of interest in alliterative poetry in the fourteenth century, e.g., *William of Palerne* (unrimed long lines similar to the alliterative verse of the Old English period), *Sir Gawain and the Green Knight* (in stanzas made up of varying numbers of long lines followed by five short rimed lines), and the "alliterative" *Morte Arthure.* See MEDIEVAL ROMANCE.

**Alliterative Verse:** A term used to characterize those old verseforms, usually Germanic in origin, in which the division of the lines and, in fact, metrical structure generally were based on periodic and regular repetition of certain initial letters or sounds within the lines. See OLD ENGLISH VERSIFICATION.

**Allusion:** A rhetorical term applied to that figure of speech making casual reference to a famous historical or literary figure or event.

> I know not where is that *Promethean heat*
> That can thy light relume.
> —Shakespeare

Biblical *allusions* are common in English literature, such as Shakespeare's "A Daniel come to judgment," in *The Merchant of Venice.* Complex literary *allusion* is characteristic of much modern poetry; a good example is T. S. Eliot's *The Waste Land* and the author's notes to the poem.

**Almanac:** In medieval times an *almanac* was a permanent table showing the movements of the heavenly bodies, from which calculations for any year could be made. *Almanacs* date from as early as the twelfth century. Later, *almanacs* or calendars for short spans of years and, finally, for single years were prepared. A further step in the evolution of the form came with the inclusion of useful information, especially for farmers. This use of the *almanac* as a storehouse of general information led ultimately to such modern works as the *World Almanac*, a compendium of historical and statistical data not limited to the single year. As early as the sixteenth century, forecasts, first of the weather and later of such human fortunes as plagues and wars, were important features of *almanacs*. Other names for *almanacs* in the sixteenth century were "prognostications," "calendars," and *"ephemerides."* At this time *almanacs* took on some features drawn from the ecclesiastical calendars and martyrologies, such as the noting of saints' days and church anniversaries.

The *almanac* figures but slightly in literature. Spenser's *Shepheardes Calender* (1579) takes its title from a French "Kalendar of Shepards" and consists of twelve poems, under the titles of the twelve months, with some attention paid to the seasonal implications. By the latter part of the seventeenth century *almanacs* contained efforts at humor, consisting usually of coarse jokes. This feature was elaborated somewhat later, with some refinements, as in Franklin's *Poor Richard's Almanac* (1732–1758), itself partly inspired by the English comic *almanac, Poor Robin*. In Germany in the eighteenth and nineteenth centuries *almanacs* included printed poetry of a high order. The Davy Crockett *almanacs*, issued in America between 1835 and 1856, recorded many frontier TALL TALES based mainly on oral tradition and helped to preserve a significant aspect of American culture.

**Ambiguity:** The expression of an idea in language of such a nature as to give more than one meaning and to leave uncertainty as to the true significance of the statement. *Ambiguity* may be intentional, as when one wishes to evade a direct reply (see Juliet's replies to her mother in Act III, Scene 5, of Shakespeare's *Romeo and Juliet*). The chief causes of *ambiguity* are undue brevity and compression of statement, "cloudy" reference of pronoun, faulty or inverted (poetical) sequence, and the use of a word with two or more meanings.

However, in literature of the highest order may be found another aspect of *ambiguity* which results from the fact that language functions in art on other levels than that of communication, where *ambiguity* is a cardinal sin. In literature words demonstrate an astounding capacity for suggesting two or more equally suitable senses in a given context, for conveying a core meaning and accompanying it with overtones of great richness and complexity, and for operating with two or more meanings at the same time. One of the attributes of the finest poets is their ability to tap what I. A. Richards has called the "resourcefulness of language" and to supercharge words with great pressures of meaning. The kind of *ambiguity* which results from this capacity of words to stimulate simultaneously several different streams of thought all of which make sense is a genuine characteristic of the richness and concentration that makes great poetry.

William Empson, in *The Seven Types of Ambiguity*, in 1931 extended and enriched the meaning of the term to include these aspects of language. Although there have been those who feel that another word than *ambiguity* should be used for these characteristics of language functioning with artistic complexity (among those suggested have been MULTIPLE MEANINGS and PLURISIGNATION), Empson's "seven types" of linguistic complexity "which adds some nuance to the direct statement of prose" have proved to be effective tools for the examination of literature. These "types of *ambiguity*" are (1) details of language which are effective in several ways at once; (2) alternative meanings that are ultimately resolved into the one meaning of the author; (3) two seemingly unconnected meanings that are given in one word; (4) alternative meanings that act together to clarify a complicated state of mind in the author; (5) a simile that refers imperfectly to two incompatible things and by this "fortunate confusion" shows the author discovering his idea as he writes; (6) a statement that is so contradictory or irrelevant that the reader is made to invent his own interpretation; and (7) a statement so fundamentally contradictory that it reveals a basic division in the author's mind.

**American Academy of Arts and Letters:** An organization parallel in purpose to certain European societies was brought into being in 1904 to recognize distinguished accomplishment in literature, art, or music. Historically, the American Academy owes its origin to the activity of the American Social Science Association, which, in 1898, realized the need for a society devoted entirely to the interests of letters and the fine arts, and organized the National Institute of Arts and Letters with a membership limited to 250. Six years later it was deemed necessary to create a smaller society composed of the most distinguished members of the Institute; accordingly, in 1904, was organized the American Academy of Arts and Letters with a membership limited to fifty. Though both men and women are

eligible, only members of the Institute may be elected to the
Academy. The society was incorporated by act of the American
Congress, April 17, 1916. The seven men first elected to membership were: William Dean Howells, Augustus Saint-Gaudens, Edmund Clarence Stedman, John LaFarge, Samuel Langhorne
Clemens, John Hay, and Edward MacDowell. "The actual work of
the Academy is to promote American literature and art by giving
the stamp of its approval of the best that both the past and the
present have to offer." This is done through public addresses and
by bringing to the United States representatives of other academies.
Annually the National Institute awards its gold medal for distinguished work in literature and the arts; every five years is conferred
the William Dean Howells medal for the best American fiction; and
annually another gold medal is awarded for good diction on the
stage.

In May of each year the Academy holds a ceremonial at which
new members are elected, the medals awarded, and fifteen $1,500
arts and letters grants given. An exhibition of the works of newly
elected members and recipients of honors is held in the art gallery
and the museum at that time. The Academy occupies its own buildings at 633 West 155th and 632 West 156th Streets, New York
City.

**American Indian Literature:** See AMERIND LITERATURE.

**American Language:** A term used to designate certain idioms and
forms peculiar to English speech in America. As is pointed out in
the *Encyclopedia Americana,* these differences usually arise in one
of three ways: some forms originate in America independent of
English speech ("gerrymander" is an example); some expressions
which were once native to England have been brought here and
have lived after they had died out in England ("fall" for "autumn");
and certain English forms have taken on modified meanings in
America (as we use "store" for "shop"). Besides these matters of
vocabulary, H. L. Mencken points out six other respects in which
American expression differs from English: syntax, intonation, slang,
idiom, grammar, and pronunciation.

Although for many years the sensitiveness of Americans made
them deny the existence of anything like an *American language,* its
existence has been recognized and its nature applauded for over a
quarter of a century. It is a unique language of American literary

art, impressively present in the work of writers like Mark Twain,.
Ring Lardner, Ernest Hemingway, and J. D. Salinger. Scholars
have given it serious attention; it is the subject of two major dictionaries, A Dictionary of American English on Historical Principles,.
edited by Sir William Craigie and J. R. Hurlbert, and A Dictionary
of Americanisms, edited by M. M. Mathews; and a group of scholars,.
led by Hans Kurath, is compiling a mammoth Linguistic Atlas of
the United States. Significant earlier studies were G. P. Krapp's.
The English Language in America and H. L. Mencken's The
American Language and its Supplements.

**American Literature, Periods of:** Any division of the literary history
of a nation is an arbitrary over-simplification. In the case of
America, where the national record long predates the development
of a self-sufficient literature, the problem is complicated further
by the fact that most divisions into early periods are based upon
political and social history and most divisions into later periods
upon the dominance of literary types or movements. Almost all.
historians of American literature have made their own systems of
period division. In this handbook American literature is treated in a
chronological pattern set against the dominant English movements
in the Outline of Literary History, and the characteristics of its own
periods are treated in the following articles:

COLONIAL PERIOD IN AMERICAN LITERATURE, 1607–1765
REVOLUTIONARY AND EARLY NATIONAL PERIOD IN AMERICAN
    LITERATURE, 1765–1830
ROMANTIC PERIOD IN AMERICAN LITERATURE, 1830–1865
REALISTIC PERIOD IN AMERICAN LITERATURE, 1865–1900
NATURALISTIC AND SYMBOLISTIC PERIOD IN AMERICAN LITERATURE,.
    1900–1930
PERIOD OF CRITICISM AND CONFORMITY IN AMERICAN LITERA-
    TURE, 1930—

If read in this sequence, these articles will give a brief history
of American writing by periods.

**Amerind Literature:** That body of writing and oral tradition developed by the various aboriginal tribes of America. The term is a
combination of syllables from American and Indian. Originally
transmitted almost entirely by word of mouth, the literature was
at first such as could easily be memorized: the rituals of annual.

festivals, tribal traditions, narrative accounts of gods and heroes. Since much of this literature grew up about the rhythmic accents of the ceremonial drum, it took on a regularity of metric pattern which gave it the quality of poetry; another part, perhaps less associated with ceremonials, was more simply natural in its recounting of events and took the form of prose. A characteristic quality of this Amerind language is its building of many ideas into one term. ("Hither-whiteness-comes-walking" being, according to Mary Austin, the Algonquin parallel for "dawn.") Most of this literature known to us today is confined to a few types: the EPIC, the folk-tale, the DRAMA, ritualistic and ceremonial exercises, and narratives of adventure. A useful collection is *The Winged Serpent: An Anthology of American Indian Prose and Poetry*, edited by Margot Astrov.

The PORTMANTEAU WORD *Amerind* is today less widely used than the longer term, *American Indian*.

**Amphibrach:** A metrical FOOT in verse consisting of three syllables, the first and last unaccented, the second accented.

Example: *ar range ment.*

**Amphigory** or **Amphigouri:** Verse that sounds well but contains little or no sense or meaning; either NONSENSE VERSE, like Edward Lear's, or nonsensical PARODY, like Swinburne's self-mockery in "Nephelidia," which begins: "From the depth of the dreamy decline of the dawn through a notable nimbus of nebulous moonshine."

**Amphimacher:** A metrical FOOT in verse, consisting of three syllables, the first and last accented, the second unaccented. Example: *at ti tude.*

**Amplification:** A figure of speech by which bare expressions, likely to be ignored or misunderstood by a hearer or reader because of their bluntness, are emphasized through restatement with additional detail. The device is used in music, oratory, and poetry quite commonly. The chief danger accompanying the use of *amplification* is that prolix writers will so elaborate a statement as to rob it even of its original meaning. Holofernes, in Shakespeare's *Love's Labour's Lost*, affords a perfect example of the evils of over-amplification:

He draweth out the thread of his verbosity finer than the staple of his argument. I abhor such fanatical phantasimes, such insociable and pointdevise companions; such rackers of orthography, as to speak doubt, fine, when he should say doubt; det, when he should pronounce debt,— d,e,b,t, not d,e,t; he clepeth a calf, cauf; half, hauf; neighbour *vocatur* nebour, neigh, abbreviated ne. This is abhominable, which he would call abominable,—it insinuateth me of insanie: *anne intelligis, domine?* To make frantic, lunatic.

**Ana:** Miscellaneous sayings, anecdotes, gossip, and scraps of information about a particular person, place, or event; or a book which records such sayings and anecdotes. Englishmen in the seventeenth century were much devoted to this type of writing and to the collecting of anecdotes. *The Table Talk of John Selden* (1689) is a typical collection of such curiosities of literature. The term also exists as a suffix, as in Goldsmith*iana*, where it denotes a collection of miscellaneous information about Goldsmith.

**Anachronism:** False assignment of an event, a person, a scene, language—in fact anything—to a time when that event or thing or person was not in existence. Shakespeare is guilty of sundry *anachronisms* such as his placing cannon in *King John,* a play dealing with a time many years before cannon came into use in England. The *anachronism,* however, is a greater sin to the realist than to the romanticist, and may or may not be important according to its effect on the literary structure as a whole. Humorists sometimes use *anachronisms* as comic or satiric devices. Mark Twain's *A Connecticut Yankee in King Arthur's Court* rests on a sustained, satirically humorous *anachronism.*

**Anacoluthon:** The failure, accidental or deliberate, to complete a sentence according to the structural plan on which it was started. Used accidentally, anacoluthic writing is, of course, a vice; used deliberately for emotional or rhetorical effect it is a recognized figure of speech, effective especially in oratory. The term is also applied to units of composition larger than the sentence when there is within the unit an obvious incoherency among the parts. Browning is very much given to this sort of construction; the following stanza from *A Toccata of Galuppi's* will serve as an illustration:

> Ay, because the sea's the street there; and
>  'tis arched by . . . what you call
> . . . Shylock's bridge with houses on it,
>    where they kept the carnival:
> I was never out of England—it's as if I
>    saw it all.

# Anacreontic Poetry

Anacreontic Poetry: Verse in the mood and manner of the lyrics of the Greek poet Anacreon; that is, poems characterized by an erotic, amatory, or Bacchanalian spirit. The characteristic *Anacreontic* STANZA consists of four lines rhyming *abab,* each line composed of three trochaic feet with one long syllable added at the end of the line: — ⏑ | — ⏑ | — ⏑ | —.

Anacrusis: A term denoting one or more extra unaccented syllables at the beginning of a VERSE before the regular RHYTHM of the line makes its appearance. Literally an upward or back beat. R. M. Alden in his *English Verse* cites the third verse of the following stanza from Shelley as an example:

> What thou art we know not;
> What is most like thee?
> *From* rainbow clouds there flow not
> Drops so bright to see
> As from thy presence showers a rain of melody.

Anagnorisis: In drama, the DISCOVERY OR RECOGNITION that leads to the PERIPETEIA or reversal.

Anagoge (or **Anagogy**): In Biblical and allegorical interpretation, the mystical or spiritual meaning of words or passages. For example, when certain passages in Virgil were interpreted in the Middle Ages as foretelling the coming of Christ they were being given anagogical interpretations. It is the highest of the FOUR SENSES OF INTERPRETATION, the others being the literal, the allegorical, and the moral. Thus, Jerusalem is literally a city in Palestine, allegorically the Church, morally the believing soul, and anagogically the heavenly City of God. These levels of meaning are regularly applied to Dante's *Divine Comedy.*

Anagram: A word or phrase made by transposing the letters of another word or phrase, as "cask" is an *anagram* of "sack," *Anagrams* have usually been employed simply as an exercise of one's ingenuity, but deserve mention here since writers have sometimes used them in verses and other work to conceal proper names or veiled messages. It is said, too, that some of the astronomers of the seventeenth century used *anagrams* to conceal certain of their discoveries until such time as it was convenient to announce their findings. *Anagrams* have been used rather frequently as a means of coining pseudonyms, as "Calvinus" became "Alcuinus", "Byran

Waller Procter" became "Barry Cornwall, poet", and "Arouet, l.j."
(*le jeune*) is said to have given the name "Voltaire" to the world.
*Erewhon* is an instance of an *anagram* as a book title. A variety of
the *anagram*, the PALINDROME, is an arrangement of letters which
gives the same meaning whether read forward or backward and is
illustrated in the remark by which Adam is alleged to have introduced himself to his wife upon her first appearance before him:
"Madam, I'm Adam."

**Analecta** (**Analects**): Literary gleanings, fragments, or selected
passages from the writings of an author or different authors; also
the title for a collection of choice extracts, e.g., *Analects from
Confucius*.

**Analogue:** This word, meaning something that is analogous to or
like another given thing, has two special uses of interest to the
student of literature: (1) philologically, an *analogue* may mean a
cognate or word in one language coresponding with one in another,
as the English word "mother" is an *analogue* of the Latin word
*mater*—kinship or common origin is usually implied; (2) in literary
history two versions of the same story may be called *analogues,*
especially if no direct relationship can be established though a remote one is probable. Thus the story of the pound of flesh in *Gesta
Romanorum* may be called an *analogue* of the similar plot in *The
Merchant of Venice.*

**Analogy:** A comparison of two things, alike in certain respects;
particularly a method of EXPOSITION by which one unfamiliar object
or idea is explained by comparing it in certain of its similarities with
other objects or ideas more familiar. In ARGUMENTATION and logic
*analogy* is also frequently used to establish contentions, it being
argued, for instance, that since A works certain results, B, which
is like A in vital respects, will also accomplish the same results.
*Analogy,* however, is often a treacherous weapon since few *different*
objects or ideas are essentially the *same* to more than a superficial
observer or thinker.

**Analytical Criticism:** A term applied to criticism which views the
work of art as an autonomous whole and believes that its meaning,
nature, and significance can be discovered by applying rigorous and
logical systems of analysis to its several parts and their organization.

The work of the NEW CRITICS is often called *analytical criticism*. See NEW CRITICS; CRITICISM, TYPES OF.

**Anapest:** A metrical FOOT in verse, consisting of three syllables, with two unaccented syllables followed by an accented one ( ⌣ ⌣ — ). The following lines from Shelley's *Cloud* are anapestic:

> Lĭke ă chīld frŏm thē womb, lĭke ă ghōst frŏm thē tomb,
> Ĭ arīse ănd ŭnbuīld ĭt agāin.

**Anaphora:** One of the devices of REPETITION, in which the same expression (word or words) is repeated at the beginning of two or more lines, clauses, or sentences. It is one of the most obvious of the devices used in the poetry of Walt Whitman.

**Anastrophe:** A rhetorical term signifying inversion of the usual, normal, or logical order of the parts of a sentence. *Anastrophe* is deliberate rather than accidental and is used, as in verse, to secure RHYTHM or to gain EMPHASIS or EUPHONY.

> Not fierce Othello in so loud a strain
> Roar'd for the handkerchief that caus'd his pain.
> —Pope

**Anathema:** A formal and solemn denunciation or imprecation, particularly as pronounced by the Greek or Roman Catholic Church against an individual, an institution, or a doctrine. The form conventionally reads: *Si quis dixerit*, etc., *anathema sit*, "If any one should say (so and so) let him be anathema." One of its most notable appearances in English literature is in Sterne's *Tristram Shandy* (Vol. III, Ch. XI, pp. 171–177 in the Odyssey edition).

**Anatomy:** Used even as early as Aristotle in the figurative sense of logical dissection or analysis, this term, which originally meant "dissection" in a medical sense, came into common use in England late in the sixteenth century in the meaning thus explained by Robert Burton in his *Anatomy of Melancholy* (1621): "What it is, with all the kinds, causes, symptoms, prognostickes, and severall cures of it." There are several pieces in English literature preceding Burton in which the medical sense of *anatomy* is still less evident, such as Thomas Nash's *Anatomy of Absurdity*, and John Lyly's *Euphues, the Anatomy of Wit*. The *anatomies* anticipated to some degree the characteristics of the essay and philosophical and scientific treatises of the seventeenth century. The term is also used by Northrop Frye, in his *Anatomy of Criticism,* to designate the kind of narrative prose work organized around ideas and dealing with intellectual themes and attitudes by piling up masses of erudition around the theme, after the manner of Menippean satire. Sterne's *Tristram Shandy* is an example, as are the whaling chapters in Melville's *Moby Dick.*

**Ancients and Moderns, Quarrel of the:** In a broad sense, every age has its battle of the "ancients" and the "moderns" in the conflict between old ideas and standards of taste and new ones. Specifically, the phrase is used in literary history to designate the complicated controversy which took place in France and England in the late seventeenth and early eighteenth centuries over the relative merits of classical and contemporary thinkers, writers, and artists. Some of the forces which stimulated the dispute were the RENAISSANCE in Western Europe, which produced both a reverence for classical authority and a desire to emulate classical writers; the growth of the new science in the seventeenth century; and the interest in such philosophical ideas as the doctrine of progress.

The dispute in France centered about the vigorous advocacy of the cause of the moderns by Charles Perrault, whose position received support from Fontenelle, Thomas Corneille, P. Perrault, and others. These moderns were opposed by Boileau, Racine, La Fontaine, La Bruyère, and others. Perrault in his poem (1687) lauding the age of Louis XIV and in his famous *Parallèles des anciens et des modernes* (1688–1697) and Fontenelle in his *Digression sur les anciens et des modernes* (1688) held that in art and poetry the efforts of the moderns showed superior taste and greater polish of form as compared with those of the ancients. The moderns were said to profit from improved methods of reasoning, scientific inventions, and Christianity. The philosophical doctrines of Descartes (1596–1650), who had rejected Aristotle, lent support to the moderns. The long-established assumption of the superiority of classical thought and art was thus vigorously challenged (see HUMANISM, CLASSICISM).

In England, the "battle of the books" began with the publication of Sir William Temple's *An Essay upon the Ancient and Modern Learning* (1690). Temple, who rejected the doctrine of progress and criticized the "pretensions" and "visions" of the members of the Royal Society, upheld the claims of the ancients in many fields and could not see that they were inferior to the moderns in knowledge or genius. The new inventions had not led to practical improvements. Modern students are not agreed as to whether Temple's work was an outgrowth of the French quarrel or was a natural result of the opposition which had existed in England for some forty years to the "advanced" thinkers who, under the inspiration of Bacon's writings and the ardent leadership of the Royal Society, had broken with the past and were espousing the new philosophy and the new science (Richard Boyle, Joseph Glanvil, Thomas Sprat, and others). Temple was answered in 1694 by William Wotton in an ambitious treatise, *Reflections upon Ancient and Modern Learning*, in which he gave the palm to the moderns in most, though not all, branches of learning. The scientific as opposed to the literary aspects of the quarrel were particularly stressed in England, the English moderns generally being willing to admit the superiority of the ancients in such fields as poetry, oratory, and art.

An episode which aroused much interest arose over the *Letters of Phalaris*, which Temple listed as a praiseworthy ancient work. Soon thereafter, Charles Boyle, an Oxford man, published a new edition of the "Phalaris" letters, taking occasion to attack the Cambridge classical scholar Dr. Thomas Bentley for an alleged slight. When Wotton published a second edition of his essay (1697), Bentley included in it an appendix which not only criticized Boyle's edition, but presented evidence, later elaborated in his famous *Dissertation* (1699), for believing that the Phalaris letters were spurious. Thus a classical scholar appeared as a champion of the moderns; in fact, Bentley employed the methods of the new science in the field of classical literature itself, and his study went far toward initiating modern historical scholarship. Jonathan Swift, in the "digressions" of the *Tale of a Tub* (written *ca.*1696) and in his famous *Battle of the Books* (written *ca.*1697, pub. 1704)—the most important literary document produced by the controversy in England—undertook the defense of his patron Temple, though Swift's satire is not altogether one-sided. Perhaps the most significant result of the whole dispute lies in the impetus it gave to the liberalizing forces which were attempting to stimulate progress through the emancipation of the human spirit from the depressing effect of a too unyielding devotion to established tradition.

**Anecdote:** A short narrative detailing particulars of an interesting EPISODE or event. In careful usage the term most frequently refers to a narrated incident in the life of an important person and should lay claim to an element of truth. Though *anecdotes* are often used by writers as the basis for short stories, an *anecdote* definitely differs from a SHORT STORY in that it lacks complicated PLOT and is unified in its presentation of time and place elements and in its relation of a single EPISODE. At one time the term connoted secret and private details of a man's career given forth in the spirit of gossip, though now it is used generally to cover any brief narrative of particulars. Anecdotic literature has a long heritage extending from ancient through modern times and comprising books as different as the *Deipnosophistae* of Athenaeus, the *Lives* of Plutarch, the *Anecdotes* of Percy, and the *Anecdota* of Procopius. The term still retains something of its original sense of an unpublished item.

**Anglicism:** A peculiarity of expression or IDIOM characteristic of the English language and distinguishing it from other languages. The term is also given to foreign expressions when taken over into English and forced to conform to English usage and syntax. Any form of expression peculiar to the English. In the United States it is used also to refer to a word or expression used particularly in England but not in common use in the United States.

**Anglo-Catholic Revival:** See OXFORD MOVEMENT.

**Anglo-French:** See ANGLO-NORMAN (LANGUAGE).

**Anglo-Irish Literature:** Literature produced in English by Irish writers, especially those living in Ireland and actuated by a conscious purpose to utilize Celtic materials, often employing an English style flavored by Irish idioms, called "Hibernian English" or "Anglo-Irish." See CELTIC RENAISSANCE.

**Anglo-Latin:** A term applied to the learned literature produced in Latin by Englishmen or others dwelling in England during the MIDDLE ENGLISH period. It is largely in prose and includes CHRONICLES, serious treatises on theology, philosophy, law, history, and science, though SATIRE (like Walter Map's *De Nugis Curialium*) and LIGHT VERSE (like the GOLIARDIC SONGS) were also written, as well as hymns and prayers and religious plays. See ANGLO-NORMAN PERIOD and MIDDLE ENGLISH PERIOD.

**Anglo-Norman (Language).** The term *Anglo-Norman* (also *Anglo-French*) is applied to the French language as it was used in England in the period following the Norman Conquest (*ca.*1100–1350) and also to the literature written in *Anglo-Norman*. The relations of France and England were so close during this period that it is difficult to be certain in all cases whether a given writer or work is to be classed as *Anglo-Norman* or merely as French. Although the terms *Anglo-Norman* and *Anglo-French* are commonly used interchangeably, some writers make distinctions that have given each term special meanings. Thus *Anglo-French* is sometimes used to designate French that shows the definite influence of English idioms. *Anglo-Norman* is often restricted to the early period of Norman times (1066 and immediately following) and is sometimes used to denote pieces written in England by persons of Norman descent using the Norman dialect of French. A third term *Franco-Norman* is also used in this latter sense. See ANGLO-NORMAN PERIOD.

**Anglo-Norman Period:** The period in English literature between 1100 and 1350, so-called because of the dominance of Norman-French culture, art, and language. The period is also often called the Early Middle English Period and is frequently dated from the triumph of William the Conqueror at the Battle of Hastings in 1066, although it was early in the twelfth century before the impact of Norman culture was marked on the English or before the Norman conquerors began to think of themselves as inhabitants of the British Isles.

    In Europe this was the age of the great crusades and the period of the dominance of French literature. In England, under Henry I, Stephen, and the Plantagenet Kings Henry II, Richard the Lion-Hearted, and John, the conquered Saxon natives and the Norman lords were establishing the working pattern of government that reached its epitomizing statement in the *Magna Charta* of 1215. Throughout the period the characteristics that are usually associated with England were developing. Feudalism was established. Parliament came into being, with a movement toward definite limits on the power of the monarchy. Oxford and Cambridge rose as strong universities. The Old English language, for a period after the Conquest the tongue of conquered slaves, not only survived in the period but blended with the French dialect of the Norman victors. Gradually it emerged as the language of England, a fact that King John's successor, Henry III, recognized when in 1258 he used English as well as French in a proclamation. By 1300 English was becoming again the language of the upper classes and was beginning to displace French in schools and legal pleadings. Henry III was succeeded in 1272 by the first of the three Edwards, who ruled England for over a hundred years (until 1377).

Latin was the language used for learned works, French for courtly literature, and English chiefly for popular works—religious plays, METRICAL ROMANCES, and popular BALLADS. On the continent Dante, the *Chanson de Roland*, and Boccaccio flourished. In England and France the body of legend and artful invention that gave England its national hero, Arthur, was coming into being in French, Latin, and English through the work of writers like Chrétien de Troyes, Wace, Geoffrey of Monmouth, Walter Map, and Layamon. (See ARTHURIAN LEGEND.)

Writings in native English were few. The last entry in the *Anglo-Saxon Chronicles* was made at Petersborough in 1154. About 1170 a long didactic poem in FOURTEENERS, the *Poema Morale*, appeared. Early in the twelfth century English METRICAL ROMANCES using English themes began to appear, the first being *King Horn*. Such ROMANCES flourished throughout the period. The DRAMA made its first major forward leaps in this period. The first recorded MIRACLE PLAY in England, *The Play of St. Catherine*, was performed at Dunstable about 1100. By 1300 the MYSTERY PLAYS were moving outside the churches and into the hands of the town guilds. The establishment of the Feast of Corpus Christi in 1311 led to the great extension of the CYCLIC DRAMAS and to the use of movable stages or PAGEANTS. The Chester CYCLE was composed around 1328.

Native English poetry, both in the older alliterative tradition and in the newer French forms, continued to develop. About 1250 came "The Owl and the Nightingale," the most famous English DÉBAT poem; about the same time lyric verse was getting under way with "Sumer is Icumen in." About 1300 came the heavily didactic *Cursor Mundi*, and around 1340 the popular *The Pricke of Conscience*, describing the misery of earth and glory of heaven and often ascribed to Richard Rolle of Hampole.

But significant as these works are in the developing strength of native English writing, the period between 1100 and 1350 is predominantly the age of the Latin CHRONICLE and of the glories of French and Anglo-Norman writings. Throughout the period, but particularly in the twelfth century, a veritable cultural renaissance was occurring which expressed itself in England primarily through imaginative literature written in ANGLO-NORMAN. In general it follows the lines of the contemporary literature of France itself and embraces (to follow Professor Schofield's list) ROMANCES, tales, historical works, political poems and SATIRES, LEGENDS and SAINTS' LIVES, didactic works, LYRICS and DÉBATS, as well as religious DRAMA. The rich culture of the court of Henry II proved a fertile field for these works, and the problem of deciding which shall be classed as ANGLO-NORMAN and which French today defies solution. By 1350, however, the French qualities of grace, harmony, humor, and chivalric idealism together with its many lyric forms, worldly subjects, and accentual meters had been absorbed into the mainstream of English writing; and in folk BALLAD, in CYCLE PLAY, in both alliterative verse and accentual poem, England was ready for a new flowering of native literary art. See *The Outline of Literary History*, under "Anglo-Norman Period."

**Anglo-Saxon:** A Teutonic tribal group resident in England in post-Roman times. In the fifth and sixth centuries the Angles and Saxons from the neighborhood of what is now known as Schleswig-Holstein, together with the Jutes, invaded and conquered Britain. From the Angles came the name England (Angle-land). After Alfred (ninth century), king of the West Saxons, conquered the Danish-English people of the Anglian territory, the official name for his subjects was, in Latin, *Angli et Saxones* (the English themselves were inclined to use the term *Engle* and call their language *Englisc*). In later times the term *Anglo-Saxons* came to be used to distinguish the residents of England from the Saxons still resident in Europe proper. The term is now broadly used to distinguish the English peoples whether resident in England, America, or the various possessions. See OLD ENGLISH PERIOD, ENGLISH LANGUAGE.

**Anglo-Saxon Versification:** See OLD ENGLISH VERSIFICATION.

**Animal Epic:** See BEAST EPIC.

**Annals:** Narratives of historical events recorded year by year. Such records in Rome in Cicero's time were known as *annales maximi* because they were kept by the pontifex maximus. Anglo-Saxon monks in the seventh century developed another sort of *annals* by recording in ecclesiastical calendars after given dates important events of the year. This practice developed into such records as the *Anglo-Saxon Chronicles*. Both *annals* (as in Ireland) and CHRON-ICLES (as in England) were frequently written long after the events recorded had taken place, the dating being sometimes more or less speculative, especially when efforts were being made to "synchronize" events in secular and in Biblical or ecclesiastical history. The term *annals* in modern times is sometimes used rather loosely for historical narrative not recorded by years and for digests and records of deliberative bodies and of scientific and artistic organizations, like *Annals of Congress, Annals of Music, Annals of Mathematics*. Although *annals* and CHRONICLES are often used interchangeably, the term *annals* technically implies a greater emphasis upon the progress or succession of events from year to year. When used in a figurative sense, the term implies events of great moment, as in Gray's reference to "The short and simple annals of the poor," and Carlyle's statement that "happy are the people whose annals are blank." See CHRONICLE.

**Annuals:** Books appearing in successive numbers at intervals of one year and usually reviewing the events of the year within specified fields of interest, as college *annuals*. The term is sometimes applied also to such compendiums as the *World Almanac*, embracing historical data and miscellaneous statistics covering a long range of years. In nineteenth century England and America the term was used to designate yearly compilations of tales, poems, and essays, illustrated with plates and handsomely bound, issued in the fall of the year for sale around Christmas as GIFT-BOOKS. They were popular in England between 1822 and 1856, and they were equally successful in America. They are significant in literary history in America because they were the best American market in the first half of the nineteenth century for short fiction, and a number of the distinguished works of writers like Hawthorne, Poe, and Simms first appeared in them. They bore descriptive and sentimental titles, such as *The Gift, Friendship's Offering, The Odd-Fellow's Offering*, and *The Token*.

**Antagonist:** The character in FICTION or DRAMA who stands directly opposed to the PROTAGONIST. A rival or opponent of the PROTAGO-NIST. See PROTAGONIST.

**Anthem:** In its popular use refers to any song of praise, rejoicing, or reverence. These emotions when related to one's country find expression in national *anthems;* when in praise of one's deity, in religious *anthems.* More restrictedly, an *anthem* is an arrangement of words from the Bible, usually from the Psalms, planned for church worship. Formerly it was essential that the music for an *anthem* be arranged for responsive singing, either by two choirs, a priest and a choir, or in another of various similar combinations.

**Anthology:** Literally "a gathering of flowers," the term is used to designate a collection of writing, either poetry or prose, usually by various authors. Although *anthologies* are made by many different principles of selection and to serve a wide variety of purposes, one of the most important of their uses is the introduction of contemporary, unknown writers to the public. *The Anthology,* perhaps the most famous of all such collections, is a gathering of some 4,500 short Greek poems composed between 490 B.C. and A.D. 1000. *The Bible* is sometimes considered an *anthology,* as is also *The Koran.* A number of *anthologies* have been important in English literary history, among them *Tottel's Miscellany* (1559), which published the chief works of Wyatt and Surrey; *England's Helicon* (1602), which published works of Sidney and Spenser; Percy's *Reliques of Ancient English Poetry* (1765); and Palgrave's *Golden Treasury* (1861), a collection of standard works of English poets.

**Anticlimax:** The arrangement of descriptive or narrative details in such an order than the lesser, the trivial, or the ludicrous confronts the reader at the point where he expects something greater and more serious. When unintentionally done in plotting, the effect is badly destructive. The term is customarily used to describe a stylistic effect resulting from a sudden or gradual decrease in interest or importance in the items of a series of two or more statements. The opposite of climactic order. *Anticlimax* is both a weakness and a strength in writing; when effectively and intentionally used it greatly increases emphasis through its humorous effect; when unintentionally employed its result is bathetic (see BATHOS). An example of its deliberate use is found in Pope's *Rape of the Lock:*

> Not youthful kings in battle seiz'd alive,
> Not scornful virgins who their charms survive
> Not ardent lovers robb'd of all their bliss,

> Not ancient ladies when refus'd a kiss,
> Not tyrants fierce that unrepenting die,
> *Not Cynthia when her manteau's pinn'd awry,*
> E'er felt such rage, resentment and despair,
> As thou, sad virgin! for thy ravish'd hair.

Unintentional *anticlimax* may be illustrated by this sentence (if it *is* unintentional): "The duty of a sailor in the navy is to protect his country and to peel potatoes."

**Antimasque:** A grotesque, usually humorous dance interspersed among the beautiful and serious actions and dances of a MASQUE. It was often performed by professional actors and dancers and served as a foil to the MASQUE proper, performed by courtly amateurs. The development and possibly the origin of the *antimasque* are due to Ben Jonson. See MASQUE.

**Antiphrasis:** IRONY, the satirical or humorous use of a word or phrase to convey an idea exactly opposite to its real significance. Thus in Shakespeare's *Julius Caesar* Antony ironically refers to Caesar's murderers as "honorable men."

**Antiquarianism:** The study of old times through any available relics, especially literary and artistic. The antiquarian impulse is associated with history, folklore, social customs, patriotism, religion, and other interests. It is widespread in its manifestations and has existed among all nations, even in their primitive periods. The medieval CHRONICLES and SAINTS' LIVES reflect it, as does such a specific movement as the revival of the native English ALLITERATIVE VERSE in the fourteenth century. *Antiquarianism* as an organized effort in England, however, is associated with the sixteenth century. In 1533 Henry VIII appointed John Leland the "King's Antiquary" and sent him throughout England to examine and collect old documents from libraries, cathedrals, colleges, abbeys, and monasteries. Leland's notes were of much use to later writers like Holinshed, and his work formed the basis for the Society of Antiquaries (1572–1605), of which Sir Walter Raleigh, John Donne, and other literary men were members. Much of the literature of the RENAISSANCE, such as the CHRONICLES, HISTORY-PLAYS, topographical poems (like Drayton's *Polyolbion*), and patriotic EPICS (like Spenser's *Faerie Queene*), reflects the antiquarian movement. William Camden was one of the greatest of Elizabethan antiquarians.

In the seventeenth century Fuller's *Worthies,* John Aubrey's *Lives,* Sir Thomas Browne's *Vulgar Errors,* and the books of Anthony à Wood (historian of Oxford University) are antiquarian in spirit. In the eighteenth century *antiquarianism* was largely motivated by the philosophical interest in primitive man, and explains in part Bishop Percy's *Reliques of Ancient English Poetry* (a collection of old ballads), the CELTIC REVIVAL, and the LITERARY FORGERIES of Chatterton and Macpherson. Indeed, the antiquarian interest formed an important phase of the ROMANTIC MOVEMENT. The GOTHIC ROMANCES and the HISTORICAL NOVELS and METRICAL ROMANCES of Scott reflect it, and even Wordsworth's famous theories about the relation of poetry to the emotions and language of simple men are sometimes traced partly to the effect of the antiquarian impulse.

**Antistrophe:** One of the three stanzaic forms of the Greek choral ODE, the others being STROPHE and EPODE. It is identical with the STROPHE, which precedes it, in METER. As the chorus sang the STROPHE they moved from right to left; in singing the *antistrophe* they exactly retraced these steps, moving back to the original position. In rhetoric, the term describes the reciprocal conversion of the same words in succeeding phrases or clauses, as, "the master of the servant, the servant of the master." See ODE.

**Antithesis:** A figure of speech characterized by strongly contrasting words, clauses, sentences, or ideas. A balancing of one term against another for impressiveness and emphasis. An attractive device when used within reason, antithetical expression with some authors becomes a vice. Certain writers make a mannerism of it. Pope, in the *Rape of the Lock* for example, relies on this figure so frequently that its significance, which lies in the quality of surprise afforded by the sudden contrast, is likely to be lost in the regularity of its recurrence. "Man proposes, God disposes" is an example of *antithesis,* as is the second line of the following characteristic Pope couplet:

> The hungry judges soon the sentence sign,
> *And wretches hang that jury-men may dine.*

True antithetical structure demands that there be not only an opposition of idea, but that the opposition in different parts be manifested through similar grammatical structure,—the noun "wretches" being opposed by the noun "jury-men" and the verb "hang" by the verb "dine" in the above example.

**Aphorism:** A concise statement of a principle or precept given in pointed words. The term was first used by Hippocrates, whose *Aphorisms* were tersely worded medical precepts, synthesized from experience. It was later applied to statements of general principle briefly given in a variety of practical fields, such as law, politics, and art. *Aphorism* implies specific authorship and compact, telling expression. The opening sentence of Hippocrates' *Aphorisms* is a justly famous example: "Life is short, art is long, opportunity fleeting, experimenting dangerous, reasoning difficult."

**Apocryphal:** Now commonly means "spurious," because "apocrypha," which originally meant hidden or secret things, became the term used to denote Biblical books not regarded as inspired, and hence excluded from the sacred CANON. Saint Jerome (A.D. 331–420) is said to be the first writer to apply the term to the uncanonical books now known as the Apocrypha. *Apocryphal* books connected with both the Old and the New Testament circulated in great numbers in the early Middle Ages. Almost all literary types found in the Bible are represented by *apocryphal* compositions. Examples of Old Testament apocrypha include: The Book of Enoch (vision), Life of Adam and Eve (legend), The Wisdom of Solomon (wisdom book), The Testament of Abraham (testament), and the Psalter of Solomon (hymns). New Testament types include: Acts of Matthew (apostolic "acts"), Third Epistle to the Corinthians (epistle), Apocalypse of Peter (vision), and Gospel of Peter (gospel). These books abound in miracles, accounts of the boyhood of Jesus, reported wise sayings of sacred character, and martyrdoms. Influence of *apocryphal* literature, blended with authentic Biblical influence, was exerted on such medieval literary types as saints' legends, visions, sermons, and even ROMANCES. Certain books accepted by the medieval church but rejected by Protestants became *apocryphal* in the sixteenth century, such as Ecclesiasticus, Baruch, and Maccabees, though they were usually printed in Protestant Bibles as useful for edification but not authoritative in determining doctrine. Writings that have been attributed to authors but have not been generally accepted in the CANON of their works are also called *apocryphal.* Thus there are Shakespeare apocrypha and Chaucer apocrypha. See CANON.

**Apologue:** A fictitious narrative about animals or inanimate objects, which, by acting like human beings, reflect the weaknesses and follies of mankind. A more bookish term for FABLE. See FABLE.

**Apology:** Two special uses of the word may be noted. It often appears in literature, especially in literary titles, in its older sense of "defense," as in Stevenson's *Apology for Idlers* and Sidney's *Apologie for Poetrie.* The Latin form *apologia* is also used in this sense, as in Cardinal Newman's *Apologia pro Vita Sua.* No admission of wrong-doing or expression of regret is involved. *Apology* is also an old spelling for APOLOGUE, a fable.

**Apophasis:** A rhetorical figure denoting that convention in speech or writing wherein one makes an assertion even while he seems or pretends to suppress or deny it. "Were I not aware of your high reputation for honesty, I should say that I believe you connived at the fraud yourself."

**Aposiopesis:** The deliberate failure to complete a sentence. As a figure of speech the form is frequently used to convey an impression of extreme exasperation or to imply a threat, as, "If you do that, why, I'll ———." *Aposiopesis* differs from ANACOLUTHON in that the latter completes a sentence in irregular structural arrangement; the former leaves the sentence incomplete.

**Apostrophe:** A figure of speech in which someone (usually, but not always absent), some abstract quality, or a non-existent personage is directly addressed as though present. Characteristic instances of *apostrophe* are found in the invocations to the muses in poetry—

> And chiefly Thou, O Spirit, that dost prefer
> Before all temples the upright heart and pure,
> Instruct me, for Thou know'st;

Or, to quote Milton again:

> Hail, Holy Light, offspring of Heaven firstborn!

The form is frequently used in patriotic oratory, the speaker addressing some glorious leader of the past and invoking his aid in the present. Since *apostrophe* is chiefly associated with deep emotional expression, the form is readily adopted by humorists for purposes of PARODY and SATIRE.

**Apothegm:** A sharply pointed and often startling maxim, more particularly centered and practical than an APHORISM, although like it in other respects. A famous example is Johnson's "Patriotism is the last refuge of a scoundrel." See APHORISM.

**Apprenticeship Novel:** A NOVEL which recounts the youth and young manhood of a sensitive PROTAGONIST who is attempting to learn the nature of the world, discover its meaning and pattern, and acquire a philosophy of life and "the art of living." Goethe's *Wilhelm Meister* is the archetypal *apprenticeship novel;* noted examples in English are Samuel Butler's *The Way of All Flesh*, James Joyce's *A Portrait of the Artist as a Young Man*, Somerset Maugham's *Of Human Bondage*, and Thomas Wolfe's *Look Homeward, Angel*. The *apprenticeship novel* is sometimes called a *bildungsroman*. (For a detailed statement of its characteristics, see Susanne Howe, *Wilhelm Meister and His English Kinsmen*, Ch. I.)

**Arcadian:** Arcadia, a picturesque plateau region in Greece, the reputed home of PASTORAL poetry, was pictured by PASTORAL poets as a land of ideal rural peace and contentment. *Arcadian* suggests an idealized rural simplicity and contentment such as shepherds in conventional PASTORAL poetry exhibited. It is sometimes used as synonymous with BUCOLIC or PASTORAL. Sir Philip Sidney, following Italian precedent, uses *Arcadia* as the title of his PASTORAL ROMANCE. See ECLOGUE, PASTORAL, IDYL.

**Archaism:** Obsolete DICTION, phrasing, IDIOM, or syntax. Used intentionally and effectively an archaic STYLE is valuable in recreating the atmosphere and spirit of the past, as in Spenser's *The Faerie Queene;* unless carefully controlled, however, *archaisms* result in an artificial and affected STYLE so absurd as to defeat the purpose of the writer.

**Archetype:** A term brought into literary criticism from the depth psychology of Carl Jung, who holds that behind each individual's "unconscious"—the blocked-off residue of his past—lies the "collective unconscious" of the human race—the blocked-off memory of our racial past, even of our prehuman experiences. This unconscious racial memory makes powerfully effective for us a group of "primordial images" shaped by the repeated experience of our ancestors and expressed in MYTHS, religions, dreams, fantasies, and powerfully in literature. T. S. Eliot says, "The pre-logical mentality persists in civilized man, but becomes available only to or through the poet." The "primordial image" which taps this "pre-logical mentality" is called the *archetype*.

The literary critic applies the term to an IMAGE, a descriptive detail, a PLOT pattern, or a character type that occurs frequently in literature, MYTH, religion, or folklore and is, therefore, believed to evoke profound emotions in the reader because it awakens a primordial image in his unconscious memory and thus calls into play illogical but strong responses. The archetypal critic studies the poem, play, or novel in terms of the images or patterns it has in common with other poems, plays, or novels, and thus by extension as a portion of the total human experience. In this sense the *archetype* is, as Northrop Frye defines it, "a symbol, usually an image, which recurs often enough in literature to be recognizable as an element of one's literary experience as a whole." (For an extensive treatment, see Maud Bodkin's *Archetypal Patterns in Poetry*.)

**Architectonics:** A critical term which expresses collectively those structural qualities of proportion, UNITY, EMPHASIS, and scale which make a piece of writing proceed logically and smoothly from beginning to end with no waste effort, no faulty omissions. The requirements of *architectonics*, a term borrowed from architecture, are felt to have been fulfilled when a piece of literature impresses a reader as a building, carefully planned and constructed, impresses the spectator. Currently the term is used to describe the successful achieving of organic unity, of "the companionship of the whole," in which the parts are not only perfectly articulated but are combined into an integrated whole, so that the work has meaning not through its parts but through its total organism.

**Areopagus:** The "hill of Ares (Mars)," the seat of the highest judicial court in ancient Athens. By association the name has come to represent any court of final authority. In this sense Milton used the term in his *Areopagitica*, addressed to the British parliament on the question of censorship and the licensing of books.

"The Areopagus" is the name used for what some literary historians believe was a sort of literary club existing in London shortly before 1580, supposed to be analogous with the *Pléiade* group in France. Whether there was a formal club or not is doubtful, but it is true that certain writers and critics, including Gabriel Harvey,

Sir Philip Sidney, Edmund Spenser, and Sir Edward Dyer were engaged in a "movement" to reform English versification on the principles of classical prosody. In their best work, however, Sidney and Spenser abandoned these experiments in classical measures in favor of Italian, French, and native English forms.

**Argument:** A prose statement summarizing the plot or stating the meaning of a long poem or occasionally of a play. The best known English examples are Milton's *Arguments* to each of the books of *Paradise Lost* and Coleridge's MARGINALIA to *The Rime of the Ancient Mariner*. The term is sometimes used by the NEW CRITICS to describe the paraphrasable idea of a poem.

**Argumentation:** One of the four chief "forms of discourse," the others being EXPOSITION, NARRATION, and DESCRIPTION. Its purpose is to convince a reader or hearer by establishing the truth or falsity of a proposition. It is often combined with EXPOSITION. It differs from EXPOSITION technically in its aim, EXPOSITION being content with simply making an explanation.

**Aristotelian Criticism:** Literally, criticism by Aristotle, as in the *Poetics*, or criticism which follows the method of analysis used by Aristotle in the *Poetics*, although the exact nature of the Aristotelian method has been a subject of much debate (see CRITICISM, HISTORICAL SKETCH). In present day critical parlance, however, the term *Aristotelian criticism* is frequently used as a contrast to the term PLATONIC CRITICISM, particularly by the NEW CRITICS. In this sense, the term implies a judicial, logical, formal criticism that is centered in the work rather than in its historical, moral, or religious context, and finds its values either within the work itself or inseparably linked to the work; the term is roughly synonymous with *intrinsic*. See CRITICISM, TYPES OF; PLATONIC CRITICISM; AUTOTELIC.

**Arminianism:** An anti-Calvinistic theology, founded by Jacobus Arminius in Holland in the early seventeenth century. It opposes the Calvinistic doctrines of election, reprobation, and absolute predestination, asserting that the human will can forfeit divine grace after receiving it and denying that predestination is absolute. It was a strong element in the theological arguments in England and America in the seventeenth and eighteenth centuries. In America Jonathan Edwards was its most powerful attacker. See CALVINISM.

**Arsis:** In METRICS, the term is usually applied today to a stressed syllable. In Greek usage, however, *arsis* was the name of the unstressed syllable. See ACCENT.

**Art Ballad:** A term occasionally used to distinguish the modern or literary BALLAD of known authorship from the early BALLADS of unknown authorship. Some successful *art ballads* are *La Belle Dame sans Merci* by Keats, *Rosabelle* by Scott, and *Sister Helen* by Rossetti. Possibly the most famous poem imitating the BALLAD manner is *The Rime of the Ancient Mariner* by Coleridge.

**Art Epic:** A term sometimes employed to distinguish such an EPIC as Milton's *Paradise Lost* or Virgil's *Aeneid* from so-called FOLK EPICS such as *Beowulf, Nibelungenlied,* and the *Iliad* and *Odyssey*. The FOLK EPIC is so named because it deals with tradition closely associated with the people or "folk" for whom it was written and whose credulity it commanded. The *art epic* is supposed to be more sophisticated, more highly idealized, and more consciously moral in purpose than is the FOLK EPIC, which it imitates. The author takes greater liberties with the popular materials he is treating and exhibits and expects less credulity. The events he narrates are in the more remote past. The present-day tendency to discredit the theories of epic origins advanced by the romantic critics of the eighteenth century is resulting in a breaking down of the assumed distinction between the two kinds, as the FOLK EPICS are now viewed as the work of single poets who worked according to traditional artistic technique. See EPIC.

**Article:** A type of ESSAY that is impersonal and largely factual. In an *article* the author writes as an authority on a subject and presents his argument and information in a systematic fashion. The term is applied to informative pieces for such widely varying places of publication as newspapers, magazines, learned and scholarly journals, and encyclopedias. The longer entries in this volume are *articles*. See ESSAY.

**Art Lyric:** This is not so much an individual LYRIC type or form as it is a particular *manner*. The *art lyric* is characterized by a minuteness of subject, great delicacy of touch, careful perfection in phrasing, artificiality of sentiment, and formality. For its subject this kind of LYRIC avoids the passionate outbursts of a Burns, harking back, rather, to the sort of thing Horace and Petrarch wrote about, the tilt of a lady's eyebrow, the glow of a cheek. With Herrick and Lovelace and Jonson and Herbert, Elizabethan and seventeenth-century English writers made much of the manner, polishing and perfecting their songs to gem-like brightness; with Shelley and Keats the *art lyric* began to carry ABSTRACT ideas. In brief, it may be said that the *art lyric* differs from the ordinary LYRIC in the degree to which the poet's self-conscious struggle for perfection of FORM dominates the spontaneity of his emotion. Certain French lyric forms, the TRIOLET, BALLADE, RONDEAU, and RONDEL, are instances of this highly polished manner of the ART LYRIC.

**Art Theatre:** See LITTLE THEATRE MOVEMENT.

**Arthurian Legend:** The question often asked, "Is King Arthur a historical person?" cannot be answered by a plain yes or no. It is probable that the LEGEND of Arthur grew up out of the deeds of some historical person. He was probably not a king and it is more than doubtful whether his name was Arthur. He was presumably a Welsh or Roman military leader of the Celts in Wales against the Germanic invaders who overran Britain in the fifth century. Just as stories in later time grew up about Robin Hood or George Washington, the stories of the great deeds of this Welsh hero gradually grew into a great body of romantic story. He provided a glorious past for the Britons to look back upon, and there is some evidence that his glorification in twelfth-century writings was due to the desire of the Norman kings to strengthen the national background by treating Arthur as an illustrious predecessor on the throne of Britain. When Arthur had developed into a great king, he yielded his position as a personal hero to a great group of knights who surrounded him. These knights of the Round Table came to be representative of all that was best in the age of chivalry, and the stories of their deeds make up the most popular group ("Matter of Britain") of the great CYCLES of MEDIEVAL ROMANCE.

There is no mention of Arthur in contemporary accounts of the Germanic invasion, but a Roman citizen named Gildas who lived in Wales mentions in his *De Excidio et Conquestu Britanniae* (written between 500 and 550) the Battle of Mt. Badon, with which later accounts connect Arthur, and a valiant Roman leader of a Welsh rally, named Ambrosius Aurelianus. About 800, Nennius, a Welsh chronicler, in his *Historia Britonum* uses the name Arthur in referring to a leader (*dux bellorum*) against the Saxons. About a century later an addition to Nennius' history called *Mirabilia* gives further evidences of Arthur's development as a hero, including an allusion to a boar-hunt of Arthur's which is told in detail in the later Welsh story of Kulwch and Olwen (in the *Mabinogion*). There are other references to Arthur in the annals of the tenth and eleventh centuries, and William of Malmesbury in his *Gesta Regum Anglorum* (1125) who treats Arthur as an historical figure, identifies him with the Arthur whom the Welsh "rave wildly about" in their "idle tales." A typical British Celt at this time was ready to fight for his belief that Arthur was not really dead but would return.

About 1136 Geoffrey of Monmouth wrote his *Historia Regum Britanniae*, professedly based upon an old Welsh book. Geoffrey adds a wealth of matter to the Arthurian legend—how much of it he invented can not now be determined—such as the stories of Arthur's supernatural birth, his weird "Passing" to Avalon to be healed of his wounds, and the abduction of Guinevere by Modred. Arthur figures as a world-conqueror who exacts tribute of even the Romans. It is probable that Geoffrey was attempting to create for the Norman kings in England a glorious historical background. He traces the history of the Britons from Brut, a descendant of Aeneas, to the great Arthur. Soon after Geoffrey's time additions to the story were made by the French poet Wace in his *Roman de Brut,* and a little later appear the famous ROMANCES of Chrétien de Troyes, in Old French, in which Arthurian themes are given their first known highly literary treatment. About 1205 the English poet Layamon added some details in his *Brut.* By this time Arthurian legend had taken its place as one of the great themes of MEDIEVAL ROMANCE.

The great popularity of Arthurian tradition continued through the Middle Ages, reaching its climax in medieval English literature in Malory's *Le Morte Darthur* (printed 1485), a book destined to transmit Arthurian stories to many later English writers, notably Tennyson. Spenser professedly used an Arthurian background for his great romantic EPIC *The Faerie Queene* (1590), and in the next century Milton contemplated a national EPIC on Arthur. Interest in Arthur decreased in the eighteenth century, but Arthurian topics were particularly popular in the nineteenth century, the best known treatment appearing in Tennyson's *Idylls of the King.* Tennyson's version, as well as E. A. Robinson's *Tristram,* shows how different generations have modified the Arthurian stories to make them express contemporary modes of thought and individual artistic ends. Arthurian themes received powerful and sympathetic musical treatment in an opera by Dryden with music by Purcell, *King Arthur*, and in Richard Wagner's operas, *Lohengrin, Tristan,* and *Parsifal.* The burlesquing treatment of chivalry in Mark Twain's *A Connecticut Yankee in King Arthur's Court* is in contrast to the usual romantic idealization, as is T. W. White's trilogy of novels published under the collective title, *The Once and Future King,* which is a powerful tribute to the continuing strength of the Arthurian legend. See MEDIEVAL ROMANCE, CHRONICLE.

**Artificial Comedy:** A term sometimes used (as by Lamb) for comedy reflecting an artificial society, like the COMEDY OF MANNERS.

**Artificiality:** In CRITICISM a term used to characterize a work that is consciously and deliberately mannered, elaborate, or conventional. *Artificiality* describes a quality which the critic senses as being studied and self-conscious; what is specifically meant by the term varies greatly from critic to critic. There is little question, however, that the style of John Lyly is artificial and that the style of Burns is not; about writers like Donne and Hemingway, however, debate can and does rage.

**Assonance:** Resemblance or similarity in sound between vowels followed by different consonants in two or more stressed syllables. *Assonance* differs from RIME in that RIME is a similarity of vowel and consonant. "Lake" and "fake" demonstrate RIME; "lake" and "fate" *assonance.*

*Assonance* is a common substitution for end-rime in the popular BALLAD, as in these lines from "The Twa Corbies":

>—In behint yon auld fail dyke,
>I wot there lies a new-slain Knight.

Such substitution of *assonance* for END-RIME is also characteristic of Emily Dickinson's verse, and is used extensively by many contemporary poets.

As an enriching ornament within the line, *assonance* is of great use to the poet. Poe and Swinburne used it extensively for musical effect. Gerard Manley Hopkins introduced modern poets to its wide use. The skill with which Dylan Thomas manipulates *assonance* is one of his high achievements. Note its complex employment in the first STANZA of Thomas' "Ballad of the Long-Legged Bait":

> The bows glided down, and the coast
> Blackened with birds took a last look
> At his thrashing hair and whale-blue eye;
> The trodden town rang its cobbles for luck.

*Assonance* is involved in "bows" and "down"; "blackened," "last," "thrashing," "hair," "whale," and "rang"; "took" and "look"; and "trodden" and "cobbles." (In passing one might also note the pattern of ALLITERATION in this stanza and that the riming of "look" with "luck" is an example of CONSONANCE.) See RIME.

**Asyndeton:** A form of condensed expression in which words or short phrases, usually joined by conjunctions, are presented in series, separated only by commas. Perhaps the most famous example is Caesar's *"Veni, vidi, vici."*

**Atmosphere:** The prevailing tone or mood of a literary work, particularly—but not exclusively—when that mood is established in part by setting or landscape. It is, however, not simply setting but rather the emotional aura which the work bears and which establishes the reader's expectations and attitudes. Examples are the sombre mood established by the description of the prison door in the opening chapter of Hawthorne's *The Scarlet Letter*, the brooding sense of fatality engendered by the description of Egdon Heath at the beginning of Hardy's *The Return of the Native*, the sense of "something rotten in the state of Denmark" established by the scene on the battlements at the opening of *Hamlet*, or the more mechanical but still effective opening stanza of Poe's "The Raven."

**Attic:** Writing characterized by a clear, simple, polished, and witty STYLE. Attica, a province of Greece today, was formerly one of the ancient Greek states. With Athens as its capital city, Attica arose to such fame for its culture and art as to survive in the term *Attic*, an adjective denoting grace and culture and the classic in art. Joseph Addison is a favorite example of an English author who may be said to have written *Attic* prose.

**Attic Salt:** *Salt* in this sense means WIT. *Attic salt* is writing distinguished by its classic refinement, its intellectual sharpness, and its elegant but stinging WIT. See ATTIC.

**Aubade:** A LYRIC about dawn or a morning serenade. A French form originally, it differs from the Provençal ALBA in usually being joyous, whereas the ALBA is a lament. Shakespeare's "Hark! Hark! the Lark" and Browning's "The Year's at the Spring" are good English examples. See ALBA.

**Augustan:** Specifically refers to the age of the Emperor Augustus of Rome (ruled 27 B.C. to A.D. 14), but since the time of Augustus was notable for the perfection of letters and learning, the term has, by analogy, been applied to other epochs in world history when literary culture was high. As Virgil and Horace made the *Augustan* age of Rome, so Addison and Steele, Swift and Pope are said to have made the *Augustan* age of English letters. In a narrow sense the term *English Augustan Age* applies only to the reign of Queen Anne (1702–1714); in a broader sense it is sometimes given the dates of Pope—1688–1744. The writers of the age were self-consciously "Augustan," aware of the parallels of their writing to Latin literature, given to comparing London to Rome, and, in the case of Pope, addressing George II satirically as "Augustus." See NEO-CLASSIC PERIOD, and *The Outline of Literary History*, where the period 1700–1750 is designated "The Augustan Age."

**Augustinianism:** The doctrines of St. Augustine of Hippo (354–430), author of *Confessions*, the first extended and completely honest self-analysis in literary history, and of the monumental *De Civitate Dei (The City of God)*, as well as a vast amount of other writing. He strongly defended the orthodox view of God and man against the heresies of Pelagius, who held that there is no original sin, that the human will is absolutely free, and that the grace of God is universal but not indispensable. In opposing PELAGIANISM, St. Augustine exalted the glory of God, stressed original sin, and asserted the necessity of divine grace. His is the essential view of man which, in the RENAISSANCE and in America, became known as CALVINISM. See CALVINISM.

**Autobiography:** The story of a person's life written by himself. Although a common loose use of the term includes under autobiographical writings MEMOIRS, DIARIES, JOURNALS, and LETTERS, distinctions among these forms need to be made. DIARIES, JOURNALS, and LETTERS are not extended, organized narratives prepared for the public eye; *autobiographies* and MEMOIRS are. But whereas

MEMOIRS deal at least in part with public events and noted personages other than the author himself, an *autobiography* is a connected narrative of the author's life, with some stress laid upon introspection. Notable great *autobiographies*—and works which tend
to clarify the distinction made above—are St. Augustine's *Confessions*, Benvenuto Cellini's *Autobiography*, Franklin's *Autobiography*,
and *The Education of Henry Adams*. Simulated *autobiography* is a
device often used in the NOVEL, as in Defoe's *Moll Flanders*, and
the NOVEL can on occasion be *autobiography* in the guise of FICTION,
as in those of Thomas Wolfe and in Joyce's *A Portrait of the Artist
as a Young Man*. See BIOGRAPHY.


**Autotelic:** A term applied to a work that is non-didactic; that is,
one whose end-purpose or intention is within itself and not dependent upon the achievement of objectives outside the work. The
term is used by the NEW CRITICS to indicate a poem that speaks its
own truth in its own terms rather than referring for its value to
some external truth. See BELIEF, THE PROBLEM OF.


**Awakening, The Great:** A phrase applied to a great revival of emotional religion in America which took place about 1735–1750, the
movement being at its height about 1740–1745 under the leadership of Jonathan Edwards. It arose as an effort to reform religion
and morals. Religion, under the "PURITAN hierarchy" led by the
Mathers, had become rather formal and cold, and the clergy somewhat arrogant. The low morals and the lack of religious zeal which
prevailed were traceable in part to the general anti-PURITAN reaction in England after 1660, the increasingly diverse character of the
population in the colonies, the hard conditions of pioneer life, and
the general reaction against the horror of the Salem Witchcraft.
The revival meetings began as early as 1720 in New Jersey. In 1734
Edwards held his first great revival at Northampton, Mass. In 1738
the famous English evangelist George Whitefield began his meetings in Georgia and in 1739–1740 made a spectacular evangelistic
tour of the colonies, reaching New England in 1740. Whitefield's
meetings were marked by great emotional manifestations, such as
trances, shoutings, tearing of garments, faintings. In 1740–1742
Edwards conducted a long "revival" at Northampton, preached in
other cities, published many sermons, including *Sinners in the
Hands of an Angry God* (1741). The conservatives or "Old Lights,"

representing the stricter Calvinists, led by the faculties of Harvard
and Yale, protested against the emotional excesses of the movement;
they were answered by Edwards in his *Treatise on the Religious
Affections* (1746). Yet Edwards himself opposed the more extreme
exhibitions of emotionalism and by 1750 a reaction against the
movement was under way. See CALVINISM, DEISM, PURITANISM.

**Bacchius:** In METRICS, a three-syllable FOOT, with the first syllable
unaccented and the last two accented but with the ICTUS on the
first accented syllable. Examples: $\breve{a}\ \overline{bove}'\ \overline{board},\ \breve{a}\ \overline{bout}'\ \overline{face}.$

**Background:** A term, like many others used in literary discussion,
borrowed from the kindred art of painting, where it signifies those
parts of the painting against which the principal objects are portrayed. In literature the term is rather loosely used to specify either
the SETTING of a piece of writing or the TRADITION and point of
view from which an author presents his ideas. Thus one might speak
either (1) of the Russian *background* (SETTING) of *Anna Karenina*
or (2) of the *background* of education, philosophy, and convictions
from which Tolstoy wrote the novel.

**Baconian Theory:** The theory, now generally discredited, that the
plays of William Shakespeare were written by Francis Bacon. The
theory grew out of an eighteenth century English suggestion that
Shakespeare, an unschooled countryman, could not have written
the plays attributed to him. In the nineteenth century the idea that
the plays were by Bacon developed both in England and in America,
with the American Delia Bacon being a particularly influential advocate of Baconian authorship. Other authors for the plays than
Bacon have been suggested, among them the Earl of Oxford, Sir
Walter Raleigh, and Christopher Marlowe (who, according to this
theory, was not murdered in 1593). The evidence offered in support of any or all of these theories is fragmentary and inconclusive
at best, at its worst it is absurd; and our steadily growing scholarly
knowledge of Shakespeare and his world increasingly discredits
these theories without silencing their advocates.

**Balance:** In rhetoric refers to that structure in which parts of a
sentence—as words, phrases, or clauses—are set off against each
other in position so as to emphasize a contrast in meaning.

The memory of other authors is kept alive by their works; but the
memory of Johnson keeps many of his works alive.

—Macaulay

As a critical term *balance* is often used to characterize nicety of
proportion among the various elements of a given piece of writing.
A story, for example, wherein SETTING, CHARACTERIZATION, and action are carefully planned, with no element securing undue emphasis, might be said to have fine *balance*.

**Ballad:** A form of verse adapted for singing or recitation and primarily characterized by its presentation in simple narrative form of
a dramatic or exciting EPISODE. A famous definition is that of F. B.
Gummere who describes the *ballad* as "a poem meant for singing,
quite impersonal in material, probably connected in its origins with
the communal dance, but submitted to a process of oral tradition
among people who are free from literary influences and fairly ho-
mogeneous in character." Though the *ballad* is a form still much
written, the so-called "popular *ballad*" in most literatures properly
belongs to the early periods before written literature was highly developed. They still develop, however, in isolated sections and among
illiterate and semi-literate peoples. In America the folk of the southern Appalachian mountains have maintained a *ballad* tradition, as
have the cowboys of the western plains, and people associated with
labor movements, particularly when they were marked by violence.
In Australia the "bush" *ballad* is still vigorous and popular. In the
West Indies the "Calypso" singers produce something close to the
*ballad* with their impromptu songs. Debate still rages as to whether
the *ballad* originates with an individual composer or as a group or
communal activity. Whatever the origin, it is true that the folk
*ballad* is, in almost every country, one of the earliest forms of literature. Certain common characteristics of these early *ballads* should
be noted: the supernatural is likely to play an important part in
events, physical courage and love are frequent themes, the incidents
are usually such as happen to common people (as opposed to the
nobility) and often have to do with domestic episodes; slight attention is paid to CHARACTERIZATION or DESCRIPTION, transitions are
abrupt, action is largely developed through DIALOGUE, tragic situations are presented with the utmost simplicity, INCREMENTAL REPE-
TITION is common, IMAGINATION though not so common as in the
ART BALLAD nevertheless appears in brief flashes, a single EPISODE
of highly dramatic nature is presented, and, often enough, the *bal-*

*lad* is brought to a close with some sort of summary STANZA. The greatest impetus to the study of *ballad* literature was given by the publication in 1765 of Bishop Percy's *Reliques of Ancient English Poetry.* The standard modern collection is *The English and Scottish Popular Ballads* edited by Francis James Child. See ART BALLAD, BALLAD STANZA.

**Ballad-Opera:** A name given to a sort of burlesque OPERA which flourished on the English stage for several years following the appearance of John Gay's *The Beggar's Opera* (1728), the best known example of the type. Modeled on Italian OPERA, which it burlesqued, it told its story in songs set to old tunes and appropriated various elements from FARCE and COMEDY. See OPERA, COMIC OPERA.

**Ballad Stanza:** The STANZAIC form of the folk or popular BALLAD. Usually it consists of four lines, riming *abcb*, with the first and third lines carrying four accented syllables and the second and fourth carrying three. There is great variation in the number of unaccented syllables. The RIME is often approximate, with ASSO-NANCE and CONSONANCE frequently appearing. A REFRAIN is not uncommon. This stanza from "Willy Drowned in Yarrow" is typical:

> Yestreen I made my bed fu' braid,
> The night I'll mak' it narrow,
> For a' the live-lang winter night
> I lie twined o' my marrow.

**Ballade:** One of the most popular of the artificial French verse forms. The *ballade* should not, however, be confused with the BALLAD, which is commonly folk-poetry, since the *ballade* is essentially so-phisticated.

For a fixed conventional verse-type the *ballade* form has been rather liberally interpreted. Perhaps early usage most frequently demanded three STANZAS and an ENVOY, though the number of lines to the STANZA and of syllables to the line seems to have varied. Typical earmarks of the *ballade* have been: (1) the REFRAIN (uni-form as to wording) carrying the MOTIF of the poem and recurring regularly at the end of each STANZA and of the ENVOY; (2) the ENVOY, by nature a peroration of climactic importance and likely to be addressed to a high member of the court or to the poet's patron; and (3) the use of only three (or at the most four) RIMES in the entire poem, occurring at the same position in each STANZA and

with no rime-word repeated except in the REFRAIN. STANZAS of
varied length have been used in the *ballade,* but the most common
one is an eight-line STANZA riming *ababbcbc* with *bcbc* for the
ENVOY. A good example of early use of English *ballade* form is Chaucer's "Balade de bon conseyl," while one of the best known modern
*ballades* is Rossetti's rendering of François Villon's "Ballade of
Dead Ladies."

**Barbarism:** A mistake in the form of a word, or a word which results from such a mistake. Strictly speaking, a *barbarism* results
from the violation of an accepted rule of derivation or inflection,
as *hern* for *hers, goodest* for *best, shooted* for *shot.* Originally it
referred to the mixing of foreign words and phrases in Latin or
Greek. See SOLECISM.

**Bard:** Commonly, in modern use, simply a "poet." Historically,
however, the term refers to those poets who recited verses usually
glorifying the deeds of heroes and leaders, to the accompaniment
of a musical instrument such as the harp. *Bard* technically refers
to the early poets of the Celts, as TROUVÈRE refers to those of Normandy, SKALD to those of Scandinavia, and TROUBADOUR to those of
Provence. See WELSH LITERATURE.

**Baroque:** A term of uncertain origin applied first to the architec-
tural style which succeeded the classic style of the RENAISSANCE
and flourished, in varied forms in different parts of Europe, from
the late sixteenth century until well into the eighteenth century. One
writer (Geoffrey Scott) has explained the *baroque* style as a blending of the "picturesque" elements (the unexpected, the wild, the
fantastic, the accidental) with the more ordered, formal, idealistic,
and logical style of the "high Renaissance." The *baroque* stressed
movement, energy, and realistic treatment. Scott points out that although the *baroque* is bold and startling, even fantastic, it is not
truly wild or accidental, since its "discords and suspensions" are
consciously and logically employed. Another writer (Croll) describes the change to the *baroque* as "a radical effort to adapt the
traditional modes and forms of expression to the uses of a self-
conscious modernism." In its considered efforts to avoid the effects
of repose, tranquillity, and complacency, it sought to startle by the
use of the unusual and unexpected. This led sometimes to grotesqueness, obscurity, and contortion. Indeed, the student will often

come upon the term in its older or "popular"' sense of the highly
fantastic, the whimsical, the bizarre, the DECADENT.

The realization that the *baroque* arose naturally from existing
conditions and is a serious and sincere STYLE, resting upon a sober
intellectual basis and designed to express the newer attitudes of its
period, has had the effect not only of causing the *baroque* to be
regarded with more sympathy and seriousness than formerly, but
also of extending the use of the term to literature as well as to
painting and sculpture. The student of literature may encounter the
term (in its older English sense) applied unfavorably to a writer's
literary STYLE; or he may read of the *baroque* period or "age of
*baroque*" (late sixteenth, seventeenth, and early eighteenth centuries); or he may find it applied descriptively and respectfully to
certain stylistic features of the *baroque* period. Thus the broken
rhythms of Donne's verse and the verbal subtleties of the English
METAPHYSICAL poets have been called *baroque* elements. Richard
Crashaw is said to have expressed the *baroque* spirit supremely in
verse. Perhaps the most influential recent student of the *baroque*
style is the German art critic Heinrich Wölfflin, some of whose followers have made ambitious efforts to explain literature on the basis
of his theories. Wölfflin's works and those of Sacheverell Sitwell
may be consulted, as well as Geoffrey Scott's *The Architecture of
Humanism*. An example of the use of the term in literary criticism
may be found in M. W. Croll's essay on "The Baroque Style in
Prose," in *Studies in English Philology in Honor of Frederick
Klaeber*. See ROCOCO, CONCEIT, METAPHYSICAL VERSE.

**Basic English:** A simplified form of English for non-English speaking peoples, consisting of a vocabulary of 850 words, of which 600
are nouns, 150 adjectives, and 100 "operators" (verbs, adverbs,
prepositions, and conjunctions). It was set up by C. K. Ogden,
acting on a suggestion in the works of Jeremy Bentham. In
America its strongest advocate has been I. A. Richards. The New
Testament and certain of Plato's works have been "translated" into
*Basic English*.

**Bathos:** The effect resulting from an unsuccessful effort to achieve
dignity or pathos or elevation of style; an unintentional ANTICLIMAX,
dropping from the sublime to the ridiculous; the depth of stupidity.
The term gained currency from Pope's treatment of it in one of the
"Martinus Scriblerus" papers in which he ironically defended the

commonplace effects of the English "poetasters" on the ground that depth (*bathos*) was a literary virtue of the moderns, as contrasted with the height (*hypsos*) of the ancients. Two examples of *bathos* given by Pope may be quoted:

> Advance the fringed curtains of thy eyes,
> And tell me who comes yonder.

Here the author (Temple) is felt to fail because of the (unintentional) ANTICLIMAX resulting from the effort to treat poetically a commonplace, prosaic idea. Richard Blackmore, in his *Job*, thus describes a great crowd gathering about Job:

> A waving sea of heads was round me spread,
> And still fresh streams the gazing deluge fed.

Here again the extravagant or inept IMAGERY, though seriously intended, defeats its own purpose, and *bathos* results. The PATHETIC FALLACY is sometimes responsible for a "bathetic" effect. If a NOVEL or a play or a cinema tries to make the reader or spectator weep and succeeds only in making him laugh, the result is *bathos*. The term is sometimes, though not accurately, applied to the deliberate use of ANTICLIMAX for satiric or humorous effect.

**Battle of the Books, The:** See ANCIENTS AND MODERNS, QUARREL OF THE.

**Beast Epic:** A favorite medieval literary form consisting of a series of linked stories grouped about animal characters and often presenting satirical comment on contemporary life of church or court by means of human qualities attributed to beast characters. Scholars still find a nice quarrel in trying to decide the exact origin of the *beast epic*, some holding that the stories developed from popular tradition and were later given literary form by monastic scholars and TROUVÈRES who molded the material at hand, others finding the origin in the writing of Latin scholastics. The oldest example known seems to be that of Paulus Diaconus, a cleric at the court of Charlemagne, who wrote about 782–786. Whether the form first developed in Germany or France is still question for scholarly combat, though there is no doubt that in the twelfth and thirteenth centuries the *beast epics* were very popular in North France, West Germany, and Flanders. The various forms of the *beast epic* agreed in having one EPISODE generally treated as the nucleus for the story: the healing of the sick lion by the fox's prescription that he wrap

himself in the wolf's skin. Some of the other animals common to
the form, besides Reynard the Fox, the lion, and the wolf, are the
cock (Chanticler), the cat, the hare, the camel, the ant, the bear,
the badger, and the stag. The best known of the *beast epics*—and
the most influential—is the *Roman de Renard,* a poem of 30,000
lines comprising twenty-seven sets or "branches" of stories growing
up in France between 1130 and 1250, the composition of which is
probably to be credited to the influence of the Latin *beast epic,*
modified in turn by the ecclesiastics and the French TROUVÈRES. Two
other important forms of the *beast epic* are: the German *Reinhart
Fuchs,* the work of Heinrich der Glichezare about 1180, a poem of
2,266 lines, and the Flemish form, *Van den vos Reinaerde,* the
work of two men, Arnout and Willem, a poem of 3,476 lines. This
last version, which contained rather more than the usual amount
of SATIRE, was published in translation by Caxton in 1481, a fact
which made the Flemish form of the *beast epic* perhaps the most
significant in England. For evidences of the influence in English
literature, see Spenser's *Mother Hubberds Tale* and Chaucer's
*Nun's Priest's Tale.* A full discussion of the *beast epic* and its
probable history is given in Lucien Foulet's *Le Roman de Renard.*

**Beast Fable:** A short TALE in which the principal actors are animals.
See FABLE.

**Beat Generation:** A term applied to a group of contemporary poets
and novelists who are in romantic rebellion against the culture and
the value systems of present-day America, and express their revolt
through literary works of loose STRUCTURE and slang DICTION asserting the essentially valueless nature of existence. Their leaders are
the poet Allen Ginsberg and the novelist Jack Kerouac. The term is
also used to describe the coterie groups into which these writers
tend to form.

**Beginning Rime:** RIME that occurs in the first syllable or syllables
of a VERSE.

**Belief, The Problem of:** The critical question of the degree to which
the aesthetic value of a literary work for a given reader is necessarily or properly affected by the acceptability to that reader of its
doctrine or philosophic or religious assumptions. Although the
question is certainly as old as Plato, it has assumed an unusual

relevance in present-day criticism because the traditional answer—
that doctrinal acceptability is one of the necessary conditions for
aesthetic value—has been brought into serious question by a group
of critics, notably those usually designated NEW CRITICS. See
AUTOTELIC.

**Belles-Lettres:** Literature, more especially that body of writing,
comprising DRAMA, POETRY, FICTION, CRITICISM, and ESSAYS which
lives because of inherent imaginative and artistic rather than
scientific or intellectual qualities. Lewis Carroll's *Alice in Wonderland,* for example, belongs definitely to the province of *belles-
lettres,* while the mathematical works of the same man, Charles
Lutwidge Dodgson, do not. Now sometimes used to characterize
light or artificial writing.

**Bestiary:** A type of literature, particularly popular during the
medieval centuries, in which the habits of beasts, birds, and
reptiles were made the text for allegorical and mystical Christian
teachings. These *bestiaries* often ascribed human attributes to
animals and were designed to moralize and to expound church
doctrine. The natural history employed is fabulous rather than
scientific and has helped to make popular in literature such ab-
normalities as the phoenix, the siren, and the unicorn. Many of
the qualities literature familiarly attributes to animals owe their
origin to the *bestiaries.* The development of the type is first attributed to Physiologus, a Greek sermonizer of about A.D. 150, but
the form was rapidly taken over by Christian preachers and hom-
ilists throughout Europe. The *bestiary* in one form or another has
been current in various world literatures: Anglo-Saxon, Arabic,
Armenian, English, Ethiopic, French, German, Icelandic, Provençal,
Spanish.

**Bible:** Derived from a Greek term meaning "little books," *Bible* is
now applied to the collection of writings known as the Holy Scriptures, the sacred writings of the Christian religion. Of the two chief
parts, the Old Testament consists of the sacred writings of the
ancient Hebrews, and the New Testament of writings of the early
Christian period. The Jewish Scriptures include three collections—
The Law, The Prophets, and Writings—written in ancient Hebrew
at various dates in the pre-Christian era. The New Testament books

were written in the Greek DIALECT employed in Mediterranean countries about the time of Christ. An important Greek form of the Hebrew Bible is the Septuagint, dating from the Alexandrian period (third century B.C.). Latin versions were made in very early times, both of the Old and New Testament books, including many of the "Apocrypha" (see APOCHRYPHAL), the most important being that made by St. Jerome about A.D. 400, known as the Vulgate—the Bible of the Middle Ages. See next three topics.

**Bible as Literature:** The high literary value of many parts of the Bible has been almost universally recognized. Such English authors as Milton, Wordsworth, Scott, Carlyle, and many others have paid tribute to Biblical literature, Coleridge even rating the style of Isaiah and the Epistle to the Hebrews as far superior to that of Homer or Virgil or Milton. The literary qualities of the Bible are accounted for partly by the themes treated, partly by the poetic character of the Hebrew tongue, and partly by the literary skill exhibited by Biblical writers. Professor Cook calls the themes of Biblical literature "the greatest that literature can treat": God, man, the physical universe, and their interrelations. Such problems as human morality, man's relation to the unseen world, and ultimate human destinies are treated with a simplicity, sincerity, intensity, and vigor seldom matched in world literature. The character of the Hebrew language, abounding in words and phrases of CONCRETE sensuous appeal and lacking the store of ABSTRACT words characteristic of the Greek, imparted an emotional and imaginative richness to Hebrew writings of a sort which lends itself readily to translation (the idea of pride, for example, is expressed by "puffed up"). The Bible is partly in prose and partly in verse, the principles of Hebrew verse being ACCENT and PARALLELISM rather than meter. The literary types found in the Bible have been variously classified. A few examples may be given: the short story, Ruth, Jonah, Esther; biographical narrative, the story of Abraham in Genesis; love LYRIC, Song of Solomon; the battle ODE, the song of Deborah (Judges, v); EPIGRAM, in Proverbs and elsewhere; devotional LYRIC, Psalms; dramatic philosophical poem, Job; ELEGY, lament of David for Saul and Jonathan (II Samuel, i, 19–27); LETTERS, the epistles of Paul; etc.

**Bible, English Translations of:** From Caedmon (seventh century) to Wycliffe (fourteenth century) there were from time to time TRANSLATIONS and PARAPHRASES in OLD ENGLISH and in MIDDLE ENGLISH of various parts of the BIBLE. They were all based upon the Latin Vulgate edition. Some were in prose and some in verse. The parts most frequently translated were the Gospels, the Psalms, and the Pentateuch. The Caedmonian paraphrases (seventh century) are extant, but Bede's prose translation of a portion of the gospel of St. John (seventh century) is not preserved. From the ninth century come some GLOSSES of the Book of Psalms and prose translations by King Alfred. The West Saxon Gospels and the GLOSSES in the Lindisfarne Gospels date from the tenth century, while Aelfric's incomplete translations of the Old Testament date from the late tenth and early eleventh centuries. The subordinate position occupied by the English language for some time after the eleventh century perhaps accounts for the lack of translations in MIDDLE ENGLISH times until the fourteenth century, when there was some renewed activity in preparing English versions and commentaries, notably by Richard Rolle of Hampole. In 1382 came the first edition of the Wycliffe Bible, largely the work of Wycliffe himself. A revision of this work, chiefly the work of John Purvey, 1388, though interdicted by the Church from 1408 to 1534, circulated freely in manuscript form for the next 150 years.

Printed English Bibles first appeared in the sixteenth century, products of the new learning of the HUMANISTS and the zeal of the Protestant Reformation. They were mainly based upon Greek and Hebrew manuscripts, or recent translations of such manuscripts. A list of important English translations follows: (1) William Tyndale —the New Testament (1525–26), the Pentateuch (1530), Jonah (1531). Tyndale is credited with the creation of much of the picturesque phraseology which characterizes his and later English translations. (2) Miles Coverdale, first complete printed English Bible (1535), based upon Tyndale and a Swiss-German translation. (3) "Matthew's" Bible (1537), probably done by John Rogers, based upon Tyndale and Coverdale, is important as a source for later translations. (4) Taverner's Bible (1539), based on "Matthew's" Bible, but revealing a tendency to greater use of native English words. Not influential. (5) The Great Bible (1539), sometimes called Cranmer's Bible, because Cranmer sponsored it and wrote a preface for the second edition (1540)—a very large volume designed to be chained to its position in the churches for the use of the public. Coverdale superintended its preparation. It

is based largely on "Matthew's" Bible. (6) The Geneva Bible
(1560), the joint work of English Protestant exiles in Geneva, including Coverdale and William Whittington, who had published in
1557 in Geneva an English New Testament which was the first
version in English divided into the familiar chapters and verses. The
Geneva Bible was dedicated to Queen Elizabeth and included
woodcuts, maps, tables, and marginal notes. It became the great
Bible of the Puritans and ran through sixty editions between 1560
and 1611. The phraseology was colored by Calvinistic tendencies.
(7) Bishops' Bible (1568), prepared by eight bishops and others
and issued to combat the Calvinistic, anti-episcopal tendencies of
the Geneva Bible. (8) The Rheims-Douai Bible (1582), a Catholic
translation based upon the Vulgate, issued to counteract the Puritan
Geneva Bible and the Episcopal Bishops' Bible. The Old Testament
section was not actually printed till 1609.

By far the most important and influential of English Bibles is
the "Authorized" or King James Version (1611). It is a revision
of the Bishops' Bible and was sponsored by King James I. The
translators, about fifty of the leading Biblical scholars of the time,
including PURITANS, made use of Greek and Hebrew texts. This
version is still the most widely read English Bible and it exerted a
most profound influence upon the language and literature of the
English and American peoples through the seventeenth, eighteenth,
and nineteenth centuries.

The Revised Version (1885) and the standard American edition
of the Revised Version (1901), the joint work of English and
American scholars, were modern versions which aimed chiefly at
scholarly accuracy.

A group of American Biblical scholars produced in 1946 an
extensive revision of the King James Version of the New Testament,
bringing to bear upon it the wealth of textual discovery and
scholarship which we now have, and in 1952 they added the Old
Testament. This translation, known as the Revised Standard Version,
although generally considered inferior to the King James Version
from a literary point of view, has already attained wide usage because of its greater accuracy and clarity. A number of renderings
into contemporary and idiomatic English have been made in this
century of the whole or parts of the Bible. Notable among them are
the translations into American idiom by James Moffatt and by
Edgar Goodspeed and the translations into British idiom by J. B.
Phillips and by Father Ronald Knox.

**Bible, Influence on Literature:** The unparalleled influence of the BIBLE upon English literature, though widely recognized, is so subtly pervasive that it can merely be suggested, not closely traced. Much of its influence has been indirect—through its effect upon language and upon the mental and moral interests of the English and American people. J. R. Green (*Short History of the English People*, Ch. viii) notes the fact that the first English Bibles of the sixteenth century brought to the common people a new world by the revival of ancient Hebrew literature: "Legend and annal, war-song and psalm, state-roll and biography, the mighty voices of the prophets, the parables of the evangelists, stories of mission journeys, of perils by the sea and among the heathen, philosophic arguments, apocalyptic visions, all were flung broadcast over minds unoccupied for the most part by any rival learning." The picturesque imagery and phraseology were an enriching element in the lives of the people, and profoundly affected not only their conduct but their language and literary tastes. "As a mere literary monument, the English version of the Bible remains the noblest example of the English tongue, while its perpetual use made it from the instant of its appearance the standard of our language."

Great authors commonly show a familiarity with the Bible, and few great English and American writers of the seventeenth, eighteenth, nineteenth, and twentieth centuries can be read with satisfaction by one ignorant of Biblical literature. Professor Cook suggests the various ways in which the Authorized Version of the Bible has affected subsequent English literature: use of Scriptural themes (Milton's *Paradise Lost*, Bunyan's *Pilgrim's Progress*, Byron's *Cain*); use of Scriptural phraseology; allusions or modified quotations (as "selling birthright" for a "mess of pottage"); incorporation, conscious or unconscious, of Biblical phraseology into common speech ("highways and hedges," "thorn in the flesh," "a soft answer," etc., etc.). The Bible is thought to have been highly influential in substituting pure English words for Latin words (Tyndale's vocabulary is 97 per cent English, that of the Authorized Version, 93 per cent). The style of many writers has been directly affected by study of the Bible, as has Bunyan's, Lincoln's, and Hemingway's. Whitman's prosodic methods as well as his vocabulary demonstrate a great debt to the Hebrew poets and prophets. Novelists of twentieth-century America are increasingly turning to the Bible for themes and plots; among the many examples are Hemingway's *The Sun Also Rises*, Faulkner's *Light in August* and *A Fable*, and Steinbeck's *The Grapes of Wrath* and *East of Eden*.

**Bibliography:** Used in several senses. The term may be applied to a SUBJECT BIBLIOGRAPHY; this is a list of books or other printed (or manuscript) material on any chosen subject. A SUBJECT BIBLIOGRAPHY may aim at comprehensiveness, even completeness; or it may be selective, intended to list only such works as are most important, or most easily available, or most closely related with a book or article to which it may be attached. *Bibliographies* following a serious essay, for example, may be merely a list of sources used by the writer of the essay, or they may be meant to point out to the reader sources of additional information on the subject. In a related use, the word designates a list of works of a particular country, author, or printer ("national" and "trade" *bibliography*). *Bibliographies* of these kinds are sometimes called ENUMERATIVE BIBLIOGRAPHIES. The process of making such lists either by students or by professional bibliographers is also referred to as *bibliography*.

In the historical sense, as used by book collectors, bibliophiles, and scholars, *bibliography* means the history of book production, history of writing, printing, binding, illustrating, and publishing. It involves a consideration of the details of book-making. *Bibliography* in this sense is sometimes used by scholars in textual criticism —the employing of bibliographical evidence to help "settle such questions as that of the order and relative value of different editions of a book; whether certain sections of a book were originally intended to form part of it or were added afterwards; whether a later edition was printed from an earlier one, and from which . . . and a number of other problems of a similar kind, which may often have a highly important literary bearing."[1] This sort of bibliographical work has been much stressed in the twentieth century, especially by members of the London Bibliographical Society, one striking result being the discovery of the forged dates on certain QUARTOS of Shakespeare's plays, actually printed in 1619 but assigned earlier dates on the title pages.

Another use of the term *bibliography* is to denote the methods of work of student and author: reading, research, taking of notes, compilation of *bibliography*, preparation of manuscript for the press, publication, etc. These last two uses of the word are of especial interest to advanced students who take university courses in *bibliography*.

"A *bibliography* of *bibliographies*" means a list of lists of works

[1]Ronald B. McKerrow, "Notes on Bibliographical Evidence," etc., *Transactions of the Bibliographical Society,* Vol. XII, 1914.

dealing with a given subject or subjects. An "annotated *bibliography*" is one in which some or all of the items listed are followed by brief descriptive or critical comment.

R. B. McKerrow's *An Introduction to Bibliography for Literary Students* and Fredson Bowers' *The Principles of Bibliographical Description* deal extensively and authoritatively with the entire subject.

**Billingsgate:** Coarse, vulgar, violent, abusive language. The term is derived from the fact that the fish-wives in Billingsgate fish market in London achieved a certain distinction from the scurrility of their language.

**Biography:** For over a thousand years *biography* has held a place of varying importance in the ANNALS of English literature. It is natural that this should be, since *biography*, as a literary form, satisfies three inherent promptings of man: the commemorative instinct, the didactic or moralizing instinct, and, perhaps most important of all, the instinct of curiosity. From these three motives *biography* derives its impetus.

*Biography Distinguished from Allied Forms.*—With *biography* have come several related forms—LETTERS, MEMOIRS, DIARIES and JOURNALS, AUTOBIOGRAPHY—which, though they spring from these same desires of men, must be distinguished from *biography* proper. MEMOIRS, DIARIES, JOURNALS, and AUTOBIOGRAPHY are closely related to each other in that each is recollection written down by the subject himself. The writer tells those items of his career which he is willing to share with others and recalls those enthusiasms which seem to him to have dictated his activity. LETTERS afford a different angle to the subject's life. Usually collected by a literary executor after the decease of the subject, they are likely to be colored by various prejudices and purposes. The subject himself may or may not have been spontaneous in his correspondence. The editor may or may not be completely honest in his printing of the letters. Delightful as this kind of thing often is, it falls short of *biography* in that the reader sees the subject only at certain times and under special conditions. Nearer the *biography* than any of these forms —and yet not an exact parallel—is the "life and times" book. In this kind of writing the author is concerned with two points: the life of his central figure and the period in which this figure lived. The writer may do a very fascinating book, one both interesting and instructive, but pure *biography*, in the more modern sense, does not look two ways; it centers its whole attention on the character and career of its subject.

*What Is Biography?*—Since *biography*, then, is not to be confused with these other forms, it is well to see exactly what it is. In England the word *biography*, as a term denoting a form of writing, first came into use with Dryden, who, in 1683, defined it as "the history of particular men's lives." But the matter is hardly so simple as this. Since its earliest appearance as a written form— and it existed long before Dryden—*biography* has meant different things to different people. A definition of *biography* in the eighteenth century would not fit the conception held in, say, the sixteenth. And during the first quarter of the twentieth century very different qualities have been insisted upon. A "history of particular men's lives" may serve, perhaps, as a unifying principle for the numerous theories of *biography*, but it falls short of a definition of the term in the twentieth century.

Today the term carries with it certain definite demands. It must be a HISTORY, but an accurate HISTORY; one which paints not only one aspect of the man but all important aspects. It must be the life of a "particular" man focused clearly on that man with more casual reference to the background of the social and political institutions of his time. It must present the facts accurately and must make some effort to interpret these facts in such a way as to present character and habits of mind. It must avoid panegyric and the didactic as the man himself might have avoided the plague. But, on the other hand, it must emphasize personality. And this personality must be the central thesis of the book. If the biographer looks at the times, it must be only with the purpose of presenting a well-constructed and unified impression of the personality of his subject; if he introduces LETTERS and ANECDOTES (as he surely will) it will be only such anecdotes and letters as reflect this central conception of personality. *Biography* today, then, may be defined as the accurate presentation of the life history from birth to death of an individual, this presentation being secured through an honest effort to interpret the facts of the life in such a way as to offer a unified impression of the character, mind, and personality of the subject.

*The Development of English Biography: The Commemorative Purpose.*—Just how this modern attitude differs from past conceptions may best be appreciated after a brief survey of the history of the *biography* as a literary type. Harold Nicolson, in his *De-*

*velopment of English Biography*, states that "we can trace the ancestry of English biography to the ancient runic inscriptions which celebrated the lives of heroes and recorded the exploits of deceased and legendary warriors." He reports it again as an element in such early Anglo-Saxon verse as *Beowulf* and the *Widsith* fragment. And in these early manifestations we find what was, probably, the first conception of *biography*—the commemorative instinct, the "cenotaph-urge." These accounts were written to glorify, and glorification, in far too many *biographies*, has remained as a prominent intent of the biographer. It has taken years to shake that conception off; indeed even now it is often present.

*The Didactic Purpose.*—This desire to commemorate greatness was, later on, united with a second purpose—the encouragement of morality. This purpose accounts for HAGIOGRAPHY, records of saints. The church took a hand. Great men and women were commemorated for their virtue, their vices being conveniently overlooked. The lives of the saints occupied the attention of scholars in the monasteries. One list of early English historical material reports 1,277 writings, almost all of which were devoted to the glorification of one or another Irish or British saint. Even Bede (who died in 735) was little more than a hagiographer. It was not until Bishop Asser (893) wrote his *Life of Alfred the Great* that anything appears which very closely resembles *biography*. Here was the life narrative of a layman told in Latin; but here, too, were the two early purposes of the biographer —commemoration and didactic moralizing.

*The Beginnings of Pure Biography.*—With Monk Eadmer of the twelfth century English *biography* reached another milestone. Eadmer, in his *Vita Anselmi*, somehow managed to humanize his subject beyond the capacity of former biographers. He introduced LETTERS into his narrative to make his points; he reported ANECDOTES and conversation in a way which definitely brightened his pages. He wrote, in short, what Nicolson considers the first pure *biography* in England. This same century, the twelfth, saw the dying out—though not the disappearance—of the hagiographer and moralizing motive. Romance was coming to the front. Living began to take on some joy. And with this lighter mood of the fourteenth and fifteenth centuries *biography* gradually became somewhat less serious, less commemorative, less didactic.

*Biography Definitely "Arrives."*—For the purposes of this brief survey, however, this summary need not pause again until the middle of the sixteenth century when William Roper (1496–1578), More's son-in-law, wrote what is now most often referred to as the first English *biography*, his *Life of Sir Thomas More*, and George Cavendish (1500–1561) wrote his *Life of Wolsey*. With these two books, English *biography* had most certainly arrived as a recognized form of literature. The didactic purpose was still obvious, the commemorative spirit was still present. But both books make a greater effort to avoid prejudice than had before manifested itself in English *biography*. Both books resorted to EPISODE and ANECDOTE and fairly vivid DIALOGUE. Both books devoted their space to the life of one man, the *Wolsey* beginning with the birth of the subject and ending with the death. But most important of all, both books made an avowed declaration to follow the truth. HAGIOGRAPHY and commemoration are present, but no writer before these two had made such general efforts to strike a fair balance, to write adversely of their subjects when adverse comment was necessary. And with this gesture toward the truth *biography* came more definitely into its own as a field of literature.

*The Seventeenth Century: Biographic Brevities.*—The next century, the seventeenth, did little to advance *biography*. It was, in general, a time of brevities. The character sketch, the ANA, flourished. People were interested in ethical motives of one sort or another. The CHARACTER was the contemporary enthusiasm. John Aubrey wrote his frank, gossipy *Minutes of Lives* as brief estimates of his contemporaries. Thomas Fuller wrote his *Worthies*. DIARIES, LETTERS, and MEMOIRS were plentiful;—the *Memoirs of Lady Fanshawe* and the *Memoirs of Colonel Hutchinson* serve as examples. The first worth-while AUTOBIOGRAPHY, perhaps, is that of Lord Herbert. But were it not for Izaak Walton's *Lives* the century would be almost a complete loss so far as *biography* is concerned. Walton, who wrote his *Lives* from 1640 to 1678, has been considered by some the first English professional biographer since he attempted the form deliberately and sustained it over a long period. Walton, too, contributed breeziness to the form, reverting to the manner of Monk Eadmer in his use of LETTERS and adding for himself supposititious conversations between his subject and others. Opposed to Walton and his biographical manner there was Thomas Sprat, whose *Life of Cowley* appeared in 1668. Sprat is important to our purpose for his manner. To him it is that the Victorian demand for "decency" in *biography* seems largely due, for Sprat wrote a life that was a cold and dignified thing, formal and proper, emasculated and virtuous. "The tradition of 'discreet' biography," writes one critic, "owes its wretched origin to him."

*The Eighteenth Century: Biography at Its Best.*—If *biography* almost stood still during the seventeenth century, the eighteenth saw it march forward to the greatest accomplishment it has enjoyed. Boswell's *Life of Johnson* stands, probably for all time, at the head of any list of *biographies*. Two lesser luminaries were Roger North and William Mason—North (*Lives of the Norths*), who insisted that panegyric be avoided and wrote brightly and colloquially, and Mason (*Life and Writings of Gray*), who carried further the use of letters and pretty largely left his reader to deduce the sort of man his subject was by a simple placing before the reader of a wide range of illustrative material. Dr. Johnson himself dignified *biography* by developing a philosophy for the writing of the form and by his insistence that to a real biographer truth was much more important than respect for a dead man or his relatives. To Dr. Johnson probably more than to any other critic of the form goes the credit of having raised *biography* to the rank of literature and art. In his *Lives of the Poets* he himself practiced his doctrines. The writing of the supreme English *biography* was, however, reserved for Johnson's biographer—James Boswell. This is no place to estimate anew that frequently praised book. What is important is the new twist which Boswell gave to biographic method. He used most of the methods developed by earlier writers, but he wrought of them a new combination. Humor of a sort was here; here was introduced a great wealth of petty detail from which the reader might make for himself his deductive analysis; here, too, were the ANECDOTE and ANA elements of the seventeenth century; and, greatest of all, here were intimacy and personal comment. To Boswell was given the privilege of making *biography* actual, real, convincing. Here at last were the commemorative elements subordinated; the didactic qualities minimized. In the work of James Boswell *biography* painted a living, breathing human being.

*Victorian Biography Becomes Discreet.*—The Boswell tradition was in a fair way of being accepted when Victorianism, with its tedious studiousness, its two-volume "life and letters" *biography*, its "authorized" biographers more or less controlled by the family and relatives of the hero, blurred the picture. True enough, in the nineteenth century before Victorianism stultified *biography*, there had been Tom Moore's *Life of Sheridan* and *Letters and Journals of Lord Byron;* as well as Lockhart's *Life of Scott.* But on the whole the freedom which Boswell had brought to this writing was restricted and confined by the Victorians. Religious orthodoxy, piety, and moral judgments again were in the saddle. Tennyson spoke for the epoch when he thundered, "What business has the public to know about Byron's wildnesses? He has given them fine work and they ought to be satisfied." HAGIOGRAPHY had returned.

*The Twentieth Century Becomes Objective and Psychological.*— The growing scientific attitude had become operative on *biography* by the early years of the twentieth century, and it brought with it not only a rejection of the polite reticence of the Victorian biographer but also a direct attack upon the admiration of famous men. Lytton Strachey, in *Eminent Victorians* (1918) and *Queen Victoria* (1921), wrote lives that were brief, ironic, artistically shaped and (his critics declare) too often inaccurate. Coupled with Strachey's method have been the assumptions of the depth psychologists, particularly of Freud, and our century has seen a host of biographical studies which are virtually attempts to read the hidden emotional life and even the unconscious experiences and motives of the subject. Van Wyck Brooks' studies of Mark Twain and of Henry James as the products of frustration are particularly significant for the American literary student, although Gamaliel Bradford's "psychographs" may have more enduring value as *biography.* Philip Guedalla in England and Carl Sandburg and Douglas Southall Freeman in America have made the twentieth century not only a period in which *biography* has been popular and widely read and written but also one in which at its best it has achieved high distinction. (See Donald A. Stauffer, *English Biography Before 1700* and *The Art of Biography in Eighteenth Century England;* Harold Nicholson, *Development of English Biography;* and John A. Garraty, *The Nature of Biography.*)

**Blank Verse:** *Blank verse* may be said to consist of unrimed lines of ten syllables each, the second, fourth, sixth, eighth, and tenth syllables bearing the ACCENTS (IAMBIC PENTAMETER). This form has generally been accepted as that best adapted to dramatic verse in English and is commonly used for long poems whether dramatic, philosophic, or narrative. Because of its freedom it appears easy to write, but good *blank verse* probably demands more artistry and genius than any other verse form. The freedom gained through lack of RIME is offset by the demands for richness to be secured through its privileges. This richness may be obtained by the skillful poet through a variety of means: the shifting of the CAESURA, or pause, from place to place within the line; the shifting of the STRESS among syllables; the use of the run-on line, which permits of thought-grouping in large or small blocks (these thought-groups being variously termed verse "paragraphs" or verse STANZAS); variation in tonal qualities by changing DICTION from passage to passage; and, finally, the adaptation of the form to reproduction of differences in the speech of characters in dramatic and narrative verse and to differences of emotional expression.

Alden attributes the development of *blank verse* as an English form to the influence of classical HUMANISM "the representatives of which grew skeptical as to the use of rime, on the ground that it was not found in classical poetry." It appears to have first found general favor in England as a medium for dramatic expression, but with Milton it was turned to EPIC use and since then has been employed in the writing of IDYLLS and LYRICS. The distinction of the first use of *blank verse* in English, though the claims are not quite clear, is generally given to Surrey, who used the form in his translation of parts of the *Aeneid* (made prior to 1547). The earliest dramatic use of *blank verse* in English was in Sackville and Norton's *Gorboduc*, 1565; the earliest use in didactic verse was in Gascoigne's *Steel Glass*, 1576; but it was only with Marlowe (prior to 1593) that the form first reached the hands of a master capable of using its range of possibilities and passing it on for Shakespeare and Milton to develop to its ultimate perfection. In more recent times some critics have manifested a willingness to extend the meaning of the term to include almost any metrical unrimed form, and not to restrict its use to verses of ten syllables and five accents.

**Blues:** An Afro-American folk-song of recent development among the Negroes of the southern United States. A *blues* is characteristically short (three-line STANZA), melancholy in tone, and marked by frequent REPETITION. Probably each *blues* was originally the composition of one person, but so readily are *blues* appropriated and changed that in practice they are a branch of folk literature. The following is an example:

Gwine lay my head right on de railroad track,
Gwine lay my head right on de railroad track,
'Cause my baby, she won't take me back.

For a full discussion of the subject, see *Blues,* by W. C. Handy, himself the author of the most famous of *blues* songs, "The St. Louis Blues."

**Bluestockings:** A term which suggests women of the intellectual type. It gained currency after 1750 as a result of its application (for reasons not now easy to establish beyond dispute) to a group of women of literary and intellectual tastes who held in London assemblies or "conversations" to which "literary and ingenious men" were invited. It was the English equivalent of the French *salon.* There was no formal organization and the personnel of the group changed from time to time, so that no "membership" list can be given with assurance or completeness. Among the women *bluestockings* were Mrs. Elizabeth Montagu (the "Queen of the Blues"), Hannah More, Fanny Burney, and Mrs. Hester Chapone. Horace Walpole was one of the male "members," and Dr. Samuel Johnson, Edmund Burke, and David Garrick were at times frequent visitors. The activities of the group were directed toward encouraging an interest in literature and fostering the recognition of literary genius (see PRIMITIVISM), and hence helped remove the odium which had attached to earlier "learned ladies." It is used today as a term of opprobrium to describe pretentiously intellectual and pedantic females.

**Blurb:** A term applied in the American book trade to the descriptive matter printed on the jackets of new books, usually extravagant in its claims. The term was invented by Gelett Burgess in 1914.

**Bombast:** Ranting, insincere, extravagant language. Grandiloquence. Elizabethan TRAGEDY, especially early SENECAN plays, contains much bombastic style, marked by extravagant IMAGERY. An example may be quoted from Shakespeare's *Hamlet* (Act II, Sc. 2):

Roasted in wrath and fire,
And thus o'er-sized with coagulate gore,
With eyes like carbuncles, the hellish Pyrrhus
Old grandsire Priam seeks.

**Bon mot:** A witty REPARTEE or statement. A clever saying.

**Book Sizes:** To understand the terms, QUARTO, OCTAVO, and the rest, used in describing *book sizes*, it is first of all necessary to know the principle determining these sizes. This principle is best understood by imagining before one a sheet of paper, "foolscap" size, 17 inches by 13½ inches.

When this paper is folded along 1–2, 3–4, and 5–6, the resulting folds mark off the sizes of book pages cut from the large foolscap sheet. Thus 1–2–7–8 represents one of two leaves cut from the original foolscap and is, therefore, a FOLIO (Latin for *leaf*) sheet or page; 2–3–4–7 represents one fourth of the original sheet and, therefore, gives us a QUARTO page; 2–3–5–6 constitutes one eighth of the original and gives us an OCTAVO page. A book size, then, is determined by the number of book leaves cut from a single large sheet. To determine the number of pages cut from the original sheet count the number of pages to a SIGNATURE; this may often be done by noting the occurrence of the SIGNATURE marks (themselves sometimes called SIGNATURES) which appear at regular intervals at the foot of a page. These symbols are usually numerals or letters and may be found regularly in early printed books and sometimes in recently printed ones. They indicate the beginning of new signatures. *The number of leaves (not pages) in a single* SIGNATURE *shows the number of leaves cut from the original sheet and is, therefore, the indication of the book size.* When there are two leaves to the SIGNATURE, the book is a FOLIO; when there are four leaves, it is a QUARTO; and so on. The table below shows in convenient outline form the principle explained above as it manifests itself in the more frequently used book sizes.

| No. of Leaves | Pages to Signature | Name |
|:---:|:---:|:---|
| 2 | 4 | Folio |
| 4 | 8 | Quarto (4to) |
| 8 | 16 | Octavo (8vo) |
| 12 | 24 | duodecimo (12mo) |
| 16 | 32 | sixteenmo (16mo) |
| 32 | 64 | thirty-twomo (32mo) |
| 64 | 128 | sixty-fourmo (64mo) |

This would all be very simple but for the fact that in modern printing there is a variety of sizes of original stock. In addition to the "foolscap 8vo" in our example, we may have Post 8vo, Demy 8vo, Crown 8vo, Royal 8vo, etc., the terms Demy, Crown, and the others referring to varying sizes of original sheets which, in turn, give varying sizes of book pages even when the number of leaves cut from the sheets is the same. So complicated has the whole question of book sizes become that expert bibliographers urge more attention to the position of the watermark on the page (a guide to book measurements too complicated to discuss here) and even then frequently give up the question in despair. Publishers arbitrarily use 12mo., OCTAVO, etc., for books of certain sizes regardless of the number of pages to the signature. For a full discussion of the subject see *An Introduction to Bibliography,* Ronald B. McKerrow, p. 164.

**Bourgeois Drama:** A loose term applied to plays in which the life of the common folk rather than that of the courtly or the rich is depicted. Such widely differing kinds of plays as Heywood's *Interludes, Gammer Gurton's Needle,* Dekker's *Shoemaker's Holiday* (REALISTIC COMEDY), and Lillo's *The London Merchant* (DOMESTIC TRAGEDY) are embraced in the term.

**Bourgeois Literature:** Literature produced primarily to appeal to the middle-class reader. Compare BOURGEOIS DRAMA, where *bourgeois* does not denote the class of readers but the social sphere of the action of the play.

**Bowdlerize:** To expurgate a book or piece of writing by omitting all offensive, indecorous passages. *Bowdlerize* derives its significance from the fact that Thomas Bowdler, an English physician, published (in 1818) an expurgated edition of Shakespeare.

**Brahmins:** Members of the highest caste among the Hindus; by ironic extension applied to the literary figures of New England in the last half of the nineteenth century and the early years of the twentieth, because they were considered to be clinging to the mid-century attitudes of Lowell, Holmes, and Longfellow long after their vitality was gone; the major supporters of the GENTEEL TRADITION.

**Breve:** The name of the symbol ( ‿ ) used to indicate a short syllable in the SCANSION of QUANTITATIVE VERSE.

**Brief:** A condensed statement, a résumé, of the main arguments or ideas presented in a speech or piece of writing. In legal practice, a formal summary of laws and authorities bearing on the main points of a case; in church history, a papal letter less formal than a bull.

**British Museum:** Of importance to students of literature since it houses probably the most important library in the world. The collection, founded in 1753 through a bequest from Sir Hans Sloane, now embraces over 5,000,000 items. It is located in Great Russell Street, in Bloomsbury, London. The *British Museum* is particularly wealthy in its collection of valuable manuscripts including, besides the famous Harleian and Cottonian MSS., a series of documents from the third century to the present. Particularly noteworthy are its collections comprising English historical chronicles, Anglo-Saxon materials, charters, Arthurian romances, the Burney Collection of classical MSS., Greek papyri, Irish, French, and Italian MSS., and the genealogical records of English families. From time to time it has been given by bequest special libraries such as Archbishop Cranmer's Collection, the Thomas Collection, the C. M. Cracherode Collection, and the Sir Joseph Banks Collection. Other important features are its assortment of items from American, Chinese and Oriental, Hebrew, and Slavonic literatures. Some four thousand newspapers are filed and bound. According to the British copyright law the Museum was to secure copies of every publication seeking copyright protection. The result of all this is an astonishing grouping together in one place of the learning and literatures of the world, so important a grouping that every advanced student of English and world literatures hopes for an opportunity to work in its archives.

**Broadside Ballad:** Soon after the development of printing in England BALLADS were prepared for circulation on FOLIO sheets, printed on one side only, two pages to the sheet, and two columns to the page. Because of their manner of publication these were termed *broadsides*. In quality these BALLADS ranged from reproductions of old popular BALLADS of real literary distinction to semi-illiterate screeds with little poetic quality. The subjects of these *broadsides* were of wide variety: accidents, dying speeches of criminals, miraculous events of one sort or another, religious and political harangues. They were often satirical in nature and frequently personal in their invective. In the sixteenth century, the heyday of their popularity, they served, as one critic states, as a "people's yellow journal." A few of the many modern collections of *broadside ballads* may be cited: *Roxburghe Ballads,* 9 vols.; *A Pepysian Garland* and *The Pack of Antolycus,* both edited by H. E. Rollins.

**Broken Rime:** A term describing the breaking of a word at the end of a verse in order to produce a RIME. Although the effect is apt to be comic, it is also used by serious poets, notably Gerard Manley Hopkins. The opening lines of his "The Windhover" illustrate *broken rime:*

> I caught this morning morning's minion, king-
> dom of daylight's dauphin, dapple-dawn-drawn Falcon, in
> his riding
> Of the rolling level underneath him steady air, and striding
> High there, how he rung upon the rein of a wimpling wing.

**Brook Farm:** A UTOPIAN experiment in communal living, sponsored by the Transcendental Club of Boston. The farm, located at West Roxbury, Massachusetts, nine miles from Boston, was taken over in 1841 by a joint stock company, headed by George Ripley. The full name of the organization was "The Brook Farm Institute of Agriculture and Education." The basic reasons for the scheme were efforts to provide for the residents opportunity for cultural pursuits and leisure at little cost, the farm being supposed, through the rotation of labor of the members, to support the residents who, in most of their time, were to be free to attend lectures, read, write, and discuss intellectual problems. No doubt the project was much influenced by the doctrines of François Fourier and Robert Owen. It should be noted that while many transcendentalists manifested an active interest in the enterprise, the movement was in no proper sense the outgrowth of a general activity on the part of all transcendentalists. Hawthorne (see the *Blithedale Romance*) was there for a period as were other prominent leaders, but such people as Emerson, Alcott, and Margaret Fuller never actively took part. Dissension among the members, the discovery that the soil was not fertile enough to bring the necessary return from the labor expended, and the burning of a new and uninsured "phalanstery," were some of the reasons which in 1846 brought about the failure of the project. See TRANSCENDENTALISM.

**Bucolic:** A term used to characterize PASTORAL writing, particularly poetry, concerned with shepherds and rural life. The treatment is usually rather formal and fanciful. In the plural, *bucolics,* the term refers collectively to the PASTORAL literature of such writers as Theocritus and Virgil. In the present loose usage the expression connotes simply poetry of rustic background and is not necessarily restricted to verse with the conventional PASTORAL elements. See PASTORAL.

**Burlesque:** A form of comic art characterized by ridiculous exaggeration. This distortion is secured in a variety of ways: the sublime may be made absurd, honest emotions may be turned to SENTIMENTALITY, a serious subject may be treated frivolously or a frivolous subject seriously. Perhaps the essential quality which makes for *burlesque* is the discrepancy between subject-matter and STYLE. That is, a STYLE ordinarily dignified may be used for nonsensical matter, or a STYLE very nonsensical may be used to ridicule a weighty subject. *Burlesque,* as a form of art, manifests itself in sculpture, painting, and even architecture, as well as in literature. This type of writing has an ancient lineage in world literature: an author of uncertain identity used it in the *Battle of the Frogs and Mice,* to TRAVESTY Homer. Aristophanes made *burlesque* popular, and in France, under Louis XIV, nothing was sacred to the satirist. Chaucer in *Sir Thopas* burlesqued MEDIEVAL ROMANCE as did Cervantes in *Don Quixote.* One of the best known uses of *burlesque* in DRAMA is Gay's *The Beggar's Opera.* In recent use the term—already broad —has been broadened to include musical plays light in nature

though not essentially *burlesque* in tone or manner. A distinction between *burlesque* and PARODY is commonly made, in which *burlesque*
is a TRAVESTY of a literary form and PARODY a TRAVESTY of a particular work. See TRAVESTY, PARODY.

**Burletta:** A term used in the late eighteenth century for a variety of
musical dramatic forms, somewhat like the BALLAD-OPERA, the EX-
TRAVAGANZA, and the PANTOMIME. One of its sponsors (George Colman, the younger) asserted that the proper use of the word was for
"a drama in rhyme, entirely musical—a short comick piece consisting of *recitative* and *singing*, wholly accompanied, more or less,
by the orchestra."

**Buskin:** A boot, thick-soled and reaching halfway to the knee, worn
by Greek tragedians with the purpose of increasing their stature,
even as comedians wore socks for the opposite purpose. By association *buskin* has come to mean TRAGEDY. Milton used "the buskin'd
stage" and "Jonson's learned SOCK" to characterize TRAGEDY and
COMEDY respectively.

**Cabal:** See ACROSTIC.

**Cacophony:** The opposite of EUPHONY; a term used to characterize
a harsh, unpleasant combination of sounds or tones. Though most
specifically a term used in the CRITICISM of POETRY, the word is
also employed to indicate any disagreeable sound effect in other
forms of writing. *Cacophony* may be an unconscious flaw in the
poet's music, resulting in harshness of sound or difficulty of articulation, or it may be used consciously for effect, as Browning and Eliot
often use it. See EUPHONY.

**Cadence:** Measured, rhythmical movement either in prose or verse.
The recurrence of EMPHASIS or ACCENT often accompanied by rising
and falling modulations of the voice. *Cadence* is related to RHYTHM,
but exists usually in larger and looser units of syllables than the
formal, metrical movement of regular verses. Properly used, *cadence*
can be made one of the most subtle and pleasing of stylistic qualities.
See FREE VERSE.

**Cæsura:** A pause or break in the metrical or rhythmical progress
of a line of VERSE. Originally, in classical literature, the *cæsura* char-

acteristically divided a FOOT between two words. Usually the *cæsura* has been placed near the middle of a VERSE. Some poets, however, have sought diversity of rhythmical effect by placing the *cæsura* anywhere from near the beginning of a line to near the end. Examples of variously placed *cæsuras* follow:

> Sleepst thou, Companion dear, || what sleep can close
> Thy eye-lids? || and remembrest what Decree
> Of yesterday, || so late hath past the lips
> Of Heav'ns Almightie. || Thou to me thy thoughts
> Wast wont, etc.
>
> —Milton

Viewed in another sense, the *cæsura* is an instrument of prose rhythm which cuts across and by varying, enriches the regularity of accentual verse. The interplay of prose sense and VERSE demand can be observed in the selection given above. Metricists who follow closely the classical distinctions use *cæsura* to indicate a pause within a FOOT and DIERESIS to indicate a pause that coincides with the end of the FOOT. This distinction is seldom made in English METRICS, where *cæsura* is employed as the generic term.

**Calendar:** See ALMANAC.

**Calligraphy:** The art of beautiful writing. In literature the significance of the term springs from the development of the art during the Middle Ages when the monks so generally gave their attention to the copying of ancient manuscripts. Much literature was preserved through their skillful penmanship.

**Calvinism:** Throughout the whole course of Western European Christian culture (and American culture as well), religious ideas and systems have profoundly affected, both directly and indirectly, literature and literary history. The great conflict of medieval times was between AUGUSTINIANISM, which would exalt the glory of God at the expense of the dignity of man (stressing original sin and the necessity of divine grace), and PELAGIANISM, which asserted man's original innocence and his ability to develop moral and spiritual power through his own efforts. ARMINIANISM was somewhat of a compromise between these positions, insisting upon the part both God and man must play in human redemption. *Calvinism* was a RENAISSANCE representative of the Augustinian point of view. At no time in the last four hundred years has the literature of England or America been free from reflections of Calvinistic thought and conduct.

Some understanding of the teachings of *Calvinism*—the charter of which is John Calvin's famous *Institutes of the Christian Religion* (1536)—is therefore important to the student of literature. Calvinistic doctrines have been summarized as follows (not all "Calvinists," of course, accepted unequivocally *all* of them): 1. God is a God of power, conceived as a king or ruler. 2. Hence the chief duty of man is to aid in making the will of God prevail. 3. This will of God can be discovered through the study of the Bible. 4. But this involves much mental work—hence the emphasis upon logical processes. The Bible furnishes the premises: man must reason from them. 5. Human nature was corrupted by Adam's sin and man therefore inherits a totally depraved nature, even infants being wholly sinful and subject to damnation. 6. Man can be saved only through God's grace by means of the Atonement. But this salvation is effective only for certain chosen ones. 7. Hence the famous doctrine of election or predestination. God must determine beforehand which individuals are to be saved, which condemned. The "elect" discover their good fortune through the inner voice or witness of the spirit. Those not chosen develop their evil natures through the agency of Satan and thus merit their hard fate. 8. Though the church and state are theoretically separate, the Church might advise the state (in New England this came to mean that only the elect might enjoy the rights of citizenship). The essential doctrines of the system are frequently summed up in the famous FIVE POINTS: (1) total depravity, man's natural inability to exercise free will, since he inherited corruption from Adam's fall; (2) unconditional election, which manifests itself through God's election of those to be saved, despite their inability to perform saving works; (3) prevenient and irresistible grace, made available in advance but only to the elect; (4) the perseverance of saints, the predetermined elect inevitably persevering in the path of holiness; and (5) limited atonement, man's corruption being partially atoned for by Christ, this atonement being provided the elect through the Holy Spirit, giving them the power to attempt to obey God's will as it is revealed in the Bible.

This system developed both zeal and intolerance on the part of the elect. It fostered education, however, which in early New England was regarded as a religious duty, and thereby profoundly affected the development of American culture. To this attitude of the

Calvinistic PURITANS may be traced much of the inspiration for such things as: the founding of many colleges and universities, the creation of a system of public schools, and the great activity of early printing presses in America—as well as the development of religious sects. Historically, especially in Europe, it is probably true that the political effects of *Calvinism* have been in the main calculated to encourage freedom and popular government.

In New England the COVENANT THEOLOGY early softened and modified *Calvinism*, but the term PURITAN in America usually refers, at least in a philosophical sense, to a belief in the doctrines of *Calvinism*. See AUGUSTINIANISM, ARMINIANISM, COVENANT THEOLOGY, PELAGIANISM.

**Canon:** (1) A standard of judgment; a criterion; (2) the authorized or accepted list of books belonging in the Christian Bible. APOCRYPHAL books are uncanonical. The term is often extended to mean the accepted list of books of any author, such as Shakespeare. Thus *Macbeth* belongs without doubt in the *canon* of Shakespeare's work, while *Sir John Oldcastle*, though printed as Shakespeare's soon after his death, is not canonical, because the evidence of Shakespeare's authorship is unconvincing. A similar use of the word is illustrated in the phrase "the Saints' *Canon*," the list of Saints actually authorized or "canonized" by the Church. See APOCRYPHA.

**Cant:** Insincere, specious language calculated to give the impression of piety and religious fervor. In critical writing the term is also used to signify the special language and phraseology characteristic of a profession or art, as "the pedagogue's cant," "the artist's cant." In this sense of a special language, the term indicates any technical or special vocabulary or dialect, as "thieves' cant," "beggars' cant," etc. More loosely still, the word signifies any insincere, superficial display of language, planned to convey an impression of conviction, but devoid of genuine emotion or feeling; that is, language used chiefly for display or effect.

**Canto:** A section or division of a long POEM. Derived from the Latin *cantus* (song) the word originally signified a section of a narrative POEM of such length as to be sung by a minstrel in one singing. Byron's *Childe Harold's Pilgrimage* is divided into *cantos*.

**Canzo:** A love song of the TROUVÈRES.

*Canzone:* A lyrical POEM, a song or BALLAD. In several ways the *canzone* is similar to the MADRIGAL. The *canzone* is a short poem consisting of equal STANZAS and an ENVOY of fewer lines than the STANZA. It is impossible to be specific as to the mechanics of the verse form since different writers have wrought rather wide variations in structure. The number of lines to the STANZA ranges from seven to twenty, and the ENVOY from three to ten. Petrarch's *canzoni* usually consisted of five or six STANZAS and the ENVOY. In general it may be said that the *canzone* form is not unlike the CHANT ROYAL though its conventions are less fixed. The *canzone* is generally conceded to have first developed in Provence during the Middle Ages and Giraud de Borneil is credited with having first evolved the pattern which has proved very popular in Italy. Others than Petrarch who have written *canzoni* are Dante, Tasso, Leopardi, Chiabrera, and Marchetti. Frequent subjects used were love, nature, and the wide range of emotional reactions to life, particularly if sad, which poets commonly present. The term and the aspects of the medieval form it designates are used by contemporary poets on occasion for poems of considerable complexity of structure.

**Caricature:** Descriptive writing which seizes upon certain individual qualities of a person and through exaggeration or distortion produces a BURLESQUE, ridiculous effect. *Caricature* more frequently is associated with drawing (cartoons) than with writing, since for writing the related types—SATIRE, BURLESQUE, and PARODY—are more generally used. *Caricature,* unlike the highest SATIRE, is likely to treat *personal* qualities, though, like SATIRE, it lends itself to the ridicule of political, religious, and social foibles.

*Carmen Figuratum:* A poem so written that the form of the printed words suggests the subject matter; the device is not common in English poetry, and is usually considered a form of false WIT. Examples are Herbert's "Easter Wings," the humorous "long and sad tail of the Mouse," in *Alice in Wonderland,* and several poems of Dylan Thomas, notably "Vision and Prayer."

**Carol (*Carole*):** In medieval times in France a *carole* was a dance, the term later being applied to the song which accompanied the dance. The leader sang the STANZAS, the other dancers singing the REFRAIN. The *carole* became very popular, and in the twelfth and thirteenth centuries spread through other European countries and was instrumental in extending the influence of the French LYRIC. Later, *carol* was used to mean any joyous song, then a HYMN of religious joy, and finally was used to designate Christmas HYMNS in particular. Some *carols*, such as "Joseph was an old man," were definitely popular, belonging to the culture of the folk, while later ones, such as Charles Wesley's "Hark, the Herald Angels Sing," are the product of more conscious and sophisticated literary effort. The Christmas HYMN is called a *noël* in France.

**Caroline:** Applied to whatever belonged to or was typical of the age of Charles I of England (1625–1642), but more particularly to the spirit of the court of Charles. Thus *Caroline* literature might mean all the literature of the time, both Cavalier and PURITAN, or it might be used more specifically to suggest that of the royalist group, such as the CAVALIER LYRISTS. *Caroline* literature was in some senses a decadent carry-over from the ELIZABETHAN and JACOBEAN periods. Melancholy not only characterized the work of the META-PHYSICAL POETS but permeated the writings of both the conflicting groups, PURITAN and Cavalier. DRAMA was decadent; ROMANTICISM was in decline; CLASSICISM was advancing; the scientific spirit was growing in spite of the absorption of the people in violent religious controversies. It was in *Caroline* times that the PURITAN migration to America was heaviest. The last segment of the RENAISSANCE in England, if the COMMONWEALTH is considered an interregnum between the RENAISSANCE and the NEO-CLASSIC PERIOD. See RENAISSANCE for a sketch of the literature; see BAROQUE, JACOBEAN, CAVALIER LYRISTS; see also "The Caroline Age" in *The Outline of Literary History.*

**Carpe diem:** "Seize the day." The phrase was used by Horace and has come to be applied generally to literature, especially to lyric POEMS, which exemplify the spirit of "Let us eat and drink, for tomorrow we shall die." The theme was a very common one in sixteenth- and seventeenth-century English love poetry; lover-poets continually were exhorting their mistresses to yield to love while they still had their youth and beauty, as in Robert Herrick's famous

> Gather ye rosebuds while ye may,
> Old Time is still a-flying;
> And this same flower that smiles today,
> Tomorrow will be dying.

**Catalexis** (adj.—**Catalectic**): Incompleteness of the last FOOT at the end of a verse; TRUNCATION at the close of a line of poetry by omission of one or two final syllables; the opposite of ANACRUSIS. *Catalexis* is one of the many ways in which the poet secures variety of metrical effects. The term ACATALECTIC is used to designate particular lines where *catalexis* is *not* employed. In the following lines written in DACTYLIC DIMETER, the second and fourth are *catalectic* because the second FOOT of each lacks the two unaccented syllables which would normally complete the DACTYL. The first and third lines, in which the unaccented syllables are *not* cut off and which therefore are metrically complete, are ACATALECTIC.

> One more unfortunate,
> Weary of breath,
> Rashly importunate,
> Gone to her death!
> —Thomas Hood

*Catalexis* is also applied to the TRUNCATION of an initial unstressed syllable; the resulting line is called HEADLESS.

**Catastasis:** In DRAMA, the heightening; the third of the four parts into which the ancients divided a play. See DRAMATIC STRUCTURE.

**Catastrophe:** The conclusion of a play, particularly a TRAGEDY; the last of the four parts into which the ancients divided a play. It is the final stage in the FALLING ACTION, ending the dramatic CONFLICT, winding up the PLOT and consisting of the actions that result from the CLIMAX. Since it usually is used in connection with a TRAGEDY and involves the death of the hero, it is sometimes used by extension to designate an unhappy ending (or event) in nondramatic FICTION and even in life. In the strict sense of DRAMATIC STRUCTURE, however, every DRAMA has a *catastrophe;* see the line in *King Lear* which reads: "Pat, he comes, like the catastrophe of the old comedy." Today, however, DÉNOUEMENT is more commonly used than *catastrophe* in this sense. See DRAMATIC STRUCTURE, DÉNOUEMENT.

**Catharsis** (or **Katharsis**): In the *Poetics* Aristotle, in defining TRAGEDY, speaks of its "through pity and fear effecting the proper purgation [*catharsis*] of these emotions," but he fails to explain what he means by "proper purgation." That a physiological METAPHOR has been used to describe the effect produced upon the emotions of the spectator by the witnessing of the tragic action is clear, but the implications of that METAPHOR—and indeed its accurate translation into concept—have been much debated in the history of CRITICISM. Two widely differing interpretations are customary today: one is that the spectator, by vicariously participating in the actions of the hero, learns through the effects upon him of fear and pity that the evil emotions of the hero are destructive and thereby has learned to avoid them in his own life (this is a didactic interpretation); the other is that the spectator's emotional conflicts are temporarily resolved and his inner agitations stilled by having an opportunity vicariously to expend fear and pity upon the tragic hero. This latter is a psychological interpretation that has undergone great subtlety of elaboration and qualification in recent years. R. B. Sharpe, in *Irony in the Drama*, suggests that the hero of a TRAGEDY comes before its conclusion to represent to the spectator "what Jung calls a symbol and Fraser a scapegoat—that is, a human figure upon whom we are able to load our emotions, from our loftiest to our lowest, our hopes, and our sins, through such a deep and complete emotional identification that he can carry them away with him into heaven or the wilderness and so free us of the burden and the tension of keeping them for ourselves. This empathic identification is . . . catharsis." See TRAGEDY.

**Cavalier Lyric:** The sort of light-hearted poem characteristic of the CAVALIER LYRISTS; gay in tone; graceful, melodious, and polished in manner; artfully showing Latin classical influences; sometimes licentious and cynical or epigrammatic and witty. At times it breathed the careless braggadocia of the military swashbuckler, at times the aristocratic ease of the peaceful courtier. Many of the poems were OCCASIONAL in character, as Suckling's charming if doggerel-like "Ballad upon a Wedding" or Lovelace's pensive "To Althea from Prison." The themes were love and war and chivalry and loyalty to the king. The term *Cavalier Lyric* is also applied to a poem of a later age but intended to illustrate the spirit or the times of the CAVALIER LYRISTS, such as Browning's "Boot, Saddle, to Horse and Away."

**Cavalier Lyrists:** The followers of Charles I (1625–1649) were called Cavaliers, as opposed to the supporters of Parliament, who were called ROUNDHEADS. The *Cavalier Lyrists* were a group of these Cavaliers who composed gay and light-hearted poems, especially Thomas Carew, Richard Lovelace, and Sir John Suckling. These men were soldiers and courtiers first and the authors of CAVALIER LYRICS only incidentally. Robert Herrick, although he was a country parson and not a courtier, is often classed with the *Cavalier Lyrists,* because many of his poems included in *Hesperides* are in the vein of the Cavaliers. See CAVALIER LYRIC.

**Celtic Literature:** Literature produced by a people speaking any one of the Celtic DIALECTS. Linguistically, the Celts are divided into two main groups. The "Brythonic" Celts include the Ancient Britons, the Welsh, the Cornish (Cornwall), and the Bretons (Brittany); while the Goidelic (Gaelic) Celts include the Irish, the Manx (Isle of Man), and the Scottish Gaels. At one time the Celts, an important branch of the Indo-European family, dominated Central and Western Europe. The Continental Celts (including the Bretons, who came from Britain) have left no literatures. The Celts of Great Britain and Ireland, however, have produced much literature of interest to students of English and American literature. See IRISH LITERATURE, WELSH LITERATURE, SCOTTISH LITERATURE, CELTIC RENAISSANCE.

**Celtic Renaissance** (or **Irish Renaissance**): A general term for the great movement of the late nineteenth and early twentieth centuries which in its various phases and sometimes conflicting "movements" aimed at the preservation of the Gaelic language (the GAELIC MOVEMENT), the reconstruction of early Celtic history and literature, and the stimulation of a new literature authentically Celtic (esp. Irish) in spirit. From before the middle of the nineteenth century there had been a growing interest in Celtic, especially Irish, antiquities, and much work was done in the collection and study, and later in printing and translation, of early Irish manuscripts embodying the history and literature of ancient Ireland. Along with this was developed the practice of collecting and printing folk-tales still preserved in oral tradition. In the 1890's came the GAELIC MOVEMENT, which stressed the use of the Gaelic language itself. More fruitful was the contemporaneous Anglo-Irish movement, which stimulated the production of a new literature in English (or "Anglo-Irish") by Irish writers on Irish themes and in the Irish spirit. Standish Hayes O'Grady's imaginative treatment of Irish history (1880) provided much impetus to the movement, and themes drawn from ancient Irish tradition were exploited in verse and drama. Fortunately, some genuine poetic geniuses were at hand to further the project, such as W. B. Yeats, George W. Russell ("A.E."), George Moore, J. M. Synge, and (later) James Stephens, Lord Dunsany, and Padraic Colum. From the beginning Lady Gregory was an enthusiastic worker—as collector, popularizer, essayist, and playwright. A striking phase of the renaissance was its dramatic manifestation. In 1899 under the leadership of Yeats, Moore, Edward Martyn, Lady Gregory, and others the Irish Literary Theatre was founded in Dublin. Though this theatre was inspired by the more or less cosmopolitan LITTLE THEATRE MOVEMENT, Yeats and Martyn did write for it some plays employing Irish folk-materials. Later Yeats joined another group more devoted to the exploitation of native elements, The Irish National Theatre Society, to which he attracted J. M. Synge, the most gifted playwright of the movement, whose *Playboy of the Western World* (1907) and *Deirdre of the Sorrows* (1910) attracted wide recognition. Later exemplars of dramatic activity were Lord Dunsany and Sean O'Casey. The *Celtic Renaissance* produced little of importance in Wales. In Scotland it is perhaps best represented by the work of "Fiona Macleod" (William Sharp).

**Celtic Revival:** A term sometimes used for the GAELIC MOVEMENT, the CELTIC RENAISSANCE, or the IRISH LITERARY MOVEMENT, as well as for the eighteenth-century movement described below.

**Celtic Revival, The (Eighteenth Century):** A literary movement of the last half of the eighteenth century which stressed the use of the historical, literary, and mythological traditions of the ancient Celts, particularly the Welsh. Through confusion Norse mythology was included in "Celtic." The movement was a part of the ROMANTIC MOVEMENT, since it stressed the primitive, the remote, the strange and mysterious, and since it aided the revolt against pseudo-classicism by supplying a new mythology for the overworked classical myths and figures. Specifically it was characterized by an intense interest in the druids and early Welsh bards, numerous translations and imitations of early Celtic poetry appearing in the wake of the discovery of some genuine examples of early Welsh verse. The most influential and gifted poet in the group was Thomas Gray, whose "The Bard" (1757) and "The Progress of Poesy" (1757) reflect early phases of the movement. The most spectacular figure in the group of "Celticists" was James Macpherson, whose long poems, *Fingal* (1762) and *Temora* (1763)—chiefly his own invention but partly English renderings of genuine Gaelic pieces preserved in the Scottish Highlands—he published as TRANSLATIONS of the poems of a great Celtic poet of primitive times, Ossian. Both Gray's and Macpherson's work influenced a host of minor poets, who were especially numerous and active in the last two decades of the century. There was also a considerable reflection of the movement in the DRAMA, e.g., Home's *The Fatal Discovery* (acted 1769) and Brooke's *Cymbeline* (1778). Late in the century the gloomy SENTIMENTALISM of Macpherson was less influential. (See E. D. Snyder, *The Celtic Revival in English Literature.*)

**Cento:** A literary patchwork, usually in verse, made up of scraps from one or many authors. An example is a fifth-century life of Christ by the Empress Eudoxia, which is in verse with every line drawn from Homer.

**Chanson:** A song. Originally composed of two-line STANZAS of equal length (couplets), each STANZA ending in a REFRAIN, the *chanson* is now more broadly interpreted to include almost any poem intended to be sung, and written in a simple style.

**Chanson de geste:** A "song of great deeds." A term applied to the early French EPIC. There is some uncertainty as to the ultimate origin of the form. The earliest and best existing example, the *Chanson de Roland*, dates probably from *ca.*1100. The early *chansons de geste* are written in ten-syllable lines marked by ASSONANCE and grouped in STANZAS of varying length. CYCLES developed, such as that of Charlemagne (*geste du roi*); that of William of Orange, which reflects the efforts of Christian heroes against the invading Saracens; and that dealing with the strife among the rebellious Northern barons. The stories generally reflect chivalric ideals with little use of love as a theme. The form flourished for several centuries, a total of about eighty examples being extant. These epic tales supplied material ("Matter of France") for MEDIEVAL ROMANCE, including English ROMANCES. See MEDIEVAL ROMANCE.

**Chant:** Loosely used to mean a SONG, but more particularly the term signifies the intoning of words to a monotonous musical measure of few notes. The words of the *chants* in the English Church are drawn from such Biblical sources as the Psalms. CADENCE is an important element, and usually one note (the "reciting note") is used for a series of successive words or syllables. DIRGES are often chanted. Repetition of a few varying musical phrases is a characteristic, and the intonation of the voice plays an important rôle. *Chants* are generally considered less melodious than SONGS.

**Chant royal:** One of the more complex, and therefore less used, French verse forms. The tradition for this verse form demands a dignified, heroic subject such as can best be expressed in rich DICTION and courtly formalities of speech. The *chant royal* consists of sixty lines arranged in five STANZAS of eleven VERSES each and an ENVOY of five VERSES, the ENVOY ordinarily starting with an invocation in the manner of the BALLADE. The RIME SCHEME usually followed is ababccddede for the stanza and ddede (as in the last five lines of the stanza) for the ENVOY. The italicized e above indicates the recurrence of a complete line as a REFRAIN at the end of each STANZA and at the close of the ENVOY. All STANZAS must be the same in all details and no rime-word may appear twice.

**Chantey (Shanty):** A sailors' SONG marked by strong RHYTHM and, in the good old days of sail, used to accompany certain forms of hard labor (such as weighing anchor) performed by seamen working in a group. The leader of the singing was referred to as the "chantey man," his responsibility being to sing a line or two introductory to a REFRAIN joined in by the whole group.

**Chapbook:** Literally "cheap" book; a small book or pamphlet, usually a single SIGNATURE of sixteen or thirty-two pages, poorly printed and crudely illustrated, which was sold to the common people in England and America through the eighteenth century by pedlers or "chapmen." *Chapbooks* dealt with all sorts of topics and incidents: travel tales, murder cases, prodigies, strange occurrences, witchcraft, biographies, religious legends and tracts, stories of all sorts. They are of interest to the literary historian because of their reflection of contemporary attitudes toward themes and situations treated in literature. The term has been revived in America this century as the title for miscellaneous small books and pamphlets.

**Character:** A literary form which flourished in England and France
in the seventeenth and eighteenth centuries. It is a brief descriptive
sketch of a personage who typifies some definite quality. The
person is described not as an individualized personality but as an
example of some vice or virtue or type, such as a busybody, a
superstitious fellow, a fop, a country bumpkin, a garrulous old man,
a happy milkmaid, etc. Similar treatments of institutions and inanimate things, such as "the character of a coffee house," also employed
the term, and late in the seventeenth century, by a natural extension of the tradition, *character* was applied to longer compositions, sometimes historical, as Viscount Halifax's *Character of
Charles II.* The vogue of *character*-writing followed the publication
in 1592 of a Latin translation of Theophrastus, an ancient Greek
writer of similar sketches. Though the *character* may have influenced Ben Jonson in his treatment of the man of HUMOURS in
comedy, the first English writer to cultivate the form as such was
Bishop Joseph Hall in his *Characters of Virtues and Vices* (1608).
Two of his successors were Sir Thomas Overbury (1614) and John
Earle (1628). Later, under the influence of the French writer
La Bruyère, *characters* became more individualized and were
combined with the ESSAY, as in the periodical essays of Addison
and Steele. Subjects of *characters* were given fanciful proper names,
often Latin or Greek, such as "Croesus." Good modern collections
of *characters* are Gwendolen Murphy's *A Cabinet of Characters* and
Richard Aldington's *A Book of 'Characters.'* See ESSAY.

**Characterization:** In the LYRIC, the ESSAY, and the AUTOBIOGRAPHY,
the author reveals aspects of his own character; in the BIOGRAPHY
and the HISTORY, he presents the characters of actual persons other
than himself; and in FICTION (the DRAMA, the NOVEL, the SHORT
STORY, and the NARRATIVE POEM), he reveals the characters of
imaginary persons. The creation of images of these imaginary
persons so credible that they exist for the reader as real within the
limits of the FICTION is called *characterization.* The ability to
characterize the people of his imagination successfully is one of the
primary attributes of a good novelist, dramatist, or short-story
writer.

There are three fundamental methods of *characterization* in
FICTION: (1) the explicit presentation by the author of the
character through direct EXPOSITION, either in an introductory block
or more often piece-meal throughout the work, illustrated by

action; (2) the presentation of the character in action, with little or no explicit comment by the author, in the expectation that the reader will be able to deduce the attributes of the actor from the actions; and (3) the representation from within a character, without comment on the character by the author, of the impact of actions and emotions upon his inner self, with the expectation that the reader will come to a clear understanding of the attributes of the character.

It is difficult to distinguish among these methods of *characterization* without discussing them in terms of narrative POINT OF VIEW. Usually the explicit method results when the story is told by a first-person NARRATOR, such as Dickens' David Copperfield or Sterne's Tristram Shandy, or by an OMNISCIENT AUTHOR, such as Fielding in *Tom Jones* or Thackeray in *Vanity Fair*. The success of the explicit method of *characterization* rests at least in part upon the personality of the NARRATOR or OMNISCIENT AUTHOR. The presentation of characters through actions is essentially the dramatic method. It is the traditional way of establishing character in the DRAMA; so much so, in fact, that only by changing some of the DRAMATIC CONVENTIONS, as in the use of a CHORUS, or EXPRESSIONISM, or in plays like O'Neill's *Strange Interlude*, can other methods of *characterization* than this be used in the theater. We know Hamlet through what he says and does; the riddle of what Shakespeare intended his true character to be is eternally unanswerable. The NOVEL and the SHORT STORY in this century have frequently adopted the dramatic technique by making objective presentations of characters in action without authorial comment, to such an extent that the SELF-EFFACING AUTHOR is today a fictional commonplace. Writers of the REALISTIC NOVEL, such as Bennett, Galsworthy, and Howells, usually employ this method of character presentation. The presentation of the impact upon the PROTAGONIST's inner self of external events and emotions begins with the novels of Henry James, whose *The Ambassadors* is an excellent example, and continues into the STREAM OF CONSCIOUSNESS NOVEL where, through INTERIOR MONOLOGUES, the subconscious or unconscious mind of the character is revealed, as in Joyce's *Ulysses* or Faulkner's *The Sound and the Fury*.

But regardless of the method by which a character is presented, the author may concentrate upon a dominant trait to the exclusion of the other aspects of the character's personality or he may attempt to present a fully rounded personality. If the presentation of a single dominant trait is carried to an extreme, not a believable character but a CARICATURE will result. If this method is handled with skill, it can produce two-dimensional characters that are striking and interesting but lack depth. Mr. Micawber in *David Copperfield* comes close to being such a two-dimensional character through the emphasis that Dickens puts upon a very small group of characteristics. Sometimes such characters are given descriptive names, such as Mr. Deuceace, the gambler in *Vanity Fair*. On the other hand the author may present us with so convincing a congeries of personality traits that a complex rather than a simple character emerges; such a character is three-dimensional or, in E. M. Forster's term, "round." As a rule, the major characters in a FICTION need such three-dimensional treatment, while minor characters are often handled two-dimensionally.

Furthermore, a character may be either STATIC or DYNAMIC. A STATIC CHARACTER is one who changes little if at all in the progress of the narrative. Things happen *to* such a character without things happening *within* him. The pattern of action reveals the character rather than showing the character changing in response to the actions. Sometimes a STATIC CHARACTER gives the appearance of changing simply because our picture of him is revealed bit by bit; this is true of Uncle Toby in *Tristram Shandy*, who does not change, although our view of him steadily changes. A DYNAMIC CHARACTER, on the other hand, is one who is modified by the actions through which he passes, and one of the objectives of the work in which he appears is to reveal the consequences of these actions upon him. Most great DRAMAS and NOVELS have DYNAMIC CHARACTERS as PROTAGONISTS. SHORT STORIES are more likely to reveal STATIC CHARACTERS through action than to show changes in characters resulting from actions.

Ultimately every successful character represents a fusion of the universal and the particular and becomes an example of the CONCRETE UNIVERSAL. It is in this dramatic particularization of the typical and universal that one of the essences of the dramatic and of *characterization* is to be found. Our minds may delight in abstractions and ideas, but it is our emotions that ultimately give the aesthetic and dramatic response, and they respond to the personal, the particular, the CONCRETE. This is why a NOVEL speaks to us more permanently than an ALLEGORY, why Hamlet has an authority forever lacking the "Indecisive Man" in a seventeenth-century character. See POINT OF VIEW, NOVEL, SHORT STORY, DRAMA, PLOT, CONCRETE UNIVERSAL.

**Chartism:** A definite political movement in England just before the middle of the nineteenth century, the object of which was to secure for the lower classes more social recognition and improved material conditions. The Chartists advocated universal suffrage, vote by ballot, annual parliaments, and other reforms. This platform is given in the *People's Charter* (1838). Carlyle's *Chartism* (1839) is an attack upon the movement. The chartist agitation is favorably reflected in some of Kingsley's novels. See INDUSTRIAL REVOLUTION.

**Chiasmus:** A type of rhetorical BALANCE in which the second part is syntactically balanced against the first but with the parts reversed, as in Coleridge's line, "Flowers are lovely, love is flower-like," or Pope's "Works without show, and without pomp presides."

**Chivalric Romance:** MEDIEVAL ROMANCE reflecting the customs and ideals of CHIVALRY. See MEDIEVAL ROMANCE, ARTHURIAN LEGEND, COURTLY LOVE, CHIVALRY IN ENGLISH LITERATURE.

**Chivalry in English Literature:** The system of manners and morals known as *chivalry*, chiefly a fruit of the feudal system of the Middle Ages, because it had been presented in MEDIEVAL ROMANCE in a highly idealized form amounting almost to a religious system for the upper classes, has furnished so much color and atmosphere and inspiration for later literature that some knowledge of its characteristics is essential to the student. The medieval knight, seen in the more brilliant light of literary idealization (as a matter of fact the typical medieval knight had many unlovely character-istics), has been portrayed not only by the many writers, known and unknown, of MEDIEVAL ROMANCE, but by later poets like Chaucer, with his "parfit, gentle knight" and Spenser, who fills the forests and plains of his *The Faerie Queene* with a brilliant procession of courteous and heroic Guyons and Scudamores and Calidores. Knights whose high oaths bind them to fidelity to God and king, truth to their lady-loves, and ready service for all ladies in distress or other victims of unjust tyrants, cruel giants, or fiendish monsters, have become commonplaces of romantic literature.

Their sketchily drawn but noble personalities impart a vigor and glow to the action of such HISTORICAL NOVELS as Scott's *Ivanhoe* and find a somewhat unreal but earnestly sympathetic treatment in the *Idylls of the King* of Tennyson. Tennyson's poem *Guinevere*, indeed, includes the following poetic statement of the ideals of knighthood (King Arthur is speaking):

> I made them lay their hands in mine and swear
> To reverence the King, as if he were
> Their conscience, and their conscience as their King,
> To break the heathen and uphold the Christ,
> To ride abroad redressing human wrongs,
> To speak no slander, no, nor listen to it,
> To honor his own word as if his God's,
> To lead sweet lives in purest chastity,
> To love one maiden only, cleave to her,
> And worship her by years of noble deeds,
> Until they won her.

A more faithful picture may perhaps be found in the pages of Malory's *Le Morte Darthur*, where the romantic glamour of knighthood, with all the effort to idealize Lancelot and Arthur and find in the "good old days" a perfect pattern for later times, is not allowed to obscure some of the less pleasing realities of medieval knighthood. So glorious a thing as *chivalry* has not, of course, gone unnoticed by the satirists. The early seventeenth century not only produced the immortal *Don Quixote* in Spain but Beaumont and Fletcher's dramatic BURLESQUE *The Knight of the Burning Pestle* in England, while modern America has brought forth not only its broadly comic *A Connecticut Yankee in King Arthur's Court* (Mark Twain) but its more subtly mocking *Galahad* (John Erskine). Some pieces of English literature which make use of chivalric elements are described in W. H. Schofield's *Chivalry in English Literature*.

**Choriambus:** In METRICS a FOOT in which two accented syllables flank two unaccented syllables: __ ◡ ◡ __. This FOOT is sometimes used in a VERSE form called *choriambics*, in which the line begins with a TROCHEE, three *choriambics* follow, and it closes with an IAMBUS. Swinburne used the form, as did Rupert Brooke, whose line: "Ī hăve / tēnd ĕd ănd lōved / yēar ŭp ŏn yēar, / Ī ĭn the sōl / ĭ tŭde" illustrates the *choriambic* line.

**Chorus:** In ancient Greece, the groups of dancers and singers who participated in religious festivals and dramatic performances. Also the songs sung by the *chorus*. At first the choral songs made up the bulk of the play, the spoken MONOLOGUE and DIALOGUE being interpolated. Later, however, the *chorus* became subordinate, offering inter-act comments. Finally, it became a mere LYRIC used to take up the time between ACTS. In Elizabethan drama the role of the *chorus* was often taken by a single actor, who recited PROLOGUE and EPILOGUE and gave inter-act comments which linked the ACTS and foreshadowed coming events. So in Sackville and Norton's *Gorboduc,* the "first" English TRAGEDY, the *chorus* consists of a few STANZAS accompanied by a DUMB SHOW, the latter foreshadowing the coming action. In Kyd's *Spanish Tragedy* the part of the *chorus* is played by a ghost and the figure Revenge, the ghost urging Revenge to inspire the actors to hasten the vengeance demanded by the action. Shakespeare sometimes employed the *chorus,* as in *Pericles,* where the old poet Gower, accompanied by a DUMB SHOW, provides PROLOGUE and inter-act comment, and in *King Henry the Fifth,* where the *chorus* comments on the action, explains change of scene, and PROLOGUE-like begs for a sympathetic attitude on the part of the spectators. Sometimes, within the play proper, one of the characters, like the Fool in *King Lear,* is said to play a "chorus-like" role when he comments on the action.

Although not commonly used, the *chorus* is still employed occasionally by the modern playwright, notably T. S. Eliot in *Murder in the Cathedral.* Sometimes a *chorus*-character—one whose role in the drama is to comment on the action—is used; such a character is Seth Beckwith in O'Neill's *Mourning Becomes Electra.* Novelists, too, have used the *chorus,* sometimes as a group of characters who comment on action, sometimes as a single character. Both Scott and Hardy often used *choruses* of rustic characters, and the CONFIDANTE of the Henry James novel is a *chorus*-character.

**Christianity, Established in England:** Although evidence for dating the introduction of *Christianity* into England is lacking, it is certain that there were Christians in Roman Britain as early as the third century, and it is probable that there was an organized church as early as A.D. 314, when the bishops of London and York are said to have attended a church council in Gaul. After the lapse into barbarism which followed the Germanic invasions of the fifth century, *Christianity* was reintroduced directly from Rome by St. Augustine, who landed in Kent in A.D. 597. It flourished in southeastern England under Ethelbert, spread northward, and gained a foothold in Northumbria under Edwin (d. 633), who had married a Kentish princess. Another group of missionaries soon came into Northumbria from the celebrated Celtic monastery of Iona, an island off the west coast of Scotland. Iona had been established in A.D. 563 by St. Columba, a missionary from Ireland, where a form of *Christianity* reflecting the monastic ideals of Bishop Martin of Tours (flourished *ca.*371–*ca.*400) had been introduced from Gaul in the fourth or early fifth century. The Celtic and Roman churches thus brought into contact differed in certain doctrines and customs (such as the date for Easter, the form of baptism, and style of tonsure for priests). The resulting disputes were settled at the famous Synod of Whitby in 664 in favor of the Roman party.

The establishment of *Christianity* in England of course had powerful and far-reaching effects upon literature, since the Church was for centuries the chief fosterer of learning. The pagan literature which survived from early Germanic times passed through the medium of Christian authors and copyists, who gave a Christian coloring to such literature as they did not wholly reject. For centuries most of the new writings owed both their inspiration and direction to Christian zeal and to the learning fostered by the Church. The Christianization in the thirteenth century of the great body of Arthurian romances is an outstanding example of the dominance of *Christianity* over medieval literary activity.

**Chronicle:** A name given to certain forms of historical writing. One authority has said that *chronicles* differ from ANNALS in their comprehensive or universal character—their concern with world history. Though there were prototypes in Hebrew, Greek, Latin, and French, it is the medieval *chronicles* in English and their RENAIS-SANCE successors that are of chief interest to the student of English literature. The *Anglo-Saxon Chronicle*, begun under King Alfred late in the ninth century and carried on by various writers in a number of monasteries in succeeding centuries, has been called the "first great book in English prose." The record begins with 60 B.C. and closes with 1154 ("Peterborough" version). Alfred and his helpers revised older minor *chronicles* and records and wrote first-hand accounts of their own times. The work as a whole is a sort of historical miscellany, sometimes sketchy in detail and detached in attitude, at other times spirited, partisan, and detailed. An important Old English poem preserved through its inclusion in the *Anglo-Saxon Chronicle* is the spirited *Battle of Brunanburh.* A famous Latin prose *chronicle* is Geoffrey of Monmouth's *History of the Kings of Britain* (*ca.*1136), which not only records legendary British history but also romantic accounts of King Arthur. The earliest important verse *chronicle* in Middle English is Layamon's *Brut* (*ca.*1205), based upon Wace's French poetic version of Geoffrey. Layamon's book illustrates the literary interest of the medieval *chronicle.* It is a long poem composed in an imaginative, often dramatic, vein, and exhibits a picturesque STYLE that is sometimes reminiscent of the best Old English poetry.

Later Middle English *chronicles* include those of Robert of Gloucester (late thirteenth century), Robert Manning of Brunne (1338), Andrew of Wyntoun (*Original Chronicle of Scotland,* early fifteenth century), John Hardyng (late fifteenth century), and John Capgrave (fifteenth century). With the rise of the Tudor dynasty came a long-sustained wave of patriotic nationalism, one result of which was the production in the sixteenth century of innumerable *chronicles*—some in Latin prose, some in English verse; some mere abstracts, some very voluminous; some new compositions, some retellings of older ones. Some of the more important *chronicles* of Elizabeth's time, besides the famous *Mirror for Magistrates,* a series of "tragedies" (for this special meaning of "tragedy" see p. 489) embodying *chronicle* material, are Richard Grafton's (1563), John Stowe's (1565, 1580, 1592), and Ralph Holinshed's (1578). Not only are portions of this mass of *chronicle*-writing themselves of genuine literary value, full of lively anecdote and description, but some of them were important as sources for Shakespeare and other dramatists. See CHRONICLE PLAY.

**Chronicle Play:** A type of DRAMA flourishing in the latter part of Elizabeth's reign which drew its English historical materials from the sixteenth century CHRONICLES, such as Holinshed's, and which stressed the nationalistic spirit of the times. It enjoyed increasing popularity with the outburst of patriotic feeling which resulted from the defeat of the Spanish Armada (1588) and served as a medium for teaching English history to the uneducated portions of the London populace. The structure of the earlier *chronicle plays* was very loose, UNITY consisting mainly in the inclusion of the events of a single king's reign. The number of characters was large. Much use was made of pageantry (coronations, funerals) and other spectacular elements, such as battles on the stage. The serious action was often relieved by comic scenes or sub-plots, as in Shakespeare's famous Falstaff plays (*Henry IV*, 1, 2; *Henry V*). The tendency to merge with ROMANTIC COMEDIES appeared as early as Greene's *James IV* (*ca*.1590); in Shakespeare's *Cymbeline* (*ca*.1610) the CHRONICLE material is completely subordinated to the demands of ROMANTIC COMEDY. The relation of the *chronicle play* to TRAGEDY is still more important, Shakespeare's *Richard III* (*ca*.1593) being an early example of the tendency of the *chronicle play* to develop into TRAGEDY of character, a movement which culminates in such plays as *King Lear* (1606) and *Macbeth* (1606). The term HISTORY PLAY is sometimes applied to a restricted group of *chronicle plays* like Shakespeare's *Henry V*, which are unified but are neither COMEDY nor TRAGEDY. The earliest true *chronicle play* is perhaps *The Famous Victories of Henry V* (*ca*.1586). Peele's *Edward I* (1590–91) and Marlowe's *Edward II* (1592) are among the best pre-Shakespearean *chronicle plays*.

**Chronique scandaleuse:** A type of writing presenting intrigues, love affairs, and petty gossip, and usually associated with life at court. As a rule these writings give the impression of having been written by an eye-witness. The personal element is important, and scandal is the food upon which such CHRONICLES thrive. *The History of Louis XI* (1460–1483) of France, a *chronique scandaleuse* credited to Jean de Troyes, is an example. This same interest in gossip about the intimate, personal life of the great and of the near-great survives today in the tabloids and in the stories, for instance, which are told of the life of moving-picture stars in Hollywood.

**Chronological Primitivism:** The belief that, on the whole, the life and actions of man were more admirable and desirable at an earlier stage of his history than at present. See PRIMITIVISM.

**"Ciceronians":** A group of Latin stylists in the RENAISSANCE who would not use any Latin word that could not be found in Cicero's writings. See PURIST.

**Classic** (noun): In the singular usually used for a piece of literature which by common consent has achieved a recognized position in literary history for its superior qualities; also an

# Classic, Classical

author of like standing. Thus, *Paradise Lost* is a *classic* in English literature. The plural is used in the same sense, as in the phrase "the study of English *classics*"; it is also used collectively to designate the literary productions of Greece and Rome, as in the statement, "A study of the *classics* is an excellent preparation for the study of modern literature."

**Classic, Classical** (adjectives): Used in senses parallel with those given under CLASSIC (noun); hence, of recognized excellence or belonging to established tradition, as a *classical* piece of music or such as bids fair to win such recognition, as "a *classic* pronouncement"; used specifically to designate the literature or culture of Greece and Rome or later literature which partakes of its qualities. "*Classical* literature" may mean Greek and Roman literature, or it may mean literature that has gained a lasting recognition, or it may mean literature that exhibits the qualities of CLASSICISM. When it is used to describe the attributes of a literary work it usually implies objectivity in the choice and handling of the theme, simplicity of style, clarity, restraint, and formal structure.

**Classical Tragedy:** This term may refer to the TRAGEDY of the ancient Greeks and Romans, as Sophocles' *Antigone;* or to tragedies based upon Greek or Roman subjects, as Shakespeare's *Coriolanus;* or to modern tragedies modeled upon Greek or Roman TRAGEDY or written under the influence of the critical doctrines of CLASSICISM. The earliest extant English TRAGEDY, Sackville and Norton's *Gorboduc* (acted 1562), is sometimes called *classical* because it is written in the manner of the SENECAN TRAGEDIES. Ben Jonson's tragedies *Catiline* and *Sejanus* not only are based upon Roman themes but are *classical* in their conscious effort to apply most of the "rules" of tragic composition derived from Aristotle and Horace. In the Restoration period John Dryden, under the influence of the French *classical tragedies* of Racine, advocated classical rules and applied them in part to his *All for Love,* which contrasts with Shakespeare's romantic treatment of the same story in *Antony and Cleopatra.* In the next century Joseph Addison's *Cato* has been referred to as "the triumph of *classical tragedy.*" See CLASSICISM, TRAGEDY, SENECAN TRAGEDY, UNITIES, ROMANTIC TRAGEDY.

**Classicism:** As a critical term, a body of doctrine which is thought to be derived from or to reflect the qualities of ancient Greek and

Roman culture, particularly literature, philosophy, art, or CRITICISM. It is commonly opposed to ROMANTICISM and REALISM, although it is important to remember that these terms overlap in their "characteristics" and are not, strictly speaking, mutually exclusive. It is particularly dangerous to classify writers or types as perfect exponents of *classicism*. Ben Jonson, for example, was a self-proclaimed advocate of *classicism* as a critic and dramatist, yet his CLASSICAL TRAGEDIES contain some definitely non-classical elements, such as COMIC RELIEF and violation of one or more of the UNITIES. Likewise some of the "romanticists" of the eighteenth century cultivated classical qualities, just as such a "neo-classicist" as Pope exhibited some "romantic" traits.

It is true, however, that *classicism* does stand for certain definite ideas and attitudes, mainly drawn from the critical utterance of the Greeks and Romans or developed through an imitation of ancient art and literature. Some of them may be suggested by the following words and phrases: restraint; restricted scope; dominance of reason; sense of FORM; UNITY of design and aim; clarity; simplicity; BALANCE; attention to structure and logical organization; chasteness in STYLE; severity of outline; moderation; self-control; intellectualism; DECORUM; respect for tradition; IMITATION; conservatism; "good sense."

A glance at certain aspects of the Greek mind will put these terms in the proper perspective. The Greeks were notable for their clarity of thought, an attribute that found expression in lucid, direct, simple expression, and that placed a premium on communication *among* men rather than self-expression *by* a man. UNITY was a dominating idea in the minds of the Greeks, and they naturally constructed buildings and works of art around central ideas, and expended great effort in making the structures symmetrical, logical, balanced, harmonious, and well-proportioned. They had a marked sense of appropriateness or DECORUM and in structure, style, and subject worked with what was fitting and dignified. Restraint of the passions, emphasis upon the common or generic attributes of men and states, and a dispassionate objectivity made them the natural foes of enthusiasm, of uniquely personal states and emotions, and of excessive subjectivity. Although not all Greek or Roman writers displayed all these characteristics, some complex of these qualities is what is usually implied when in English we use the term *classicism*.

*Classicism* in English literature has been an important force, often an "issue," since RENAISSANCE times. The humanists became conscious advocates of CLASSICAL doctrine, and even such an essentially romantic artist as the poet Spenser fell strongly under its influence, not only drawing freely upon CLASSICAL materials but definitely espousing CLASSICAL doctrines and endeavouring to "imitate" such CLASSICAL masters as Virgil and Homer. Shakespeare, though he has left no formal statement of his critical attitude and though he is essentially a "romantic" dramatist, undoubtedly reflects CLASSICAL influence. Sir Philip Sidney, though he wrote PASTORAL ROMANCES, speaks mainly as a classicist in his critical essay, *The Defence of Poesie*. Ben Jonson stands as the stoutest RENAISSANCE advocate of *classicism*, both in dramatic CRITICISM and in his influence upon English poetry. Milton has been said to show a perfect balance of ROMANTICISM and *classicism*. The CLASSICAL attitude, largely under French inspiration, triumphed in the RESTORATION and AUGUSTAN AGES, and John Dryden, Joseph Addison, and Alexander Pope, together with Doctor Samuel Johnson of the next generation, stand in English literary history as exemplars of the CLASSICAL (or NEO-CLASSIC) spirit in literature and criticism. Though nineteenth-century literature was largely romantic (or in its later phases realistic), the vitality of the CLASSICAL attitude is shown by the critical writings of such men as Francis Jeffrey, Matthew Arnold, and Walter Pater. In the twentieth century there has been a strong revival of CLASSICAL attitudes in the literary practice and the critical principles of men like T. E. Hulme, T. S. Eliot, and Ezra Pound, and much of our most distinguished and sophisticated poetry and criticism is today redolent of *classicism*. See HUMANISM, NEO-CLASSICISM, CLASSICAL, ROMANTICISM, REALISM, NEW CRITICISM.

**Clerihew:** A form of LIGHT VERSE which in two COUPLETS of irregular METER touches off a well-known person whose name forms one of the RIMES. It was invented by Edmund Clerihew Bentley, who, while in school listening to a chemistry lecture, wrote:

> Sir Humphrey Davy
> Abominated gravy.
> He lived in the odium
> Of having discovered sodium.

**Cliché:** From the French word for a stereotype plate; a block for printing. Hence any expression so often used that its freshness and clearness have worn off is called a *cliché*, a stereotyped form. Some examples are: "bigger and better," "loomed on the horizon," "the light fantastic," "stood like a sentinel," "sadder but wiser."

**Climax:** In rhetoric a term used to indicate the arrangement of words, phrases, and clauses in sentences in such a way as to form a rising order of importance in the ideas expressed. Such an arrangement is called climactic and the item of greatest importance is called the *climax*. Originally the term meant such an arrangement of succeeding clauses that the last important word in one is repeated as the first important word in the next, each succeeding clause rising in intensity or importance.

In larger pieces of composition—the ESSAY, the SHORT STORY, the DRAMA, or the NOVEL—the *climax* is the point of highest interest, the point at which the reader makes his greatest emotional response. The term used in this sense is an index of emotional response in the reader or the spectator. However, in DRAMATIC STRUCTURE *climax* is a term used to designate the turning point in the action, the place at which the RISING ACTION reverses and becomes the FALLING ACTION. In Freytag's five-part view of DRAMATIC STRUCTURE, the *climax* is the third part or third ACT. Both narrative FICTION and DRAMA have tended to move the *climax*, both in the sense of turning action and in that of highest response, nearer the end of the work and thus have produced structures less symmetrical than those that follow Freytag's pyramid. In speaking of DRAMATIC STRUCTURE, the term *climax* is synonymous with CRISIS. However, CRISIS is used exclusively in the sense of STRUCTURE, whereas *climax* is used as a synonym for CRISIS *and* as a description of the intensity of interest in the reader or spectator. In this latter sense *climax* sometimes occurs at other points than at the CRISIS. See CRISIS, DRAMATIC STRUCTURE.

**Cloak and Sword Romance:** The term comes from the Spanish *comedia de capa y espada*, a dramatic type of which the ingredients were gallant cavaliers, lovely ladies, elegance, adventure, and intrigue. In English it refers to swashbuckling plays or NOVELS characterized by much action and presenting gallant heroes in love with fair ladies, a glamorous color thrown over all. Settings and characters are often, though not necessarily, Spanish, Italian, or French, the manners are courtly and gracious, the plot full of intrigue resulting most commonly in duels.

Dumas' *The Three Musketeers* and many currently popular television plays are good examples. *Cloak and sword romances* were very popular in America in the period between 1890 and 1915.

**Closed Couplet:** Two successive VERSES riming *aa* and containing within the two lines a complete, independent statement. It is "closed" in the sense that its meaning is complete within the two verses and does not depend on what goes before or follows for its grammatical structure or thought. Example:

> One prospect lost, another still we gain;
> And not a vanity is giv'n in vain;
> —Pope

**Closet Drama:** A play (usually in verse) designed to be read rather than acted. Notable examples are Milton's *Samson Agonistes,* Shelley's *The Cenci,* Browning's *Pippa Passes,* and the ONE-ACT PLAYS that W. D. Howells wrote for the *Atlantic Monthly*. Giving the term a broader meaning, some writers include in it such dramatic poems as Swinburne's *Atalanta in Calydon* and other products of the effort to write a literary DRAMA by imitating the style of an earlier age, such as Greek DRAMA. T. H. Dickinson indeed says that the *closet drama* "arises from the application of the standards of one day to the art of a later day"—an effort to continue the TRADITION of Shakespeare or the TRADITION of the Greeks after the stage itself had lost both the TRADITIONS. Such poetic DRAMAS as Tennyson's *Becket* and Browning's *Strafford* are not infrequently called *closet dramas* because, though their authors meant them to be acted, they actually are more successful as literature than acted DRAMA. In English literature the nineteenth century was noted for the production of *closet drama,* perhaps because the actual stage was so monopolized by BURLESQUE, MELODRAMA, OPERETTA, and such light forms that literary men were stimulated either to attempt to provide more worthy DRAMAS for the contemporary stage or at least to preserve the TRADITION of literary DRAMA by imitating earlier masterpieces. See DRAMATIC POETRY, POETIC DRAMA, PASTICHE.

**Cockney School:** A derogatory title applied by *Blackwood's Magazine* to a group of nineteenth-century writers including Hazlitt, Leigh Hunt, Keats, and Shelley, because of their alleged poor taste in such matters as DICTION and RIME. Some offending rimes were *name* and *time, vista* and *sister,* words which, the suggestion was, could rime only to a cockney ear. One sentence from the denounce-ment printed in *Blackwood's Magazine* must serve as illustrative of the whole spirit of his attack: "They [the writers above] are by far the vilest vermin that ever dared to creep upon the hem of the majestic garment of the English muse." The attack reflected the Tory view that men of "low" or "cockney" birth and breeding would inevi-tably have cockney politics and write cockney verse. The famous attack on Keats (August, 1818) associates his "bad" verse with his radical political friends and his "lowly" beginnings as an apothecary's apprentice.

**Coherence:** A fundamental principle of composition demanding that the parts of any piece of writing be so arranged and bear such a relationship one to the other that the meaning of the whole may be immediately clear and intelligible. Words, phrases, clauses, within the sentence; and sentences, paragraphs, and chapters in larger pieces of writing are the units which, by their progressive and logical arrangement, make for *coherence* or, contrariwise, by an illogical arrangement, result in incoherence.

**Coined Words:** Words consciously and arbitrarily manufactured "out of whole cloth," as opposed to those which enter the language as a result of one of the more natural processes of language develop-ment. Many words which were originally *coined words* (such as *telephone, airplane,* and *kodak*) have become accepted terms. Constantly occurring examples of such words are those fabricated by commercial firms for advertising purposes: "Nabisco" (National Biscuit Company), "Socony" (Standard Oil Company of New York). Frowned upon as a literary practice, word coining is never-theless constantly affecting our language. See NEOLOGISM.

**Collaboration:** The association of two or more people in a given piece of literary work. Beaumont and Fletcher afford one of the most famous instances of *collaboration* in the field of English literature.

**Collate:** To compare in detail two texts, versions, editions, or printings in order to determine and record the points of agreement and disagreement; also to verify the order of the sheets or SIGNA-TURES of a book before binding.

**Colloquialism:** An expression used in informal conversation but not accepted as good usage in formal speech or writing. A *colloquialism* lies between the upper speech level of dignified formal, or "literary" language and the lower level of slang. It may differ from more formal language in pronunciation, grammar, vocabulary, imagery, or connotative quality. As in the case of slang, a colloquial expression eventually may be accepted as "standard" usage. "I'll be right over," is a permissable colloquial expression in an intimate telephone conversation, though formal style might call for a more dignified and "correct" phrase. *Fix* may be used as a *colloquialism* for "mend." See SLANG, PROVINCIALISM, DIALECTS.

**Colloquy:** A conversation or DIALOGUE, especially when it is in the nature of a formal discussion or a conference; used in this sense occasionally in literary titles, as Erasmus' *Colloquies*. See DIALOGUE.

**Colonial Period in American Literature, 1607–1765:** From the founding of the colony at Jamestown, which began the colonial period in America, until the Stamp Act in 1765 finally forced the colonists into a widespread consciousness of themselves as separate from their mother land, the writing produced in America was generally utilitarian, polemical, or religious. Three major figures emerged in this period: Edward Taylor, whose religious METAPHYSICAL POETRY, written at the close of the seventeenth and the beginning of the eighteenth centuries, did not see publication until 1937; Jonathan Edwards, whose religious and philosophical treatises have not been surpassed by an American; and Benjamin Franklin, whose Addisonian rephrasings of the teachings of the Enlightenment are the stylistic epitome of the period.

That BELLES-LETTRES should not have come is hardly surprising. Whether PURITANS of the North or ROYALISTS of the South, the colonists were uniformly engaged throughout the period in possessing the land, cultivating it, making it safe and fruitful. Wilderness, Indians, and disease were common foes that demanded the strict attention of the early colonists. Wealth, government, progress, political rights absorbed a major portion of the attention of the Americans of the later colonial period.

The seventeenth century was the age of travel and personal records, DIARIES, historical and descriptive accounts, sermons, and a little verse—largely instructive, like Wigglesworth's *The Day of Doom*, or religious, like the *Bay Psalm Book* and the numerous funeral elegies. Only Anne Bradstreet, "The Tenth Muse Lately Sprung Up in America," raised a thin and faltering but true poetic voice.

In the eighteenth century, the dangers of early colonization were over, but the colonial attitude persisted. Religious controversy was prevalent. Newspapers and ALMANACS flourished. Jonathan Edwards both in the pulpit and in his writing demonstrated his greatness as a thinker and a didactic writer. Benjamin Franklin created what was perhaps the first fully realized and widely popular American fictional character in Richard Saunders of *Poor Richard's Almanac*. William Byrd wrote with CAVALIER grace and urbanity of his life and neighbors in Virginia and North Carolina. But little important verse and no native DRAMA emerged. As the period in which Americans had thought and acted like colonials of the British crown drew to a close in the 1760's, a vast amount of writing had been done in America, some of it of a high quality, but very little that did not self-consciously take English authors as models and even less that could merit the term *belletristic*. See the section on "The Colonial Period in American Literature," in *The Outline of Literary History*.

**Colophon:** A publisher's symbol or device formerly placed at the end of a book but now more generally used on the title page or elsewhere near the beginning. The function of *colophons* is to identify the publisher. *Colophons* at different times and with different publishers have incorporated one or more of these items: title and author of book, the printer, the date and place of manufacture. The earliest known use of *colophons* was in the fifteenth century, at which time they were likely to be complete paragraphs wherein the author addressed the reader in a spirit of reverence—now that he had completed his work. Sir Thomas Malory, for example, closed his *Le Morte Darthur* with the statement that it "was ended in the ix yere of the reygne of Kyng Edward the fourth," and asks that his readers "praye for me whyle I am on lyue that God sende me good delyuerance, and whan I am deed I praye you all praye for my soule." The term is also applied to any device, including the words "The End" or "Finis," that marks the conclusion of any printed work.

**Comedy:** As compared with TRAGEDY, *comedy* is a lighter form of DRAMA which aims primarily to amuse and which ends happily. It differs from FARCE and BURLESQUE by having a more sustained

PLOT, more weighty and subtle DIALOGUE, more natural characters, and less boisterous behavior. The border-line, however, between *comedy* and other dramatic forms cannot be sharply defined, as there is much overlapping of technique, and different "kinds" are frequently combined. Even the difference between *comedy* and TRAGEDY tends to disappear, as Allardyce Nicoll points out, in their more idealistic forms. HIGH COMEDY and LOW COMEDY may be further apart from each other in nature than are TRAGEDY and some serious *comedy*. Psychologists have shown the close relation between laughter and tears, and *comedy* and TRAGEDY alike sprang, both in ancient Greece and in medieval Europe, from diverging treatments of ceremonial performances.

Since *comedy* strives to provoke smiles and laughter, both WIT and HUMOR are utilized. In general the comic effect arises from a recognition of some incongruity of speech, action, or character revelation. The incongruity may be merely verbal as in the case of a play on words, exaggerated assertion, etc.; or physical, as when stilts are used to make a man's legs seem disproportionately long; or satirical, as when the effect depends upon the beholder's ability to perceive the incongruity between fact and pretense exhibited by a braggart. The range of appeal here is wide, varying from the crudest effects of LOW COMEDY to the most subtle and idealistic reactions aroused by some HIGH COMEDY. The "kinds" of comedy and, in part, the relation between *comedy* and TRAGEDY are thus accounted for. As one writer says: "We have seen that comic effects have a common basis in incongruity, contrast; that the incongruity may lie principally in the realm of events, and we have comic intrigue, or in the realm of appearances, and we have comic character; while usually both these are found in conjunction, but with preponderating emphasis on one or the other, which gives us farce or intrigue comedy on the one hand and character comedy on the other. . . . Comedy itself varies according to the attitude of the author or recipient, tending, where it becomes judicial, toward satire; where it becomes sympathetic, toward pathos and tragedy."[1]

English *comedy* developed from native dramatic forms growing out of the religious DRAMA, the MORALITY PLAYS and INTERLUDES, and possibly folk games and plays and the performances of wandering entertainers, such as dancers and jugglers. In the RENAISSANCE the rediscovery of Latin *comedy* and the effort to apply the rules of

[1]E. Woodbridge (Morris), *The Drama, Its Law and Its Technique*, Allyn and Bacon, 1898, p. 67. Reprinted by permission of the publishers.

classical CRITICISM to DRAMA profoundly affected the course of English *comedy*. Foreign influences also have at times been important, as the French influence on Restoration *comedy* or the Italian influence upon Jacobean PASTORAL DRAMA. The more ambitious *comedy* of the earlier Elizabethans was ROMANTIC, while the *comedy* of the seventeenth century, both Jacobean and Restoration, was prevailingly REALISTIC (though the Fletcherian TRAGI-COMEDY flourished early in the century). SENTIMENTAL COMEDY was dominant in the eighteenth century, but was opposed late in the period by a revival of the realistic COMEDY OF MANNERS. In the early nineteenth century such light forms as BURLESQUE and OPERETTA were popular, serious *comedy* again appearing late in the century. Some of the more prominent authors of English *comedy* are: John Lyly, Robert Greene, George Peele, William Shakespeare, Ben Jonson, George Chapman, Thomas Middleton, Thomas Heywood, John Fletcher, Philip Massinger (Elizabethans and Jacobeans); Sir George Etheredge, William Congreve, and Thomas Shadwell (Restoration); Richard Steele, Richard B. Sheridan, Oliver Goldsmith (eighteenth century); T. W. Robertson (mid-nineteenth century); H. A. Jones, Oscar Wilde, A. W. Pinero, G. B. Shaw, J. M. Barrie, Philip Barry, S. N. Behrman (late nineteenth and twentieth centuries).

Attention may be called to a special use of the word *comedy* in medieval times, when it was applied to non-dramatic literary compositions marked by a happy ending and by a less exalted style than was found in TRAGEDY. Dante's *Divine Comedy*, for example, was so named by its author because of its "prosperous, pleasant, and desirable" conclusion, and because it was written in the vernacular (Italian) "in which women and children speak." The nomenclature employed in describing different kinds of *comedy* is somewhat confused, and it is impossible in this handbook to include all the terms employed by the many writers on the subject. An effort has been made to include the most important ones, however. See HIGH COMEDY, LOW COMEDY, REALISTIC COMEDY, ROMANTIC COMEDY, COURT COMEDY, TRAGI-COMEDY, SENTIMENTAL COMEDY, COMEDY OF MANNERS, INTERLUDE, TRAGEDY, DRAMA, WIT AND HUMOR.

**Comedy of Humours:** A term applied to the special type of REALISTIC COMEDY which was developed in the closing years of the sixteenth century by Ben Jonson and George Chapman and which derives its comic interest largely from the exhibition of "humourous" characters; that is, persons whose conduct is controlled by some one characteristic or whim or HUMOUR. Some single HUMOUR or exaggerated trait of character gave each important figure in the action a definite bias of disposition and supplied the chief motive for his actions. Thus in Jonson's *Every Man in His Humour* (acted 1598), which made this type of play popular, all the words and acts of Kitely are controlled by an overpowering suspicion that his wife was unfaithful; George Downright, a country squire, must be "frank" above all things; the country gull in town determines his every decision by his desire to "catch on" to the manners of the city gallant. In his "Induction" to *Every Man out of His Humour* (1599) Jonson explains his character-formula thus:

> Some one peculiar quality
> Doth so possess a man, that it doth draw
> All his affects, his spirits, and his powers,
> In their confluctions, all to run one way.

The *comedy of humours* owes something to earlier vernacular COMEDY, but more to a desire to imitate the classical COMEDY of Plautus and Terence and to combat the vogue of ROMANTIC COMEDY. Its satiric purpose and realistic method are emphasized and lead later into more serious character studies, as in Jonson's *The Alchemist*. It affected Shakespeare's art to some degree—the "humorous" man appearing now and again in his plays (Leontes in *Winter's Tale* is a good example)—and it is perhaps worth mentioning that most of Shakespeare's tragic heroes are such because they allow some one trait of character (ambition, jealousy, contemplation, etc.) to be overdeveloped and thus to destroy the balance necessary to a poised, well-rounded, and effective personality. The *comedy of humours* was closely related to the contemporary COMEDY OF MANNERS and exerted an important influence upon the COMEDY of the Restoration period. See COMEDY OF MANNERS.

**Comedy of Intrigue:** A COMEDY in which the manipulation of the action by one or more characters to their own ends is of more importance than are the characters themselves. Another name for COMEDY OF SITUATION.

**Comedy of Manners:** A term most commonly used to designate the REALISTIC, often satirical, COMEDY of the Restoration period, as practiced by Congreve and others. It is also used for the revival, in modified form, of this COMEDY a hundred years later by Goldsmith and Sheridan, as well as for a revival late in the nineteenth century. Likewise the REALISTIC COMEDY of Elizabethan and Jacobean times is sometimes called *comedy of manners*. In the stricter sense of the term, the type is concerned with the manners and conventions of an artificial, highly sophisticated society. The fashions, manners, and outlook on life of this social group are reflected. The characters are more likely to be types than individualized personalities. PLOT, though often involving a clever handling of situation and intrigue, is less important than ATMOSPHERE and DIALOGUE and SATIRE. The prose DIALOGUE is witty and finished, often brilliant. The appeal is intellectual but not imaginative or idealistic. SATIRE is directed in the main against the follies and deficiencies of typical characters, such as fops, would-be wits, jealous husbands, coxcombs and others who fail somehow to conform to the conventional attitudes and manners of the elegant society of the time. As this SATIRE is directed against the aberrations of social behavior rather than of human conduct in its larger aspects, true HUMOR can hardly be said to be present. A distinguishing characteristic of the *comedy of manners*, too, is its emphasis upon an illicit love duel, involving at least one pair of witty and often amoral lovers. This prevalence of the immoral "love game" is partly explained by the manners of the time and social groups concerned, and partly by the special satirical purpose of the comedy itself. In its SATIRE and REALISM and employment of "humours" the *comedy of manners* was somewhat indebted to Elizabethan and Jacobean comedy. It owed something, of course, to the French COMEDY OF MANNERS as practiced by Molière.

The reaction against the questionable morality of the plays and a growing sentimentalism brought about the downfall of this type of COMEDY near the close of the seventeenth century and it was largely supplanted through most of the eighteenth century by SENTIMENTAL COMEDY. Purged of its objectionable features, however, the *comedy of manners* was revived by Goldsmith and Sheridan late in the eighteenth century, and in a somewhat new garb by Oscar Wilde late in the nineteenth century. The *comedy of manners* has been popular in the twentieth century in the works of playwrights like Noel Coward, Somerset Maugham, and Philip Barry.

A few typical *comedies of manners* are: Etheredge, *The Man of Mode* (1676); Wycherley, *The Plain Dealer* (1674); Congreve, *The Way of the World* (1700); Goldsmith, *She Stoops to Conquer* (1773); Sheridan, *The Rivals* (1775) and *The School for Scandal* (1777); Wilde, *The Importance of Being Earnest* (1895); Maugham, *The Circle* (1921); Coward, *Private Lives* (1931);

Barry, *The Philadelphia Story* (1939). See HIGH COMEDY, REALISTIC COMEDY, COMEDY OF HUMOURS.

**Comedy of Situation:** A COMEDY which depends for its interest chiefly upon ingenuity of PLOT rather than upon character interest; COMEDY OF INTRIGUE. Background, too, is relatively unimportant. There is much reliance upon ridiculous and incongruous situations, a heaping up of mistakes, plots within plots, disguises, mistaken identity, unexpected meetings, etc. A capital example is Shakespeare's *The Comedy of Errors,* a play in which the possibilities for confusion are multiplied by the use of twin brothers who have twins as servants. In each case the twins look so much alike that at times they doubt their own identity. A COMEDY of this sort sometimes approaches FARCE. Ben Jonson's *Epicene* and Middleton's *A Trick to Catch the Old One* are later Elizabethan *comedies of situation* or intrigue. A modern example is Shaw's *You Never Can Tell.* The phrase *comedy of situation* is sometimes used also to refer merely to an incident, such as Falstaff's description of his fight with the robbers in Shakespeare's *King Henry IV,* Part I. See FARCE-COMEDY.

**Comic Opera:** An OPERETTA, or comedy opera, stressing spectacle and music but employing spoken DIALOGUE. An early example is Sheridan's *The Duenna* (1775). The best known *comic operas* are those of Gilbert and Sullivan produced in London, chiefly at the Savoy (constructed for the purpose) in the 1870's and 1880's, e.g., *The Mikado* (1885). See BALLAD-OPERA.

**Comic Relief:** A humorous scene, incident, or speech in the course of a serious FICTION or DRAMA. Such comic intrusions are usually consciously introduced by the author to provide relief from emotional intensity and at the same time, by contrast, to heighten the seriousness of the story. When properly employed, they can enrich and deepen the tragic implications of the action; notable examples are the drunken porter scene in *Macbeth* (see De Quincey's essay, "On the Knocking at the Gate in Macbeth"), the gravedigger scene in *Hamlet,* and Mercutio's role in *Romeo and Juliet.* Although not a portion of Aristotle's formula for a TRAGEDY, *comic relief* has been almost universally employed by English playwrights.

**Commedia dell' arte:** Improvised COMEDY; a form of Italian LOW COMEDY dating from very early times, in which the actors, who usually performed conventional or stock parts, such as the "pantaloon" (Venetian merchant), improvised their DIALOGUE, though a PLOT or SCENERIO was provided them. A "harlequin" interrupted the action at times with low buffoonery. A parallel or later form of the *commedia dell' arte* was the MASKED COMEDY, in which conventional figures (usually in masks) each spoke his particular dialect (as the Pulcinella, the rogue from Naples). There is some evidence that the *commedia dell' arte* colored English LOW COMEDY from early times, but its chief influence on the English stage came in the eighteenth century in connection with the development of such spectacular forms as the PANTOMIME.

**Common Measure:** See COMMON METER.

**Common Meter:** A STANZA form consisting of four lines, the first and third being IAMBIC TETRAMETER (eight syllables, $\smile$ __ $\smile$ __ $\smile$ __ $\smile$ __) and the second and fourth IAMBIC TRIMETER (six syllables, $\smile$ __ $\smile$ __ $\smile$ __). An example:

> He either fears his fate too much,
> Or his deserts are small,
> That dares not put it to the touch
> To gain or lose it all.
> —Marquis of Montrose.

It is distinguished from the BALLAD STANZA principally by its metrical regularity. Often it is called COMMON MEASURE and is designated by the abbreviation *C.M.*

**Commonplace Book:** A classified collection of quotations or arguments prepared for reference purposes. Thus, a reader interested in moral philosophy might collect thoughts and quotations under such heads as truth, virtue, or friendship. *Commonplace books* were utilized by authors of ESSAYS, theological arguments, and other serious treatises. The *Commonplace Book* of John Milton is still in existence. The term is also sometimes applied to private collections of favorite pieces of literature such as the poetical miscellanies of Elizabethan times. R. W. Stallman's *The Critic's Notebook* is an excellent *commonplace book* of the NEW CRITICISM.

**Commonwealth Interregnum:** The period between the execution of Charles I in 1649 and the restoration of the monarchy under Charles

II in 1660, during which England was ruled by Parliament under the control of the PURITAN leader, Oliver Cromwell, whose death in 1658 marked the beginning of the end of the Commonwealth. John Milton was Latin Secretary in the Commonwealth government. Although the theatres were closed in 1642, dramatic performances continued more or less openly, but only Davenant's *The Siege of Rhodes* (1656), a spectacle play heralding the HEROIC DRAMA of the RESTORATION, was a significant new DRAMA. It was an age of major prose works: Milton's political pamphlets, Hobbes' *Leviathan* (1651), Jeremy Taylor's *Holy Dying* and *Holy Living* (1650, 1651), Walton's *The Compleat Angler* (1653), and works by Sir Thomas Browne and Thomas Fuller. The age delighted in translations of the contemporary French prose romances, and in 1654 Roger Boyle published *Parthenissa*, in the style of Mlle. de Scudéry, a precursor of the NOVEL. In poetry Vaughan, Waller, Cowley, Davenant, and Marvell flourished; the metaphysical strain continued; and two attempts at the EPIC were made, Davenant's *Gondibert* (1650) and Cowley's *Davideis* (1656), but both are incomplete. By the end of the *Commonwealth Interregnum*, John Dryden's poetic career was under way. He and Marvell, both of whose best work was to come later, shared with Milton the honor of being the best poets of a troubled time, although they wrote little poetry during it.

**Compensation:** In METRICS a means of supplying omissions in a line; a form of SUBSTITUTION. Such omissions are usually unstressed syllables; the customary means of compensating for their absence is the pause, which has the effect of a *rest* in music. It is illustrated in Tennyson's lines:

> Break, break, break,
> On thy cold grey stones, O Sea!

Each of these lines has three stressed syllables; and metrically they are approximately equivalent, despite the fact that there are only three syllables in the first but seven in the second. The pronounced pauses following each word of the first line compensate for the unstressed syllables that have been omitted. See SUBSTITUTION.

**Complaint:** A LYRIC poem, frequent in the Middle Ages and the RENAISSANCE, in which the poet (1) laments the unresponsiveness of his mistress, as in Surrey's "A Complaint by Night of the Lover

Not Beloved"; (2) bemoans his unhappy lot and seeks to remedy it, as in "The Complaint of Chaucer to His Empty Purse"; or (3) regrets the sorry state of the world, as in Spenser's *Complaints*. In a *complaint,* which usually takes the form of a MONOLOGUE, the poet commonly explains his sad mood, describes the causes of it, discusses possible remedies, or appeals to some lady or divinity for help from his distress.

**Complication:** That part of a dramatic or narrative PLOT in which the entanglement of affairs caused by the conflict of opposing forces is developed. It is the tying of the knot to be untied in the RESOLUTION. In the five-part idea of DRAMATIC STRUCTURE it is synonymous with RISING ACTION. The second ACT of a five-act TRAGEDY is often called "the act of *complication.*" See DRAMATIC STRUCTURE, ACT.

**Conceit:** Originally the term was almost synonymous with "idea" or "conception," and implied something made or conceived in the mind. Its later specialized uses in describing a type of poetic METAPHOR still retain the essential sense of the original meaning, in that *conceit* implies intellectual ingenuity whether applied to the Petrarchan conventions of the ELIZABETHAN PERIOD or the elaborate and witty analogies of the writers of METAPHYSICAL VERSE.

The term is used to designate an ingenious and fanciful notion or conception, usually expressed through an elaborate ANALOGY, and pointing to a striking parallel between two seemingly dissimilar things. A *conceit* may be a brief METAPHOR but it usually forms the framework of an entire poem. In English there are two basic kinds of *conceits:* the PETRARCHAN CONCEIT, most often found in love poems and SONNETS, in which the subject of the poem is compared extensively and elaborately to some object, a rose, a ship, a garden, etc.; and the METAPHYSICAL CONCEIT, in which complex, startling, and highly intellectual analogies are made.

In the eighteenth and nineteenth centuries, the term was used in a derogatory sense, the *conceit* being considered strained, arbitrary, and false. Dr. Johnson was particularly devastating on the METAPHYSICAL CONCEIT. Today the term is more nearly neutral, being used to describe the unhappy over-reaches of poets as well as their striking and effective comparisons. In contemporary verse the *conceit* is again a respected vehicle for the expression of witty perceptions and telling analogies. It is used with great effect by Emily Dickinson, T. S. Eliot, Allen Tate, and John Crowe Ransom. See

Metaphysical conceit, Petrarchan conceit, metaphysical verse, baroque, Gongorism, Marinism.

**Concrete Terms:** The converse of abstract terms; although *concrete terms* are close to specific terms or particular terms, the phrase carries with it significantly the sense of describing something that has actual existence and can be palpably known or experienced. A *concrete* noun evokes an image of something with an objective existence; a *concrete* illustration brings what is abstract into the range of personal, usually sensory, experience. As abstract terms form the language of philosophy and science by reducing the particular instance to the general case or quality, so *concrete terms,* with their emphasis on the sensory and the tangible and their address to the emotional response, form the basic language of the literary arts. As Arthur Quiller-Couch said of Shakespeare, so may we say to some degree of all literary artists: "He chooses the concrete word, in phrase after phrase forcing you to touch and see." See abstract terms, concrete universal, allegory.

**Concrete Universal:** A critical term used to designate the idea that a work of art expresses the universal through the concrete and the particular. The quarrel between the universal and the particular in literature is at least as old as Aristotle, who declared poetry to be more universal than history. The writers in periods of classicism and neo-classicism tend to stress the universal aspects; the writers in periods of romanticism and realism the particular aspects. Yet if literature is "knowledge brought to the heart" it must talk ultimately of universals and express them in concrete and particular instances. See universality, archetype, allegory, abtract terms, concrete terms.

**Confidant** (feminine, **Confidante**): A character in a novel or a drama who takes little part in the action but is a close friend of the protagonist and who receives the confidences and intimate thoughts of the protagonist. The use of the *confidant* enables a dramatist to reveal the thoughts and intentions of the protagonist without the use of asides or soliloquies or the point of view of an omniscient author. Well-known *confidants* are Horatio in *Hamlet,* Dr. Watson in the Sherlock Holmes stories, and Maria Gostrey in James' *The Ambassadors.* See chorus.

**Conflict:** The struggle which grows out of the interplay of the two opposing forces in a PLOT. It is *conflict* which provides the elements of interest and suspense in any form of FICTION, whether it be a DRAMA, a NOVEL, or a SHORT STORY. At least one of the opposing forces is usually a person, or, if an animal or an inanimate object, is treated as though it were a person. This person, usually the PROTAGONIST, may be involved in *conflicts* of four different kinds: (1) he may struggle against the forces of nature, as in Jack London's "To Build a Fire"; (2) he may struggle against another person, usually the ANTAGONIST, as in Stevenson's *Treasure Island* and most MELODRAMA; (3) he may struggle against society as a force, as in the novels of Dickens and George Eliot; or (4) two elements within him may struggle for mastery, as in the RESTORA-TION HEROIC DRAMA or in *Macbeth*. A fifth possible kind of *conflict* is often cited, the struggle against Fate or destiny; however, except where the gods themselves actively appear, such a struggle is realized through the action of one or more of the four basic *conflicts*. Seldom do we find a simple, single *conflict* in a PLOT, but rather a complex one partaking of two or even all the elements given above. For example, the basic *conflict* in *Hamlet* may be interpreted to be a struggle within Hamlet himself, but it is certainly also a struggle against his uncle as ANTAGONIST, and, if the Freudian interpretations of motive are accepted, even a struggle against nature. Dreiser's *Sister Carrie* records a girl's struggle against society, as represented by the city, and yet it is a struggle against her basic nature and even partly within herself. Even so seemingly simple a story as London's "To Build a Fire," in which the PROTAGONIST battles the cold unsuccessfully, is also the record of an inner *conflict*. The term *conflict* not only implies the struggle of a PROTAGONIST against someone or something, it also implies the existence of some MOTIVATION for the *conflict* or some goal to be achieved by it. *Conflict* is the raw material out of which PLOT is constructed. See PLOT, MOTIVATION, PROTAGONIST, ANTAGONIST, DRAMATIC STRUCTURE.

**Connecticut Wits:** See HARTFORD WITS.

**Connotation:** The cluster of implications that words or phrases may carry with them, as distinguished from their denotative meanings. *Connotations* may be (1) private and personal, the result of individual experience, (2) group (national, linguistic, racial), or (3) general or universal, held by all or most men. The scientist and the philosopher attempt to hold words to their denotative meaning; the literary artist relies upon *connotation* to carry his deepest meanings. See DENOTATION, AMBIGUITY, CONCRETE TERMS, ABSTRACT TERMS.

**Consonance:** The use at the ends of VERSES of words in which the final consonants in the stressed syllables agree but the vowels that precede them differ, as "add-read," "bill-ball," and "born-burn." Contemporary poets frequently use *consonance*. In this stanza by Emily Dickinson

> A quietness distilled,
> As twilight long begun,
> Or Nature, spending with herself
> Sequestered afternoon,

the linking of "begun" and "afternoon" is an example of *consonance*. It is also sometimes called HALF RIME and SLANT RIME. See ASSONANCE.

**Contemporary Period in English Literature:** The contemporary period in English literature may be considered to begin with the first World War in 1914, to be marked by the strenuousness of that experience and by the flowering of talent and experiment that came during the boom of the twenties and then fell away during the ordeal of economic depression in the 1930's. The second World War, making England an embattled fortress, had catastrophic effects on all of English life. It was followed by a period of desperate re-adjustment, a period whose literature was marked by a groping uncertainty. In very recent times, this uncertainty has given way to the anger and the protest against their elders of the "Angry Young Men," such as John Wain, Colin Wilson, Kingsley Amis, and John Osborne.

In the early years of the period the novelists of the EDWARDIAN AGE continued as major figures, with Galsworthy, Wells, Bennett, Forster, and Conrad dominating the scene, and to be joined before the 'teens were over by Somerset Maugham. A new fiction, centering itself in the experimental examination of the inner self was coming into being in the works of writers like Dorothy Richardson and Virginia Woolf. It reached its peak in the publication in 1922 of James Joyce's *Ulysses,* a book perhaps as influential as any prose work by a British writer in this century. In their highly differing ways D. H. Lawrence, Aldous Huxley, and Evelyn Waugh protested against the nature of modern society; and the maliciously witty NOVEL, as Huxley and Waugh wrote it in the twenties and thirties, was typical of the attitude of the age and is probably as truly representative of the English NOVEL in the contemporary period as is the NOVEL exploring the private self through the STREAM OF CONSCIOUSNESS. In the thirties and forties, Joyce Cary and Graham Green produced a more traditional fiction of great effectiveness, and Henry Green made comedy of the everyday life of man. Today in writers like Elizabeth Bowen, Angus Wilson, and Ivy Compton-Burnett the English novel continues its urbane and sharply witty way, while the "Angry Young Men" write fictional accounts of their deep dissatisfaction. Throughout the period English writers have practiced the SHORT STORY with distinction; notable examples being Katherine Mansfield and Somerset Maugham, working in the tradition of Chekhov.

The theatre saw the social plays of Galsworthy, Jones, and Pinero, the play of ideas of Shaw, and the COMEDY OF MANNERS of Maugham—all well established in the EDWARDIAN AGE—continue and be joined by Noel Coward's COMEDY, the proletarian DRAMA of Sean O'Casey, the serious verse plays of T. S. Eliot and Christopher Fry, and the high craftsmanship of Terence Rattigan. John Osborne, of the "Angry Young Men," has had marked success in the theatre in recent years.

Perhaps the greatest changes in literature, however, came in poetry and criticism. In 1914 Bridges was poet laureate, to be succeeded in 1930 by John Masefield. Wilfred Owen was one of the most powerful poetic voices of the early years of the contemporary period, but his career ended with an untimely death in the first World War. Through the period Yeats continued poetic creation, steadily modifying his style and subjects to his late form. At the time of his death in 1939 he probably shared with T. S. Eliot the distinction of being the most influential poet in the British Isles. Yet Eliot's *The Waste Land,* although its author was American, was the most important single poetic publication in England in the period. In the work of Yeats and Eliot, of W. H. Auden, of Stephen Spender, of C. Day Lewis, of Edith Sitwell, and of Gerard Manley Hopkins, whose poems were posthumously published in 1918, a new poetry came emphatically into being. The death at thirty-nine

of Dylan Thomas in 1953 silenced a powerful lyric voice, which had
already produced fine poetry and gave promise of doing even finer
work. T. S. Eliot and I. A. Richards, along with T. E. Hulme, Herbert Read, F. R. Leavis, Cyril Connolly, and others, have created
an informed, essentially anti-Romantic, analytical criticism, centering its attention on the work of art itself.

England in the twentieth century has watched her political and
military supremacy gradually dissipate, and since the second
World War she has found herself greatly reduced in the international scene and torn by internal economic and political troubles.
Her writers during these turbulent and unhappy years have turned
inward for their subject matter and have expressed bitter and often
despairing cynicism. Her major literary figures in the present age,
as they were in the EDWARDIAN AGE, have often been non-English.
Her chief poets have been Irish, American, and Welsh; her most influential novelists, Polish and Irish; her principal dramatists, Irish
and American. Yet in the very young and the very talented writers
beginning work as the decade of the fifties ends may be seen a
promise of new strength and new assurance. See *Outline of Literary
History.*

**Contrast:** A rhetorical device by which one element (idea or
object) is thrown into opposition to another for the sake of emphasis or clearness. The effect of the device is to make both contrasted ideas clearer than either would have been if described
by itself. The principle of *contrast,* however, is useful for other
purposes than to make definitions or to secure clearness. Skillfully
used by an artist, *contrast* may become, like colors to the painter or
chords to the musician, a means of arousing emotional impressions
of deep artistic significance.

**Controlling Image:** An IMAGE or METAPHOR which runs throughout
and determines the form or nature of a literary work. The *controlling image* of the following poem by Edward Taylor is the
making of cloth:

> Make me, O Lord, thy Spinning Wheele compleat;
>     Thy Holy Worde my Distaff make for mee.
> Make mine Affections thy Swift Flyers neate,
>     And make my Soule thy holy Spoole to bee.
>     My Conversation make to be thy Reele,
>     And reele the yarn thereon spun of thy Wheele.

Make me thy Loome then, knit therein this Twine:
And make thy Holy Spirit, Lord, winde quills:
Then weave the Web thyselfe. The yarn is fine.
Thine Ordinances make my Fulling Mills.
Then dy the same in Heavenly Colours Choice,
All pinkt with Varnish't Flowers of Paradise.

Then cloath therewith mine Understanding, Will,
Affections, Judgment, Conscience, Memory;
My Words and Actions, that their shine may fill
My wayes with glory and thee glorify.
Then mine apparell shall display before yee
That I am Cloathed in Holy robes for glory.

See FUNDAMENTAL IMAGE, CONCEIT, METAPHYSICAL CONCEIT, IMAGE.

**Convention:** A literary *convention* is any device or style or subject matter which has become, in its time and by reason of its habitual use, a recognized means of literary expression, an accepted element in technique. The use of ALLITERATIVE VERSE among the Anglo-Saxons and of the HEROIC COUPLET in the time of Dryden or Pope are conventions in this sense. The personified virtues of the MORALITY PLAYS, the braggart soldier of the Elizabethan stage, and the fainting heroine of sentimental fiction are examples of conventional STOCK CHARACTERS. Features which later become *conventions* usually arise from freshness of appeal, acquire a pleasing familiarity at the hands of good writers, and eventually, through excessive or unskillful use, become distasteful and fall into disuse. Sometimes, however, discarded *conventions* are revived when apparently dead, as when the French poet Villon revived successfully the BALLADE. Poetic IMAGERY tends to become conventional, as when a "code" of EPITHETS, adjectives, METAPHORS, and SIMILES came to be regarded by the Augustans as "poetic." Not infrequently *conventions* depart so far from the realities and probabilities of life that literature could not employ them if custom had not made them acceptable, as in the case of the SOLILOQUY in drama. In real life men do not talk to themselves in long, rhetorical MONOLOGUES in which they analyze their thoughts and motives. Yet the device has become so conventional in DRAMA that Shakespeare could rely upon it as a medium for some of his finest effects, and such a modern playwright as Eugene O'Neill can have his characters speak their thoughts in the presence of other characters who are supposed to hear nothing, an illustration of how an impossibility in real life can become accepted in literature because of its conventional character. For an illuminating discussion of some aspects of the subject see J. L. Lowes, *Convention and Revolt in Poetry*. See TRADITION, STOCK CHARACTERS, MOTIF, DRAMATIC CONVENTIONS.

**Copyright:** The exclusive legal right to publish or reproduce for sale works of literature or art. Such rights are protected for the author or publisher by an Act of March 4, 1909, in the United States, and by the Copyright Act of 1911 in England. International *copyright* was established in 1891 but it is generally considered inadequate. In America a *copyright* is for twenty-eight years, renewable once, making a maximum period of protection of fifty-six years. In England the *copyright* protects a work for fifty years after the author's death, regardless of the date of initial publication of the work. Secondary rights—rights to serialize, adapt for motion pictures, stage, or television—create a complicated problem. Detailed information on both British and American *copyright* can be found in Appendices II and III of the *Oxford Companion to English Literature*. See PIRATED EDITIONS.

**Coronach:** A song of lamentation; a funeral DIRGE. A Gaelic word reflecting a custom in Ireland (where "keening" is the more commonly used term) and in the Scottish Highlands. The word means a "wailing together," and judging from Sir Walter Scott's presentation a typical *coronach* was sung by the Celtic women. In one of his novels he says, "Their wives and daughters came, clapping their hands, and crying the coronach, and shrieking." In *The Lady of the Lake* (Stanza xvi of Canto III) appears a *coronach* of Scott's own composition:

> He is gone on the mountain,
> He is lost to the forest,
> Like a summer-dried fountain,
> When our need was the sorest, . . .

**Corpus Christi Plays:** Medieval religious plays based upon the Bible and performed by town guilds on movable wagons as a part of the procession on Corpus Christi day. See MYSTERY PLAYS.

**Counterplayers:** The characters in a DRAMA who plot against the hero or heroine, e.g., Claudius, Polonius, Laertes, and their associates in *Hamlet*. See ANTAGONIST.

*Coup de théâtre:* An unexpected, usually unmotivated, surprising turn in a DRAMA, which produces a sensational effect; by extension any piece of claptrap or anything designed solely for effect.

**Couplet:** Two lines of VERSE with similar END-RIMES. Formally, the *couplet* is a two-line STANZA form with both grammatical structure and idea complete within itself, but the form has gone through numerous adaptations, the most famous of which is HEROIC VERSE. In French literature *couplet* is sometimes used in the sense of STANZA. It is customary but not essential that the length of each line be the same. *Couplets* are usually written in octosyllabic and decasyllabic lines. See CLOSED COUPLET, HEROIC VERSE.

**Court Comedy:** The characteristics of this type of COMEDY are explained by the fact that it was written to be performed at the royal court. *Love's Labour's Lost* is a *court comedy* belonging to Shakespeare's early period. Some years before Shakespeare came to London, the Elizabethan *court comedy* had been developed to a high degree of effectiveness by John Lyly in such plays as *Endimion* and *Campaspe*. Characteristics include: artificial PLOT; little action; much use of mythology; pageantry; elaborate costuming and scenery; prominence of music, especially songs; lightness of tone; characters numerous and often balanced (arranged in contrasting pairs); STRUCTURE artificial; STYLE marked by WIT, grace, verbal cleverness, quaint IMAGERY, PUNS; prose DIALOGUE; pages prominent, being witty and saucy; eccentric characters such as braggarts, witches, and alchemists often employed; much farcical action; allegorical meanings sometimes embodied in the characters and action. Though some of these traits of the Lylian *court comedy* dropped out later, *court comedy* in the seventeenth century retained many of them and was always operatic in tone and spectacular in presentation. See MASQUE.

**Courtesy Books:** A name given to a class of books which flourished in late RENAISSANCE times and which dealt with the ideals and training of the "courtly" person. Often in DIALOGUE form, the *courtesy book* discussed such questions as the qualities of a gentleman or court lady, what constituted a gentleman, the etiquette of COURTLY LOVE, the education of the future courtier or prince, and the duties of the courtier as a state counsellor. The *courtesy book* originated in Italy, the most famous example being Castiglione's

*Il Cortegiano,* "The Courtier" (1528), which exerted great influence on English writers, especially after its translation into English by Sir Thomas Hoby in 1561. The earliest English *courtesy book* is Sir Thomas Elyot's *Book of the Governour* (1531).

Somewhat similar to the *courtesy books,* but not to be confused with them, were the numerous etiquette books written not to explain the character of the noble or royal person but to deal with the problems of conduct confronting the well-bred citizen as well as the "gentleman." One of the best is *Galateo* by the Italian Della Casa. Early English examples of this type are *The Babees Book* and Caxton's *Book of Courtesy.*

Many books of the seventeenth century carried on the tradition established by the RENAISSANCE books of courtesy and etiquette, such as: John Cleland's *Institution of a Young Nobleman,* 1607 (Puritan); Henry Peacham's *Compleat Gentleman,* 1622 (courtly); Richard Brathwaite's *The English Gentleman,* 1630 (Puritan); and Francis Osborne's *Advice to a Son,* 1658 (a precursor of Lord Chesterfield's *Letters*). By extension the term *courtesy book* can be applied to a poem like Spenser's *The Faerie Queene,* since one of the objects of the work is to portray the moral virtues. A similar extension has applied the term to Franklin's *Autobiography,* since that work was written to instruct his son in the ways of the world.

**Courtly Love:** A philosophy of love and a code of love-making which flourished in chivalric times, first in France and later in other countries, especially in England. The exact origins of the system cannot now be completely traced, but fashions set by the Provençal TROUBADOURS and ideas drawn from the Orient and especially from Ovid were probably the chief sources. The conditions of feudal society and the veneration of the Virgin Mary, both of which tended to give a new dignity and independence to woman, also affected it. The method of debate or SOLILOQUY by which the doctrines of *courtly love* are given expression in literature was probably indebted to current scholastic philosophy.

According to the system, falling in love is accompanied by great emotional disturbances; the lover is bewildered, helpless, tortured by mental and physical pain, and exhibits certain "symptoms," such as pallor, trembling, loss of appetite, sleeplessness, sighing, weeping, etc. He agonizes over his condition and indulges in endless self-questioning and reflections on the nature of love and his own wretched state. His condition improves when he is accepted, and he is inspired by his love to great deeds. He and his lady pledge each other to secrecy, and they must remain faithful in spite of all obstacles. Andreas Capellanus wrote a treatise late in the twelfth century in which he summarized prevailing notions of *courtly love* through imaginary conversations and through his thirty-one "rules." According to the strictest code, true love was held to be impossible in the married state. Hence some authorities distinguish between true *courtly love* as it is illustrated in the story of Lancelot and Guinevere in Chrétien's "The Knight of the Cart," and Ovidian love. Basically, *courtly love* was illicit and sensual, but a sort of Platonic idealism soon appeared and is found in the usual literary presentation, this modification being doubtless due to the softening influence of Christianity and polite society.

*Courtly love* ideas abound in medieval ROMANCE and are perhaps not unconnected with the later (Renaissance) Petrarchan and Platonic love doctrines as found, for example, in Eizabethan sonnet-sequences. The system of *courtly love* largely controls the behavior of the characters in Chaucer's *Troilus and Criseyde*. C. S. Lewis has made a detailed study of *courtly love* in *The Allegory of Love*.

**"Courtly Makers":** A phrase applied to the court poets in the reign of Henry VIII who introduced the "new poetry" from Italy and France into England. "*Maker*" was used in the sixteenth century, both in Scotland and England, for poet, the use of the term arising from the concept of the poet as a creator (the word *poet* itself comes from a Greek word meaning *maker* or *do-er*). The "*courtly makers*" were given credit by the Elizabethans for "reforming" or polishing the "rude and homely manner" of earlier English poetry. Their work was imitative and experimental, based upon forms and fashions already developed by the Italians. They were most successful perhaps in poetic TRANSLATIONS or PARAPHRASES and in SONGS, even Henry VIII himself being credited with the authorship of both words and music of several graceful songs. The introduction of the SONNET and of BLANK VERSE into English is due to the efforts of the two most important poets of the group, Sir Thomas Wyatt and the Earl of Surrey. Other "*courtly makers*" were William Cornish, Lord Vaux, Lord Rochford (George Boleyn), Sir Anthony St. Leger, Lord Morley (Henry Parker), Sir Francis Bryan, Sir Thomas Chaloner, John Heywood, Robert Fairfax, and Robert Cooper. Most of the work of these men has probably perished, as their ideas of "gentlemanly" conduct did not lead them to publish their work, poetry being cultivated as an incidental grace. Manuscript collections were made for private libraries, however, one of which, now commonly known as *Tottel's Miscellany,* was published in 1557 and exerted a powerful influence on Elizabethan poetry. In fact, the chief importance of the *"courtly makers"* lies in the pioneer character of their work, as their efforts were brought to a perfect flowering by the poetic generations which followed them. Sometimes the term *"courtly maker"* is applied to any court poet.

**Courts of Love:** A phrase applied to supposed tribunals for settling questions involved in the system of COURTLY LOVE. The judge, a court lady or Venus herself, would hear debate on such questions as: "Can a lover love two ladies at once?" "Are lovers or married couples more affectionate?" Though it was once generally believed that such courts were actually held in high society in chivalric times, modern scholarship is inclined to regard the *courts of love* as mere literary conventions. The term *court of love* is also sometimes extended to include allegorical and processional pageants such as the Masque of Cupid passage in Spenser's *The Faerie Queene* (Book III, Cantos xi–xii). The phrase, too, is sometimes used loosely as a synonym for COURTLY LOVE.

**Covenant Theology:** A modification of the doctrines of CALVINISM made in the seventeenth century and particularly important in New England. It substitutes for divine decrees as a basis for election the idea of a contractual relationship between God and man. In the *Covenant theology* it is held that God promised Adam and his posterity eternal life in exchange for absolute obedience. When Adam broke this covenant, he incurred punishment as a legal responsibility for himself and his posterity. However, God made another covenant with Abraham, promising man the ability to struggle toward perfection. During THE GREAT AWAKENING Jonathan Edwards attacked the *Covenant theology* and urged a return to CALVINISM. See CALVINISM; AWAKENING, THE GREAT.

**Crisis:** In a FICTION or a DRAMA the point at which the opposing forces that create the CONFLICT interlock in the decisive action on which the PLOT will turn. *Crisis* is applied to the EPISODE or incident wherein the situation in which the PROTAGONIST finds himself is sure either to improve or grow worse. Since *crisis* is essentially a structural element of PLOT rather than an index of the emotional response which an event may produce in a reader or spectator, as CLIMAX is, the *crisis* and the CLIMAX do not always occur together. (See CLIMAX on this point.) The actual turning point in the action may result in events which produce climactic effects without themselves being of compelling interest. See CLIMAX, PLOT, CONFLICT, DRAMATIC STRUCTURE.

**Critic:** One who estimates and passes judgment on the value and quality of literary works. The term is used for a great variety of persons ranging from the writers of brief reviews and notices in the popular press to expounders of the aesthetic principles that define the nature and function of art. A *critic* may employ any of many different types of CRITICISM and support any of many different theories of art. See CRITICISM, HISTORICAL SKETCH and CRITICISM, TYPES OF.

**Criticism, Historical Sketch:** *Classical Criticism.*—The first important critical treatise, the *Poetics* of Aristotle (fourth century B.C.), has proved to be the most influential. This Greek philosopher defined POETRY as an idealized representation of human action, and TRAGEDY as a serious, dramatic representation or IMITATION of some magnitude, arousing pity and fear wherewith to accomplish a CATHARSIS of such emotions; tragedies should have UNITY and completeness of PLOT, with beginning, middle, and end. The *Poetics* also treats the element of character in TRAGEDY and the relation of TRAGEDY to EPIC poetry as well as the relation of imaginative literature to such other forms as history and philosophy. Aristotle's treatise on the Homeric EPIC has not survived. The great attention given by the ancients to "rhetoric" is also important critically, though developed largely because of the interest in oratory. The great influence of the *Poetics* began in the RENAISSANCE. Aristotle's criticism has been much debated by modern students and not infrequently misunderstood. It may be studied conveniently with the aid of a commentary such as that of Butcher or Humphry House.

Another Greek document of primary significance is the treatise of Longinus, *On the Sublime* (date uncertain, perhaps third century after Christ). Very different from the *Poetics* of Aristotle in content and spirit, this work acclaims sublimity, height, and imagination in a style that is itself enthusiastic and eloquent.

Longinus finds the sources of the Sublime in great conceptions, noble passions, and elevated diction.

The foremost Latin critic was Horace, whose *Art of Poetry*, written as an informal EPISTLE in verse, has exercised considerable power. It discusses types of POETRY and of character, stresses the importance of Greek models, emphasizes the importance of DECORUM, and advises the prospective poet to write both for entertainment and instruction. Many of Horace's phrases have entered into the common language of criticism, such as *ut pictura poesis*, "poetry is like painting"; *labor limae*, "the labor of the file" (i.e., revision); and *aut prodesse aut delectare*, "either to profit or to please." The influence of Horace's criticism was especially great in England in the sixteenth and seventeenth centuries. Quintilian's *Institutes of Oratory* is, after Horace's epistle, perhaps the most important Latin critical treatise. Other ancient critics include Plato, Dionysius of Halicarnassus, Plutarch, and Lucian among the Greeks; and Cicero, the Senecas, Petronius, and Macrobius among the Latin writers. The art of rhetoric constituted an integral part of this literary criticism.

*The Middle Ages.*—So far as known, there was little interest in criticism in the Middle Ages. Much of what there was dealt perfunctorily with Latin versification, rhetoric, and grammar. The ecclesiastical theologians who dominated the intellectual life were inclined to regard literature as a servant of theology and philosophy, and there was consequently a reduced interest in imaginative literature as such. Classical pagan literature was generally neglected or little known, and there was not much contemporary literature of a sort to arouse critical interest. The rhetoricians dealt in great detail with technical matters of vital interest to the creative writer: the use and nature of FIGURATIVE LANGUAGE; organization; beginnings; endings; development (amplification, condensation); STYLE—especially the adaptation of STYLE to type of composition; ornamentation, etc. The very great influence of such teachings upon the early work of Chaucer has been demonstrated in detail. Certain passages in Chaucer's poetry, too, show that he was conscious of the principles controlling literary composition.

The influence of St. Augustine (*d.* 430), who condemned the poets because they pictured the gods as vicious, doubtless contributed to the general distrust of literature on moral and religious grounds which persisted through the Middle Ages into modern times. It must be noted, however, that St. Augustine's attack on imaginative writing produced replies which anticipate later critical attitudes and arguments: the literary and the moral points of view should not be confused; the ancients should be followed, etc. Isidore of Seville (sixth and seventh centuries) listed the types and kinds of literature (based on Biblical forms).

But it was not until the end of the medieval period that a really great critic appeared in the person of the Italian poet Dante, whose *De Vulgari Eloquentia* (early fourteenth century) discusses the problems of vernacular literature. Dante reflects classical ideas on DECORUM, IMITATION, and the nature of the poet. He discusses diction, sentence-structure, STYLE, versification, and dialects. Petrarch and Boccaccio, great Italian scholars and writers of the fourteenth century, produced critical works which belong in part to the medieval period and in part to the RENAISSANCE which they helped to usher in. Boccaccio's famous defense of poetry in Books XIV and XV of his *Genealogia Deorum Gentilium* is particularly important to students of later criticism.

*The Renaissance: Italy and France.*—The RENAISSANCE reacted against the theological interpretation of poetry current in the Middle Ages and attempted a justification of it as an independent art, along lines suggested by humanistic ideals. In Italy, Vida, Robertelli, Daniello, Minturno, Giraldi Cinthio, J. C. Scaliger, Castelvetro, and many others were concerned with such topics as: poetry as a form of philosophy and an imitation of life; the doctrine of verisimilitude (reproduction of actual conditions of life); pleasurable instruction as the object of poetry; the theory of DRAMA, especially TRAGEDY—the tragic hero and the UNITIES were much debated; and the theory of the EPIC poem. The causes for the growth of CLASSICISM have been assigned (by Spingarn) to HUMANISM, Aristotelianism, and RATIONALISM—with PLATONISM, medievalism, and nationalism acting as ROMANTIC forces. These tendencies toward CLASSICISM actuated Italian criticism of the sixteenth century and French criticism of the seventeenth. The first French critical works were rhetorical and metrical, the most important being Sibilet's *Art of Poetry* (1548); but the first highly significant French criticism centered around the *Pléiade*, a group interested in refining the French language and literature by borrowings and imitations of the classics, Ronsard being its most famous writer and Du Bellay being the author of its manifesto, his epochal *Defence and Illustration of the French Language* (1549). Among the prominent seventeenth-century French critics were

Malherbe, who reacted strongly against the *Pléiade*, Chapelain, Corneille, Saint-Evremond, d'Aubignac, Rapin, Le Bossu, and Boileau, whose influence was especially powerful. These writers illustrate the course of French criticism in the direction of CLASSICISM, a rational crystallizing of poetic theory, and a codification of the principles of literary structure.

*The English Renaissance.*—In Renaissance England the earliest critical utterances were directed toward matters of rhetoric and diction, as in the "prefaces" of the printer William Caxton (late fifteenth century) and the rhetorics of Leonard Cox (*ca.*1530) and Thomas Wilson (1553). As early as Sir Thomas Elyot's *Book of the Governour* (1531) the claims of English as a vehicle for literature were being urged against the extreme humanist opposition to the vernacular as crude and not permanent. The actual development of a native literature was accompanied by discussions of how best to build up the English vocabulary, the extreme humanists and INKHORNISTS, who favored the introduction of heavy Latin and Greek words, being opposed by those who stressed native words (see PURIST). Much attention was given to the requirements of DECORUM and IMITATION. The first technical treatise on English versification was Gascoigne's *Certain Notes of Instruction* (1575). Verse forms already developed in English, including RIME, were perfected in the face of the critical impulse to insist upon such classical verse forms as the unrimed HEXAMETER. Practice ran ahead of theory in this matter, as may be seen by comparing the actual practices of Sidney and Campion with their serious critical condemnation of RIME. Campion's essay, *Observations in the Art of English Poesie* (1602), was promptly and effectively answered by Samuel Daniel in his *A Defence of Rime*. Similarly, Shakespearean RO-MANTIC TRAGEDY developed in spite of the prevailing critical insistence upon the UNITIES.

But perhaps the most vital critical issue centered about the effort to justify literature in the face of the PURITAN attack based upon moral grounds, a movement which attacked the DRAMA in particular, as in Stephen Gosson's *The School of Abuse* (1579). Many of these critical questions were treated in Sidney's *Defence of Poesie* (pub. 1595), the most significant piece of criticism of the period. Sidney stressed the high function of the poet, exalted poetry above philosophy and history, answered the objections to poetic art, examined the types of poetry, and assigned praise and blame among the writers of the preceding generation on the basis of their conformity to classical principles as expressed by the Italian critics. Important critical expressions came from Francis Bacon (*Advancement of Learning*, 1605) and Ben Jonson (*Timber: or Discoveries*). In Jonson, a man of vast learning and uncommon common sense, we may see the definite tendency toward the NEO-CLASSICISM that was to become the center of English criticism for more than a century.

*The Restoration: Dryden.*—The next master was John Dryden, with his numerous prefaces and essays, the greatest of which is the *Essay of Dramatick Poesie* (1668). This treatise, written in dialogue form with ease and vigor, fairly presents the claims of "ANCIENTS AND MODERNS," of French and English dramatists; RIME, TRAGI-COMEDY, and the UNITIES receive consideration; the influence of Corneille is apparent; while much applied criticism keeps the essay from being entirely theoretical. In his *Preface to the Fables* (1700) Dryden gives a noteworthy estimate of the genius of Chaucer. Other Restoration critics include: Sir Robert Howard, Thomas Rymer, the Earls of Mulgrave and Roscommon, and Sir William Temple. The foreign influence was predominantly French.

*The Eighteenth Century: Pope, Addison, Johnson.*—Alexander Pope was not merely the first poet of his generation, but also its most significant critic, what with the prefaces to his translation of Homer and his edition of Shakespeare, and his *Essay on Criticism* (1711), by far the leading piece of verse criticism in the language. In this work Pope set forth the NEO-CLASSIC principles of following nature and the ancients, outlined the causes of bad criticism, described the good critic, and concluded with a short history of criticism. Addison's critical papers in the *Spectator* (1711–1712) on TRAGEDY, WIT, BALLADS, *Paradise Lost*, and the pleasures of the imagination were designed for a popular audience, but they exerted a strong influence upon formal criticism and aesthetic theory. The neo-classical critics in general devoted themselves to such topics as reason, correctness, WIT, taste, *genres*, rules, IMITATION, the classics, the function of the imagination, the status of emotion, and the dangers of enthusiasm. RATIONALISM and CLASSICISM and the "school of taste" were held in a balance that often proved precarious. Gradually, however, the sway of authority was weakened; the historical point of view gained in general acceptance; textual criticism became more scientific. But Samuel Johnson remained the defender of the older order; his large body of critical expression may be gleaned from his periodical essays, the preface to his edition of Shakespeare, and his *Lives of the Poets*. The personality of Doctor Johnson stimulated orthodoxy as much as did his writings.

*Early Romantic Tendencies.*—But there were dissenters who were foreshadowing the romantic ideals of the coming era—the Wartons, Edward Young, Bishop Hurd, and others. Joseph Warton (*Essay on the Genius and Writings of Pope,* 1756, 1782) refused Pope the highest rank among poets because of insufficient emotion and imagination; Thomas Warton (*Observations on The Faerie Queene of Spenser,* 1754) emphasized the emotional quality of the great Elizabethan poet; Young (*Conjectures on Original Composition,* 1759) spoke in favor of independence and against the imitation of other writers; Hurd (*Letters on Chivalry and Romance,* 1762) justified Gothic manners and design, Spenser's poetry, and the Italian poets; and attacked some of the main tenets of the AUGUSTANS. Other eighteenth-century critics of note were John Hughes, John Dennis, Henry Fielding, Edmund Burke, Goldsmith, Lord Kames, Hugh Blair, and Sir Joshua Reynolds.

*Romanticism: Wordsworth, Coleridge, Shelley, Lamb.*—The volume of poems by Wordsworth and Coleridge entitled *Lyrical Ballads* (1798) is frequently cited as formally ushering in the Romantic Movement. For the second edition (1800) Wordsworth wrote a preface that acted as a manifesto for the new school and set forth his own critical creed. It was his object to "choose incidents and situations from common life," to use "language really used by men." Wordsworth was reacting from what he considered the artificial poetic practice of the preceding era; he condemned the use of personification and "poetic diction." There could be "no essential difference between the language of prose and metrical composition." Wordsworth defined the poet as a "man speaking to men" and poetry as "the breath and finer spirit of all knowledge," "the spontaneous overflow of powerful feelings" which takes its origin from emotion "recollected in tranquillity." Though not ideally equipped for the rôle of critic, Wordsworth here produced a document, free from inherited critical jargon and replete with illustrious passages. It is of prime importance in the history of English literature and criticism. His own poetic practice is not always consistent with his theory.

Coleridge, with his superior philosophical training and profundity of thought, became one of England's greatest critics, despite his digressiveness and verbosity. The *Biographia Literaria* (1817) is both autobiographical and critical. Therein he explained the division of labor in the *Lyrical Ballads:* his own endeavors "should be directed to persons and characters supernatural, or at least romantic; yet so as to transfer from our inward nature a human interest and a semblance of truth sufficient to procure for these shadows of imagination that willing suspension of disbelief for the moment, which constitutes poetic faith"; while Wordsworth was "to propose to himself as his object, to give the charm of novelty to things of every day, and to excite a feeling analogous to the supernatural, by awakening the mind's attention to the lethargy of custom, and directing it to the loveliness and the wonders of the world before us; an inexhaustible treasure, but for which, in consequence of the film of familiarity and selfish solicitude, we have eyes, yet see not, ears that hear not, and hearts that neither feel nor understand." These two fundamental romantic points of view were applied to *The Rime of the Ancient Mariner* of Coleridge and *Lucy Gray* of Wordsworth. Coleridge disagreed, however, with Wordsworth's statements about the principles of METER and POETIC DICTION: rustic life is not favorable to the formation of a human diction; poetry is essentially ideal and generic; the language of Milton is as much that of real life as is that of the cottager; art strives to give pleasure through beauty. Coleridge subtly expounded the nature of beauty and the conditions for its existence. His discussion of the IMAGINATION and the FANCY is penetrating. In his lectures on Shakespeare Coleridge did much to spread the romantic worship of the Bard's genius in all its aspects, though, like Lamb and Hazlitt, he contributed little new to Shakespearean criticism. The English romanticism of Coleridge and others found considerable support in the philosophy, aesthetics, and literature of German romanticism.

Other critics of importance in the first half of the nineteenth century were Lamb, Hazlitt, and Leigh Hunt. Lamb's criticism was charming and enthusiastic but eccentric, capricious, and unorganized; it showed good taste, great originality of thought as well as keenness of phrase; and it stimulated the appreciation of earlier English literature. Hazlitt is more remarkable for many happy phrases, sound judgment, and an infectious spirit than for any systematic philosophy. Hunt is a most catholic and readable critic. The poet Shelley's *Defence of Poetry* (1821) is an abstract *apologia* reminiscent of RENAISSANCE treatises. Other critics of this period are: William Blake, Cardinal Newman, Carlyle, De Quincey, Landor, Henry Hallam, and Macaulay. The review journals, the

Whig *Edinburgh Review* (ed. Francis Jeffrey) and the Tory *Quarterly Review* (ed. William Gifford), voiced fundamentally conservative opinions and dominated periodical criticism.

*The Nineteenth Century: Arnold, Pater; Realism.*—Matthew Arnold was the leading critic of the last half of the nineteenth century. He thought of poetry as a "criticism of life" and of criticism itself as the effort to "know the best that is known and thought in the world and by in its turn making this known, to create a current of true and fresh ideas." Criticism should seek absolute truth. Form, order, and measure constituted the classical qualities which Arnold admired. He sought to judge literature by high standards; he used specimens (or "touchstones") of great poetry as well as his own sensitive taste in forming judgments. "The grand style," he said, "arises in poetry, when a noble nature, poetically gifted, treats with simplicity or with severity a serious subject." The greatness of a poet "lies in his powerful and beautiful application of ideas to life." Arnold was primarily interested in the true and the great; he subordinated the historical method. His vigorous and lucid style and his high ideals of life and literature have made him an extremely powerful figure in the history of criticism. Three of his better known critical essays are *The Function of Criticism* (1865), *The Study of Poetry* (1888), and *On Translating Homer* (1861).

In the later nineteenth century we find the tenets of ROMANTICISM still in the field and the principles of REALISM and of IMPRESSIONISM gaining ground. The expansion of natural science helped the progress of realistic and naturalistic criticism (see NATURALISM), which was a reaction against both CLASSICISM and ROMANTICISM. HISTORICAL CRITICISM, the attempt to understand a work in the light of "the man and the *milieu*," had been in process of development for at least two centuries and at last was crystallized in the writings of the Frenchmen Sainte-Beuve and Taine. IMPRESSIONISM grew out of ROMANTICISM and obtained an eloquent advocate in Walter Pater. Victorian critics discussed such topics as the function and nature of art and literature, the rôle of morality, the place of the IMAGINATION, the problems of STYLE, the province of the NOVEL, and the theory of the comic. Though there were no real schools of critics, the tendency of criticism was away from the application of standards toward the use of impressionistic methods. The German influence yielded ground to the French. Significant contributions were made by Thackeray on the English humorists; John Stuart

Mill on the nature of poetry; Walter Bagehot on pure, ornate, and grotesque art in poetry; Pater on style and on hedonism in art; George Meredith on the comic spirit; Leslie Stephen on the eighteenth century; and Swinburne on the Elizabethan and Jacobean dramatists.

M. H. Abrams, in *The Mirror and The Lamp*, has pointed out that all critical theories, whatever their language, discriminate four elements in "the total situation of a work of art," and he discriminates both the kinds of criticism and the history of critical theory and practice in terms of the dominance of one of these elements. They are: the *work*, that is, the thing made by the maker, the poem produced by the poet, the artifact created by the artificer; the *artist*, the maker, the poet, the artificer; the *universe*, that is, the "nature" that is imitated, if art is viewed as IMITATION, the materials of the real world or the world of ideal entities out of which the work may be thought to take its subject; and the *audience*, the readers, spectators, or listeners to whom the work is addressed. If the critic views art basically in terms of the *universe*, in terms of what is imitated, he is using the MIMETIC THEORY. If the critic views art basically in terms of its effect on the *audience*, he is using the PRAGMATIC THEORY. If the critic views art basically in terms of the *artist*, that is, views it as expressive of the maker, he is using the EXPRESSIVE THEORY. If the critic views art basically in its own terms, seeing the *work* as a self-contained entity, he is using an OBJECTIVE THEORY.

A backward glance over the history of criticism in the light of these theories is revealing. The MIMETIC THEORY is characteristic of the criticism of the classical age, with Aristotle as its great expounder. Horace, however, introduced the idea of instruction—*utile et dulce*—and thereby put the effect upon the audience in the center of his view of art. From Horace through most of the eighteenth century, the PRAGMATIC THEORY was dominant, although the NEO-CLASSIC critics revived a serious interest in IMITATION. Indeed, as M. H. Abrams asserts, "the pragmatic view, broadly conceived, has been the principal aesthetic attitude of the Western world." At the same time, it is true that criticism through the eighteenth century was securely confident of the imitative nature of art. With the beginnings of ROMANTICISM came the EXPRESSIVE THEORY, in a sense the most characteristic of the ROMANTIC attitudes. When Wordsworth calls poetry "the spontaneous overflow of powerful feeling," the *artist* has moved to the center. Now the poet's IMAGINATION is a new force in the world and a source of unique knowledge, and expression is the true function of art. Beginning in the nineteenth century and becoming dominant in the twentieth has been the "poem *per se* . . . written solely for the poem's sake," as Poe expressed it. Here FORM and STRUCTURE, patterns of IMAGERY and SYMBOLS, become the center of the critic's concern, for he looks at the work of art as a separate cosmos. However, increasing interest in psychology has kept the contemporary critic also aware of the fact that the *audience* functions in the work of art, and views of the MYTH current today tend to bring the *artist* back to a central position and at the same time to value in terms of the *audience* the truth he speaks through his ARCHETYPAL patterns and IMAGES from his racial unconscious.

These views of criticism will help us chart the history of the craft in America in the nineteenth century and in England and America in the twentieth.

*American Criticism in the Nineteenth Century.*—Criticism in America, besides reflecting, sometimes tardily, European attitudes, has been concerned with questions peculiar to a literature growing out of a transplanted culture. To what extent is American literature derivative and imitative? How can American literature develop a purely American spirit? What is this spirit? What of the effect of PURITAN ethical conceptions upon American literature? How has the frontier affected it?

Early nineteenth-century criticism, as evidenced by the earlier numbers of the *North American Review* (estab. 1815), was conservative and NEO-CLASSIC. Pope reigned. Later, the ROMANTIC attitude triumphed, and Byron, Scott, Wordsworth, and eventually Shelley, Keats, Coleridge, Carlyle, and Tennyson were exalted. The earlier writer-critics were in the main ROMANTIC, Poe, Lowell, and Emerson. Poe, however, stressed workmanship, technique, structure, the divorce of art and morality; was highly rational; and enunciated independent theories of the LYRIC and the SHORT STORY. Emerson believed art should serve moral ends; asserted that all American literature was derivative; and assumed the ROMANTIC attitude toward nature and individualism. Lowell is first IMPRESSIONISTIC and ROMANTIC; at times professedly REALISTIC; and eventually CLASSICAL and ethical, after his revolt against SENTIMENTALISM.

After the Civil War a strong critical movement toward REALISM developed, and it had two powerful critical spokesmen, William

Dean Howells and Henry James. Interested almost exclusively in FICTION and particularly in the NOVEL, they advanced a theory that the fidelity of the *work* to the *universe*, with universe defined in a materialistic or psychological-social sense, was the object of art. "Realism" was defined by Howells as "neither more nor less than the truthful treatment of material." Yet there were aspects of the PRAGMATIC THEORY here, for he saw a moral obligation resting on the *artist* in terms of the *effects* of his works on the *audience*. At the close of the century, under the influence of the French, particularly Zola, a group of American novelists were advancing a theory of art that was frankly MIMETIC; this is the application of scientific method, even of scientific law, to enhance the seriousness and increase the depth of the portraying of the actual by the artist. The theory is NATURALISM, and Frank Norris was its most vocal expounder as the century ended. However, Henry James, in critical essays already written and in the prefaces which he prepared for the collected edition of his NOVELS in the first decade of the twentieth century, was to make the most significant formulation of critical principles about the NOVEL, centering in craftsmanship, that an American has produced. James and Poe emerge from nineteenth century America as the most powerful and original American critics of the age. Other important critics were Hamlin Garland and H. H. Boyesen.

*Twentieth Century Criticism.*—In England and America the first decade of the twentieth century saw a continuation of the concern with REALISM and NATURALISM, but little serious critical examination of them. IMPRESSIONISM and "appreciation," led in England by Walter Pater and his followers and in America by James Huneker, ruled the day. In the second decade, a group of Americans, under the leadership of Van Wyck Brooks, attacked the cultural failures of America and began the search for a "usable past," a search which was to occupy men like Randolph Bourne, Lewis Mumford, and Bernard De Voto down to the present and which saw in 1927–1930 in Vernon L. Parrington's monumental *Main Currents in American Thought* one of the major documents in critical scholarship in the century. At the same time, in England two young Americans, Ezra Pound and T. S. Eliot, were learning from T. E. Hulme to distrust ROMANTIC expressionism and to turn to formalism and objectivity. In the 1920's the impact of the new psychologies was deeply felt in England, particularly in the work of I. A. Richards, whose reaction against IMPRESSIONISM expressed itself in efforts to make an exact science of the examination of how literature produced psychological states in its reader. He was followed by Herbert Read and William Empson. And in America Freudian psychology was applied to literary problems by a variety of critics, but the strong movement was the NEW HUMANISM, which, under the leadership of Irving Babbit and Paul Elmer More, formulated a critical position resting on the traditional moral and critical standards of the humanists.

In the 1930's, as a partial aftermath of the financial collapse, came a wave of critics espousing Marxist and near-Marxist ideas—a specialized form of PRAGMATIC THEORY—both in England and America. The major English Marxist was Christopher Caudwell; while no Americans approached him in excellence, critics like Granville Hicks and V. F. Calverton strongly espoused the reading of literature in the light of radical social views. During the 1930's in America, reacting both against the NEW HUMANISTS and the Marxist critics came a group, drawn largely from the AGRARIANS, who vigorously embraced an OBJECTIVE THEORY of art. Led by John Crowe Ransom, who gave them a name and something resembling a credo in his book *The New Criticism,* these essentially conservative and anti-romantic writers—Allen Tate, Robert Penn Warren, Donald Davidson, Yvor Winters, and later Cleanth Brooks, started from the position of T. S. Eliot and Ezra Pound and quickly formed themselves into a powerful force in the formal criticism of literature. At the same time a similar group, though much less organized, were practicing a stringent and aesthetically centered criticism in England, among them being Eliot himself, F. R. Leavis, and Cyril Connolly. Both in England and America, the theories of Carl Jung about the racial unconscious (see ARCHETYPE) have been operative and have received vigorous expression by writers like Maud Bodkin and Eliot in England and Susanne Langer and Francis Fergusson in America. The twentieth century is often called an age of criticism and in the richness and complexity of its systems, the rigor of its application, and the enthusiasm of its espousal of the cause of the literary arts it can wear that title with honor. Today these many movements are fusing into a healthy eclecticism, and readers and writers alike are benefited by it. For a distinguished short survey of the history of criticism, see W. K. Wimsatt, Jr., and Cleanth Brooks, *Literary Criticism: A Short History* and for American criticism, see Floyd Stovall (ed.), *The Development of American Literary Criticism.* See the articles on various kinds of criticism as listed under CRITICISM, TYPES OF.

**Criticism, Types of:** *Criticism* is a term which has been applied since the seventeenth century to the description, justification, analysis, or judgment of works of art. There are many ways in which *criticism* may be classified. Some of the more common classifications are given here, as supplementary to M. H. Abrams' discrimination among the major critical theories as MIMETIC, PRAGMATIC, EXPRESSIVE, and OBJECTIVE (see CRITICISM, HISTORICAL SKETCH, beginning at "The Nineteenth Century"). One common dichotomy for *criticism* is ARISTOTELIAN VS. PLATONIC. In this sense, ARISTOTELIAN implies a judicial, logical, formal *criticism* that tends to find the values of a work either within the work itself or inseparably linked to the work; and PLATONIC implies a moralistic, utilitarian view of art, where the values of a work are to be found in the usefulness of art for other and non-artistic purposes. Such a view of PLATONIC CRITICISM is narrow and in part inaccurate, but those who hold it point to the exclusion of the poet from Plato's Republic. Essentially what is meant by the ARISTOTELIAN-PLATONIC dichotomy is an intrinsic-extrinsic separation.

A separation between *relativistic criticism* and *absolutist criticism* is also often made, in which the *relativistic* critic employs any or all systems which will aid him in reaching and elucidating the nature of a work of art, whereas the *absolutist* critic holds that there is one proper critical procedure or set of principles and no others should be applied to the critical task.

There is also an obvious division between THEORETICAL CRITICISM, which attempts to arrive at the general principles of art and to formulate inclusive and enduring aesthetic and critical tenets, and PRACTICAL CRITICISM (sometimes called "applied" criticism), which brings these principles or standards to bear upon particular works of art.

*Criticism* may also be classified according to the purpose which it is intended to serve. The principal purposes which critics have had are: (1) to justify one's own work or to explain it and its underlying principles to an uncomprehending audience (Dryden, Wordsworth, Henry James); (2) to justify imaginative art in a world that tends to find its value questionable (Sidney, Shelley, the NEW CRITICISM); (3) to prescribe rules for writers and to legislate taste for the audience (Pope, Boileau, the Marxists); (4) to interpret works to readers who might otherwise fail to understand or appreciate them (Edmund Wilson, Matthew Arnold); (5) to judge works by clearly defined standards of evaluation (Samuel Johnson, T. S. Eliot); (6)

to discover and to apply the principles which describe the foundations of good art (Coleridge, Addison, I. A. Richards).

*Criticism* is also often divided into the following types in literary and critical histories: (1) IMPRESSIONISTIC, which emphasizes how the work of art affects the critic; (2) HISTORICAL, which examines the work against its historical surroundings and the facts of its author's life and times; (3) TEXTUAL, which attempts by all scholarly means to reconstruct the original manuscript or textual version of the work; (4) FORMAL, which examines the work in terms of the characteristics of the type or GENRE to which it belongs; (5) JUDICIAL, which judges the work by a definable set of standards; (6) ANALYTICAL, which attempts to get at the nature of the work as an object in itself through the detailed analysis of its parts and their organization; (7) MORAL, which evaluates the work in relation to human life; and (8) MYTHIC, which explores the nature and significance of the ARCHETYPES and archetypal patterns in the work.

These widely differing classification systems for *criticism* are not mutually exclusive, and there are certainly others. These will serve, however, to indicate to the student that the critic has employed a great variety of strategies in getting at the work of art and communicating what he finds there.

**Crown of Sonnets:** Seven SONNETS interlinked by having the last line of the first form the first line of the second, the last line of the second form the first line of the third, etc., with the last line of the last SONNET repeating the first line of the first. Donne's "La Corona" is an example.

**Cubist Poetry:** Poetry that attempts to do in VERSE what the cubist painters do on canvas; that is, take the elements of an experience, totally fragment them (creating what Picasso calls "destructions") and then so re-arrange them that a new and meaningful synthesis is made (Picasso's "sum of destructions"). The poetry of e. e. cummings, Kenneth Rexroth, and some of that of Archibald MacLeish fit this category.

**Cultural Primitivism:** The belief that nature (what exists undisturbed by man's artifice) is preferable and fundamentally better than any aspect of man's culture (any area of human activity where, by art or craft, man has modified or ordered nature). It is a belief that distrusts artifice, logic, social and political organizations, rules, and conventions. See PRIMITIVISM, CHRONOLOGICAL PRIMITIVISM.

**Cycle:** A word, originally meaning circle, which came to be applied to a collection of poems or ROMANCES centering about some outstanding event or character. Cyclic narratives are commonly accumulations of TRADITION given literary form by a succession of authors rather than by a single writer. "Cyclic" was first applied to a series of epic poems intended to supplement Homer's account of the Trojan War and written by a group of late Greek poets known as the Cyclic Poets. Other examples of cyclic narrative are the Charlemagne EPICS and Arthurian ROMANCE, like the "Cycle of Lancelot," etc. The MEDIEVAL religious DRAMA presents a cyclic treatment of Biblical themes.

**Cyclic Drama:** The great CYCLES of medieval religious DRAMA. See MYSTERY PLAY.

**Cynicism:** Doubt of the generally accepted standards and of the innate goodness of human action. In literature the term is important as one used from time to time to characterize groups of writers or movements distinguished by dissatisfaction with contemporary conditions. Originally the expression came into being with a group of ancient Greek philosophers, a group led by Antisthenes and including such others as Diogenes and Crates. The major tenets of the cynics were belief in the moral responsibility of the individual for his own acts and the dominance of the will in its right to control human action. Reason, mind, will, individualism were, then, of greater importance than the social or political conduct so likely to be worshiped by the multitudes. This exaltation of the individual over society it is which makes most unthinking people contemptuous of the cynical attitude. Any highly individualistic writer, scornful of the commonly accepted social standards and ideals, is, for this reason, called cynical. Almost every literature has had its schools of cynics. It is important to remember that *cynicism* is not necessarily a weakness or a vice, and that the cynics have done much for civilization. Samuel Butler's *Way of All Flesh* and W. Somerset Maugham's *Of Human Bondage* are two examples of the cynical NOVEL.

**Dactyl:** A metrical FOOT consisting of one accented syllable followed by two unaccented syllables, as in the word *mannikin*. See METER and VERSIFICATION.

**Dadaism:** A movement of young writers and artists in Paris during and just after World War I, which attempted to suppress the logical relationship between idea and statement, argued for absolute freedom, held meetings at bars and in theatres, and delivered itself of numerous nonsensical and semi-nonsensical "manifestoes." It was founded in Zurich in 1916 by Tristan Tzara (who then went to Paris) with the admittedly destructive intent of perverting and demolishing the tenets of art, philosophy, and logic and replacing them with conscious madness as a protest against the insanity of the war. Similar movements sprang up in Germany, Holland, Italy, Russia, and Spain. About 1924 the movement developed into SURREALISM. See Edmund Wilson's *Axel's Castle* and Malcolm Cowley's *Exile's Return* for accounts of the movement.

**Dark Ages:** A phrase sometimes loosely used as a synonym for the medieval period of European history. Its use is vigorously objected to by most modern students of the Middle Ages, since the phrase reflects the old, discredited view that the period in question was characterized by intellectual darkness, an idea that arose from lack of information about medieval life. The studies of modern scholars have made it certain that *dark ages* is a phrase that completely misrepresents the medieval period, which, as a matter of fact, was characterized by intellectual, artistic, and even scientific activity which led to high cultural attainments. Most present-day writers, therefore, avoid the phrase altogether. Some who do use it restrict it to the earlier part of the Middle Ages (fifth to eleventh centuries).

***Débat:*** A type of literary composition, usually in VERSE, that was highly popular in the Middle Ages, in which two persons or objects, frequently allegorical, debated some specific topic and then referred it to a judge. Possibly the *débat* reflects the influence of the "pastoral contest" in Theocritus and Virgil. The form was particularly popular in France, where the subjects debated ranged over most human interests, such as theology, morality, politics, COURTLY LOVE, and social questions. In England the *débat* tended to be religious and moralistic. The best English example is *The Owl and the Nightingale* (*ca.*12th century), whose interpretation has caused much scholarly debate.

**Decadence:** A term used in literary history and criticism to denote the decline or deterioration which commonly marks the end of a great period. Arthur Symons listed as *decadent* qualities "an intense self-consciousness, a restless curiosity in research, an oversubtilizing refinement upon refinement, a spiritual and moral perversity." It is best to remember, however, that the term is relative and can not always suggest the same qualities to the same writers and that no two periods of *decadence* can be just alike. In English dramatic history the period following Shakespeare was marked by such *decadent* qualities as a relaxing of critical standards, a breaking down of types (COMEDY and TRAGEDY merging), a lowered moral tone, sensationalism, over-emphasis upon some single interest (like plot-construction or "prettiness" of style), a decreased seriousness of purpose, and a loss of poetic power. The "silver age" of Latin literature (reign of Trajan), including such writers as Tacitus, Juvenal and Martial (satirists), Lucan, and the Plinys, is called *decadent* in relation to the preceding "golden age" of Augustus made illustrious by Virgil, Horace, Ovid, and Livy. In the last half of the nineteenth and the early years of the twentieth centuries *decadence* found a special expression in the work of a group known as the DECADENTS.

**Decadents:** A group of late nineteenth- and early twentieth-century writers, principally in France but also in England and America, who held that art was superior to nature, that the finest beauty was that of dying or decaying things, and who, both in their lives and their art, attacked the accepted moral, ethical, and social standards of their time. In France the group included Verlaine, Rimbaud, Baudelaire, Huysmans, and Villiers de l'Isle Adam. In England the *decadents* included Oscar Wilde, Ernest Dowson, Aubrey Beardsley, and Frank Harris. In America it is best represented by Edgar Saltus, although there are *decadent* qualities in Stephen Crane.

**Decorum:** A critical term describing that which is proper to a character, subject, or setting in a literary work. According to classical standards, the UNITY and harmony of a composition could be maintained by the observance of dramatic propriety. The STYLE should be appropriate to the speaker, the occasion, and the subject matter. So RENAISSANCE authors were careful to have kings speak in a "high" STYLE (such as majestic blank verse), old men in a "grave" STYLE, clowns in prose, and shepherds in a "rustic" STYLE. Puttenham (1589) cites as an example of the lack of *decorum* the case of the English translator of Virgil who said that Aeneas was fain to "trudge" out of Troy (a beggar might "trudge," but not a great hero). Beginning in the RENAISSANCE the type to which a character belonged was regarded as a most important element in determining his qualities; age, rank, and social status were often held as fundamental in the art of CHARACTERIZATION. Thus a too rigid adherence to such distinctions led to a hardening of character. But on the use of *decorum* in the *Iliad* Pope said: "The *speeches* are to be considered as they flow from the characters, being perfect or defective as they agree or disagree with the manners of those who utter them. As there is more variety of characters in *The Iliad*, so there is of speeches, than in any other poem," and "Homer is in nothing more excellent than in that distinction of characters which he maintains through his whole poem. What Andromache here says can be spoken properly by none but Andromache." *Decorum* has often been considered the controlling critical idea of the NEO-CLASSIC age in England.

**Definition:** A brief EXPOSITION of a term calculated to explain its meaning. Formal *definitions* consist of two elements: (1) the general class (*genus*) to which the object belongs, and (2) the specific ways (*differentiae*) in which the object differs from other objects within the same general class. For instance, in the first sentence above "brief exposition" lists the general class to which *definition* belongs and "calculated to explain its meaning" shows the way in which *definition* differs from other expositions which may be intended, for instance, to make clear the location of a site, the operation of a machine or any one of the various other functions which expositions in general may perform. The following examples should help to make this clear:

| *Term defined* | *General class to which it belongs* | *Specific ways in which it differs from other objects in the same general class* |
|---|---|---|
| A canoe   is a | boat | pointed at both ends and propelled by paddling. |
| A radio   is an | instrument | for receiving or transmitting wireless messages. |

Rarely are single-sentence *definitions* satisfactory in themselves. But the principle above stated guides in forming longer expositions in which both the second and third elements of the *definition* may be extended almost indefinitely.

**Deism:** The religion of those believing in a God who rules the world by established laws but not believing in the divinity of Christ or the inspiration of the Bible; "natural" religion, based on reason and a study of nature, as opposed to "revealed" religion. The scientific movement which grew out of the new knowledge of the world and the universe following upon the discoveries and theories of Columbus, Copernicus, Galileo, Francis Bacon, and later the members of the Royal Society, furthered the development of a rationalistic point of view which more and more tended to rely upon reason instead of upon revelation in the consideration of man's relation to God and the Universe. The fact that the conceptions of the physical world found in the Old Testament seemed inconsistent with the newer knowledge shook the faith of many in the doctrine of the special inspiration of the Bible. *Deism* was a product of this general point of view. It absorbed also something from the theological movements of Arianism (opposition to the doctrine of the Trinity) and ARMINIANISM (which stressed moral conduct as a sign of religion and opposed the doctrine of election; see CALVINISM). The somewhat prevalent notion that the deists believed in an "absentee" God, who, having created the world and set in motion machinery for its operation, took no further interest either in the world or in man is perhaps unfair, as it is certainly not applicable to all eighteenth-century deists, some of whom even believed in God's pardoning of the sins of a repentant individual.

The reputed "father" of the deists was Lord Herbert of Cherbury (1583–1648); later philosophical representatives of the movement included the third earl of Shaftesbury (1671–1713) and Lord Bolingbroke (1678–1751). From Shaftesbury deistic views passed to Voltaire and other French philosophers, who in turn powerfully influenced later English (and American) thought. John Toland (1670–1722), Anthony Collins (1676–1729), and Matthew Tindal (d. 1733) wrote important deistic treatises. The fact that there were groups of theological deists as well as philosophical ones, some deists not agreeing with other deists, makes it difficult to give any accurate summary of the tenets of *deism*, but the following statements perhaps fairly represent the point of view of the English deists: 1. The Bible is not the inspired word of God; it is good so far as it reflects "natural" religion and bad so far as it contains "additions" made by superstitious or designing persons. 2. Certain Christian theological doctrines are the product of superstition or the invention of priests and must be rejected; e.g., the deity of Christ, the doctrine of the Trinity, and theory of the atonement for sins. 3. God is perfect, is the creator and governor of the Universe, and works not capriciously but through unchangeable laws (hence "miracles" are to be rejected as impossible). 4. Human beings are free agents, whose minds work as they themselves choose; even God cannot control man's thoughts. 5. Since man is a rational creature, like God, he is capable of understanding the laws of the universe; and as God is perfect, so can man become perfect through the process of education. Man may learn of God through a study of nature, which shows design and must therefore be an expression of God. 6. Practical religion for the individual consists in achieving virtue through the rational guidance of conduct (as exemplified in the scheme for developing the moral virtues recorded by Franklin in his *Autobiography*). The deistic system is in some ways more optimistic than CALVINISM, with which it came into conflict. Some of the "moderate" deists attempted to reconcile *deism* with Christianity on the ground that reason and revelation never disagreed and were but two different methods of discovering the same body of truth. H. E. Cushman says that *deism* was founded on three principles: (1) the origin and truth of religion may be scientifically investigated; (2) the origin of religion is the conscience; (3) positive religions are degenerate forms of natural religion.

The effects of deistic thinking upon literature were very great and cannot be briefly traced. The *deism* of Pope's *Essay on Man* (partly inspired by Bolingbroke) illustrates the effect on the "classical" school, while the doctrine of man's perfection in Shelley's poetry and much of the Wordsworthian worship of nature are examples of deistic influences on the "romantic" school. The poet James Thomson was an acknowledged deist. Gibbon's *Decline and Fall of the Roman Empire* (1776–1788) excited much controversy because of its deistic treatment of Christianity. Tom Paine's *Age of Reason* is more deistic than atheistic. In America *deism* affected the writing of many writers of the Revolutionary period, notably Franklin and Jefferson.

**Denotation:** The specific, exact meaning of a word, independent of its emotional coloration or associations. See CONNOTATION.

*Dénouement:* The final unraveling of the PLOT in DRAMA or FICTION; the solution of the mystery; the explanation or outcome. *Dénouement* implies an ingenious untying of the knot of an intrigue, involving not only a satisfactory outcome of the main situation but an explanation of all the secrets and misunderstandings connected with the plot COMPLICATION. In DRAMA *dénouement* may be applied to both TRAGEDY and COMEDY, though the common term for a tragic *dénouement* is CATASTROPHE. The final scene of Shakespeare's *Cymbeline* is a striking example of how clever and involved a dramatic *dénouement* may be: exposure of villain, clearing up of mistaken identities and disguises, reuniting of father and children, of husband and wife, etc., etc. By some writers *dénouement* is used as a synonym for FALLING ACTION. See also CATASTROPHE, DRAMATIC STRUCTURE, SHORT STORY.

**Description:** That one of the four chief types of composition (see ARGUMENTATION, EXPOSITION, and NARRATION) which has as its purpose the picturing of a scene or setting. Though often used apart for its own sake (as in Poe's *Landor's Cottage*) it more frequently is subordinated to one of the other types of writing; especially to NARRATION, with which it most frequently goes hand in hand. Descriptive writing is most successful when its details are carefully selected according to some purpose and to a definite point of view, when its IMAGES are concrete and clear, and when it makes discreet use of words of color, sound, and motion.

**Detective Story:** A NOVEL or SHORT STORY in which a crime, usually a murder—the identity of the perpetrator unknown—is solved by a detective through a logical assembling and interpretation of palpable evidence, known as clues. This definition is the accepted one for the true *detective story,* although in practice much variation occurs. If the variations are too great, however—such as the absence of the detective, or a knowledge from the beginning of the identity of the criminal, or the absence of a process of reasoning logically from clues—the story falls into the looser category of MYSTERY STORY. The specific form *detective story* had its origin in "The Murders in the Rue Morgue," by Edgar Allan Poe (1841). In this tale, "The Purloined Letter," "The Mystery of Marie Rogêt," and "Thou Art the Man," Poe is said to have established every one of the basic conventions of the *detective story.* The form has been remarkably popular in England and America, as a form of light entertainment for the intellectual.

Generally, American *detective stories* have had greater sensationalism and action than the English ones, which have usually placed a premium on tightness of plotting and grace of STYLE. The greatest of *detective story* writers was Sir Arthur Conan Doyle, whose Sherlock Holmes stories seem to have established a character, a room, a habit, a few gestures and a group of phrases in the enduring heritage of English-speaking readers. "S. S. Van Dine" (Willard Huntington Wright) carried ingenuity of plotting to a very high level in America in the 1920's in his Philo Vance stories, a course in which he was ably followed by the authors of the Ellery Queen novels. The introduction of brutal realism coupled with a poetic but highly idiomatic STYLE in the *detective stories* of Dashiell Hammett in the 1930's has resulted in distinguished work by the Americans Raymond Chandler and Ross MacDonald. In England the continuing ingenuity of Agatha Christie and John Dickson Carr (also "Carter Dickson") and the skill and grace of Dorothy Sayers and the New Zealander Ngaio Marsh are contributions to the form. All of these practitioners have made it a point of honor to observe the fundamental rule of the *detective story* (and the rule which most clearly distinguishes it from the MYSTERY STORY): that the clues out of which a logical solution to the problem can be made be fairly presented to the reader at the same time that the detective receives them and that the detective deduce the answer to the riddle from a logical reading of these clues. See MYSTERY STORY.

**Deus ex machina:** The employment of some unexpected and improbable incident in a story or play in order to make things turn out right. In the ancient Greek theatre when gods appeared in plays they were lowered to the stage from the "machine" or stage structure above. The abrupt but timely appearance of a god in this fashion, when used to extricate the mortal characters of the drama from a situation so perplexing that the solution seemed beyond mortal powers, was referred to in Latin as the *deus ex machina* ("god from the machine"). The term is now employed to characterize any device whereby an author solves a difficult situation by a forced invention. A villian may fail to kill a hero because he has forgotten to load his revolver. A long-lost brother, given up for dead, suddenly appears on the scene provided with a fortune he has won in foreign parts, just in time to save the family from disgrace or a sister from an unwelcome marriage. The employment of the *deus ex machina* is commonly recognized as evidence of deficient skill in plot-making or an uncritical willingness to disregard the probabilities. Though it is sometimes employed by good authors, it is found most frequently in MELODRAMA. See PLOT, COUP DE THÉÂTRE.

**Dial, The:** A periodical published in Boston from 1840 to 1844 as the mouthpiece of the New England transcendentalists. Margaret Fuller was its first editor (1840–42) and Emerson its second (1842–44). Among the most famous contributors to *The Dial* were Alcott, the two Channings (William H. and William Ellery), Dana, Emerson, Margaret Fuller, Lowell, Thoreau, and Jones Very.

In 1860 another organ of TRANSCENDENTALISM named *The Dial* appeared briefly in Cincinnati, edited by Moncure Conway and with contributions by Emerson, Alcott, and Howells. From 1880 to 1929, a distinguished literary monthly (and between 1892 and 1916, a fortnightly) was published under the name *The Dial*, first in Chicago and after 1916 in New York. Until 1916 it was a conservative literary review. From 1916 to 1920, under the editorship of Conrad Aiken, Randolph Bourne, and Van Wyck Brooks, it was a radical journal of opinion and criticism, publishing writers like Dewey, Veblen, Laski, and Beard. After 1920 it became the most distinguished literary monthly in America, noted for its reproductions of modern graphic art and a powerful advocate of modern artistic movements. It published writers like Thomas Mann, T. S. Eliot, and James Stephens. Marianne Moore was editor from 1926 until it ceased publication in 1929.

**Dialects:** When the speech of two groups or of two persons representing two groups both speaking the same "language" exhibits very marked differences, the groups or persons are said to speak different *dialects* of the language. If the differences are very slight, they may be said to represent "sub-dialects" rather than *dialects*. If the differences are so great that the two groups or persons cannot understand each other, especially if they come from separate political units or countries, they are said to speak different languages. Yet the gradations are so narrow that no scientific method has been devised which will make it possible in all cases to distinguish between a language and a *dialect*. The chief cause of the development of *dialects* is isolation or separation due to lack of ease of communication. Natural barriers such as mountain ranges and social barriers caused by hostile relations tend to keep groups from frequent contact with each other with a resultant development of habitual differences in speech-habits, leading toward the formation of *dialects* or even languages. Likewise among neighboring groups the *dialect* of one group commonly becomes dominant, as did West Saxon in early England.

When the Teutonic tribes which form the basis of the English "race" (Angles, Saxons, etc.) came to England from the Continent in the fifth century, they spoke separate *dialects* of West Germanic. In Old English times (fifth to eleventh centuries) there were four main *dialects:* (1) Northumbrian (north of the Humber River) and (2) Mercian (between the Thames and the Humber), both being branches or sub-dialects of the original Anglian *dialect*; (3) the Kentish (southeastern England), based upon the language of the Jutes, and (4) the Saxon (southern England). The early literature produced in the Northern districts (seventh to ninth centuries) is preserved chiefly in Southern (West Saxon) versions of the tenth and eleventh centuries. In Middle English times the old *dialects* appear under different names and with new sub-dialects. Northumbrian is called Northern; Saxon and Kentish are called Southern; the Northern English spoken in Scotland becomes Lowland Scotch; Mercian becomes Midland, and is broken into two main sub-dialects, West Midland and East Midland. The latter was destined to become the immediate parent of modern English. Middle English literature, therefore, exists in a variety of *dialects*, more or less clearly differentiated. Layamon's *Brut* and *The Owl and the Nightingale,* for example, are in the Southern *dialect; Cursor Mundi* and *Sir Tristrem* are in Northern; the *Ormulum* is early Midland, while *Havelok the Dane, Piers Plowman,* and the poetry of Chaucer are in later Midland. The Middle English *dialects* differed in vocabulary, sounds, and inflections, so that Northerners and Southerners had difficulty in understanding each other. A few examples of the differences may be given: In Northern, "they sing" would be "they singes"; in Midland, "they singen"; in Southern, "they singeth." Northern "kirk" is Southern "church." The present participle in Northern ended in -*ande;* in Southern, in -*inde* or -*inge;* in Midland, in -*ende* or -*inge.* Though the literary language in modern times has been standardized, it must not be supposed that *dialects* no longer exist, especially in oral speech. Skeat lists nine modern *dialects* in Scotland; in England proper he finds three groups of Northern, ten groups of Midland, five groups of Eastern, two groups of Western, and ten groups of Southern.

**Dialects, American:** American *dialects* are less marked than English *dialects,* although some dialectal differences are easily discernible. However, only in areas where a local *patois,* such as Cajun in New Orleans or Gullah on the South Carolina coast, is spoken do Americans have serious difficulty in understanding one another. Three broad dialectal areas are generally recognized in the United States, although their speeches are sometimes given differing names. These areas are: New England and eastern New York, the speech of which is usually called "Eastern"; the area south of Pennsylvania and the Ohio River, extending westward beyond the Mississippi River into Texas, the speech of which is usually called "Southern"; and the broad area which extends from New Jersey on the Atlantic coast, through Pennsylvania and western New York into the middle west and the southwest and then over all the Pacific Coast, an area which comprises more than three-fourths of the American population; the speech of this area is usually called "General American" and sometimes "Western." Modern methods of transportation and mass communication are steadily leveling American speech and eradicating dialectual differences which once existed. At one time a great number of sub-dialects were recognized and exploited in LOCAL COLOR writings; most of these have today merged into the speech patterns of "General American." As a result of the work in progress on the *Linguistic Atlas of the United States* (see AMERICAN LANGUAGE), much more accurate records of remaining regional and local differences of speech are being made, although at the time when they are tending to be lost. Dialectal differences in America are matters of vocabulary, of grammatic habit, and of pronunciation.

**Dialogue:** Conversation of two or more people as reproduced in writing. Most common in FICTION, particularly in DRAMAS, NOVELS, and SHORT STORIES, *dialogue* is nevertheless used in general expository and philosophical writing (Plato). An analysis of *dialogue* as it has been employed by great writers shows that it embodies certain literary and stylistic values: (1) It advances the action in a definite way and is not used as mere ornamentation. (2) It is consistent with the character of the speakers, their social positions and special interests. It varies in tone and expression according to the nationalities, DIALECTS, occupations, and social levels of the speakers. (3) It gives the *impression* of naturalness without being an actual, *verbatim* record of what may have been said, since

FICTION, as someone has explained, is concerned with "the semblance of reality," not with reality itself. (4) It presents the interplay of ideas and personalities among the people conversing; it sets forth a conversational give and take—not simply a series of remarks of alternating speakers. (5) It varies in DICTION, RHYTHM, phrasing, sentence length, etc., according to the various speakers participating. The best writers of *dialogue* know that rarely do two or more people of exactly the same cultural and character background meet and converse, and the *dialogue* they write notes these differences. (6) It serves, at the hands of some writers, to give relief from, and lightness of effect to, passages which are essentially serious or expository in nature.

It should be noted, however, that in the Eizabethan DRAMA the CONVENTION of using BLANK VERSE and high rhetoric for noble or elevated characters and prose for underlings and comic characters modifies these rules, as did the doctrine of DECORUM in the seventeenth and eighteenth centuries. Furthermore, plays of WIT, such as those by Oscar Wilde, and plays of idea, such as those by G. B. Shaw, unhesitatingly take liberties with the idea of appropriateness to station and character in *dialogue.*

The *dialogue* is also a specialized literary composition in which two or more characters debate or reason about an idea or a proposition. There are many notable examples in the world's literature, the best known being the *Dialogues* of Plato. Others include Lucian's *Dialogues of the Dead,* Dryden's *Essay on Dramatic Poesie,* and Landor's *Imaginary Conversations.* Richard Chase's commentary on American literature, *The Democratic Vista,* is cast in *dialogue* form.

**Diary:** A day-by-day CHRONICLE of events, a JOURNAL. Usually a personal and more or less intimate record of events and thoughts kept by an individual. Not avowedly intended for publication —though it is difficult to insist on this point since many diarists have certainly kept their tongues in their cheeks—most *diaries,* when published, have appeared posthumously. Far and away the most famous *diary* in English is that of Samuel Pepys, which details events between January 1, 1660, and May 29, 1669. Other important English *diaries* are those of John Evelyn, Bulstrode Whitelocke, George Fox, Jonathan Swift, John Wesley, and Fanny Burney. Noted American diarists include Samuel Sewell, Sarah K. Knight, and William Byrd. The *diary* has, in late years, become a conscious literary form used by travelers, statesmen, politicians, etc., as a convenient method of presenting the run of daily events in which they have had a hand. See AUTOBIOGRAPHY, BIOGRAPHY.

**Diatribe:** Writing or discourse characterized by bitter invective, abusive argument. A harangue. Originally it was a treatment in DIALOGUE of a limited philosophical proposition in a simple, lively, conversational tone. Popular with the Stoic and Cynic philosophers, it became noted for the abusiveness of the speakers, a fact which led to its present-day meaning.

**Diction:** The use of words in oral or written discourse. A simple list of words makes up a vocabulary; the accurate, careful *use* of these words in discourse makes good *diction*. The qualities of proper *diction* as illustrated by the work of standard authors are: (1) the apt selection of the word for the particular meaning to be conveyed, (2) the use of legitimate words accepted as good usage (excluding all SOLECISMS, BARBARISMS, and improprieties) and (3) the use of words which are clear-cut and specific. The manner in which words are combined constitutes STYLE rather than *diction* since *diction* refers only to the selection of words employed in the discourse.

There are at least four levels of usage for words: the formal, the informal, the colloquial, and SLANG. Formal refers to the level of usage common in serious books and formal discourse; informal refers to the level of usage found in the relaxed but polite conversation of cultivated people; colloquial refers to the everyday usage of a group and it may include terms and constructions accepted in that group but not universally acceptable; and SLANG refers to a group of newly COINED WORDS which are not acceptable for polite usage as yet.

It should be noted that the accepted *diction* of one age often sounds unacceptable to another. See POETIC DICTION.

**Dictionaries:** At different times during their five hundred years of development, English *dictionaries* have emphasized different elements and have passed through an evolution as great as any of our literary forms or tools. In their modern form *dictionaries* arrange their words alphabetically, give explanations of the meanings, the derivations, the pronunciations, illustrative quotations and idioms, synonyms, and antonyms. Sometimes, however, the "dictionary" is restricted to word-lists of a special significance as *dictionaries* of law, of medicine, of art, etc.

Of the *dictionaries* available to the American student and reader, the following should be noted: There are three American "un-abridged"—that is, purporting to record the totality of words in current usage—*dictionaries: The Century* (1889), *The New Standard* (1893), and *The New International* (1898); all have been frequently revised. However, the most complete *dictionary* on the market is from England, the Oxford *New English Dictionary* (1884–1928). Three sizable shorter *dictionaries* are in wide use in America: the *American College Dictionary* (1947); *Webster's New Collegiate Dictionary* (1949), an abridgement of *The New International Dictionary;* and *Webster's New World Dictionary* (1953); all of these are frequently revised. Of special interest to the literary student are the *Dictionary of American English* (1938–1944), the *Dictionary of Americanisms* (1951), the *English Dialect Dictionary*, edited by Joseph Wright (6 volumes), and the *Dictionary of Slang and Unconventional English*, edited by Eric Partridge. H. W. Fowler's *Dictionary of Modern English Usage* is a witty and in-dispensable guide to good usage and graceful expression, and is particularly valuable for Americans in the revision by Marjorie Nicolson.

"English lexicography began," says a writer in the *Encyclopædia Britannica*, "with attempts to explain Latin words by giving English equivalents" and cites the *Promptorium Parvulorum* (1440) of Galfridus Grammaticus, a Dominican monk of Norfolk, printed by Pynson in 1499 as an early example. Just which publication deserves the distinction of being called the first English *dictionary* it is dif-ficult to say because the evolution was so gradual that the concep-tion of what constituted a good word-book differed from year to year. Vizetelly gives credit to Richard Huloet's *Abecedarium* (1552) as the first *dictionary;* the *Britannica* article credits "the first approach to success in collecting and defining all words in good usage in the English language" to Nathaniel Bailey, whose major work was not published until 1730; *The Dictionary of Syr T. Eliot, Knyght,* (1538), appears to have been the work first to establish the term "dictionary."

The evolution of the English *dictionary* is a study interesting enough to warrant the serious attention of scholars. Here only an outline can be suggested. The early word-books started off listing simply the "hard words" which people might not be expected to know; the classification was sometimes alphabetical, sometimes by subject matter. Later, the lexicographers looked upon themselves as literary guardians of national speech and listed only such words as were dignified enough to be of "good usage"; the function of these compilers was to standardize, to "fix" the national language. Illustrative of this point of view were the collections of such scholarly academies as those of Italy and France; and, indeed, Dr. Samuel Johnson, a whole academy in himself, first held and later abandoned this same sort of ideal (see list below). Archbishop Trench, a British scholar, declared roundly in 1857 that a proper *dictionary* was really an "inventory of language" including colloquial uses as well as literary uses and Trench's insistence on the philological attitude for the lexicographer probably did more to develop the modern word-book than any other single influence.

A list of some of the titles important in the evolution of the *dictionary*, exclusive of those given above, includes:

John Florio (1598), *Queen Anna's New World of Words.*
Robert Cawdrey (1604) (who used English words only), *A Table Alphabeticall Contyning and Teaching the True Writing and Understanding of Hard Usuall English Wordes.*
Randle Cotgrave (1611), *A Bundle of Words.*
John Bullokar (1616), *An English Expositor.*
Henry Cockeram (1623), *The English Dictionarie* (in which "idiote" was defined as "an unlearned asse").
Thomas Blount (1656), *Glossographia.*
Edward Phillips (1658), *The New World of English Words.*
Nathaniel Bailey (1721), *Universal Etymological English Dictionary.*
Samuel Johnson (1755), *Dictionary of the English Language* (in which 50,000 words were explained. The most pretentious volume published up to that time. The personal element injected into definitions gives us such famous explanations as that for *oats:* "a grain which in England is generally given to horses, but in Scotland supports the people," and, further, that *Whig* was "the name of a faction" while *Tory* signified "one who adhered to the antient constitution of the state and the apostolical hierarchy of the Church of England, opposed to a Whig").
Thomas Sheridan (1780), *Complete Dictionary of the English Language* (which gave special emphasis to the pronunciation of the words).
Samuel Johnson (1798?), *A School Dictionary.* The first American *dictionary.* This Johnson was not related to the earlier Dr. Samuel. This first American *dictionary* simplified some of the English spellings and began the use of phonetic marks as aids to pronunciation.
Noah Webster (1828), *American Dictionary;* the most famous name in American lexicography.
Joseph Emerson Worcester (1846), *Universal and Critical Dictionary of the English Language.*

In 1884 was begun in England the great work *A New English Dictionary on Historical Principles,* founded mainly on material accumulated by the Philological Society, and edited by James A. H. Murray, Henry Bradley, and W. A. Craigie. From Murray's part in the editing of the first volume, the work is sometimes called *Murray's Dictionary,* though it is more commonly called the *New English Dictionary* or the *Oxford English Dictionary.* It was completed in 1928. Though issued in "parts" the full work is now printed in ten large volumes or twenty "half-volumes." It is easily the greatest of all English *dictionaries* in the fullness of its illustrative examples and in its elaborate analysis of the meanings and etymologies. The citations are drawn from English writings ranging in date from the years 1200 to 1928. It is particularly valuable for its dated quotations of actual sentences showing the meanings of a word at various periods. It contains 240,165 "main words," of which 177,970 are in current use. With the addition of subordinate words, combinations, and a small number of foreign words, the total number of words entered for definition runs to 414,825. See LEXICOGRAPHY.

**Didactic Poetry:** POETRY which is intended primarily to teach a lesson. The distinction between *didactic poetry* and non-didactic poetry is difficult to make and always involves a subjective judgment of the author's purpose on the part of the critic or reader. For example, Bryant's "To a Waterfowl" is obviously concerned with an ethical or religious idea, yet it is not generally considered *didactic,* perhaps because most readers sense that the idea of a protective Providence is dramatically appropriate to the physical and emotional situation being presented—that the poet is communicating his feeling about the idea rather than communicating the idea itself. On the other hand, Pope's *Essay on Criticism* is an emphatic instance of *didactic poetry.* See DIDACTICISM.

**Didacticism:** Instructiveness in a literary work one of the purposes of which appears to be to give guidance, particularly in moral, ethical, or religious matters. Since all literary art exists in order to communicate something—an idea, a teaching, a precept, an emotion, an attitude, a fact, an autobiographical incident, a sensation—the ultimate question of *didacticism* in a literary work appears to be one of the intent of the author or of his ostensible purpose. If, of Horace's dual functions of the artist, he elects instruction as his primary goal, he is didactic in intent or we may say that the purpose of the work he produces is didactic. Another way of stating the problem is to say that if the thing to be communicated takes precedence as an act of communication over the artistic qualities of the FORM through which it is communicated the work is didactic. Viewed in still another way, a work is didactic if it would have as its ultimate effect a meaning or a result outside itself. In a sense those who divide CRITICISM into PLATONIC and ARISTOTELIAN are dividing the purposes of literary art into didactic and non-didactic. From this definition it is obvious that *didacticism* is an acceptable aspect of literature, at least up to a certain point, despite the fact that the term usually carries a derogatory meaning in CRITICISM. The objection to *didacticism* results from a feeling that, if carried too far or borne too self-righteously, it will subvert the object of literature to lesser and ignoble purposes. Among those who make didactic demands of literature today are the practitioners of MORAL CRITICISM, the Marxists, and those who measure literature by sociological standards. The most bitter foes of *didacticism* today are probably the NEW CRITICS, who do not declare poetry to be meaningless but who declare its significant meaning to be intrinsic. See AUTOTELIC; BELIEF, THE PROBLEM OF; ARISTOTELIAN CRITICISM; PLATONIC CRITICISM; NEW CRITICISM; CRITICISM, TYPES OF; CRITICISM, HISTORICAL SKETCH; PARAPHRASE, HERESY OF.

**Dieresis:** A term sometimes used in METRICS to designate the situation where the pause in a VERSE falls at the end of a FOOT; usually called CAESURA. See CAESURA.

**Digression:** The insertion of material unrelated or distantly related to the specific subject under discussion in a given work. In a work with a firm PLOT, a *digression* is a serious violation of UNITY. In the FAMILIAR ESSAY it is a standard device, and it was not infrequently used in the EPIC. The device was particularly popular in seventeenth and eighteenth century English writing, notable examples being the *digressions* in Swift's *Tale of a Tub* and Sterne's "Digression on Digressions" in *Tristram Shandy*. If a *digression* is lengthy and formal it is sometimes called an EXCURSUS.

**Dilettante:** One who follows an art for the love of it rather than as a serious profession. In literature, as with the other arts, the term has taken on a derogatory meaning, however, and is more usually employed to indicate one who reads and talks books and writers from hearsay and a careless reading, perhaps of reviews, as opposed to the student who makes a careful and critical study of a writer, period, movement, or book. Originally a *dilettante* meant an amateur; now it usually means a dabbler.

**Dimeter:** A VERSE consisting of two FEET. See SCANSION.

**Dirge:** A wailing SONG sung at a funeral or in commemoration of death. A short LYRIC of lamentation. See CORONACH, ELEGY, MONODY, PASTORAL ELEGY, THRENODY.

**Discovery:** In a TRAGEDY, the revelation of a fact previously unknown to the character, a knowledge of which now results in the turning of the action. See DRAMATIC STRUCTURE.

**Disguisings:** In medieval times (and in some places into the twentieth century) a species of game or spectacle with a procession of masked figures. *Disguisings* were usually of a popular or folk character. See MASQUE.

**Dissertation:** A formal, involved EXPOSITION written to clarify some scholarly problem. *Dissertation* is sometimes used interchangeably with THESIS but the usual practice, at least in college and university circles, is to reserve *dissertation* for the more elaborate essays and papers written "in partial fulfillment of the requirements for the doctor's degree" and to limit the use of THESIS to smaller problems, less perplexing, less involved, submitted for the bachelor's or master's degree. Of course these words as employed in academic circles are part of the CANT of college language since both THESIS and *dissertation* are commonly used off college campuses simply to signify careful, thoughtful discussions, in writing or speech, on almost any serious problem. In literature the term has been used lightly, as in Lamb's "A Dissertation on Roast Pig" and formally as in Bolingbroke's *Dissertation on Parties* or in Newton's *dissertations;* here the term implies learned formality.

**Dissonance:** Harsh and inharmonious sounds, a marked breaking of the music of a VERSE of POETRY, which may be intentional, as it often is in Browning, but if unintentional is a major poetic flaw. The term is also sometimes applied to RIMES that are almost true RIMES but fail by a slight margin to be perfect because of variations in vowel sounds too slight to earn them the name of ASSONANCE; a form of HALF-RIME or SLANT RIME.

**Distich:** A COUPLET. Any two consecutive lines in similar form and riming. An EPIGRAM or MAXIM completely expressed in couplet form. Example:

> Hope springs eternal in the human breast;
> Man never is, but always to be, blest.
> > —Pope

See -STICH.

**Distributed Stress:** A term used to describe a situation in METRICS where each of two syllables takes, or shares, the STRESS. Also called HOVERING STRESS or RESOLVED STRESS. See HOVERING STRESS.

**Dithyramb:** Literary expression characterized by wild, excited, passionate language. Its LYRIC power relates it most nearly to VERSE though its unordered sequence and development, its seemingly improvised quality, give it often the form of prose. Dithyrambic VERSE was probably originally meant to be accompanied by music and was historically associated with Greek ceremonial worship of Dionysus. It formed the original for the choral element in Greek VERSE, later developing into the finer quality which we know as Greek TRAGEDY. Rather rare in English, dithyrambic verse is most closely related to the ODE; it finds its best expression in Dryden's *Alexander's Feast*.

**Ditty:** A SONG, a REFRAIN. The term is somewhat vaguely and loosely used for almost any short, popular, simple melody. It implies something familiar and is perhaps most often applied to SONGS of the sailor. The term is also used, in the sense of THEME, to refer to any short, apt saying or idea which runs through a composition.

**Divine Afflatus, The:** A phrase used to mean poetic inspiration, particularly the exalted state immediately preceding creative composition, when the poet is felt to be receiving his inspiration directly from a divine source. The doctrine of divine inspiration for poets was advocated by Plato. Although the phrase and doctrine have been used in a serious and sincere sense by such a poet as Shelley, the term is perhaps more often used now in a somewhat contemptuous sense, to imply a sort of pretentious over-valuation in a would-be poet or a bombastic spirit in an orator, whose fervid style or manner is felt not to be justified by the actual substance of the poem or oration.

**Doctrinaire:** An adjective applied to one whose attitude is controlled by a preconceived theory or group of theories and who is inclined to disregard other points of view as well as practical considerations. His view is likely to be theoretical, narrow, and one-sided, as compared with practical and broad-minded. Criticism like Dr. Samuel Johnson's may be *doctrinaire* because controlled by a definite code of critical doctrines. Literature itself may be called *doctrinaire* when written, like some of Carlyle's books, to demonstrate such a doctrine as "hero-worship" or the "gospel of work"; or like a novel of William Godwin's, to preach a social doctrine. Politically, the word was applied to the constitutional royalists in France after 1815. See DIDACTICISM.

**Doggerel:** Jerky, rude composition in VERSE. Any poorly executed attempt at POETRY. Characteristics of *doggerel* verse are monotony of RIME and RHYTHM, cheap sentiment, and trivial, trite subject matter. Some *doggerel* does, however, because of certain humorous and BURLESQUE qualities it attains, become amusing and earns a place on one of the lower shelves of literature. Doctor Johnson's parody on Percy's "Hermit of Warkworth" is an example:

> As with my hat upon my head
> I walk'd along the Strand,
> I there did meet another man
> With his hat in his hand.

**Domestic Tragedy:** In spite of the authority of Aristotle and the examples of the great CLASSICAL and ROMANTIC TRAGEDIES of Jonson, Shakespeare, and others, the English stage at various periods has produced tragedies based not upon the lives of historical personages of high rank (see TRAGEDY) but upon the lives of everyday contemporary folk. Running contrary to the prevailing critical conceptions of the proper sphere of TRAGEDY, *domestic tragedy* was long in winning critical recognition. Indeed, Allardyce Nicoll notes that the earlier *domestic tragedy* of the eighteenth century was a purely English form, as only in England were dramatists bold enough to believe that a serious play could be contemporary and topical. In Elizabethan times were produced such powerful *domestic tragedies* as the anonymous *Arden of Feversham* (late sixteenth century), Thomas Heywood's *A Woman Killed With Kindness* (acted 1603), and *The Yorkshire Tragedy* (1608, anon.). The type failed, however, to hold its popularity in competition with other forms, and disappeared from the stage. This early Elizabethan *domestic tragedy* specialized in murder stories taken from contemporary bourgeois life. In the eighteenth century *domestic tragedy* reappeared, tinged this time with the SENTIMENTALISM of the age, as in George Lillo's *The London Merchant* (1731) and Edward Moore's *The Gamester* (1753), in the latter of which plays the tragic hero is a gambler who, falsely accused of murder, takes poison and dies just after hearing that a large amount of money has been left to him. The eighteenth-century *domestic tragedy*, however, was crowded out by other forms, though the idea was taken over by foreign playwrights and later in the nineteenth century reintroduced from abroad, especially under the influence of Ibsen, since whose time the old conception of TRAGEDY as possible only with heroes of high rank has definitely given way to plays which present fate at work among the lowly. No catalogue of these modern plays can here be attempted, though John Masefield's *Tragedy of Nan* (1909) may be noted as an important twentieth-century example of the form, as is also O'Neill's *Desire Under the Elms*, Arthur Miller's *The Death of a Salesman*, and Williams' *Cat on a Hot Tin Roof*.

**Doric:** The *Doric* DIALECT in ancient Greece was thought of as lacking in refinement, and *Doric* architecture was marked by simplicity and strength rather than by beauty of detail. So a rustic or "broad" DIALECT may be referred to as *Doric*, and such simple idyllic pieces of literature as Tennyson's *Dora* or Wordsworth's *Michael* may be said to exhibit *Doric* qualities. It is often applied to PASTORALS. Perhaps the best single synonym is "simple." See ATTIC, with which *Doric* was and is in conscious contrast.

**Double Rime:** FEMININE RIME, that is, RIME in which the similar stressed syllables are followed by identical unstressed syllables. "Stream" and "beam" are RIMES; "streaming" and "beaming" are *double rimes*.

**Drama:** Aristotle called *drama* "imitated human action." But since his meaning of IMITATION is in doubt, this phrase is not so simple or clear as it seems. Professor J. M. Manly sees three necessary elements in *drama:* (1) a story (2) told in action (3) by actors who impersonate the characters of the story. This admits such forms as PANTOMIME. Yet many writers insist that DIALOGUE must be present, e.g., Professor Schelling, who calls *drama* "a picture or representation of human life in that succession and change of events that we call story, told by means of dialogue and presenting in action the successive emotions involved." Dramatic elements have been combined and emphasized so differently in dramatic history as to make theoretical definition difficult.

*Origins: Greek and Roman Drama.*—Some account of how *drama* originated and how it has developed will perhaps throw more light upon its nature. *Drama* arose from religious ceremonial. Greek COMEDY developed from those phases of the Dionysian rites which dealt with the theme of fertility; Greek TRAGEDY came from the Dionysian rites dealing with life and death; and medieval DRAMA arose out of rites commemorating the birth and the resurrection of Christ. These three origins seem independent of each other. The word COMEDY is based upon a word meaning "revel," and early Greek COMEDY preserved in the actors' costumes evidences of the ancient phallic ceremonies. Gradually comedy developed away from this primitive display of sex interest in the direction of greater DECORUM and seriousness, though the "Old Comedy" was gross in character. SATIRE became an element of COMEDY as early as the sixth century B.C. Menander (342–291 B.C.) is a representative of the "New Comedy"—a more conventionalized form which was imitated by the great Roman writers of COMEDY, Plautus and Terence, through whose plays classical COMEDY was transmitted to the Elizabethan dramatists.

The word TRAGEDY seems to mean a "goat-song," and may reflect Dionysian death and resurrection ceremonies in which the goat was the sacrificial animal. The DITHYRAMBIC chant used in these festivals is perhaps the starting point of TRAGEDY. The possible process of development has been thus stated by Professor Nicoll: "From a common chant the ceremonial song developed into a primitive duologue between a leader, dressed probably in the robes of the god, and the chorus. The song became elaborated; it developed narrative elements, and soon reached a stage in which the duologue told in primitive wise some story of the deity. Further forward movements were introduced. Two leaders instead of one made their appearance. The chorus gradually sank into the background, no longer taking the place of a protagonist."[1] The great Greek authors of TRAGEDIES were Aeschylus (525–456 B.C.), Sophocles (496–406 B.C.), and Euripides (480–406 B.C.). Modeled on these were the Latin CLOSET-DRAMAS of Seneca (4? B.C.–A.D. 65) which exercised a profound influence upon Renaissance TRAGEDY (see SENECAN TRAGEDY).

*Rebirth of Drama in Middle Ages.*—The decline of Rome witnessed the disappearance of acted classical DRAMA. The MIME survived for an uncertain period and perhaps aided in preserving the tradition of acting through wandering entertainers (see JONGLEUR, MINSTREL). Likewise, dramatic ceremonies and customs, some of them perhaps related to the ancient Dionysian rites themselves, played an uncertain part in keeping alive in medieval times a sort of substratum of dramatic consciousness. Scholars are virtually agreed, however, that the great institution of MEDIEVAL DRAMA in Western Europe, leading as it did to modern *drama,* was a new form which developed, about the ninth and following centuries, from the ritual of the Christian Church (see MEDIEVAL DRAMA). The dramatic forms resulting from this development, MYSTERY or CYCLIC PLAYS, MIRACLE PLAYS, MORALITIES, flourishing especially in the fourteenth and fifteenth centuries, lived on into the RENAISSANCE.

*Renaissance English Drama.*—The new interests of the RENAISSANCE included TRANSLATIONS and IMITATIONS of classical DRAMA, partly through the medium of SCHOOL and UNIVERSITY PLAYS, partly through the work of university-trained professionals engaged in supplying *dramas* for the public stage or the court or such institutions as the INNS OF COURT, and partly through the influence of classical dramatic CRITICISM, much of which reached England through Italian scholars. Thus a revived knowledge of ancient *drama* united with the native dramatic traditions developed from medieval forms and technique to produce in the later years of the sixteenth century the vigorous and many-sided phenomenon known as ELIZABETHAN DRAMA, with its spectacular and patriotic CHRONICLE PLAYS, its TRAGEDIES OF BLOOD, its light-hearted COURT COMEDIES, its dreamy and delightful ROMANTIC COMEDIES, its PASTORAL PLAYS, satirical plays, and realistic presentations of London life. These *dramas*

[1]Allardyce Nicoll, *British Drama,* Thomas Y. Crowell Company, 1925, p. 15. Reprinted by permission of the publishers.

were written by playwrights who made up collectively an illustrious group of able dramatists, led by the immortal Shakespeare. All English *drama* shared the DECADENT tendencies of JACOBEAN and CAROLINE times and in 1642 the PURITANS officially closed the theatres.

*Restoration and Eighteenth-century Drama.*—The stout efforts of Ben Jonson in Elizabethan times to curb the romantic tendencies which had helped to make possible the masterpieces of Shakespeare and to insist upon the observance of classical rules of *drama* bore late fruit when in RESTORATION times, under the added influence of French *drama* and theory, English *drama* was officially revived under court auspices. NEO-CLASSIC tendencies now held sway. Shakespeare was "rewritten" for the stage. The HEROIC PLAY and the new COMEDY OF MANNERS flourished, followed in the eighteenth century first by the SENTIMENTAL COMEDY and DOMESTIC TRAGEDIES and in the latter part of the century by a chastened COMEDY OF MANNERS under Goldsmith and Sheridan.

*Nineteenth-century Drama.*—MELODRAMA and spectacle reigned through the early nineteenth century, occasional efforts to produce an actable literary *drama* proving futile. The late nineteenth century witnessed an important revival of serious *drama*, with, however, a tendency away from the established TRADITIONS of poetic TRAGEDY and COMEDY in favor of shorter plays stressing ideas or problems or situations and depending much upon DIALOGUE.

*American Drama.*—In America theatrical performances, at first produced by amateurs, appeared very early in the eighteenth century in such cities as Boston, New York, and Charleston, S. C., though no *drama* was written by an American till about the middle of the century, at which time important groups of professional actors also appeared. The early *drama* was imitative and dependent upon English originals or models. The Revolutionary War produced some political plays. The first native TRAGEDY was Thomas Godfrey's *Prince of Parthia* (acted 1767), and the first COMEDY professionally produced was Royall Tyler's *The Contrast* (1787). The early nineteenth century witnessed a growing interest in the theatre, William Dunlap and John Howard Payne (author of "Home, Sweet Home") being prolific playwrights. Increased use was made of American themes. In the middle of the century George Henry Boker produced notable ROMANTIC TRAGEDIES, and literary *drama* received some attention. American dramatic art advanced in the period following the Civil War with such writers as Bronson Howard, though it was restricted greatly by the triumph of commercial theatrical management. The early twentieth century produced several dramatists of note (William Vaughn Moody, Percy MacKaye, Josephine Peabody, Eugene O'Neill) and has witnessed a remarkable growth of the LITTLE THEATRE MOVEMENT.

*Twentieth-century Drama:* There has been a healthy rebirth of dramatic interest and experimentation in the twentieth century both in Great Britain and in the United States. In the Irish Theatre, under the leadership of people like Lady Gregory and Douglas Hyde, a vital *drama* has emerged, with original and powerful plays from men like W. B. Yeats, J. M. Synge, Padraic Colum, and Sean O'Casey (see CELTIC RENAISSANCE). Meanwhile, in England the influence of Ibsen (also important on the Irish playwrights) made itself strongly felt in the PROBLEM PLAYS and DOMESTIC TRAGEDIES of Henry Arthur Jones and Arthur Wing Pinero, in the witty and highly intellectual *drama* of G. B. Shaw, and in the REALISM of W. S. Houghton and John Galsworthy. Somerset Maugham, Noel Coward, and James Barrie have been active producers of COMEDY; John Masefield gave expression to the tragic vision in a long series of plays. T. S. Eliot and Christopher Fry revived and enriched verse *drama*. Also important is John Osborne, the leader of England's "Angry Young Men" (*Look Back in Anger*).

The twentieth century saw the development of a serious American *drama*. Early in the century REALISM, which had had its first American dramatic representation in J. A. Herne's *Margaret Fleming* in 1890, was followed, sometimes afar off, by Percy MacKaye, William Vaughn Moody, and Rachel Carothers. But it remained for the great craftsmanship, serious experimentation, and morbid imagination of Eugene O'Neill to give a truly American expression to the tragic view of experience. O'Neill is the greatest playwright America has produced and the example both of his success and of his experimentation fired a host of others. Thornton Wilder, Philip Barry, Lillian Hellman, Sidney Howard, Robert Sherwood, Tennessee Williams, and Arthur Miller have given America a serious *drama* for the first time in its history. Barry, S. N. Behrman, George Kaufman, and John van Druten have practiced the comic craft with skill. Maxwell Anderson revived the verse play successfully, and Rodgers and Hammerstein gave the musical comedy unexpected depth and beauty in *Oklahoma* and other "musicals."

Details of dramatic history are given throughout the *Outline of Literary History*. See also COMEDY, CONFLICT, CHARACTERIZATION, DRAMATIC STRUCTURE, PLOT, and TRAGEDY.

**Dramatic Conventions:** Whether one approach the DRAMA as spectator, reader, or student, he must bring to it what Coleridge aptly called "that willing suspension of disbelief for the moment which constitutes poetic faith." Although the DRAMA is, as Aristotle asserted, an IMITATION of life, the stage and the printed page present physical difficulties for the making of such IMITATIONS. The various devices which have been employed as substitutions for reality in the DRAMA and which the audience must accept as real although it knows them to be false are called *dramatic conventions.* One approaching a DRAMA must, in the first place, accept the fact of impersonation or representation. The actors on the stage must be taken as the persons of the story (though this acceptance by no means precludes a degree of detachment sufficient to enable the spectator to appraise the art of the actor). The stage must be regarded as the actual scene or geographical SETTING of the action. The intervals between ACTS or SCENES must be expanded imaginatively to correspond with the needs of the story. Moreover, one must accept special CONVENTIONS, not inherent in DRAMA as such but no less integral because of their traditional use, such as the SOLILOQUY, the "asides," the fact that ordinary people are made spontaneously to speak in highly poetic language and that actors always speak louder than would be natural, actually pitching their voices to reach the most distant auditor rather than the persons in the group on the stage, etc. Similarly one must be prepared at times to accept costuming that is conventional or symbolic rather than realistic.

In the ELIZABETHAN THEATRE, the spectator had imaginatively to picture the platform as in turn a number of different places; in the modern theatre, he must accept the idea of the invisible "fourth wall" through which he views interior actions. All means of getting inside the minds of characters—and they are many—are CONVENTIONS (even if only within the single play; see O'Neill's *Strange Interlude*) that are successful exactly to the extent that the audience is willing to believe them. Even the curtain which opens and closes the DRAMA is in its way as pure a CONVENTION as the CHORUS of a Greek TRAGEDY. See CONVENTION.

**Dramatic Irony:** The words or acts of a character in a play may carry a meaning unperceived by himself but understood by the audience. Usually the character's own interests are involved in a way he cannot understand. The IRONY resides in the contrast between the meaning intended by the speaker and the added significance seen by others. The term is occasionally applied also to non-dramatic narrative, and is sometimes extended to include any situation (such as mistaken identity) in which some of the actors on the stage or some of the characters in a story are "blind" to facts known to the spectator or reader. So understood, *dramatic irony* is responsible for much of the interest in FICTION and DRAMA, because the reader or spectator enjoys being in on the secret. For an example see TRAGIC IRONY. The complexity and the centrality of *dramatic irony* to a serious consideration of DRAMA is shown in R. B. Sharpe's detailed *Irony in the Drama*.

**Dramatic Monologue:** A LYRIC poem which reveals "a soul in action" through the conversation of one character in a dramatic situation. The character is speaking to an identifiable but silent listener in a dramatic moment in the speaker's life. The circumstances surrounding the conversation, one side of which we "hear" as the *dramatic monologue*, are made clear by implication in the poem, and a deep insight into the character of the speaker is given. Although a quite old form, the *dramatic monologue* was brought to a very high level by Robert Browning, who is often credited with its creation. Tennyson used the form on occasion, and contemporary poets have found it congenial, as witness the work of Robert Frost, E. A. Robinson, Carl Sandburg, Allen Tate, and T. S. Eliot, whose "Love Song of J. Alfred Prufrock" is a distinguished twentieth century example of a *dramatic monologue*. See SOLILOQUY.

**Dramatic Poetry:** A term that, logically, should be restricted to poetry which employs dramatic form or some element or elements of dramatic technique as a means of achieving poetic ends. The DRAMATIC MONOLOGUE is an example. The dramatic quality may result from the use of DIALOGUE, MONOLOGUE, vigorous DICTION, BLANK VERSE, or the stressing of tense situation and emotional CONFLICT. Because of the presence of dramatic elements in the poems to be included in the volume, Browning used the phrase "Dramatic Lyrics" as the subtitle of *Bells and Pomegranates*, No. III (1842). However, the phrase *dramatic poetry* is not infrequently employed broadly so as to include compositions which, like Shakespeare's *The Tempest*, may be more properly classed as POETIC DRAMA, or which, like Browning's *Pippa Passes*, are more commonly called CLOSET DRAMAS (see CLOSET DRAMA).

**Dramatic Structure:** The ancients compared the PLOT of a DRAMA to the tying and untying of a knot. The principle of dramatic CONFLICT, though not mentioned as such in Aristotle's definition of DRAMA, is implied in this figure. The technical structure of a serious play is determined by the necessities of developing this dramatic CONFLICT. Thus a well-built TRAGEDY will commonly show the following divisions, each of which represents a phase of the dramatic CONFLICT: introduction, RISING ACTION, CLIMAX or CRISIS (turning point), FALLING ACTION, and CATASTROPHE. The relation of these parts is sometimes represented graphically by the figure of a pyramid, called Freytag's pyramid, the rising slope suggesting the RISING ACTION or tying of the knot, the falling slope the FALLING ACTION or resolution, the apex representing the CLIMAX.

The *introduction* (or EXPOSITION) creates the tone, gives the setting, introduces some of the characters, and supplies other facts necessary to the understanding of the play, such as events in the story supposed to have taken place before the part of the action included in the play, since a play, like an EPIC, is likely to plunge *in medias res,* "into the middle of things." In *Hamlet,* the bleak midnight scene on the castle platform, with the appearance of the ghost, sets the keynote of the TRAGEDY, while the conversation of the watchers, especially the words of Horatio, supply antecedent facts, such as the quarrel between the dead King Hamlet and the King of Norway. The ancients called this part the PROTASIS.

The RISING ACTION, or COMPLICATION, is set in motion by the EXCITING FORCE (in *Hamlet* the ghost's revelation to Hamlet of the murder) and continues through successive stages of CONFLICT between the hero and the COUNTERPLAYERS up to the CLIMAX or turning point (in *Hamlet* the hesitating failure of the hero to kill Claudius at prayer). The ancients called this part the EPITASIS.

The downward or FALLING ACTION stresses the activity of the forces opposing the hero and while some suspense must be maintained, the trend of the action must lead logically to the disaster with which the TRAGEDY is to close. The FALLING ACTION, called by the ancients the CATASTASIS, is often set in movement by a single event called the TRAGIC FORCE, closely related to the CLIMAX and bearing the same relation to the FALLING ACTION as the EXCITING FORCE does to the RISING ACTION. In *Macbeth* the TRAGIC FORCE is the escape of Fleance following the murder of Banquo. In *Hamlet* it is the "blind" stabbing of Polonius, which sends Hamlet away from the court just as he appears about to succeed in his plans. The latter part of the FALLING ACTION is sometimes marked by an event which delays the CATASTROPHE and seems to offer a way of escape for the hero (the apparent reconciliation of Hamlet and Laertes). This is called the "moment of final suspense" and aids in maintaining interest. The FALLING ACTION is usually shorter than the RISING ACTION and often is attended by some lowering of interest (as in the case of the long conversation between Malcolm and MacDuff in *Macbeth*), since new forces must be introduced and an apparently inevitable end made to seem uncertain. RELIEF SCENES are often resorted to in the FALLING ACTION, partly to mark the passage of time, partly to provide emotional relaxation for the audience. The famous scene of the grave diggers in *Hamlet* is an example of how this RELIEF SCENE may be justified through its inherent dramatic qualities and through its relation to the serious action (see COMIC RELIEF).

The CATASTROPHE, marking the tragic failure, usually the death, of the hero (and often of his opponents as well) comes as a natural outgrowth of the action. It satisfies, not by a gratification of the emotional sympathies of the spectator but by its logical conformity, and by a final presentation of the nobility of the succumbing hero. A "glimpse of restored order" often follows the CATASTROPHE proper in a Shakespearean TRAGEDY, as when Hamlet gives his dying vote to Fortinbras as the new king.

This five-part *dramatic structure* was believed by Freytag to be reflected in a five-act structure for TRAGEDY. However, the imposing of a rigorous five-act structure upon Elizabethan TRAGEDY is questionable, since relatively few plays fall readily into the pattern of an ACT of EXPOSITION, an ACT of RISING ACTION, an ACT of CLIMAX, an ACT of FALLING ACTION, and an ACT of CATASTROPHE. It should be noted too that this structure based upon the analogy of the tying and untying of a knot is applicable to COMEDY, the NOVEL, and the SHORT STORY, with the adjustment of the use of the broader term DÉNOUEMENT for CATASTROPHE in works that are not tragic, despite the fact that technically CATASTROPHE and DÉNOUEMENT are synonymous. (See ACT, CATASTROPHE, and DÉNOUEMENT.)

During the nineteenth century conventional structure gave way to a newer technique. First, COMEDY, under the influence of French bourgeois comedy, the "well-made play" of Eugène Scribe and others, developed a set of technical CONVENTIONS all its own; and as a result of the movement led by Ibsen, serious DRAMA cast off the restrictions of five-act TRAGEDY and freed itself from conventional formality. By the end of the century the traditional five-act

*Drame*

structure was to be found only in poetic or consciously archaic TRAGEDY, whose connection with the stage was artificial and generally unsuccessful. However the fundamental elements of structure given here remained demonstrably present, though in modified form, in these newer types of plays. If at first glance it seems that Ibsen opens one of his DOMESTIC TRAGEDIES at or just before the TRAGIC FORCE, the EXPOSITION, the EXCITING FORCE, and the RISING ACTION which brought about the situation with which he opens are still present and are communicated to the audience by implication and FLASHBACK. The fundamental *dramatic structure* seems timeless and impervious to basic change. See TRAGEDY, CONFLICT, ACT, CATASTROPHE, CLIMAX, CRISIS.

**Drame:** A form of play between TRAGEDY and COMEDY developed by the French in the eighteenth century and later introduced into England, where it is often called a *"drama."* It is a serious play, of which the modern PROBLEM PLAY is an example.

**Dream Allegory** (or **Vision**): The dream was a conventional narrative frame that was widely used in the Middle Ages and is still employed on occasion. The narrator falls asleep and while sleeping dreams a dream which is the actual story told in the dream frame. In the Middle Ages the device was used for ALLEGORY. Among the major *dream allegories* are *The Romance of the Rose,* Dante's *Divine Comedy,* Chaucer's *The Book of the Duchess* and *The House of Fame, The Pearl,* and *The Vision of Piers Plowman.* The *dream allegory* forms the narrative frame for Bunyan's *Pilgrim's Progress* and Edward Bellamy's *Looking Backward.* See ALLEGORY, FRAME-STORY.

**Droll:** A short dramatic piece (also known as "drollery" or "droll humour") cultivated on the COMMONWEALTH stage in England as a substitute for full-length or serious plays not permitted by the government. A *droll* was likely to be a "short, racy, comic" scene selected from some popular play (as a Launcelot Gobbo scene from *The Merchant of Venice*) and completed by dancing somewhat in the manner of the earlier JIG.

**Dumb Show:** A pantomimic performance used as a part of a play. The term is applied particularly to such specimens of silent acting as appeared in Elizabethan DRAMA. The *dumb show* provided a spectacular element and was often accompanied by music. Sometimes it employed allegorical figures like those in the MORALITY PLAY and the MASQUE. Sometimes it foreshadowed coming events in the action and sometimes it provided comment like that of the CHORUS. Sometimes it appeared as PROLOGUE or between ACTS and sometimes it was an integral part of the action, being performed by the characters of the play proper. Whatever its origin, it seems to have appeared first in the third quarter of the sixteenth century in the Senecan plays (see SENECAN TRAGEDY). It continued in use well into the seventeenth century. More than fifty extant Elizabethan plays contain *dumb shows*. The one appearing in Shakespeare's *Hamlet* (Act III, Scene ii) is unusual in that it is preliminary to a show which is itself a "play within a play." Other well-known Elizabethan plays containing *dumb shows* are Sackville and Norton's *Gorboduc* (1562), Robert Greene's *James the Fourth* (1591), John Marston's *Malcontent* (1604), John Webster's *Duchess of Malfi* (1614), and Thomas Middleton's *The Changeling* (1623). See DISGUISINGS, MASQUE, PAGEANT, PANTOMIME.

**Duodecimo:** A BOOK SIZE, designating a book whose SIGNATURES result from sheets folded to twelve leaves or twenty-four pages. See BOOK SIZES.

**Dynamic Character:** A character in a FICTION or DRAMA who develops or changes as a result of the actions of the PLOT. See CHARACTERIZATION.

**Early Tudor Age, 1500–1557:** During the early years of the sixteenth century, the ideals of the RENAISSANCE were rapidly replacing those of the Middle Ages. The Reformation of the English church and the revival of learning known as HUMANISM were making major modifications in English life and thought. In literature it was a time of experimentation and of extensive formal borrowings from French and Italian writings. Wyatt and Surrey imported and "Englished" the SONNET and BLANK VERSE, while Barclay and Skelton continued the older satiric tradition. Sir Thomas Elyot and Sir Thomas More were the major prose writers, and the translators and the chroniclers were adding substantially both to English knowledge and to English prose style. The late medieval DRAMA was still dominant, with the MYSTERY PLAYS, MORALITIES, and INTERLUDES in great vogue, although SCHOOL PLAYS were beginning to introduce new elements into the DRAMA, notably in *Ralph Roister Doister,* the first "regular" English COMEDY. Perhaps the most important single book, from a literary point of view, was *Tottel's Miscellany* (1557), a collection of the "new poetry" which paved the way for Elizabethan poets. See THE RENAISSANCE and *Outline of Literary History.*

**Early Victorian Age, 1832–1870:** The period between the death of Sir Walter Scott and 1870 was a time of the gradual lessening of the Romantic impulse and the steady growth of REALISM in English letters. It bears to ROMANTICISM much the same relation that the AGE OF JOHNSON bears to the NEO-CLASSIC PERIOD—it is an age in which the seeds of the new movement were being sown but which was still predominantly of the old. In poetry, the voices of the major Romantics had been stilled by death, except for that of Wordsworth, and a new poetry more keenly aware of social issues and more marked by doubts and uncertainties resulting from the pains of the INDUSTRIAL REVOLUTION and the advances in scientific thought appeared. The chief writers of this poetry were Tennyson, Browning, Arnold, and the young Swinburne. In the NOVEL Dickens, Thackeray, the Brontë sisters, and Trollope flourished. In the essay Carlyle, Newman, Ruskin, Arnold, and DeQuincey did outstanding work. See ROMANTIC PERIOD IN ENGLISH LITERATURE, VICTORIAN, and *"Outline of Literary History."*

**Eclogue:** Literally, *eclogue* in Greek meant "selection" and was applied to various kinds of poems. From its application to Virgil's PASTORAL poems, however, *eclogue* came to have its present restricted meaning of a formal PASTORAL poem following the traditional technique derived from the IDYLLS of Theocritus (third century B.C.). Conventional *eclogue* types include: (1) the singing match: two shepherds have a singing contest on a wager or for a prize, a third shepherd acting as judge; (2) the rustic DIALOGUE: two "rude swains" engage in banter, perhaps over a mistress, perhaps over their flocks; (3) the DIRGE or lament for a dead shepherd (see PASTORAL ELEGY); (4) the love-lay: a shepherd may sing a song of courtship or a shepherd or shepherdess may complain of disappointment in love; (5) the EULOGY. In RENAISSANCE times, following Mantuan's Latin *eclogues* (fifteenth century) the *eclogue* was used for veiled SATIRE, particularly SATIRE against the corruptions of the clergy, against political factions, and against those responsible for the neglect of poetry. The earliest and most famous collection of conventional *eclogues* in English literature is Spenser's *The Shepheardes Calender* (1579), made up of one *eclogue* for each month. By the eighteenth century a distinction was made between *eclogue* and PASTORAL, the term *eclogue* being used to describe the FORM and PASTORAL the content. Hence *eclogue* came to mean a DRAMATIC POEM, with little action or characterization, in which sentiments are expressed in DIALOGUE or SOLILOQUY, and *eclogues* laid in towns became possible. See PASTORAL.

*Edinburgh Review:* A quarterly JOURNAL of CRITICISM founded in 1802 by Francis Jeffrey, Sydney Smith, and Henry Brougham. The first issue, consisting of 252 pages, appeared October 10, 1802, under the editorship of Sydney Smith, though Jeffrey was subsequently the editor for twenty-seven years. The state of CRITICISM and book reviewing at the time was so low that the founders determined on a vigorous, outspoken policy which not only made a successful publication (10,000 circulation after ten years), but also stirred up the whole English-reading world. Among the contributors to the *Review* were some of the most brilliant writers of the time, the list including in addition to the editors such men as Walter Scott, Henry Hallam, and Francis Horner. The motto of the publication—*Judex damnatur, cum nocens absolvitur,* "the judge is condemned when the guilty man is acquitted"—indicates clearly the rigorous policy of the founders, and, if the ire which the magazine aroused in many quarters is a criterion, it appears that not only were few guilty men acquitted, but that many innocent men were condemned. After seven years of being browbeaten, the Tories started a rival journal, the *Quarterly Review* (1809), the two publications riding literary and political prejudices hard and enlivening British CRITICISM while giving to journalism one of its most brilliant and erratic epochs.

One of the abhorrences of the *Edinburgh Review* was the "lakers" (Lake School of writers), more particularly Southey and Wordsworth. An article by Henry Brougham called *Hours of Idleness* (reviewing an early volume by Byron) provoked Byron's famous satire, *English Bards and Scotch Reviewers.* Later contributors included Macaulay, Carlyle, Hazlitt, and Arnold. *The Edinburgh Review* ceased publication in 1929.

**Edition:** "In modern times we can define *edition* as the whole number of copies of a book printed at any time or times from one setting-up of type, and IMPRESSION as the whole number of copies printed at one time (in ordinary circumstances, the total number of copies printed without removing the type or plates from the press). By ISSUE is generally meant some special form of the book in which, for the most part, the original printed sheets are used but which differs from the earlier or normal form by the addition of new matter or by some difference in arrangement. Parts of an IMPRESSION printed on different paper are also sometimes referred to as different ISSUES. The word is, however, very loosely used, and a cheap 'reissue' may merely mean the old book quite unchanged, except perhaps for the substitution of a cheaper binding, but at a reduced price."[1] As applied to old books, *edition* and IMPRESSION are practically synonymous, because of the practice of distributing type after a printing. Other uses of the term *edition* appear in such phrases as "a ten-volume *edition* of Kipling" (referring to the form of publication) and "Grosart's *edition* of Spenser" (reflecting the fact of editing).

**Editorial:** A short ESSAY, expository or argumentative in character, used in newspapers or magazines. The purpose of the *editorial* is usually to discuss current news events, and the subjects treated may range from matters of purely local importance through county, state, national, and international affairs. The usual *editorial* form falls naturally into three divisions: a statement of the event or situation to be discussed, a clarification of this situation through elaboration of the points concerned, and an expression of the opinion of the editorial office as to the significance, justice, or purpose inherent in the situation. Some publications print as *editorials* pleasant little essays on insignificant or minor situations, frankly admitting such bits to publication simply for the charm of their STYLE or the grace of their HUMOR.

**Edwardian Age:** The name usually given the period in English literature between the death of Victoria in 1901 and the beginning of the first World War in 1914, so-called after King Edward VII, who ruled from 1901–1910. It was a period marked by a strong

[1] R. B. McKerrow, *An Introduction to Bibliography for Literary Students,* p. 175. Oxford University Press. Reprinted by permission of the publishers.

reaction in thought, conduct, and art to the stiff propriety and conservatism of the Victorian age. The regular mental posture of the Edwardians was critical and questioning. There was a growing distrust of authority in religion, morality, and art, a basic doubt of the conventional "virtues," and a deep-felt need to examine critically all existing institutions. These attitudes expressed themselves in literature that was brilliant and elegant, although not always deep or enduring.

The CELTIC RENAISSANCE in Ireland awakened the dramatic talents of Lady Gregory, Douglas Hyde, Lennox Robinson, J. M. Synge, and W. B. Yeats; the intellectual DRAMA of G. B. Shaw continued the Ibsen influence; James Barrie and Lord Dunsany kept romance and whimsy alive on the stage. In England John Galsworthy was producing social plays, such as *The Silver Box, Strife*, and *Justice*.

In poetry it was an age of endings and beginnings. Victorianism lingered on in the verses of the LAUREATE, Alfred Austin (succeeded in 1913 by Robert Bridges), and in the work of men like Noyes and Kipling. George William Russell ("A.E.") and W. B. Yeats were beginning poetic careers; Masefield's first volumes appeared; and Hardy's *The Dynasts* made its ambitious appearance.

But it was predominantly an age of prose. REALISM and NATURALISM advanced steadily. In the NOVELS of Arnold Bennett were detailed pictures of the grim commonplace; in those of Galsworthy the beginnings of the SAGA of the middle classes. H. G. Wells launched his novelistic criticisms of society; and Kipling recorded the march of empire. But the greatest writers of prose in the British Isles in the *Edwardian Age* were James Joyce, whose *Dubliners* appeared in 1914, and Joseph Conrad, who during the *Edwardian Age* published distinguished work, including *Youth* and *Nostromo*.

Works of distinction or promise, other than those by authors already mentioned, included Butler's *The Way of All Flesh*, Hudson's *Green Mansions*, Stephens' *Crock of Gold*, and Barrie's *The Admirable Crichton*.

The degree to which the new strength and brilliance of English writing was moving away from its older orientations is demonstrated, perhaps, by the fact that in the *Edwardian Age* the best dramatist was an Irishman, Shaw; the best poet an Irishman, Yeats; the best novelist an expatriated Pole, Conrad; and the figure with greatest promise for the future another Irishman, Joyce.

# Effect

**Effect:** Totality of impression or emotional impact upon the reader. "The tale of *effect*" was a term used to describe GOTHIC and horror stories of the type published in *Blackwood's Magazine* in the first half of the nineteenth century. Poe considered the primary objective of the SHORT STORY to be the achieving of a unified *effect*. The *effect* striven for may be one of horror, mystery, beauty, or whatever the writer's mood dictates, but once the *effect* is hit upon, everything in the story—PLOT, CHARACTERIZATION, SETTING—must work toward this controlling purpose. One of the paragraphs in Poe's criticism of Hawthorne's *Twice-Told Tales* stands out as the best explanation of this principle of *effect*:

A skilful literary artist has constructed a tale. If wise, he has not fashioned his thoughts to accommodate his incidents; but having conceived, with deliberate care, a certain unique or single *effect* to be wrought out, he then invents such incidents—he then combines such events as may best aid him in establishing his preconceived effect. If his very initial sentence tend not to the outbringing of this effect, then he has failed in his first step. In the whole composition there should be no word written, of which the tendency, direct or indirect, is not to the one preëstablished design. And by such means, with such care and skill, a picture is at length painted which leaves in the mind of him who contemplates it with a kindred art, a sense of the fullest satisfaction. . . .

**Elaboration:** A rhetorical method for developing a THEME or picture in such a way as to give the reader a completed impression. This may be done in various ways: by repetition of the statement or idea, by a change of words and phrases, by supplying additional details, etc. Over-elaboration, however, immediately becomes a fault since it results in Polonius-like diffuseness, wordiness, and stupidity. *Elaboration* is also used as a critical term characterizing a literary, rhetorical STYLE which is rather ornate. See AMPLIFICATION.

**Elegiac:** In classical PROSODY, a METER used in the DISTICH employed for lamenting or commemorating the dead; it consists of a VERSE of DACTYLIC HEXAMETER followed by one of PENTAMETER. The ancient poets used *elegiacs* not only for THRENODIES but also for SONGS of war and love. The *elegiac* meter has been popular in Germany but rarely used in England and America. Coleridge's DISTICH will serve as an example:

> In the hexameter rises the fountain's silvery column,
> In the pentameter aye falling in melody back.

In English CRITICISM, the term *elegiac* is used as an adjective to describe poetry expressing sorrow or lamentation (as in *elegiac strains*) or belonging to or partaking of an ELEGY.

**Elegy:** A sustained and formal POEM setting forth the poet's meditations upon death or upon a grave THEME. The meditation often is occasioned by the death of a particular person, but it may be a generalized observation or the expression of a solemn mood. A classical form, common to both Latin and Greek literatures, the *elegy* originally signified almost any type of serious, subjective meditation on the part of the poet whether this reflective element was concerned with death, love, or war, or merely the presentation of information. In classic writing the *elegy* was more distinguishable by its use of ELEGIAC meter than by its subject matter. The Elizabethans used the term for love poems, particularly COMPLAINTS. Notable English *elegies* include the OLD ENGLISH poem "The Wanderer," *The Pearl*, Chaucer's *The Book of the Duchess*, Donne's *Elegies*, Gray's *Elegy Written in a Country Churchyard*, Tennyson's *In Memoriam*, and Whitman's "When Lilacs Last in the Dooryard Bloom'd." These poems indicate the variety of method, mood, and subject which is included under the term *elegy*. A specialized form of *elegy*, popular with English poets, is the PASTORAL ELEGY, of which Milton's *Lycidas* is an outstanding example. See PASTORAL ELEGY.

**Elision:** The omission of a part of a word for ease of pronunciation, for EUPHONY, or to secure a desired rhythmic effect. This is most often accomplished by the omission of a final vowel preceding an initial vowel as "th'orient" for "the orient," but *elision* also occurs between syllables of a single word as "ne'er" for "never."

**Elizabethan Age:** The name given in English literature to the segment of the RENAISSANCE which occurred during the reign of Elizabeth I (1558–1603). The meaning of the term is sometimes extended to include the JACOBEAN PERIOD (1603–1625). An age of great nationalistic expansion, commercial growth, and religious controversy, it saw the development of English DRAMA to its highest level, a great outburst of LYRIC song, and a new interest in CRITICISM. Sidney, Spenser, Marlowe, and Shakespeare flourished; and Bacon, Jonson, and Donne first stepped forward. It has justly been called the "Golden Age of English Literature." For details of its literary history, see "The Elizabethan Age" in *The Outline of Literary History;* for a sketch of its literature see RENAISSANCE.

**Elizabethan Drama:** This phrase is commonly used for the entire body of RENAISSANCE English DRAMA produced in the century preceding the closing of the theatres in 1642, although it is sometimes employed in a narrower sense to designate the DRAMA of the later years of Elizabeth's reign and the few years following it. Thus, Shakespeare is an Elizabethan dramatist, although more than one third of his active career lies in the reign of James I. Modern English DRAMA not only came into being in Elizabethan times but developed so rapidly and brilliantly that the Elizabethan era is the golden age of English DRAMA.

Lack of adequate records makes it impossible to trace the steps by which *Elizabethan drama* developed, though the chief elements which contributed to it can be listed. From MEDIEVAL DRAMA came the TRADITION of acting and certain CONVENTIONS approved by the populace. From the MORALITY PLAYS and the INTERLUDES in particular came comic elements. With this medieval heritage was combined the classical TRADITION of DRAMA, partly drawn from a study of the Roman dramatists, Seneca (tragedy) and Plautus and Terence (comedy), and partly from humanistic CRITICISM based upon Aristotle and transmitted through Italian RENAISSANCE scholarship. This classical influence appeared first in the SCHOOL PLAYS. Later it affected the DRAMA written under the auspices of the royal court and of the INNS OF COURT. Eventually it influenced the plays of the university-trained playwrights connected with the public stage. Indeed, the part played by the UNIVERSITY WITS in adapting classical dramatic materials to the demands of the popular stage seems to have advanced dramatic technique to a point where it was ready for the perfecting touch of the master dramatist himself. The modern theatre arose with *Elizabethan drama* (see PUBLIC THEATRES, PRIVATE THEATRES). For types of *Elizabethan drama* and names of dramatists see *Outline of Literary History* (pp. 532–541) and TRAGEDY, ROMANTIC TRAGEDY, CLASSICAL TRAGEDY, TRAGEDY OF BLOOD, COMEDY, COMEDY OF HUMOURS, COURT COMEDY, REALISTIC COMEDY, CHRONICLE PLAY, and MASQUE.

**Elizabethan Literature:** Literature produced in England during the ELIZABETHAN AGE; that is, 1558–1603, although the meaning is often extended to include the JACOBEAN PERIOD, and sometimes given as wide a scope as 1550–1660. See ELIZABETHAN AGE.

**Elizabethan Miscellanies:** Poetical ANTHOLOGIES made in the ELIZABETHAN AGE. See MISCELLANIES, POETICAL.

**Elizabethan Theatres:** Public and private playhouses that developed and flourished in the ELIZABETHAN AGE. See PUBLIC THEATRES, PRIVATE THEATRES.

**Ellipsis:** A figure of speech characterized by the omission of one or more words which, while essential to the grammatic structure of the sentence, are easily supplied by the reader. The effect of *ellipsis* is rhetorical; it makes for emphasis of statement. The device often traps the unwary user into difficulties, since carelessness will result in impossible constructions. The safe rule is to be sure that the words to be supplied occur in the proper grammatic form not too remote from the place the *ellipsis* occurs. In the following quotations the brackets indicate *ellipsis:*

> Where wigs [strive] with wigs, [where] with sword-knots
>                                          sword-knots strive,
> [Where] Beaus banish beaus, and [where] coaches coaches drive.
> —Pope

**Emblem Books:** An "emblem" consisted of a motto expressing some moral idea and accompanied by a picture and a short poem illustrating the idea. The poem was always short—SONNETS, EPIGRAMS, MADRIGALS, and various STANZA forms being employed. The picture (originally itself the "emblem") was symbolic. A collection of emblems was known as an *emblem book*. Emblems and *emblem books,* which owed their popularity partly to the newly developed art of engraving, were very popular in all Western European languages in the fifteenth, sixteenth, and seventeenth centuries. Examples of emblems: The motto *Divesque miserque,* "both rich and poor," illustrated by a picture of King Midas sitting at a table where everything was gold and by a verse or "posie" explaining how Midas, though rich, could not eat his gold; *Parler peu et venir au poinct,* "speak little and come to the point," illustrated by a quatrain and a picture of a man shooting at a target with a cross-bow. Edmund Spenser's earliest known literary work consisted of TRANSLATIONS of SONNETS of Du Bellay and Petrarch for *A Theatre of Worldings* (1569), a translation of a Dutch *emblem book*. Several of Spenser's poems, such as *The Shepheardes Calender* and *Muiopotmos*, show the influence of emblems. Shakespeare seems to have made much use of emblem literature, as in the casket scene in *The Merchant of Venice*. Francis Quarles is the author of an interesting seventeenth-century *emblem book*.

**Emotional Element in Literature:** Although generalizations about the nature, intent, and language of literature are at best unsatisfactory efforts to bind together a congeries of contrasting and often conflicting elements, men have usually agreed in distinguishing among scientific, philosophical, and artistic expressions. It is true that the term *literature* is sometimes applied to graceful and effective DESCRIPTIONS, EXPOSITIONS, and ARGUMENTS whose purpose is to explain, instruct, or persuade; in a stricter sense, however, *literature* is properly reserved for expressions in which the aesthetic aim is equal to or outweighs the scientific or philosophical. This is, of course, a way of asserting that the grace, beauty, and symmetry of art are more than ornaments or sugar-coating for the pill of fact or concept. In a basic sense, the scientist appeals to our sense of fact; the philosopher to our intellectual being, our powers of logic and conceptualizing; and the artist to our emotional being, our inner selves. On the simplest level of language, science employs words for their DENOTATIONS, giving them verifiable but GENERAL referents in the world of things; philosophy deals with ABSTRACT TERMS, being concerned with the conceptualizing of experience; art deals with CONCRETE TERMS, tangible, particular, specific. These CONCRETE TERMS are frequently IMAGES that evoke immediate emotional responses from the reader. (See ABSTRACT TERMS; CONCRETE TERMS; BELIEF, THE PROBLEM OF: CRITICISM, TYPES OF.)

In I. A. Richards' distinction, art uses "emotive language"—language employed for the effects it produces in emotion and attitude—as contrasted with science which uses "referential language"—language used for the sake of the reference it produces. To insist upon this emotional quality of literature is not to deny it other kinds of meaning and value, but it is to insist that literature conveys these other meanings and values in the uniquely emotive language of art. (See CONCRETE UNIVERSAL.)

Contemporary criticism has interested itself deeply in the emotional aspect of literature, with the assertion that there is an aspect of knowledge which can be conveyed by no other means than through the language and form of art (see OBJECTIVE CORRELATIVE).

**Empathy:** The act of identifying ourselves with an object and participating in its physical and emotional sensations, even to the point of making our own physical responses, as, standing before a statue of a discus-thrower, one flexes his muscles to hurl the discus. *Empathy* may be expended upon an inanimate object, an animal, or a person. It may be active, in that it results in the creative process, or it may be passive, in that it results from reading and appreciation. It is to be contrasted with "sympathy" through which we have a fellow-feeling for someone; for *empathy* implies an "involuntary projection of ourselves" into something or someone else. Some modern critics see in *empathy* the key to the nature and meaning of art (see EMOTIONAL ELEMENT IN LITERATURE). The term is a translation of Hermann Lotze's word *Einfühlung*—"feeling into"—and it entered our critical vocabulary in this century.

**Emphasis:** A principle of rhetoric dictating that important elements be given important positions and adequate development whether in the sentence, the paragraph, or the whole composition. The more important positions are, naturally, at the beginning and end. But *emphasis* may also be secured (1) by repetition of important ideas, (2) by the development of important ideas through supplying plenty of specific detail, (3) by simply giving more space to the more important phases of the composition, (4) by contrasting one element with another since such contrasts focus the reader's attention on the point in question, (5) by careful selection of details so chosen that subjects related to the main idea are included and all irrelevant material excluded, (6) by climactic arrangement, (7) by mechanical devices such as capitalization, italics, symbols, different colors of ink, etc.

**Empiricism:** In philosophy, the practice of drawing rules of practice not from theory but from experience. Hence an empirical method is sometimes equivalent to an "experimental" method. In medicine, however, an "empiric" usually means a quack. The term is sometimes borrowed by literary critics and used in a derogatory sense, an *empiric* judgment being an untrained one. The empirical method, in the sense of the experimental, is important in literary theories of NATURALISM.

**Encomium:** In Greek literature a poem or speech in praise of a living person before a select group. Today any speech or writing that is of a laudatory nature. See PANEGYRIC, EULOGY.

**End-Rime:** RIME that occurs at the ends of the VERSES. See RIME.

**End-stopped Lines:** Lines of verse in which both the grammatical structure and the sense reach completion at the end of the line. The absence of ENJAMBEMENT, or RUN-ON LINES.

> All are but parts of one stupendous whole,
> Whose body Nature is, and God the soul:
> —Pope

**English Language:** The *English language* developed from the West Germanic dialects spoken by the Angles, Saxons, and other Teutonic tribes which participated in the gradual invasion and occupation of England in the fifth and sixth centuries, a movement which resulted in the obliteration of the earlier Celtic and Roman cultures in the island. The word *English* applied to the language reflects the fact that Anglo-Saxon literature first flourished in the North and was written in the Anglian dialects (hence *Englisc,* "English") spoken in Northumbria and Mercia. Later, under King Alfred, the West Saxon region became the cultural center. The word *Englisc* was still employed as its name, however, and the earlier Anglian literature was copied in the West Saxon dialect, now commonly referred to as OLD ENGLISH, or "Anglo-Saxon." As a language West Saxon was very different from modern English. It was burdened with grammatical gender, declensions, conjugations, tense-forms, and case-endings almost equal in extent to those found in Latin. The word "stone," for example, had six forms (singular: *stān, stānes, stāne;* plural: *stānas, stāna, stānum*) representing five cases (nominative, genitive, dative, accusative, instrumental). Pronouns and verbs likewise possessed complicated inflectional systems. In addition, the four great DIALECTS of the OLD ENGLISH PERIOD (Northumbrian, Mercian, West Saxon, Kentish) differed among themselves in grammar, pronunciation, and vocabulary. The first writing was in RUNES, which were displaced later by the Roman alphabet used by the Christian missionaries. Specimens of OLD

ENGLISH have survived from as early as the eighth century, but most of the existing manuscripts are in West Saxon of the tenth and eleventh centuries. Though a few Latin and fewer Celtic words were added to the vocabulary in OLD ENGLISH times, most of the words were Teutonic, consisting of words used by the Angles and Saxons, augmented by the introduction of Danish and Norse words as the result of later invasions.

The changes which have made modern English look like a different language from OLD ENGLISH are the result of the operation of certain natural tendencies in language development, such as the progressive simplification of the grammar; and the accidents of history, such as the NORMAN CONQUEST and the growth of London as a cultural center. The greatest change took place in the earlier part of the period known as MIDDLE ENGLISH (*ca.* 1100–*ca.*1500) or a little earlier. The leveling of inflections and other simplifying forces, already under way in late OLD ENGLISH times, were accelerated by the results of the NORMAN CONQUEST, which dethroned English as the literary language, in favor of the French language spoken by the newcomers (see ANGLO-FRENCH and ANGLO-NORMAN). Left to the everyday use of the subjugated native elements of the population, English changed rapidly in the direction of modern English, as is shown in manuscripts written about 1200, when English was again coming into literary use. By late MIDDLE ENGLISH times (fourteenth century) the process of simplification had gone so far that in Chaucer's time almost all the old inflections either were lost or were weakened to a final *-e*, often unpronounced. The introduction of French words in the MIDDLE ENGLISH period proved a powerful source of enrichment to the English vocabulary. By this time, too, many Danish words, acquired much earlier, appear. In the fourteenth and fifteenth centuries a significant step toward the development of a standardized, uniform language came with the new prominence given the London DIALECT (largely East Midland), which thus became the basis for Modern English. This development came chiefly from the growing importance of London commercially and politically, the influence of the writings of Chaucer and his followers, the adoption of English instead of French in the courts and schools (fourteenth century), and the employment of this DIALECT by Caxton, the first English printer (late fifteenth century).

Modern English (*ca.*1500 on) has been marked by an enormous expansion in vocabulary, the new words being drawn from many sources, chiefly Latin and French. Since French is itself based upon Latin, English has acquired many doublets, such as "strict" and "strait," permitting further developments in shades of meaning. An examination of a dictionary will show the vast preponderance of foreign words over native English words, though the latter include the more frequently used words of everyday intercourse, such as "man," "wife," "child," "go," "hold," "day," "bed," "sorrow," "hand." The stylistic effect of English prose writing is greatly affected by the nature of the vocabulary used, particularly as between native English words and those derived from Latin, either directly or through French. The native words in general give an effect of simplicity and strength, while the Latin or Romance words impart smoothness and make possible fine distinctions in meaning. Modern English has also drawn freely upon many other sources for new words. Greek, for example, has been resorted to for scientific terms, new words being formed from Greek root-meanings, Greek prefixes, suffixes, etc. In grammar, the simplification process has been retarded in modern times by such conservative forces as grammars, DICTIONARIES, printers, and school teachers. Likewise spelling and pronunciation have become fixed in somewhat chaotic and archaic forms by the influence of the same standardizing tendencies.

Today only a quarter of the words in common usage in English are of OLD ENGLISH derivation, yet the ones which determine the nature of the language—articles, pronouns, and connecting words —are of OLD ENGLISH origin. What inflectional endings remain for pronouns, adjectives, and adverbs are OLD ENGLISH, as are our verb forms. We have retained the Germanic word order, the Germanic tendency to associate ACCENT and loudness and to stress the first syllable of nouns. We have borrowed three-fourths of our words and have always fitted them into an English frame. The result is that English remains basically a Teutonic tongue, which perpetually renews itself at the fountain of the world's languages. See OLD ENGLISH, MIDDLE ENGLISH, ANGLO-NORMAN, DIALECTS, AMERICAN ENGLISH.

**English Literature, Periods of:** The division of a nation's literary history into periods offers a convenient method for studying authors and movements, as well as the literature itself, in their proper perspectives. Hence most literary histories and anthologies are arranged by periods. In the case of English literature, there are almost as many arrangements as there are books on the subject. This lack of uniformity arises chiefly from two facts. In the first place, periods merge into one another because the supplanting of one literary attitude by another is a gradual process. Thus the earlier romanticists are contemporary with the later neo-classicists, just as the neo-classical attitude existed in the very heyday of Elizabethan romanticism. Dates given in any scheme of literary periods, therefore, must be regarded as approximate and suggestive only, even when they reflect some very definite fact, as 1660 (the Restoration of the Stuarts) and 1798 (the publication of *Lyrical Ballads*). In the second place, the names of periods may be chosen on very different principles. One plan is to name a period from its greatest or its most representative author: Age of Chaucer, Age of Spenser, etc. Another is to coin a descriptive adjective from the name of the ruler: Elizabethan Period, Jacobean Period, Victorian Period. Or pure chronology or names of centuries may be preferred: Fifteenth-Century Literature, Eighteenth-Century Literature, etc. Or descriptive titles designed to indicate prevailing critical or philosophical attitudes, or dominant fashions or "schools" of literature may be used: Neo-classicism, Romanticism, Age of Reason. Logically, some single principle should control in any given scheme, but such consistency is not always found. The table below gives the scheme used in this book:

### PERIODS OF ENGLISH LITERATURE

|  |  |
|---|---|
| 428–1100 | Old English Period |
| 1100–1350 | Anglo-Norman Period |
| 1350–1500 | Middle English Period |
| 1500–1660 | The Renaissance Period |
| 1500–1557 | Early Tudor Age |
| 1558–1603 | Elizabethan Age |
| 1603–1625 | Jacobean Age |
| 1625–1649 | Caroline Age |
| 1649–1660 | The Commonwealth Interregnum |
| 1660–1798 | The Neo-Classical Period |
| 1660–1700 | The Restoration Age |
| 1700–1750 | The Augustan Age |
| 1750–1798 | The Age of Johnson |
| 1798–1870 | The Romantic Period |
| 1798–1832 | The Age of the Romantic Triumph |
| 1832–1870 | The Early Victorian Age |

Historical sketches of the periods listed in this table are given in the Handbook, and briefer descriptions of the subdivisions of periods (here called uniformly *ages*) are also given in the Handbook. *The Outline of Literary History* follows this table and gives details of general and literary history.

**Enjambement:** The device of continuing the sense and grammatical construction of a VERSE or a COUPLET on into the next.

    *Enjambement* occurs with the presence of the RUN-ON LINE and offers contrast to the END-STOPPED LINE. The first and second lines below, carried over to the second and third for completion, are illustrations of *enjambement:*

> Or if Sion hill
> Delight thee more, and Siloa's brook, that flow'd
> Fast by the oracle of God.
>
>               —Milton

**Enthymeme:** A SYLLOGISM informally stated and omitting one of the two premises—either the major or the minor. The omitted premise is to be understood. Example: "Children should be seen and not heard. Be quiet, John." Here the obvious minor premise— that John is a child—is left to the ingenuity of the reader.

**Enumerative Bibliography:** A list of works of a particular country, author, printer, or type. See BIBLIOGRAPHY.

**Envoy (*envoi*):** A conventionalized STANZA appearing at the close of certain poems; particularly associated with the French BALLADE form. The *envoy* (1) is usually addressed to a prince, a judge, a patron, or other person of importance; (2) repeats the REFRAIN line used throughout the BALLADE; (3) consists normally of four lines (though not necessarily so limited); (4) usually employs the *bcbc* rime-scheme. See BALLADE.

**Epic:** A long narrative POEM in elevated STYLE presenting characters of high position in a series of adventures which form an organic whole through their relation to a central figure of heroic proportions and through their development of EPISODES important to the history of a nation or race. The origin of *epics* is a matter of great scholarly dispute. According to one theory, the first *epics* took shape from the scattered work of various unknown poets, and through accretion these early EPISODES were gradually molded into a unified whole and an ordered sequence. Though held vigorously by some, this theory has generally given place to one which holds that the materials of the *epic* may have accumulated in this fashion but that the *epic poem* itself is the product of a single genius who gives it STRUCTURE and expression. *Epics* without certain authorship are called FOLK EPICS, whether the scholar believes in a folk, or a single authorship theory of origins, however.

*Epics*, both FOLK and ART EPICS, share a group of common characteristics: (1) The hero is a figure of heroic stature, of national or international importance, and of great historical or legendary significance; (2) the setting is vast in scope, covering great nations, the world, or the universe; (3) the action consists of deeds of great valor or requiring superhuman courage; (4) supernatural forces—gods, angels, and demons—interest themselves in the action and intervene from time to time; (5) a STYLE of sustained elevation and grand simplicity is used; and (6) the *epic* poet recounts the deeds of his heroes with objectivity. To these general characteristics (some of which are omitted from particular *epics*), should be added a list of common devices or CONVENTIONS employed by most *epic* poets: the poet opens by stating his theme, invokes a Muse to inspire and instruct him, and opens his narrative *in medias res*—in the middle of things—giving the necessary EXPOSITION in later portions of the *epic;* he includes catalogues of warriors, ships, armies; he gives extended formal speeches by the main characters; and he makes frequent use of the EPIC SIMILE.

A few of the more important FOLK EPICS are: *The Iliad* and *The Odyssey* (by Homer), the Old English *Beowulf*, the East Indian *Mahabharata*, the Spanish *Cid*, the Finnish *Kalevala*, the French *Song of Roland*, and the German *Nibelungenlied*. Some of the best known ART EPICS are: Virgil's *Aeneid*, Dante's *Divine Comedy* (although it lacks many of the distinctive characteristics of the *epic*), Tasso's *Jerusalem Delivered*, Milton's *Paradise Lost*. American poets in the late eighteenth and early nineteenth centuries struggled to produce a good *epic* poem on the American adventure, but without success. Longfellow's *Hiawatha* is an attempt at an Indian *epic*.

Whitman's *Leaves of Grass,* considered as the autobiography of a generic American, is sometimes called an American *epic,* as is Stephen Vincent Benét's *John Brown's Body.*

In the Middle Ages there was a great mass of literature verging on the *epic* in form and purpose though not answering strictly to the conventional *epic* formula. These poems are variously referred to as *epic* and as ROMANCE. Spenser's *The Faerie Queene* is the supreme example.

**Epic Formula:** See EPIC.

**Epic Simile:** An elaborated comparison. This type differs from an ordinary SIMILE in that it is more involved, more ornate, and is a conscious imitation of the Homeric manner. The secondary object or picture is developed into an independent aesthetic object, an IMAGE which for the moment excludes the primary object with which it is compared. The following from *Paradise Lost* may serve as an example:

> Angel Forms, who lay entranced
> Thick as autumnal leaves that strow the brooks
> In Vallombrosa, where the Etrurian shades
> High over-arched embower; or scattered sedge
> Afloat, when with fierce winds Orion armed
> Hath vexed the Red-Sea coast, whose waves o'erthrew
> Busiris and his Memphian chivalry,
> While with perfidious hatred they pursued
> The sojourners of Goshen, who beheld
> From the safe shore their floating carcases
> And broken chariot-wheels.
>
> —Milton

**Epicurean:** A piece of literature may be said to be *epicurean* if it exhibits a mood or spirit of surrender to the search for pleasure, especially such sensuous pleasures as eating and drinking. The usage arose through a misunderstanding of what Epicurus, a Greek philosopher, meant by "pleasure" when he advocated the doctrine that man's legitimate aim was the pursuit of pleasure. Of course, *epicurean* may be applied to an author himself.

**Epigram:** A pointed saying; hence an epigrammatic style is concise, pointed, often antithetical, as "Man proposes but God disposes." This rhetorical use of the word is derived from certain qualities of a type of poem known as an *epigram*. Originally (in ancient

Greece) an *epigram* meant an inscription, especially an EPITAPH. Then it came to mean "a very short poem summing up as though in a memorial inscription what it is desired to make permanently memorable in a single action or situation" (Mackail). Hence the *epigram* was characterized by compression, pointedness, clarity, BALANCE, and polish. Examples of the ancient *epigram* may be found in the Greek Anthology and in the work of the Roman poet Martial (A.D. 40–104), whose work supplied the models for Ben Jonson, the greatest writer of *epigrams* in the English RENAISSANCE. Martial had used the *epigram* for various themes and purposes: EULOGY, friendship, compliment, EPITAPHS, philosophic reflection, *jeux d'esprit,* and (especially) SATIRE, particularly against sham and hypocrisy. Although numerous *epigrams* were written by sixteenth-century English writers, notably John Heywood, they did not conform closely to the classical type, reflecting rather various forms of medieval HUMOR and SATIRE. With the realistic revolt against Elizabethan ROMANTICISM just before 1600, the classical *epigram* was cultivated, chiefly as a vehicle for SATIRE. Many collections were published between 1596 and 1616, including the famous one of Sir John Harington (1615). All these reflected the current idea that an *epigram* was a pointed SATIRE. Jonson undertook to restore the wider classical use of the word and he wrote not only satirical EPIGRAMS but EPISTLES, verses of compliment, EPITAPHS, reflective verses, etc. An *epigram* of this period was typically a short poem consisting of two parts, an introduction stating the occasion or setting the tone, and a conclusion which sharply and tersely, often with the effect of surprise, gives the main point. In the eighteenth century the spirit though not the form of the *epigram* continued. Many of Pope's couplets are *epigrams* when separated from their context. Coleridge, too, indulged in the *epigram* on occasion, but Walter Savage Landor was its greatest and most persistent user after Jonson.

**Epilogue:** A concluding statement; an appendix to a composition. Sometimes used in the sense of a PERORATION to a speech, but more generally applied to the final remarks of an actor addressed to the audience at the close of the play. Opposed to PROLOGUE, a speech used to introduce the play. Puck, in *A Midsummer Night's Dream,* recites an *epilogue* which is characteristic of RENAISSANCE plays in that it bespeaks the good will of the audience and courteous treatment by critics. As the use of *epilogues* became more general, poets of reputation were often paid to contribute *epilogues* to plays much as PREFACES written by prominent authors are now sometimes paid for by publishers. *Epilogues* were an indispensable part of all major dramatic efforts in the late seventeenth century and throughout the eighteenth century, disappearing from general use about the middle of the nineteenth. They are now rarely employed.

**Episode:** An incident presented as one continuous action. Though having a UNITY within itself, the *episode* in any composition is usually accompanied by other *episodes* so woven together according to the conscious artistic purpose of the writer as to create a SHORT STORY, DRAMA, or NOVEL. Originally, in Greek DRAMA, an *episode* referred to that part of a TRAGEDY which was presented between two CHORUSES. More narrowly the term is sometimes used to characterize an incident injected into a piece of FICTION simply to illuminate character or to create background where it bears no definite relation to the PLOT and in no way advances the action.

**Episodic Structure:** A critical term applied to writing which consists of little more than a series of incidents. Simple narrative as opposed to narrative with PLOT. The *episodes* succeed each other, in this type of writing, with no very logical arrangement (except perhaps that of chronology) and without COMPLICATION or a close interrelationship. Travel books naturally fall into *episodic structure*. The term is applied also to long narratives which may contain complicated PLOTS, like the Italian ROMANTIC EPIC, if the action is made leisurely by the use of numerous *episodes* employed for the purpose of developing character or PLOT. The METRICAL ROMANCE and the PICARESQUE NOVEL are said to have *episodic structure*, since the events that occur in them have no causal relationship and are together because they happened in chronological order to a single character. As a rule, a work with *episodic structure* has little or no central PLOT.

**Epistle:** Theoretically an *epistle* is any LETTER, but in practice the term is limited to formal compositions written by an individual or a group to a distant individual or group. The most familiar use of the term, of course, is to characterize certain of the books of the New Testament. The *epistle* differs from the common LET-

TER in that it is a conscious literary form rather than a spontaneous, chatty, private composition. Ordinarily the *epistle* is associated with the scriptural writing of the past, but this is by no
means a necessary restriction since the term may be used to indicate formal LETTERS having to do with public matters and with
philosophy as well as with religious problems. It is regularly applied to the formal LETTERS of dedication that appear in books.
Pope used it to describe formal LETTERS in verse.

**Epistolary Novel:** A NOVEL in which the narrative is carried forward by LETTERS written by one or more of the characters. It has
the merit of giving the author an opportunity to present the feelings and reactions of characters without himself intruding into
the action of the NOVEL; it further gives a sense of immediacy to
the action, since the LETTERS are usually written in the thick of
the action. The *epistolary novel* also enables the author to present
multiple points of view on the same event through the use of
several correspondents' epistolary records of the occurrence. It is
also a device for creating VERISIMILITUDE, the author merely serving as "editor" for the correspondence of "actual" persons. Obvious disadvantages are the fact that the correspondents in an
*epistolary novel* become incredible and indefatigable scribblers
under the most surprising circumstances and the fact that the en-
forced objectivity of the "editor" shuts the author off from comment on the actions of his characters.

Samuel Richardson's *Pamela* (1740) is frequently considered
the first English *epistolary novel*, although the use of LETTERS to
tell stories and to give racy gossip and sage instruction goes back
in England at least as far as Nicholas Breton's *A Poste with a
Packet of Mad Letters* (1630) and includes such sentimental
analyses of the feminine heart as Aphra Behn's *Love Letters Between a Nobleman and His Sister* (1683). Richardson's *Clarissa
Harlowe* (1748) is certainly the greatest, as it is the most extended, of *epistolary novels*. The form was popular in the eighteenth century, particularly for the SENTIMENTAL NOVEL. Other
notable examples are Smollett's *Humphry Clinker* (1771) and
Fanny Burney's *Evelina* (1778). The epistolary method has not
often been successfully used in the nineteenth and twentieth
centuries, although the use of LETTERS within NOVELS has been
common. See NOVEL.

**Epitaph:** Inscription used to mark burial places. Commemorative VERSES or lines appearing on tombs or written as if intended for such use. Since the days of early Egyptian records *epitaphs* have had a long and interesting history, and while they have changed somewhat as to purpose and form, they show less development than most literary types. The information usually incorporated in such memorials includes the name of the deceased, the dates of birth and death, age, profession (if a dignified one), together with some pious motto or invocation. Many prominent writers— notably Johnson, Milton, and Pope—have left *epitaphs* which they wrote in tribute to the dead. Early *epitaphs* were usually serious and dignified—since they chiefly appeared on the tombs of the great—but more recently they have, either consciously or unconsciously, taken on humorous qualities. Certainly one of the most famous inscriptions is that marking Shakespeare's burial place:

> Good frend, for Jesus sake forbeare
> To digg the dust encloased here;
> Bleste be ye man y$^t$ spares thes stones,
> And curst be he y$^t$ moves my bones,—

But this is as much a curse as an *epitaph.* "O rare Ben Jonson" and *"Exit* Burbage" are two examples of simple and effective *epitaphs.* A famous French inscription is from Père Lachaise in Paris:

> Ci-gît ma femme: ah! que c'est bien
> Pour son repos, et pour le mien!

The *epitaph* "On the Countess Dowager of Pembroke," formerly attributed to Ben Jonson, though now credited to William Browne, deserves quotation:

> Underneath this sable hearse
> Lies the subject of all verse:
> Sidney's sister, Pembroke's mother.
> Death, ere thou hast slain another,
> Fair and learned and good as she,
> Time shall throw a dart at thee.

**Epitasis:** A term used by the ancients to designate the RISING ACTION of a DRAMA. See DRAMATIC STRUCTURE.

**Epithalamium (Epithalamion):** A bridal SONG; a SONG or POEM written to celebrate a wedding. Many ancient poets (the Greek

Pindar, Sappho, and Theocritus and the Roman Catullus) as well as modern poets (like the French Ronsard and the English Spenser) have cultivated the form. Perhaps Spenser's *Epithalamion* (1595), written to celebrate his own marriage, is the finest of the English marriage hymns. The successive STANZAS in this poem treat such topics as: invocation to the Muses to help praise his bride; bride is awakened by music; decking of the bridal path with flowers; nymphs adorn the bride; the assembling of the guests; description of the beauty of the bride, physical and spiritual; the bride at the altar; the marriage-feast; welcoming the night; asking the blessing of Diana and Juno and the stars.

**Epithet:** Strictly an adjective or adjective phrase used to point out a characteristic of a person or thing, as Goldsmith's "noisy mansions" (for schoolhouses), but sometimes applied to a noun or noun phrase used for a similar purpose, as Shakespeare's "The trumpet of the dawn" (for the cock). Many considerations enter into the success of an *epithet*, such as its aptness (indeed, *epithet* is actually used sometimes rather loosely to mean any apt phrase), its freshness, its pictorial quality, its connotative value (what it suggests rather than says), its musical value, etc. In literature rememberable *epithets* are very often figurative, as Keats' "snarling trumpets" and Milton's "laboring clouds."

The so-called HOMERIC EPITHET, often a compound adjective, as "all-seeing" Jove, "swift-footed" Achilles, "blue-eyed" Athena, "rosy-fingered" dawn, depends upon aptness combined with familiarity rather than upon freshness or variety. It is almost a part of a name. Since *epithets* often play a prominent part in the calling-of-names which characterizes INVECTIVE or personal SATIRE, some persons have the mistaken notion that an *epithet* is always uncomplimentary. A TRANSFERRED EPITHET is an adjective used to limit grammatically a noun which it does not logically modify, though the relation is so close that the meaning is left clear, as Shakespeare's "dusty death," or Milton's "blind mouths." This subtly suggestive device, often involving the PATHETIC FALLACY, is used effectively by the poets. The following phrases contain examples of *epithets:* glimmering landscape, murmuring brook, dazzling immortality, pure-eyed Faith, silver answer, prostituted muse, dark-skirted wilderness, circumambient foam, care-charmer sleep, sweet silent thought, meek-eyed peace.

**Epitome:** A summary or abridgment. A condensed statement of the content of a book. A "miniature representation" of a subject. Thus Magna Charta has been called the *epitome* of the rights of Englishmen, and Ruskin referred to St. Mark's as an *epitome* of the changes of Venetian architecture through a period of nine centuries.

**Epode:** One of the three STANZA forms employed in the PINDARIC ODE. The others are STROPHE and ANTISTROPHE. See ODE.

**Eponym:** The name of a person who is so commonly associated with some widely recognized attribute that the name comes to stand for the attribute, as Helen for beauty or Caesar for dictator.

**Equivalence:** In METRICS, a kind of SUBSTITUTION, in which a FOOT equal to the one expected but different from it is used in a VERSE. In QUANTITATIVE VERSE, one long syllable was considered the *equivalent* of two short syllables and thus a SPONDEE (two long syllables) could be substituted for an ANAPEST (two shorts and a long). See SUBSTITUTION, COMPENSATION.

**Equivocation:** The use of a word in two distinct meanings, with the intention to deceive. See EQUIVOQUE.

**Equivoque:** A kind of PUN in which the same word or phrase is so used that it has two different and incongruous meanings. If the *equivoque* is used with the intention to deceive the result is called EQUIVOCATION.

**Erotic Literature:** Amorous writing. The classification of literature as *erotic* is based on the subject matter—love—rather than the literary form employed. Consequently *erotic literature* embraces almost any form of writing—the LYRIC, the DRAMA, SHORT STORY, NOVEL, even EPIGRAMS and ELEGIES, the LYRIC proving perhaps the most popular vehicle. The lines which distinguish *erotic literature* from any writing based on the love theme are hard to draw. The classification is broad enough to include the range of writing about love from the mildly sentimental to the actually pornographic. The presentation of love in literature called *erotic* must, however, approach the fleshly quality to be placed in this category.

**Esperanto:** An artificial speech constructed from roots common to the chief European languages and designed for universal use. *Esperanto* was devised by Dr. L. L. Zamenhof, a Russian, and took its name from Zamenhof's pseudonym, "Dr. Esperanto," used in signing his first pamphlet on the subject in 1887. The account in *The Encyclopædia Britannica* summarizing the principles which should govern any truly universal language states that such a speech "should be international, easy for all, euphonious, phonetic, flexible, regular, adaptable, and must be tested by long continued practical use on a large scale," requirements which, the Esperantists argue, their language has met. Certain qualities of the language may here be pointed out: the grammar is so simple as to be clear after a few minutes' study, the spelling is strictly phonetic, the language is euphonious and adaptable, and pronunciation is simple since the ACCENT always falls on the penult. Since Zamenhof's beginning in 1887, *Esperanto* has grown in popularity, although it gives little promise today of becoming a truly universal tongue.

**Essay:** A moderately brief prose discussion of a restricted topic. Because of the wide application of the term, no satisfactory definition can be arrived at (one book on the *essay* spends forty-three pages on "What Is an Essay?"). Nor can a wholly acceptable "classification" of *essay* types be made. Among the terms that have been used in attempting classifications of the *essay* are: moralizing, critical, character, anecdotal, letter, narrative, aphoristic, descriptive, reflective, biographical, historical, periodical, didactic, editorial, whimsical, psychological, outdoor, nature, cosmical, and personal. Such a list, although depressingly long, is incomplete; obviously the task of classifying the *essay*, like that of defining it, has eluded human skill. A basic and very useful division can, however, be made: FORMAL and INFORMAL ESSAYS. The INFORMAL ESSAY, sometimes called the "true" *essay*, includes moderately brief aphoristic *essays* like Bacon's, PERIODICAL ESSAYS like Addison's, and PERSONAL ESSAYS like Lamb's. Qualities which make an *essay* INFORMAL include: the personal element (self-revelation, individual tastes and experiences, confidential manner), humor, graceful style, rambling structure, unconventionality or novelty of theme, freshness of form, freedom from stiffness and affectation, incomplete or tentative treatment of topic. The points of view and wide range of themes in the IN-

FORMAL ESSAY may be suggested by citing a few typical titles: "On the Enjoyment of Unpleasant Places" (Stevenson), "A Cure for Fits in Married Ladies" (Steele), "A Chapter on Ears" (Lamb), "A Dissertation on Roast Pig" (Lamb), "Getting Up on Cold Mornings" (Hunt), "On Going a Journey" (Hazlitt—advocating the solitary hike), "Every Man's Natural Desire to Be Somebody Else" (Crothers). Qualities of the FORMAL ESSAY include: sober seriousness of purpose, dignity, logical organization, length. The term may include both short discussions, expository or argumentative, such as the serious magazine ARTICLE, and longer treatises, like the chapters in Carlyle's *Heroes and Hero-Worship*. However, a sharp distinction between even FORMAL and INFORMAL ESSAYS can not be maintained at all times. In the following sketch the INFORMAL ESSAY will be given chief consideration, since it lies more completely in the realm of literature.

*Montaigne: Beginnings.*—When the French philosopher Montaigne retired from active life to devote himself to study and reflection (the "contemplative" life), he followed the fashion of the times in his practice of collecting pithy sayings—MAXIMS, APHORISMS, ADAGES, APOTHEGMS, PROVERBS—along with ANECDOTES and quotations from his readings in the classics. A collection of such wise sayings upon a single topic was known in France as a *leçon morale*. After a time Montaigne developed the habit of recording also the results of a searching self-analysis and became attracted by the idea that he was himself representative of man in general. He published his first collection of such writings in 1580 under the title *Essais*—the first use of the word for short prose discussions. The word means "attempts," and by the use of it Montaigne meant to indicate that his discussions were tentative or incomplete as compared with ordinary formal philosophical writings. By adding the personal element to the aphoristic *leçon morale* Montaigne created the modern *essay*. "Myself," he said, "am the groundwork of my book." The second edition (1588) gave even greater emphasis to the personal element. Mainly philosophical and ethical, the *essays* cover a wide range of topics: "Of Idleness," "Of Liars," "Of Ready and Slow Speech," "Of Smells and Odors," "Of Cannibals," "Of Sleeping," "Upon Some Verses of Vergil," etc.

*The Essay in England: Bacon and the Seventeenth Century.*— When the youthful Francis Bacon published in 1597 his first collection of aphoristic *essays*, he borrowed his title, *Essays*, from Montaigne's book—and became the first English "essayist." As a matter of fact Bacon's *essays*, which he referred to as "dispersed meditations," are less indebted to Montaigne than to earlier collections of "sentences" or wise sayings and to the wisdom literature of the Greeks and Romans, Bacon himself citing especially Seneca's *Epistles to Lucilius* as ancient examples of the type. The ten *essays* first published were short and consisted chiefly of a collection of MAXIMS on a given subject. The book was very popular, and revised, enlarged editions were issued in 1612 and 1625. The later *essays* are longer, sometimes more personal, and are developed by a wealth of illustration, quotation, and figures of speech. In fact, Bacon's STYLE achieved a compactness, clarity, imaginative richness, phrasal power, and sentence-rhythm which have made his *essays* an enduring part of the world's literature. The "aphoristic" quality of his STYLE is seen in such typical quotations as these: "The errors of young men are the ruin of business," and "He that hath a wife and children hath given hostages to fortune." In attitude and tone Bacon's *essays* are highly practical and utilitarian rather than ethically idealistic. Like the Renaissance COURTESY BOOKS they had for their chief purpose the giving of useful advice to those who wished to get on in practical life, especially as men of affairs.

After Bacon the seventeenth century contributed little to the development of the INFORMAL ESSAY, the influence of Bacon and Montaigne dominating such *essays* as were produced. Owen Felltham's *Resolves* (1620) shows the application of Bacon's method to religious topics. Sir William Cornwallis' *Essays* (1600) reflects the method of Montaigne. More worthy essayists appeared after the Restoration. Sir William Temple, the statesman, and Abraham Cowley, the poet, wrote Montaigne-like PERSONAL ESSAYS while living in retirement, Cowley's being particularly happy efforts. Though the INFORMAL ESSAY, strictly defined, received little attention in this century, there was much prose writing closely related to the INFORMAL and FORMAL ESSAY. The chapters of Sir Thomas Browne's *Religio Medici* (1642) in their STYLE and in their tendency toward self-revelation and moralizing are suggestive of the INFORMAL ESSAY, as are the miscellaneous sketches in Ben Jonson's *Timber, or Discoveries Made upon Men and Matter* (1641). Dryden's famous *Essay on Dramatic Poesy* (1668) is an example of a critical *essay* in conventional DIALOGUE form. The numerous PREFACES and books on literary CRITICISM from the late sixteenth and early seventeenth centuries are also forerunners of the later critical *essay*. Milton's great *Areopagitica,* in form an argumentative address, is a masterly example of what might now be called a FORMAL ESSAY. Not unrelated to *essay* writing, too, are such long prose treatises as Robert Burton's *Anatomy of Melancholy* (1621), Locke's *Essay on the Human Understanding* (1690), and even Izaak Walton's famous *Compleat Angler* (1653). The LETTER or formal EPISTLE as a vehicle for writing which was much like the INFORMAL ESSAY appeared in James Howell's *Familiar Letters* (1645–1655). The seventeenth century also saw the development in English of the CHARACTER, a brief character sketch of a quality or type-personality destined to become popular and exert an appreciable influence upon the PERIODICAL ESSAY of the eighteenth century, partly, to be sure, through the work of a French writer of CHARACTERS, La Bruyère, who had combined the CHARACTER with the *essay.* The EPIGRAM, as written by Ben Jonson, in its depiction of moral and social types sometimes became a sort of counterpart of the CHARACTER and may have influenced *essay* writers.

*The Periodical Essay: Eighteenth Century.*—The second great step in the history of the INFORMAL ESSAY came with the creation by Steele and Addison in the early years of the eighteenth century of the PERIODICAL ESSAY, a new art-form which achieved great popularity and attracted the genius of the best writers of the time. In 1691 there had appeared with Dunton's *Athenian Gazette* a new type of PERIODICAL, small in format and designed to entertain as well as instruct. A feature of Daniel Defoe's *A Weekly Review of Affairs in France* (1704) had been a department called "Advice from the Scandalous Club," gossipy in character. From this germ Richard Steele developed the new *essay* in his *Tatler* (1709–1711). The purpose of the papers was "to recommend truth, innocence, honor, virtue, as the chief ornaments of life." Joseph Addison soon joined Steele and the two later launched the frankly informal daily *Spectator* (1711–1712; 1714). The new *essay* was affected not only by its periodical form, which prescribed the length, but by the general spirit of the times. RENAISSANCE individualism was giving way to a centering of interest in society, and the moral reaction from the excesses of the RESTORATION AGE made timely the effort of the essayists to reform the manners of the age, refine its tastes, and provide topics for discussion at the popular coffee houses of London.

As compared with earlier *essays,* the PERIODICAL ESSAY is briefer, less aphoristic, less intimate and introspective, less individualistic, less "learned," and is more informal in STYLE and tone, making more use of HUMOR and SATIRE, and embracing a wider range of topics. The appeal is to the middle classes as well as to the cultivated few, but the city reader seems always to have been in the authors' minds. Addison referred to two types of *Spectator* papers: "serious essays" on such well-worn topics as death, marriage, education, and friendship; and "occasional papers," dealing with the "folly, extravagance, and caprice of the present age." The latter class especially aided in fixing as a tradition of the INFORMAL ESSAY that delightful informality, whimsicality, HUMOR, and grace which appears in scores of *essays* on such topics as women's fashions, dueling, witchcraft, coffee houses, and family portraits. The type developed much conventional machinery such as fictitious characters, clubs, visions, and imaginary correspondents.

The popularity of the form led to many imitations of the *Tatler* and *Spectator,* such as the *Guardian,* the *Female Tatler,* the *Whisperer,* and men like Swift, Pope, and Berkeley contributed *essays* to some of them. The novelist Fielding incorporated *essays* in his *Tom Jones.* Later in the century Dr. Samuel Johnson (in the *Rambler,* 1750–1752, and the *Idler* papers, 1758–1760), Lord Chesterfield, Horace Walpole, and Oliver Goldsmith appeared as accomplished informal essayists. Some of Goldsmith's *Letters from a Citizen of the World* (1760–1761) are noted examples of the form. After Goldsmith the *essay* declined as a literary form, though pleasant specimens of the form were written by Henry Mackenzie and Richard Cumberland.

*The Personal Essay: Nineteenth Century.*—A great revival of interest in the writing of both FORMAL and INFORMAL ESSAYS accompanied the triumph of the ROMANTIC MOVEMENT and the founding of new types of magazines in the first quarter of the nineteenth century, and brought about new forms and fashions. The informal type responded to the romantic impulses of the time. The production of the PERSONAL ESSAY, too, was stimulated greatly by the development of a new type of periodical: *Blackwood's Magazine* (1817) and the *London Magazine* (1820), which provided a market for the *essays* of Lamb, Hazlitt, Hunt, De Quincey, and others. Lamb's *Essays of Elia* (begun in 1820) exhibited an intimate STYLE, an autobiographical interest, a light and easy HUMOR and sentiment, an urbanity and unerring literary taste which have made Lamb one of the favorite essayists of all time. Even the novelists took up *essay* writing (Dickens, *Sketches by Boz,* 1836; Thackeray,

*Roundabout Papers*, 1860–1863). Though they followed in many respects their eighteenth-century predecessors, this group of nineteenth-century essayists accomplished a great change in the *essay* form. Freed from the space restrictions of the *Tatler* type and encouraged by a reading public eager for "original" work, these writers modified the Addisonian *essay* by making it more personal, longer, and more varied in theme, and by freeing it from the stereotyped features of the earlier form. Late in the century a worthy successor to Lamb appeared in Robert Louis Stevenson, for whose whimsical humor, nimble imagination, accomplished STYLE, and buoyant personality, the PERSONAL ESSAY formed an ideal medium of expression (*Virginibus Puerisque*, 1881; *Memories and Portraits*, 1887). More recent writers of the informal *essay* in England are A. C. Benson, G. K. Chesterton, and E. V. Lucas.

*The Formal Essay: Nineteenth Century.*—The FORMAL ESSAY of the early nineteenth century was largely the result of the appearance of the critical magazine, especially the *Edinburgh Review* (1802), the *Quarterly Review* (1809), and the *Westminster Review* (1824). Book reviews in the form of long critical *essays* were written by Francis Jeffrey, T. B. Macaulay, Thomas De Quincey, Sir Walter Scott, Thomas Carlyle, and later by George Eliot, Matthew Arnold, and many others. The manner of the FORMAL ESSAY appears also in the works of many other prose writers of the century. The separate chapters in the books of such men as Thomas Carlyle, John Ruskin, Walter Pater, Charles Kingsley, Leslie Stephen, Walter Bagehot, T. H. Huxley, Matthew Arnold, and Cardinal Newman are essay-like treatments of phases of the historical, biographical, scientific, educational, religious, and ethical topics concerned.

*The Essay in America.*—Though there is some reflection of *essay* literature in such early American writers as Cotton Mather, Jonathan Edwards, Benjamin Franklin, Thomas Jefferson, Alexander Hamilton, and such "itinerant" Americans as Tom Paine and J. H. St. John de Crèvecoeur, the first really great literary essayist in America is Washington Irving, whose *Sketch-Book* (1820) contains *essays* of the Addisonian type. Some of H. D. Thoreau's works (e.g., *Walden*) exhibited characteristics of the INFORMAL ESSAY, and Oliver Wendell Holmes in *The Autocrat of the Breakfast Table* (1857) was a successful writer of informal, humorous *essays*. Ralph Waldo Emerson, reminiscent of Bacon in his aphoristic style, fired with transcendental idealism, became perhaps the best known of all American essayists. James Russell Lowell (*Among My Books,* 1870, 1876) is another notable writer of *essays,* as is Edgar Allan Poe, who produced important critical *essays.* Later able essayists, formal or informal, include G. W. Curtis, C. D. Warner, W. D. Howells, Mark Twain, and John Burroughs. More recent names are those of Agnes Repplier, S. M. Crothers, Katherine Fullerton Gerould, Dallas Lore Sharp, Henry Van Dyke, William Beebe, Christopher Morley, James Thurber, E. B. White, and the writers for the *New Yorker.*

*Summary.*—In attempting to sum up the evolution of the *essay* as a form one must again note the distinction between the FORMAL and the INFORMAL ESSAY. The FORMAL ESSAY, instead of crystalliz-ing into a set literary type, has tended to become diversified in form, spirit, and length, according to the theme and serious pur-pose of its author. At one extreme it is represented by the brief, serious magazine ARTICLE and at the other by scientific or philo-sophical treatises which are books rather than *essays.* The tech-nique of the FORMAL ESSAY is now practically identical with that of all factual or theoretical prose writing in which literary effect is secondary to serious purpose. Its tradition has doubtless tended to add clarity to English prose style by its insistence upon unity, structure, and perspicacity.

The INFORMAL ESSAY, on the other hand, beginning in aphoristic and moralistic writing, modified by the injection of the personal element, broadened and lightened by a free treatment of human manners, modified and partly controlled in style and length by the limitations of periodical publication, has developed into a recognizable literary GENRE, the first purpose of which is to enter-tain, and the manner of which is sprightly, light, novel, or humor-ous. As such the form has aided in giving something of a Gallic grace to other forms of prose composition, notably letterwriting. But valuable though its contributions to prose writing have been and respected as it is today as a literary GENRE, the INFORMAL ESSAY has had few skillful or serious practitioners in the twentieth century. Perhaps our frenzied age is ill-suited to its sane, calm grace.

**Etiquette Books (Renaissance):** See COURTESY BOOKS.

**Eulogy:** A formal, dignified speech or writing, highly praising a person or a thing. See ENCOMIUM.

**Euphemism:** A figure of speech in which an indirect statement is substituted for a direct one in an effort to avoid bluntness. With the advance of REALISM in recent years strained *euphemisms* are seldom found in literature, since authors now generally realize that such expressions are taken by discriminating readers as evidences of a tendency to be insincere or even sentimental. Small-town journalistic style, however, still abounds with such locutions as "passed on" for "died," etc. Euphemistic terms have been much used by many writers in an effort to mention a disagreeable idea in an agreeable manner.

**Euphony:** A quality of good STYLE which demands that one select combinations of words which sound pleasant to the ear. Harsh, grating, cacophonous sounds violate *euphony* and make for unpleasantness in reading. Careful writers avoid such pitfalls as the juxtaposition of harsh consonants, a series of unaccented syllables, unconscious riming or repetition of similar sounds, jerky rhythm, and excessive ALLITERATION.

**Euphuism:** An affected STYLE of speech and writing which flourished late in the sixteenth century in England, especially in court circles. It took its name from *Euphues* (1579) by John Lyly, who developed the STYLE partly in an effort to refine English prose style and partly in an effort to attract, through novelty and lightness, the interest of the feminine readers whom he professed to write for. The chief characteristics of *euphuism* are: balanced construction, often antithetical and combined with ALLITERATION; excessive use of the rhetorical question; a heaping up of SIMILES, illustrations, and examples, especially those drawn from mythology and "unnatural natural history" about the fabulous habits and qualities of animals and plants. Following are some typical passages from *Euphues:* "Be sober but not too sullen; be valiant but not too venturous"; "For as the finest ruby staineth the color of the rest that be in place, or as the sun dimmeth the moon, so this gallant girl more fair than fortunate and yet more fortunate than faithful, etc."; "Do we not commonly see that in painted pots is hidden the deadliest poison? that in the greenest grass is the greatest serpent? in the clearest water the ugliest toad?" "The filthy sow when she is sick eateth the sea-crab and is immediately recured: the tortoise having tasted the viper sucketh *Organum* and is quickly revived; the bear ready to pine eateth up ants and is recovered; the dog having surfeited . . .

eateth grass and procureth remedy, etc."; "Being incensed against the one as most pernicious and enflamed with the other as most precious."

Lyly did not invent *euphuism;* rather he combined and popularized elements which others had developed. The RENAISSANCE had been greatly interested in perfecting vernacular STYLE (Italian, French, Spanish, English) in connection with the theory that modern languages were capable of being used for great literature. Important forerunners of Lyly in England were Lord Berners, in his translation of Froissart's *Chronicle* (1523, 1525); Sir Thomas North's translation (1557) of *The Dial of Princes* by Guevara (whose Spanish itself was highly colored); and George Pettie in his *A Petite Palace of Pettie his Pleasure* (1576). One of Pettie's sentences, for example, reads: "Nay, there was never bloody tiger that did so terribly tear the little lamb, as this tyrant did furiously fare with the fair Philomela."

The chief vogue of *euphuism* was in the 1580's, though it was employed much later. The court ladies cultivated it for social conversation, and such writers as Robert Greene and Thomas Lodge used it in their novels (as *Menaphon* and *Rosalynde*). Sir Philip Sidney reacted against it and was followed by many others. Shakespeare both employed it and ridiculed it in *Love's Labour's Lost.* Though the extravagance and artificiality of *euphuism* make it seem ludicrous to a modern reader, it is to be remembered that it actually played a powerful and beneficial rôle in the development of English prose. It established the idea that prose (formerly heavy and Latinized) might be written with IMAGINATION and FANCY, while its emphasis on short clauses and sentences and on balanced construction aided in imparting clearness to prose STYLE. These virtues of clearness and lightness and pleasant ornamentation remained as a permanent contribution after a better taste had eliminated the vices of extravagant artificiality. In a justly famous scene between Falstaff and Prince Hal, Shakespeare mocks the euphuistic style (*Henry IV,* Pt. I, Act II, Sc. 4).

**Exciting Force:** In a DRAMA the force which starts the CONFLICT of opposing interests and sets in motion the RISING ACTION of the play. Example: the witches' prophecy to Macbeth, which stirs him to schemes for making himself king. See DRAMATIC STRUCTURE.

**Excursus:** A formal, lengthy DIGRESSION. See DIGRESSION.

**Exemplum:** A moralized TALE. Just as modern preachers often make use of "illustrations," so medieval preachers made extensive use of TALES, ANECDOTES, and INCIDENTS, both historical and legendary, to point morals or illustrate definite doctrines. Often highly artificial and to a modern reader incredible, these "examples" seem to have appealed very strongly to medieval congregations, because of their concreteness, their narrative and human interest, as well as their moral implications. Collections of *exempla,* classified according to subject, were prepared for the use of preachers. An important book of the sort was Jacques de Vitry's *Exempla* (early thirteenth century). At times sermons degenerated into mere series of ANECDOTES, sometimes even humorous in character. Dante in thirteenth-century Italy and Wycliffe in fourteenth-century England protested against this tendency, and Wycliffe as an element in his reform program omitted *exempla* from his own sermons.

The influence of *exempla* and example-books on medieval literature was very great, as may be illustrated from several of Chaucer's poems. The *Nun's Priest's Tale,* for example, itself cast into sermon form, uses *exempla,* as when Chanticleer tells Pertelot ANECDOTES to prove that dreams have a meaning. The *Pardoner's Tale* is itself an *exemplum* to show how Avarice leads to an evil end.

**Existential Criticism:** A contemporary school of CRITICISM, led by Jean Paul Sartre, which denies the legitimacy of the traditional critical questions, and examines a literary work in terms of the ways in which it explores the *existential* questions and in terms of its existent impact on the reader. See EXISTENTIALISM.

**Existentialism:** A term applied to a group of attitudes current in philosophical, religious, and artistic thought during and after World War II, which emphasizes existence rather than essence and sees the inadequacy of the human reason to explain the enigma of the universe as the basic philosophical question. The term is so broadly and loosely used that an exact definition is not possible. In its modern expression it had its beginning in the writings of the nineteenth century Danish theologian, Søren Kierkegaard. The German philosopher Martin Heidegger is important in its formulation, and the French novelist-philosopher Jean Paul Sartre has done most to give it its present-form and popularity. *Existentialism* has found art and literature to be unusually effective methods of expression; in the NOVELS of Franz Kafka, Dostoyevski, Camus, Faulkner, and Hemingway, and in the plays and novels of Sartre, it has found its most persuasive media.

Basically the existentialist assumes that the significant fact is that we and things in general exist, but that these things have no meaning for us except as we through acting upon them can create meaning. Sartre claims that the fundamental truth of *existentialism* is in Descartes' formula, "I think; therefore, I exist." The existential philosophy is concerned with the personal "commitment" of this unique existing individual in the "human situation." It attempts to codify the irrational aspect of man's nature, to objectify non-being or nothingness and see it as a universal source of fear, to distrust concepts, and to emphasize experiential concreteness. The existentialist's point of departure is the immediate sense of awareness that man has of his situation. A part of this awareness is the sense man has of meaninglessness in the outer world; this meaninglessness produces in him a discomfort, an anxiety, a loneliness in the face of man's limitations and a desire to invest experience with meaning by acting upon the world, although efforts to act in a meaningless, "absurd" world lead to anguish, greater loneliness, and despair. Such a philosophical attitude can result in nihilism and hopelessness, as, indeed, it has with many of the literary existentialists.

On the other hand, the existential view can assert the possibility of improvement. Most pessimistic systems find the source of their despair in the fixed imperfection of human nature or of the human context; the existentialist, however, denies all absolute principles and holds that human nature is fixed only in that we have agreed to recognize certain human attributes; it is, therefore, subject to change if men can agree on other attributes or even to change by a single man if he acts bravely in contradiction to the accepted principles. Hence, for the existentialist, the possibilities of altering human nature and society are unlimited, but, at the same time, man can hope for aid in making such alterations only from within himself.

In contradistinction to this essentially atheistic *existentialism,* there has also developed a sizable body of Christian existential thought, represented by men like Karl Jaspers, Jacques Maritain, Nicolas Berdyaev, Martin Buber, and Paul Tillich. An excellent general and sympathetic treatment of the existential attitude may be found in William Barrett's *Irrational Man.*

# Expletive

**Expletive:** An interjection to lend emphasis to a sentence or, in VERSE especially, the use of a superfluous word (some form of the verb "to do," for example) to make for RHYTHM. Profanity is, of course, another form of *expletive* use. Careless speech is full of superfluous words which are *expletive* in nature. A common colloquial *expletive* is "you see" added frequently to a statement, as "I went home, you see, at ten o'clock."

*Explication de texte:* A method which originated in the teaching of literature in France; it involves the painstaking analysis of the meanings, relationships, and AMBIGUITIES of the words, IMAGES, and small units that make up a literary work. It is now one of the tools of the NEW CRITICS. See ANALYTICAL CRITICISM, AMBIGUITY, NEW CRITICISM.

**Exposition:** One of the four chief types of composition, the others being ARGUMENTATION, DESCRIPTION, and NARRATION. Its purpose is to explain the nature of an object, an idea, or a THEME. *Exposition* may exist apart from the other types of composition, but frequently two or more of the types are blended, DESCRIPTION aiding *exposition*, ARGUMENT being supported by *exposition*, NARRATION reinforcing by example an *exposition*. The following are some of the methods used in *exposition* (they may be used singly or in various combinations): identification, definition, classification, illustration, comparison and contrast, and analysis.

In DRAMATIC STRUCTURE the *exposition* is the introductory material, which creates the tone, gives the SETTING, introduces the characters, and supplies other facts necessary to an understanding of the play. See DRAMATIC STRUCTURE.

**Expressionism:** A movement affecting painting, the DRAMA, the NOVEL, and POETRY, which followed and went beyond IMPRESSIONISM in its efforts to "objectify inner experience." Fundamentally it means the willing yielding up of the REALISTIC and NATURALISTIC methods, of VERISIMILITUDE, in order to use objects in art not as representational but as transmitters of the impressions and moods of a character or of the author or artist. In painting, for instance, "childhood" might be shown not through a conventional representational picture of children at play or at school but by seemingly unarticulated and exaggerated physical details that suggest "childhood" or convey the impression which the artist has of the concept "child."

As an organized literary movement *expressionism* was strongest in the theatre in the 1920's, and its entry into other literary forms was probably through the stage. *Expressionism* had its origin in the German theatre in the early years of the century. It was a response to several different forces: the growing size and mechanism of society with its tendency to depress the value of the arts made the artists seek new ways of making art forms valuable instruments for man; at the same time the depth psychologists, notably Freud, laid bare the phantasms in the depths of the human mind and offered the artist a challenge accurately to record them; meanwhile Marxism had instructed even the non-Marxist artist that the individual was being lost in a mass society; to these pressures came the example of the dramas of Strindberg, whose plays *The Dance of Death* (1901) and *The Dream Play* (1902) employ extensive non-realistic devices. The German dramatists Wedekind, Georg Kaiser, and Ernst Toller and the Czech dramatist Karel Capek (the author of the nightmarish fantasy of the future, *R. U. R.*) were the major figures in the European expressionistic drama, which flourished in the 1920's. It was marked by unreal atmosphere, a nightmarish quality of action, distortion and over-simplification, the de-emphasis of the individual (characters were likely to be called the "Father" or the "Bank Clerk"), anti-realistic stage SETTINGS, and staccato, telegraphic DIALOGUE. The expressionistic DRAMA was strongly influential on Pirandello and Lorca. For American students it is most important in its impact on Eugene O'Neill, whose *Emperor Jones* attempts to project by symbolic scenes and sound-effects the racial memories of a modern Negro. Elmer Rice's *The Adding Machine,* which uses moving stages and other non-realistic devices to express the mechanical world seen by one cog in it named Mr. Zero, is an almost equally noted example. Elements of *expressionism* can be seen in the plays of Thornton Wilder, Arthur Miller, and Tennessee Williams.

In the NOVEL the presentation of the objective outer world as it expresses itself in the impressions or moods of a character is a device widely used. The most famous extended example is Joyce's *Finnegans Wake,* although the expressionistic intent and method is often apparent in works using the STREAM OF CONSCIOUSNESS technique, as witness the "Circe" episode in Joyce's *Ulysses.*

Probably the most complete transfer of the quality of expressionistic drama to the NOVEL, however, is to be found in the works of Franz Kafka.

The revolt against REALISM, the distortion of the objects of the outer world, and the violent dislocation of time sequence and spatial logic in an effort accurately but not representationally to show the world as it appears to a troubled mind can be found in contemporary poetry, particularly that of Robinson Jeffers and T. S. Eliot, whose "The Hollow Men" is an excellent example and whose *The Waste Land* is the poetic classic of the movement. See IMPRESSIONISM, REALISM.

**Expressive Theory of Criticism:** The term, used by M. H. Abrams, that designates a theory of art which holds the object of the artist to be the expression of his emotions, impressions, or beliefs; an essential doctrine of the ROMANTIC critics. See CRITICISM, HISTORICAL SKETCH.

**Extravaganza:** A fantastic, extravagant, or irregular composition. It is most commonly applied to dramatic compositions such as those of J. R. Planché, the creator of the dramatic *extravaganza.* Planché himself defined it as a "whimsical treatment of a poetical subject as distinguished from the broad caricature of a tragedy or serious opera, which was correctly described as burlesque." The subject was often a fairy tale. The presentation was elaborate, and included dancing and music. An example is Planché's *Sleeping Beauty* (acted 1840). A later use of *extravaganza,* still current, is to designate any extraordinarily spectacular theatrical production. The term *extravaganza* is also applied to fantastic musical compositions, especially musical CARICATURES. In literature the term is occasionally used to characterize such rollicking or unrestrained work as Butler's *Hudibras,* a CARICATURE of the PURITANS.

**Eye-Rime:** RIME that appears correct from the spelling, but is HALF-RIME or SLANT-RIME from the pronunciation, as "watch" and "match" or "love" and "move."

**Fable:** A brief TALE, either in prose or VERSE, told to point a moral. The characters are most frequently animals, but they need not be so restricted since people and inanimate objects as well are sometimes the central figures. The subject matter of *fables* has to do with supernatural and unusual incidents and often draws its origin from FOLKLORE sources. By far the most famous *fables* are those accredited to Aesop, a Greek slave living about 600 B.C.; but almost equally popular are those of La Fontaine, a Frenchman writing in the seventeenth century, because of their distinctive HUMOR and WIT, their wisdom and sprightly SATIRE. Other important fabulists are Gay (England), Lessing (Germany), Krylov (Russia). A *fable* in which the characters are animals is called a BEAST FABLE, a form that has been popular in almost every period of literary history, usually as a satiric device to point out the follies of mankind. The BEAST FABLE continues to be vigorous in such diverse works as Kipling's *Jungle Books* and *Just So Stories*, Joel Chandler Harris' Uncle Remus stories, and George Orwell's *Animal Farm*. Many critics, particularly in the NEO-CLASSIC PERIOD, have used *fable* as a term for the PLOT of a FICTION or a DRAMA. See BEAST EPIC, BESTIARY, ALLEGORY.

**Fabliau:** A humorous TALE popular in medieval French literature. The *fabliaux* gained their wide diffusion largely through the popularity of the JONGLEUR, who spread the *fabliaux* widely throughout France. The conventional form was eight-syllable VERSE. These *fabliaux* consisted of stories of various types, but one point was uppermost—their humorous, sly SATIRE on human beings. Themes frequently used in these stories, which were often bawdy, dealt familiarly with the clergy, ridiculed womanhood, and were pitched in a key which made them readily and boisterously understandable to the uneducated. The form was also present in English literature of the MIDDLE ENGLISH PERIOD, Chaucer especially leaving us examples of *fabliaux,* in tales of the Miller, Reeve, Friar, Summoner, Merchant, Shipman, and Manciple. Although *fabliaux* often had ostensible "morals" appended to them, they lack the serious intention of the FABLE, and they differ from the FABLE too in always having human beings as characters and in always maintaining a REALISTIC tone and manner.

**Fairy Tale:** A story relating mysterious pranks and adventures of supernatural spirits who manifested themselves in the form of diminutive human beings. These spirits possessed certain qualities which are constantly drawn upon for TALES of their adventures: supernatural wisdom and foresight, a mischievous temperament, the power to regulate the affairs of man for good or evil, the capacity to change themselves into any shape at any time. *Fairy tales* as such—though they had existed in varying forms before—became popular toward the close of the seventeenth century. Almost every nation has its own fairy literature, though the FOLK-LORE element embodied in *fairy tales* prompts the growth of related TALES among different nations. Some of the great source-collections are the *Pentamerone* of Basilio (Italian), the *Contes de ma Mère l'Oye* of Perrault (French), the *Cabinet des Fées* (French), and those of the Grimm brothers in German and of Keightley and Croker in English. Hans Christian Andersen, of Denmark, is probably the most famous writer of original *fairy tales*.

**Falling Action:** The second "half" or RESOLUTION of a dramatic PLOT. It follows the CLIMAX, beginning often with a TRAGIC FORCE, exhibits the failing fortunes of the hero (in TRAGEDY) and the successful efforts of the COUNTERPLAYERS, and culminates in the CATASTROPHE. See DRAMATIC STRUCTURE.

**Familiar Essay:** A term applied to the more personal, intimate type of INFORMAL ESSAY. It deals lightly, often humorously, with personal experiences, opinions, and prejudices, stressing especially the unusual or novel in attitude and having to do with the varied aspects of everyday life. Goldsmith, Lamb, and Stevenson were particularly successful in the form. See ESSAY.

**Fancy:** A critical term now used almost exclusively in the Coleridgean opposition of IMAGINATION AND FANCY, in which *fancy* is "mechanic," logical, "the aggregative and associative power," as opposed to the "organic" and "creative" IMAGINATION. See IMAGINATION AND FANCY.

**Fantastic Poets:** A term applied by Milton to the school of metaphysical poets (see METAPHYSICAL VERSE).

**Fantasy:** Though sometimes used as an equivalent of FANCY and even of IMAGINATION (see IMAGINATION AND FANCY), *fantasy* is usually employed to designate a "conscious breaking free from experienced reality," as Pellizzi defines it. The term is applied to a work which takes place in a non-existent and unreal world, such as fairyland, or concerns incredible and unreal characters, as in Maeterlinck's *The Blue Bird*, or employs physical and scientific principles not yet discovered or contrary to present experience, as in SCIENCE-FICTION and UTOPIAN fiction. *Fantasy* may be employed merely for the whimsical delight of author or reader, or it may be the means used by the author for serious comment on reality. The most sustained example of *fantasy*, combining both intentions, in recent literature are the novels of James Branch Cabell laid in the mythical kingdom of Poictesme.

**Farce:** The word developed from Late Latin *farsus*, connected with a verb meaning "to stuff." Thus an expansion or amplification in the church liturgy was called a *farse*. Later, in France, *farce* meant any sort of extemporaneous addition in a play, especially comic jokes or "gags," the clownish actors speaking "more than was set down" for them. In the late seventeenth century *farce* was used in England to mean any short humorous play, as distinguished from regular five-act COMEDY. The development in these plays of certain elements of LOW COMEDY is responsible for the usual modern meaning of *farce:* a dramatic piece intended to excite laughter and depending less on PLOT and character than on exaggerated, improbable situations, the humor arising from gross incongruities, coarse wit, or horseplay. *Farce* merges into COMEDY, and the same play (e.g., Shakespeare's *The Taming of the Shrew*) may be called by some a *farce*, by others a COMEDY. *Life Below Stairs* (1759), with the production of which Garrick was connected, has been termed the "best farce" of the eighteenth century. In the American theatre, Brandon Thomas' *Charley's Aunt* (1892), dealing with the extravagant events resulting from a female impersonation, is the best known American *farce*, although *farce* has been the stock-in-trade of motion-picture comedians. See FARCE-COMEDY.

**Farce-Comedy:** A term sometimes applied to comedies which rely for their interest chiefly on farcical devices (see FARCE, LOW COMEDY), but which contain some truly comic elements which elevate them above most FARCE. Shakespeare's *The Taming of the Shrew* and *The Merry Wives of Windsor* are called *farce-comedies* by some authorities. One writer distinguishes between the *farce-comedy* of Aristophanes (loose STRUCTURE, variety of appeal, operatic quality) and that of Plautus (careful STRUCTURE, intricate INTRIGUE, broad HUMOR).

**Federalist Age in American Literature:** The portion of American literary history between the formation of the national government and the "Second Revolution" of Jacksonian Democracy, so-called because of the dominance of the Federalist Party in American political life and thought. The period extends from 1790 to 1830. Internationally, the Age saw the emergence of the United States as a world force through the War of 1812. Internally it was an "Era of Good Feeling," with the sectional and social issues which were to plague the nation in mid-century just beginning to be felt. It was an age of rapid literary development. In 1790 the United States could boast of few distinguished writers of any kind and almost none of belletristic excellence; at its close America was clearly ready for the artistic burgeoning forth that marked the period from 1830 to the Civil War. Poetry moved from the imitative neo-classicism of Barlow and Dwight, through the limited romanticism of Freneau, to the first notable American achievements in verse in the work of Bryant. The novel, first practiced in America in 1789, saw good work by Charles Brockden Brown and H. H. Brackenridge and the establishment of a distinctively American romance with the Leatherstocking Tales of James Fenimore Cooper. Irving in his burlesque *Knickerbocker's History* and in his essays and tales found an international audience. The *North American Review*, founded in 1815, was a thriving quarterly. In the decade 1800–1810, Hawthorne, Simms, Whittier, Longfellow, Poe, and Holmes were born; and 1819 was an *annus mirabilis*, being the birth year of Lowell, Melville, and Whitman. By 1830 the neo-classic, restrained, aristocratic Federalist that America had been had given way to a romantic, exuberant, democratic young giant that was flexing its muscles and was beginning effectively to express itself in art as well as action. See *Outline of Literary History* and REVOLUTIONARY AND EARLY NATIONAL PERIOD IN AMERICAN LITERATURE.

**Feminine Ending:** An extra-metrical syllable, bearing no STRESS, added to the end of a line in IAMBIC or ANAPESTIC METER. This variation gives a sense of movement and an irregularity to the METER which make for grace and lightness. The form is perhaps most commonly used in BLANK VERSE. The second line below carries an illustration:

> O! I could play the woman with mine eyes
> And braggart with my tongue. But gentle heav*ens,*
> Cut short all intermission.
>
> —Shakespeare

**Feminine Rime (double rime):** A RIME of two syllables, one stressed and one unstressed, as *waken* and *forsaken, audition* and *rendition.* In Chaucer, the *feminine rime* was very common because of the frequent recurrence of the final *-e* in Middle English. The term "feminine" is a courtesy—either to the form or to womanhood—since it is employed to connote the lightness and grace which result from the use of this type of RIME.

> Above the pines the moon was slowly *drifting,*
>     The river sang below;
> The dim Sierras, far beyond, *uplifting*
>     Their minarets of snow.
>
> —Bret Harte

**Feudalism:** The system of social and political organization that prevailed in Western Europe during a large part of the medieval period. It developed from the anarchy which followed the fall of Charlemagne's empire in the ninth century. In feudal theory every landholder was merely the tenant of some greater landlord. Thus, the barons or powerful prelates were the tenants of the king; the lesser lords, knights, and churchmen were tenants of the barons and prelates; while the serfs and "villeins" were tenants of the lesser nobles. In practice—as the whole system was based upon force—the relations were more complicated: even kings sometimes owed allegiance to a great churchman or baron. As rent the various groups paid to their immediate superiors "service," which might consist of visible property or of military aid. Socially, there were two sharply defined classes: the workers (villeins or free renters; serfs or bondmen); and the "prayers and fighters" (knights, upper clergy, lords). *Feudalism* broke down in the fifteenth century. The ideals of chivalry (see CHIVALRY IN ENGLISH LITERATURE) grew out of *feudalism* and powerfully affected the character of much medieval and even RENAISSANCE literature, notably the ROMANCES and ROMANTIC EPICS. The feudal social order is pictured in Chaucer's *Canterbury Tales* and its evils set forth in the *Vision of Piers Plowman* (fourteenth century).

**Fiction:** Narrative writing drawn from the IMAGINATION of the author rather than from history or fact. The term is most frequently associated with NOVELS and SHORT STORIES, though DRAMA and NARRATIVE POETRY are also FORMS of *fiction,* and FABLES, PARABLES, FAIRY TALES, and FOLKLORE contain fictional elements.

Sometimes authors weave fictional episodes about historical characters, epochs, and settings and thus make "historical *fiction*." Sometimes authors use imaginative elaborations of incidents and qualities of a real person in a BIOGRAPHY, resulting in a type of writing popular in recent years, the "fictional BIOGRAPHY." Sometimes the actual events of the author's life are presented under the guise of imaginative creations, resulting in "autobiographical *fiction*." Sometimes actual persons and events are presented under the guise of *fiction*, resulting in the ROMAN À CLEF. The chief function of *fiction* is to entertain, to be "interesting" in Henry James' phrase; but it often serves also to instruct, to edify, to persuade, or to arouse. It is one of the chief devices by which man communicates his vision of the nature of reality in CONCRETE TERMS.

Since *fiction* is a subject matter rather than a type of literature, one interested in any of the particular forms which *fiction* assumes should turn to the articles on specific types, such as NOVEL, SHORT STORY, DRAMA, NARRATIVE POEM, FABLE, for details of the history and STRUCTURE of these types.

**Figurative Language:** Intentional departure from the normal order, construction, or meaning of words in order to gain strength and freshness of expression, to create a pictorial effect, to describe by ANALOGY, or to discover and illustrate similarities in otherwise dissimilar things. *Figurative language* is writing that embodies one or more of the various FIGURES OF SPEECH, the most common of which are: ANTITHESIS, APOSTROPHE, CLIMAX, HYPERBOLE, IRONY, METAPHOR, METONYMY, PERSONIFICATION, SIMILE, SYNECDOCHE. These figures are often divided into two classes: TROPES, literally meaning "turns," in which the words in the figure undergo a decided change in meaning, and "figures of thought," in which the words retain their literal meaning but their rhetorical pattern is changed. An APOSTROPHE, for example, is a "figure of thought," and a METAPHOR is a TROPE. See IMAGERY, METAPHOR, TROPE.

**Figures of Speech:** The various kinds of departure from normal construction or meaning of language when it is employed figuratively. See FIGURATIVE LANGUAGE.

*Filidh* (*pl. fili*): Early Irish professional poets. See IRISH LITERATURE.

*Fin de siècle:* "End of the century," a phrase often applied to the last ten years of the nineteenth century. The eighteen-nineties were a transitional period, one in which writers and artists were consciously abandoning old ideas and conventions and attempting to discover and set up new techniques and artistic objectives. One writer (Holbrook Jackson) has noted three main characteristics of the decade in art and literature: DECADENCE, exemplified in Oscar Wilde and Aubrey Beardsley; REALISM or "sense of fact," represented by Gissing, Shaw, and George Moore, with their reaction against the sentimental; and radical or revolutionary social aspirations, marked by numerous new "movements" (including the "new woman," who dared ride a bicycle and seek political suffrage) and by a general sense of emancipation from the traditional social and moral order. See EDWARDIAN AGE.

**Final Suspense, Moment of:** A dramatic term used to indicate the ray of hope sometimes appearing just before the CATASTROPHE of a TRAGEDY. Thus Macbeth's continued faith that he cannot be hurt by any man born of woman keeps the reader or spectator in some suspense as to the apparently inevitable tragic ending. See DRAMATIC STRUCTURE.

**Five Points of Calvinism:** See CALVINISM.

**Flashback:** A device by which the writer of a FICTION or a DRAMA presents SCENES or INCIDENTS that occurred prior to the opening scene of the work. It is a method of presenting EXPOSITION dramatically. Various devices may be used, among them recollections of the characters, narration by the characters, dream sequences, and reveries. Notable examples in the theatre occur in Elmer Rice's *Dream Girl* and Arthur Miller's *Death of a Salesman.* Maugham used the *flashback* skillfully and effectively in *Cakes and Ale,* and it is employed consistently in the novels of John P. Marquand. See EXPOSITION.

**Fleshly School of Poetry, The:** The title of a critical ESSAY published in the *Contemporary Review,* October, 1871. The article was signed "Thomas Maitland" (a pseudoym); actually it was written by Robert W. Buchanan. The critic took to task the poets Swinburne, Morris, and Rossetti, though most of the article is couched as a review of Rossetti's poems and Rossetti himself draws most of the fire. Buchanan accused the three of being in league to praise each other's work and refers to them as the "Mutual Admiration School." The following passage will make clear the general tone and trend of Buchanan's criticism:

The fleshly gentlemen have bound themselves by solemn league and covenant to extol fleshliness as the distinct and supreme end of poetic and pictorial art, to aver that poetic expression is greater than poetic thought, and by inference that the body is greater than the soul, and sound superior to sense; and that the poet, properly to develop his poetic faculty, must be an intellectual hermaphrodite. . . .

Rossetti replied to this denunciation by an attack called "The Stealthy School of Criticism" which was published in *The Athenaeum* (December 16, 1871).

**Folio:** A BOOK SIZE, designating a book whose SIGNATURES result from sheets folded to two leaves or four pages. *See* BOOK SIZES.

**Folk Drama:** In its stricter and older sense, as usually employed by folklorists, the term means dramatic activities of the folk—the unsophisticated treatment of folk themes by the folk themselves, particularly activities connected with popular festivals and religious rites (for the development of ancient Greek drama from such forms, see DRAMA). For a treatment of medieval *folk drama* of this sort, the student may consult the first volume of Sir Edmund Chambers's *Mediaeval Stage* and the same writer's *The English Folk-Play*, in which such forms as the sword dance, the St. George play, the mummers' play are described. The MEDIEVAL religious DRAMA, though sophisticated in the sense of being based upon Scriptural materials and a religion with a fully developed written theology, is by some folklorists regarded as a form of *folk drama*, and the "folk" character of such twentieth-century plays as Marc Connelly's *Green Pastures* is commonly recognized. The religious DRAMA of the Middle Ages (see MEDIEVAL DRAMA), however, is treated by historians of the DRAMA as a special form, not as *folk drama*.

Another sense in which the term *folk drama* is being employed, especially in America, includes plays which, while written by sophisticated and consciously artistic playwrights, reflect the customs, language, attitudes, and environmental difficulties of the folk. These plays are commonly performed, not by the folk themselves, but by amateur or professional actors. They tend to be realistic, close to the soil, and sympathetically human. The plays of J. M. Synge, Lady Gregory, and other authors of the CELTIC RENAISSANCE and the American plays by Paul Green and others published in the several volumes of *Carolina Folk-Plays* are examples. The latter reflect especially the life of the Negro and the Southern "mountain folk."

**Folk Epic:** An EPIC by an unknown author or authors or of doubtful attribution or assumed to be the product of communal composition. See EPIC, ART EPIC.

**Folklore:** A term first used by W. J. Thomas in the middle of the nineteenth century as a substitute for "popular antiquities." The existence of varied conceptions of the term makes definition difficult. The one adopted by the Folklore Society of London about 1890 is: "The comparison and identification of the survivals of archaic beliefs, customs, and traditions in modern ages." A book on *folklore* published by an American scholar in 1930 affirms that *folklore* "limits itself to a study of the unrecorded traditions of the people as they appear in popular fiction, custom and belief, magic and ritual." The same writer (Krappe) regards it as the function of *folklore* to reconstruct the "spiritual history of man" from a study of the ways and sayings of the folk as contrasted with sophisticated thinkers and writers. Although concerned primarily with the psychology of early man or with that of the less cultured classes of society, some of the forms of *folklore* (e.g., superstitions and proverbial sayings) belong also to the life of modern man, literate as well as illiterate, and may, therefore, be transmitted by written record as well as by word of mouth. *Folklore* includes MYTHS, LEGENDS, stories, RIDDLES, PROVERBS, nursery rimes, charms, spells, omens, superstitions of all sorts, popular BALLADS, cowboy songs, plant lore, animal lore, and customs dealing with marriage, death, and amusements. The relations of *folklore* to sophisticated literature are important, but not always easy to trace. A folk tale may be retold by an author writing for a highly cultivated audience, and later in a changed form again be taken over by the folk. Folk customs are associated with the development of dramatic activity, because of the custom of performing plays at folk festivals.

Literature is full of elements taken over from *folklore,* and some knowledge of the formulas and CONVENTIONS of *folklore* is often an aid to the understanding of great literature. The acceptance of

the rather childish love-test in *King Lear* may rest upon the fact
that the MOTIF was an already familiar one in *folklore*. The effects
of such works as Coleridge's *Christabel* or Keats' *Eve of St. Agnes*
depend upon the recognition of popular superstitions, while some
familiarity with fairy lore is necessary if one is to catch in full the
charm of James Stephens' *The Crock of Gold*. The fine MEDIEVAL
ROMANCE of *Sir Gawain and the Green Knight*, written for a cultivated audience, centers round the folk-formula of the challenging
of a mortal by a supernatural being to a beheading contest: the
binding force of the covenant between Gawain and the Green
Knight is explained by primitive attitudes rather than by rational
rules of conduct. Shakespeare's *Hamlet* is a retelling of an old popular tale of the "exile-and-return" formula.

The study of *folklore* in America, particularly that of the cowboy, the mountaineer, and the Negro, has received increasing attention in the twentieth century.

**Foot:** The unit of RHYTHM in a VERSE, whether accentual or QUAN-
TITATIVE. A FOOT usually consists of one stressed or long syllable
and one or more unstressed or short syllables; however, the SPONDEE
consists of two stressed syllables, the PYRRHIC of two unstressed
syllables. The following are the common patterns in English accentual VERSE: IAMBUS ( ‿ — ), TROCHEE ( — ‿ ), ANAPEST
( ‿ ‿ — ), and DACTYL ( — ‿ ‿ ).

**Forgeries, Literary:** See LITERARY FORGERIES.

**Form:** A term used in CRITICISM to designate the organization of
the elements of a work of art in relation to its total EFFECT. VERSE
*form* refers to the organization of rhythmic units in a line. STANZA
*form* refers to the organization of the VERSES. The *form* of the
IMAGES refers to the interrelationships existing among the IMAGES
in a work. The *form* of the ideas refers to the organization or structure of thought in the work.

In a common division, critics distinguish between *form* and content, *form* being the pattern or STRUCTURE or organization which
is employed to give expression to the content. A similar distinction
is often made between "conventional" *form* and organic *form*. This
is the difference between what Coleridge called "mechanic" *form*
and *form* that "is innate; it shapes, as it develops, itself from within,
and the fullness of its development is one and the same with the

perfection of its outward form." Another way of expressing this difference is to think of "conventional" *form* as representing an ideal pattern or shape which precedes the content and meaning of the work and of organic *form* as representing a pattern or shape that develops as it is because of the content and meaning of the work. "Conventional" *form* presupposes certain characteristics of organization or pattern which must be present in the work and which are used as tests for the ultimate merit of the work as art—the chief one usually being UNITY. Organic *form* asserts that each poem has, as Herbert Read has said, "its own inherent laws, originating with its very invention and fusing in one vital unity both structure and content."

*Form* is also used to designate the common attributes that distinguish one GENRE from another. In this sense *form* becomes an ABSTRACT TERM describing not one work but the commonly held qualities of many. This abstract *form* in NEO-CLASSIC periods tends to become a legislative device, a congeries of "rules" to be followed. See STRUCTURE, GENRE.

**Formal Criticism:** CRITICISM which examines a work of art in terms of the characteristics of the type or GENRE to which it belongs. See CRITICISM, TYPES OF; FORM.

**Formal Essay:** A serious, dignified, logically organized ESSAY, written to inform or persuade. See ESSAY.

**Four Senses of Interpretation:** The levels frequently used in interpreting Scriptural and allegorical materials; they are the literal, the allegorical, the moral, and the anagogical. See ANAGOGE.

**"Fourteeners":** A verse form consisting of fourteen syllables arranged in IAMBIC feet. George Chapman, for instance, has a translation of the *Iliad* in this meter, but in recent years the form has fallen into disuse.

**Frame-story:** A story within a narrative setting or *frame,* a story within a story. This is a convention frequently used in classical and modern writing. Perhaps the best known examples are found in the *Arabian Nights,* the *Decameron,* and the *Canterbury Tales.* Chaucer, for example, introduced in his Prologue a group of people making a pilgrimage. Here we are told something of each of his characters, how they meet at the Tabard Inn, and how they proceed on their journey. This general setting may be thought of as the *frame;* the stories which the various pilgrims tell along the way are stories within the general framework, or *frame-stories.*

**Franco-Norman:** See ANGLO-NORMAN (LANGUAGE).

**Free Verse:** Often called *vers libre* and *polyrhythmic verse.* It is to be distinguished from conventional VERSE chiefly by its irregular metrical pattern, its use of CADENCE rather than uniform metrical feet. Even though *free verse* does not follow the regular RHYTHM of the usual poetry, it has great possibilities for subtle effects; in fact this freedom to secure a variety of rhythmical effects instead of one is the chief justification for the existence of the form. *Free verse* lives in greater rhythmical units than conventional verse. In conventional verse the unit is the FOOT, or, perhaps, the line; in *free verse* the unit is the STANZA or STROPHE.

The recent enthusiasm for *vers libre* may make us forget the history of the form and think of it as a twentieth-century contribution. To do this, however, is to forget the fact that Hebrew verse (like much Oriental poetry) is based on large rhythmical units and that our familiar *Psalms* and *Song of Solomon* are as definitely *free verse* as anything Carl Sandburg has written. Nor is the form new to European literature: France has practised it for many years; Heinrich Heine used it in his *The North Sea;* W. E. Henley and Matthew Arnold practised it in England; Walt Whitman shocked America with it before 1860. Stephen Crane employed it before Amy Lowell. It is idle to talk of the superiority of one form over another since both are manifestations of poetic mood and temper. What is important is that the experimentation with *free verse* in the twentieth century has done much to free poetry from certain formal conventions which might, conceivably, have mechanized it beyond all spontaneity and life.

**French Forms:** (Sometimes referred to as the "fixed" poetic forms.) A name given to certain definitely prescribed VERSE patterns which originated in France largely during the time of the TROUBADOURS. The more usual French forms are: BALLADE, CHANT ROYAL, PANTOUM, RONDEAU, RONDEL, ROUNDEL, SESTINA, TRIOLET, and VILLANELLE. These are all explained in their proper places in this Handbook.

**Frontier Literature:** In America, writing done by and on the frontier or having as its subject the frontier and frontier life. Up to 1890, when the free lands had all been pretty generally claimed, one aspect of American history was the steady westward movement of the frontier. Cooper, for example, could write of the frontier as being in New York State; Brackenridge in *Modern Chivalry* saw the wilds of Pennsylvania as the outer edge of cultivation; Simms in his border romances could see Georgia and Alabama as untamed wildernesses. Mark Twain in *Roughing It* could picture a primitive West. The extent to which this westward moving frontier colored and shaped American thought and life and the extent to which its passing marked a sharp turn in the character of the American are matters of great debate among historians and literary scholars. But whatever one may think of Frederick Turner's much-praised and often-attacked thesis that the frontier has been the dominant influence in American history, there is little question that it has consistently found literary expression in a virile, humorous, often crude body of songs, tales, and books which have been marked by a realistic view of life, a sanguine contemplation of violence, and an immense gusto. Much of the writing of this frontier was subliterary, confined to oral tradition and to newspapers, but it kept constantly alive in America a hearty HUMOR and a healthy REALISM, even in the face of the GENTEEL TRADITION. Important writers in the frontier tradition have been Timothy Flint, Augustus Baldwin Longstreet, Joseph Glover Baldwin, Artemus Ward, Caroline Kirkland, Joseph Kirkland, Bret Harte, Mark Twain, and Hamlin Garland. Whether the ultimate effect of the frontier on writers growing up in it was good or bad was a question that precipitated one of the most bitter critical controversies in American literary history, that between Van Wyck Brooks and Bernard De Voto over Brooks' thesis that the frontier was one of the stifling and frustrating influences that bridled Mark Twain's genius.

**Fundamental Image:** A central or controlling figure around which a work is organized. When the controlling figure is a METAPHOR, it is called a CONTROLLING IMAGE, a device often used in META-PHYSICAL VERSE. *Fundamental image* is used to designate the simpler, non-metaphorical use of some important aspect or feature of an object being described or discussed. This reduction of the complex whole to one main feature or unifying principle simplifies and focuses the description in such a way as to make for clearness. The famous description of the battle of Waterloo, in which Victor Hugo employed the outline of the letter A as illustrative of the position of the various armies, is a notable example of the clarifying value of the *fundamental image*. See CONTROLLING IMAGE.

**Gaelic Movement:** The movement begun late in the nineteenth century, especially as embodied in the Gaelic League, founded by Douglas Hyde in 1893, which aimed at the preservation of the Gaelic language. This native Celtic speech had been gradually giving way to English since the seventeenth century and had not been permitted in the new schools established in the middle of the nineteenth century. The *Gaelic Movement* attempted to foster the production of a new native Irish literature in Gaelic. Hyde himself wrote plays in Gaelic. Though the movement attracted wide attention and some controversy, it has not been notably successful in stopping the advance of English as a spoken language in Ireland, and on the literary side has been overshadowed by the IRISH LITERARY MOVEMENT, which encouraged the use of English in creating a new Irish literature exploiting Irish materials. See CELTIC RENAISSANCE.

**Gallicism:** A word or phrase or idiom characteristic of the French language, or a custom or turn of thought suggestive of the French people. Thus when an Englishman uses the phrase "reason for existence" or "stroke of policy," he is probably imitating the French idiomatic phrases *raison d'être* and *coup d'état*. The term is applied to any borrowing from the French language in which the borrower stops short of using the French word without disguise. Although *Gallicisms* have obviously enriched and enlivened the language, the danger is that they will be used as a form of affectation.

**Gasconade:** Since the natives of Gascony (in France) were considered inveterate boasters, *gasconade* came to be used to mean bravado or boastful talk. Vainglorious fiction may be called *gasconade*.

**General Terms:** A *general term* refers to a group, a class, a type, whereas a SPECIFIC WORD refers to a member of that group, class, or type. Obviously the distinction between *general terms* and

SPECIFIC WORDS is relative, not absolute. For example, "dog" is SPECIFIC if compared to "animal," but *general* if compared to "chihuahua," while "chihuahua" is SPECIFIC if compared to "dog," but *general* if compared to "Sancho," one particular chihuahua.

**Generic Words:** See GENERAL TERMS, ABSTRACT TERMS, CONCRETE TERMS.

**Genre:** A term used in literary criticism to designate the distinct types or categories into which literary works are grouped according to FORM or technique. The term comes from French, where it means "kind" or "type." In its customary application, it is used loosely, since the varieties of literary "kinds" and the principles on which they are made are numerous. The traditional *genres* include such "kinds" as TRAGEDY, COMEDY, EPIC, LYRIC, PASTORAL. Today a division of literature into *genres* would also include NOVEL, SHORT STORY, ESSAY, and, perhaps, RADIO or TELEVISION PLAY. The difficulty resulting from the loose use of the term is easily illustrated: NOVEL designates a *genre*, but so does PICARESQUE NOVEL; LYRIC designates a *genre*, but so does SONNET, as do both ELEGY and PASTORAL ELEGY.

*Genre* classification implies that there are groups of formal or technical characteristics existing among works of the same "kind" regardless of time or place of composition, author, or subject matter; and that these characteristics, when they define a definite group of works, are of basic significance in talking about literary art. Prior to the ROMANTIC AGE in England, there was a tendency to assume that literary "kinds" had an ideal existence and obeyed "laws of kind," these laws being criteria by which works could be judged. In the ROMANTIC AGE, *genre* distinctions were often looked upon merely as restatements of CONVENTIONS and were suspect. Today critics frequently regard *genre* distinctions as useful descriptive devices but rather arbitrary ones.

In painting the term *genre* is applied to works that depict ordinary, everyday life in realistic terms. By extension, the term is sometimes used in literary criticism to designate a poem that deals with commonplace or homely situations in subdued tones. By this usage, Whittier's "Snow-Bound" is often called "a *genre* study."

Northrop Frye's *Anatomy of Criticism* contains a detailed and provocative treatment of the theory of *genres*. See FORM.

**Genteel Comedy:** A term employed by Addison to characterize such early eighteenth-century COMEDY as Cibber's *The Careless Husband*. This COMEDY was a sort of continuation of the Restoration COMEDY OF MANNERS, adapted to the polite, genteel manners of the age of Anne. Compared with Restoration COMEDY, the moral tone was higher, the motives of the characters more artificial, the wit less brilliant, and the general atmosphere sentimentalized.

**Genteel Tradition:** A tradition of correctness and conventionality that was active in American writing in the latter part of the nineteenth and the early part of the twentieth centuries. It was largely, although not exclusively, associated with New England. Both REALISM and NATURALISM were in differing ways reactions against the *Genteel Tradition*. Among its leading figures were R. H. Stoddard, Bayard Taylor, E. C. Stedman, T. B. Aldrich, and E. R. Sill. See BRAHMINS.

**Georgian:** Pertaining to the reigns of the four Georges (1714–1830). The romantic poets from Wordsworth to Keats have been called "Georgians" in this sense. A group of minor poets including Thomas Lovell Beddoes, W. M. Praed, and Thomas Hood are sometimes styled the "second Georgian school," as opposed to the earlier group. They are looked upon as representing a transition from the romantic to the Victorian poets. From 1911 to 1922 there appeared four anthologies of modern verse entitled *Georgian Poetry*, *Georgian* here referring to the reign of George V (1910–1936). These volumes, according to their editor, E. H. Marsh, reflect a belief that English poetry was "once again putting on new strength and beauty" and beginning a new "Georgian" period. W. W. Gibson, Rupert Brooke, and John Masefield are representative of the poets included. The term is, in fact, so varied in its applications as to be of questionable usefulness.

**Gest:** An old word occasionally found in English, especially in literary titles from the medieval period, meaning a tale of war or adventure, as the *Gest Historiale of the Destruction of Troy* (fourteenth century). This use of the word is probably borrowed from the more common word in Old French, *geste*, as in the CHANSON DE GESTE. The corresponding Latin word appears in a somewhat similar sense in the title of the famous collection of stories written in Latin about 1250, the *Gesta Romanorum*, "deeds of the Romans."

**Ghost-writer:** One who does journalistic writing which is published under the name of another. Businessmen, artists, athletes—in fact almost anyone who is much in the public eye but who is also either unskilled or uninterested in writing—often allow their names to be attached to articles and stories relating to their special fields and written by journalists employed for the purpose. Ghost-writing is more frequently employed in the preparation of newspaper and magazine articles than in the writing of books.

**Gift-Books:** Miscellaneous collections of literary materials—SHORT STORIES, ESSAYS, POETRY—published annually in book form for purchase as gifts. They were popular in England and America in the nineteenth century. Their value in American literary history has been great. See ANNUALS.

**Gleeman:** A musical entertainer among the Anglo-Saxons. *Gleemen* were usually traveling professionals who recited poetry (especially stories) composed by others, though some of them were original poets. They were sometimes attached to kings' courts, but occupied a less dignified and permanent position than the SCOP. In the main, the SCOP composed and the *gleeman* sang or recited the SCOP's compositions, to the accompaniment of the harp or other instrument. Some writers, however, both medieval and modern, use the term loosely for any kind of medieval composer or reciter.

**Gloss:** An explanation. A hard word in a text might be explained by a marginal or interlinear word or phrase, usually in a more familiar language. Thus Greek manuscripts were "glossed" by Latin copyists and readers who gave the Latin word or phrase equivalent to the difficult one in Greek. Similar bilingual *glosses* were inserted in medieval manuscripts by scribes who would explain Latin words by native, vernacular words. Some of the earliest examples of written Irish, for example, are found in the margins and between the lines of Latin manuscripts written in the early Middle Ages. Later the word came to have a broader use in E. K.'s "Gloss" to Spenser's *The Shepheardes Calendar* (1579), which undertakes not only to explain the author's purpose and to comment on the degree of his success, but also to supply "notes" explaining difficult words and phrases and giving miscellaneous "learned" comments. The marginal *gloss* which Coleridge supplied in 1817 for his early *Rime of* *the Ancient Mariner* is little more than a summary of the story, slightly colored by the poet's effort to clarify the meaning.

The word is sometimes used in a bad sense, as when to "gloss" a passage means to misinterpret it and "to gloss over" is used in the sense of "explain away" or excuse. "Glossaries" developed from the habit of collecting *glosses* into lists.

**Gnomic:** Aphoristic, moralistic, sententious. The "Gnomic Poets" of ancient Greece (sixth century B.C.) arranged their wise sayings in series of MAXIMS; hence the term *gnomic* was applied to all poetry which dealt in a sententious way with ethical questions, such as the "wisdom" poetry of the Bible, the Latin *sententiae*, the Saemundian *Edda*, and the *gnomic* verses in Old English. Although more properly applied to a style of poetry, as to some of the verse of Francis Quarles, prose style such as characterizes Bacon's early essays is also called *gnomic* when marked by the use of APHORISMS.

**Goliardic Verse:** Lilting Latin VERSE, usually satiric, composed by university students and wandering scholars in Germany, France, and England in the twelfth and thirteenth centuries. *Goliardic verse* celebrated wine, women, and song; was often licentious; and was marked by irreverent attacks on church and clergy. Its dominant theme was CARPE DIEM. Its name comes from a legendary bishop and "archpoet" Golias. Another of the Goliardic poets was Walter Map, to whom more verses have been attributed than he could possibly have written.

**Gongorism:** A highly affected style taking its name from Luis de Góngora y Argote, a Spanish poet (1561–1627), whose writings exhibited in a high degree the various qualities characteristic of the stylistic extravagances of the time, such as the introduction of new words (NEOLOGISMS), innovations in grammar, BOMBAST, PUNS, PARADOXES, CONCEITS, and obscurity. It reflects both cultism (affected language) and conceptism (strained figures, obscure references). It has some of the qualities of EUPHUISM. See MARINISM, CONCEIT.

**Gothic:** Though the Goths were a single Germanic tribe of ancient and early medieval times, the meaning of *Gothic* was broadened to signify Teutonic or Germanic and, later, "medieval" in general. In architecture, *Gothic*, though it may mean any style not classic, is more specifically applied to the style which succeeded the Romanesque in Western Europe, flourishing from the twelfth to the sixteenth centuries. It is marked by the pointed arch and vault, a tendency to vertical effects (suggesting aspiration), stained windows (mystery), slender spires, flying buttresses, intricate traceries, and especially by wealth and variety of detail and flexibility of spirit. Applied to literature the term was used by the eighteenth-century neo-classicists as synonymous with "barbaric" to indicate anything which offended their classic tastes. Addison said that both in architecture and literature those who were unable to achieve the classic graces of simplicity and dignity and UNITY resorted to the use of foreign ornaments, "all the extravagances of an irregular fancy." The romanticists of the next generation, however, looked with favor upon the *Gothic;* to them it suggested whatever was medieval, natural, primitive, wild, free, authentic, "romantic." Indeed, they praised such writers as Shakespeare and Spenser because of their *Gothic* elements—variety, richness, mystery, aspiration. See GOTHIC NOVEL.

**Gothic Novel:** A form of NOVEL in which magic, mystery, and chivalry are the chief characteristics. Horrors abound: one may expect a suit of armor suddenly to come to life, while ghosts, clanking chains, and charnel houses impart an uncanny atmosphere of terror. Although anticipations of the *Gothic novel* appear in Smollett (esp. in *Ferdinand, Count Fathom,* 1753), Horace Walpole was the real originator, his famous *Castle of Otranto* (1764) being the first. Its setting is in a medieval castle (hence the term "Gothic") which has long underground passages, trap-doors, dark stairways, and mysterious rooms whose doors slam unexpectedly. William Beckford's *Vathek, an Arabian Tale* (1786) added the element of Oriental luxury and magnificence to the species. Mrs. Anne Radcliffe's five romances (1789–1797), especially *The Mysteries of Udolpho,* added to the popularity of the form. Her emphasis upon setting and story rather than upon character-delineation became conventional, as did the types of characters she employed. Succeeding writers who produced Gothic romances include: Matthew ("Monk") Lewis, William Godwin, and Mary Wollstonecraft Shelley, whose *Frankenstein* is a striking performance in the tradition. The form spread to practically every European literature, being especially popular in Germany. In America the type was cultivated early by Charles Brockden Brown. The *Gothic novels* are not only of interest in themselves but have exerted a significant influence upon other forms. This influence made itself felt in the poetry of the Romantic period, as in Coleridge's *Christabel* and *Kubla Khan*, Wordsworth's *Guilt and Sorrow*, Byron's *Giaour*, and Keats' *Eve of St. Agnes*. Some of the ROMANCES were dramatized, and some DRAMAS not based on ROMANCES, like Byron's *Manfred* and Morton's *Speed the Plough*, have Gothic elements. The novels of Scott, Charlotte Brontë, and others, as well as the mystery and horror type of SHORT STORY exploited by Poe and his successors, contain materials and devices traceable to the *Gothic novel*. The term *Gothic novel* is today often applied to works which lack the Gothic setting or the medieval atmosphere but which attempt to create the same ATMOSPHERE of brooding and unknown terror which the true *Gothic novel* does.

**"Graveyard School":** A phrase sometimes used in designating the group of eighteenth-century poets who wrote long, gloomy poems on death and immortality. The "graveyard" poetry was related to early stages of the English romantic movement, reflecting the tendency to cultivate melancholy for its own sake and to react against the fastidious "niceness" of the Augustans, who took care to avoid the "shadow of the grave" and the "mystery of the future." The graveyard poets, far from shrinking from these themes, tried to get the atmosphere of "pleasing gloom" by realistic efforts to call up not only the horrors of death but the very "odor of the charnel house." An early exemplar or forerunner of the school was Thomas Parnell, whose *Night-Piece on Death* (1722) not only anticipates some of the sentiment of Gray's famous *Elegy Written in a Country Churchyard* (1751)—the most famous poem produced by the group—but whose "long palls, drawn hearses, cover'd steeds, and plumes of black" show an approach to the phraseology of Robert Blair's *The Grave* (1743), one of the most typical poems of the movement, and of the *Night-Thoughts* (1742) of Edward Young, an influential writer of melancholy verse. These last two writers, says W. L. Phelps, reflect "the joy of gloom, the fondness for bathing one's temples in the dank night air and the musical delight of the screech owl's shriek." While their defenders have insisted that the *graveyard school* was philosophically contemplating immortality, the lasting effect of their poetry, with the exception of a few pieces such as Gray's *Elegy*, has been one element in the GOTHIC aspect of ROMANTICISM. In America the poetry of the *graveyard school* was reflected in Philip Freneau's "The House of Night"

(1779) and most notably in William Cullen Bryant's famous "Thanatopsis" (1817).

**Great Awakening, The:** See AWAKENING, THE GREAT.

**Grub Street:** Because struggling writers and literary "hacks" lived in Grub Street in London (now Milton Street), the phrase *Grub Street*, since the eighteenth century, has meant either the "tribe" of poor writers living there or the qualities which characterized such authors. *Grub Street* poets were bitterly attacked by Pope, and *Grub Street* has been used contemptuously by Doctor Johnson, Byron, and others to suggest "literary trash."

**Hagiography:** The lives of the saints, particularly those devoted to the glorification of one or another Irish or British saint. Hence, by extension, a BIOGRAPHY which greatly overpraises the virtues of its subject. See BIOGRAPHY.

**Haiku** (sometimes written **Hokku**): A form of Japanese poetry which states in three lines of five, seven, and five syllables a clear picture designed to arouse a distinct emotion and suggest a specific spiritual insight. Since the Second World War, a number of American writers have been interested in Japanese poetry. Earlier in the century it was a formative influence on the IMAGISTS.

**Half-Rime:** Imperfect RIME, the result usually of CONSONANCE, but occasionally of ASSONANCE. See RIME, SLANT RIME, ASSONANCE, CONSONANCE.

**Hamartia:** The "great error or frailty" through which the fortunes of the hero of a TRAGEDY are reversed. Aristotle asserts that the PROTAGONIST of a TRAGEDY should be "a man who is not eminently good or just, yet whose misfortune is brought about not by vice or depravity, but by some error or frailty." This *hamartia*, often called the "tragic flaw," may be caused by bad judgment, bad character, inherited weakness, or any of several other possible causes of error; it must, however, express itself through a definite action, or failure to perform a definite action. See TRAGEDY.

**Harlequinade:** A play in which a "harlequin" or buffoon stars. See COMMEDIA DELL' ARTE, PANTOMIME.

**Hartford Wits:** A group of Connecticut writers, many of whom were graduates of Yale, active about the period of the American Revolution. The three most prominent were Joel Barlow, Timothy Dwight, and John Trumbull; some others in the group were Richard Alsop, Theodore Dwight, and Lemuel Hopkins. Naturally conservative in politics and philosophy, these men were, as well, conservative in their literary models, following Addison and Pope, the two literary gods of their century. Some of the best-known works of these writers are Trumbull's *M'Fingal*, Dwight's *Conquest of Canaan* (an epic poem of eleven books mingling Christian and Revolutionary history), and Barlow's *Columbiad*, planned as another American EPIC, a ten-book recitation of the glories of the future America as revealed to Columbus in prison. They are also known as the CONNECTICUT WITS.

**Headless Line:** A line of VERSE from which an unstressed syllable has been dropped at the beginning. See CATALEXIS.

**Hebraism:** The attitude toward life which subordinates all other ideals to those of conduct, obedience, and ethical purpose. It is opposed to the Hellenistic conception of life which subordinates everything to the intellectual. The two terms, *Hebraism* and *Hellenism*, have each taken on a special and limited significance—neither of which is fully fair to all the facets of the genius of the two peoples—as the result of critical discussion long centering about the question of conduct and wisdom in living. In modern literature the most notable discussion of the two conflicting ideals is found in the fourth chapter of Matthew Arnold's *Culture and Anarchy*. The following quotations in explanation of the terms are cited from Arnold:

> We may regard this energy driving at practice, this paramount sense of the obligation of duty, self-control, and work, this earnestness in going manfully with the best light we have, as one force. And we may regard the intelligence driving at those ideas which are, after all, the basis of right practice, the ardent sense for all the new and changing combinations of them which man's development brings with it, the indomitable impulse to know and adjust them perfectly, as another force. And these two forces we may regard as in some sense rivals,—rivals not by the necessity of their own nature, but as exhibited in man and his history,— and rivals dividing the empire of the world between them. And to give these forces names from the two races of men who have supplied the most signal and splendid manifestations of them, we may call them respectively the forces of Hebraism and Hellenism. Hebraism and

Hellenism,—between these points of influence moves our world. . . .
The final aim of both Hellenism and Hebraism, as of all great spiritual
disciplines, is no doubt the same: man's perfection of salvation. . . .
The governing idea of Hellenism is *spontaneity of consciousness:* that of
Hebraism, *strictness of conscience.*

**Hedge Club:** See TRANSCENDENTAL CLUB, TRANSCENDENTALISM.

**Hellenism:** See HEBRAISM.

**Hemistich:** A half-line of VERSE. See -STICH.

**Hendecasyllabic Verse:** A VERSE of eleven syllables, frequent in
Greek and Latin poetry and a standard line in Italian poetry. The
form was originated by Catullus. Its English users have been few,
chief among them being Tennyson.

**Heptameter:** A line of VERSE consisting of seven FEET. See SCANSION.

**Hero or Heroine:** The central character (masculine or feminine)
in a work of FICTION or a DRAMA. The terms are applied to the
characters who are the focal points of the readers' or the spectators'
interest, often without reference to the superiority of the moral
qualities of one character over another. Used as a technical term in
describing a work of FICTION, *hero* (or *heroine*) refers to a relationship of character to action; therefore, the more neutral term PRO-
TAGONIST is probably preferable. See PLOT, STRUCTURE, PROTAGO-
NIST.

**Heroic Couplet:** IAMBIC PENTAMETER lines rimed in pairs. The
favorite METER of Chaucer—*The Legend of Good Women* is an
instance—this verse form did not come into its greatest popularity,
however, until the middle of the seventeenth century (with Waller
and Denham); after which time it was for several years the dominant mold for the POETIC DRAMA. The distinction of having made
first use of the *heroic couplet* in dramatic composition is variously
given to Orrery's *Henry V,* in which it was used throughout, and
Etherege's *The Comical Revenge,* in which it was employed for
most passages of dramatic action. Both of these plays date from
1664. D'Avenant had as early as 1656 made some use of the *heroic
couplet* in his *Siege of Rhodes.* It was with Dryden, however, that

the form became best known, Dryden using it in such plays as
*Tyrannick Love, Almanzor and Almahide,* and *Aureng-Zebe.* Some
other seventeenth-century dramatists who adopted the couplet now
that it was the accepted form were: Sedley, Settle, Otway, Lee.
With Pope the *heroic couplet* became so important and fixed a
form—for various purposes—that its influence dominated English
verse for many years and was not broken down until the Romanticists dispelled the tradition in their demand for a new freedom.
An example of the *heroic couplet:*

> But when to mischief mortals bend their will,
> How soon they find fit instruments of ill!
>
> —Pope

In the NEO-CLASSIC PERIOD, the *heroic couplet* was usually made
up of a rimed pair of END-STOPPED LINES, the couplet forming
something resembling a short STANZA. The use of marked CAESURAS
in the lines and a highly symmetrical grammatical structure made
the *heroic couplet* a form well adapted to epigrammatic expression
and to balanced sentences marked by symmetry and antithesis. In
the ROMANTIC AGE, poets like Keats, in *Endymion,* retained rimed
pairs of IAMBIC PENTAMETER lines but abandoned the other restrictions of the *heroic couplet,* although Byron both used and defended
Pope's graceful lines.

**Heroic Drama:** A type of TRAGEDY and TRAGI-COMEDY that developed in England during the RESTORATION. It was characterized by
excessive spectacle, violent emotional conflicts in the main characters, extravagant bombastic DIALOGUE, and more or less EPIC personages as chief characters. The heroic play usually had its setting
in some distant land such as Mexico, Morocco, or India. Its hero
rivals Achilles in warlike deeds and easily surpasses him in love.
This hero is constantly torn between his passion for some lady
(more than likely a captive princess or the daughter of his greatest
enemy) and his honor or duty to his country. If he is able to satisfy
both the demands of love and duty, the play ends happily for hero
and heroine and unhappily for the villain and villainess. The heroine
is always a paragon of virtue and honor, often torn between her
loyalty to her villain-father and her love for the hero. The villain
is usually a tyrant and usurper with an overweening passion for

power or else with a base love for some beautiful and virtuous lady. The villainess is the dark, violently passionate rival of the heroine. The hero's rival in love is sometimes the villain and sometimes the hero's best friend. All are unreal, all speak in HYPERBOLE, all rant and rage. Since the HEROIC COUPLET developed at the same time as did the *heroic drama,* the writers of heroic plays commonly, though not always, wrote in HEROIC COUPLETS. The action of the play was grand, often revolving around the conquest of some empire. The scenery used in producing the heroic play was elaborate.

The influences that combined to produce the *heroic drama* were the romantic plays of the Jacobeans, especially those of Beaumont and Fletcher; the development of OPERA in England; and the French court romances by de Scudéry and La Calprenède, some of which were brought to England by the court of Charles II. Though elements of the heroic play appear in Davenant's *Siege of Rhodes* (1656), the Earl of Orrery perhaps wrote the first full-fledged *heroic drama, The General* (1662). Dryden, however, is the greatest exponent of the type, his *Conquest of Granada* typifying all that is best and all that is worst in the species. Elkanah Settle, Nahum Tate, Nathaniel Lee, Sir Robert Howard, John Crowne, and Thomas Otway are other playwrights who cultivated the *heroic drama.* Although the faults of the type were recognized early, the most brilliant attack being the satirical play of George Villiers, Duke of Buckingham (and others), *The Rehearsal* (1671), the plays flourished until about 1680, and the extravagances that characterized them affected eighteenth-century TRAGEDY.

**Heroic Verse:** Poetry composed of IAMBIC PENTAMETER feet and rimed in line-pairs. Also called HEROIC COUPLETS.

**Hexameter:** A line of six metrical FEET. As a classical verse form in Latin or Greek poetry, in which languages the *hexameter* was the conventional medium for EPIC and DIDACTIC POETRY, the term was definitely restricted to a set pattern: six feet, the first four of which were DACTYLS or SPONDEES, the fifth almost always a DACTYL (though sometimes a SPONDEE in which case the verse is called spondaic), the sixth a SPONDEE or TROCHEE. True *hexameters* are scarce in English poetry because of the rarity of actual SPONDEES in our language. However, poets writing in English, notably Longfellow in *Evangeline,* have variously modified the classical form to adapt it to the exigencies of our language and have left us *hexameters* much less strictly patterned than the classical. See ALEXANDRINE, ELEGIACS.

**Hiatus:** A pause or break between two vowel sounds not separated by a consonant. It is the opposite of ELISION, which prompts the sliding over of one of the vowels, whereas a *hiatus* occurs only when in a break between two words the final vowel of the first and the initial vowel of the second are each carefully enunciated. In logic *hiatus* signifies the omission of one of the logical steps in the process of reasoning.

**High Comedy:** Pure or serious COMEDY, as contrasted with LOW COMEDY. *High comedy* rests upon an appeal to the intellect and arouses "thoughtful" laughter by exhibiting the inconsistencies and incongruities of human nature and by displaying the follies of social manners. The purpose is not consciously didactic or ethical, though serious purpose is often implicit in the SATIRE which is not infrequently present in *high comedy*. Thoughtful amusement is aimed at. Emotion, especially SENTIMENTALITY, is avoided. If a man makes himself ridiculous by his vanity or ineffective by his stupid conduct or blind adherence to tradition, *high comedy* laughs at him. Some ability to perceive promptly the incongruity exhibited is demanded of the audience, so that *high comedy* has been said to be written for the few. As George Meredith suggests in his essay on *The Idea of Comedy* (a classic pronouncement on the nature of *high comedy*), care must be taken that the laughter provoked be not derisive, but intellectual. Laughing at an exhibition of poverty, for example, since it ridicules our unfortunate nature instead of our conventional life, is not truly comic. "But when poverty becomes ridiculous" by attempting "to make its rags conceal the bareness in a forlorn effort at decency," or foolishly tries to rival the ostentation of the rich, it becomes a fit theme for comic presentation. Although *high comedy* actually offers plenty of superficial laughs which the average playgoer or reader can perceive, its higher enjoyment demands a certain intellectual acumen and poise and philosophic detachment. "Life is a comedy to him who thinks." But the term *high comedy* is used in various senses. In NEO-CLASSIC times a criterion was its appeal to and reflection of the "higher" social class and its observance of DECORUM, as illustrated in Etherege and Congreve. In a broader sense it is applied to some of Shakespeare's plays, like *As You Like It*, and to modern comedies of G. B. Shaw. See COMEDY, COMEDY OF MANNERS, COMEDY OF HUMOURS, REALISTIC COMEDY.

**Historical Criticism:** Criticism that examines a work and describes and evaluates it in terms of the social and historical context in which it was produced and the facts of its author's life and of its composition. The historical critic attempts to re-create through the historical process the meaning and the values which the work had for its own time; his objective is not to elucidate the meaning the work has for the present so much as it is to lead the reader in the present into a responsive awareness of the meaning the work had for its own age. See CRITICISM, TYPES OF.

**Historical Fiction:** See FICTION, HISTORICAL NOVEL.

**Historical Novel:** A NOVEL which reconstructs a personage, a series of events, a movement, or the spirit of a past age and pays the debt of serious scholarship to the facts of the age being re-created. The classic formula for the *historical novel*, as evolved by Scott and given expression in his numerous prefaces and introductions to the Waverley Novels, calls for an age when two cultures are in conflict, one dying and the other being born; into this cultural conflict, fictional personages are introduced who participate in actual historical events and move among actual personages from history; these fictional characters undergo and give expression to the impact which the historical events had upon people living through them, with the result that a picture of a bygone age is given in personal and immediate terms. *Ivanhoe*, with its disinherited Saxon hero in a Norman world is a striking example. *Historical novels* which take this task seriously have been called NOVELS OF MANNERS laid in the past.

The extent to which actual historical events of some magnitude must be present, the extent to which actual historic personages must be actors in the story, the time which must have elapsed between the events of the story and its writing are among the questions to which both historical novelists and critics of the form have given varying answers. There has been little dispute, however, over the responsibility of the historical novelist to give a truthful picture of the age he describes or over the fact that the *historical novel* is often centered in a social context. Two tendencies to depart from the "formula" should be noted: one is "the costume romance," in which history is exploited as a background for a series of adventurous or sexual exploits; the other is the "novel of character" laid in the past, in which the setting and the age are of secondary importance to the representation of a group of characters; *The Scarlet Letter* is a classic example of the latter.

Although writers have combined fiction and history since time began and although literary historians have found adumbrations of the *historical novel* in many forms and works, it required the development of a serious view of history before a serious *historical novel* could develop. This view came in the eighteenth century, and various writers began seriously to attempt works which correspond to the ideals of the *historical novel*, but it remained for Sir Walter Scott in *Waverley* in 1814 to establish the form. Among his noted successors have been Thackeray, Alexander Dumas, Victor Hugo, Tolstoi, James Fenimore Cooper, Bulwer-Lytton, Charles Reade, Hervey Allen, and Kenneth Roberts. See NOVEL.

**History Play:** See CHRONICLE PLAY.

**Holy Grail:** The cup from which Christ is said to have drunk at the Last Supper and which was used to catch his blood at the Crucifixion. It became the center of a tradition of Christian mysticism and eventually was linked with Arthurian ROMANCE as an object of search on the part of Arthur's knights. The *grail* as it appears in early Arthurian literature (Chrétien's *Perceval*) is perhaps of pagan origin, some sort of magic object not now to be traced with assurance. In the poems of Robert de Boron (*ca.*1200) it appears as a mystic symbol and is connected with Christian tradition (having been brought to England by Joseph of Arimathea). In the Vulgate Romances (see VULGATE), two great CYCLES are devoted to the *grail*, the first or "History" dealing with the Joseph tradition, the second or "Quest" dealing with the search for it by Arthurian knights. Perceval, the first hero of the quest, because he was not a pure knight, and Lancelot, because he was disqualified by his love for Guinevere, gave place to Galahad, the wholly pure knight, conceived as Lancelot's son and Perceval's kinsman. The pious quest for the *grail*, no less than the sinful love of Lancelot and Guinevere, helped bring about the eventual downfall of the Round Table fellowship. See ARTHURIAN LEGEND.

**Homeric Epithet:** See EPITHET.

**Homeric Simile:** See EPIC SIMILE.

**Homily:** A form of oral religious instruction given by an ordained minister with a church congregation as audience. The *homily* is sometimes distinguished from the sermon in that the sermon usually is on a theme drawn from a scriptural text and a *homily* usually gives practical moral counsel rather than discussion of doctrine. The distinction is by no means rigorously maintained. OLD ENGLISH literature contains *homilies* by Aelfric and Wulfstan.

**Horatian Ode:** Horace applied the term *ode* to comparatively informal poems written in a single stanzaic form. The term *Horatian Ode* is, therefore, often applied to such poems. Notable examples are Marvell's "Horatian Ode upon Cromwell's Return from Ireland," and Keats' "Ode on a Grecian Urn." See ODE.

**Hornbook:** A kind of primer common in England from the sixteenth to the eighteenth centuries. On a sheet of vellum or paper were printed the alphabet, combinations of consonants and vowels commonly used in making up syllables, the Lord's Prayer, and a list of Roman numerals. The sheet was mounted on wood and covered (for protection) by transparent horn (hence *hornbook*). Its most famous use in literature is in *The Gull's Hornbook* by Thomas Dekker, an amusing and satirical "primer" of instructions for the young dandy of early seventeenth-century London. The *hornbook* here supplies a framework for a social SATIRE.

**Hovering Stress:** A term designating the metrical effect that results from two adjacent syllables sharing the ICTUS, so that the STRESS appears to hover over both syllables. It is also called DISTRIBUTED STRESS and RESOLVED STRESS, and it appears often in the work of Gerard Manley Hopkins and is sometimes considered a metrical device used by Whitman.

**Hubris** or **Hybris:** Overweening pride which results in the misfortune of the PROTAGONIST of a TRAGEDY. It is the particular form of HAMARTIA, or tragic flaw, which results from excessive pride, ambition, and overconfidence. *Hubris* leads the PROTAGONIST to break a moral law or ignore a divine warning with calamitous results. The excessive ambition of Macbeth is a standard example of *hubris* in English drama. See HAMARTIA, TRAGEDY.

**Hudibrastic Verse:** The OCTOSYLLABIC COUPLET as adapted by Samuel Butler in his satiric poem, *Hudibras*. In this long poem, published in three parts between 1663 and 1678, Butler satirized the PURITANS of England. *Hudibras* was conspicuous for its HUMOR, its BURLESQUE elements, its MOCK-EPIC FORM, and its wealth of satiric EPIGRAM. The meter is IAMBIC TETRAMETER riming in couplets, *aa—bb*, etc. It is filled with outrageous RIMES that are often double and even triple. The term is used today to characterize VERSE following Butler's general manner and particularly his shocking RIMES.

**Humanism:** Broadly, this term suggests any attitude which tends to exalt the human element or stress the importance of human interests, as opposed to the supernatural, divine elements—or as opposed to the grosser, animal elements. So a student of human affairs may be called a *humanist*, and the study of man as man, i.e., of the human race rather than of individual human beings, has been called *humanism*. In a more specific sense, *humanism* suggests a devotion to those studies supposed to promote most effectively human culture—in particular, those dealing with the life, thought, language, and literature of ancient Greece and Rome. In literary history, indeed, the most important use of the term is to designate the revival of classical culture which accompanied the RENAISSANCE. This use of the term is justified not only by the fact that the RENAISSANCE humanists found in the classics a justification for their tendency to exalt human nature and build a new and highly idealistic gospel of progress upon it, but also by the fact that they found it necessary to break sharply with medieval attitudes which had subordinated one aspect of human nature by exalting the supernatural and divine. The RENAISSANCE humanists agreed with the ancients in asserting the dignity of man and the importance of the present life, as against such medieval thinkers as looked upon the present life as chiefly useful as a preparation for a future life.

RENAISSANCE *humanism* developed first in the fourteenth and fifteenth centuries in Italy and was marked by a passion for rediscovering and studying ancient literature. It spread to other Continental countries and finally to England, where a series of efforts to develop humanistic activities culminated successfully late in the fifteenth century with the introduction of the study of Greek at Oxford (see OXFORD REFORMERS). Early humanists in England applied themselves first to a mastering of the Greek as well as the Latin language and then to applying their new methods to theology, statecraft, education, and finally to criticism and literature. Unlike some Continental humanists the English group, though they reacted against medieval asceticism and scholasticism and sharply attacked current abuses in the Church, retained their faith in Christianity. Indeed, they entered enthusiastically upon a program of human development based upon the assumption that the best of classical culture could be fused with Christianity—a faith which accounts in part for what at first seem to be incongruous mixtures of paganism and Christianity in much RENAISSANCE literature, notably the poetry of Spenser and Milton. The zealous efforts of such men as Dean John Colet and Erasmus to reform church conditions and theology through education and an appeal to reason were checked by the success of the more vigorous and radical Lutheran movement. The "modern" character of this *humanism* may be indicated by recalling a few of its political and educational doctrines: political institutions are of human, not divine, origin and exist for human good, the monarch's "duties" being of greater concern than his "rights"; war is unchristian and inhumane and should be resorted to only when approved by the people themselves; the highest human happiness can come only through the virtuous life, which in turn can best be achieved through the control of reason, buttressed by education; women should be educated; nature should be employed as an educational tool; physical education is of the utmost importance; schoolmasters should be learned and gentle.

A later phase of humanistic activity was its interest in literary criticism, through which it affected powerfully the practice of RENAISSANCE authors. The validity of critical ideas drawn from Aristotle and Horace was asserted and the production of a vernacular literature which imitated the classics was advocated. Though this led to some unfortunate and unsuccessful efforts to restrict the English vocabulary and to repress native VERSE FORMS in favor of classical words and forms, in general humanistic criticism exerted a wholesome effect upon literature by lending it dignity (as in the EPIC and TRAGEDY) and grace (as in the Jonsonian LYRIC) and by stressing restraint and FORM. Its influence was especially great in the DRAMA, where, though writers like

Shakespeare rejected the three UNITIES, it aided in establishing unified STRUCTURE. The texture of RENAISSANCE literature, too, was greatly enriched by the humanistically inspired familiarity with the incidents, characters, motives, and IMAGERY of classical mythology, history, and literature. Sidney's *Defence of Poesie*, a humanistic document, is generally taken as the first major document in English criticism, and the establishment of the classical attitude (see CLASSICISM) through the influence of Jonson and (later) Dryden and Pope and others was itself a fruit of RENAISSANCE *humanism*. In fact, a tracing of the effects of *humanism* upon the literature of the seventeenth and eighteenth centuries would largely coincide with the history of CLASSICISM and NEO-CLASSICISM. One of the phases of the reaction against ROMANTICISM in the nineteenth century was a revival of *humanism*, as exemplified in Matthew Arnold. See HUMANISM, THE NEW.

**Humanism, The New:** A philosophical-critical movement called *The New Humanism* took place in America between 1910 and 1930 inspired in large part by the humanist position assumed by Matthew Arnold. Its leaders were Irving Babbitt, Paul Elmer More, Norman Foerster, and Robert Shafer. *The New Humanism* was in large part a reaction against certain forms of REALISM and particularly of NATURALISM, which the new humanists believed overstressed the animal elements in human nature. The movement was a protest against the philosophies and psychologies of "our professedly scientific time." No complete codification of the tenets of the new humanists can be made, but the following summary, based on Foerster's *American Criticism*, suggests their general attitudes: Humanism assumes (1) that assumptions are unavoidable, (2) that the essential quality of experience is not natural but ethical, (3) that there is a sharp dualism between man and nature, and (4) that man's will is free. On these premises the following doctrines are based: (1) an adequate human standard demands the cultivation of every part of human nature; (2) but these parts must be cultivated harmoniously and discriminatingly, not impulsively and uncritically; (3) the scale of values so implied consists of the normally or typically human—is concerned with the universal and permanent rather than with the temporary code of a conventional society; (4) the nearest approach toward such a standard is found in the great ages of the past, especially of Greece, but humanism draws also upon Christianity, Oriental philosophy, and such modern writers as Shakespeare, Milton, and Goethe; (5) unlike romanticism, humanism is faithful to the Hellenic doctrine of reason, applied to the whole of human experience, even the extra-scientific; (6) it departs from the narrowly "scientific" method by supplementing the reason with the intuitive and imaginative; (7) the ultimate ethical principle is that of restraint or control, whereby humanism avoids the anarchy of the "self-expression" cult, yet recognizes the necessity of freedom, defined as "liberation from outer constraints and subjection to inner law"; (8) though this center is the reality which gives rise to religion, humanism declines to accept a formal theology, holding that the value of intuition must be tested by the intellect.

This reaction against the tenets of an age of science and artistic self-expression, however, failed to achieve a large following outside academic circles. The popular critic Stuart Sherman was active in it for a while, and the poet-critic T. S. Eliot was an interested observer. After 1930 it fell before attacks by two enemies, the sociological critics and the advocates of the NEW CRITICISM, a movement that effectively raised the New Humanists' standard of the validity of the art object in an age of science and yet one that began partially as a reaction against the strict morality and the intolerance of the contemporary in art which *New Humanism* had often displayed. See HUMANISM; NEW CRITICISM; CRITICISM, HISTORICAL SKETCH.

**Humanitarian Novel, The:** See SOCIOLOGICAL NOVEL.

**Humor:** A term used in English since the early eighteenth century to denote one of the two major types of writing (*humor* and WIT) whose purpose is the evoking of some kind of laughter. It is derived from the physiological theory of HUMOURS, and it was used to designate a person with a peculiar disposition which led to his readily perceiving the ridiculous, the ludicrous, and the comical and effectively giving expression to this perception. In the eighteenth century it was used to name a comical mode that was sympathetic, tolerant, and warmly aware of the depths of human nature, as opposed to the intellectual, satiric, intolerant quality associated with WIT. However, it is impossible to discuss *humor* separately from WIT, and the reader is referred to the article on WIT AND HUMOR.

**Humours:** In the old theory of physiology the four chief liquids of the human body, blood, phlegm, yellow bile, and black bile, were known as *humours.* They were closely allied with the four elements. Thus blood, like *air,* was hot and moist; yellow bile, like *fire,* was hot and dry; phlegm, like *water,* was cold and moist; black bile, like *earth,* was cold and dry. Both physical diseases and mental and moral dispositions ("temperaments") were caused by the condition of the *humours.* Disease resulted from the dominance of some element within a single *humour,* or from a lack of balance or proportion among the *humours* themselves. The *humours* gave off vapors which ascended to the brain. An individual's personal characteristics, physical, mental, and moral, were explained by his "temperament" or the state of his *humours.* The perfect temperament resulted when no one *humour* dominated. The sanguine man has a dominance of blood, is beneficent, joyful, amorous. The choleric man is easily angered, impatient, obstinate, vengeful. The phlegmatic man is dull, pale, cowardly. The melancholic man is gluttonous, backward, unenterprising, thoughtful, sentimental, affected. A disordered state of the *humours* produced, further, more exaggerated characteristics. These facts explain how the word *humour* in Elizabethan times came to mean "disposition," then "mood," or "characteristic peculiarity," later specialized to "folly," or "affectation." By 1600 it was common to use *humour* as a means of classifying characters. The influence on Elizabethan literature of the doctrines based on *humours* was very great, and familiarity with them is a great aid in understanding such characters as Horatio, Hamlet, and Jacques in Shakespeare. Many passages often taken as figurative may have had a literal meaning to the Elizabethans, as "my liver melts." See COMEDY OF HUMOURS.

**Hymn:** A LYRIC POEM expressing religious emotion and generally intended to be sung by a CHORUS. Church and theological doctrine, pious feeling, and religious aspiration characterize the ideas of these lyrics, though originally the term referred to almost any song of praise whether of gods or famous men. The early Greek and Latin Christian churches developed many famous *hymn* writers, and the importance of *hymns* during the Dark and Middle Ages can hardly be exaggerated since they gave to the great mass of people a new verse form as well as a means of emotional expression. The twelfth and thirteenth centuries saw the greatest development of Latin *hymns* (*Dies Irae,* etc.). The wide use of *hymns* during these centuries helped to destroy certain literary conventions of the past and exerted an important influence on the versification of English and German poetry as well as that of the romance languages. Some famous *hymn* writers of England were Wesley, Cowper, Watts, Toplady, Newman; of America, Whittier and Holmes. For a concise and careful statement regarding this form see the article on *hymns* in the *Encyclopædia Britannica*. See ANTHEM, TROPE.

**Hypallage:** A figure of speech in which an EPITHET is moved from the more natural to the less natural one of a group of nouns, as when Virgil writes of "the trumpet's Tuscan blare" when the normal order would be "the Tuscan trumpet's blare."

**Hyperbole:** A figure of speech in which conscious exaggeration is used without the intent of literal persuasion. It may be used to heighten effect or it may be used to produce comic effect. Macbeth is using *hyperbole* in the following lines:

> No; this my hand will rather
> The multitudinous seas incarnadine,
> Making the green one red.

**Iambus (iamb):** A metrical FOOT consisting of an unaccented syllable and an accented ( $\smile$ ＿ ). The most common metrical measure in English verse. A line from Marlowe will serve as an illustration:

> Come live | with me | and be | my love

**Ictus:** In VERSIFICATION, the ACCENT or STRESS that falls on a syllable; *ictus* does not refer to the stressed syllable but to the stress itself. See ACCENT.

**Idiom:** A use of words, a grammatic construction peculiar to a given language, an expression which cannot be translated literally into a second language. "To carry out" may be taken as an example. Literally it means, of course, to carry something out (of a room perhaps), but idiomatically it means to see that something is done, as "to carry out a command." *Idioms* in a language usually arise from a peculiarity which is syntactical or structural or from the veiling of a meaning in a METAPHOR (as in the above instance).

**Idyll** (or **Idyl**): Not so much a definite poetic GENRE (like the SONNET, for instance) as a descriptive term which may be applied to one or another of the poetic GENRES which are short and possess marked descriptive, narrative, and PASTORAL qualities. In this popular sense, Whittier's "Maud Muller" might be called an *idyll*. PASTORAL and descriptive elements are usually the first requisites of the *idyll*, although the PASTORAL element is usually presented in a conscious literary manner. The point of view of the *idyll* is that of a civilized and artificial society glancing from a drawing-room window over green meadows and gamboling sheep, or of the week-end farm viewed through a picture window. Historically the term goes back to the *idylls* of Theocritus, who wrote short pieces depicting the simple, rustic life in Sicily to please the civilized Alexandrians. It has also been applied to long descriptive and narrative poems, particularly Tennyson's *Idylls of the King*. See PASTORAL.

**Image:** Originally a sculptured, cast, or modeled representation of a person; even in its most sophisticated critical usage, this fundamental meaning is still present, in that an *image* is a literal and concrete representation of a sensory experience or of an object that can be known by one or more of the senses. It functions, as I. A. Richards has pointed out, by representing a sensation through the process of being a "relict" of an already known sensation. The *image* is one of the distinctive elements of the "language of art," the means by which experience in its richness and emotional complexity is communicated, as opposed to the simplifying and conceptualizing processes of science and philosophy. The *image* is, therefore, a portion of the essence of the meaning of the literary work, not ever properly a mere decoration."

*Images* may be either "tied" or "free," a "tied" *image* being one so employed that its meaning and associational value is the same or nearly the same for all readers; and a "free" *image* being one not so fixed by context that its possible meanings or associational values are limited; it is, therefore, capable of having various meanings or values for various people.

*Images* may also be either literal or figurative, a literal *image* being one that involves no necessary change or extension in the obvious meaning of the words, one in which the words call up a sensory representation of the literal object or sensation; and a figurative *image* being one that involves a "turn" on the literal meaning of the words. An example of a collection of literal *images* may be seen in Coleridge's "Kubla Khan":

> In Xanadu did Kubla Khan
> A stately pleasure-dome decree:
> Where Alph, the sacred river, ran
> Through caverns measureless to man
> Down to a sunless sea.

These *images* apparently represent a literal scene. The literal *image* is one of the basic properties of prose FICTION, as witness such different writers as Joseph Conrad and Ernest Hemingway, both of whose works are noted for the evocative power of their literal *images*. The opening lines of this Wordsworth sonnet show both kinds of *images*, literal and figurative:

> It is a beauteous evening, calm and free;
> The holy time is quiet as a Nun
> Breathless with adoration; the broad sun
> Is sinking down in its tranquillity.

The two middle lines are highly figurative, whereas the first and fourth lines are broadly literal, although there are figurative "turns" present by implication in "free" and "tranquillity."

The qualities usually found in *images* are particularity, concreteness, and an appeal to sensuous experience or memory. See IMAGERY, SYMBOL, METAPHOR, ABSTRACT TERMS, CONCRETE TERMS, FIGURATIVE LANGUAGE.

**Imagery:** A term used widely in contemporary criticism, *imagery* has a great variety of meanings. In its literal sense it means the collection of IMAGES within a literary work or a unit of a literary work. In a broader sense it is used as synonymous with TROPE or FIGURE OF SPEECH. Here the TROPE designates a special usage of words in which there is a change in their basic meanings. There are four major types of TROPES: IMAGES, which are literal and sensory and properly should not be called TROPES at all; SYMBOLS, which combine a literal and sensuous quality with an abstract or suggestive aspect; SIMILE, which describes by expressed ANALOGY; and METAPHOR, which describes by implied ANALOGY. Not only do these four types of TROPES define the meaning of *imagery*, they also suggest the ranges of possible application that are to be found in the term.

Many contemporary critics are deeply concerned over the

"structure of IMAGES," "the IMAGE-clusters," "IMAGE patterns," and "thematic *imagery*." Such patterns of *imagery*, often without the conscious knowledge of author or reader, are sometimes taken to be keys to the "deeper" meaning of a literary work or pointers to the unconscious motivations of its author. A few critics tend to see the "IMAGE pattern" as indeed being the basic meaning of the work and a sounder key to its values and interpretation than the explicit statements of the author or the more obvious events of PLOT or action. One of the notable contributions of the NEW CRITICS has been their awareness of the importance of the relationships among IMAGES to the nature and meaning of LYRIC poetry.

A study of the *imagery* of a literary work may center itself on the physical world which is presented through the language of the work; upon the rhetorical patterns and devices by which the TROPES in the work are achieved; upon the psychological state which produced the work and gave it its special and often hidden meaning; upon the ways in which the pattern of its IMAGES reinforces (or on occasion contradicts) the ostensible meaning of statement, PLOT, and action in the work; or upon how the IMAGES strike responsively upon resonant points in the racial unconscious producing the emotive power of ARCHETYPES and MYTH. See IMAGE, METAPHOR, FIGURATIVE LANGUAGE, NEW CRITICISM, ALLEGORY.

**Imagination and Fancy:** The theories of poetry advanced by the ROMANTIC critics of the early nineteenth century (Wordsworth, Coleridge, and others) led to many efforts to distinguish between *imagination* and *fancy*, terms which had formerly been used as virtually synonymous. The word *imagination* itself, according to one student (Bray), already had passed through three stages of meaning in England. In RENAISSANCE times it was opposed to reason and regarded as the "means by which poetical and religious conceptions could be attained and appreciated." Thus Bacon cited it as the one of the three faculties of the rational soul: "history has reference to the memory, poetry to the imagination, and philosophy to the reason"; and Shakespeare says the poet is "of imagination all compact." In the NEO-CLASSIC PERIOD it was the faculty by which IMAGES were called up, especially visual IMAGES (see Addison's *The Pleasures of the Imagination*), and was related to the process by which "IMITATION of nature" might take place. Because of its tendency to transcend the testimony of the senses, the poet who might draw upon *imagination* must subject it to the check of reason, which should determine its form of presentation. Later in the eighteenth century the *imagination,* opposed to reason, was conceived as so vivid an imaging process that it affected the passions and formed "a world of beauty of its own," a poetical illusion which served not to affect conduct but to produce immediate pleasure.

The ROMANTIC critics, however, conceived the *imagination* as a blending and unifying of the powers of the mind which enabled the poet to see inner relationships, such as the identity of truth and beauty. So Wordsworth says that poets

> Have each his own peculiar faculty,
> Heaven's gift, a sense that fits him to perceive
> Objects unseen before . . .
> An insight that in some sort he possesses, . . .
> Proceeding from a source of untaught things.

This new conception of *imagination* necessitated a distinction between it and *fancy.* Coleridge (*Biographia Literaria*) especially stressed, though he never fully explained, the difference. He called *imagination* the "shaping and modifying" power, *fancy* the "aggregative and associative" power. The former "struggles to idealize and to unify," while the latter is merely "a mode of memory emancipated from the order of time and space." To illustrate the distinction Coleridge remarked that Milton had a highly imaginative mind, Cowley a very fanciful one. Leslie Stephen (1879) stated the distinction briefly, "fancy deals with the superficial resemblances, and imagination with the deeper truths that underlie them."

While *imagination* is usually viewed as a "shaping" and ordering power, the function of which is to give art its special authority, the assumption is almost always present that the "new" creation shaped by the *imagination* is a new form of reality, not a FANTASY nor a fanciful projection. When Shakespeare writes

> As imagination bodies forth
> The forms of things unknown, the poet's pen
> Turns them to shapes and gives to airy nothing
> A local habitation and a name,

his reference is properly made to *imagination,* not to that power of inventing the novel and unreal by recombining the elements found in reality, which we commonly call *fancy* and which expresses itself in FANTASY. See FANCY.

**Imaginative Element in Literature:** See IMAGE, IMAGERY, EMO-
TIONAL ELEMENT IN LITERATURE, ROMANTICISM, IMAGINATION
AND FANCY.

**Imagists:** The name applied to a group of poets who rose to
prominence in America between 1909 and 1918. Their name came
from the French title, *Des Imagistes,* given to the first anthology
of their work (1914); this, in turn, having been borrowed from a
critical term which had been applied to some few French pre-
cursors of the movement. The most conspicuous figures of the
*imagist* movement were Ezra Pound, "H.D.," John Gould Fletcher,
Amy Lowell, Carl Sandburg, and William Carlos Williams. Im-
agism was a spirit of revolt against conventionalities of the time
rather than a goal set up as in itself a permanently lasting objective.
The best volume speaking critically for the group is Amy Lowell's
*Tendencies in Modern American Poetry* (1917); the major objectives of the movement, as suggested in this volume, were: (1) to
use the language of common speech, but to employ always the
exact word—not the nearly-exact; (2) to avoid all cliché expressions; (3) to create new rhythms as the expressions of a new
mood—and not to copy old rhythms which merely echo old moods;
(4) to allow absolute freedom in the choice of subject, since the
*Imagists* believed passionately in the artistic value of modern life;
(5) to present an IMAGE (that is to be concrete, firm, definite in
their pictures—harsh in outline); (6) to strive always for concentration which, they were convinced, was the very essence of
poetry; (7) to suggest rather than to offer complete statements.
The *Imagists* were influenced by Chinese poetry and particularly
by the Japanese HAIKU, with its single sharp IMAGE.

**Imitation:** The concept of art as *imitation* has its origin with the
classical critics. Aristotle said at the beginning of his *Poetics* that
all arts are modes of *imitation,* and he defines a TRAGEDY as an
*imitation* of an action. Aristotle seems here (and elsewhere) to be
defending art against Plato's charge that it is twice removed from
truth or reality. On the other hand, the Greek and Roman schools
of rhetoric used the *imitation* of literary models as an accepted
form of composition. Both views of *imitation* have been persistently
present in English literary history.

The concept of Aristotelian *imitation*—that art *imitates* "Nature"
—was pervasively present in English critical thought until the end

of the eighteenth century. This *imitation* of Nature came to be regarded as a realistic portrayal of life, a reproduction of natural objects and actions. Moreover, admiration of the success with which the greater classic writers had followed Nature bred a practice and bolstered the rhetorical theory of following in their footsteps. Critics in the RENAISSANCE and the NEO-CLASSIC PERIOD accepted *imitation* in this rhetorical sense of copying models in the various types of poetry. They did not believe that *imitation* should replace genius, but an adherence to classical models was considered a safe method of avoiding literary vices and attaining virtues. *Imitation* of this sort had several varieties: writing in the spirit of the masters and using merely their general principles; borrowing from the ancients with the necessity of accommodating the material to the poet's own age; the collection and use of special "beauties" in thought and expression from the works of the best poets; the exercise of PARAPHRASE and free TRANSLATION. *Imitation* as a copying of other writers was discussed and employed in all degrees of dependence, from the most dignified to the most servile.

In the ROMANTIC AGE, the MIMETIC THEORY OF ART was replaced by the EXPRESSIVE THEORY, and the meaning of Aristotle's term *imitation* underwent serious change as the concept of NATURE had been undergoing change. NATURE then became the creative principle of the universe, and Aristotlelian *imitation* was considered to be "creating according to a true idea," and a work of art was "an idealized representation of human life—of character, emotion, action—under forms manifest to sense."

With the rise of REALISM and NATURALISM, a renewed emphasis on the accurate portrayal of the palpable actual returned, although the term *imitation* was not often used. Among contemporary critics there is some interest in the implications for the theory of *imitation* of the depth psychologies. See CRITICISM, HISTORICAL SKETCH and CRITICISM, TYPES OF.

**Impression:** The total number of copies of a book printed at one time or without removing the type or plates from the press. See EDITION.

**Impressionism:** A highly personal manner of writing in which the author presents characters or scenes or moods as they appear to his individual temperament at a precise moment and from a particular vantage point rather than as they are in actuality. The term is one borrowed from painting. About the middle of the nineteenth century the French painters Manet, Monet, Degas, Renoir, and others revolted from the conventional and academic conceptions of painting and held that it was more important to retain the impressions an object makes on the artist than meticulously to present the appearance of that object by precise detail and careful, realistic finish. Their especial concern was with the use of light on their canvases. They suggested the chief features of an object with a few strokes; they were more interested in atmosphere than in perspective or outline. "Instead of painting a tree," says Lewis Mumford, the impressionist "painted the effect of a tree." The movement had its counterpart in literature, writers accepting the same conviction that the personal attitudes and moods of the writer were legitimate elements in depicting character or setting or action. Briefly, the literary impressionist holds that the expression of such elements as these through the fleeting impression of a moment is more significant artistically than a photographic presentation of cold fact. The object of the impressionist, then, is not to present his material as it is to the realist but as it is *seen* or *felt* to be by himself in a single passing moment. He employs highly selective details, the "brush-strokes" of sense-data that can suggest the impression made upon him or upon some character in the story or poem. In poetry *impressionism* was an important aspect of the work of the IMAGISTS; in FICTION it is present in the works of writers like Dorothy Richardson and Virginia Woolf and in the "Camera Eye" sections of Dos Passos' *U.S.A. Impressionism* differs from EXPRESSIONISM significantly in avoiding conscious distortion and abstraction. See EXPRESSIONISM, IMAGISTS.

**Impressionistic Criticism:** A type of criticism that attempts to communicate what the critic sees and feels in the presence of a work of art. Anatole France called *impressionistic criticism* "the adventures of a sensitive soul among masterpieces." See CRITICISM, TYPES OF; CRITICISM, HISTORICAL SKETCH.

**Incremental Repetition:** A form of iteration found frequently in the BALLAD. To quote Miss Louise Pound: "By incremental repetition is meant the ballad repetition not in the refrain way but structurally or for emphasis by which successive stanzas reveal a situation or advance the interest by successive changes of a single phrase or line. A stanza repeats a preceding one with variation but adds something to advance the story."[1] A common form which this sort of repetition takes is the question and answer, the answer repeating in large part the phrasing in the question itself. Some students of BALLAD structure believe that this repetition is the result of the old BALLAD's being sung as an accompaniment to the dance, and grew out of the recurrence of certain movements and rhythms of the dance. Two stanzas from *Child Waters* will serve as illustration of *incremental repetition:*

> There were four and twenty ladies
> Were playing at the ball,
> And Ellen, was the fairest lady,
> Must bring his steed to the stall.
>
> There were four and twenty ladies
> Was a playing at the chess,
> And Ellen, she was the fairest lady,
> Must bring his horse to grass.

**Incunabulum:** A term applied to any book printed in the last part of the fifteenth century (before 1501). Since the first printed books resembled in size, form, and appearance the medieval manuscript, which had been developed to a high degree of artistic perfection, *incunabula* are commonly large and ornate. As examples of early printing, *incunabula* are prized by modern collectors. From an historical and literary point of view they are interesting as reflecting the intellectual and literary interests of the late fifteenth century. The number of existing *incunabula* is large, including about 360 printed in England. Among famous English *incunabula* are Caxton's edition of Chaucer's *Canterbury Tales* and *Le Morte Darthur* of Malory. Modern libraries containing important collections of *incunabula* are the Bodleian at Oxford, the Cambridge University Library, the John Rylands Library in Manchester, the British Museum in London, the Bibliothèque Nationale in Paris, the Library of Congress in Washington, the Henry Huntington Library in San Marino, California, the Newberry Library in Chicago, and the Pierpont Morgan Library in New York.

**Induction:** An old word for *introduction.* This term was sometimes used in the sixteenth century to denote a framework intro-

---

[1] From Louise Pound's *Poetic Origins and the Ballad.* By permission of The Macmillan Company.

duction (see FRAME-STORY). Thus Sackville's "Induction" to a portion of *The Mirror for Magistrates* tells how the poet was led by Sorrow into a region of Hell where dwelt the shades of the historical figures whose tragic lives are the subject of the *Mirror*. In the book proper each "shade" relates his own sad tale; the *induction* supplies the framework much as the famous "Prologue" supplies the framework for the stories making up Chaucer's *Canterbury Tales*. In *The Taming of the Shrew* Shakespeare employs an *induction* in which a drunken tinker is persuaded that he is a lord, for whose amusement is performed a play—the play is *The Taming of the Shrew* itself.

**Industrial Revolution:** A term used to characterize the social-political-economic struggle which characterized life in England for a hundred years or more but which was most intensified in the last quarter of the eighteenth and first quarter of the nineteenth centuries. Invention, scientific discovery, changing economic, political, and social ideas and ideals all contributed to the furor that was England during these years. By 1760 blast furnaces had begun to promote the manufacture of iron; the textile industry grew by leaps and bounds with the invention of the spinning jenny and the power loom (1785). The number of English looms increased in less than two decades from three thousand to one hundred thousand. James Watt made even greater strides possible through his perfection of the steam engine. Roads, canals, and railroads increased transportation facilities. Agriculture was all but deserted; by 1826 not a third of the former population was left on the farms. Hundreds of thousands of men wandered through the country, many dying, impoverished and diseased. The sweat shop was born; the master craftsman found his trade taken from him by the machine. Home work gave way to factory work. Industry and commerce flourished in cities which grew rapidly. The villages were all but deserted. A middle-class capitalistic group developed almost overnight, and progressed at the expense of men, women, and children whom they overworked in their mills. All England turned her attention to making money.

Such industrial changes as these are related to literature since the writers of the period definitely concerned themselves with these contemporary problems. The bewilderment which came with the new industry called for explanation, understanding, and attempts at solution. Crabbe in such pieces as *The Village* and *The*

*Borough* set forth pictures of the conditions; Charles Kingsley in such novels as *Yeast* and *Alton Locke* and Mrs. Gaskell in *Mary Barton, a Tale of Manchester Life,* presented the struggles and unfairness of the times in fiction. Dickens turned his attention to the relief of the poor. Ruskin and Carlyle sought to point the way to reform; Arnold in his *Essays* condemned a Philistine England which measured her greatness by her wealth and her numbers. Mill (*Principles of Political Economy*), Bentham (*Radical Reform*), Robert Owen (*New View of Society*), and Malthus (*Principles of Political Economy*) wrestled with the problems of the time from the point of view of the social sciences. One stanza from Thomas Hood's "Song of the Shirt" (1843) will show the sympathetic attitude with which literature regarded suffering during the *Industrial Revolution:*

> Work—work—work!
>   My labor never flags;
> And what are its wages? A bed of straw,
>   A crust of bread—and rags.
> That shattered roof—and this naked floor—
>   A table—a broken chair—
> And a wall so blank, my shadow I thank
>   For sometimes falling there!

**Informal Essay:** As distinguished from the FORMAL ESSAY, the *informal essay* is less obviously serious in purpose, usually shorter, freer of STRUCTURE, easier of STYLE, and is written to please and entertain rather than to instruct. See ESSAY.

**Inkhornists:** A group in the RENAISSANCE PERIOD who favored the introduction of heavy Latin and Greek words into the standard English vocabulary. See PURIST and CRITICISM, HISTORICAL SKETCH.

**Inns of Court:** The four voluntary, unchartered societies or legal guilds in London which have the privilege of admitting persons to the bar. They take their names from the buildings they occupy— the Inner Temple, the Middle Temple, Lincoln's Inn, and Gray's Inn, buildings which they have occupied since the fourteenth century. Though the origin of these societies is lost in the medieval inns of law, it is clear that in late medieval times they became great law schools and so continued for centuries: today they are little more than lawyers' clubs, though they do exert considerable influence in guarding admissions to the bar. The *Inns of Court* were educational institutions and cultural centers in the sixteenth and seventeenth centuries. Their libraries as well as their spirit of fellowship fostered literary interests. Regular DRAMA, as well as MASQUES and INTERLUDES, was nurtured by the Inns. Shakespeare's *Comedy of Errors* was acted before the fellows of Gray's Inn during the Christmas season of 1594. The Inns, like the universities, saw much playwriting and amateur acting on the part of "gentlemen" who would scorn connection with the early PUBLIC THEATRES. Many English authors have received their education, in whole or in part, in the *Inns of Court*. Chaucer may have belonged to one; Sir Thomas More was a Lincoln's Inn product; George Gascoigne and Francis Bacon were admitted to law practice from Gray's Inn; Thomas Shadwell and Nicholas Rowe were members of the Inner Temple, etc. Charles Dickens was living in one of the old buildings of Lincoln's Inn when he published *The Pickwick Papers*. A vivid description of life in the Inns appears in Thackeray's *Pendennis*.

**Innuendo:** An insinuation or indirect suggestion, often with harmful or sinister connotation.

**Intentional Fallacy:** In contemporary criticism, a term used to describe the error of judging the success and the meaning of a work of art by the author's expressed or ostensible intention in producing it. The term was introduced by W. K. Wimsatt, Jr., and M. C. Beardsley (see *The Verbal Icon*, by Wimsatt) to insist that "the poem is not the critic's own and not the author's. . . . What is said about the poem [by the author] is subject to the same scrutiny as any statement in linguistics or in the general science of psychology or morals." The *intentional fallacy*, like the AFFECTIVE FALLACY, is an error in judgment when viewed from an OBJECTIVE THEORY OF ART, for holders of the OBJECTIVE THEORY tend—at least in their extreme statements—to see the work of art as AUTOTELIC. The degree to which biographical facts, data regarding linguistic change, and knowledge of the social and intellectual climate in which the work was produced become relevant factors, along with the author's statement of intention, are matters of sharp disagreement among contemporary critics. It should be noted that Wimsatt and Beardsley say, "The author must be admitted as a witness to the meaning of his work." It is merely that they would subject his testimony to rigorous scrutiny in the light of the work itself. See AFFECTIVE FALLACY, AUTOTELIC, HISTORICAL CRITICISM.

**Interior Monologue:** One of the techniques by which the STREAM OF CONSCIOUSNESS of a character in a NOVEL or a SHORT STORY is presented. It records the internal, emotional experience of the character on any one level or on combinations of several levels of consciousness, reaching downward to the non-verbalized level where IMAGES must be used to represent non-verbalized sensations or emotions. It assumes the unrestricted and uncensored portrayal of the totality of interior experience on the level or levels being represented. It gives, therefore, the appearance of being illogical, associational, free of authorial control. There are two distinct forms which an *interior monologue* may take: direct, in which the author seems not to exist and the interior self of the character is given directly, as though the reader were overhearing an articulation of the stream of thought and feeling flowing through the character's mind; and indirect, in which the author serves as selector, presenter, guide, and commentator. The Molly Bloom section at the close of Joyce's *Ulysses* is the best known example of a direct *interior monologue* in English; the novels of Virginia Woolf are excellent illustrations of the indirect *interior monologue.* It is generally agreed that Édouard Dujardin, in *Les Lauriers sont coupés* (1887), first used the *interior monologue* extensively. The term is often, although erroneously, used as a synonym for STREAM OF CONSCIOUSNESS. See STREAM OF CONSCIOUSNESS, IMPRESSIONISM.

**Interlude:** A kind of DRAMA that developed in late fifteenth- and early sixteenth-century England and that played an important part in the secularization of the DRAMA and in the development of REALISTIC COMEDY. The word may mean a play brief enough to be presented in the interval of a dramatic performance, entertainment, or feast (e.g., Medwall's *Fulgens and Lucres, ca.*1497), or it may mean a play or DIALOGUE between two persons. Some *interludes* imitate French FARCE and do not exhibit symbolic technique and didactic purpose, while others appear to have developed from the MORALITY PLAY, and still others from the Latin SCHOOL DRAMA: the two latter types are likely to be moralistic. Professor Tucker Brooke has stressed the aristocratic character of the *interlude* and says that the *interlude* was understood in Tudor times to mean a short play exhibited by professionals at the meals of the great and on other occasions where, later, MASQUES would have been fashionable. The essential qualities are brevity and WIT. Some writers, however (like F. E. Schelling), regard such an episode as that of the sheep-stealing Mak in the Towneley *Second Shepherd's Play* as an *interlude*. The chief developers of the *interlude* were John Heywood and John Rastell, the first English dramatists, so far as known, to recognize that a play might be justified on the single test of ability to amuse. Heywood's *interludes* were produced in the 1520's and 1530's, the most famous being *The Four P's* (the Palmer, the Pardoner, the Pothecary, and the Pedlar, who engage in a sort of lying contest managed as a satire against women), and *The Merry Play of John John the Husband, Tyb His Wife, and Sir John the Priest* (in which the priest and Tyb hoodwink the husband). Rastell's *interludes* include *The Nature of the Four Elements, The Field of the Cloth of Gold*, and *Gentilness and Nobility*. Homely details and realistic treatment are significant features of the *interludes*, which still followed the allegorical pattern of the MORALITY and yet represented the growth away from the abstract and toward the individual and particular.

**Internal Rime:** See RIME, LEONINE RIME.

**Intrigue Comedy:** A COMEDY in which the major interest is in PLOT complications resulting from scheming by a character or characters. See COMEDY OF SITUATION.

**Introduction:** The opening sentences or paragraphs of a piece of writing. All literary combinations have been said to have three parts: beginning, middle, end. On this basis the *introduction* is the beginning to the beginning. Sometimes the term is applied to an ESSAY printed at the beginning of a book—much like a preface—to explain the author's chief ideas, purposes, hopes, and disillusions regarding the book he has written. See INDUCTION, PROLEGOMENON.

**Invective:** Harsh, abusive language directed against a person or cause. Vituperative writing. The *Letters* of Junius and the open letter written by Stevenson in defense of Father Damien have qualities of *invective*.

**Invention:** Originality in thought, STYLE, DICTION, IMAGERY, or PLOT. In this present-day sense the term implies creative power of an independent sort. But the use of the term by early English critics often is colored by an older meaning of the term and by the implications of the theory of IMITATION, and the student will do well to remember that RENAISSANCE and NEO-CLASSIC critics in their use of the term may have in mind the older idea of the "discovery" of literary material as something to be IMITATED or represented. In Latin rhetoric *inventio* meant the "finding" of material and was applied, for example, to an orator's "working up" of his case before making a speech. According to the Aristotelian doctrine of IMITATION an author did not create his materials "out of nothing"; he found them in Nature. A critic writing under the control of these classical conceptions could not think of *invention* in its narrower, modern sense. Yet the idea of ORIGINALITY, of using "new" devices, and of avoiding the trite expression appears in the use of the term in England as early as RENAISSANCE times. As the term was used somewhat loosely for several centuries, it is not possible to give a single definition which will explain all the passages in which the term appears in writings of the sixteenth, seventeenth, and eighteenth centuries. In the ROMANTIC AGE and since, *invention,* in the sense of the discovery of an original or organizing principle, has been replaced by IMAGINATION.

**Inversion:** The placing of a sentence element out of its normal position either to gain EMPHASIS or to secure a so-called "poetic effect." *Inversion* used with restraint and care is an effective rhetorical device, but used too frequently or so grotesquely as to distort the language, it will immediately work ruin with a STYLE and result in artificiality. A simple illustration is the command the small boy gives his dog: "Rover, go home," a command generally considered more efficient than "Go home, Rover," which is, perhaps, the more natural. Probably the most offensive common use of *inversion* is the placing of the adjective after the noun in such expressions as "home beautiful," etc.

The device is often happily employed in poetry. Where the writer of prose might say: "I saw a vision of a damsel with a dulcimer" Coleridge writes:

> A damsel with a dulcimer
> In a vision once I saw.

**Invocation:** An address to a deity for aid. In classical literature convention demanded an opening address to the muses, an *invocation* bespeaking their assistance in the writing. EPICS, particularly, were likely to begin in this way. Milton, in *Paradise Lost,* accepts the tradition, but instead of invoking one of the muses of poetry addresses the

> Heavenly Muse, that, on the secret top
> Of Oreb, or Sinai, didst inspire
> That shepherd who first taught the chosen seed
> In the beginning how the heavens and earth
> Rose out of Chaos: . . .

**Ionic:** A classical FOOT with two long and two short syllables. When it is occasionally attempted in English, stressed syllables are used for the long ones and unstressed for the short.

*Ipse dixit:* Any dogmatic statement. Literally the Latin means: "He himself has said." Hence the term is used to characterize any edict or brief statement emphatically uttered, but unsupported by proof.

**Irish Literary Movement, Irish Literary Revival, Irish Renaissance:** Variant terms for the movement which encouraged the production of Anglo-Irish literature. See CELTIC RENAISSANCE.

**Irish Literature:** The early literature of Ireland is of particular interest because it is greater in bulk, earlier in date, and more striking in character than any other preserved vernacular Western European literature, and because it has furnished a storehouse of literary materials for later writers, especially those of the early ROMANTIC PERIOD and of the CELTIC RENAISSANCE. It is possible, too, that it supplies a clue to the obscure origins of ARTHURIAN LEGEND. The development of this extensive native literature, as well as the remarkable flourishing of Latin learning in Ireland in the early Middle Ages, is due in part to the fact that the Teutonic invasions which destroyed Roman power in the fifth century failed to reach Ireland, which became a refuge for European scholars and for several centuries the chief center of Christian culture in Western Europe. The Irish clerics, too, seemed to be unusually tolerant of native pagan culture and therefore aided in preserving a great mass of native, often primitive, legendary and literary tradition of great interest to the student of FOLKLORE and literary origins.

Although much poetry in Irish was doubtless written in very early times, definite metrical forms employing ALLITERATION and RIME having been developed as early as the seventh century, the great bulk of early Irish literature is in prose. In fact, the early Irish EPICS are distinguished from most other early epic literature by their employment of prose instead of verse (though the Irish prose EPICS frequently include poetic PARAPHRASES or commentaries, "rhetorics," scattered throughout the text). The basic stories of the chief EPIC CYCLE reflect a state of culture prevailing about the time of Christ. Verbally preserved from generation to generation for centuries, they seem to have been written down as early as the seventh and eighth centuries. These early copies of the old stories were largely destroyed and scattered as a result of the Norse invasion (eighth and ninth centuries), the stories being imperfectly recovered and again recorded in manuscripts by the patriotic antiquarians of the tenth and later centuries. Two large manuscripts of the twelfth century containing these retellings of ancient story are still in existence, the *Book of the Dun Cow* (before 1106) and the *Book of Lenster* (before 1160).

The early SAGA literature is divided into three great CYCLES: the "mythological," based on early Celtic myths and historical legends concerning population groups or "invasions"; the Ulster Cycle, or "Red Branch," of which Cuchullin is the central heroic figure; and the Fenian Cycle, concerned with the exploits of Finn mac Cool and his famous companions. The Ulster Cycle was more aristocratic than the Fenian and is therefore preserved in greater volume in the early manuscripts. The chief story is the *Táin bó Cualnge*, "The Cattle Raid of Cooley," the greatest of the early Irish epics. Other important stories of this cycle are *The Feast of Bricriu* (containing a beheading game like that in *Sir Gawain and the Green Knight*), *The Wooing of Etaine* (a fairy mistress story), and *The Exile of the Sons of Usnech* (the famous Deirdre story). The Fenian stories, perhaps later in origin than the Ulster tales, have shown greater vitality in oral tradition, many of them still being current among the Gaelic peasants of Ireland and Scotland. They were utilized by the famous James Macpherson in the eighteenth century (see LITERARY FORGERIES).

Early Irish professional poets (*fili*) or story-tellers were ranked partly by the extent of their repertory of tales, the highest class being able to recite no less than 350 separate stories. These stories were divided into numerous classes or types, such as cattle raids, wooings, battles, deaths, elopements, feasts, exiles, destructions, slaughters, adventures, voyages, visions, etc.

In addition to the romantic or SAGA literature there has been preserved (partly in Latin) a vast amount of historical, legal, and religious literature, the latter including a great many SAINTS' LIVES (romantically told), as well as HYMNS, martyrologies, and one of the earliest examples of medieval biographical writing, Adamnan's *Vita Sancti Columbae,* "The Life of Saint Columba" (before A.D. 700).

The traditional literary technique of the native Irish writers was much altered after the spread of English power and culture in Ireland in the seventeenth century, and the decline in the employment of the Irish language since that time has been accompanied by a lowering and lessening of literary activity. For "revivals" of Gaelic literature and culture see CELTIC RENAISSANCE, CELTIC REVIVAL, GAELIC MOVEMENT.

**Irony:** A figure of speech in which the actual intent is expressed in words which carry the opposite meaning. *Irony* is likely to be confused with SARCASM but it differs from SARCASM in that it is usually lighter, less harsh in its wording though in effect probably more cutting because of its indirectness. It bears, too, a close relationship to INNUENDO. The ability to recognize *irony* is one of the surest tests of intelligence and sophistication. Its presence is marked by a sort of grim HUMOR, an "unemotional detachment" on the part of the writer, a coolness in expression at a time when the writer's emotions are really heated. Characteristically it speaks words of praise to imply blame and words of blame to imply praise, though its inherent critical quality makes the first type much more common than the second. The great effectiveness of *irony* as a literary device is the impression it gives of great restraint. The writer of *irony* has his tongue in his cheek; for this reason *irony* is more easily detected in speech than in writing since the voice can, through its intonation, so easily warn the listener of a double significance. One of the most famous ironic remarks in literature is Job's "No doubt but ye are the people, and wisdom shall die with you." Antony's insistence, in his oration over the dead Caesar, that "Brutus is an honorable man" bears the same ironic imprint. Goldsmith, Jane Austen, Thackeray—these authors have in one novel or another made frequent use of this form; Jonathan Swift is an arch-ironist;

his "Modest Proposal" for saving a starving Ireland, by suggesting that the Irish sell their babies to the English landlords, is perhaps the most savagely sustained ironic writing in our literature. The novels of Thomas Hardy and Henry James are elaborate artistic expressions of the ironic spirit, for *irony* applies not only to statement but also to event, SITUATION, and STRUCTURE. In DRAMA, *irony* has a special meaning, referring to knowledge held by the audience but hidden from the relevant actors. In contemporary criticism, *irony* is used to describe a poet's "recognition of incongruities" and his controlled acceptance of them. Among the devices by which *irony* is achieved are HYPERBOLE, UNDERSTATEMENT, and SARCASM. See DRAMATIC IRONY.

**Irregular Ode:** An ODE that does not follow either the pattern of STROPHE, ANTISTROPHE, and EPODE of the PINDARIC ODE or the repetition of STANZAS of the HORATION ODE, but freely alters its stanzaic forms both in number and in length. It was introduced by Abraham Cowley in the seventeenth century. Wordsworth's "Ode on Intimations of Immortality" is a noted example. See ODE.

**Issue:** A special form of a book in which the original sheets are used but with added material or new arrangement. See EDITION.

**Italian Sonnet:** A SONNET divided into an OCTAVE always riming *abbaabba* and a SESTET usually riming *cdecde*. See SONNET.

**Jacobean Age:** That portion of the RENAISSANCE PERIOD which fell during the reign of James I (1603–1625), so-called from the Latin form of James, *Jacobus*. Early Jacobean literature was in reality a rich flowering of Elizabethan literature, while late Jacobean writing showed the attitudes characteristic of the CAROLINE AGE. During the *Jacobean Age* the breach between Puritan and Cavalier steadily widened and there was a widespread growth of REALISM in art and CYNICISM in thought. It is the greatest period for the English DRAMA; Shakespeare wrote his greatest TRAGEDIES and his TRAGI-COMEDIES; Jonson flourished, producing CLASSICAL TRAGEDY, REALISTIC COMEDY, and MASQUES; and Beaumont and Fletcher, Webster, Chapman, Middleton, and Massinger were at their peaks. In poetry, Shakespeare published his *Sonnets*, Drayton his *Poems*, and Donne his METAPHYSICAL VERSE. In prose, it saw the publication of the King James translation of the Bible, Bacon's major work, Donne's

# Jargon

sermons, Burton's *Anatomy of Melancholy*, the CHARACTER essays, and Dekker's realistic "novels." See RENAISSANCE PERIOD and *Outline of Literary History*.

**Jargon:** Confused speech, resulting particularly from the mingling of several languages or dialects. The term is also used to refer to any strange language which sounds uncouth to us; in this sense outlandish speech. Sometimes *jargon* means simply nonsense or gibberish. *Jargon*, like CANT, also signifies the special language of a group or profession, as the legal *jargon*, pedagogic *jargon*, thieves' *jargon*, etc.

**Jest-books:** A name applied to collections of humorous, witty, or satirical anecdotes and jokes which had some vogue in England and Germany and other European countries in the sixteenth and succeeding centuries. The "jests" in these miscellanies owe something to the Latin *facetia*, something to the medieval FABLIAU and EXEMPLUM, and borrow also from the EPIGRAM, the PROVERB, and ADAGE. They are usually short and often end with a "moral." Coarseness, ribaldry, REALISM, SATIRE, and CYNICISM often characterize the witty turns. The material in the *jest-books* probably is similar in character to the stock-in-trade of the medieval MINSTRELS, the printing press making possible the dissemination of such matter in book form. Women, friars, cuckolds, Welshmen, courtiers, tradesmen, foreigners, military officers, doctors, students, travelers, and many other classes are butts of the WIT or victims of practical jokes. The earliest English *jest-book* is *A Hundred Merry Tales* (ca.1526). Another famous one was *The Gests of Skoggan* (ca.1565), which illustrates a tendency of *jest-books* to be "biographical" in making the jokes cluster about a single man. Thus the *Merie Tales of Master Skelton* was partly responsible for the poor reputation of John Skelton after his death. So there were in the seventeenth and eighteenth centuries *jest-books* on Ben Jonson. One famous court jester, Archie Armstrong (under James I and Charles I), published his own *jest-book, A Banquet of Jests and Merry Tales* (1630). It is divided into "Court Jests," "Camp Jests," "College Jests," "City Jests," and "Country Jests."

**Jesuits:** Members of the Society of Jesus, a Catholic religious order founded by Saint Ignatius Loyola in 1534. In contrast with the ascetic ideals of the medieval Catholic orders, the *Jesuits* were conceived as a band of spiritual soldiers living under strict military discipline who were expected to engage actively in affairs. The discipline was strict, the individual having no rights as such but vowing to serve God through the Society of Jesus. The members were bound by personal vows of poverty, chastity, and obedience. The head of the Order is called the "general," lives in Rome, and is subject to the Pope. The *Jesuits* became famous as schoolmasters and made effective efforts to raise the educational as well as spiritual standards of the clergy. Their activities as missionaries are well known; the letters of *Jesuit* missionaries in America give important pictures of early life in the colonies. They were very active in New France. Although political activities were technically forbidden, the objectives of the Order actually led the *Jesuits* into political intrigue and it is this fact that has led to much criticism of the Order, which is often accused of duplicity and casuistry, a charge perpetuated unjustly in the use of the term Jesuitical as a derogatory adjective. English poetry has been enriched by the poetic work of some *Jesuit* poets, notably Robert Southwell (1561–1595), whose *Saint Peter's Complaint* and his more brilliant short poems such as *The Burning Babe*, anticipate both the seriousness of Milton and the CONCEITS of Donne, and Gerard Manley Hopkins (1844–1899), whose *Poems*, posthumously published in 1918, demonstrated an intensity of feeling and a mastery of experimental poetic devices which have made him a master figure in modern poetry.

**Jeu d'esprit:** A witty playing with words, a clever sally. Much of Thomas Hood's verse, for example, may be said to be marked by a happy *jeu d'esprit*. The term is also applied to brief, clever pieces of writing, such as Benjamin Franklin's "Bagatelles."

**Jig:** A non-literary farcical dramatic performance, the words being sung to the accompaniment of dancing. It was popular on the Elizabethan stage, often being used as an afterpiece. "He's for a jig, or a tale of bawdry," Hamlet says of Polonius. See DROLL.

**Johnson's Circle:** See LITERARY CLUB.

**Jongleur:** A French term for a professional musical entertainer of medieval times, analogous to the Anglo-Saxon GLEEMAN and the later MINSTREL. Though primarily one who sang or recited the LYRICS, BALLADS, and stories of such original poets as the TROUBA-

DOUR and the TROUVÈRE, the *jongleur* sometimes composed and sometimes supplied non-musical forms of entertainment, such as juggling and tumbling. The dissemination of literary forms and materials from nation to nation in the Middle Ages is due partly to the activities of the *jongleur* and the MINSTREL.

**Journal:** A form of autobiographical writing, in which a day-by-day account of events and a record of personal impressions are kept. It is usually less intimate than a DIARY and more obviously chronological than an AUTOBIOGRAPHY. The term *journal* is also applied to any periodical publication that contains news or deals with matters of current interest in any particular sphere, as *The Journal of Southern History.*

**Judicial Criticism:** A kind of criticism that, in contradistinction to IMPRESSIONISTIC CRITICISM, attempts by the rigorous application of general standards and objective criteria to analyze, classify, define, and evaluate works of art. See CRITICISM, TYPES OF.

**Kailyard School:** A name given to a group of Scottish writers whose work dealt idealistically with ordinary people in modern village life in Scotland. DIALECT was an important element in their writing. J. M. Barrie and "Ian Maclaren" are two of the best known members of the "school," which was popular toward the close of the nineteenth century. *Kailyard* is a Scottish term for a cabbage garden.

**Katharsis:** See CATHARSIS.

**Kenning:** A stereotyped figurative phrase used in OLD ENGLISH and other Germanic tongues as a synonym for a simple noun. *Kennings* are often picturesque metaphorical compounds. Specimen *kennings* from *Beowulf* are "the bent-necked wood," "the ringed prow," "the foamy-necked," "the sea-wood," and the "sea-farer," for *ship;* "the swan-road" and "the whale-road" for the *sea;* the "leavings of the file" for the *sword;* the "twilight-spoiler" for the *dragon;* the "storm of swords" for *battle;* and "peace-bringer among nations" for the *queen.*

**Kind:** A term widely used during the NEO-CLASSIC PERIOD for GENRE or literary type. Implicit in the use of the term is the assumption that literary GENRES have an objective, absolute existence analogous to the "kinds" of the natural world and that they obey "the laws of kind." See GENRE.

**Kit-Cat Club:** A club generally believed to have existed in London between 1703 and 1733, founded by members of the Whig Party and dedicated in part to the insuring of a Protestant succession to the throne. Among its members were Addison, Steele, Congreve, Vanbrugh, and Marlborough. It met at the "Cat and Fiddle" pastry-shop, kept by Christopher Cat, from whom it is generally assumed to have taken its name, although Addison in the *Spectator* (No. IX) says the name came from the pies served by Christopher Cat and called "kit-cats." In the summer it met in a room with a very low ceiling at the home of the publisher Jacob Tonson. When Sir Godfrey Kneller painted the portraits of the members to hang in this room, he was forced to use small canvasses, 36 by 28 inches, and this size was later called kit-cat size.

**Knickerbocker Group:** A name given to a group writing in and about New York during the first half of the nineteenth century. The name "Knickerbocker" was made famous by Washington Irving in his *Knickerbocker's History of New York*. The heyday of the group was the first third of the century, although it was represented in the *Knickerbocker Magazine* (1833–1865); the remnants of the Knickerbocker school were pilloried in Poe's *The Literati of New York City*. Journalism, editorship, the frontier, poetry, novels, songs, and, in the case of Byrant at least, translation from the classics, were the sorts of things which claimed the attention of these writers. The term "school" is, for them, a misnomer, since they consciously held few tenets in common and worked to no deliberate purpose as a group. Their association was one of geography and chance rather than of close organization. At the turn into the nineteenth century New York was forging ahead of Boston as a center of activity and of population, a fact which meant that naturally the city was becoming more important as a literary center. The more illustrious members of the school were: Washington Irving (*Salmagundi* papers, written in collaboration with others, *Knickerbocker's History of New York, Sketch Book, Tales of a Traveller*, etc.), James Fenimore Cooper (*The Spy, The Pioneers, The Pilot, Last of the Mohicans, Pathfinder, Deerslayer*, etc.), William Cullen Bryant (*Poems*, and translation of Homer), Joseph Rodman Drake (*The*

*Culprit Fay*), Fitzgreene Halleck (*Marco Bozzaris*), John Howard
Payne (*Home Sweet Home*), Samuel Woodworth (*The Old Oaken
Bucket*), George P. Morris (*Woodman, Spare That Tree*).

**Koran:** A Moslem collection of scriptural writings. The text is believed to have been revealed to Mohammed from time to time over
a period of years, and, after many changes and much editing, took
shape in an official transcription after Mohammed's death (A.D.
632). The book is the sacred scripture of millions of followers, and
presents—in addition to matters of theology—moral teaching,
liturgical directions, and advice as to religious conduct and ceremonials. The speaker is usually God.

*Lai:* See LAY.

**Lake School:** A name used to characterize Coleridge, Wordsworth,
and Southey—three poets who at the beginning of the nineteenth
century were living in the Lake District (Cumberland, Westmor-
land, and Lancashire). The name "lakers" is credited to the *Edinburgh Review*, which for several years adopted a very contemptuous attitude toward the poets. There was, properly, no "school"
in the sense of the three all working for common objectives, but
it is true that Coleridge and Wordsworth had certain convictions in
common and on occasion worked together.

**Lament:** A poem expressing some great grief, usually more intense
and more personal than that expressed in a COMPLAINT. *Deor's Lament*, an early Anglo-Saxon poem, for instance, presents the plain-
tive regret of the SCOP at his changed status after a rival had usurped
his place in the esteem of a patron. The separate "tragedies" in
such collections as the sixteenth-century *Mirror for Magistrates*, in
which the ghosts of dead worthies tell the stories of their fall
from fortune, were called *laments* in Renaissance times, an example
being Sackville's "Lament" of the Duke of Buckingham. See COM-
PLAINT.

**Lampoon:** Writing which ridicules and satirizes the character or
personal appearance of a person in a bitter, scurrilous manner.
*Lampoons* were written in either verse or prose. Lampooning became a dangerous sport and fell into disuse with the development
of the libel laws. See EPIGRAM.

**Late Victorian Age, 1870–1901:** The period between 1870 and the death of Queen Victoria saw the full flowering of the movement toward REALISM which had set in as early as the 1830's but which had been subordinated to the dominant ROMANTICISM of the first half of Victoria's reign. George Eliot and Thomas Hardy carried the realistic NOVEL to new heights. Spencer, Huxley, Newman, Arnold, and Morris, in the ESSAY, argued the meaning of the new science, the new religion, and the new society. The DRAMA, which had been sleeping for more than a century, awoke under the impact of the influence of Ibsen and the CELTIC RENAISSANCE. Stevenson, W. H. Hudson, and Kipling revived romantic fiction. Oscar Wilde and the "decadents" wrote witty poetry and DRAMA. Walter Pater advanced the doctrine of "Art for Art's sake." The tendency to look with critical eyes on man, society, and God, to ask pragmatic questions, and to seek utilitarian answers—a tendency which had begun in the second quarter of the century—had become the dominant mode of thought and of writing by the time that Queen Victoria died. See REALISTIC PERIOD IN ENGLISH LITERATURE, VICTORIAN, and *Outline of Literary History.*

**Laureate:** See POET LAUREATE.

**Lay** (*lai*): A SONG or short NARRATIVE POEM. The word has been applied to several different poetic forms in French and English literature. The earliest existing French *lais* were composed in the twelfth century and were professedly based upon earlier songs or verse-tales sung by Breton minstrels on themes drawn from Celtic legend; hence the term "Breton lay." Though some of the early French *lais* were LYRIC, most of them were NARRATIVE, like those of Marie de France, who wrote at the court of the English King Henry II about A.D. 1175. A few of Marie's *lais* are related to ARTHURIAN LEGEND, the *Lay of Lanval,* for example, in which Arthur and Gawain appear. The prevailing verse-form of the early French *lais* was the eight-syllabled line riming in COUPLETS. Later French *lais,* such as those of the RENAISSANCE, developed more complicated metrical forms.

The word *lay* was applied to English poems written in the fourteenth century in imitation of the French "Breton *lais.*" Though a few of them follow the short COUPLET form, more use the popular TAIL-RIME STANZA. Any short narrative poem similar to the French *lai* might be called a "Breton *lay*" by the English poets. Actually themes from various sources were employed, classical, Oriental, Celtic, etc. Some of the best-known English Breton *lays* are the *Lay of Launfal, Sir Orfeo, Sir Gowther,* and Chaucer's *Franklin's Tale.*

Since the sixteenth century, *lay* has been used by English writers as synonymous with *song.* In the early nineteenth century, *lay* sometimes meant a short historical BALLAD, as Scott's *Lay of the Last Minstrel* and Macaulay's *Lays of Ancient Rome. Lais* as used by François Villon for the title of the poems now known as *Petit Testament* (1456) is a different word, corresponding to modern French *legs,* "bequest."

**Legend:** A NARRATIVE or TRADITION handed down from the past. A *legend* is distinguished from a MYTH in that the *legend* has more of historical truth and perhaps less of the supernatural. *Legends* often indicate the lore of a people, and, in this way, serve as at least a partial expression of the racial or national spirit. *Saints' legends* are narratives of the lives of the early church heroes. Loosely a *legend* is any brief explanatory comment accompanying paintings, maps, etc.

**Leonine Rime:** A particular form of INTERNAL RIME (see RIME) characterized by the riming of the syllable preceding the CÆSURA with the last syllable of the line. Ordinarily *Leonine rime* is restricted to PENTAMETERS and HEXAMETERS, but less rigidly the term is applied to verses such as the "Stabat Mater" of the Church. The expression is said to be derived from the name of a writer of the Middle Ages, Leoninus, canon of St. Victor in Paris, who wrote ELEGIAC lines containing this variety of INTERNAL RIME. An example of *Leonine rime* is italicized in the following:

Ex rex Ed*vardus,* debacchans ut Leo*pardus.*

Also called INTERNAL RIME.

**Letter-press:** Used to distinguish the reading matter, or the "text," of a book from the illustrative matter. This use of the term may have derived from the fact that, in the older processes of printing, the letter-press printed directly from type instead of from the plates, woodcuts, or blocks used for illustrations. The term is also employed to refer to the typography of a work, or to printing in a general sense.

**Letters:** A general name sometimes given to literature (see BELLES-LETTRES). More specifically, of course, the classification refers to notes and EPISTLES exchanged between acquaintances, friends, or commercial firms. A great body of informal literature is preserved through collections of actual *letters*. The correspondence of such figures as Lord Byron, Jane and Thomas Carlyle, Lord Chesterfield, Charles Dickens, Edward FitzGerald, William Hazlitt, Charles Lamb, Mary Wortley Montague, Thomas Gray, Horace Walpole, Sydney Smith, and Robert Louis Stevenson—to mention a few of the great letter writers—constitutes one of the pleasantest of by-ways in the whole realm of literature. *Letters,* in this sense, are distinguished from EPISTLES in that they present personal and natural relationships among friends, whereas EPISTLES are more usually formal documents prepared with a view to their being read by some public. See EPISTLE.

**Lexicography:** The art of making DICTIONARIES or LEXICONS. The most ancient DICTIONARY extant is said to be a Greek LEXICON called *Homeric Words,* prepared by Apollonius the Sophist in the reign of Augustus (27 B.C.–A.D. 14). The technique of making LEXICONS and DICTIONARIES developed slowly from the mere explanation of hard words by simpler ones in the same language to the preparation of elaborate lists, alphabetically arranged, with derivations, pronunciation, spellings, and illustrative quotations, and meanings, either in the same or other languages. For English *lexicography,* see DICTIONARIES, ENGLISH.

**Lexicon:** A word list or wordbook; a vocabulary; one of the standard terms for DICTIONARY, although it is usually applied only to dictionaries of Greek or Hebrew. See LEXICOGRAPHY.

**Libretto:** The text or book, containing the story, TALE, or PLOT of an OPERA or of any long musical composition—a cantata, for instance. It is the diminutive form of the Italian *libro,* a book.

**Light Opera:** A form of OPERA which lacks the dignity and seriousness of grand OPERA and usually stresses sentiment rather than passion. It is unlike COMIC OPERA in that spoken DIALOGUE is not commonly employed. An example is M. W. Balfe's *The Bohemian Girl* (1843).

**Light Verse:** Short LYRIC poems, gay and bantering in tone, sportive in mood, and often sophisticated in subject and formal in treatment. There are many varieties of *light verse:* PARODY, LIMERICK, OC-CASIONAL VERSE, EPIGRAMS, VERS DE SOCIÉTÉ, CLERIHEWS, NONSENSE VERSE. Grace and ease of expression, fancifulness and will to delight, charming but mordant WIT, and frequently some serious or satiric intent are characteristic of a kind of poetry that has been practiced with grace and honor by Aristophanes, Shakespeare, Goethe, Milton, Jonson, the CAVALIER LYRISTS, Swift, Pope, Dorothy Parker, Lewis Carroll, Edward Lear, W. S. Gilbert, T. S. Eliot, Phyllis McGinley, Christopher Morley, and Helen Bevington. Writers of *light verse* often employ difficult and challenging FORMS, delighting in particular in the FRENCH FORMS.

**Limerick:** A form of LIGHT VERSE, a particularly popular type of NONSENSE-VERSE. Its composition follows a rather definite pattern: five anapestic lines of which the first, second, and fifth, consisting of three feet, RIME; and the third and fourth lines, consisting of two feet, RIME. Sometimes a *limerick* is written in four lines, but when so composed, its third line bears an INTERNAL RIME and might easily be considered two lines.

The origin of the *limerick* is not definitely known. Though originally a kind of epigrammatic song, passed around orally, *limericks* increased the range of their subject matter to encompass every possible theme, nothing being sacred to their HUMOR. They were chiefly concerned, however, with the manners, morals, and peculiarities of people. Their first recorded appearance in print was in 1821, when Loane's *History of Sixteen Wonderful Old Women* was published, but they reached the peak of their vogue when Edward Lear published his *Book of Nonsense* in 1846. The following, taken from Lear's volume, illustrates the accepted *limerick* form:

> There was an old Man of the Dee,
> Who was sadly annoyed by a Flea;
>   When he said, "I will scratch it!"
>   They gave him a hatchet
> Which grieved that old Man of the Dee.

**Litany:** A ritualistic form of supplication commonly used in the Catholic Church. A solemn prayer. The form is sometimes adopted by writers for original poetic expression.

**Literal:** Accurate to the letter, without embellishment. Thus, in the first sense, the word is used, as in a "literal translation," to signify accuracy and thoroughness in presenting the exact meaning of the original—a TRANSLATION which is according to the usual meaning of the words and allows no freedom of expression or imagination to the translator. Quite different from PARAPHRASE. In the second sense, the term is frequently used to distinguish language which is matter of fact and CONCRETE from language which is given to much use of FIGURES OF SPEECH. *Literal* language is the opposite of FIGURATIVE.

**Literary Ballad:** See ART BALLAD.

**Literary Club, The (Doctor Johnson's Circle):** A club formed in London in 1764 at the suggestion of Sir Joshua Reynolds, famous painter, and with the coöperation of Dr. Samuel Johnson. Among the seven other charter members were Edmund Burke and Oliver Goldsmith. Famous men admitted to membership during Johnson's lifetime included Bishop Percy (ballad collector), David Garrick (actor), Edward Gibbon (historian), Adam Smith (economist), and James Boswell (Johnson's biographer). At first the members met at a weekly supper, and later at a fortnightly dinner during Parliament. At these meetings there was much free and spirited discussion of books and writers, classic and contemporary, Doctor Johnson frequently dominating the conversation. Johnson became a sort of literary dictator and the Club itself was a formidable power: whole editions of a book were sold off in one day by its sanction. Though commonly thought of only in connection with late eighteenth-century literature, the Club has continued in existence, its later membership including fifteen prime ministers and such authors as Scott, Macaulay, Hallam, and Tennyson.

**Literary Forgeries:** The plagiarist tries to get the world to accept as his own what someone else has written. The literary forger, on the contrary, tries to make the world accept as the genuine writing of another what he has himself composed. His motive may be to supply authority for some religious or political doctrine or scheme, or it may be to cater to some prevailing literary demand (as when spurious BALLADS were composed in the eighteenth century in response to the romantic interest in old BALLADS), or it may be, as

Bacon would say, "for the love of the lie itself." *Literary forgeries* seem to be numerous in all countries and in all ages. A book of nearly 300 pages by J. A. Farrer gives accounts of many famous *literary forgeries,* yet, as Andrew Lang says, several additional volumes would be needed to make the account of known forgeries complete. It is possible here to call attention to but a few cases.

The Greek statesman, Solon, inserted forged verses in the revered *Iliad* to further his political purposes. A forged "diary" of a supposed soldier in the Trojan War, Dares the Phrygian, actually composed by some Roman about the fourth century after Christ, had the effect of turning the sympathy of European peoples from the Greeks to the Trojans and of supplying an account of the war which for over a thousand years was accepted as more "authentic" than Homer's. In addition it supplied the kernel for what developed into one of the most famous love stories of all time, that of Troilus and Cressida. A famous Italian scholar, Carlo Sigonio, about 1582 composed what pretended to be the lost *Consolatio* of Cicero. The imitation was so clever and the genuineness of the document so effectively argued by Sigonio himself that although there was always some doubt, it was not till 200 years later that the facts were discovered.

In English literary history an example is afforded by the tragic story of Thomas Chatterton (1752–1770), the "boy poet," who wrote "faked" poems and prose pieces supposed to have been written by a fifteenth-century priest. Although Chatterton was but twelve years old when he began his forgeries, his imitation of medieval English was so clever and his actual poetic gifts were so high that his efforts attracted wide attention before his suicide at the age of eighteen. About the same time came another famous case of an effort to supply the current romantic interest in the medieval and the primitive with supposedly ancient pieces of literature, James Macpherson's "Ossianic" poems (1760–1765). Macpherson seems to have made some use of genuine Celtic tradition but in the main to have composed the epic *Fingal* himself, which he claimed had been written in the third century by Ossian, son of Fingal. Macpherson's public was sharply divided between those who accepted this "discovery" as genuine and those who, like Doctor Johnson, denounced him as an impostor. The episode is referred to as the OSSIANIC CONTROVERSY.

Just as it is not easy for editors and publishers to detect all plagiarized writing presented to them, so it is difficult for them to avoid being exploited by literary forgers, who sometimes mix the authentic and the spurious so cleverly that not only the editors and publishers, but the general public and the professional critics are deceived. And this is as true of the twentieth century as of the eighteenth. See PLAGIARISM.

**Literary Magazines:** A selected bibliography of literary journals in Great Britain and the United States which have been most influential in the development of the literature of the two countries follows.

A Selected List of Some Representative
American Literary Magazines
(Arranged in the order of their founding)

| | | | |
|---|---|---|---|
| 1803–1811 | Monthly Anthology | 1865– | Nation |
| 1815–1940 | North American Review | 1866–1878 | Galaxy |
| | | 1868–1875 | Overland Monthly |
| 1821– | Saturday Evening Post | 1870–1881 | Scribner's Monthly |
| | | 1870–1932 | Outlook |
| 1824–1826 | United States Literary Gazette | 1880–1929 | Dial (Reorganized) |
| | | 1881–1930 | Century Magazine |
| 1828–1832 | Southern Review | 1883– | Ladies' Home Journal |
| 1830–1898 | Godey's Lady's Book | 1883–1935 | Overland Monthly |
| 1831–1835 | New England Magazine | 1886– | Cosmopolitan |
| | | 1886–1940 | Forum |
| 1833–1865 | Knickerbocker | 1886–1939 | Scribner's Magazine |
| 1834–1864 | Southern Literary Messenger | 1889–1929 | Munseys' |
| 1837–1859 | United States Democratic Review | 1889– | Poet Lore |
| | | 1890–1937 | Review of Reviews |
| 1840–1844 | Dial | 1892– | Sewanee Review |
| 1841–1858 | Graham's | 1892– | Yale Review |
| 1842–1857 | Southern Quarterly Review | 1893–1924 | McClure's |
| | | 1895–1933 | Bookman |
| 1844–1907 | Eclectic Magazine | 1899–1929 | Everybody's |
| 1844–1941 | Living Age | 1902– | South Atlantic Quarterly |
| 1850– | Harper's Magazine | | |
| 1853–1870 | Putnam's | 1906–1919 | Bellman |
| 1857–1916 | Harper's Weekly | 1906–1956 | American |
| 1857– | Atlantic Monthly | 1912– | Poetry |
| 1865– | Catholic World | 1914– | New Republic |

| | | | |
|---|---|---|---|
| 1916– | Theatre Arts Magazine | 1925– | New Yorker |
| 1920–1924 | Freeman | 1934– | The Partisan Review |
| 1921–1925 | Reviewer | 1935–1942 | Southern Review |
| 1924– | American Mercury | 1939– | The Kenyon Review |
| 1924– | Saturday Review of Literature | 1948– | The Hudson Review |
| 1925– | Virginia Quarterly Review | | |

## A Selected List of Some Representative British Literary Magazines
### (Arranged in the order of their founding)

| | | | |
|---|---|---|---|
| 1731–1907 | Gentleman's Magazine | 1869–1916 | Academy |
| 1802–1929 | Edinburgh Review | 1877– | Nineteenth Century, now Twentieth Century |
| 1809– | Quarterly Review | | |
| 1817– | Blackwood's Magazine | 1890–1936 | Review of Reviews |
| 1824–1914 | Westminster Review | 1891–1934 | Bookman |
| 1828–1921 | Athenaeum | 1891– | Strand Magazine |
| 1828– | Spectator | 1893– | Canadian Magazine |
| 1830–1882 | Fraser's | 1894–1897 | Yellow Book |
| 1836– | Dublin Review | 1902– | Times Literary Supplement |
| 1841– | Punch | 1907–1931 | Nation |
| 1845–1886 | British Quarterly Review | 1908–1937 | English Review |
| 1853– | London Quarterly Review | 1912– | Poetry Review |
| | | 1913– | New Statesman |
| 1855– | Saturday Review | 1914–1919 | Egoist |
| 1859–1907 | Macmillan's | 1919–1939 | London Mercury |
| 1860–1939 | Cornhill Magazine | 1922–1939 | Criterion |
| 1865–1901 | Argosy | 1923– | Adelphi |
| 1865– | Fortnightly Review | 1928– | Life and Letters Today |
| 1866– | Contemporary Review | 1932–1953 | Scrutiny |
| | | 1951– | Essays in Criticism |
| | | 1953– | Encounter |

**Literary Periods:** See ENGLISH LITERATURE, PERIODS OF; AMERICAN LITERATURE, PERIODS OF; and *Outline of Literary History.*

Litotes: A form of UNDERSTATEMENT in which a thing is affirmed by stating the negative of its opposite. To say "He was not unmindful" when one means that "He gave careful attention" is to employ *litotes*. Although a common device in ironic expression, *litotes* was also one of the characteristic FIGURES OF SPEECH of Old English poetry.

*Litterateur:* A literary man, one who occupies himself with the writing or criticism or appreciation of literature. Although the term means one who is engaged in literary work or who has adopted literature as a profession, in practical usage it has a connotation of the DILETTANTE or of the "precious."

Little Magazine: A term used to designate literary journals of small circulation, very limited capital, and usually quite short lives, dedicated to the fostering of avant-garde aesthetic ideas and to publishing experimental poetry and prose. Notable early examples were *The Yellow Book* (1894–1897) and *The Savoy* (1896) which gave expression to the English revolt against Victorian ideas, ideals, and materialism. Early American *little magazines* were *The Lark* (1895–1897) and *The Chap-Book* (1894–1898), but the most influential of all such American journals has been *Poetry: A Magazine of Verse*, founded by Harriet Monroe in Chicago in 1912 and still in existence.

The heyday of the *little magazine* came between World War One and the depression of the thirties. In England, in the United States, and particularly in Paris, a generation of artists in revolt against their culture and its standards found in the *little magazine* a sounding board, however small, for their ideas. *The Little Review* (1914–1929), *The Seven Arts* (1916–1917), *The Fugitive* (1922–1925), *The Dial* (after its move to New York in 1916 and to its end in 1929), *Hound and Horn* (1927–1934), *Secession* (1922–1924), *transition* (1927–     ), *Broom* (1921–1924), and *The Double Dealer* (1921–1925) were among the best of hundreds of such publications.

After the depression young writers tended to desert avant-garde aesthetic positions for radical social postures, and the *little magazines* were in large measure casualties of the depression. In the post-World-War-Two world, experimental writing and criticism has found an effective sounding board in university circles, and the present day equivalent of the *little magazine* is frequently a joint student-faculty production operating under a grant from the parent institution.

Thousands of pages of bad experimental poetry, fiction, and criticism were published in the *little magazines* in their heyday, but these debits were more than offset by the fact that James Joyce, T. S. Eliot, Sherwood Anderson, Ernest Hemingway, William Faulkner, Edgar Lee Masters, Ezra Pound, Hart Crane, e. e. cummings, Edmund Wilson, the NEW CRITICS, Gertrude Stein, Thornton Wilder, John Crowe Ransom, and Allen Tate, among many others, found in the pages of the *little magazines* their first sympathetic publication media.

**Little Theatre Movement:** A term applied to a succession of definite efforts to encourage the writing and production of significant plays, as opposed to the more highly commercialized productions designed primarily for long runs and box-office success. The movement was originated by André Antoine in Paris in 1887 for the purpose of trying out certain dramatic experiments in a methodical way. There gathered about Antoine, himself a gifted actor, a group of young authors, whose plays he produced at the *Théâtre Libre* before a select audience of season ticket holders. His attempts to advance the cause of good DRAMA included also the introduction of notable foreign plays by such writers as Tolstoy, Ibsen, Hauptmann, Björnson, Strindberg, and Turgenev. Though Antoine achieved only a limited success, his experiment aided in the development of certain French dramatists (Henri Lavedan, Paul Hervieu, Jules Lemaître, and E. Brieux) and influenced the founding of two other French *little theatres:* Lugné-Poë's *Théâtre de l'Œuvre* (1893) and Jacques Copeau's *Vieux Colombier* (1914). Likewise in Germany there was established in 1889 the *Freie Bühne.* It was followed by a rapid development of native talent: Hauptmann, Max Halbe, Otto Erich Hartlehen, and others.

In England the movement had its beginning in the opening of the Independent Theatre (1891) under the management of Jacob Grein. Shaw, Jones, Pinero, Barrie, Galsworthy, and Barker were to some degree products of the movement in England. In Ireland the Little Theatre (1899) made attempts to encourage new Irish writers and the use of Irish themes. William Boyle, Lennox

Robinson, J. M. Synge, Lady Gregory, and William Butler Yeats wrote for the Abbey players (see CELTIC RENAISSANCE). The beginning of the *little theatre movement* in America came in 1906 and 1907 when three groups were organized in Chicago: The New Theatre, the Robertson Players, and the Hull House Theatre, the latter being especially vigorous. In 1911–1912 came additional establishments: The Little Theatre of Maurice Brown (Chicago), Mrs. Lyman Gale's Toy Theatre (Boston), and the Festival Players of the Henry Street Settlement, the Provincetown Players, and the Washington Square Players (New York). Members of the Washington Square Players formed the Theatre Guild, which operated with spectacular success and was able by 1925 to build its own million-dollar playhouse. A splinter from the Guild formed the Group Theatre, which produced plays by writers like Paul Green and Clifford Odets. Despite these professional successes, however, the *little theatre movement* in America remained essentially local and amateur, spread over thousands of groups in towns and cities across the nation. It sometimes had a strong university flavor, coming largely from the work of George P. Baker at Harvard and later at Yale and Frederich H. Koch at the University of North Carolina. The *little theatre movement* successfully established a flexible theatre for serious writing and acting, brought the DRAMA to thousands who might never otherwise have seen it, and developed men of such talent as Eugene O'Neill, Paul Green, Philip Barry, Thornton Wilder, and R. E. Jones.

A significant outgrowth of the *little theatre movement* came in 1936 with the establishment of the Federal Theatre Project, which annually employed over 13,000 theatre workers and in its three years of existence produced more than 1200 plays. Its purpose was to supplement the commercial stage with serious and experimental DRAMA at low prices.

**Liturgical Drama:** A term sometimes applied to the early phase of MEDIEVAL religious DRAMA when the MYSTERY PLAYS were performed as a part or an extension of the liturgical service of the church. In their earliest form they were in Latin, and were operatic in character, the lines being chanted or sung rather than spoken. The name *liturgical drama* is also sometimes used for the MYSTERY PLAYS developed from the liturgy. See MYSTERY PLAY, MEDIEVAL DRAMA.

**Local Color Writing:** Writing which exploits the speech, dress, mannerisms, habits of thought, and topography peculiar to a certain region. Of course all FICTION has a locale, but *local color writing* exists primarily for the portrayal it presents of the people and life of a geographical setting. About 1880 this interest became dominant in American literature; what was called a "local color movement" developed. The various sectional divisions of America were "discovered." Bret Harte, Mark Twain, and Joaquin Miller wrote of the West; George Washington Cable, Lafcadio Hearn, Mary Noailles Murfree, and Joel Chandler Harris spoke for the South; Sarah Orne Jewett and Mary E. Wilkins Freeman interpreted New England.

*Local color writing* was marked by the attempt at accurate DIALECT reporting, a tendency toward the use of eccentrics as characters, and the use of sentimentalized pathos or whimsical humor in plotting. A subdivision of REALISM, *local color writing* lacked the basic seriousness of true REALISM; by and large it was content to be entertainingly informative about the surface peculiarities of special regions. It emphasized verisimilitude of detail without being concerned often enough about truth to the larger aspects of life or human nature. Although local color NOVELS were written, the bulk of the work done in the movement was in the SKETCH and the SHORT STORY, aimed at the newly developing mass-circulation magazine audience. See REGIONAL LITERATURE.

**Locution:** A term applied to a word or a group of words that constitutes a meaning group. It is also applied to a style of speech or verbal expression, particularly when it involves some peculiarity of IDIOM or manner.

**Lollards:** The name applied to the followers of John Wycliffe, who inspired a popular religious reform movement in England late in the fourteenth century. Lollardism sprang from the clash of two ideals—that of worldly aims, upheld by the rulers of church and state, and that of the self-sacrificing religion, separated from worldly interests, upheld by the humbler elements among the clergy and the laity. Wycliffe himself died in 1384 after sponsoring and aiding in the translation of parts of the Bible into English; but the movement continued to gain strength. In 1395 the *Lollards* presented a petition to Parliament demanding reform in the church. Though King Richard opposed the petition strongly and it was not successful, its terms are important as early expressions of the attitude which triumphed with the Reformation movement in the sixteenth century. It denounced the riches of the clergy, asked that war be declared unchristian, and expressed disbelief in such important Catholic doctrines and practices as transubstantiation, image-worship, and pilgrimages. Though suppressed early in the fifteenth century Lollardism lived on secretly and later flared up in time to furnish a strong native impetus to the Lutheran Reformation in England early in the sixteenth century. This survival of Lollardism helps explain the fact that the English Reformation movement in its early stages was a popular movement rather than a scholarly one. Some *Lollards* were burned as heretics. Early Lollardism is reflected in *Piers Plowman's Creed* (popular attitude). Chaucer's country parson, so sympathetically described in the *Prologue* to the *Canterbury Tales,* was accused by the Host of being a "Loller." Lollardist attitudes find late expression in many of the pamphlets of the Reformation controversy.

**Long Measure:** A STANZA form consisting of four lines of IAMBIC TETRAMETER and riming either *abcb* or *abab.* Compare with BALLAD STANZA, COMMON MEASURE.

**Loose Sentence:** A sentence grammatically complete at some point (or points) before the end; the opposite of a PERIODIC SENTENCE. A simple *loose sentence* consists of an independent clause followed by a dependent clause. Most of the complex sentences we use are loose (the term implies no fault in structure), the PERIODIC SENTENCE being usually reserved for emphatic statements and to secure variety. The constant use of the PERIODIC SENTENCE would impose too great a strain on the reader's attention. *Loose sentences,* however, which are composed of too many dependent clauses, become "stringy."

**Lost Generation:** A term applied to the American writers, most of whom were born around 1900, who fought in the first World War, and who constituted a group reacting against the tendencies of the older writers in the 1920's. Although many of them spent much of their time in Paris, others lived and worked in New York, and some remained in the Middle West and the South. They were very active in the publication of LITTLE MAGAZINES. The term "Lost Generation" came from Gertrude Stein's remark to Hemingway that "You are all a lost generation." Hemingway used it as a motto in his novel *The Sun Also Rises,* whose hero, the emasculated Jake Barnes, is often considered the archetypal man of the generation. It was widely applied to such figures as F. Scott Fitzgerald, Hemingway, Hart Crane, Louis Bromfield, and Malcolm Cowley, as descriptive of the traditional values which had been lost to them as a result of the war and the nature of the modern world.

**Low Comedy:** The opposite of HIGH COMEDY, *low comedy* has been called "elemental comedy," in that it is lacking in seriousness of purpose or subtlety of manner, having little intellectual appeal. Some typical features of *low comedy* are: quarreling, fighting, noisy singing, boisterous conduct in general, boasting, BURLESQUE, trickery, buffoonery, clownishness, drunkenness, coarse jesting, servants' chatter (when unrelated to the serious action), scolding, shrewishness, etc. In English dramatic history *low comedy* appears first as an incidental expansion of the action, often originated by the actors themselves, who speak "more than is set down for them." Thus in MEDIEVAL religious DRAMA Noah's wife exhibits stubbornness and has to be taken into the ark by force and under loud protest, or Pilate or Herod engage in uncalled-for ranting. In the MORALITY PLAYS the elements of *low comedy* became much more pronounced, and the antics of the Vice and other boisterous horse-play were introduced to lend life to the plays. In Elizabethan drama such elements persisted, in spite of their violation of the law of DECORUM, because they were demanded by the public; but playwrights like Shakespeare frequently made them serve serious dramatic purposes (such as relief, marking passage of time, echoing main action). A few of the many examples of *low comedy* in Shakespeare are: the porter scene in *Macbeth,* Launcelot Gobbo and old Gobbo in *The Merchant of Venice,* the Audrey-William love-making scene in *As You Like It,* and the Trinculo-Stephano-Caliban scene in *The Tempest.* The famous Falstaff scenes in *King Henry the Fourth* are examples of how Shakespeare could lift *low comedy* into pure COMEDY by stressing the human and character elements and by infusing an intellectual content into what might otherwise be mere buffoonery. *Low comedy* is not a recognized special type of play, as is the COMEDY OF HUMOURS, for example, but may be found either alone or combined with various sorts of both COMEDY and TRAGEDY. See COMEDY, FARCE, VAUDEVILLE.

**Lyric:** A brief subjective POEM strongly marked by IMAGINATION, melody, and emotion, and creating for the reader a single, unified impression. The early Greeks distinguished between *lyric* and choric poetry by terming that poetry *lyric* which was the expression of the emotion of a single singer accompanied by a lyre, and "choric" those verses which were the expression of a group and were sung by a CHORUS. This distinction has now quite disappeared, though the conception of the *lyric* as the individual and personal emotion of the poet still holds and is, perhaps, the chief basis for discriminating between the *lyric* and other poetic forms. No longer primarily designed to be sung to an accompaniment, the *lyric* nevertheless is essentially melodic since the melody may be secured by a variety of RHYTHM patterns and may be expressed either in rimed or unrimed verses. Subjectivity, too, is an important element of a form which is the personal expression of personal emotion imaginatively phrased. It partakes, in certain high examples, of the quality of ecstasy. With a record of existence for thousands of years in every literature of the world, the *lyric* has naturally been different things to different people at different times. Strict definition is impossible. After devoting a full volume to the record and forms of the *lyric*, Ernest Rhys recognizes frankly the freedom and mobility of the type as a means of poetic expression, but speaks of it ideally as "a carol or love-song in three passages: first, the theme; then an access of emotion, a pensive variation, or an enlargement of the theme; and lastly, the recoil, or the fulfilment, of the melody."

The history of the *lyric* in English literature starts almost with the beginnings of our literature. In that earliest EPIC, *Beowulf,* certain passages clearly have *lyric* qualities. *Deor's Lament* we may call essentially lyrical in purpose. Later the introduction of Latin HYMNS and the NORMAN CONQUEST brought in French and Italian elements. By about 1280 we have in the famous "Sumer is icumen in" what would pass the strictest critic today as a lyrical expression. By 1310 a manuscript collection of poems was made which, in addition to Southern European forms, presented some forty English *lyrics.* Before 1400 Chaucer had written a fair body of *lyrics,* particularly those modeled on French forms. The TROUBADOUR of France had done his work well and had so awakened interest in lyrical forms as to make them common to the various European literatures. Later, Petrarch made current the SONNET. Thomas Wyatt and the Earl of Surrey popularized in England these

Italian lyrical forms, particularly the SONNET, and by the time Tottel's *Miscellany* appeared (1557) the body of English *lyrics* was notably large and creditable. In Elizabethan England the *lyric* burst into full bloom at the touch of such poets as Sidney, Spenser, Daniel, and Shakespeare. SONGS, MADRIGALS, airs, became the very stuff of poetry. Jonson and Herrick carried the tradition further. To seventeenth-century England Cowley introduced the IRREGULAR ODE (a *lyric* form), and later Dryden adopted the form. The romantic revival brought English literature some of its noblest poetry in the ODES of Gray, Collins, Wordsworth, and Coleridge. Burns raised the *lyric* to new power. Coleridge and Wordsworth made it the vehicle of ROMANTICISM. Scott, Byron, Shelley, and Keats molded the form to new perfection. Bryant, Emerson, Whittier, Longfellow, and Poe gave it expression in a new land. Victorian poets spoke through it most frequently. Tennyson, Browning, Rossetti, William Morris, Swinburne— England's greatest poets of the period—were also some of our greatest lyricists. And in twentieth-century England and America the *lyric*—in its various types—is still the most frequently used poetic expression.

The *lyric* is perhaps the most broadly inclusive of all the various types of VERSE. In a sense it could be argued, perhaps, to be not so much a form as a manner of writing. Subjectivity, IMAGINATION, melody, emotion—these qualities have been fairly persistently adhered to by the poets. But as the *lyric* spirit has flourished, the manner has been confined in various ways with the result that we have, within the *lyric* type, numerous sub-classifications. The *lyric* is a genus with many species. HYMNS, SONNETS, SONGS, BALLADS, ODES, ELEGIES, VERS DE SOCIÉTÉ, the whole host of FRENCH FORMS, BALLADE, RONDEL, RONDEAU—all these are varieties of lyrical expression classified according to differing qualities of form and subject matter and mood.

**Lyrical Drama:** A term used for a dramatic poem (see DRAMATIC POETRY) in which the form of DRAMA is used to express LYRIC themes (author's own emotions or ideas of life) instead of relying upon a story as the basis of the action.

*Mabinogion:* A term applied to a collection of old Welsh tales translated by Lady Charlotte Guest from the *Red Book of Hergest,* a Welsh manuscript written in the thirteenth or fourteenth century containing tales written centuries earlier. Only four of these tales, *Pwyll, Prince of Dyved; Branwen, Daughter of Llyr; Manawyddan, Son of Llyr;* and *Math, Son of Mathonwy* (the so-called "four branches"), are in the strictest sense of the word included in the term *mabinogion.* Although some modern authors follow Lady Charlotte Guest in explaining this word as meaning "a collection of tales for the young," later authorities explain *mabinogion* as the plural of *mabinogi,* "a collection of tales every young poet should know," a *mabinog* being a sort of literary apprentice, a young man receiving instruction from a qualified BARD. For a classification of the contents of the *Mabinogion* and for the possible relation of the tales to Arthurian romances, see WELSH LITERATURE.

**Macaronic Verse:** A type of humorous VERSE which mingles two or more languages. More especially it refers to poems incorporating modern words (given Latin or Greek endings) with Latin or Greek. The origin of this pleasing sort of nonsense is credited to a Benedictine monk, Teofilo Folengo (1491–1544), who wrote a MOCK HEROIC called *Liber Macaronicus.* Verse of the sort was soon written in France and other European countries; the best example in English is said to be the *Polemo-Middinia* credited to William Drummond of Hawthornden. The following, by "E.C.B.," will be a self-explanatory example to anyone who knows his Latin (or his Mother Goose):

> Cane carmen SIXPENCE, pera plena rye,
> De multis atris avibus coctis in a pie:
> Simul hæc apert'est, cantat omnis grex,
> Nonne permirabile, quod vidit ille rex?
> Dimidium rex esus, misit ad reginam
> Quod reliquit illa, sending back catinum.
> Rex fuit in aerario, multo nummo tumens;
> In culina Domina, bread and mel consumens;
> Ancell' in horticulo, hanging out the clothes,
> Quum descendens cornix rapuit her nose.

**Macron:** The name of the symbol ($^-$) used to indicate a long syllable in QUANTITATIVE VERSE or, frequently, the stressed syllable in accentual verse.

**Madrigal:** A short LYRIC, usually dealing with love or a PASTORAL theme and designed for—or at least suitable for—a musical setting. In the ELIZABETHAN PERIOD the term was used to describe a kind of SONG sung without accompaniment by five or six voices with intricate interweaving of words and melody. The Italian *madrigal* usually consisted of six to thirteen lines based on three RIMES. Today the term is used quite loosely. Shakespeare's "Take, O, take those lips away" from *Measure for Measure* is a *madrigal*.

**Magazine:** A term applied to any of several kinds of periodical miscellanies containing various kinds of material by several authors. See LITERARY MAGAZINES for a listing of *magazines* of importance to literary study.

*Magnum opus:* A great work, a masterpiece. Formerly the term was used in all seriousness, but nowadays it often carries with it a suggestion of IRONY or SARCASM.

**Malapropism:** An inappropriateness of speech resulting from the use of one word for another which has some similarity to it. The term is derived from a character, Mrs. Malaprop, in Sheridan's *The Rivals,* who was constantly giving vent to such expressions as the following: "as headstrong as an allegory on the banks of the Nile," "a progeny of learning," "illiterate him, I say, quite from your memory."

**Malediction:** A curse. The opposite of benediction since it invokes evil rather than good. The famous "Cursed be he that moves my bones" used as an epitaph for Shakespeare is an example.

**Manners, Comedy of:** See COMEDY OF MANNERS.

**Manners, Novel of:** See NOVEL OF MANNERS.

**Manuscript, Medieval:** As the precursor of the modern printed book and as the medium through which both classical and medieval literatures were preserved for modern times, the *medieval manuscript* has much interest. The art of manuscript-making was highly developed; the finer existing "illuminated" manuscripts and early printed books modeled on them show an artistry perhaps superior to that of the best examples of modern book-making. The Gutenberg Bible (1456), for example, has been called the finest printed book in existence. As no mechanical means such as printing existed for multiplying copies, each manuscript required for its manufacture an infinite amount of skilled labor. Parchment was first employed, the finest kind being vellum (made from calf-skin), though paper was employed in the later Middle Ages. The actual writing was done chiefly in the monasteries, first by ordinary monks and later by professional scribes. The process of making the book included (1) the copying of the text by the scribe on separate sheets, (2) the inspection by the corrector, (3) the insertion of the capital letters and rubrics and other colored decorative matter by the rubricator and illuminator, (4) the binding by a binder who arranged the sheets (usually by folding a group of four sheets once to make a "quire" of eight leaves of sixteen pages) and completed the binding by the use of wooden boards, leather, and velvet. The result was a substantial "manuscript" in form much like a modern book of large size but far sturdier in construction. The illuminator did his work with great care. Favorite colors were gold and red and blue, though green and purple and yellow were frequently employed. In spite of losses by fire, war, robbery, and neglect, thousands of *medieval manuscripts* are still in existence and are carefully preserved in numerous public and private libraries. Early printed books (see INCUNABULUM) were modeled on the manuscript. In England, many *medieval manuscripts,* perhaps containing literature now lost, are thought to have been destroyed as a result of the suppression of the monasteries during the Protestant Reformation.

**Marinism:** An affected poetic STYLE practiced by the Italian poet G. Marini[1] (1569–1625) and his followers. It is the manifestation in Italy of a general tendency toward a strained, flamboyant, or shocking STYLE which accompanied the later phases of the RENAISSANCE in Western Europe, in some respects analogous to the BAROQUE in art. Marini expressed this aspect of his creed thus:

> Astonishment's the poet's aim and aid:
> Who cannot startle best had stick to trade.
> (Fletcher's translation)

A typical conceit of Marini is his calling stars "blazing half-dimes of the celestial mint." Another aspect of *Marinism* was its "effeminate voluptuousness," stressed by Professor J. B. Fletcher. Though it is not probable that Marini's influence affected Donne, some other English METAPHYSICAL poets were influenced; e.g.,

[1]Or Marino.

Lord Herbert of Cherbury, Thomas Stanley, Sir Edward Sher-
burne, and Richard Crashaw. (On this point the works of the
Italian scholar Mario Praz may be consulted.) See EUPHUISM,
CONCEIT, GONGORISM, METAPHYSICAL VERSE, BAROQUE.

**Marprelate Controversy:** In the 1580's the Puritan opposition to
the bishops of the established church in England, whose power
was greatly strengthened by state support, expressed itself in
outspoken pamphlets. Some of the authors of these Puritan tracts
were severely punished—one ultimately executed—and in 1585 the
censorship over such publications was made more rigid by a pro-
vision limiting printing rights to London and the two universities.
In defiance of these regulations the Puritan party began issuing, in
1588, a series of violent attacks on the episcopacy, printed sur-
reptitiously and signed by the pen-name "Martin Marprelate." The
attacks were answered with corresponding scurrility by the conservatives, including Robert Greene, John Lyly, and Thomas Nash.
The authorship of the Marprelate pamphlets has never been
definitely established, but whoever the author was or whoever
the authors were, they and their opponents supplied interesting
examples of spirited prose SATIRES. The controversy was suppressed
by the death in prison of one alleged author and the execution in
1593 of two others.

**Masculine Rime:** RIME that falls on the stressed and concluding
syllables of the rime-words. See RIME, FEMININE RIME.

**Masked Comedy:** See COMMEDIA DELL' ARTE.

**Masque:** In England as well as in other European countries there
existed in medieval times (partly at least as survivals or adaptations
of ancient pagan seasonal ceremonies) species of games or spectacles characterized by a procession of masked figures. In these
DISGUISINGS or MUMMINGS, which were usually of a popular or
folk character, a procession of masquers would go through the
streets, enter house after house, silently dance, play at dice with
the citizens or with each other, and pass on. Adopted by the
aristocracy, these games, modified by characteristics borrowed
from civic pageants, chivalric customs, sword-dances, and the
RELIGIOUS DRAMA, developed into elaborate and costly spectacles,
which themselves evolved into the magnificent entertainments

known as *masques*. Because of this gradual evolution of the form and the scanty character of the records it is impossible to say with assurance just when the *masque* actually came into existence. The famous Epiphany spectacle of 1512, given by and participated in by Henry VIII, is sometimes referred to as the first English *masque*.

The chief development of the *masque* came, however, in the latter part of Elizabeth's reign and, especially, in the reigns of James I and Charles I. In the first third of the seventeenth century the *masque* reached its climax under such poets as Daniel, Beaumont, Middleton, Ben Jonson, and others. The greatest development was due to the poetic and dramatic genius of Jonson, poet laureate, and Inigo Jones, famous court architect and deviser of stage machinery. The "essential" *masque*, as distinguished from the "literary" *masque* (e.g., *Comus*), has been described by the Rev. Ronald Bayne as "the appeal of the moment to the eye and the ear, the blaze of colour and light, the mist of perfume, the succession of rapidly changing scenes and tableaux crowded with wonderful and beautiful figures. All the gods of Olympus, all the monsters of Tartarus, all the heroes of history, all the ladies of romance, the fauns, the satyrs, the fairies, the witches—all these were presented to the eye, while every kind of musical instrument charmed the ear, and eye and ear together were delighted by an elaboration of dance and measured motion which has never been known since."[1]

*Masques* became increasingly expensive of production, almost unbelievable amounts being expended in costumes, scenery, properties, and for professional musicians, dancers, actors, etc. In the *masque* proper, which was the arrival and set dancing of masked figures, the actors were amateurs drawn from courtly society itself—princes and princesses, even queens and kings, taking part. With the development by Jonson of the ANTIMASQUE, the dramatic and literary qualities increased. Mythological and PASTORAL elements were emphasized, Jonson maintaining (against Daniel and Jones) that the *masque* should be based upon some poetic idea and the action should be significant as well as spectacular, so that Milton's *Comus* (1634), one of the best known of all *masques*, represents a legitimate development of what was originally little but spectacle. The *masque* commonly was a feature of some celebra-

[1]From *Cambridge History of English Literature* (American edition), Vol. VI, p. 371. Reprinted by permission of The Macmillan Company.

tion, such as a wedding or coronation, and served as a formal preliminary entertainment to a court ball, and was frequently employed at the entertainments in the INNS OF COURT. *Masques* exerted much influence upon the poetry and DRAMA of the RENAISSANCE. Spenser, for example, incorporates masque-like episodes in his *The Faerie Queene* (e.g., the procession of the Seven Deadly Sins in Book I, Canto iv, and the *masque* of Cupid in III, xii). The effect upon the popular DRAMA itself was probably great, since some dramatists wrote for both the court and the London stage, and the latter gradually took on refinements imitated from courtly performances. Peele's *Arraignment of Paris* is a PASTORAL play much like a *masque*. Many of Shakespeare's plays show the influence; the betrothal *masque* in *The Tempest* is an example. *As You Like It* has been called a mere "series of tableaux and groupings," masque-like in the lack of serious action, in the prominence of music, and in the spectacular appearance of Hymen as a DEUS EX MACHINA at the end. The glorious era of the *masque* ended with the triumph of the Puritan Revolution (1642). See ANTIMASQUE.

**Maxim:** A short, concise statement, usually drawn from experience and inculcating some practical advice; an ADAGE. "When in doubt, win the trick," a saying of Hoyle's, is an example of a *maxim* in bridge. See APHORISM, PROVERB.

**Medieval Drama:** A general term used to include all forms of DRAMA in the Middle Ages, though the religious drama and its allied forms are usually meant by the phrase. The medieval religious drama was an outgrowth of the liturgical services of the church. As early as the tenth century, perhaps in Northern France, TROPES or musical elaborations of the church services, particularly of the Easter Mass, developed into true DRAMA when the Latin lines telling the story of the Resurrection, instead of being sung antiphonally by the two parts of the choir, were sung or spoken by priests who impersonated the two angels and the three Marys in the scene at the tomb of Christ.

Such dramatic TROPES later become detached from the liturgical service, and *medieval drama* was born. That such performances appeared early in England is shown by the existence of the famous *Concordia Regularis* (ca.975), a complete set of instructions (stage directions) supplied to the Benedictine monks by the Bishop of Winchester. This record is earlier than any similar record from the Continent. The conscious dramatic intent is shown in the first few lines of the *Concordia:* "While the third lesson is being chanted, let four brethren vest themselves. Let one of these, vested in an alb, enter as though to take part in the service, and let him approach the sepulchre without attracting attention and sit there quietly with a palm in his hand . . . and let them all . . . stepping delicately as those who seek something, approach the sepulchre" (Chambers' translation). Dramatic TROPES developed around the Christmas and Easter services.

This use of the dramatic method for the purpose of making vivid religious rites and instruction must have struck a responsive chord in the medieval audience, and it was not long till further important developments, the stages of which cannot now be exactly traced, took place. The performances were transferred from the church to the outdoors; Latin gave way to native language everyone could understand; and eventually the performances became secularized when the town authorities, utilizing the trade guilds as dramatic companies, took charge of the production of the plays. Eventually great CYCLES of Scriptural plays developed in which the whole plan of salvation was dramatically set forth (see MYSTERY PLAY). Plays employing the same technique as the Scriptural plays but based upon the lives of saints, especially miracles performed by saints including the Virgin Mary (MIRACLE PLAYS, or SAINTS' PLAYS), also developed about A.D. 1100, though they seem not to have been numerous in England. Much later (*ca.*1400) the MORALITY PLAY (dramatization of a moral ALLEGORY) became popular and with the somewhat similar play known as INTERLUDE became an immediate precursor of ELIZABETHAN DRAMA. There was also a considerable body of FOLK DRAMA in the late Middle Ages, performed out of doors on such festival days as Hock Tuesday—Robin Hood plays, Sword-dance Plays, MUMMINGS and DISGUISINGS. Perhaps also there were plays based on MEDIEVAL ROMANCES. But as these forms were often non-literary, the existing records make it difficult to estimate their extent or the exact nature of their influence upon subsequent dramatic tradition.

The CYCLIC DRAMA (MYSTERY PLAYS) and the MORALITIES doubtless played an important part in supplying entertainment and instruction in the later Middle Ages, becoming so secularized as to bring on the disapproval of the church. The development of secular elements, especially the stressing of comic features such as the shrewish behavior of Noah's wife or the addition of comic scenes not demanded by the serious action, such as the sheep-stealing episode in the Towneley *Second Shepherd's Play*, led definitely toward Elizabethan COMEDY. Though it is difficult to analyze the full influence exerted by *medieval drama* upon later DRAMA, it is certain, as Professor Schelling remarks, that "on the upgrowth of the literatures of modern Europe the old sacred drama exercised no small or inappreciable effect," and that in England "it was in the ruins and débris of the miracle play and morality that ELIZABETHAN DRAMA struck its deepest roots."[1] Professor Nicoll, too, observes, "There is freshness of fancy here, a free treatment of the material, a rich fund of humour, and at times a true sense of the profound and tragic. If with the mysteries we are but on the border of drama proper, we can see clearly the various traditions which later were brought to culmination in the time of Queen Elizabeth."[2] For the method of performance of the medieval religious drama see MYS-TERY PLAY. See DRAMA, MIRACLE PLAY, LITURGICAL DRAMA, TROPE, MORALITY PLAY, FOLK DRAMA, INTERLUDE.

**Medieval Manuscript:** See MANUSCRIPT, MEDIEVAL.

**Medieval Romance:** For the application of the word "romance" to this type of narrative, see ROMANCE. A useful definition by Dorothy Everett (*Essays and Studies,* 1929) may be quoted: "Medieval romances are stories of adventure in which the chief parts are played by knights, famous kings, or distressed ladies, acting most often under the impulse of love, religious faith, or, in many, the mere desire for adventure." Though the origin of the *medieval romance* cannot be traced with confidence, it appears in Old French literature of the twelfth century as a form which supplants in popularity the older CHANSON DE GESTE, an EPIC form. In distinguishing the *romance* from the EPIC one may note that the EPIC reflects an heroic age whereas the *romance* reflects a chivalric age; the EPIC has weight and solidity, whereas the *romance* exhibits mystery and fantasy; the EPIC does not stress rank or social distinctions, important in the *romance;* the tragic seriousness of the EPIC is not matched in the lighter-hearted *romance;* the heroic figures of the

---

[1] F. E. Schelling, *Elizabethan Drama,* Houghton Mifflin Company, Vol. I, 1908, p. 1. Reprinted by permission of and arrangement with the publishers.

[2] Allardyce Nicoll, *British Drama,* Thomas Y. Crowell Company, 1925, p. 29. Reprinted by permission of the publishers.

EPIC are more consistently conceived than the heroes of *romance;* where the EPIC hero aims at high achievement, the hero of *romance* is usually satisfied with more or less aimless adventure; the EPIC observes narrative UNITY, whereas the STRUCTURE of the *romance* is loose; love is absent or of minor interest in the EPIC, whereas it is supreme in the *romances;* EPIC fighting is serious and well motivated, whereas fighting in the *romances* is spontaneous; the EPIC uses the dramatic method of having the characters speak for themselves, whereas the reader of a *romance* is kept conscious of a NARRATOR. The *romances* became extremely popular in Western European countries, occupying a place comparable with that of the NOVEL in modern literature. The earliest *romances* were in VERSE (hence the term METRICAL ROMANCES), but prose was also employed later. The materials for the early French *romances* were drawn chiefly from the Charlemagne material or CHANSONS DE GESTE ("Matter of France"), ancient history and literature ("Matter of Rome the Great"), and Celtic lore, especially Arthurian material ("Matter of Britain").

*Romances,* most of them based upon French originals, were being produced in English as early as the thirteenth century. They flourished in the fourteenth century, and continued to be produced in the fifteenth and sixteenth centuries, though the disfavor which they met at the hands of RENAISSANCE HUMANISTS caused them to lose standing, and RENAISSANCE versions as well as versions appearing in seventeenth- and eighteenth-century CHAPBOOKS are frequently degenerate forms, written to appeal chiefly to the middle and lower social classes. Middle English *romances* may be grouped on the basis of their subject-matter. The "Matter of England" includes stories based upon Germanic (including English) tradition and embraces *King Horn* (ca.1225), *Richard Lionheart* (before 1300), *Beves of Hampton* (ca.1300), *Havelock the Dane* (ca.1300), *Guy of Warwick* (ca.1300), and *Athelstan* (ca.1350). The "Matter of France" includes stories of Charlemagne and William of Orange, drawn from the CHANSONS DE GESTE. Important *romances* of the group are *Sir Ferumbras* (ca.1375), *Otuel* (ca. 1300), *The Song of Roland* (late fourteenth century), and *Huon of Bordeaux* (fifteenth century). The "Matter of Antiquity" includes various legends of Alexander the Great, legends of Thebes, and legends of Troy (including Chaucer's famous *Troilus and Criseyde*). The "Matter of Britain" includes the important Arthurian literature and is represented by such classics as the fourteenth-century MET-

RICAL ROMANCE, *Sir Gawain and the Green Knight* and the fifteenth-century prose *Le Morte Darthur* of Malory. The Arthurian *romances* developing about the legend of the pseudo-historical King Arthur (see ARTHURIAN LEGEND) had eventually developed into great CYCLES of stories in Old French literature, some of the heroes of which, such as Tristram and Lancelot, did not belong to the original legend of Arthur. They were greatly elaborated in the bulky thirteenth-century French prose *romances* ("VULGATE Romances") which became the chief sources for such English treatments of Arthurian themes as Malory's. A fifth group might include *romances* of miscellaneous origin, especially Oriental. Examples are *Amis and Amiloun* (before 1300), *Floris and Blanchefleur* (*ca.* 1250), *Sir Isumbras* (1350–1400), and *Ipomydon* (fourteenth century).

The MIDDLE ENGLISH *romances* are largely in verse, a few alliterative, others in COUPLETS or stanzaic forms borrowed from France. In comparison with French *romances* they usually show inferior artistry, less attention to psychological treatment (as COURTLY-LOVE characteristics), less sophistication, more credulity and use of the grotesque (like Richard's eating the lion's heart), and a higher moral tone. See ROMANCE, ARTHURIAN LEGEND, COURTLY LOVE, MIDDLE ENGLISH.

**Meiosis:** Intentional UNDERSTATEMENT for humorous or satiric effect and occasionally for emphasis. See UNDERSTATEMENT, LITOTES, IRONY.

**Melodrama:** A play based on a romantic PLOT and developed sensationally, with little regard for convincing MOTIVATION and with a constant appeal to the emotions of the audience. The object is to keep the audience thrilled by the awakening, no matter how, of strong feelings of pity or horror or joy. POETIC JUSTICE is superficially secured, the characters (who are either very good or very bad) being rewarded or punished according to their deeds. Though typically a *melodrama* has a happy ending, TRAGEDIES which use much of the same technique are sometimes referred to as melodramatic. Likewise by a further extension of the term stories are sometimes said to be melodramatic in character. T. H. Dickinson has listed the qualities of *melodramas:* (1) they are governed by force rather than by sentiment or emotion; (2) the story is developed by action, circumstance, and "machinery" rather than by the tracing of motives or personal revelation; (3) the characters are types; (4) within the types the characters are arranged by the most rudimentary of moral divergencies, the struggle always being between the good and the bad; (5) the action takes place on a plastic stage, with rapid changes of scene and action requiring the aid of the imagination.

The term literally means "a play with music," and at one time it was applied to the OPERA in a broad sense. *Melodrama* came into widespread use in England in the nineteenth century as a device to circumvent the Licensing Act, which restricted "legitimate" plays to the PATENT THEATRES but which allowed musical entertainments in other theatres. The use of songs, recitative, and incidental music disguised the dramatic nature of popular stage pieces, and they came to be known as *melodramas*. The first English *melodrama* is believed to have been Thomas Holcroft's *A Tale of Mystery*, produced in 1802. These *melodramas* usually exhibited the deplorable characteristics already listed, and finally the term by extension was applied to these characteristics independent of the presence or absence of music.

**Memoirs:** A form of autobiographical writing dealing with the recollections of prominent people or people who have been a part of or have witnessed significant events. *Memoirs* differ from AUTOBIOGRAPHY proper in that they are usually concerned with personalities and actions other than those of the writer himself, whereas the AUTOBIOGRAPHY lays a heavier stress on the inner and private life of its subject.

**Mesostich:** See ACROSTIC.

**Metaphor:** An implied ANALOGY which imaginatively identifies one object with another and ascribes to the first one or more of the qualities of the second or invests the first with emotional or imaginative qualities associated with the second. It is one of the TROPES; that is, one of the principal devices by which poetic "turns" on the meaning of words are achieved. I. A. Richards' distinction between the TENOR and the VEHICLE of a *metaphor* has been widely accepted and is very useful. The TENOR is the idea being expressed or the

# Metaphor

subject of the comparison; the VEHICLE is the IMAGE by which this idea is conveyed or the subject communicated. When Shakespeare writes

> That time of year thou mayst in me behold
> When yellow leaves, or none, or few, do hang
> Upon those boughs which shake against the cold,
> Bare ruined choirs, where late the sweet birds sang,

the TENOR is old age, the VEHICLE is the season of late fall or early winter, conveyed through a group of IMAGES unusually complex in their implications. The TENOR and VEHICLE taken together constitute the FIGURE OF SPEECH, the TROPE, the "turn" in meaning which the *metaphor* conveys. The purposes for using *metaphors* can vary widely. At one extreme, the VEHICLE may merely be a means of decorating the TENOR; at the other extreme, the TENOR may merely be an excuse for having the VEHICLE. ALLEGORY, for example, may be thought of as an elaborate and consistently constructed extended *metaphor* in which the TENOR is never expressed. In the simplest kinds of *metaphors* there is an obvious direct resemblance that exists objectively between the TENOR and the VEHICLE, and in some *metaphors,* particularly those which lend themselves to elaborate CONCEITS, the relationship between TENOR and VEHICLE is in the mind of the maker of the *metaphor.* The first kind tends to be sensuous and the second witty.

Aristotle praised the *metaphor* as "the greatest thing by far" for the poet, and saw it as the product of his insight which permitted him to find the similarities in seemingly dissimilar things. Modern criticism follows Aristotle in placing a similarly high premium on the poet's abilities in the making of *metaphors,* and ANALYTICAL CRITICISM tends to find almost as much rich suggestiveness in the differences between the things compared as it does in the recognition of surprising but unsuspected similarities. Cleanth Brooks uses the term "functional *metaphor*" to describe the way in which the *metaphor* is able to have "referential" and "emotive" characteristics and to go beyond them and become a direct means in itself of representing a truth incommunicable by any other means. Clearly when a *metaphor* performs this function, it is behaving as a SYMBOL.

*Metaphors* may be simple, that is, may occur in the single isolated comparison, or a large *metaphor* may function as the CONTROLLING IMAGE of a whole work (see Edward Taylor's poem quoted in the article on CONTROLLING IMAGE), or a series of VE-

HICLES may all be associated with a single TENOR, as in Hamlet's "To be or not to be" soliloquy. In this last kind of case, however, unless the IMAGES can harmoniously build the TENOR without impressing the reader with a sense of their incongruity, the danger of a MIXED FIGURE is grave.

The whole nature of our language is highly metaphorical. Most of our modern speech, which now seems prosaic enough, was once largely metaphorical. Our ABSTRACT TERMS are borrowed from physical objects. Natural objects and actions have passed over into abstractions because of some inherent metaphorical significance. Thus "transgression"—which today signifies a misdemeanor, an error, or mistake—formerly meant "to cross a line." The metaphorical significance has been lost—is said to be "dead"—and the former figure of speech now stands simply for an abstraction. (It is thus, in fact, that ABSTRACT TERMS possibly first came into language; early man was necessarily content simply to name the objects about him which he could see and feel and smell.) See IMAGE, TROPE, FIGURE OF SPEECH, CONTROLLING IMAGE, ALLEGORY.

**Metaphysical Conceit:** A highly ingenious kind of CONCEIT widely used by the metaphysical poets, who explored all areas of knowledge to find in the startlingly esoteric or the shockingly commonplace telling and unusual analogies for their ideas. The use of such unusual CONCEITS as CONTROLLING IMAGES in their poems is a hallmark of the writers of METAPHYSICAL POETRY. The *metaphysical conceit* often exploits verbal logic to the point of the grotesque, and it sometimes achieves such extravagant turns on meaning that it becomes absurd, as when Richard Crashaw writes of Mary Magdalene's eyes as

> Two walking baths; two weeping motions,
> Portable and compendious oceans.

But when a *metaphysical conceit* strikes from our minds the same spark of recognition which the poet had, so that it gives us a perception of a real but previously unsuspected similarity that is enlightening, it speaks to both our minds and our emotions with force, as in Donne's "The Flea" or his comparison of the union of himself with his lover in the figure of a draftsman's compass in "A Valediction Forbidding Mourning" or in Taylor's "Huswifery" (quoted in the article on CONTROLLING IMAGE). See METAPHYSICAL POETRY, CONCEIT, CONTROLLING IMAGE, METAPHOR.

**Metaphysical Poetry:** Sometimes used in the broad sense of philosophical poetry, VERSE dealing with metaphysics, poetry "unified
by a philosophical conception of the universe and of the rôle assigned to the human spirit in the great drama of existence"
(H. J. C. Grierson). In this sense Lucretius and Dante wrote *metaphysical poetry*. Herbert Read sees it as the "emotional apprehension of thought," *felt thought*, to be contrasted with the LYRIC, and
regards some of the poetry of Chapman and Wordsworth, as well
as that of John Donne and his followers, as *metaphysical*.

Commonly, however, the term is used to designate the work of
the seventeenth-century writers referred to as the "Metaphysical
Poets." They formed a school in the sense of employing similar
methods and of being actuated by a spirit of revolt against the romantic conventionalism of Elizabethan love poetry, in particular
the PETRARCHAN CONCEIT. Their tendency toward psychological
analysis of the emotions of love and religion, their penchant for
the novel and the shocking, their use of the METAPHYSICAL CONCEIT,
and the extremes to which they sometimes carried their techniques
resulted frequently in obscurity, rough VERSE, and strained IMAGERY.
These faults gave them a bad reputation in the NEO-CLASSIC PE-
RIOD. However, there has been a twentieth century revival of interest
in their work and admiration for their accomplishments. Consequently the reader will find the word *metaphysical* used in both a
derogatory and a complimentary sense.

The characteristics of the best *metaphysical poetry* are logical
elements in a technique intended to express honestly, if unconven-
tionally, the poet's sense of the complexities and contradictions of
life. The poetry is intellectual, analytical, psychological, disillu-
sioning, bold; absorbed in thoughts of death, physical love, religious
devotion. The DICTION is simple as compared with that of the
ELIZABETHAN or the NEO-CLASSIC PERIODS, and echoes the words
and the cadences of common speech. The IMAGERY is drawn from
the commonplace or the remote, actual life or erudite sources, the
figure itself often being elaborated with self-conscious ingenuity.
The FORM is frequently that of an argument with the poet's lover,
with God, or with himself. The metaphysical poets wrote of God
and of theology, of the court and of the church, of love and of
nature—often elaborately, it is true—but usually with a high regard for FORM and the more intricate subtleties of METER and
RIME. Yet the VERSE is often intentionally rough; Ben Jonson thought
Donne "deserved hanging" for not observing ACCENT. The rough-

ness may be explained in part by the dominance of thought over strict FORM, in part by the fact that ruggedness or irregularity of movement goes naturally with a sense of the seriousness and perplexity of life, with the realistic method, with the spirit of revolt, and with the sense of an argument cast in speech rather than song.

If the results of the metaphysical manner are not always happy, if the unexpected details and surprising figures are not always integrated imaginatively and emotionally, it must be remembered that these poets were attempting a more difficult task than confronts the complacent writer of conventional VERSE. Their failures appear most strikingly in their fantastic METAPHYSICAL CONCEITS. When they succeed—as they often do—their poetry, arising out of their own sense of incongruity and confusion, is an effective "emotional apprehension of thought," hauntingly real to us in our perplexing world.

The term *metaphysical* was first applied to Donne in derogation of his excessive use of philosophy by Dryden in 1693, but its present use to designate a special poetic manner originated with Samuel Johnson's description of *metaphysical poetry* in his "Life of Cowley."

No exact list of metaphysical poets can be drawn up. Donne was the acknowledged leader. Crashaw and Cowley have been called the most typically *metaphysical*. Some were Protestant religious mystics, like Herbert, Vaughan, and Traherne; some Catholic, like Crashaw; some were CAVALIER LYRICISTS, like Carew and Lovelace; some were satirists, like Donne and Cleveland; one was an American clergyman, Edward Taylor. The new recognition that has come to the metaphysical poets has arisen from a realization of the seriousness of their art, an interest in their spirit of revolt, their REALISM, their intellectualism, and other affinities with modern interests, as well as from the fact that they produced some fine poetry. T. S. Eliot, John Crowe Ransom, and Allen Tate are modern poets affected by the metaphysical influence. See CONCEIT, METAPHYSICAL CONCEIT, CONTROLLING IMAGE, BAROQUE, MARINISM.

**Meter:** The recurrence in poetry of a rhythmic pattern, or the RHYTHM established by the regular or almost regular occurrence of similar units of RHYTHM. In poetry there are four basic kinds of rhythmic patterns: (1) QUANTITATIVE, in which the RHYTHM is established through units containing regular successions of long syllables and short syllables; this is the classical *meter;* (2) accentual,

# Metonymy

in which the occurrence of a syllable marked by STRESS or ACCENT determines the basic unit regardless of the number of unstressed or unaccented syllables surrounding the stressed syllable; OLD ENGLISH VERSIFICATION employs this kind of *meter,* and so does SPRUNG RHYTHM; (3) syllabic, in which the number of syllables in a line is fixed, although the ACCENT varies; much Romance versification employs this *meter;* and (4) accentual-syllabic, in which both the number of syllables and the number of ACCENTS are fixed or nearly fixed; when the term *meter* is used in English it usually refers to accentual-syllabic RHYTHM.

The rhythmic unit within the line is called a FOOT. In English accentual-syllabic VERSE, the standard feet are: IAMBIC ($\smile$ —), TROCHAIC (— $\smile$), ANAPESTIC ($\smile$ $\smile$ —), DACTYLLIC (— $\smile$ $\smile$), SPONDAIC (— —), and PYRRHIC ($\smile$ $\smile$), although others sometimes occur. The number of feet in a line forms another means of describing the *meter.* The following are the standard English lines: MONOMETER, one foot; DIMETER, two feet; TRIMETER, three feet; TETRAMETER, four feet; PENTAMETER, five feet; HEXAMETER, six feet, also called the ALEXANDRINE; HEPTAMETER, seven feet, also called the "FOURTEENER" when the feet are IAMBIC. See ACCENT, SUBSTITUTION, CATALEXIS, OLD ENGLISH VERSIFICATION, QUANTITATIVE VERSE, FOOT, SCANSION.

**Metonymy:** A common FIGURE OF SPEECH which is characterized by the substitution of a term naming an object closely associated with the word in mind for the word itself. In this way we commonly speak of the king as "the crown," an object closely associated with kingship thus being made to stand for "king." So, too, in the book of Genesis we read, "In the sweat of thy face shalt thou eat bread," a FIGURE OF SPEECH in which "sweat" represents that with which it is closely associated, "hard labor." See HYPALLAGE, SYNECDOCHE.

**Metrical Accent:** The ACCENT demanded by the RHYTHM pattern of a VERSE of poetry. See ACCENT.

**Metrical Romance:** A romantic TALE in VERSE. The term is applied both to such medieval verse ROMANCES as *Sir Gawain and the Green Knight* and to the type of verse ROMANCES produced by Sir Walter Scott (*The Lady of the Lake, Marmion*) and Lord Byron (*Bride of Abydos, The Giaour*). The latter kind reflects the ten-

dencies of ROMANTICISM in its freedom of technique and its preference for remote settings (the past in Scott, the Near East in Byron)
as well as in its sentimental qualities. See MEDIEVAL ROMANCE.

**Metrics:** The systematic examination of the patterns of RHYTHM
in poetry, and the formulation of principles describing their nature;
another term for PROSODY.

**Middle English:** English as spoken and written in the period following the NORMAN CONQUEST and preceding the Modern English
period beginning at the RENAISSANCE. The dates most commonly
given are 1100 to 1500, though both are approximate dates, as the
NORMAN CONQUEST came in 1066 and some writings earlier than
1500 (e.g., Malory's *Le Morte Darthur*) may properly be called
"modern" English. For the changes in the language which mark
*Middle English,* see ENGLISH LANGUAGE.

**Middle English Period:** The period in English literature between
the replacement of French by MIDDLE ENGLISH as the language of
court and art and the early appearances of definitely modern English writings, roughly the period between 1350 and 1500. The Age
of Chaucer (1350–1400) was marked by political and religious unrest, the Black Death (1348–1350), Wat Tyler's Rebellion (1381),
and the rise of the LOLLARDS. The fifteenth century was badly torn
by the Wars of the Roses. There was a steadily increasing nationalistic spirit in England, and at the same time early traces of HUMANISM
were appearing.

The great CYCLES of MYSTERY PLAYS flourished, and toward the
end of the period the MORALITY came into existence, and the last
years of the fifteenth century saw the arrival of the INTERLUDE,
while the FOLK DRAMA was popular among the common people.
In prose it was the period of Wycliffe's sermons and his translation
of the Bible, of Mandeville's *Travels,* of the medieval CHRONICLES,
of prose ROMANCES, and, supremely, of Malory's *Le Morte Darthur.*
ROMANCES, both prose and metrical, continued to be popular, with
*Sir Gawain and the Green Knight,* as the finest example. The period
between 1350 and 1400 was a rich poetic age: it saw the first truly
major English poet, Chaucer, as well as poetry like *The Pearl, The
Vision of Piers Plowman,* and Gower's *Confessio Amantis.* There
was a revival of ALLITERATIVE VERSE, although the accentual-syllabic
METERS of Chaucer and his school eventually carried the day. The

fifteenth century was a weak poetic age; its poetry consisted chiefly of Chaucerian imitations, and only Hoccleve, Skelton, and James I of Scotland gave it any distinction. The popular BALLAD flourished. With the establishment of the Tudor Kings on the English throne in 1485, however, England once more had internal peace, and it possessed a flexible language that was very close to modern English and had a powerful dramatic tradition. The glories of the RENAISSANCE were almost ready to burgeon forth.

*Miles gloriosus:* The braggart soldier, a STOCK CHARACTER in COMEDY. The type appeared in Greek COMEDY, was stressed by the Roman playwrights (Terence's *Thraso* and Plautus' *Miles Gloriosus*), and adopted by RENAISSANCE dramatists. An early example is Ralph Roister Doister, central figure in the play named after him (the "first" English COMEDY). Examples in ELIZABETHAN DRAMA are Captain Bobadil in Jonson's *Everyman in his Humour,* Quintiliano in Chapman's *May Day,* and Shakespeare's Sir John Falstaff (*King Henry IV,* 1, 2), Don Armado de Adriano (*Love's Labour's Lost*), Parolles (*All's Well*), and Ancient Pistol (*King Henry V*). Although the treatments differ in different examples, the *miles gloriosus* is likely to be cowardly, parasitical, bragging, and subject to being victimized easily by practical jokers.

**Mime:** A form of popular COMEDY developed by the ancients (fifth century B.C. in Southern Italy). It portrayed the events of everyday life by means of dancing, imitative gestures, and witty DIALOGUE. It finally degenerated into sensual displays and the performers sank to a low social level. The Christian Church frowned upon the performances and they were largely driven from the public stage. They were kept alive, however, by wandering entertainers. In England, the exhibitions seem to have consisted generally of low forms of buffoonery. The *mime* aided in preserving the comic spirit in DRAMA, its influence possibly being apparent in the medieval MYSTERY PLAY and the Renaissance INTERLUDE—perhaps also the Renaissance "DUMB SHOW" and through it the modern PANTOMIME. Many elements of modern VAUDEVILLE are in direct line of descent from the *mime.* The *mime* is not regarded as a true link between ancient CLASSICAL DRAMA and modern DRAMA, though it perhaps did aid in keeping alive the tradition of dramatic method and of the acting profession in the so-called dark ages.

**Mimesis:** The Greek word for IMITATION, often used in criticism to indicate Aristotle's theory of IMITATION.

**Mimetic Theory of Art:** A theory of art which places a primary emphasis upon the actuality which is imitated in the art work. See CRITICISM, HISTORICAL SKETCH.

**Minnesinger:** "Singer of love," a medieval German LYRIC poet whose art was perhaps inspired by that of the TROUBADOUR. Though the German poets reflect the love system known as COURTLY LOVE, their poetry in general is more wholesome than that of the TROUBADOURS. They flourished in the twelfth and thirteenth centuries. Walther von der Vogelweide is regarded as the greatest of the class.

**Minor Plot:** See SUBPLOT.

**Minstrel:** A musical entertainer or traveling poet of the later Middle Ages who carried on the tradition of the earlier GLEEMAN and JONGLEUR. *Minstrels* flourished especially in the late thirteenth and the fourteenth centuries and played a prominent part in the cultural life of the time. The typical *minstrel* may be thought of as a gifted wandering entertainer, skilled with the harp and tabor, singing songs, reciting ROMANCES, and carrying news from town to town, castle to castle, country to country, delighting all classes of society, from kings and knights to priests and burgesses and laborers. Love LYRICS, BALLADS, LEGENDS, and ROMANCES were so composed and disseminated. They were at once the actors and journalists and poets and orchestras of their time. The *Lay of Havelok the Dane* is a good example of the "minstrel ROMANCE." Flourishing in Chaucer's day, minstrelsy declined in the fifteenth century and tended to disappear with the increase of literacy following the introduction of printing. In their enthusiasm for "primitive" or untutored poetic genius and for medievalism in general, the poets and novelists of the romantic school, such as Beattie and Scott, imparted a somewhat idealized meaning to *minstrel* and "minstrelsy," as they did to BARD.

**Miracle Play:** Although this term is used by many authorities on English drama in a broad sense which includes the Scriptural

CYCLIC DRAMA (see MYSTERY PLAY), it is restricted by others to its early sense of a non-Scriptural play based upon the legend of some saint or upon a miracle performed by some saint or sacred object (such as the sacramental bread). However common *miracle plays* in this stricter sense may have been in medieval England, very few have been preserved. It is known that a play of St. Catherine, probably in Latin or ANGLO-NORMAN, was performed at Dunstable about A.D. 1100. At this time *miracle plays* on St. Nicholas were being produced in France. A play called *Dux Moraud* (thirteenth or fourteenth century), in English, which exists in a fragmentary form, may have been a *miracle play*, possibly one in which the Virgin Mary supplied the DEUS EX MACHINA (Virgin Play). Other extant English plays that either are *miracle plays* or plays of very similar character are the *Play of the Sacrament* (late fifteenth century) and the *Conversion of St. Paul* and *Mary Magdalene* (*ca.*1500). An interesting modern example of a miracle play is Maeterlinck's *Sister Beatrice*. See MYSTERY PLAY.

**Miscellanies, Poetical:** The collection of poems by Wyatt, Surrey, and others published by Richard Tottel in 1557 as *Songs and Sonnets,* commonly known as *Tottel's Miscellany* (see COURTLY MAKERS), set a fashion that resulted in the publication of nearly twenty *poetical miscellanies* within the next half-century, usually under highly figurative or alliterative titles and varying greatly in quality and kind of VERSE printed. Some are posthumous publications of COMMONPLACE BOOKS such as the *Paradise of Dainty Devices* of Richard Edwards (1576), a very popular collection of poems of a serious character. Some *miscellanies* have a specialized character, like the *Handful of Pleasant Delights* (1584), a collection of BALLADS. Some of the later ones, like *England's Parnassus* (1600), are collections not of complete poems but of poetical quotations. One, *The Passionate Pilgrim* (1599), was published as Shakespeare's, and does contain some of Shakespeare's verse. Frequently the *miscellany* was made up of poems selected from other *miscellanies* or from manuscript sources. Much of the verse is anonymous, some is falsely ascribed, and some indicates authorship by initials not now understandable. Much uncertainty and some intentional mystification are connected with the parts played by collectors or editors. New poems were frequently printed along with old ones, and old ones sometimes appear in variant forms. The *miscellanies* are important as reflecting the great poetical activity of the time, particularly of the years preceding the appearance of Spenser, Sidney, and other major figures. They reflect, too, the metrical experiments of this earlier period. The poems in *A Gorgeous Gallery of Gallant Inventions* (1578), for example, make free use of ALLITERATION and employ a wide variety of metrical forms. Such poet-dramatists as Shakespeare borrowed LYRICS from the earlier *miscellanies* and lived to see their own verse appear in the later ones. Aside from *Tottel's*, particularly important *miscellanies* are *The Phoenix Nest* (1593) and *England's Helicon* (1600). The former, assembled by "R.S.," contains poems by Sidney, Spenser, Lodge, and others. The latter, the best of them all, is a veritable store-house of Elizabethan poetry selected from many poets, great and small.

The practice of publishing *poetical miscellanies* thus begun in the sixteenth century, of course, has continued to the present time. Professor Arthur E. Case, in his *Bibliography of English Poetical Miscellanies, 1521–1750*, lists several hundred titles of various sorts of poetical collections.

*Mise en scène:* The stage setting of a play, including the use of scenery, properties, etc., and the general arrangement of the piece. Modern DRAMA relies far more upon *mise en scène* for its effects than did earlier DRAMA. Indeed, the lack of scenery has been given as a partial explanation of the high literary quality of ELIZABETHAN DRAMA, the playwright being forced to rely upon his language for his descriptive effects; while the increased dependence upon scenery is said to be one of the reasons for the decreased attention to purely literary devices on the modern stage. By extension the term *mise en scène* is applied to the total surroundings of any event.

**Mixed Figures:** The mingling of one FIGURE OF SPEECH with another immediately following with which the first is incongruous. A notable example is the sentence of Castlereagh: "And now, sir, I must embark into the feature on which this question chiefly hinges." Here, obviously, the sentence begins with a nautical figure ("embark") but closes with a mechanical figure ("hinges"). The effect is grotesque. Mixed imagery, however, is sometimes deliberately used by master writers with great effectiveness, when the differing figures contribute cumulatively to a single referent which is increasingly illuminated as they pile up. It is important, however, that the cumulative effect of the various IMAGES not be one of incongruity. See METAPHOR, TENOR, VEHICLE.

**Mock Epic** or **Mock Heroic:** Terms frequently used interchangeably to designate a literary form which burlesques EPIC poetry by treating a trivial subject in the "grand style," or which uses the EPIC FORMULAS to make ridiculous a trivial subject by ludicrously overstating it. Usually the characteristics of the classical EPIC are employed, particularly the invocation to a deity; the formal statement of theme; the division into books and CANTOS; the grandiose speeches (challenges, defiances, boastings) of the heroes; descriptions of warriors (especially their dress and equipment), battles, and games; the use of the EPIC or Homeric SIMILE; and the employment of supernatural machinery (gods directing or participating in the action). When the mock poem is much shorter than a true EPIC some prefer to call it *mock heroic,* a term also applied to poems which mock ROMANCES rather than EPICS. Ordinary usage, however, employs the terms interchangeably. Chaucer's *Nun's Priest's Tale* is partly *mock heroic* in character as is Spenser's finely wrought *Muiopotmos,* "The Fate of the Butterfly," which imitates the opening of the *Aeneid* and employs elevated STYLE for trivial subject-matter. Swift's *Battle of the Books* is an example of a cuttingly satirical *mock epic* in prose. Pope's *The Rape of the Lock* is perhaps the finest *mock heroic* poem in English, satirizing in polished verse the trivialities of polite society in the eighteenth century. The cutting of a lady's lock by a gallant is the central act of heroic behavior, a card game is described in military terms, and such airy spirits as the sylphs hover over the scene to aid their favorite heroine. For a detailed treatment of the *mock heroic,* see Richmond P. Bond, *English Burlesque Poetry, 1700–1750.*

**Monody:** A DIRGE or LAMENT in which a single mourner expresses individual grief, e.g., Arnold's *Thyrsis, A Monody.* See DIRGE, ELEGY, THRENODY.

**Monologue:** A composition, oral or written, presenting the discourse of one speaker only. A SOLILOQUY. Any speech or narrative presented wholly by one person. Sometimes loosely used to signify merely any lengthy speech. See DRAMATIC MONOLOGUE, INTERIOR MONOLOGUE.

**Monometer:** A line of VERSE consisting of only one FOOT. See SCANSION, METER.

**Montage:** A device, probably borowed from motion pictures, used in IMPRESSIONISM to establish a scene or an atmosphere by a series of brief pictures or impressions following one another quickly without apparent logical order. The "Newsreels" in Dos Passos' *U.S.A.* are examples of *montages.* The device is sometimes used in the INTERIOR MONOLOGUE.

**Mood:** The tone (as "pensive," "reflective," "rollicking") which prevails in a piece of literature. See EMOTIONAL ELEMENT IN LITERATURE.

**Mora, Morae:** Terms used to designate periods of duration in QUANTITATIVE VERSE, the *mora* being the duration of a short syllable and the *morae* being that of a long syllable. The symbol ($\smile$) which indicates a *mora* is called a BREVE, that ($-$) which indicates a *morae* is called a MACRON.

**Moral Criticism:** Criticism which evaluates a work of art in moral terms, judges it in terms of the ethical principles which, the critic feels, should govern human life. See CRITICISM, TYPES OF.

**Morality Play** ("Morality"): A kind of POETIC DRAMA which developed in the late Middle Ages (probably late fourteenth century) and which was distinguished from the religious DRAMA proper, such as the MYSTERY PLAY, by the fact that it was a dramatized ALLEGORY in which the abstract virtues and vices (like Mercy, Conscience, Perseverance, and Shame) appear in personified form, the good and the bad usually being engaged in a struggle for the soul of man. One student of the drama (A. H. Tolman) has distinguished two classes. The "full-scope" *morality* is one in which the theme is the saving of man's soul, and the central figure is man in the sense of humanity in general. The best-known example is *Everyman* (*ca.*1500). The "limited-scope" *morality* is one which deals with a single vice or moral problem or a situation applicable to a certain person. Thus Skeleton's *Magnificence* has for its theme the dangers of uncontrolled expenditures and was possibly written as advice to Henry VIII. Later, pedagogical and political themes as well as theological became quite common. The limited-scope *morality* developed later than the full-scope and is perhaps superior dramatically because of its independence and greater concreteness and REALISM. *Morality plays* have also been classified by content or purpose, as religious (*Everyman*), doctrinal (John Bale's *King Johan*), didactic-pedagogical (*Wyt and Science*), political (Skelton's *Magnificence*), etc. By the sixteenth century some of the *morality plays* had admitted so much realistic, farcical material that they had begun to establish a tradition of English COMEDY, and doubtless contributed much to the INTERLUDE. In fact, INTERLUDE and *morality* became more or less interchangeable in describing plays. Such comic figures as the Vice and the Devil were especially well-developed and were influential upon later COMEDY. Though morality themes were widely employed in RENAISSANCE drama of the sixteenth century, the *morality plays* as such lost their popularity in Elizabethan times.

*Motif* (**Motive**): A simple element which serves as a basis for expanded NARRATIVE; or, less strictly, a conventional situation, device, interest, or incident employed in FOLKLORE, FICTION, or DRAMA. The carrying off of a mortal queen by a fairy lover is a *motif* about which full stories were built in MEDIEVAL ROMANCE. In the BALLAD called *The Elfin Knight* the "fairy music" *motif* appears when the sound of the knight's horn causes the maiden to fall in love with the unseen hero. In music and art the term is used in various other senses, as for a recurring melodic phrase, a prevailing idea or design, or a subject for detailed sculptural treatment.

**Motivation:** The justification of the action of a character in a PLOT by the presenting of a convincing and impelling cause for that action. The chief difference, perhaps, between amateurish, puerile FICTION and great works of imaginative power lies in this very question of *motivation*. The story or drama of action is sometimes content to unfold a series of thrilling, unnatural EPISODES, exciting in themselves, but growing out of no inherent purpose of the author other than his desire to excite his reader. Motivated action, however, is action justified by the make-up of the character partaking in the activity. Hamlet is slow to resolve and refuses to kill Claudius when he finds him at prayer; Othello is intensely jealous and proud—and smothers Desdemona when he thinks her unfaithful; Falstaff is more of a wit than a hero—and runs from the scene of the robbery. All this is *motivation* through character. *Motivation* usually consists of a combination of psychological traits and external events. If it is worked out satisfactorily, it leaves the reader with a recognition of those emotive and circumstantial forces which made the action inevitable.

**Movement:** A critical term denoting action or incident. Thus a play is spoken of as having, or not having, *movement*, implying that the dramatic action is strong or weak, rapid or slow. The term is also used to indicate a new development in literary activity or interest, as the OXFORD MOVEMENT, the FREE-VERSE movement.

**"Muckrakers":** A term applied derisively to a group of American writers who between 1902 and 1911 worked actively to expose the dishonest methods and unscrupulous motives operative in big business and in city, state, and national government. A group of MAGAZINES—*The Arena, Everybody's, McClure's,* the *Independent, Collier's,* and the *Cosmopolitan*—led the movement, publishing the writings of the leading *"muckrakers"*—Ida Tarbell, Lincoln Steffens, T. W. Lawson, Mark Sullivan, and Samuel H. Adams. Upton Sinclair's novel *The Jungle* and some of the novels of Winston Churchill and of D. G. Phillips are "muckraking" books. The term comes from a character in Bunyan's *Pilgrim's Progress,* who is so busy raking up muck that he does not see a celestial crown held over him. It was applied to this group of writers as a derogatory epithet by Theodore Roosevelt.

**Multiple meanings:** A term sometimes used by contemporary critics as a substitute for AMBIGUITY when that word is used to designate the capacity of words to stimulate several quite different streams of thought, all of which make sense. See AMBIGUITY.

**Mummery:** A simple dramatic performance usually presented by players masked or disguised. A farcical presentation, a sort of PANTOMIME. See MASQUE.

**"Mummings":** See MASQUE.

**Muses:** Goddesses represented as presiding over song, the various departments of literature, and the liberal arts. They were nine in number and are generally considered the daughters of Zeus and Mnemosyne (memory). In literature, their traditional significance is that of inspiring and helping poets. In various periods of Greek history, the *muses* were given different names and attributes, but the conventionally accepted list and the realm of interest ascribed to each are as follows: Calliope (epic poetry), Clio (history), Erato (lyrics and love poetry), Euterpe (music), Melpomene (tragedy), Polyhymnia (sacred poetry), Terpsichore (choral dance and song), Thalia (comedy), and Urania (astronomy).

**Musical Comedy:** Closely related, especially in its earlier forms, to BURLESQUE and VAUDEVILLE, *musical comedy* developed in the early twentieth century in England and America into one of the most popular of all dramatic forms. Though much use is made of music, both vocal and orchestral, the DIALOGUE is spoken, not sung. The success of the form depends partly upon the acting, partly upon the success of the songs, and partly upon the spectacular staging. Satirical "hits" at current figures and interests are features. The comic effects are sometimes farcical (see FARCE) in character.

**Mystery Play:** A medieval religious play based upon Biblical history; a Scriptural play. *Mystery plays* originated in the liturgy of the Church and developed from LITURGICAL DRAMAS into the great CYCLIC PLAYS, performed outdoors and ultimately upon movable PAGEANTS. They were the most important forms of the MEDIEVAL DRAMA of Western Europe and flourished in England from the late Middle Ages until well into RENAISSANCE times. They seem to have developed about three nuclei: (1) Old Testament plays treating such events as the Creation, the fallen angels, the fall of man, the death of Abel, the sacrifice of Isaac, etc., and the Prophet plays, which prepared for (2) the New Testament plays dealing with the birth of Christ—the Annunciation, the birth, the visit of the wise men, the shepherds, and the visit to the temple; and (3) the Death and Resurrection plays—entry to Jerusalem, the betrayal by Judas, trial and crucifixion, lamentation of Mary, sepulchre scenes, the resurrection, appearances to disciples, Pentecost, and sometimes the Day of Judgment. So the whole scheme of salvation was presented. They were often known as CORPUS CHRISTI PLAYS because of the habit of performing the plays on PAGEANTS in connection with the Corpus Christi processional. The great CYCLES whose texts have been preserved to us are the York, the Chester, the Coventry, and the Wakefield (or "Towneley"). They differ in length and in the list of plays or scenes included as well as in literary and dramatic value, the Towneley plays being especially important in dramatic development.

After the plays left the Church and became "secularized," they were performed by trade guilds, sometimes on fixed stages or stations (the crowds moving from station to station), sometimes on movable PAGEANTS. A writer of the sixteenth century, Archdeacon Rogers, who witnessed a late production of the Chester cycle at Whitsuntide, has left the following oft-quoted description:

Every company had its pageant, or part, which pageants were a high scaffold with two rooms, a higher and a lower, upon four wheels. In the lower they appareled themselves, and in the higher room they played, being all open on the top, that all beholders might hear and see them. The places where they played them was in every street. They began first at the Abbey gates, and when the first pageant was played it was wheeled to the high cross before the mayor, and so to every street; and so every street had a pageant playing before them at one time, till all the pageants for the day appointed were played: and when one pageant was near ended, word was brought from street to street, that so they might come in place thereof exceeding orderly, and all the streets have their pageants afore them all at one time playing together; to see which players there was great resort, and also scaffolds and stages made in the streets in those places where they determined to play their pageants.

The word *mystery* was first applied to these plays by an eighteenth-century editor (Robert Dodsley, 1744), on the analogy of the French *mystère*, a Scriptural play; medieval writers were more likely to refer to the plays as CORPUS CHRISTI PLAYS, "Whitsuntide plays," "PAGEANTS," etc., and possibly as MIRACLE PLAYS, the term preferred for them by many modern authorities. See MEDIEVAL DRAMA, MIRACLE PLAYS, LITURGICAL DRAMA, PAGEANT, DRAMA.

**Mystery Story (or Novel):** A term used to designate a work of prose FICTION in which the element of mystery or terror plays a controlling part. It is applied to such various types of FICTION as the DETECTIVE STORY, the GOTHIC NOVEL, the story of strange or frightening adventure, the "supense" novel, the tale of espionage, the tale of crime, and the story in which the PROTAGONIST, usually a woman, is relentlessly pursued by some unknown but alarming menace. See DETECTIVE STORY.

**Mysticism:** The theory that a knowledge of God or immediate reality is attainable through the use of some human faculty that transcends intellect and does not use ordinary human perceptions or logical processes. *Mysticism* takes many different forms and does not yield itself readily to definition. Objective studies of *mysticism* are impossible, since one not himself a mystic must be content to receive as fact the autobiographical or artistic record of an experience that is, by its very nature, ineffable. There are two broad types of *mysticism;* in one God is seen as transcendent, outside the human soul, and union with Him is achieved through a series of steps or stages; in the other God is immanent, dwelling within the soul and to be discovered by penetrating deeper into the inner self. The terminology of *mysticism*, since it is forced to be figurative, is often difficult and obscure. A conventional statement of the Christian mystic's progress on the path to God is as follows: the soul undergoes a purification (the purgative way), which leads to a sense of illumination in the love of God (the illuminative way), and after a period the soul enters into a union with God (the unitive way), and progresses into a final ecstatic state of perfect knowledge of God (the spiritual marriage), during some period of which there comes a time of alienation and loss in which the soul cannot find God at all (the soul's dark night).

Aspects of *mysticism* and the mystical experience are common in English and American literature, although to call any single writer—with a few exceptions like Richard Rolle of Hampole and William Blake—a mystic is to invite a challenge. Clearly, however, there are mystical elements in the work of Richard Crashaw, George Herbert, John Bunyan, William Cowper, William Wordsworth, S. T. Coleridge, P. B. Shelley, Thomas Carlyle, the New England TRANSCENDENTALISTS, Walt Whitman, and W. V. Moody.

**Myth:** Anonymous stories having their roots in the primitive folk-beliefs of races or nations and presenting supernatural episodes as a means of interpreting natural events in an effort to make concrete and particular a special perception of man or a cosmic view. *Myths* differ from LEGENDS in that they have less of historical background and more of the supernatural; they differ from the FABLE in that they are less concerned with moral didacticism and are the product of a racial group rather than the creation of an individual. Every country and literature has its mythology; the best known to English readers being the Greek, Roman, and Norse. But the mythology of all groups takes shape around certain common themes; they all attempt to explain the creation, divinity, and religion, to guess at the meaning of existence and death, to account for natural phenomena, and to chronicle the adventures of racial heroes.

They also have a startlingly similar group of MOTIFS, characters, and actions, as a number of students of *myth* and religion, particularly Sir James Frazer, have pointed out. Although there was a time when *myth* was a virtual synonym for error, notably in the NEO-CLASSIC PERIOD, the tendency today is to see *myths* as dramatic or narrative embodiments of a people's perception of the deepest truths. Various modern writers have insisted on the necessity of *myth* as a material with which the artist works, and in varying ways and degrees have appropriated the old *myths* or created new ones as necessary substances to give order and a frame of meaning to their personal perceptions and images; notable among such "mythmakers" have been William Blake, W. B. Yeats, T. S. Eliot (particularly in *The Waste Land*), James Joyce, and Wallace Stevens.

Since the introduction of Jung's concept of the "racial unconscious" (see ARCHETYPE) and of Ernst Cassirer's theories of language and *myth*, contemporary critics have found in the *myth* a useful device for examining literature. There is a type of imagination, Philip Wheelwright insists, that can properly be called "the Archetypal Imagination, which sees the particular object as embodying and adumbrating suggestions of universality." The possessors of such imagination arrange their works in archetypal patterns, and present us with naratives which stir us as "something at once familiar and strange." They thus give concrete expression to something deep and primitive in us all. Thus those critics—and they are many—who approach literature as *myth* see in it vestiges of primordial ritual and ceremony, or the repository of racial memories, or a structure of unconsciously held value systems, or an expression of the general beliefs of a race, social class or nation, or a unique embodiment of a cosmic view. One significant difference should be noted, however; *myth* in its traditional sense is an anonymous, non-literary, essentially religious formulation of the cosmic view of a people who approach its formulations not as representations of truth but as truth itself; *myth* in the sophisticated literary sense in which it is currently used is the intelligible and often self-conscious use of such primitive methods to express something deeply felt by the individual artist which will, he hopes, prove to have universal responses. The MYTHOPOEIC poet attempts to return to the role of the prophet-seer, by creating a *myth* which strikes resonant points in the minds of his readers and speaks with something of the authority of the old *myths*. See ARCHETYPE, MYTHOPOEIC.

**Mythic Criticism:** Criticism which explores the nature and significance of the ARCHETYPES and archetypal patterns in a work of art. See MYTH; ARCHETYPE; CRITICISM, TYPES OF.

**Mythopoeic:** A term applied to writers who, suffering the lack of an acceptable or widely believed body of mythic material to give order to their imaginative restatements of experience, set about consciously to make a mythic frame for their works. Notable *mythopoeic* writers have been Blake, Yeats, Joyce, and Eliot.

**Naïve Narrator or Hero:** A disingenuous character who is the ostensible author (often the oral NARRATOR) of a narrative whose implications are much plainer to the reader than they are to the NARRATOR himself. The *naïve narrator* can be a device for IRONY, either gentle or savage, or it can be a device for PATHOS, as it frequently is when a child narrates with open-eyed innocence events whose implications are tragic or horrible. The *naïve narrator* is used a great deal by Sherwood Anderson in short stories like "I'm a Fool" and "The Egg"; Swift employs the device in "A Modest Proposal" with savage effectiveness; Mark Twain's *The Adventures of Huckleberry Finn* and Ring Lardner's "Hair-Cut" are also well-known examples of the use of the *naïve narrator*.

**Narration:** That one of the four types of composition (see ARGUMENTATION, DESCRIPTION, and EXPOSITION) the purpose of which is to recount an event or a series of events. *Narration* may exist, of course, entirely by itself, but it is most likely to incorporate with it considerable description. There are two forms of *narration: simple narrative,* which is content to recite an event or events and is largely chronological in its arrangement of details—as in a newspaper account of a fire; and *narrative with plot,* which is less often chronological and more often arranged according to a preconceived artistic principle determined by the nature of the PLOT and the type of story intended (see PLOT). The chief purpose of *narration* is to interest and entertain, though, of course, it may be used to instruct and inform.

**Narrative Essay:** An INFORMAL ESSAY in narrative form—ANECDOTE, INCIDENT, or ALLEGORY. It differs from a SHORT STORY not only in its simpler STRUCTURE, but especially in its ESSAY-like intent, the story being a means of developing an idea rather than being an end in itself. Addison's *Vision of Mirzah* is an example. See ESSAY.

**Narrative Poem:** A non-dramatic poem which tells a story or presents a narrative, whether simple or complex, long or short. EPICS, BALLADS, and METRICAL ROMANCES are among the many kinds of *narrative poems.*

**Narrator:** In the broadest sense, anyone who recounts a narrative, either in writing or orally. In FICTION the term is used in a more technical sense, as the ostensible author or teller of a story. In FICTION presented in the first person, the "I" who tells the story is the *narrator;* he may be in any of various relations to the events, he describes, ranging from being their center (the PROTAGONIST) through various degrees of minor importance (MINOR CHARACTERS) to being merely a witness. In FICTION told from an OMNISCIENT-AUTHOR POINT OF VIEW, the author himself acts self-consciously as narrator, recounting the story and freely commenting on it. A *narrator* is always present, at least by implication, in any work of FICTION, except a story in which a SELF-EFFACING AUTHOR relates events with apparent OBJECTIVITY; yet even there the *narrator* exists in fact, although we and the author act as though he did not. See POINT OF VIEW.

**Naturalism:** A term sometimes applied to writing that demonstrates a deep interest in NATURE, such as Wordsworth and other Romantic writers had; and sometimes used to describe any form of extreme REALISM, although this usage is a very loose one. It should properly be reserved for use as the designation of a movement in the NOVEL in the late nineteenth and early twentieth centuries in France, America, and England.

In its simplest sense *naturalism* is the application of the principles of scientific determinism to FICTION. It draws its name from its basic assumption that everything that is real exists in NATURE, NATURE being conceived as the world of objects, actions, and forces which yield the secrets of their causation and being to objective scientific inquiry. The fundamental view of man which the naturalist takes is of an animal in the natural world, responding

# Naturalism

to environmental forces and internal stresses and drives, over none of which he has either control or full knowledge. It tends to differ from REALISM, not in its attempt to be accurate in the portrayal of its materials but in the selection and organization of those materials, selecting not the commonplace but the representative and so arranging the materials that the structure of the novel reveals the pattern of ideas—in this case, scientific theory—which forms the author's view of the nature of experience. In this sense, *naturalism* shares with ROMANTICISM a belief that the actual is important not in itself but in what it can reveal about the nature of a larger reality; it differs sharply from ROMANTICISM, however, in finding that reality not in transcendent ideas or absolute ideals but in the scientific laws which can be revealed through the action of individual instances. This distinction may be illustrated in this way. Given a block of wood and a force pushing upon it, producing in it a certain acceleration: REALISM will tend to concentrate its attention on the accurate description of that particular block, that special force, and that definite acceleration; ROMANTICISM will tend to see in the entire operation an illustration or symbol or suggestion of a philosophical truth and will so represent the block, the force, and the acceleration—often with complete fidelity to fact—that the idea or ideal that it bodies forth is the center of the interest; and *naturalism* will tend to see in the operation a clue or a key to the scientific law which undergirds it and to be interested in the relationship between the force, the block, and the produced acceleration, and will so represent the operation that Newton's first law of motion (even on occasion in its mathematical expression— $F \propto ma$) is demonstrated or proved by this representative instance of its universal occurrence in nature.

In this sense *naturalism* is the novelist's response to the revolution in thought that modern science has produced. From Newton it gains a sense of mechanistic determinism; from Darwin (the greatest single force operative upon it) it gains a sense of biological determinism and the inclusive METAPHOR of the lawless jungle which it has used perhaps more often than any other; from Marx it gains a view of history as a battleground of vast economic and social forces; from Freud it gains a view of the determinism of the inner and subconscious self; from Taine it gains a view of literature as a product of deterministic forces; from Comte it gains a view of social and environmental determinism. In the most influential statement ever made of the theory of *naturalism*, Émile

Zola's *Le roman expérimental,* the ideal of the naturalist is stated as the selection of truthful instances subjected to laboratory conditions in a novel, where the hypotheses of the author about the nature and operation of the forces that work upon man can be put to the test. Zola's term *expérimental,* usually translated "Experimental," is more properly translated "Empirical."

Although the fidelity to detail and the disavowal of the assumptions of the Romanticists give *naturalism* obvious affinities with REALISM, so that it is often confused in its origins with that movement and Balzac and Flaubert are credited with being naturalists, the Goncourt Brothers and Zola are generally recognized as having begun the naturalistic novel and codified its theory. Strong elements of *naturalism* are to be seen in the work of George Eliot and of Thomas Hardy, but American novelists have been generally more receptive to its theories than the English have. Frank Norris (1870–1902) wrote naturalistic novels in conscious imitation of Zola and made an American critical defense of the school, *The Responsibilities of the Novelist,* in which he saw that its real enemy was REALISM and not ROMANTICISM. Stephen Crane (1871–1900) used the devices of IMPRESSIONISM in producing naturalistic novels. Jack London (1876–1916) wrote naturalistic novels with Nietzschean "supermen" (and "superdogs") as PROTAGONISTS. But the greatest American naturalist—after Zola perhaps the greatest naturalist—was Theodore Dreiser (1871–1945), whose *An American Tragedy* is an archetypal American example. James T. Farrell and James Jones, among others, have kept the school alive in America.

The novels produced in this school have tended to emphasize either a biological determinism, with an emphasis on the animal nature of man, particularly his heredity, portraying him as an animal engaged in the endless and brutal struggle for survival, or a socio-economic determinism, portraying man as the victim of environmental forces and the product of social and economic factors beyond his control or his full understanding. Occasionally, as in the novels of Thomas Hardy, man is seen as the victim of "destiny" or "fate." But whichever of these views is taken, the naturalist strives to be objective, even documentary, in his presentation of material; to be amoral in his view of the struggle in which the human animal finds himself, neither condemning nor praising man for actions which he cannot control; to be pessimistic in his view of human capabilities—life, he seems to feel, is a vicious trap, a cruel game; to be frank and almost clinically direct in his portrayal of man as an animal driven by fundamental urges—fear, hunger, and sex; to be deterministic in his portrayal of human actions, seeing them as explicable in cause-and-effect relationships; and to exercise a bias in the selection of characters and actions, frequently choosing primitive characters and simple, violent actions as best giving him "experimental conditions." No single naturalistic novel displays completely this catalogue of qualities, but taken together they tend to define the directions and intentions of *naturalism.*

**Naturalistic and Symbolistic Period in American Literature:** The period between 1900 and 1930 in America was the age of the birth of contemporary attitudes and contemporary writing. It is sharply divided by the World War, the first part being a time dominated by NATURALISM, and the part after the War being marked by a growing international awareness, a sensitivity to European literary models, and a steadily developing SYMBOLISM in poetry and FICTION. The first decade of the twentieth century was an age of the "muckraking" magazine exposé and the "muckraking" NOVEL. During this decade, Henry James, living in England, probably carried American REALISM to its greatest height in *The Ambassadors, The Wings of the Dove,* and *The Golden Bowl;* Mark Twain, although still alive, was no longer producing works comparable to those of the 1880's and his pessimism was growing more darkly marked; Howells, too, was still producing his NOVELS and his amiable critical ESSAYS but without the strength of his heyday. Frank Norris, Theodore Dreiser, and Jack London were producing crude but powerful examples of the naturalistic NOVEL. William Vaughn Moody was writing a socially conscious VERSE and extremely popular DRAMA; and Edwin Arlington Robinson had launched the career that was to flower into great distinction in the second and third decades of the century.

The second decade saw the virtual birth of modern American poetry, with the founding of *Poetry* magazine in Chicago in 1912 by Harriet Monroe, the emergence of the IMAGISTS, the beginning of the careers of Frost, Pound, Eliot, Sandburg, and Masters. The realistic NOVEL continued in the work of Howells, Ellen Glasgow, Willa Cather, and Edith Wharton. As the decade ended the plays of Eugene O'Neill gave promise of a theatrical revival to match the growing LITTLE THEATRE MOVEMENT and the development of the FOLK DRAMA. Prior to the twentieth century American criticism had been sporadic and uncertain, but the work of W. C. Brownell, James Huneker, and a group of young critics demanding a "usable past"—among them, Randolph Bourne and Van Wyck Brooks—joined with the developing artistic concern of the avant-garde groups and the LITTLE MAGAZINES to produce an increasingly sensitive body of critical work as the second decade of the century drew toward a close.

The First World War produced a major dislocation of a number of talented young men, most of them born between 1895 and 1902, who became volunteer ambulance and ammunition truck drivers in the French and Italian armies, came early in contact with European culture, and emerged from the War disillusioned with American "idealism" and with the crassness of American culture. This postwar generation, considering itself self-consciously as a "LOST GENERATION," set about a repudiation of American culture in three ways: one group, largely from the East, went back to Europe and there published LITTLE MAGAZINES, waited upon Gertrude Stein, took part in DADAISM, and formulated a polished and *symbolistic* style—among them were F. Scott Fitzgerald, Ernest Hemingway, Edmund Wilson, e. e. cummings, Malcolm Cowley, and Sherwood Anderson, and, on the English side of the channel, Ezra Pound and T. S. Eliot; another group, largely from the Middle West, came east and in Cambridge, New Haven, and Greenwich Village, produced a literature that was realistic, satiric, and critical, aimed at the standardized mediocrity of the American village—among them were Ring Lardner and Sinclair Lewis; and another group, largely Southern, repudiated the meaningless mechanism of capitalistic America by looking backward to a past that had had tradition and order—these were the poets and critics who published the *Fugitive* in Nashville and were AGRARIANS, and others who contributed to magazines like the *Double Dealer* in New Orleans. Out of this last group have come the contemporary Southern NOVEL and much of the NEW CRITICISM; the group includes John Crowe Ransom, Allen Tate, Robert Penn Warren, and William Faulkner.

All of these groups—expatriates, revolters against the village, and seekers of a tradition of order—sought for art forms and critical standards different from those of the traditional American writer, and they found them in the methods of the French *symbolists*, in the work of Joyce and Proust, in the complex intellectual poetry of the seventeenth century "Metaphysicals," and in the kind of experimentation that the LITTLE MAGAZINES existed to foster. By the end of the period, a group of academic critics, the NEW HUMANISTS, were formulating a doctrine of life and art that repudiated the contemporary artist, and in the late fall of 1929 the collapse of the stock-market, signaling the beginning of the depression, marked an effective end to a period in which most of the seeds of contemporary American writing had been sown.

**Nature:** Few terms are so important to the student of literature—or so difficult—as this one. Since conformity with *nature*—the resort to *nature* as a norm or standard for judging artistic expression—long permeated critical thinking (see MIMETIC THEORY OF ART), some knowledge of the "normative" meanings of the term is necessary to the understanding of much criticism and literature. Professor A. O. Lovejoy found as many as sixty different meanings for "*nature*" in its normative functions. Both neo-classicists and romanticists would "follow *Nature*"; but the former drew from the term ideas of order, regularity, and universality, both in "external" *nature* and in human *nature*, while the latter found in *nature* the justification for their enthusiasm for irregularity ("wildness") in external *nature* and for individualism in human *nature*. Other contradictory senses may be noted: the term *nature* might mean, on the one hand, human *nature* (typical human behavior); or, on the other hand, whatever is antithetical to human *nature* and man's works—what has not been "spoiled" by man.

The neo-classic view of *nature* as implying universal aesthetic validity led to a reverence for "rules" drawn from long-continued acceptance by human beings, such acceptance being taken as an evidence of their basis in what is universal in human *nature*. The rules were based upon proved models. Opposed to this was the romantic tendency to regard as "natural" the primitive, the unsophisticated, the naïve—a conception which justified the *disregard* of rules and precedents and the exaltation of the freedom of individual expression which characterizes much "romantic" literature. Among some neo-classic writers the words "reason" and "nature" were closely allied in meaning, because both were closely related to the idea of "order" (John Dennis said that *nature* was order in the visible world, while reason was order in the invisible realm). The distinction between *nature* and WIT (in one of its senses) was not always clear, since both provided tests of excellence, though, properly, WIT was specific, while *nature* was generic, thought of as an ultimate, as indicated in the familiar lines from Pope's *Essay on Criticism:*

> True Wit is Nature to advantage dressed,
> What oft was thought, but ne'er so well expressed.

The serious student of the literature of the RENAISSANCE, of NEO-CLASSICISM, and of ROMANTICISM may well consult A. O. Lovejoy's *Essays in the History of Ideas.*

For the general student of literature, *nature* in the sense of "external nature"—the objects of the natural world such as mountains, trees, rivers, flowers, and birds—is of particular interest since it has supplied so large a part of the imaginative substance of literature, especially poetry, from the earliest times to the present day. Some survey, therefore, of the attitudes toward external *nature* may be useful. One writer (Shairp) lists the following different uses which poets make of external *nature:* (1) they express childlike delight in the open-air world; (2) they use *nature* as the background or setting to human action or emotion; (3) they see *nature* through historic coloring; (4) they make *nature* sympathize with their own feelings; (5) they dwell upon the infinite side of *nature;* (6) they give description of *nature* for its own sake; (7) they interpret *nature* with imaginative sympathy; (8) they use *nature* as a symbol of the spirit.

The greatest attention to *nature* in English literature came in the ROMANTIC PERIOD, when the revolt against the strained conventionalities of neo-classic fashions led to much theorizing about the relation of man to external *nature* and the production of a vast amount of poetry putting the new theories into practice. To be sure, earlier English literature had made much use of *nature.* The comparatively small amount of Anglo-Saxon literature remaining reflects both a simple love of *nature* and a power for picturesque description—as in the "Riddles" (see RIDDLE) and such poems as the *Wife's Complaint* and the *Husband's Message*—and especially a sense of mystery and awe in the presence of *nature,* as in *Beowulf.* Late medieval literature—Chaucer and the ROMANCES—was apt to present *nature* in idyllic, conventionalized forms, a pleasant garden or "bower" on a May morning. In the RENAISSANCE there was sometimes a genuine, subjective response to natural surroundings, as in some of Surrey's poems, though often the treatment was conventional in character, as in the PASTORALS and the SONNETS. Shakespeare, of course, though no theorist like Wordsworth, shows a wide knowledge of *nature* and an unsurpassed faculty for drawing upon subjects from *nature*, whether conventional or fresh, to give appropriate settings and to impart an air of reality to dramatic situations and human moods—from the romantic "How sweet the moonlight sleeps upon this bank" of the Lorenzo-Jessica love-scene to the tragic and powerfully passionate responses of the distracted Lear to the rumblings of the storm which breaks over him as a terrible echo to his growing insanity.

The eighteenth century brought the great conflict between the neo-classicists and the romantics, and nowhere were the issues sharper between the two schools than in their treatment of external *nature*. In their zeal to follow "correct" models, to restrain enthusiasm, and in their preference of city to rural life, the neo-classicists found little room for recording intimate observations of *nature*, though they did, of course, employ natural imagery, usually conventionalized, and use *nature* descriptions as settings and as a basis for philosophical reflections. For the wilder aspects of *nature* they expressed strong abhorrence. Winter was "the deformed wrong side of the year," while mountains were a positive blemish upon the landscape and the ocean was a dangerous, wearying waste of waters—a far cry from the passionate warmth of Byron's famous apostrophe in *Childe Harold's Pilgrimage:* "And I have loved thee, Ocean," etc. The writers who adumbrated the coming change, such as Lady Winchilsea, John Dyer, James Thomson (especially *The Seasons*, 1726–1730), were giving voice to the new enthusiasm for *nature* while NEO-CLASSICISM was at its height, and the movement grew with Gray and Collins and Cowper and others till a little later readers were quite ready to respond to the charming presentation of the beauties of the homelier aspects of *nature* as sung by Robert Burns.

With Wordsworth came the climax of the nature-cult in English poetry, *nature* now being recognized as closely akin to man, able to minister to his spiritual needs and to reveal God to him (see *Tintern Abbey* for a classic poetic statement of the progressive phases of Wordsworth's responses to *nature*). Coleridge, too, gave climactic expressions to the romantic enthusiasm for the wilder, disordered aspects of *nature* which the neo-classicists could not brook. Observe the sharp contrast between the following passages, the first from Pope, and the second from Coleridge:

> Here hills and vales, the woodland and its plain,
> Here earth and water seem to strive again;

Not chaos-like together crushed and bruised,
But, as the world, harmoniously confused:
Where order in variety we see,
And where, though all things differ, all agree.
Here waving groves a chequered scene display,
And part admit, and part exclude the day;
As some coy nymph her lover's warm address
Nor quite indulges, nor can quite repress.
                                    (*Windsor Forest*)

But oh! that deep romantic chasm which slanted
Down the green hill athwart a cedarn cover!
A savage place! as holy and enchanted
As e'er beneath a waning moon was haunted
By woman wailing for her demon lover!
                                    (*Kubla Khan*)

The poetry of the other great romantic poets, Shelley, Keats, and Byron, is shot through with intimate, subjective presentations of *nature* in all its forms, from the delicate and mysterious to the grotesque and awful. This attitude was not only reflected widely in American literature (Bryant, Lowell, Whittier, Emerson, Thoreau) but persisted in much of the verse of the great Victorians, notably Tennyson.

The widespread acceptance of the Darwinian concepts of *nature* and of a natural struggle for existence has colored and modified the view of *nature*, and Wordsworth's gentle instructor in beauty can become a "nature red in tooth and claw" in Tennyson's *In Memoriam*, although that is not his persistent attitude. With the development of NATURALISM a view of *nature* as a raw and primitive jungle within which the struggle for survival relentlessly continues came into being, with *nature* viewed as a scientific fact, devoid of meaning in philosophical terms. However, in its calmer moments, it still can minister to the human spirit, as can be seen in Hemingway's "Big Two-Hearted River" or the fishing scenes in *The Sun Also Rises* or in Faulkner's *The Bear*. *Nature* is for the contemporary writer what it has always been for the writer, not an objective fact, but the "world's body" through which he speaks in concrete terms his perceptions of himself and the world, and it is capable of having fluctuating meanings in the same author's work and at the same time of speaking with authority. Emerson's *nature*, in his essay *Nature*, exists for five uses: as commodity, beauty, language, discipline, and, finally, ideal symbol. These varying uses are found by one man writing from a pronounced point of view. The reader is, therefore, well warned that *nature*, like one of Humpty Dumpty's words in *Alice in Wonderland,* means exactly what its user intends it to mean, just that, and nothing more!

**Negative Capability:** A term used by Keats to describe the objective and impersonal aspect of Shakespeare. Shakespeare had "innate universality," Keats asserted. "A poet has no Identity . . . he is continually . . . filling some other Body." The term has since been applied widely to the qualities in an artist's work which enable him to avoid in it the expression of his own personality. See AESTHETIC DISTANCE, OBJECTIVE CORRELATIVE.

**Neo-Classicism:** The term applied to the CLASSICISM which dominated English literature in the RESTORATION AGE and in the eighteenth century. It draws its name from the fact that it found in classical literature and in contemporary French neo-classical writings models for its literary expressions and a group of attitudes toward life and art. It was, at least in part, the result of the reaction against the dying fires of enthusiasm which had blazed extravagantly in the RENAISSANCE. Upon the RENAISSANCE idea of the limitless potentiality of man was imposed a view of man as limited, dualistic, imperfect; upon the intensity of his responses were imposed a reverence for order and a delight in reason and rules; upon the burgeoning of his imagination into new and strange worlds was imposed a distrust of innovation and invention; upon his expanding individualism was imposed a view that saw him most significantly in his generic qualities and his group activities; upon the enthusiasms of religious MYSTICISM was imposed the restrained good sense of DEISM. From the French critics, from Horace, from Virgil, and from other writers of classical literature came the artistic ideals of order, logic, restrained emotion, accuracy, "correctness," "good taste," and DECORUM. A sense of symmetry, a delight in design, and a view of art as centered in man, with man as its primary—although not its exclusive—subject matter, and the belief that literature should be judged in terms of its service to man (see PRAGMATIC THEORY OF ART) resulted in the seeking of proportion, unity, harmony, and grace in literary expressions that aimed to delight and to instruct and correct man, primarily as a social animal. It was the great age of the ESSAY, of the LETTER, of SATIRE, of moral instruction, of PARODY, and of BURLESQUE. The play of mind upon life was regarded as more important than the play of feeling, with the result that a polite, urbane, witty, intellectual art developed.

A few of the concrete effects of neo-classic ideals upon literature may be mentioned. POETIC DICTION and IMAGERY tended to become conventional with details subordinated to design. The appeal to the intellect rather than to the emotions resulted in a fondness for WIT and the production of much SATIRE, both in prose and verse. The irregular or unpleasant aspects of external NATURE, such as mountains, ocean, winter, were less frequently utilized than the pleasanter phases as represented in stars, flowers, or a formal garden. A tendency to REALISM marks the presentation of life with the generic qualities and common attributes and actions of men being stressed. Literature exalted form—polish, clarity, brilliance. It avoided the obscure or the mysterious. It valued the classical critical requirements of universality and DECORUM. It "imitated" (see IMITATION) the classics and cultivated classical literary forms and types, such as SATIRE and the ODE. The earlier English authors whose works were produced in a "less cultivated" age either were ignored or were admired more for their genius than for their art. Didactic literature flourished. Though BLANK VERSE and the SPENSERIAN STANZA were cultivated, rimed COUPLETS were the favorite form of verse. Although many of the attitudes and mannerisms of the neo-classicists were swept aside by the great tide of ROMANTICISM, the movement exerted a permanently wholesome effect upon literature in its clarifying and chastening effect upon English prose style and in its establishing in English literature the importance of certain classical graces, such as recognition of order and good form, unified structure, clearness, conciseness, and restraint. Poetic technique as developed by Pope, too, has become a permanent heritage, even such romanticists as Byron having learned at his feet. Indeed, imitations of Pope's verse have been innumerable in eighteenth- and nineteenth-century English and American literature. In the twentieth century there has been a strong neo-classical tendency in much of the best poetry and criticism, growing out of a reaction against ROMANTICISM and out of a growing distrust of the potentialities of man, together with a new respect for the place of intellect in life and art. Writers like T. E. Hulme, T. S. Eliot, and the NEW CRITICS are on many issues, *mutatis mutandis,* at one with *neo-classicism.*

**Neo-Classic Period:** The period in English literature between the return of the Stuarts to the English throne in 1660 and the full assertion of ROMANTICISM which came with the publication of *Lyrical Ballads* by Wordsworth and Coleridge in 1798. It falls into three relatively distinct segments: the RESTORATION AGE (1660–1700), the AUGUSTAN AGE (1700–1750), and the AGE OF JOHNSON (1750–1798).

In the RESTORATION AGE, England underwent a strong reaction against the Puritanism of the COMMONWEALTH INTERREGNUM; its already strong interest in scientific investigation and philosophical thought increased; and NEO-CLASSICISM, with particularly strong French influences, developed steadily. The HEROIC COUPLET became a major verse form; the ODE was a widely used poetic GENRE; and the poetic muse usually served didactic or satiric purposes. In prose, despite the tendency toward utilitarian goals, the "modern" style was developing, notably in Dryden's work. In DRAMA, the re-opening of the theatres and the establishment of the PATENT THE-ATRES led to the development of the HEROIC DRAMA in COUPLETS and the COMEDY OF MANNERS in prose. Milton, Bunyan, and Dryden were the principal writers of the period, with *Paradise Lost* and *Pilgrim's Progress,* although atypical of the spirit of license and re-volt dominant in the age, perhaps its major achievements in litera-ture. Dryden's accomplishments, although none of them reached the individual heights of Milton or Bunyan, were signally fine, and pointed forward toward the AUGUSTAN AGE. Otway, Wycherley, and Congreve enriched the stage, while the prose of Locke found its way into a permanent place in English thought.

In the AUGUSTAN AGE, NEO-CLASSICISM found its highest English expression. The classical ideals of taste, polish, "common sense," and reason (drawn from the ancients, from France, and from the RESTORATION AGE, and modified by current philosophical and sci-entific activities) were more important than emotion and IMAGINA-TION. DEISM was advancing steadily, and the same rule of reason resulted in a literature that was realistic, satirical, moral, correct, and affected strongly in its origins and its expressions by politics and intrigue. Poetry sparkled with the polished COUPLETS of Pope. It was concerned with truth, with the satiric, and the didactic. The MOCK EPIC and the verse ESSAY were common forms. In the work of James Thomson was to be found, in BLANK VERSE and in the SPENSERIAN STANZA, a growing concern with nature and science; and in the "GRAVEYARD SCHOOL" a sentimental melancholy.

On the stage the HEROIC DRAMA was no more, being replaced by the DOMESTIC TRAGEDY of writers like Lillo and imitations of CLASSI-

CAL TRAGEDY such as Addison's *Cato*. SENTIMENTAL COMEDY replaced the less "moral" COMEDY OF MANNERS, in the work of men like Cibber and Steele. The Licensing Act of 1737 imposed a stifling political censorship on the English theatre.

It was a great age of prose. The essay PERIODICAL was adumbrated in JOURNALS like Defoe's *Review*, and attained its epitome in *The Tatler* and *The Spectator*—journals that had a profound influence on English prose style and were followed by a host of imitators. The prose SATIRES of Swift were among the glories of the age. The prose FICTION of Defoe, and the early NOVELS of Richardson, Fielding, and Smollett had all appeared before the mid-century mark.

The AGE OF JOHNSON was a period of transition that was still dominated by the critical energies and the prose vigor of a great representative of the passing tradition, Dr. Samuel Johnson. The developing interest in human freedom, the developing impact of German ROMANTICISM, the widening range of intellectual interests and human sympathies, the developing appreciation of external NATURE and the country life, the developing cult of the primitive—all joined with political events like the American and the French revolutions and religious occurrences like the rise of Methodism to establish the bedrock upon which English ROMANTICISM was to rest.

In poetry Gray, Cowper, Burns, and Crabbe flourished. An interest in folk literature and popular BALLADS developed. In the DRAMA Goldsmith and Sheridan returned laughter to the stage with the COMEDY OF MANNERS, although SENTIMENTAL COMEDY still flourished. Shakespeare was immensely popular on the stage; and the BURLESQUE, the PANTOMIME, and the MELODRAMA—forms that freed the DRAMA (although at a high price) from the sharp restrictions of the PATENT THEATRES—developed. In prose, the NOVEL advanced steadily. In the works of Sterne and Mackenzie developed the sentimental NOVEL; in those of Walpole, Mrs. Radcliffe, and Clara Reeves the GOTHIC NOVEL. By the end of the century Brooke and Godwin were producing novels of political and philosophical purpose.

In the AGE OF JOHNSON the greatest literary figures were Johnson himself, as poet, critic, novelist, journalist, and lexicographer—an embodiment of the ideals of the *Neo-Classic Period*—and Robert Burns, as poet of the common people, the Scottish soil, and the Romantic soul—an adumbration of the coming ROMANTIC PERIOD.

By 1798, Wordsworth, Coleridge, and Blake had already launched their careers; Johnson and Burns were dead; and Shelley, Byron, and Keats had been born.

See the *Outline of Literary History*, AUGUSTAN AGE, RESTORATION AGE, and the AGE OF JOHNSON.

**Neologism:** A word newly introduced into a language, especially as a means of enhancing literary style. There was much conscious use of *neologisms*, especially from Greek and Latin sources, in RENAISSANCE times, partly as a result of a definite critical attitude toward the enrichment of the native English vocabulary. But the practice is not confined to any one period. Too often authors employ *neologisms* in a somewhat "cheap" effort to give their style an atmosphere of freshness or erudition (see PEDANTRY), but the variety and flexibility and resourcefulness of the modern English vocabulary are largely the cumulative result of the successful use of *neologisms*. A vast number of *neologisms*, of course, employed by individual authors or by stylistic "schools" (see EUPHUISM, GONGORISM) have not gained permanent foothold in the vocabulary. See COINED WORDS.

**Neo-Platonism:** A system of belief which originated in Alexandria in the third century, composed of elements of PLATONISM mixed Oriental beliefs and with some aspects of Christianity. Its leading representative was Plotinus. See PLATONISM.

**New Criticism, The:** In a strict sense, the term is applied to the criticism written by John Crowe Ransom, Allen Tate, R. P. Blackmur, Robert Penn Warren, and Cleanth Brooks, and it is derived from Ransom's book, *The New Criticism*, published in 1941, which discussed a movement in America in the 1930's which paralleled movements in England led by critics like T. S. Eliot, I. A. Richards, and William Empson. Generally the term is applied, however, to the whole body of contemporary criticism which centers its attention in the work of art as an object in itself; finds in it a special kind of language opposed to—or at least different from—the languages of science or philosophy; and examines it through a process of close analysis. The New Critics constitute the school in contemporary criticism which most completely employs the OBJECTIVE THEORY OF ART. The movement has varied sources; among them are I. A. Richards' *The Principles of Literary Criticism* (1924), Wil-

liam Empson's *Seven Types of Ambiguity* (1930), the work of
Remy de Gourmont, the anti-romanticism of T. E. Hulme, the
French EXPLICATION DE TEXTE, the psychological theories of the
ARCHETYPE, the concepts of order and tradition of the Southern
AGRARIANS, and the work of Ezra Pound and T. S. Eliot.

Not even the group to which the term can be applied in its
strictest sense has formed a school subscribing to a fixed dogma;
when to this group are added others like Yvor Winters and Kenneth Burke, it can be seen that the *New Criticism* is really a cluster
of attitudes toward literature rather than an organized critical system. The primary concern of these critics has been to discover the
intrinsic worth of literature, to demonstrate that worth to intelligent
readers, and to defend that worth against the types of attack they
believe to be inherent in contemporary thought. Indeed, the *New
Criticism* is primarily a protest against the conventional and traditional ways of viewing life and art. The New Critics are protesting
against the mechanistic and positivistic nature of the modern
world; and their protest is framed in terms of a cultural tradition,
a religious order, and sometimes an aristocratic social system. They
are protesting against a view of life and knowledge that rests on
fact and inference from fact alone; and their protest takes the
form of an insistence on literature as a valid form of knowledge and as a communicator not of the truths of other languages
but of the truths incommunicable in other terms than those of
the language of literature itself. They are protesting against
ROMANTICISM with its doctrines of self-expression, its EXPRESSIVE
THEORY OF ART, and its philosophy of perfectibility; and their protest takes the form of the OBJECTIVE THEORY OF ART, of the impersonal artist, and of neo-classic restraint. They are protesting
against IMPRESSIONISM in criticism; and their protest takes the form
of intense methodological concern and often of semantic analysis.
They were originally protesting against the NEW HUMANISM of Babbitt and More; and their protest took the form of an insistence that
the morality and value of a work of art is a function of its inner
qualities and that literature cannot be evaluated in general terms
or terms not directly related to the work itself. Their concern has
been with the IMAGE, the SYMBOL, the "meaning," and only infrequently with GENRE, with PLOT, or with CHARACTER. This aspect
of the *New Criticism* has led to attacks by critics interested in GENRE
or FORM and who assert that the New Critics reduce literature to a
linguistic or symbolic monism that makes the significant discrimina-

tion among types impossible. In actual practice, the *New Criticism* has most often been applied, and has worked best when applied, to the LYRIC; it has been less successful when applied to extended works of FICTION or DRAMA. See CRITICISM, TYPES OF; INTENTIONAL FALLACY; AFFECTIVE FALLACY; IMAGERY; EXPLICATION DE TEXTE; AUTOTELIC; ARCHETYPE; MYTH; OBJECTIVE THEORY OF ART.

**New Humanism, The:** See HUMANISM, THE NEW.

**Nine Worthies, The:** Late medieval and early RENAISSANCE literature reflects the widespread tradition or classification of the heroes known as the "nine worthies." Caxton lists them in his preface to Malory's *Le Morte Darthur* in the conventional three groups: Hector, Alexander, Julius Caesar (pre-Christian pagans); Joshua, David, Judas Maccabeus (pre-Christian Jews); Arthur, Charlemagne, Godfrey of Boulogne (Christians). They are personated in the burlesque play incorporated in Shakespeare's *Love's Labour's Lost*.

**Nobel Prize:** A large sum of money awarded annually to the person having produced during the year the most eminent piece of work in the field of idealistic literature. This award, granted through the Swedish Academy in Stockholm, was made possible by Alfred Bernhard Nobel (1833–1896), a Swedish chemist and engineer. Nobel willed the income from practically his entire estate for the establishment of such annual prizes and the endowment of research foundations, not only in the field of literature but also in physics, chemistry, medicine or physiology, and for the promotion of world peace. The amount of each prize varies with the income from the main fund, but averages about $40,000. Nationality does not enter into consideration at all in the awarding of the prizes, which was begun on December 10, 1901, the fifth anniversary of Nobel's death. A further stipulation of Nobel's will empowers the Swedish Academy, which awards the prize for literature, to withhold the grant for any one year; if no work during that year is deemed worthy of the recognition, the amount of the prize reverts to the main fund. The winners of the prize in literature have been as followers: 1901, René François Armand Sully-Prudhomme; 1902, Theodore Mommsen; 1903, Björnstjerne Björnson; 1904, equally divided between Frédéric Mistral and José Echegaray; 1905,

Henryk Sienkiewicz; 1906, Giosué Carducci; 1907, Rudyard Kipling; 1908, Rudolf Eucken; 1909; Selma Lagerlöf; 1910, Paul Heyse; 1911, Maurice Maeterlinck; 1912, Gerhart Hauptmann; 1913, Rabindranath Tagore; 1915, Romain Rolland; 1916, Verner von Heidenstam; 1917, divided equally between Karl Gjellerup and Henrik Pontoppidan; 1919, Carl Spitteler; 1920, Knut Hamsun; 1921, Anatole France; 1922, Jacinto Benavente; 1923, William Butler Yeats; 1924, Vladislav St. Reymont; 1925, George Bernard Shaw; 1926, Grazia Deledda; 1927, Henri Bergson; 1928, Sigrid Undset; 1929, Thomas Mann; 1930, Sinclair Lewis; 1931, Erik Axel Karlfeldt; 1932, John Galsworthy; 1933, Ivan Bunin; 1934, Luigi Pirandello; 1936, Eugene O'Neill; 1937, Roger M. duGard; 1938, Pearl Buck; 1939, Eemil Sillanpaa; 1944, Johannes V. Jensen; 1945, Lucila Godoy y Alcayaga (Gabriela Mistral); 1946, Herman Hesse; 1947, André Gide; 1948, T. S. Eliot; 1949, William Faulkner; 1950, Bertrand Russell; 1951, Par Lagerkvist; 1952, François Mauriac; 1953, Winston Churchill; 1954, Ernest Hemingway; 1955, Halldor Kiljan Laxness; 1956, Juan Ramon Jimenez; 1957, Albert Camus; 1958, Boris Pasternak; 1959, Salvatore Quasimodo. No awards were made in literature in 1914, 1918, 1935, and 1943. The giving of the prizes was suspended in the period 1940–1942.

**Nocturne:** A poetic and often sentimental composition, expressing moods supposed to be especially appropriate to evening or night time. A SERENADE; a SONG.

*Nom de plume* (**pen name**): A fictitious name adopted by a writer for professional use or to disguise his true identity. For example, Sidney Porter assumed the pen name "O. Henry"; and Madame Amantine Lucile Aurore Dudevant, almost unknown by her real name, was famous as the French novelist, George Sand.

**Nonsense Verse:** A variety of LIGHT VERSE entertaining because of its strong rhythmic quality and lack of logic or consecutive development of thought. In addition to the marked RHYTHM, *nonsense verse* is often characterized by the presence of coined nonsense words ("frabjous day") a mingling of words from various languages (MACARONIC VERSE), "tongue twisters," and a calling upon the printer for unbelievably freakish arrangement of type to portray Christmas trees, pipes, men falling downstairs—anything which occurs to the fancy of the versifier. LIMERICKS are a popular nonsense verse form. Edward Lear and Lewis Carroll have built large reputations through writing *nonsense verse*.

**Norman Conquest:** The conquest of England by the Normans following the victory of William I in 1066 at the Battle of Senlac (Hastings). It affected English literature and the English language drastically by the introduction of Norman-French cultural and racial characteristics and ideals and by the introduction of the French language. It was followed by three centuries of social, political, and linguistic readjustment, out of which modern England was to come. See ANGLO-NORMAN (LANGUAGE), ANGLO-NORMAN PERIOD, ENGLISH LANGUAGE, MIDDLE ENGLISH, MIDDLE ENGLISH PERIOD.

**Novel:** The term *novel* is used in its broadest sense to designate any extended fictional prose narrative. In practice, however, its use is customarily restricted to narratives in which the representation of character occurs either in a static condition or in the process of development as the result of events or actions (see CHARACTERIZATION). Often the term implies that some organizing principle—PLOT or THEME or idea—should be present in a narrative that is called a *novel*. Almost without exception, *novel* refers to a prose work; although Chaucer's *Troilus and Criseyde* has frequently been called a *novel*. The term *novel* is an English transliteration of the Italian *novella*, a short, compact, broadly realistic tale popular in the medieval period and perhaps best represented by the tales in the *Decameron*. In most European countries the word *roman* is used rather than *novel*, thus linking the *novel* with that body of legendary, imaginative, and poetic material associated with the older ROMANCE, of which, in one sense the *novel* is a modern extension. The conflict between the imaginative and poetic recreation of experience implied in *roman* and the realistic representation of the soiled world of common men and action implied in *novel* has been present in the form from its beginning, and it accounted for a distinction often made in the eighteenth and nineteenth centuries between the ROMANCE and the *novel*, in which the ROMANCE was the tale of the long ago or the far away or the imaginatively improbable; whereas the *novel* was bound by the facts of the actual world and the laws of probability.

All *novels* are representations in fictional narrative of life or experience but the form is itself as protean as life and experience themselves have proved to be. Serious FICTION deals with man in significant action in his world. The world which appears to be a significant stage for such action varies greatly from author to author. An author's world may be only within the lowest recesses of the human unconscious; it may be the haunted deck of a whaling ship; it may be the fixed social structure of an aristocratic society; it may be the jungle of Africa or of a vast city; it may be the ideal structure of a Utopian dream. And man in his essential self can be viewed in an endlessly varying series of guises. Basically what we are saying here is that the subject matter of the *novel* defies cataloging or analysis; it may range from the puckish recollections of *Tristram Shandy* to the complex and seemingly total actuality of *War and Peace*.

In shaping this various material to the formal demands of FICTION, the novelists have displayed an equal variety. The *novel* may concentrate upon character, almost to the exclusion of incident or PLOT. It may be merely a series of incidents strung together like beads on a string, as the PICARESQUE NOVEL tends to be. It may be firmly plotted, with a structure as firm and sure as that of a TRAGEDY (see DRAMATIC STRUCTURE). It may attempt to present the details of life with a scientist's detached and objective completeness, as in NATURALISM; or it may try by IMAGE and linguistic and syntactic modification to reproduce the unconscious flow of the emotions, as in the STREAM-OF-CONSCIOUSNESS NOVEL. It may be episodic, loose in structure, epic in proportions—what is called "panoramic"—or it may be as tightly knit as a well-made play, bringing its material forward in dramatic orderliness—what is called "scenic."

But however diffuse and various the *novel* is as a form, it has always submitted itself to the dual test of artistic success and imitative accuracy or truth. It has, therefore, proved to be a continuing problem to the critic, while it has spoken with unique authority to the average reader of the past two centuries. Its best definition is ultimately the history of what it has been.

The English *novel* is essentially an eighteenth-century product. However, without the richness of literary activity which had preceded the eighteenth century, the *novel* could not have matured. The narrative interest developed in the stories of Charlemagne and Arthur, the various romantic CYCLES, the FABLIAUX; the descriptive values and appreciation of nature found in the PASTORALS; the historical interest of DIARIES and JOURNALS; the enthusiasm for character portrayal developed in sketches and BIOGRAPHIES; the use of suspense in TALES and MEDIEVAL ROMANCES—all these had to be familiar and understood before writers could evolve the *novel*, a form which draws certain elements from many of the literary types which preceded it.

*The Roots of the English Novel.*—But the matter is hardly as simple as this situation may suggest. Classical literature of Greece and Italy had its forms of the modern *novel*. In the second century B.C., Aristides wrote a series of tales of his home town, Miletus, a collection which was called *Milesiaka* but which is not known to scholars today, though Edmund Gosse ventures to say that it "was probably the beginning of the modern novel." Six centuries later Heliodorus, a Syrian, wrote *Aethiopica*—a love story at least somewhat true to life. *Daphnis and Chloe* (Greek), attributed to Longus of the third century, can be, says the same critic, "strictly called a novel." In Latin there were various contributory works of which only two will be mentioned here, the *Golden Ass* of Apuleius, a translation from the Greek, and the *Satyricon* of Petronius which presented the life and customs of the time of Nero.

But the NOVELLA of Italy is one of the earlier literary forms to which the modern *novel* is deeply indebted both for its narrative form and for its name. The appearance of *Cento Novelle Antiche* just before the opening of the fourteenth century gave great vogue to the NOVELLA form. These NOVELLE were stories of scandalous love, of chivalry, of mythology and morals, of the type best known to modern English readers, perhaps, through the gay stories of Boccacio's *Decameron* (*ca.*1348). Loose women, unscrupulous priests, rough peasants, and high-born nobles, formed the central figures of most of these tales. A few of the more famed collections of NOVELLE are: Sacchetti's *Trecente Novelle*, Fiorentino's *Il Pecorone*, Masuccio's *Novellino*, and Bandello's *Novelle*.

From Spain came at least two works which were major influences on the development of the *novel:* the *Lazarillo de Tormes* of 1554 and Cervantes' *Don Quixote* of 1605 (see PICARESQUE NOVEL).

France, like Italy, was greatly given to the short tale, the NOVELLA form. About 1450 was written the *Quinze Joies du Mariage* (anonymous) in the manner of the Italian. Antoine de la Sale's *Cent Nouvelles Nouvelles* and Bonaventure Despériers' *Nouvelles Récréations* carried on this interest. In 1535 appeared the *Gargantua* of Rabelais, which, while not at all a *novel*, nevertheless has certain sustained narrative interest which warrants its inclusion in this summary. Honoré d'Urfé's *Astrée* (1610) has more definitely the qualities we demand in a *novel* today and by the middle of the seventeenth century Mlle. de Scudéry (1607–1701) was writing romances which might pass muster—if interests had not changed so much—even in the twentieth century. The romantic qualities of Scudéry called forth a realistic reaction from Scarron, who wrote *Roman Comique*. Some literary historians assign to Marguerite de la Vergne the honor of having created the first full-blown French *novels* in her *Princesse de Montpensier* and *Princesse de Clèves* written during the 1660's. Other French works important in the development of the *novel* were: La Fontaine's *Psyché* (1669), Fénelon's *Télémanque* (1669), Le Sage's *Gil Blas* (1715, Books I–III), Marivaux's *Marianne* (1731), and Prévost's *Manon Lescaut* (1731).

English writers of the eighteenth century, then, had as a background the whole experience of continental Europe. The classical literature of Greece and Rome, the CYCLES of ROMANCE, PASTORAL literature, the PICARESQUE tale of adventure, the interest in human character portrayed through the ANA—all these elements and others held in solution the material which was eventually to crystallize into the English *novel*. In addition to these beginnings from Europe, the English novelists had native parallels of their own—the Arthurian materials, the *Euphues* of Lyly (1579), the *Arcadia* of Sir Philip Sidney, the narrative interest in Lodge's *Rosalynde* (1590), the picaresque element in Nash's *Jack Wilton* (1594), the humanitarian sympathy for the slave and the narrative chronicle of Aphra Behn's *Oroonoko* (1688), the extended narrative of moral significance in John Bunyan's *Pilgrim's Progress* (1678–1684), and the character element present in the *Spectator* papers of Addison and Steele. Defoe, in *Robinson Crusoe* (1719) and *Moll Flanders* (1722), using very loose narrative structures, and Swift, in *Gulliver's Travels* (1726), using satiric ALLEGORY, had brought VERISIMILITUDE to adventure and to the chronicling of human life, two vital component parts of the later *novel* form.

*The Novel Matures.*—With these narrative qualities then already rooted in various types of English and European writing, the ground was fertile, tilled, and seeded when Samuel Richardson, in 1740, issued his *Pamela: or Virtue Rewarded*, the first English book which practically all critics and historians are willing to call a clearly realized *novel*. Richardson's three *novels, Pamela, Clarissa*

*Harlowe* (1747–1748), and *Sir Charles Grandison* (1753) are chiefly in the EPISTOLARY form and have one eye full upon the ethics of the time.

After Richardson's success with *Pamela*, followed rapidly other significant *novels:* Henry Fielding started his *Joseph Andrews* (1742) as a SATIRE on the niceness of *Pamela*, but before going far he forgot his ironical intent and told a vigorous story of his own. In 1748 Smollett published *Roderick Random;* in 1749 came Fielding's greatest *novel, Tom Jones,* important for its development of PLOT and its realistic interpretation of English life; in 1751 both Smollett and Fielding repeated, the first with *Peregrine Pickle* and the second with *Amelia.* Defoe, Richardson, Fielding, Smollett— these men stand at the very source of the English *novel.* The succeeding years brought other *novels* and novelists, but the first real impetus to long fiction was given by these four. Sterne wrote *Tristram Shandy* (1760–1767), a work which broke, even this early, the narrative form of the *novel* and, applying Locke's psychological theories, undertook the exploration of the inner self. Horace Walpole made much of the GOTHIC mysteries in his *Castle of Otranto* (1764). Two years later Oliver Goldsmith wrote the *Vicar of Wakefield.* And then came such *novels* as Fanny Burney's *Evelina* (1778) and Ann Radcliffe's *Mysteries of Udolpho* (1794).

The nineteenth century saw the flowering of the English *novel* as an instrument portraying a middle-class society. Jane Austen produced NOVELS OF MANNERS and Scott virtually created the HISTORICAL NOVEL and carried it to a high point in the first quarter of the century. The great Victorian novelists—Dickens, Thackeray, and Trollope—created vast fictional worlds loaded with an abundance of social types and actions and arranged in complex and intricate melodramatic plots. In Thomas Hardy and George Eliot the last half of the century found writers who, in differing degrees, applied the tenets of NATURALISM to the *novel.*

In the twentieth century the English *novel* has probed more and more deeply into the human mind, there to find the materials with which to work. Virginia Woolf, Dorothy Richardson, and James Joyce, writing STREAM-OF-CONSCIOUSNESS NOVELS, have greatly expanded and deepened the subject matter of the *novel* and modified the techniques of FICTION so that this new subject matter may be dealt with. This century has been marked, too, by a growing concern over critical and technical issues in FICTION.

*The Novel in America.*—Not for fifty years after Richardson published *Pamela* were *novels* written in America, although *Pamela* appeared in an American edition within two years of its English publication. However, before the close of the eighteenth century *novels* were being written in America. *The Power of Sympathy*, a moralistic tale of seduction, by William Hill Brown (1789) must stand alone here as an early example. With Charles Brockden Brown, though, America produced her first important novelist. Brown, who wrote chiefly in the GOTHIC manner, was the author of four readable tales: *Arthur Mervyn* (1799), *Ormond* (1799), *Wieland* (1798), and *Edgar Huntley* (1799), as well as others less well known. Some twenty years later James Fenimore Cooper was publishing *The Spy* (1821), *The Pioneers* (1823), *The Pilot* (1824). The Leatherstocking Series included, in addition to *The Pioneers*, already mentioned, *The Deerslayer* (1841), *The Last of the Mohicans* (1826), *The Pathfinder* (1840), and *The Prairie* (1827). By 1850, when Hawthorne's *Scarlet Letter* appeared, the American *novel* had come into its full powers, a fact made abundantly clear by the publication in 1851 of Herman Melville's *Moby-Dick*. In the last half of the nineteenth century, REALISM, articulated as a theory by William Dean Howells and well exemplified in his work, and made the basis of a highly self-conscious art by Henry James, dominated the American *novel*. This control gave way in the early years of the twentieth century to the NATURALISM of Norris and Dreiser. After the first World War, a group of talented young novelists introduced a number of ideas drawn from the French realists and symbolists into American FICTION and produced a new, vital, but essentially ROMANTIC *novel* with strong naturalistic overtones. Important among them were Ernest Hemingway and William Faulkner. Today the American *novel* is a varied form practiced with self-conscious skill by a number of novelists and read by large audiences more earnestly than is any other serious literary form.

Attempts to classify the *novel* usually come to logical grief, however helpful they may be, for the terms are by no means mutually exclusive. In this Handbook special forms of the *novel* are discussed in separate entries, broadly classified by subject matter. They are DETECTIVE NOVEL, PSYCHOLOGICAL NOVEL, SOCIOLOGICAL NOVEL, SENTIMENTAL NOVEL, PROPAGANDA NOVEL, HISTORICAL NOVEL, NOVEL OF MANNERS, NOVEL OF CHARACTER, NOVEL OF INCIDENT, NOVEL OF THE SOIL, REGIONAL NOVEL, PICARESQUE NOVEL, GOTHIC NOVEL, APPRENTICESHIP NOVEL, STREAM-OF-CONSCIOUSNESS NOVEL, PROBLEM NOVEL, EPISTOLARY NOVEL. The principal modes in which novelists write are the general modes of their ages; such modes are the products of style, literary convention, and the author's attitude toward life. They are defined in this Handbook under the general terms such as REALISM, ROMANTICISM, IMPRESSION-ISM, EXPRESSIONISM, NATURALISM.

**Novel of Character:** A NOVEL which places its major emphasis upon the representation and development of character rather than upon exciting EPISODE, as in the NOVEL OF INCIDENT, or unity of PLOT or STRUCTURE. See NOVEL, CHARACTERIZATION.

**Novel of Incident:** A term applied to NOVELS in which action and more or less unrelated EPISODES dominate, and PLOT and character are subordinate. In this type of NOVEL the PLOT structure is loose and easy; emphasis is on interest and thrilling incident rather than on CHARACTERIZATION or sustained SUSPENSE. If one may call Defoe's *Robinson Crusoe* a NOVEL, then it may be used to illustrate this *novel of incident* type. Here the EPISODES of the shipwreck, the meeting with Friday, the clash with visiting natives—these and other incidents follow each other chronologically but they are more or less independent of each other and each does not contribute to the SUSPENSE with which the next is read. Dumas' *Three Muske-teers* is also a *novel of incident,* though here the PLOT is more developed than in Defoe's story.

**Novel of Manners:** A NOVEL, among the dominant forces of which are the social customs, manners, conventions, and habits of a definite social class at a particular time and place. In the true *novel of manners* the social mores of a specific group are defined and described in detail and with great accuracy, and these mores become powerful controls over characters. The *novel of manners* is often, although by no means always, satiric; it is always realistic in manner, however. The HISTORICAL NOVEL is sometimes called the *"novel of manners* laid in the past." The NOVELS of Jane Austen, Edith Wharton, and John P. Marquand are *novels of manners*. See NOVEL.

**Novel of Sensibility:** A NOVEL in which the characters have a heightened and highly emotional response to events, actions, and sentiments. The author attempts to produce in the reader a similar heightened emotional response to actions. Sterne's *Tristram Shandy* is a major example and Mackenzie's *Man of Feeling* unconsciously carries the idea of intensity of character response beyond the limits of reason. See SENTIMENTAL NOVEL.

**Novel of the Soil, The:** A special kind of REGIONALISM in the NOVEL, in which the lives of people struggling for existence in remote rural sections are starkly portrayed. Examples are Ellen Glasgow's *Barren Ground,* O. E. Rölvaag's *Giants in the Earth,* and Elizabeth Madox Roberts' *Time of Man.* It should be emphasized that the term *novel of the soil* refers primarily to a subject matter rather than to a manner; however, the term is usually restricted to portrayals of country life in the manner of REALISM or NATURALISM.

**Novelette:** A work of prose FICTION of intermediate length, longer than a SHORT STORY and shorter than a NOVEL. Since, however, there is little agreement on maximum length for any of these types, the distinction that in general the *novelette* displays the customarily compact structure of the SHORT STORY with the greater development of character, THEME, and action of the NOVEL is perhaps useful. Melville's *Billy Budd,* Stevenson's *Dr. Jekyll and Mr. Hyde,* Henry James' *The Turn of the Screw,* and Conrad's *Heart of Darkness* are examples.

**Novella:** A TALE or SHORT STORY. The term is particularly applied to the early tales of Italian and French writers—such as the *Decameron* of Boccaccio and the *Heptameron* of Marguerite of Valois. The form is of especial interest to students of English literature for two reasons: (1) many of these early *novelle* were used by English writers as sources for their own work, and (2) it was from this form that the term *novel* as a designation of a form of prose FICTION developed. The *novelle* were among the significant formative influences on the English NOVEL.

**Obiter dicta:** Things said "by the way"; incidental remarks: opposed to statements based upon calculated, deliberate judgment. Though legal in origin, the term is sometimes used in literary association, as in speaking of one author's *obiter dicta* being weightier and wiser than another's serious, labored expressions.

**Objective Correlative:** A term first used by T. S. Eliot to describe a pattern of objects, actions, or events, or a situation which can serve effectively to awaken in the reader the emotional response which the author desires without being a direct statement of that emotion. It is an impersonal or objective means of communicating feeling. Eliot calls the *objective correlative* "the only way of expressing emotion in the form of art" and defines it as "a set of objects, a situation, a chain of events which shall be the formula of that *particular* emotion, such that when the external facts, which must terminate in sensory experience, are given, the emotion is immediately evoked." The term has had wide currency in this sense among contemporary critics. It had been used by Washington Allston in a lecture on art as early as 1850 to describe the process by which the external world produces pleasurable emotion, but Eliot's usage gave it new meaning and made of it a new term. See NEGATIVE CAPABILITY, AESTHETIC DISTANCE.

**Objective Theory of Art:** A critical term used by M. H. Abrams to describe the view which holds the literary work to be most significant as an object in itself, independent of the facts of its composition, the actuality it imitates, its author's stated intention, or the effect it produces on its audience. See CRITICISM, HISTORICAL SKETCH; AUTOTELIC; NEW CRITICISM.

**Objectivity:** A quality in a literary work of impersonality, of freedom from the expression of personal sentiments, attitudes, or emotions by the author. In contemporary criticism *objectivity* is a highly desirable quality in art. See AESTHETIC DISTANCE, OBJECTIVE CORRELATIVE, NEGATIVE CAPABILITY.

**Occasional Verse:** Poetry written to grace or commemorate a social, historical, or personal event. Although the term includes VERS DE SOCIÉTÉ, it usually designates writing of more serious and more dignified purpose. POETS LAUREATE are called upon to produce *occasional verse* in the discharge of their responsibilities. Among notable examples of *occasional verse* are Spenser's "Epithalamion," celebrating his marriage; Dryden's "Astraea Redux," celebrating the return to the throne of Charles II; Marvell's "Horatian Ode upon Cromwell's Return from Ireland," and Milton's "Lycidas," upon the death of Edward King.

**Octameter:** A line of VERSE consisting of eight FEET. See SCANSION.

**Octave:** An eight-line STANZA. The chief use of the term, however, is to denote the first eight-verse division of the Italian SONNET as separate from the last six-verse division, the SESTET. In the strict SONNET usage the *octave* rimes *abbaabba*, serves to state a generalization later applied or resolved in the SESTET, and comes to such a complete close at the end of the eighth line as to be marked by a full stop.

**Octavo:** A BOOK SIZE designating a book whose SIGNATURE results from sheets folded to eight leaves or sixteen pages. See BOOK SIZES.

**Ode:** "Any strain of enthusiastic and exalted lyrical verse, directed to a fixed purpose, and dealing progressively with one dignified theme." (Gosse.) The term connotes certain qualities both of manner and form. In manner, the *ode* is an elaborate LYRIC, expressed in language dignified and sincere and definitely imaginative and intellectual in tone. In form the *ode* is much more complicated than most of the LYRIC types. Perhaps the essential distinction of form is the division into STROPHES: the STROPHE, ANTISTROPHE, and EPODE. Originally a Greek form used in dramatic poetry, the *ode* was then choral in quality. Accompanied by music, the CHORUS of singers moved up one side during the STROPHE, down the other during the ANTISTROPHE, and stood in place during the EPODE. In a general way this movement emphasized the rise and fall of emotional power. In English poetry there are three types of *odes:* the PINDARIC (regular), the HORATIAN or homostrophic, and the IRREGULAR type. The PINDARIC ODE is characterized by the three-STROPHE division, the STROPHE and the ANTISTROPHE alike in form, the EPODE different from the other two. The metrics and verse lengths may vary within any one STROPHE of the *ode,* but when the movement is repeated the metrical scheme for corresponding divisions should be similar though accompanied by new RIMES. It is not essential that STROPHE, ANTISTROPHE, and EPODE alternate regularly since the EPODE may be used at the end or inconsistently between the STROPHE and the ANTISTROPHE (*Ode to Liberty,* Collins). The second *ode*-form, the HORATIAN or homostrophic, consists of only one STANZA type, and that type may be almost infinitely varied within its pattern (*Ode to France,* Coleridge). The third form of the *ode,* the IRREGULAR, is credited to the poet Cowley, who seems to have thought he was writing PINDARIC ODES. Like the second type considered, freedom within the STROPHE is the characteristic earmark of this form. But here the STROPHES are rules unto themselves and all pretense at STANZA pattern may be discarded. The length of the lines may vary, the number of lines in each STROPHE may vary widely, the RIME pattern need not be carried over from STANZA to STANZA, and the metrical movement will quicken and slacken with the mood of the poet and the emotional intensity. Much more flexible than the two other forms considered, the IRREGULAR ODE affords greatest freedom of expression to the poet and, consequently, greatest license. In English poetry, these three forms are well represented in the following poems: Gray's "The Bard," an example of the strict PINDARIC ODE; Collin's "Ode to Evening," an example of the HORATIAN ODE; and Wordsworth's "Ode on the Intimations of Immortality," an example of the IRREGULAR ODE. In contemporary poetry, the public nature, solemn diction, and stately gravity of the *ode* have on occasion been effectively used for ironic overtones, as in Allen Tate's "Ode on the Confederate Dead."

**Old English (Language):** That form of language spoken in the British Isles between the Anglo-Saxon invasions in the fifth century and the NORMAN CONQUEST in the eleventh; a Germanic dialect. See ENGLISH LANGUAGE.

**Old English Period:** The period in English history and literature between the invasion of England by the Teutonic tribes of Angles, Saxons, and Jutes, beginning about 428, and the establishment of the Norman rule of England around 1100, following the triumphant Conquest of England by the Norman French under William the Conqueror. Saxon monarchies were established in Sussex, Wessex, and Essex in the fifth and sixth centuries; Anglian monarchies in Northumbria, East Anglia, and Mercia in the sixth and seventh centuries. Christianity was introduced early and gradually won out over the pagan culture. It was an age of intertribal conflict and, in the ninth century, of struggles with the invading Danes. The greatest of the rulers of the period was Alfred, who, in the ninth century, effected a unification of the Teutonic groups.

Learning and culture flourished in the monasteries, with Whitby the cradle of English poetry in the North and Winchester that of English prose in the South. Although much writing throughout the period was in Latin, Christian monks began writing in the vernacular which we call OLD ENGLISH about 700. In the earliest part of the period the poetry, written in accentual METER and linked with ALLITERATION (see OLD ENGLISH VERSIFICATION) was centered on the life of the Germanic tribes and was basically pagan, although Christian elements were early incorporated. The best of these poems which have survived are the great EPIC *Beowulf* (*ca.*700), "The Seafarer," "Widsith," and "Deor's Lament." Early poetry of a more emphatically Christian nature included Caedmon's "Song," Biblical paraphrases such as *Genesis, Exodus, Daniel, Judith;* religious narratives such as the *Crist, Elene, Andreas;* and the allegorical *Phoenix* (a translation from Latin). Literature first flourished in Northumbria, but in the reign of Alfred the Great (871–901) West Saxon became the literary DIALECT. Under Alfred, much Latin literature was translated into English prose, such as Pope Gregory's *Pastoral Care,* Boethius' *Consolation of Philosophy,* and Bede's *Ecclesiastical History;* and the great *Anglo-Saxon Chronicle* was revised and expanded. A second prose revival took place in the HOMILIES of Aelfric and Wulfstan (tenth and eleventh centuries), works noted for the richness of their style, reflecting Latin models. Late examples of Anglo-Saxon verse are the "Battle of Maldon" and the "Battle of Brunanburgh," heroic poems. The NORMAN CONQUEST (1066) put an end to serious literary work in the OLD ENGLISH LANGUAGE. See OLD ENGLISH (LANGUAGE), OLD ENGLISH VERSIFICATION, ENGLISH LANGUAGE.

**Old English Versification:** The metrical system employed by English poets in the period before 1100. It is essentially an accentual system (see METER), consisting of equal numbers of accented syllables to the line and varying numbers of unaccented syllables. The normal Old English line fell into two HEMISTICHS, each having two accented syllables and with the HEMISTICHS separated by a heavy CAESURA. The ACCENTS are grammatical; that is, they fall on syllables which would normally carry stress in that particular construction. The HEMISTICHS are bound by ALLITERATION, one or both the accented syllables of the first alliterating with the first accented syllable of the second and much more rarely with the second accented syllable. Variant lines were: the rare "short line," which contains only two stressed syllables and no CAESURA, the stressed syllables being bound by ALLITERATION; and the "hypermetrical line" in which three or more stressed syllables may appear in each HEMISTICH. To go beyond such a schematic outline is to enter an area of great scholarly uncertainty and controversy. The reader is referred to Kemp Malone's excellent summary in Chapter III, "The Old Tradition: Poet Form," in *A Literary History of England*, edited by A. C. Baugh (New York, 1948).

**Omniscient Point of View:** A term used to describe the POINT OF VIEW in a work of FICTION in which the author is capable of knowing, seeing, and telling whatever he wishes in the story, and exercises this freedom at will. It is characterized by freedom in shifting from the exterior world to the inner selves of a number of characters and by a freedom in movement both in time and place; but to an even greater extent it is characterized by the freedom of the author to comment upon the meaning of actions and to state the thematic intentions of the story whenever and wherever he desires. See POINT OF VIEW.

**One-Act Play:** A form of DRAMA which has been attracting an increasing amount of attention since about 1890. Before that date *one-act plays* had been used chiefly on VAUDEVILLE programs and as curtain-raisers on the "legitimate" stage. About that time especial attention to the *one-act play* came with the LITTLE THEATRE MOVE-MENT and the practice of relying upon a group of such short plays for a single evening's entertainment. The fact that the form was adopted by playwrights of high ability (J. M. Barrie, A. W. Pinero, Gerhart Hauptmann, G. B. Shaw) furthered its development. A widening circle of authors has produced *one-act plays* in the twentieth century, both in England and America, including John Masefield, Lord Dunsany, Lady Gregory, J. M. Synge, John Galsworthy, A. A. Milne, Percy MacKaye, Eugene O'Neill, Paul Green, Thorton Wilder, Noel Coward, Tennessee Williams, and Arthur Miller. The technique of the *one-act play* is highly flexible, the most important demand being for unity of EFFECT, with consequent vigor of DIALOGUE, stressing of character, and economy of narrative materials. Its relation to the "regular" or longer DRAMA has often been likened to that of the SHORT STORY to the NOVEL.

**Onomatopoeia:** The use of words which in their pronunciation suggest their meaning. Some onomatopoeic words are "hiss," "slam," "buzz," "whirr," "sizzle." However, *onomatopoeia* in the hands of a poet becomes a much more subtle device than simply the use of such words when, in an effort to suit sound to sense, he creates verses which themselves carry their meaning in their sounds. A notable example is quoted from *The Princess* by Tennyson:

> The moan of doves in immemorial elms,
> And murmuring of innumerable bees.

The RHYTHM of the lines, the succession of sounds, the effectiveness of RIMES all contribute to the effect by which the poem as a pattern of sounds echoes the sense which its words denote. Perhaps the idea, accepted by some linguists, that front vowels tend to suggest light, small, or airy things and back vowels dark, large, and heavy things operates in producing the total onomatopoeic effect of a poem. Pope's lines in *An Essay on Criticism* may well be quoted:

> 'Tis not enough no harshness gives offense,
> The sound must seem an echo to the sense:
> Soft is the strain when Zephyr gently blows,
> And the smooth stream in smoother numbers flows;
> But when the loud surges lash the sounding shore,
> The hoarse, rough verse should like the torrent roar:
> When Ajax strives some rock's vast weight to throw,
> The line too labors, and the words move slow.

**Opera:** Though the primary interest in *opera* is musical, the fact that it is a dramatic form which has exerted a considerable influence upon English stage history and has employed important literary themes gives it an interest to the student of literature. Only its connection with English DRAMA will be noticed here. *Opera* is musical DRAMA in the sense that the DIALOGUE instead of being spoken is sung, to the accompaniment of instrumental music, now always an orchestra. A play in which incidental music is stressed may be called "operatic," but is not true *opera* if the DIALOGUE is spoken. Greek DRAMA contained DIALOGUE sung to the accompaniment of the lyre or flute and is therefore a precursor, in fact somewhat of a model, for modern *opera*, which developed in Italy about 1600 as a result of amateur efforts to recapture the quality of the musical effects of Greek TRAGEDY by means of musical recitation instrumentally accompanied. The form was at first a MONODY, as in Jacopo Peri's *Euridice* (1600), the first public production in the new style. From these beginnings developed the important form now known as grand *opera*. Italian *opera* reached England soon after 1700, but before this date certain definite advances in the direction of *opera* had taken place on the English stage. To some degree an outgrowth of the Renaissance MASQUE, Sir William Davenant's *Siege of Rhodes* (1656) is a precursor of the English *opera*, since it was "a musical entertainment . . . written in rime and designed on the lines of Italian *opera* to be sung in recitative and aria" (Allardyce Nicoll). The attention to scenery as well as the songs and orchestral accompaniment were suggestive of later English *opera*. During the RESTORATION AGE operatic versions of some of Shakespeare's plays (*The Tempest, Macbeth*) were called "dramatic *operas*," but the DIALOGUE was spoken, not sung. About 1689 Henry Purcell and Nahum Tate brought out *Dido and Aeneas*, in which the DIALOGUE was in recitative. Early in the eighteenth century Italian *operas* were "translated" and sung by English singers, as *Arsinoë, Queen of Cypress* (Drury Lane, 1705), and *Camilla* (1705–1707). Later "bilingual" *operas* appeared, in which Italian singers sang part of the DIALOGUE in Italian while English singers sang the rest in English. The first completely Italian *opera* sung in Italian in England was *Almahide* (1710), which established the success of the form in England. About this time George Frederick Handel came to England. He produced *Rinaldo* in 1711, and exerted a powerful influence for many years thereafter. From the first the efforts to employ Italian singers and *opera* met with much disfavor, as evidenced by Addison's SATIRE and by the famous BURLESQUE *opera* by John Gay, *The Beggar's Opera* (1728). The success of *opera* and various forms of BURLESQUE *opera* at this time probably had much to do with the decay of "legitimate" DRAMA and the growth of the tendency toward lyrical and spectacular elements on the English stage in the eighteenth and nineteenth centuries. See BALLAD-OPERA.

*Opéra bouffe:* A French term for a very light form of COMIC OPERA developed from VAUDEVILLE music and said to be the ancestor of the COMIC OPERAS of Gilbert and Sullivan.

**Operetta:** See COMIC OPERA.

**Oration:** A formal speech intended to inspire to some action. Carefully prepared and delivered in an impassioned manner, the *oration* carries its greatest power in the emotional appeal it makes. Although a major cultural interest in classical days and even up to a few decades ago, the *oration* has lost its popular appeal and is now but rarely heard in legislative halls, the court room, the church.

**Originality:** The use of new subject matter or forms or styles by an author, rather than the employment of traditional or conventional subject matters, forms, or styles. At various periods in literary history the value placed upon *originality* by authors, readers, and critics has fluctuated greatly. See INVENTION.

**Ossianic Controversy:** See LITERARY FORGERIES.

**Otiose:** A term used in literary criticism to characterize a STYLE which is verbose, redundant, pleonastic. Literally it implies *leisure* and, in the special sense here employed, it designates idle, useless, inefficient writing, the use of language which is so very much at leisure that it performs no useful function.

***Ottava rima:*** A STANZA pattern consisting of eight IAMBIC PENTAMETER lines riming *ababbcc*. Boccaccio is credited with originating this pattern, which was much used by Tasso and Ariosto. Some of the English poets making important use of *ottava rima* are Spenser, Milton, Keats, and Byron. The illustration is from *Don Juan:*

> But words are things, and a small drop of ink
>   Falling like dew, upon a thought, produces
> That which makes thousands, perhaps millions, think;
>   'Tis strange, the shortest letter which man uses
> Instead of speech, may form a lasting link
>   Of ages; to what straits old Time reduces
> Frail man, when paper—even a rag like this,
> Survives himself, his tomb, and all that's his!

In its original Italian form *ottava rima* lines were HENDECASYLLABIC, that is, had eleven syllables.

**Oxford Movement:** Also known as "Tractarian Movement" and "Anglo-Catholic Revival." During the first third of the nineteenth century the English Church had become somewhat lax in urging the ancient doctrines, in enforcing discipline, in carrying out ritual, and in keeping up the church edifices. In 1833 a movement for reform got under way at Oxford following a sermon on "national apostasy" by John Keble. The leader was John Henry (later Cardinal) Newman, who wrote the first of the ninety papers (*Tracts for the Times,* 1833–1841) in which the ideas of the group were advocated. Other leaders were R. H. Froude, Isaac Williams, Hugh James Rose (a Cambridge man), and E. B. Pusey. The reformers aimed primarily at combating liberalism and skepticism and restoring to the Church and to church worship the dignity, beauty, purity, and zeal of earlier times. They hoped also to protect the Church from the encroachment of the State, as threatened by the Whig Reform Bill of 1832 and other measures looking toward reducing the revenues of the Church and curbing its authority.

To provide a solid foundation for their reforms, the sponsors of the movement undertook to prove the divine origin of the Church and the historical continuity connecting the early Church with the Church of England. This led them to an espousal of certain doctrines regarded by some as purely Roman Catholic, and after the publication of Newman's final tract in 1841 a storm of criticism arose, as a result of which Newman lost his position at Oxford, became a layman, and finally (1845) joined the Roman Catholic Church, later becoming a Cardinal. When Charles Kingsley attacked his sincerity, Newman replied with the famous *Apologia pro Vita Sua* (1864), a full statement of his spiritual and mental history, the candor and beauty and force of which won for Newman the high regard which his personality and literary art have enabled him to retain ever since. Though some of Newman's followers also became Catholics, the main movement, led now by Pusey, continued, though in its later stages it became less controversial and theoretical and more practical, furthering the establishment of guilds, improvement of church music, revival of the ritual, building and beautifying of church buildings. Besides stimulating the work of one of the finest of English prose writers, the movement attracted the attention of various literary men, Carlyle heaping disdain upon it, Arnold attacking it, etc. Also the sponsors of the movement wrote a number of propagandist novels, like Newman's *Loss and Gain* and Charlotte M. Yonge's *The Heir of Redclyffe*. The Episcopal Church in the United States reflects much of the reform doctrine of the Tractarians.

**Oxford Reformers:** A term applied to a group of humanist scholars whose associations began at Oxford University in early RENAISSANCE times, particularly the three close friends John Colet, Sir Thomas More, and the great Dutch scholar Erasmus. Though Erasmus, who had come to Oxford to study Greek and who spent part of his life in England, was the most famous member of the group and More the best loved, Colet seems to have been the real leader. The group was zealously interested in effecting certain reforms in Church and State based upon current humanist ideas. Moral training and moral reform were to be accomplished through rational rather than emotional processes. Reason should dominate. Humanity should be uplifted through education and the consequent improvement of individual character. The church should be reformed from within by purging it of corrupt practices and by improving the standards, moral and educational, of the clergy. The group advocated the historical method in the study of the Bible, opposed medieval scholasticism and asceticism, and strongly advocated education as a means of improving religion, private character, and political institutions. Their activities can be merely hinted at here. More recorded his dream of a perfect human society and government in his *Utopia* (1516); Colet when dean of St. Paul's founded with his own funds the St. Paul's school for boys, where new methods of instruction were developed and where sons of the common folk might be admitted; Erasmus outlined his ideals of state in his *Institutes of a Perfect Prince.* Keenly interested in purging the church of the evils which Luther a few years later rebelled against, the *Oxford Reformers* were unwilling to follow either Luther or Henry VIII in breaking with Rome, and died good Catholics, though disappointed idealists.

**Oxymoron:** Etymologically, "pointedly foolish"; a rhetorical AN-TITHESIS bringing together two contradictory terms. Such a contrast makes for sharp emphasis. Examples are: "cheerful pessimist," "wise fool," "sad joy," "eloquent silence."

**Pæan:** A SONG of praise or joy. Originally the term was restricted to ODES sung by a Greek CHORUS in honor of Apollo; later the term was broadened to include praise sung to other deities of antiquity. In modern times, the word has come to mean simply any song of joy. Homer indicates, too, that *pæans* were frequently sung on military occasions: before an attack, after a victory, when a fleet set sail, etc.

**Pæon:** In METRICS, a FOOT consisting of one long or stressed syllable and three short or unstressed syllables. *Pæons* are named in terms of the one of the four syllables which is long or stressed, a "first *pæon*" being ― ◡ ◡ ◡, a "second" being ◡ ― ◡ ◡, etc. Although not common in English verse, this essentially classic

FOOT does occasionally appear, notably in the poetry of Gerard Manley Hopkins.

**Pageant:** Used in three senses: (1) a scaffold or stage on which DRAMAS were performed in the Middle Ages; (2) plays performed on such stages; (3) modern dramatic spectacles designed to celebrate some historical event, often of local interest. The medieval *pageant,* constructed on wheels for processional use, as in celebrating Corpus Christi day, was designed for the use of a particular guild for the production of a particular play and usually reflected this special purpose. Thus the *pageant* of the fisherman, designed to present the play of Noah, would be constructed and painted to represent the Ark. For a contemporary description of the medieval *pageant* and its use, see MYSTERY PLAY. Though the modern *pageant* is an outgrowth of a very ancient tradition which includes primitive religious festivals, Roman "triumphs," etc., its recent remarkable development in England and especially in America makes it essentially a twentieth-century spectacle. It is usually understood to mean an outdoor exhibition consisting of several scenes presented with recitation (PROLOGUES, etc.), usually with DIALOGUE, with historically appropriate costumes, sometimes with musical features, the whole being designed to commemorate some event which appeals to the emotional loyalties of the populace. Sometimes the *pageant* is processional, with a series of "floats," uniformed marchers, mounted officials, etc., while it is sometimes presented in an outdoor theatre of some sort, such as an athletic stadium. The true *pageant* is thought of as an outdoor exhibition, closely connected with the folk-drama movement.

**Palimpsest:** A writing surface, whether of vellum, papyrus, or other material, which has been used twice or more for manuscript purposes. Before the invention of paper, the scarcity of writing material made such substances very valuable and the vellum surfaces were often scraped or rubbed or the papyrus surfaces washed. With material so used a second time it frequently happened that the earlier script either was not completely erased or that, with age, it showed through the new. In this way many documents of very early periods have been preserved for posterity. In one instance, for example, a Syriac text of St. Chrysostom of perhaps the tenth century was found to be superimposed on a sixth-century grammatical work in Latin, which again had covered some fifth-century Latin records. Modern chemical methods make it possible today to recover many of the original texts.

**Palindrome:** A word, sentence, or VERSE which reads the same from left to right and from right to left. See ANAGRAM.

**Palinode:** A piece of writing recanting or retracting a previous writing, particularly such a recanting, in VERSE form, of an earlier ODE.

**Panegyric:** A formal written or oral composition lauding a person. In Roman literature *panegyrics* were usually presented in praise of a living person though in Greek literature they were more likely to be reserved for praise of the dead. This was a popular form of oratory among fulsome speakers who resorted to this sort of composition in praise of living emperors. Two famous *panegyrics* are those of Gorgias, the *Olympiacus,* and of Pliny the Younger delivered when he became consul, a speech praising Trajan. The term is now often used with a derogatory connotation. See ENCOMIUM.

**Pantheism:** A philosophic-religious attitude which finds the spirit of God manifest in all things and which holds that whereas all things speak the glory of God it is equally true that the glory of God is made up of all things. Finite objects are at once both God and the manifestation of God. The term is impossible of exact, formal definition since it is so personal a conviction as to be differently interpreted by different philosophers and religionists, but for its literary significance it is clearly enough described as an ardent faith in NATURE as both the revelation of deity and deity itself. The word was first used in 1705 by the deist John Toland who called himself a pantheist (from *pan* meaning "all" and *theos* meaning "deity"). The pantheistic attitude, however, is much older than the eighteenth century, since it pervades the primitive thought of Egypt and India, was common in Greece long before the time of Christ, was taken up by the Neo-platonists of the Middle Ages, and has played an important part in Christian and Hebraic doctrine. Spinoza is, from the philosophic point of view, the great spokesman of *pantheism,* as Goethe is, perhaps, the great poet of the idea. In literature *pantheism* finds frequent expression. Wordsworth in England and Emerson in America may be selected from many as giving typical expression to the pantheistic conception. The following, from Wordsworth's *Lines Composed a Few Miles above Tintern Abbey* is, perhaps, as clear an expression of the idea as is found in modern literature:

> . . . a sense sublime
> Of something far more deeply interfused,
> Whose dwelling is the light of setting suns,
> And the round ocean and the living air
> And the blue sky, and in the mind of man;
> A motion and a spirit, that impels
> All thinking things, all objects of all thought,
> And rolls through all things.

**Pantomime:** In its broad sense the term means silent acting; the form of dramatic activity in which silent motion, gesture, facial expression, and costume are relied upon to express emotional or narrative situations. The war dances of primitive society are thus pantomimic. Partly pantomimic was the Roman MIME and completely so the English DUMB SHOW. In English stage history, *pantomime* usually means the spectacular dramatic form which flourished from the early years of the eighteenth century. Though "*pantomime* proper" (no speaking) is said to have been introduced by a dancing master in 1702 at the Drury Lane Theatre, the usual form of *pantomime*, as sponsored at Lincoln's Inn Fields theatre by John Rich some years later, was somewhat more varied: "In the first place, there was usually a serious legendary story told by means of dancing and songs—in fact, a short opera. . . . In these plots moved the figures of the *commedia dell' arte*, burlesquing in silent movement the action of the more serious tale. All of this was laid upon a background of the most spectacular description, with the lavish use of 'machinery' and countless changes of scene to please the ravished spectators."[1] The *pantomime* flourished throughout the eighteenth century and, along with other related forms, till near the close of the nineteenth century, its popularity frequently diverting the activities of great actors (as David Garrick) from serious drama and affecting unfavorably the tradition of "legitimate" drama through its tendency to lower the public taste.

**Pantoum:** Usually considered as one of the sophisticated FRENCH FORMS though, as a matter of fact, the *pantoum* was taken over

[1] Allardyce Nicoll, *British Drama*, Thomas Y. Crowell Company, 1925, p. 270. Reprinted by permission of the publishers.

from the Malaysian by Victor Hugo and other French poets. This primitive origin is evident in the monotonous repetition of lines, a monotony possibly derived from the rhythmic beating of the Oriental tom-tom. The *pantoum* may consist of an indefinite number of four-line STANZAS, but in any case the second and fourth VERSES of one STANZA must reappear as the first and third lines of the following STANZA. The STANZAS are quatrains, the rime scheme being monotonously *abab, abab.* In the final STANZA the first and third lines of the first STANZA are repeated in reverse order, the poem thus ending with the same line with which it began.

**Parable:** An illustrative story answering a question or pointing a moral or lesson. A true *parable,* however, is much more than an anecdote since, implicitly at least, detail for detail in the *parable* is parallel with the situation which calls forth the *parable* for illustration. *Parables* are, in this sense, allegories (see ALLEGORY). Naturally in Christian countries the most famous *parables* are those told by Christ, such for instance as the *parable* of the sower.

**Paradox:** A statement which while seemingly contradictory or absurd may actually be well-founded or true. *Paradox* is a rhetorical device used to attract attention, to secure emphasis. Bentley's statement that there are "none so credulous as infidels" is an illustration. *Paradox* is a common element in epigrammatic writing, as the work of G. K. Chesterton, for instance, will give evidence.

**Parallelism:** A structural arrangement of parts of a sentence, sentences, paragraphs, and larger units of composition by which one element of equal importance with another is equally developed and similarly phrased. The principle of *parallelism* simply dictates that coördinate ideas should have coördinate presentation. Within a sentence, for instance, where several elements of equal importance are to be expressed, if one element is cast in a relative clause the others should be expressed in relative clauses, etc. Conversely, of course, the principle of *parallelism* demands that unequal elements should *not* be expressed in similar constructions. Practiced writers are not likely to attempt, for example, the comparison of positive and negative statements, of inverted and uninverted constructions, of dependent and independent clauses. And, for an example of simple *parallelism,* the sentence immediately above may serve. *Parallelism* is characteristic of Oriental poetry, being notably present in the Psalms, as in

> The Heavens declare the glory of God;
> And the firmament sheweth his handywork.

It is also characteristic of the songs and chants of the American Indians. *Parallelism* seems to be the controlling principle of the poetry of Walt Whitman. It shapes the following poem of his on almost every level from that of the word to that of the central idea:

A noiseless patient spider,
I mark'd where on a little promontory it stood isolated,
Mark'd how to explore the vacant vast surrounding,
It launch'd forth filament, filament, fflament out of itself.
Ever unreeling them, ever tirelessly speeding them.

And you O my soul where you stand,
Surrounded, detached, in measureless oceans of space,
Ceaselessly musing, venturing, throwing, seeking the spheres to connect
  them.
Till the bridge you will need be form'd, till the ductile anchor hold,
Till the gossamer thread you fling catch somewhere, O my soul.

**Paraphrase:** A restatement of an idea in such a way as to retain the meaning while changing the diction and form. A *paraphrase* is usually an amplification of the original for the purpose of clearness, though the term is also used for any rather general restatement of an expression or passage. Thus one might speak of a *paraphrase* from the French meaning a loose statement of the idea rather than an exact translation, or of a *paraphrase* of a poem indicating a prose explanation of a difficult passage of verse. In contemporary criticism the paraphrasing of works of literary art is frowned upon, and the followers of the NEW CRITICISM often condemn what they call the "heresy of the *paraphrase*," a term suggesting their stand that the essential nature of a poem is incommunicable in other terms than its own. Allen Tate states it succinctly when he says, "We know the particular poem, not what it says that we can restate."

**Parenthesis:** An explanatory remark thrown into the body of a statement and frequently separated from it by ( ). However, any comment which is an interruption of the immediate purpose is spoken of as a *parenthesis* whether it be a word, phrase, clause, sentence, or paragraph. Commas and dashes are substituted for the *parenthesis* marks when the interruption is not so abrupt as to demand the ( ). Brackets [ ] are used for parenthetical material more foreign to the subject of the sentence than *parentheses* will control and also to enclose material injected into a statement by some editorial hand. Modern novelists, interested in accurately reporting the fluid and unstable nature of thought and feeling, frequently employ *parentheses,* although often without formal punctuation. Joyce and Faulkner are noted examples. Others, anxious to qualify and define precise shades of meaning find the extensive use of parenthetical material helpful, as does Henry James.

**Parnassus:** The name of a mountain in Greece famed as the haunt of Apollo and the Muses. The word has also been used as a title for a collection or ANTHOLOGY of poems or poetical extracts, e.g., *England's Parnassus* (1600).

**Parody:** A composition burlesquing or imitating another, usually serious, piece of work. It is designed to ridicule in nonsensical fashion, or to criticize by brilliant treatment, an original piece of work or its author. When the *parody* is directed against an author or his style, it is likely to fall simply into barbed witticisms, often venting personal antagonisms of the parodist against the one parodied. When the subject matter of the original composition is parodied, however, it may prove to be a valuable indirect criticism or it may even imply a flattering tribute to the original writer. Often a *parody* is more powerful in its influence on affairs of current importance—politics, for instance—than an original composition. The *parody* is in literature what the CARICATURE and the cartoon are in art. Known to have been used as a potent means of SATIRE and ridicule even so far back as Aristophanes, *parody* has made a definite place for itself in literature and has become a popular type of literary composition. See BURLESQUE.

**Paronomasia:** An old term for a PUN or play on words.

***Pastiche:*** A French word for a PARODY or literary imitation. Perhaps for humorous or satirical purposes, perhaps as a mere literary exercise or *jeu d'espirit,* perhaps in all seriousness (as in some CLOSET DRAMAS), a writer imitates the style or technique of some recognized writer or work. Amy Lowell's *A Critical Fable* (1922) might be

called a *pastiche,* since it is written in the manner of James Russell
Lowell's *A Fable for Critics.* In art, a picture is called a *pastiche*
when it manages to catch something of a master's peculiar style. In
music, *pastiche* is applied to a medley or assembly of various pieces
into a single work. The term is also applied to literary patchworks
formed by piecing together extracts from various works by one or
several authors. See CENTO, PARODY.

**Pastoral:** A poem treating of shepherds and rustic life, after the
Latin word for shepherd, *pastor.* The *pastoral* began in the third
century B.C. when the Sicilian poet Theocritus included poetic
sketches of rural life in his *Idylls.* The Greek *pastorals* existed in
three forms: the DIALOGUE or singing-match, usually between two
shepherds, often called the ECLOGUE because of the number of
singing-matches in Virgil's "Selections"; the MONOLOGUE, often the
plaint of a lovesick or forlorn shepherd lover or a poem praising
some personage; and the ELEGY or LAMENT for a dead friend. The
*pastoral* early became a highly conventionalized form of poetry, the
poet (Virgil is an example) writing of his friends and acquaintances
as though they were poetic shepherds moving through rural scenes.
The form is artificial and unnatural—the "shepherds" of the *pastoral*
often speaking in courtly language and appearing in dress more
appropriate to the drawing room than to rocky hills and swampy
meadows. In this connection G. P. Marsh noted that "pastoral poetry
affects the manner or matter of rustic life, not for accurate description, but as a purely artistic device for conveying the interests and
emotions of the poet himself, of the society not rural in which he
lives." Between 1550 and 1750 this conventionalized *pastoral* was
much written in England under the influence of the classical revival. In modern use the term is often loosely construed to mean
any poem of rural people and setting (Untermeyer, for instance,
speaks of Robert Frost as a "pastoral" poet). Since this classification is based on subject matter and manner rather than on FORM,
we often use the term in association with other poetic types; we
thus have *pastoral* LYRICS, ELEGIES, DRAMAS, or even *pastoral* EPICS.
Milton's *Lycidas,* Shelley's *Adonais,* and Arnold's *Thyrsis* are examples of English *pastorals,* as is Spenser's *The Shepheardes Calender.*
Many twentieth-century critics employ a highly sophisticated
concept of the *pastoral* which was advanced by William Empson.
In this specialized usage, the *pastoral* is considered a device for literary INVERSION, a means of "putting the complex into the simple"

—of expressing complex ideas through simple personages, for example. Empson, using this specialized definition, finds *pastoral* elements in such widely differing works as the proletarian NOVEL (whose hero undergoes an INVERSION of function) and *Alice in Wonderland.* See IDYLL, BUCOLIC, ECLOGUE, PASTORAL DRAMA, PASTORAL ELEGY.

**Pastoral Drama:** The PASTORAL conventions so popular at times in poetry (as the ECLOGUE) and in the PASTORAL ROMANCE are reflected also in a form of DRAMA occasionally cultivated by English dramatists. Whether the *pastoral drama* originated in simple dramatic ECLOGUES (as W. W. Greg thinks) or is more closely related to such fifteenth-century mythological plays as Politian's *Orfeo,* it is certain that the type developed in Italy in the sixteenth century and was affected by the PASTORAL ROMANCE. Tasso's *Aminta* and Guarini's *Il Pastor Fido* (1590) were models for English RENAISSANCE pastoral plays, as cultivated by Samuel Daniel, John Fletcher, and Ben Jonson. The best is Fletcher's *The Faithful Shepherdess* (acted 1608–1609). Some of Shakespeare's ROMANTIC COMEDIES, such as *As You Like It,* are strongly affected by the PASTORAL influences and are sometimes called PASTORAL plays. The eighteenth-century stage saw some translations and imitations of Italian *pastoral drama,* and PASTORAL conventions were utilized along with the mythological in the more spectacular forms of dramatic activity which flourished in the eighteenth and nineteenth centuries.

**Pastoral Elegy:** A poem employing conventional PASTORAL imagery, written in dignified, serious language, and taking as its theme the expression of grief at the loss of a friend or important person. The form represents a combining of the PASTORAL ECLOGUE and the ELEGY. The conventional divisions, as evidenced in Milton's *Lycidas,* are: the invocation of the muse, an expression of the grief felt in the loss of a friend, a procession of mourners, a digression (on the church), and, finally, a consolation in which the poet submits gracefully to the inevitable and declares his conviction that, after all, everything has turned out for the best. Other conventions often present include: appearance of the poet as shepherd, praise of the dead "shepherd," the PATHETIC FALLACY, flower symbolism, invective against death, reversal of the ordinary processes of nature as result of the death, bewilderment caused by grief, declaration of belief in some form of immortality, use of a REFRAIN and of the

RHETORICAL QUESTION. Moschus' lament for Bion (third century B.C.), the November ECLOGUE of Spenser's *The Shepheardes Calender*, and Shelley's *Adonais* are examples of the form. See ECLOGUE, ELEGY, PASTORAL.

**Pastoral Romance:** A prose narrative, usually long and complicated in PLOT, in which the characters bear PASTORAL names and in which PASTORAL conventions dominate. It often contains interspersed songs. Though the Greek *Daphnis and Chloë* of Longus (third century) is classed as a *pastoral romance*, the form was reborn in the RENAISSANCE with Boccaccio's *Ameto* (1342). Montemayor's *Diana Enamorada* (1552) is an important Spanish *pastoral romance*. Typical English examples are Sir Philip Sidney's *Arcadia* (1590) and Thomas Lodge's *Rosalynde* (1590)—the source for Shakespeare's *As You Like It*. See ECLOGUE, PASTORAL, and PASTORAL DRAMA.

*Pastourelle:* A medieval type of DIALOGUE poem in which a shepherdess is wooed by a man of higher social rank. In the Latin *pastoralia* a scholar does the courting; in the French and English, a poet. The body of the poem is the DIALOGUE in which the case is argued. Sometimes the suit is successful, but often a father or brother happens along and ends the wooing. In the English forms the poet asks permission to accompany the maid to the fields; she refuses and threatens to call her mother. The *pastourelle* possibly developed from popular wooing-games and wooing-songs, though one of Theocritus' IDYLLS (no. 27) is much like the medieval *pastourelle*. The form seems to have influenced the PASTORAL dialogue-lyrics of the Elizabethans and may have figured in the development of early ROMANTIC DRAMA in England.

**Patent Theatres:** The removal of the ban against theatrical performances in England in 1660 resulted in much rival activity among groups seeking to operate playhouses. Before August, three independent companies were established at three old theatres, the Red Bull, the Cockpit, and Salisbury Court. At this time Sir William Davenant and Thomas Killigrew secured from Charles II a "patent" granting them the privilege of censorship of plays and the right to organize two companies and erect two theatres which should have a monopoly. Though opposed by the jealous master of the revels, Sir Henry Herbert, and by some of the independent managers, Davenant and Killigrew succeeded in enforcing their rights. Davenant's company, the "Duke of York's Company," occupied in 1661 a new theatre in Lincoln's Inn Fields and later one at Dorset Garden. Killigrew's company, the "King's Company," erected the Theatre Royal, the first of a famous succession of houses on this spot, all known as Drury Lane, since 1663. The theatres used by these two favored companies are known as *"patent" theatres*. The companies united in 1682, but in 1695 Betterton led a rebellious group of actors to a second theatre in Lincoln's Inn Fields. After a generation of confusion, Parliament passed a licensing act in 1737, reaffirming the patent rights and establishing the monopoly of Drury Lane and Covent Garden (erected 1732). Despite strenuous efforts of rival managers to encroach upon the privileges of the patentees, this act remained in force until 1843, when it was repealed and the patents revoked. Among the managers of Drury Lane after Killigrew are Cibber, Garrick, and Sheridan; of Covent Garden, John Rich (the builder), the elder Colman, and John P. Kemble. See PRIVATE THEATRES.

**Pathetic Fallacy:** A phrase coined by Ruskin to denote that tendency of poets and writers of impassioned prose to credit nature with the emotions of human beings. In a larger sense the *pathetic fallacy* is any false emotionalism in writing resulting in a too impassioned description of nature. It is the carrying over to inanimate objects of the moods and passions of a human being. This crediting of nature with human qualities is a constant device of poets. A frequently occurring expression of the imagination, it becomes a fault when it is overdone to the point of absurdity, in which case it approaches the CONCEIT. A passage from Ruskin (*Modern Paintters,* Vol. 3, Part IV, Chap. xii) in which he discusses the *pathetic fallacy* is quoted:

> They rowed her in across the rolling foam—
> The cruel, crawling foam.

The foam is not cruel, neither does it crawl. The state of mind which attributes to it these characters of a living creature is one in which the reason is unhinged by grief. All violent feelings have the same effect. They produce in us a falseness in all our impressions of external things, which I would generally characterize as the "pathetic fallacy."

**Pathos:** From the Greek root for suffering or deep feeling, *pathos* is the quality in art and literature which stimulates pity, tenderness, or sorrow in the reader or viewer. Although in its strict meaning it is closely associated with the pity which TRAGEDY is supposed to evoke, in common usage it describes an acquiescent or relatively helpless suffering or the sorrow occasioned by unmerited grief, as opposed to the stoic grandeur and awful justice of the tragic hero. In this distinction, Hamlet is a tragic figure and Ophelia a pathetic one; Lear's fate is tragic, Cordelia's pathetic. See BATHOS.

**Pedantry:** A display of learning for its own sake. The term is often used in critical reproach of an author's style when that style is marked by a superfluity of quotations, foreign phrases, ALLUSIONS, etc. Holofernes in Shakespeare's *Love's Labour's Lost* can hardly open his lips without giving expression to *pedantry:*

> Most barbarous intimation! yet a kind of insinuation, as it were, *in via,* in way, of explication; *facere,* as it were, replication, or, rather, *ostentare,* to show, as it were, his inclination,—after his undressed, unpolished, uneducated, unpruned, untrained, or rather, unlettered, or, ratherest, unconfirmed fashion,—to insert again my *haud credo* for a deer.

**Pegasus:** The winged horse of Grecian fable said to have sprung from Medusa's body at her death. *Pegasus* is associated with the inspiration of poetry (though in modern times in a somewhat jocular vein) because he is supposed by one blow of his hoof to have caused Hippocrene, the inspiring fountain of the Muses, to flow from Mount Helicon. As a symbol of poetic inspiration poets have sometimes invoked the aid of *Pegasus* instead of the Muses.

**Pelagianism:** A theological doctrine asserting man's original innocence and his capacity to achieve moral and spiritual power through his own unaided efforts. See CALVINISM, AUGUSTINIANISM.

**Pentameter:** A line of VERSE consisting of five feet. See SCANSION.

**Periodical:** A term applied to any publication that appears at regular intervals; it includes such publications as JOURNALS, MAGAZINES, and REVIEWS, but customarily not newspapers. See MAGAZINE.

**Periodical Essay:** A term applied to an ESSAY written for publication as the principal or only item in an issue of a PERIODICAL. The most notable *periodical essays* were written for *The Tatler* and *The Spectator,* but the form was very popular throughout most of the eighteenth century. See ESSAY.

**Periodic Sentence:** A sentence not grammatically complete before the end; the opposite of a LOOSE SENTENCE. The characteristic of a *periodic sentence* is that its construction is such as constantly to throw the mind forward to the idea which will complete the meaning. The *periodic sentence* is effective when it is desired to arouse interest and curiosity, to hold an idea in suspense before its final revelation is made. Periodicity is accomplished by the use of parallel phrases or clauses at the opening; by the use of dependent clauses preceding the independent clause, and by the use of such correlatives as *neither . . . nor, not only . . . but also,* and *both . . . and.* "Because it was raining, I went into the house" is an example of a *periodic sentence* composed of a dependent clause preceding the independent clause.

**Period of Criticism and Conformity in American Literature:** The year 1930 marked a decided turning point in American social and cultural history as well as the beginning of the period in literary history in which we still live. In October, 1929, the stock-market crash heralded the end of the prosperous twenties, and by the end of 1930 the impact of the depression was being felt in most areas of American life and thought. As the depression intensified, the social and economic revolution called the New Deal occurred, and a steadily increasing concern with sociological issues occupied the serious writer. Shortly after the depression began the expatriate group which had in Paris made a religion of art came back to America and joined the radical movements that earned the thirties the name of "The Red Decade."

Hemingway's career had been launched in the twenties, and his work in the thirties added little to his stature; but Faulkner was to produce in the first half of the decade the largest single body of his best work. Dos Passos wrote his trilogy, *U.S.A.;* and James T. Farrell, Thomas Wolfe, and John Steinbeck acquired fame and did their best work. A radical social point of view was present in most of these writers, a critical approach to American institutions. In the meantime, the poets who had in the twenties produced the *Fugitive* magazine in Nashville reacted strongly against the radical political thought and the sociological literary orientations of their world; they expressed their politico-economic reaction through the principles of AGRARIANISM and their rejection of sociological concerns in the artist through the formulation of the NEW CRITICISM. Edwin Arlington Robinson, Robert Frost, T. S. Eliot, Edna St. Vincent Millay, and Carl Sandburg continued their dominant position in poetry, and e.e. cummings, Robinson Jeffers, Archibald Macleish, and William Carlos Williams raised newer strong poetic voices. Maxwell Anderson, Eugene O'Neill, Clifford Odets, and Thornton Wilder dominated the stage.

The signing of the Russo-German pact in 1939 and the coming of the second World War put an effective end to the radicalism of the thirties. The War and its aftermath resulted in an age of conformity and conservatism, bolstered by a burgeoning economy. American life, thought, and writing in the forties and the fifties were marked by a tendency to conformity, to traditionalism, and to reverence for artistic form and restraint; while, at the same time, the period was marked by informality in social conduct and freedom of subject matter in art.

The postwar DRAMA revealed the strong new talents of Arthur Miller and Tennessee Williams, while Thornton Wilder was doing his most mature work and Eugene O'Neill was at the end of his career dramatizing with powerful effectiveness the tragic nature of his own experience. Both poetry and criticism tended to retreat to the critical quarterlies, where each operated with a high level of technical skill and without great distinction or vitality. The major figures in the NOVEL were still Hemingway and Faulkner, both of whom received the Nobel Prize, although neither of them was producing work of the quality of that they had done in the twenties and the thirties. Of the newer novelists, Robert Penn Warren showed skill, seriousness, and virtuosity, and John P. Marquand carried the satirical NOVEL OF MANNERS to a high level of accomplishment. In James Jones and a group of other young neo-naturalists a strong, frank, and formless kind of fiction appeared. But the remark which, perhaps, best characterizes the literature of America from the second World War to the present is that its major works and its major literary events were produced by writers whose careers had been firmly established in the twenties and the thirties and who had done their best work then. The chaos of a hot war and the constraint of a cold one conspired to produce a literature of conformity. See the *Outline of Literary History*.

**Periods of English and American Literary History:** See ENGLISH LITERATURE, AMERICAN LITERATURE, and *Outline of Literary History*.

**Peripety:** The REVERSAL of fortune for the PROTAGONIST in a dramatic or fictional PLOT, whether to his fall in a TRAGEDY or to his success in a COMEDY. See DRAMATIC STRUCTURE.

**Periphrasis:** An indirect, abstract, roundabout method of stating ideas; the application to writing or speech of the old conviction that "the longest way 'round is the shortest way home." Used with restraint and with deliberate intent *periphrasis* may be a successful rhetorical device, but the danger is that it will be overdone and will result in mere Polonius-like verbosity. Fowler cites as an objectionable use of *periphrasis* (for "No news is good news") the periphrastic circumlocution "The absence of intelligence is an indication of satisfactory developments." Authors frequently use the form to secure humorous effects; for example, Shenstone refers to pins as "the cure of rents and separations dire, and chasms enormous."

**Peroration:** The conclusion of an ORATION or discourse in which the discussion is summed up, and the speaker endeavors to enforce his arguments by a pointed and rhetorical appeal to the emotions of his audience; a recapitulation of the major points of any speech.

**Persiflage:** Light, inconsequential chatter, written or spoken; gay, satirical banter; a trifling, flippant manner of dealing with any theme or subject matter.

**Personal Essay:** A kind of INFORMAL ESSAY which utilizes an intimate style, some autobiographical content or interest, and an urbane conversational manner. See ESSAY.

**Personification:** A figure of speech which endows animals, ideas, abstractions, and inanimate objects with human form, character, or sensibilities; the representing of imaginary creatures or things as having human personalities, intelligence, and emotions; an impersonation in DRAMA of one character or person, whether real or fictitious, by another person. Keats's *personification* of the Grecian urn as the

> Sylvan historian, who canst thus express
> A flowery tale more sweetly than our rhyme:

is an obvious *personification* as are his earlier references to the urn as an "unravished bride of quietness" and as a "foster child of silence and slow time." *Personification* as a figure of speech is also called PROSOPOPOEIA. See ALLEGORY.

**Persuasion:** That one of the major types of composition the purpose of which is to convince of the wisdom of a certain line of action. *Persuasion* is really a phase of ARGUMENTATION and resembles it in that its purpose is to establish the truth or falsity of a proposition, but is somewhat distinct from it in that it is calculated to arouse to some action. *Persuasion* may draw on the other types of composition—ARGUMENTATION, DESCRIPTION, EXPOSITION, and NARRATION—for support, and in fact does incorporate within itself elements of each. Its chief reason for consideration as a separate type is simply that it uses these forms to a specific goal—that of arousing action through the conviction it carries to the reader or hearer. The most common form of *persuasion* is the ORATION, and the most effective form is that which combines the appeal to the intellect with an appeal to the emotions.

**Petrarchan Conceit:** The kind of CONCEIT used by the Italian poet Petrarch in his love sonnets and widely imitated by RENAISSANCE English sonneteers. It rests upon elaborate and exaggerated comparisons expressing in extravagant terms the beauty, cruelty, and charm of the beloved and the suffering, sorrow, and despair of the forlorn lover. Hyperbolic analogies to ships at sea, marble tombs, wars, and alarums are used; OXYMORON is common. Shakespeare in "Sonnet 130," which begins,

> My mistress' eyes are nothing like the sun;
> Coral is far more red than her lips' red:
> If snow be white, why then her breasts are dun;
> If hairs be wires, black wires grow on her head,

satirizes the Petrarchan conventions while giving a reasonably accurate catalogue of some of the more common ones.

**Philippic:** In modern usage, any speech or harangue bitterly invective in character; a discourse filled with denunciations and accusations. The term comes from the twelve orations of Demosthenes in which he berated Philip II of Macedon as an enemy of Greece.

**Philistinism:** The worship of material and mechanical prosperity, the disregard of culture, beauty, and spiritual things. The term was made popular by Matthew Arnold's use of it in his essay, "Sweetness and Light," which appeared as the first chapter of *Culture and Anarchy.* In this paper Arnold writes:

> If it were not for this purging effect wrought upon our minds by culture, the whole world, the future as well as the present, would inevitably belong to the Philistines. The people who believe most that our greatness and welfare are proved by our being very rich, and who most give their lives and thoughts to becoming rich, are just the very people whom we call Philistines. Culture says: "Consider these people, then, their way of life, their habits, their manners, the very tones of their voices; look at them attentively; observe the literature they read, the things which give them pleasure, the words which come forth out of their mouths, the thoughts which make the furniture of their minds, would any amount of wealth be worth having with the condition that one was to become just like these people by having it?"

**Philology:** In its general sense *philology* means the scientific study of both language and literature. Thus there are *philological* clubs and journals of *philology* devoted to linguistic and literary research. The late Professor A. S. Cook even went so far as to say: "The ideal philologist is at once antiquary, palaeographer, grammarian, lexicologist, expounder, critic, historian of literature, and, above all, lover of humanity." *Philology* is also sometimes used in a narrower sense to mean the scientific study of language. A *philologist* in this sense is a specialist in linguistics, and courses in *philology* are linguistic courses, such as the study of Anglo-Saxon or Hebrew as distinguished from courses in literature. There is a tendency to discard this use of the word in favor of "linguistics."

**Picaresque Novel, The:** A CHRONICLE, usually autobiographical, presenting the life story of a rascal of low degree engaged in menial tasks and making his living more through his wits than his industry. Episodic in nature, the *picaresque novel* is, in the usual sense of the term, structureless. It presents little more than a series of thrilling incidents impossible to conceive as happening in one life. The *picaro,* or central figure, through the nature of his various pranks and predicaments and by virtue of his associations with people of varying degree, affords the author an opportunity for SATIRE on the social classes. Romantic in the sense of being a story of adventure, the *picaresque novel* nevertheless is strongly marked by realistic methods in its faithfulness to petty detail, its utter frankness of expression, and its drawing of incidents from low life.

From earliest times, of course, the rogue has been a favorite character in story and picture. As far back as the *Satyricon,* Petronius at the court of Nero recognized the possibilities of the type. In the Middle Ages the FABLES continued the manner though it transferred roguery from man to animals. Reynard is a typical picaroon. He lives by his wits; gets into trouble and out of it, but always interests the reader. It was not until the sixteenth century that this rogue literature crystallized and became a definite type. A NOVEL called *La Vida de Lazarillo de Tormes y de sus fortunas y adversidades,* probably dating from 1554, brought this about. So popular did this work become and through so many different editions did it pass, that it was one of the most-read books of the century. Cervantes took up the manner. And before long French imitators sprang up. Of all the French NOVELS Le Sage's *Gil Blas* (1715) was by far the most popular. So definitely was the type fixed as a Spanish form that the French writers—Le Sage among them—gave their characters Spanish names, placed their EPISODES in Spain, and paid the early Spanish writers the compliment of borrowing extensively the incidents used in their books.

It was inevitable, with all this enthusiasm, that the type should undergo modifications. Feminine characters assumed the role of the picaroon. In one prominent NOVEL a nun figured as the central character. Episodes became more and more scandalous in the effort to attract more and more readers. Moralists appeared who avowed their intention of pointing out the evils of the rogue's life by presenting especially revolting and villainous incidents.

The English, as well, adopted the picaresque manner. In 1594 appeared *The Unfortunate Traveller: or, The Life of Jack Wilton* by Thomas Nash—the first important *picaresque novel* in the language. With Daniel Defoe in the eighteenth century the type became really important in English literature. His *Moll Flanders* presents the life record of a female picaroon. Fielding in *Jonathan Wild* and Smollett in *Ferdinand, Count Fathom,* lent dignity to the type through the importance of their literary reputation.

There are, perhaps, seven chief qualities distinguishing the *picaresque novel.* (1) First of all, it chronicles a part or the whole of the life of a rogue. It is likely to be done in the first person—as AUTOBIOGRAPHY—but this is by no means essential. (2) The chief figure is drawn from a low social level and is of "loose" character, according to conventional standards. The occupation of this central figure, should he tolerate employment at all, is menial in nature. (3) The NOVEL presents little PLOT. Rather is it a series of EPISODES only slightly connected. (4) There is little character interest. Progress and development of character do not take place. The central figure starts as a *picaro* and ends as a *picaro*, manifesting the same aptitudes and qualities throughout. When change occurs, as it sometimes does, it is external change brought about by the man's falling heir to a fortune or by his marrying a rich widow. Internal character development is not a quality of the *picaresque novel*. (5) The method is realistic. While the story may be romantic in itself, it is presented with a plainness of language, a freedom in vocabulary, and a vividness of detail such as the realist only is permitted. (6) SATIRE is a prominent element. Thrown with people from every class and often from different parts of the world, the *picaro* serves them intimately in one lowly capacity or another and learns all their foibles and frailties. The *picaresque novel* may in this way be made to satirize both social casts and national or racial peculiarities. (7) The hero of the *picaresque novel* usually stops just short of being an actual criminal. The line between crime and petty rascality is a hazy one, but somehow the *picaro* always manages to draw it. Carefree, unmoral perhaps, he avoids actual crime and turns from one peccadillo to disappear down the dust of the road in search of another.

**Pindaric Ode:** The regular ODE, characterized by a division into units containing three parts—the STROPHE and ANTISTROPHE, alike in form, and the EPODE, different from the other two. See ODE.

**Pirated Edition:** An unauthorized edition of a work, stolen from one country and produced for sale in another. It represents an infringement of COPYRIGHT resulting in an illegal publication. The term is most often applied to the period before the establishment of modern international COPYRIGHT conventions, when the use without permission or payment of literary works copyrighted in another nation was a common practice. See COPYRIGHT.

**Plagiarism:** Literary theft. A writer who steals the PLOT of some obscure, forgotten story and uses it as new in a story of his own is a plagiarist. *Plagiarism* is more noticeable when it involves a stealing of language than when substance only is borrowed. From flagrant exhibitions of stealing both thought and language *plagia-*

*rism* shades off into less serious things such as unconscious borrowing, borrowing of minor elements, and mere IMITATION. In fact, the critical doctrine of IMITATION, as understood in Renaissance times, often led to what would nowadays be called *plagiarism*. Thus, Spenser's free borrowings from other romantic EPICS in composing his *Faerie Queene* were by him regarded as virtues, since he was "following" a predecessor in the same type of writing. A modern dramatist could not with impunity borrow PLOTS from other DRAMAS and from old stories in the way in which Shakespeare did. With *plagiarism* compare LITERARY FORGERIES, its converse, where an author pretends that another has written what he has actually written himself. See GHOST-WRITER.

**Plaint:** VERSE expressing grief or tribulation; a chant of lamentation; a LAMENT; an expression of sorrow. See COMPLAINT.

**Platonic Criticism:** A term often used by contemporary critics to describe a type of criticism which finds the values of a work of art in its extrinsic rather than its intrinsic qualities, in its usefulness for non-artistic purposes. The term is currently used in opposition to ARISTOTELIAN CRITICISM, which finds the value of a work of art within the work itself. See ARISTOTELIAN CRITICISM; CRITICISM, TYPES OF.

**Platonism:** The idealistic philosophical doctrines of Plato, because of their concern with the aspirations of the human spirit, their tendency to exalt mind over matter, their mystical and optimistic grappling with the great problems of the universe and of man's relation to the great cosmic forces, and their highly imaginative elements, have appealed strongly to certain English authors, particularly the poets of the RENAISSANCE and of the ROMANTIC PERIOD. Plato himself declined to "codify" his philosophical views and perhaps altered them much during his own life. He left expressions of them in his great DIALOGUES or conversations, in which various great Greeks (such as Socrates, Alcibiades, and Aristophanes) are made to discuss philosophical problems, particularly those involving problems of the universe and man's relation to it, the nature of love and beauty, the constitution of the human soul, the relation of beauty to virtue, etc. Unlike Aristotelian philosophy, which tends to be systematic, formal, scientific, logical, and critical, and which occupies itself chiefly with the visible universe, the natural world, and mankind, *Platonism* is flexible, interested in the unseen world, and concerned with man's possibilities and destinies. It has been called an "intellectual vision" rather than a cold, philosophical system. Plato founded his famous "Academy" in 380 B.C., where for a third of a century he taught students attracted from far and near (including Aristotle himself). Later leaders of the Academy and other followers now known as "Neo-platonists" modified and expanded Plato's teachings and it is difficult even now to distinguish the purely Platonic elements from elements added by later Platonists. Among the "Neo-platonists" there were two groups of especial importance. (1) The Alexandrian school. This group, especially Plotinus (third century), stressed the mystical elements and amalgamated them with many ideas drawn from other sources. Their NEO-PLATONISM was in fact a sort of religion, which, though itself supplanted by Christianity, supplied medieval Christian thinkers (including Boëthius and St. Augustine) with many ideas. (2) The Neo-platonists of the Italian RENAISSANCE. Under the leadership of Marsilio Ficino (1433–1499), who led the Platonic Academy at Florence and who translated and explained Plato, a highly complex and mystical system developed, one of the aims of which was the fusing of Platonic philosophy and Christian doctrine. It was this particular kind of NEO-PLATONISM which kindled the imagination of such RENAISSANCE poets as Sidney and Spenser.

Important Platonic doctrines found in English literature include:

1. The doctrine of ideas (or "forms"). True reality is found not in the realm of sense but in the higher, spiritual realm of the ideal and the universal. Here exist the "ideas" or images or patterns of which material objects are but transitory symbols or expressions.

2. The doctrine of recollection. This implies the preëxistence and immortality of the soul, which passes through a series of incarnations. Most of what the soul has seen and learned in "heaven" it forgets when imprisoned in the body of clay but it has some power of "recalling" ideas and images. Hence human knowledge.

3. The doctrine of love. There are two kinds of love and beauty, a lower and a higher. The soul or lover of beauty in its quest for perfect beauty ascends from the sensual gradually, through a process of idealization, to the spiritual, and thereby develops all the virtues both of thought and of action. Beauty and virtue become identified.

An interesting exposition of the Neo-platonic doctrines of love may be read in the fourth book of Castiglione's *The Book of the Courtier*. Representative English poems embodying Platonic ideas include: Spenser's *Hymn in Honor of Beauty*, Shelley's *Hymn to Intellectual Beauty*, and Wordsworth's *Ode on the Intimations of Immortality from Recollections of Early Childhood*.

**Pléiade:** A term originally applied to an ancient group of seven authors (named after the constellation of the Pleiades), and to several later groups, the most important of which for the student of English literature is the group of critics and poets which flourished in France in the second half of the sixteenth century. The leading figures were Ronsard, Du Bellay, and (later) Desportes. The poetic manifesto of the "school" is Du Bellay's *Défense et Illustration de la Langue Française* (1549). It shows an interest in developing a new vernacular literature following the types cultivated by classical writers. The popular and the medieval were to be avoided, except that certain medieval courtly pieces were to be rewritten. The native language was to be enriched by coining words, by borrowing from the Greek and Latin, and by restoring to use lost native words, so that a literary language might be produced which would make possible the creation of a new French literature comparable with classical literature. The high function of the poet and of poetry was stressed. The influence of the group was a constructive and important one upon Elizabethan poets, notably Spenser, and the more or less mythical AREOPAGUS has been regarded as an English counterpart of the *Pléiade*, since Sidney and his group were enthusiastically engaged in the effort to refine the English language and to create a new national literature based upon humanistic ideals.

**Pleonasm:** The superfluous use of words. *Pleonasm* may consist of needless repetition, or of the addition of unnecessary words in an effort to express an idea completely, or of a combination of the two. For example, in the sentence, "He walked the entire distance to the station on foot," the last two words are pleonastic. Although *pleonasm* is a violation of correct grammatical usage, it is employed occasionally to add emphasis, and in such instances its use may be considered legitimate. See TAUTOLOGY.

**Plot:** A planned series of interrelated actions progressing, because of the interplay of one force upon another, through a struggle of opposing forces to a climax and a *dénouement*. However, such abstract terms as the above mean little; it is perhaps more helpful to describe *plot* than to define it with generalities. The incidents which are part of a *plot* are, it has been said, (1) *planned;* they are preconceived by the author; they spring from his conscious thought; they are not simply taken over from life. No matter how realistic an author may be, he must arrange and select his incidents according to a *plot* purpose since life itself only rarely, if ever, unfolds according to the plans of a fiction *plot*. *Plot* is, too, (2) a *series of actions* moving from a beginning through a logically related sequence to a logical and natural outcome. One incident—an afternoon's cruise—does not make a *plot*, no matter how interesting the afternoon may have been. Several incidents—if the story is one of action—are essential. There must at least be a beginning, a middle, and an end in the interplay of the opposing forces and, most frequently, this means three or more EPISODES. And these incidents grow one upon another; incident two following by a causal relationship from incident one, and incident three following, by this same relationship, from two. The difference between a simple narrative and a story of *plot* is the difference between a calendar and a knitted scarf. In the calendar the pages follow one another logically, but in the scarf the texture is the result of weaving one thread over and under another. In a story with closely knit *plot* the removal of one incident would bring the whole structure down upon one's head much as though he had removed an important prop from the scaffolding for a building. In a story of mere unrelated incidents, the removal of one incident would leave, simply, a gap. (3) This interrelationship of action is the result, as has been said, of the *interplay of one force upon another*. Without CONFLICT, without opposition, *plot per se* does not exist. We must have a Claudius flouting a Hamlet, an Iago making jealous an Othello, if we are to have *plot*. These forces may be physical (or external), or they may be spiritual (or internal); but physical or spiritual they must afford an opposition. And this opposition it is, which knits one incident to another, which dictates the causal relationship, which develops the struggle. This struggle between the forces, moreover, comes to a head in some one incident—the CRISIS—which forms the turning-point of the story and which usually marks the point of greatest SUSPENSE. In this climactic EPISODE the RISING ACTION comes to a termination, the FALLING ACTION begins; and as a result of this incident some DÉNOUEMENT or CATASTROPHE is bound to follow.

*Plot* is, in this sense, an artificial rather than a natural ordering of events. Its function is to simplify life by imposing order upon it. It would be possible, though most tedious, to recite *all* incidents, *all* events, *all* thoughts which pass through the minds of one or more characters during a period of, say, a week. And somewhere in this recital might be buried a story. But the demands of *plot* stipulate that the author *select* from this welter of event and reflection those items which have a certain UNITY, which point to a certain end, which have a common interrelationship, which represent not more than two or three threads of interest and activity. *Plot* brings order out of life; it selects only one or two emotions out of a dozen, one or two conflicts out of hundreds, only two or three people out of thousands, and a half-dozen EPISODES from possible millions. In this sense it focuses life.

And it usually focuses with one principal idea in mind—character. The most effective incidents are those which spring naturally from the given characters, the most effective *plot* presents struggle such as would engage these given characters, and the most effective emotion for the *plot* to present is that inherent in the quality of the given characters. The function of *plot*, from this point of view, is to translate character into action.

The use of a DEUS EX MACHINA to solve a COMPLICATION is now pretty generally condemned as a weakness in *plot* structure since it is now generally conceded that *plot* action should spring from the innate quality of the characters participant in the action. But *fate*, since it may be interpreted as working through character, is, with the development of the realistic method, still very popular. The one great weakness good writers of FICTION avoid is the use of incident and EPISODE which are extraneous to the essential purposes of the *plot* pattern. *Plot*, it need hardly be added, is an element common to various forms of FICTION: the NOVEL, the SHORT STORY, the DRAMA being the types of writing most frequently making use of the interest which springs from the SUSPENSE which *plots* develop. See DRAMATIC STRUCTURE, CHARACTERIZATION.

**Plurisignation:** A term sometimes used by contemporary critics to describe the kind of AMBIGUITY which results from the capacity of words to stimulate several different streams of thought. See AMBIGUITY.

**Poem:** A composition characterized by the presence of IMAGINATION, emotion, truth (significant meaning), sense impressions, and a dignified and concrete language; expressed rhythmically and with an orderly arrangement of parts and possessing within itself a UNITY; the whole written with the dominant purpose of giving aesthetic or emotional pleasure. A formal and final definition of POETRY is, of course, impossible; it means different things to different people at different times. See POETRY.

**Poet Laureate:** In medieval universities there arose the custom of crowning with laurel a student who was admitted to an academic degree, such as the bachelor of arts. Later the phrase *poet laureate* was used as a special degree conferred by a university as a recognition of skill in Latin grammar and versification. There also existed in the late Middle Ages the custom of bestowing a crown of laurel on a poet for distinctive work, Petrarch being so honored in 1341. Independent of these customs and usages was the ancient practice of kings and chieftains, both in educated and barbarous nations, of maintaining "court poets," persons attached to the prince's household and maintained for the purpose of celebrating the virtues of the royal family or singing the praises of military exploits. Court poets of this type included the SCOP among Anglo-Saxon peoples, the SKALD among the Scandinavian, the FILIDH among the Irish, and the higher ranks of BARDS among the Welsh. An example of a court poet in classical antiquity is Theocritus (third century B.C.), who served as such both at the court of Ptolemy Philadelphus in Alexandria and the Tyrant Hiero in Syracuse. The modern office of *Poet Laureate* in England resulted from the application of the academic term *poet laureate* to the traditional court poet.

The present official laureateship was established in the seventeenth century, though there were interesting anticipations earlier. Henri d'Avranches, for example, was an official *versificator regis* for Henry III and received an annual grant of wine as part of his stipend. Later, at the courts of Henry VII and Henry VIII, an academic *poet laureate* named Bernardus Andreas of Toulouse (a blind poet) was officially recognized as a *Poet Laureate*, wrote Latin odes for his masters, and received a pension. The tradition was not carried on after the poet's death. The first officially appointed *Poet Laureate* was John Dryden, though Spenser, Daniel, Drayton, Ben Jonson, and William Davenant are often included in the list, the latter two with strong justification. Spenser, Daniel, and Drayton were court poets of the same sort Chaucer was and were in no sense *Poets Laureate*. Jonson, however, received a pension, a grant of wine, and was an official (though not exclusive) writer of MASQUES for James I and Charles I. Moreover, his contemporaries called him "the *Poet Laureate*" and he was ambitious to be so known. After Jonson's death in 1637 Davenant was hailed as Jonson's successor and at the RESTORATION (1660) he was informally recognized even at court as Jonson's successor as *Poet Laureate*, though he seems not to have received any official designation as such during his lifetime. Upon Davenant's death, however, Dryden received (1670) an official appointment to the office, the warrant mentioning the office as "void by the death of Sir William Davenant." Davenant thereby received a sort of *ex post facto* official recognition and actually was informally recognized during his life, but Dryden was the first whose official appointment is recorded. After the Revolution Dryden was displaced, and in 1689 Thomas Shadwell was appointed *Poet Laureate*. Successive laureates were: Nahum Tate (1692–1715), Nicholas Rowe (1715–1718), Laurence Eusden (1718–1730), Colley Cibber (1730–1757), William Whitehead (1757–1785), Thomas Warton (1785–1790), Henry James Pye (1790–1813), Robert Southey (1813–1843), William Wordsworth (1843–1850), Alfred Tennyson (1850–1892), Alfred Austin (1892–1913), Robert Bridges (1913–1930), John Masefield (1930–    ).

The early, primary duty of the laureate was to render professional service to the royal family and the court. The practice of composing ODES in celebration of royal birthdays, New Year's, and other occasions developed in the seventeenth century and became obligatory upon the laureate in the eighteenth century. Each year such an ODE was sung at a formal court reception held to wish the king a happy New Year. This custom lapsed during the illness of George III and was abolished in Southey's time. Sometimes the laureate has served as a "poet-defender" of the king in personal and political as well as national disputes (for example, Dryden). Later the more appropriate custom of expecting a poem in times of national stress or strong patriotic feeling developed, though since Southey the writing of verse for special occasions has not been obligatory. Two of the best-known "laureate" poems are Tennyson's "Ode" written to be sung at the funeral of the Duke of Wellington and the same writer's "Charge of the Light Brigade."

The servile or perfunctory character of the laureate's duties often prevented the appointment of the best living poets, though since Wordsworth's time the appointment has been regarded as a recognition of poetic distinction. Gray, Scott, and Samuel Rogers declined appointments as *Poet Laureate*. Gray actually asserted that a poet accepting the post was certain to be humiliated either by having his poor verses advertised or by incurring the active enmity of jealous versifiers. Until recent times the custom of satirizing the *Poet Laureate* was almost as traditional as the annual gift of a butt of wine; it grew out of the character of some of the appointees and their perfunctory duties. Cibber, who was much jibed at for his servile flattery, admitted to Pope that he wrote "more to be fed than to be famous."

**Poetics** (noun): A system or body of theory concerning the nature of POETRY. The principles and rules of poetic composition. The term is used in two forms, *poetic* and *poetics*, with *poetics* the more common, both referring to the body of principles promulgated or exemplified by a poet or critic. The classic example, of course, is Aristotle's *Poetics* and the first paragraph of that work indicates that it is Aristotle's purpose to treat of "poetry in itself and of its various kinds, noting the essential quality of each; to inquire into the structure of the plot as requisite to a good poem; into the number and nature of the parts of which a poem is composed; and similarly into whatever else falls within the same inquiry."

**Poetic Diction:** Words chosen for a supposedly inherent poetic quality. At one time poets and critics in England sought for and admired a special language for POETRY which differed from the language of common speech. Spenser sought in ARCHAISMS, for example, the materials out of which to fashion a diction properly poetic; the poets of the AUGUSTAN AGE subjected poetic language to the test of DECORUM and evolved a special vocabulary for POETRY. The Romantic poets, led by Wordsworth, denied the essential difference between the proper language of POETRY and that of prose or everyday speech. The tendency in our own time is to allow the poet the widest possible vocabulary range, but to use a consciously *poetic diction* only for ironic effect.

**Poetic Drama:** A term properly restricted to poetic plays written to be acted. It is thus distinguished from DRAMATIC POETRY and CLOSET DRAMA, although some writers treat *poetic drama* as synonymous with DRAMATIC POETRY, and some use *poetic drama* to designate CLOSET DRAMA.

**Poetic Justice:** Loosely, that ideal judgment which rewards virtue and punishes vice among the characters of a narrative.

The use of "poetic" in the term, however, does not so much imply that the phrase is restricted to POETRY as that it is based on a philosophic system of POETIC. The eighteenth century particularly interested itself in the question. John Dennis and Joseph Addison were the proponents of the two points of view.

I conceive that every Tragedy ought to be a very solemn Lecture, inculcating a particular Providence, and showing it plainly protecting the good, and chastizing the bad, or at least the violent: and that if it is otherwise, it is either an empty amusement, or a scandalous and pernicious Libel upon the government of the world.

—Dennis

The *English* Writers of Tragedy are possessed with a Notion, that when they represent a virtuous or innocent Person in Distress, they ought not to leave him till they have delivered him out of his Troubles, or made him triumph over his Enemies. This Error they have been led into by a ridiculous Doctrine in Modern Criticism, that they are obliged to an equal Distribution of Rewards and Punishments, and an impartial Execution of Poetical Justice.

—Addison

Aristotle announced that "the mere spectacle of a virtuous man brought from prosperity to adversity moves neither pity nor fear; it merely shocks us." And here is, really, the heart of the whole question. Suffering as an end in itself is intolerable dramatically. Hamlet dead with poison, Desdemona smothered, Juliet dead— all these placed before us on the stage unmotivated, unexplained, constitute not TRAGEDY but sheer pain. Such scenes would be exhibitions of fate over which the characters have had no control and for which they were in no sense responsible; they would be, had not Shakespeare been the artist he was, mere *accidents* and as such would have no claim to *poetic justice*. But, in a higher, a more spiritual, a more *dramatic* sense, *poetic justice* may be said to have been attained since, as Shakespeare *wrote* the plays, the actions moved logically, thoughtfully, consistently to some such CATASTROPHES as those which awaited these three tragic characters. *Poetic justice*, then, in this higher sense, is something greater than the mere rewarding of virtue and the punishment of vice; *it is the logical and motivated outcome of the given conditions and terms of the tragic plan as presented in the earlier acts of the drama even though, from a worldly sense, virtue meets with disaster and vice seems temporarily rewarded.* With CATASTROPHES less fatal than those which visited Hamlet and Desdemona, TRAGEDY would be in danger of becoming COMEDY; DRAMA, in its purest sense, would disappear. For the reader of poetic TRAGEDY, the beauty of sorrow, the CATHARSIS which comes with the spectacle of the mysteries of life, are greater values than the knowledge that Claudius had perhaps been exiled and Iago hanged, or that Hamlet had been married to Ophelia and Othello had lived to look upon Desdemona's wrinkled cheek. In its modern sense, then, *poetic justice* may be considered as fulfilled when the outcome, however fatal to virtue, however it may reward vice, is the logical and necessary result of the action and principles of the major characters as they have been presented by the dramatist. It should be noted that such an outcome as that described here presupposes a universe in which the author sees order and organizing principles. In the absence of such principles in the author's world view even this *poetic justice* as the motivated and logical outcome of the given conditions and terms of the narrative is impossible, as witness Kafka's *The Trial.*

**Poetic License:** The privilege, sometimes claimed by poets, of departing from normal order, DICTION, RIME, or pronunciation in order that their verse may meet the requirements of their metrical pattern. The best poets rarely resort to the excuse of *poetic license* since they take enough care with their writing to avoid such distortions. Readers of POETRY should not be too hasty in setting down as *license* an irregularity—such as the use of an archaic word or the departure from normal word order—which may have been deliberately planned by the poet to establish a desired poetic effect. If one applies the strict demands of prose to POETRY, of course most poetic expression will, from such a point of view, consist of *poetic license.* The decision is largely relative. Prose, for instance, would state boldly: "Kubla Khan decreed that a stately palace be built in Xanadu." Coleridge, however, has it that

> In Xanadu did Kubla Khan
> A stately pleasure-dome decree:

The Coleridge form includes (1) INVERSION of order (since "in Xanadu" precedes the subject and predicate), (2) the expletive use of "did" for the simple past tense form "decreed," and (3) a coined expression, "pleasure-dome," for "palace" or "pavilion." The reader who has no POETRY in his soul will condemn such methods as nonsense and hail it all as *poetic license.* Yet all that is distorted is the normal *prose* form; as POETRY the lines are readily acceptable to the tolerant reader of verse. And, after all, the poet uses his *license* as a poet only when it is necessary to distort DICTION or grammar for the sake of form.

**Poetical Miscellanies:** See MISCELLANIES, POETICAL.


**Poetry:** A term applied to the many forms in which man has given a rhythmic expression to his most imaginative and intense perceptions of his world, himself, and the interrelationship of the two. Such a definition, however inadequate, points to the impossibility of binding in a simple formula a mode of expression and communication as primary and as enduring and still as eternally changing as *poetry* is. Only through an examination of other efforts at definition, at its origins, and at certain aspects of its nature can anything significant be said about *poetry.* This is not strange; indeed, it would be strange if man's most concrete form of expression yielded itself easily to abstract definition.

The origin of poetic expression is concealed in the dim past of man. No literary historian will presume to point out the earliest beginnings of *poetry,* though it is conceded on all sides that the first conscious literary expression took the form of primitive VERSE. The fact that VERSE is inherently emotional and that man, under emotional stress, breaks naturally into rhythmic expression establishes this point. Further evidence pointing to the same inference comes from early tribal ceremonials; races which have no written literature nevertheless employ poetic and rhythmic forms in their tribal ceremonies. In fact, it is evident that the first *poetry* was associated with the other arts of music and the dance. When a tribe or a people experienced any great event, a war, a migration, a flood, it seemed natural to chronicle and preserve these episodes in dance and song. Until recent years it had been frequently assumed that the earliest *poetry* was communal in origin, was the work not of one conscious literary artist, but rather of a group working together to commemorate some event. (See BALLAD.) The point is now made by some literary historians, that it is absurd to imagine a group doing as a whole what any single member of that group could not do as an individual.

The following attempts to define *poetry* are noteworthy:

I would define the poetry of words as the rhythmical creation of beauty. Its sole arbiter is taste. With the intellect or with the conscience it has only collateral relations. Unless incidentally, it has no concern whatever either with duty or with truth.

—Edgar Allan Poe

Poetry is the imaginative expression of strong feeling, usually rhythmical . . . the spontaneous overflow of powerful feelings recollected in tranquillity.

—William Wordsworth

The proper and immediate object of Science is the acquirement or communication of truth; the proper and immediate object of Poetry is the communication of pleasure . . . I wish our clever young poets would remember my homely definitions of prose and poetry; that is, *prose:* words in their best order; *poetry:* the best words in the best order.

—Samuel Taylor Coleridge

Poetry . . . a criticism of life under the conditions fixed for such a criticism by the laws of poetic truth and beauty.

—Matthew Arnold

Poetry is the utterance of a passion for truth, beauty, and power, embodying and illustrating its conceptions by imagination and fancy, and modulating its language on the principle of variety in uniformity.

—Leigh Hunt

By poetry we mean the art of employing words in such a manner as to produce an illusion of the imagination, the art of doing by means of words what the painter does by means of colors.

—Macaulay

Absolute poetry is the concrete and artistic expression of the human mind in emotional and rhythmical language.

—Theodore Watts-Dunton

Poetry, therefore, we will call musical Thought.

—Carlyle

Poetry is the record of the best and happiest moments of the best and happiest minds.

—Shelley

. . . speech framed . . . to be heard for its own sake and interest even over and above its interest of meaning.

—Gerard Manley Hopkins

An actual poem is the succession of experiences—sounds, images, thoughts, emotions—through which we pass when we are reading as poetically as we can.

—Andrew Bradley

. . . the rhythmic, inevitably narrative, movement from an overclothed blindness to a naked vision.

—Dylan Thomas

. . . the presentment, in musical form, to the imagination, of noble grounds for the noble emotions.

—Ruskin

If I read a book and it makes my whole body so cold no fire can ever warm me, I know that it is poetry. If I feel physically as if the top of my head were taken off, I know that it is poetry.

—Emily Dickinson

Poetry is language that tells us, through a more or less emotional reaction, something that cannot be said. All poetry, great or small, does this.

—Edwin Arlington Robinson

The art which uses words as both speech and song to reveal the realities that the senses record, the feelings salute, the mind perceives, and the shaping imagination orders.

—Babette Deutsch

Reading over any such list of statements, brings us, time and again, certain words, certain qualities, certain ideas: *emotion, imagination, idea* (or *thought*), *truth* (or *meaning*), *sentiment, passion, power, sense impression, interpretation* ("criticism of life"), *beauty, dignity, rhythm, freshness of expression, orderly arrangement, concreteness, pleasure.* And a further consideration of these words and phrases shows that they fall rather naturally into three classifications and point the way to three qualities common to all *poetry:* (1) It has a particular *content,* (2) it has a more or less particular *form,* and (3) it has a particular *effect.*

This three-fold aspect of *poetry* it is which makes the term so impossible of acceptable definition. Poets, critics, readers are of varying natures and prejudices. To some content is all important; to others form is the *sine qua non;* and to others all is to be judged by effect. A Carlyle will emphasize thought, a Poe beauty, a Matthew Arnold interpretation.

We shall do well, then, to limit our discussion of the nature of *poetry* to a consideration of these three qualities: *content, form,* and *effect.*

*The Content of Poetry.*—*Poetry* is definitely emotional. It presents the emotions of the poet as they are aroused by some scene of beauty, some experience, some attachment. For this reason it is often rich in sentiment and passion. Almost any LYRIC of Robert Burns is an instance of this emotional, passionate element. (See EMOTIONAL ELEMENT IN LITERATURE.) The content of *poetry* is, equally, IMAGINATIVE. The poet, as someone has said, does not speak the accurate language of science, does not, for example, refer to water as $H_2O$ but as "rippling," a "mirror," or "blue," using, not the elements which compose water but the effect which water creates in his imaginative mind and wanting the reader to respond to "water" as physical fact rather than abstract concept. It is this emotional, imaginative quality which Shakespeare had in mind in *A Midsummer Night's Dream:*

> The poet's eye, in a fine frenzy rolling,
> Doth glance from heaven to earth, from earth to heaven:
> As imagination bodies forth
> The forms of things unknown, the poet's pen
> Turns them to shapes and gives to airy nothing
> A local habitation and a name.
> Such tricks hath strong imagination,
> That, if it would but apprehend some joy,
> It comprehends some bringer of that joy.

Again, our series of statements concerning the nature of *poetry* emphasizes the elements of truth, thought, idea, meaning. *Poetry* must have significance; it must somehow contribute to the store of human knowledge or experience. This is what Matthew Arnold meant when he wrote of it as a "criticism of life"; what Watts-Dunton meant when he called it an "artistic expression of the human mind"; what Carlyle meant by "musical Thought." This insistence on the presence of meaning was probably in E. A. Robinson's mind when he said that *poetry* tries to tell us "something that cannot be said." The existence of an idea, a significance, a meaning, an attitude, or a feeling distinguishes *poetry* from DOGGEREL. However, the fact that *poetry* is concerned with meaning does not make it necessarily DIDACTIC. Great didactic *poetry* exists, but *poetry* is not great because it is DIDACTIC. In the words of Leigh Hunt, *poetry* is a "passion for truth, beauty, and power." To Wordsworth it meant "strong feeling," to Ruskin "noble grounds for noble emotions." Emily Dickinson's test was that real *poetry* left her whole body so cold no fire could ever warm her. All these requisites indicate the need for honesty of emotion, for depth of passion and feeling, for, in short, *power*.

Another key to the content of *poetry* can be found in *beauty*. All poets will agree to this element although by no means will all poets agree as to what is beautiful. To Shelley beauty meant the song of the skylark; Carl Sandburg finds it in a brickyard; Whitman in a leaf of grass. But beauty, of some degree, must be present. If it is a new, strange beauty of some familiar object so much the better. The poet, like the artist and the musician, is different from most other people because of his sensitivity to beauty in all its various forms; he is, in short, a poet chiefly because of this sensitivity. "Poetry," says Shelley, "turns all things to loveliness; it exalts the beauty of that which is most beautiful, and it adds beauty to that which is most deformed . . . ; it strips the veil of familiarity from the world, and lays bare the naked and sleeping beauty, which is the spirit of its forms," an idea which Dylan Thomas expresses as the "movement from overclothed blindness to a naked vision."

*Poetry* is usually dignified. In poetic composition life tends to be on parade—grand, magnificent, and marching with a fanfare. *Poetry* usually lives in Carcassone, although the nature of Carcassone—its language, manners, and rules of DECORUM—changes from age to age. The content of *poetry* is usually *emotional, imaginative,* compact with *meaning*, marked by *power, beauty,* and *dignity*.

*The Form of Poetry*.—The second element with which we are concerned in an examination of the nature of *poetry* is *form*. If *poetry* can be set off from other writing by its *content*, the distinction of *form* is even more clear-cut. While it is true that in some forms of writing (POLYPHONIC PROSE, for example) *poetry* borders closely upon the form of PROSE and PROSE upon the form of VERSE, for most cases this distinction of form is serviceable enough. The first characteristic of *poetry*, from the standpoint of form, is the presence of RHYTHM. Of course all good PROSE has a more or less conscious RHYTHM, but the RHYTHM of *poetry* is marked by a degree of regularity far surpassing that of PROSE (see PROSE RHYTHM). In fact, one of the chief rewards of reading *poetry* is the satisfaction which comes from finding "variety in uniformity," a shifting of RHYTHMS which, nevertheless, constantly return to the basic pattern (see RHYTHM and METER). The ear recognizes the existence of recurring ACCENTS at stated intervals and recognizes, too, variations from these RHYTHM patterns. Whatever the pattern,

IAMBIC PENTAMETER, DACTYLLIC DIMETER, or any one of the many possible combinations in any of the other rhythmic systems (see METER), there is a regularity of recurrence which is more uniform than in PROSE. Frequently, of course, RIME affords an obvious difference by which one may distinguish the form of *poetry* from that of PROSE. Another key is *arrangement, order*. The demands of the VERSE pattern—the combinations of RHYTHM and RIME—often exact a "poetic" arrangement of the phrases and clauses. INVERSION is more justified in *poetry* than in PROSE; SYNCOPE is more common. The poet is granted a license (though modern poets hesitate to avail themselves of it) in sequence and syntax which is denied the prose-writer. Since most *poetry* is relatively short it is likely to be characterized by compactness of thought and expression, to possess an intense UNITY, to be carefully arranged in climactic order. The distinction between *poetry* and PROSE on these points is not so much the presence of these qualities as the degree to which they are respected. A vital element of all great *poetry* is its *concreteness*. Here, again, the form is different from that of most PROSE. PROSE is satisfied, usually, to state a fact baldly and in general or ABSTRACT TERMS. *Poetry* insists on the specific, the concrete. The point may be made more obvious by quoting the following lines by Shakespeare:

> Our revels now are ended. These our actors,
> As I foretold you, were all spirits, and
> Are melted into air, into thin air:
> And, like the baseless fabric of this vision,
> The cloud-capp'd towers, the gorgeous palaces,
> The solemn temples, the great globe itself,
> Yea, all which it inherit, shall dissolve,
> And, like this insubstantial pageant faded,
> Leave not a rack behind. We are such stuff
> As dreams are made on; and our little life
> Is rounded with a sleep.

Here almost every line presents a concrete IMAGE or shows a picture-quality. The lines are alive with specific language. In a passage on the imagination Shakespeare has himself written imaginatively. What does it all mean? PROSE would express the idea simply and bluntly; it might, indeed, be content with the first five words of the passage. And here is one of the qualities of VERSE which makes so many people pretend to dislike it. "Why can't poets say exactly what they mean?" people who like to call themselves "practical" ask. The answer is, of course, that they do say what they mean; it is no fault of theirs if subtlety of expression, beauty of IMAGERY, and music of words fall on deaf ears.

One more distinction between the form of *poetry* and the form of PROSE must be cited—*language*. In addition to this concreteness, this IMAGERY already mentioned, the very language of *poetry* usually differs from that of PROSE. To Milton the language of *poetry* was "simple, sensuous, and impassioned." Since the function of *poetry* is to present concretely the IMAGES of the poet, it is the responsibility of the poet to select language which succeeds in making his IMAGES concrete. The specific word, the word rich in connotative value, the word carrying implications of sound and color and action—these are the especial stock of the true poet. Modern *poetry* tends to throw overboard the special vocabulary which was once thought of as the special language of *poetry*, the *thees* and *thous* and *e'ers* (see POETIC DICTION). The language of the poet is more rich in the figures of speech, in METONOMY, SYNECDOCHE, and METAPHOR, than is the language of the prose-writer. And so we find that the *form* of *poetry*, as well as the *content*, serves to distinguish *poetry* from PROSE.

*The Effect or Purpose of Poetry.*—There remains only one further distinction to make—that based on *effect*. PROSE is, of course, written with a hundred purposes in the minds of authors. It may be to please, as in FICTION; or it may be to instruct, as in this reference book, in a geography, a history, or a volume of philosophy. Again, PROSE is used to convince, to persuade to a line of action: to explain and to expound, to describe a scene or to narrate an action. All of these purposes may be blended together, any combination of them may exist together, or any one of them may stand almost alone. But with *poetry*, the chief, the ultimate purpose must be *to please*. The various senses of sight and sound and color may be appealed to, the various emotions of love and fear and appreciation of beauty may be called forth by the poet, but *whatever the immediate appeal, the ultimate effect of poetry is that of giving pleasure.*

With the advance of the years from the dim past wherein *poetry* found its origin, the art of poetic composition has undergone a long process of refinement. From its general or racial interest it has become intensely individualistic; from the ceremonial recounting of tribal and group movements it has become the vehicle for DRAMA, for history, for personal emotion. It is, however, still common today to classify *poetry* into three great type-divisions; the *epic*, the *dramatic*, and the *lyric*.

*Forms and Types of Poetry.*—The three types just mentioned are, in turn, broken up into further classifications. With the development of conscious artistry, numerous set patterns such as the SONNET, the ODE, the ELEGY have evolved. Further subdivisions have been made on the basis of mood and purpose, such as the PASTORAL, and SATIRIC and DIDACTIC *poetry*. All of these types and manners are discussed in their proper position in this Handbook.

**Point of View:** A term used in the analysis and criticism of FICTION to describe the way in which the reader is presented with the materials of the story, or, viewed from another angle, the vantage point from which the author presents the actions of the story. If the author serves as an all-knowing maker, not restricted to time, place, or character, and free to move and to comment at will, the *point of view* is usually called OMNISCIENT. At the other extreme, a character within the story—major, minor, or merely a witness— may tell the story as he experienced it, saw it, heard it, and understood it. Such a character is usually called a first-person NARRATOR; if he does not comprehend the implications of what he is telling he is called a NAÏVE or disingenuous NARRATOR. The author may tell the story in the third person and yet present it as it is seen and understood by a single character—major, minor, or merely witness—restricting information to what that character sees, hears, feels, and thinks; such a *point of view* is said to be limited to one character. The author may employ such a limited *point of view* and restrict the materials presented to the interior responses of the *point of view* character, resulting in the INTERIOR MONOLOGUE. The author may present his material by a process of narrative exposition, in which actions and conversations are presented in summary rather than in detail; such a method is usually called *panoramic*. On the other hand, he may present actions and conversations in detail, as they occur, and objectively—without authorial comment; such a method is usually called *scenic*. If the scenic method is carried to the point where the author never speaks in his own person and does not ostensibly intrude himself into the scenes he presents, he is said to be a SELF-EFFACING AUTHOR. In extended works of FICTION authors frequently employ combinations of several of these methods. The concern with *point of view* in current criticism and the experimentation with *point of view* by many current novelists are both very great. Since Henry James's critical essays and Prefaces, *point of view* has often been considered the technical aspect of FICTION which leads the critic most readily into the problems and the meanings of a NOVEL or a SHORT STORY. See NARRATOR.

**Polyphonic Prose:** According to Amy Lowell, who made considerable use of the form, not really PROSE at all, but VERSE. She defined the term as follows: " 'Polyphonic' means—many voiced—and the form is so called because it makes use of all the 'voices' of poetry, namely: metre, *vers libre*, assonance, alliteration, rhyme, and return." Printed as PROSE, this form, when read aloud as Miss Lowell suggested, reveals fleeting glimpses of the various poetic practices.

**Popular Ballad:** See BALLAD.

**Portmanteau Words:** Words concocted by accident or for deliberate humorous effect by telescoping two words into one, as the making of "squarson" (attributed to Bishop Wilberforce) from "squire" and "parson." *Portmanteau words* was a name given by Lewis Carroll to this type of fabrication, a type which he himself used in *Through the Looking Glass.* An example of Carroll's manner occurs in his famous "Jabberwocky" poem where, for instance, he made "slithy" of "lithe" and "slimy." In his *History of the Snark* Carroll explained the system by which such words were made: "For instance, take the two words 'fuming' and 'furious.' Make up your mind that you will say both words, but leave it unsettled which you will say first. Now open your mouth and speak. If your thoughts incline ever so little towards 'fuming' you will say 'fuming-furious'; if they turn by even a hair's breadth towards 'furious,' you will say 'furious-fuming'; but if you have that rarest of gifts, a perfectly balanced mind, you will say 'frumious.' " James Joyce in *Ulysses* and particularly in *Finnegans Wake* employs many *portmanteau words* to enrich and deepen the AMBIGUITY of his works.

**Posy (Posie):** Sometimes used in the sense of "a collection of flowers" to indicate an ANTHOLOGY. The term also signifies a motto, usually in verse, inscribed on a ring. When the "mouse-trap" play begins and the PROLOGUE has been spoken Hamlet asks Ophelia: "Is this a prologue, or the posy of a ring?"

**Pot-boiler:** A SLANG term given to a book or an article written solely for the income derived from it. It is writing which will "keep the pot boiling" and thus supply sustenance, presumably, for more worthy work.

**Poulter's Measure:** A metrical pattern, now rarely used, consisting of a COUPLET composed of a first line in IAMBIC HEXAMETER and a second line in IAMBIC HEPTAMETER. The term is said to have originated from a custom of the London poulterers of giving the customer twelve eggs to the dozen in the first dozen bought, and fourteen in the second dozen. Wyatt and Surrey, Sidney, Nicholas Grimald, and Arthur Brooke are some of the poets who have used this form. *Poulter's measure* exists today in a modified form; it is a four-line STANZA composed of IAMBIC TRIMETER verses for the first, second, and fourth lines, and an IAMBIC TETRAMETER for the third. The opening lines of Arthur Brooke's *Romeus and Juliet* afford an example of *poulter's measure:*

> There is beyond the Alps, a town of ancient fame,
> Whose bright renown yet shineth clear, Verona men it name;
> Built in a happy time, built on a fertile soil,
> Maintainéd by the heavenly fates, and by the tarnished toil.

**Practical Criticism:** Criticism in which the critic's principles of art and aesthetic beliefs are applied to specific works of art; often called "applied criticism," the term is used in opposition to THEORETICAL CRITICISM, in which general principles and broad tenets are sought. See CRITICISM, TYPES OF.

**Pragmatic Theory of Art:** A theory of art, according to M. H. Abrams, in which the critic's major interest is in the effect that the art object produces in its audience. See CRITICISM, HISTORICAL SKETCH.

**Pragmatism:** A term, first used by C. S. Peirce in 1878 in an article in *Popular Science Monthly* to describe a philosophical doctrine that determines value and meaning through the test of consequences or utility. Its principal exponents have been William James and

John Dewey, through whose work and influence it has made itself pervasively felt in America. The *pragmatist* insists that no questions are significant unless the results of answering them in one way rather than another have practical consequences in human affairs. In William James's words: "The 'whole meaning' of a conception expresses itself in practical consequences, consequences either in the shape of conduct to be recommended, or in that of experience to be expected, if the conception be true." John Dewey and his followers have emphasized the implications of *pragmatism* upon logical processes, insisting that logical thinking must be subordinate to practical life and that thought aims not at truth but at satisfying some practical end that life demands. The world of the pragmatists is pluralistic, interested in context, relativistic in its beliefs about truth and value systems, devoid of the metaphysical concerns except as they have practical consequences. On the other hand, it places a high premium upon conduct, upon ethical concerns. In literature, *pragmatism* found its most vigorous expression in the REALISM that developed in America after 1870.

**Preamble:** An introductory portion of a written document. In formal sets of "resolutions" there is usually a *preamble* which sets forth the occasion for the resolutions. This *preamble* is introduced by one or more statements beginning with "Whereas" and is followed by the resolutions proper, each article of which is introduced by the word "Therefore."

**Preciosity:** A critical term sometimes applied to writing which is consciously "pretty," labored or affected in STYLE, fastidious in DICTION, over-refined in manner.

**Preface:** A short introductory statement printed at the beginning of a book or article—and separate from it—in which the author states his purpose in writing, makes necessary acknowledgments of assistance, points out difficulties and uncertainties in connection with the writing of the book, and, in general, informs the reader of such facts as he thinks pertinent to a reading of the text. Some writers, notably Dryden and Shaw, have written *prefaces* which were really extended ESSAYS.

**Prelude:** A short poem, introductory in character, prefixed to a long poem or to a section of a long poem. Lowell's *The Vision of*

*Sir Launfal* contains *preludes* of the latter sort. Rarely, as in the case of Wordsworth's famous *Prelude*, a poem so entitled may itself be lengthy.

**Pre-Raphaelitism:** The Pre-Raphaelite movement originated with the establishment in 1848 of the Pre-Raphaelite brotherhood by Dante Gabriel Rossetti, Holman Hunt, John Everett Millais, and other artists as a protest against the conventional methods of painting then in use. The Pre-Raphaelites wished to regain the spirit of simple devotion and adherence to NATURE which they found in Italian religious art before Raphael. Ruskin asserted that *Pre-Raphaelitism* had but one principle, that of absolute uncompromising truth in all that it did, truth attained by elaborating everything, down to the most minute detail, from NATURE and from NATURE only. This meant the rejection of all conventions designed to heighten effects artificially. Several of the group were both artists and poets, and the effect of the cult was therefore felt in English literature. Rossetti was the most influential. His "Blessed Damozel," published in 1850 in one of the four issues of *The Germ,* the organ of the group, is a religious narrative with pictorial qualities. In general, the characteristics of Pre-Raphaelite poetry are: pictorial elements, SYMBOLISM, sensuousness, tendency to metrical experimentation, attention to minute detail, and an interest in the medieval and the supernatural. By certain critics, who deemed sensuousness the dominant characteristic of their poetry, the Pre-Raphaelites were styled the "FLESHLY SCHOOL." The chief literary products of the movement were Rossetti's translation of Dante, his sonnets, and his ballad-like verse; Christina Rossetti's lyrics; and the poems of William Morris, such as *The Earthly Paradise* and *The Defense of Guinevere.* Morris' practical application of medieval craftsmanship to business effected a great change in public taste in home decoration.

**Primitivism:** The doctrine that primitive man, because he had remained closer to NATURE and had been less subject to the corrupt influences of society, was nobler and more nearly perfect than is civilized man. The idea flourished in eighteenth-century England and France and was an important element in the creed of the "sentimentalists" of the romantic movement. Though it is perhaps not possible to trace all the forces which aided in the development and promulgation of the primitivistic doctrine, a few may be suggested. The rationalistic philosopher, the third Earl of Shaftesbury (*fl. ca.* 1710), in his effort to show that God had revealed himself completely in NATURE—and that NATURE was therefore perfect—reasoned that primitive peoples were close to God and therefore essentially moral. Man is by nature prone to do good: his evil comes from self-imposed limitations of his freedom. Romantic accounts of savage peoples by writers of travel literature added impetus to the movement, as did also the linguistic researches into the origin of language by such men as Lord Monboddo (*The Origin of Language,* 1773–1792), and the effort of various scholars to find the reason for Homer's greatness in his assumed primitive surroundings. Tremendous impetus from France was given the movement by the writings of Rousseau, whose slogan of "Return to Nature" was based upon his belief that man was potentially perfect and that his faults were due to the vicious effect of the type of society he had developed, one which tended progressively to restrict the freedom and hence lessen the moral goodness of man.

One of the most interesting phases of the primitivistic movement in English literature was its doctrine that the best poetry should be natural or instinctive, not cultivated. There was therefore a feverish search not only for a perfect primitive man but for a perfect "untutored" poet. Among the many savages brought by the primitivists to England in their search for the perfect natural man the enthusiasts searched for evidence of poetic genius. The "inspired peasant" was sought for, too, among the unlettered population of Great Britain, and many such "geniuses" were fêted by high society till their fame wore out: Henry Jones, the poetical bricklayer; James Woodhouse, the poetical shoemaker; and Ann Yearsley, the poetical milk-woman of Bristol, who signed her poems "Lactilla" and was sponsored by the BLUESTOCKINGS. Gray's *The Bard* (1757) and James Beattie's *The Minstrel* (1771–1774) reflect the doctrine of primitive poetic genius, and no lover of English poetry can forget "some mute inglorious Milton" of Gray's famous *Elegy.* For a time the forged "Ossian" poems of James Macpherson (see LITERARY FORGERIES) seemed an answer to the romantic prayer for the discovery in Britain of the work of some primitive epic poet. When, finally, Robert Burns appeared, the doctrine of the peasant poet seemed proved, and the Scotch BARD was received with extravagant enthusiasm, especially in Edinburgh.

Of course, all England did not go primitivistic. The craze was ironically attacked by such conservatives as Doctor Johnson and Edmund Burke. The "noble savage" idea produced the idealized American Indian, as in Cooper's novels, and American life was exploited as ideal because primitive, as in Crèvecoeur's *Letters from an American Farmer* and Gilbert Imlay's novel of pioneer life, *The Emigrants*. (For the later reaction against these idealized treatments of the Indian and the pioneer see Francis Parkman's *The Oregon Trail* and Hamlin Garland's *Main Travelled Roads* or his *A Son of the Middle Border*.) It has been seriously asserted that the enthusiastic reception of Benjamin Franklin in Paris was partly attributable to the interest in Americans stirred by the primitivists. Elements of *primitivism,* related to the idea of natural goodness, appear throughout American writing in the nineteenth century.

A common and useful distinction is made between CULTURAL PRIMITIVISM and CHRONOLOGICAL PRIMITIVISM, CULTURAL being used for the *primitivism* that prefers the natural to the man-made, the uninhibited to the controlled, the simple and primitive to that upon which man has worked, NATURE to art; and CHRONOLOGICAL being used for the *primitivism* that looks backward to a "Golden Age" and sees man's present sad state as the product of what culture and society have done to him. If this distinction is made—and it should be recognized that the terms are not mutually exclusive—it becomes apparent that many of the political doctrines of the American founding fathers were influenced by CHRONOLOGICAL PRIMITIVISM, while CULTURAL PRIMITIVISM has been a powerful, although silent, force in American REALISM. See PROGRESS.

**Printing, Introduction into American Colonies:** Although the Spaniards had brought printing presses to Mexico and elsewhere much earlier, the real beginning of printing in America dates from 1639, when, according to Governor Winthrop's *Diary*, a printing house was begun by Stephen Daye. In reality, Daye was the printer, not the proprietor. The first thing printed was the freeman's oath, the next an ALMANAC, and the next the famous "Bay Psalm Book" (1640), the earliest surviving American book. William Bradford was printing in Philadelphia as early as 1683. Later he moved to New York and became the government printer. The introduction of printing into Virginia was opposed by Governor Berkeley and a printing establishment was suppressed in 1682, though printing was reintroduced not long thereafter.

**Printing, Introduction into England:** The debt which literature owes to the art of printing is so great that every reader of books should acquaint himself with its history. The development of printing in the fifteenth century was not only encouraged by the new intellectual curiosity of the RENAISSANCE but itself supplied a powerful stimulus to the revival of learning and the literature which followed in its wake. The first generation or so of printers busied themselves chiefly with the reproduction of the great works of the past, medieval and classical, and with ecclesiastical documents. By the first decade of the sixteenth century printers were beginning to be of service to contemporary writers by supplying them with a vastly enlarged potential audience, and the glorious harvest in literature produced by the RENAISSANCE could hardly have been possible without the aid of the printing press. Relations between printers and writers became increasingly close, and it was a publisher (Richard Tottel) rather than a professional man of letters who supplied a great impetus to creative poetic work in England by publishing a large collection of manuscript poems of Wyatt and Surrey and others just before the beginning of Elizabeth's reign (*Tottel's Miscellany,* 1557). By making literature salable, the printers helped create the professional man of letters. The circumstances surrounding the invention and development of printing in Western Europe (the Chinese and Japanese had practised a simple form of printing centuries before) are so lost in obscurity that it is impossible now to assign the invention to any country or person or exact date. Although there seems to have been some sort of forerunner of the printed book in Holland, it is fairly certain that the most important development of the art took place in Mainz, Germany, during the forties and fifties of the fifteenth century. The earliest existing book which can be dated is an "Indulgence" (Mainz, 1454); the most famous existing early book is the so-called Gutenberg Bible (Mainz, 1456). On the authority of fifteenth-century writers, John Gutenberg of Mainz is commonly given credit for the invention.

From Mainz the art spread to Italy, France, Holland, and other countries, reaching England in 1476, when William Caxton set up his famous press at Westminster. Caxton had learned printing on the Continent, and at Bruges, probably in 1475, had brought out the first book printed in English, the *Recuyell of the Histories of Troy.* The first printed books in England were perhaps pamphlets, some of them in Latin, but the first dated English book printed in England was Caxton's *Dictes or Sayings of the Philosophers* (1477).

Before his death Caxton had printed about a hundred separate books. He did much to direct the public taste in reading. He specialized in translations, poetry, and romances, two of his most important books being his edition of Chaucer's *Canterbury Tales* (1483) and his publication of Malory's *Le Morte Darthur* (1485). Other early presses in England include one at Oxford (1478) and one at St. Albans (1479), both devoted chiefly to learned works. Caxton himself was succeeded by his assistant, Wynken de Worde, a printer without literary talent but important because he published, during his long career, about 800 books, some of them of literary interest. An important contemporary was Richard Pynson (*fl.*1490–1530).

**Private Theatres:** This term seems to have arisen about 1596, when the Blackfriars theatre was so described by its sponsors who were seeking privileges not granted to the PUBLIC THEATRES. The name is misleading, since the *private theatres,* though they charged a higher admission fee and attracted in general a higher class of spectators than did their "public" rivals, were open to all classes. They did differ from the PUBLIC THEATRES in that they were indoor institutions, artificially lighted, smaller, and typically rectangular. As the *private theatre* was connected in its origin with companies of child actors, so in its maturity it was used chiefly (not exclusively) by the companies of child actors. The Elizabethan *private theatres* were the Blackfriars, Paul's School, the Cockpit (or Phoenix), and Salisbury Court, the latter two being known also as "court theatres." Shakespeare's company in the early seventeenth century controlled both the Blackfriars, the chief *private theatre,* and the Globe, the chief PUBLIC THEATRE. The *private theatres,* being indoor institutions of a somewhat aristocratic character, became of increasing importance in the seventeenth century, when the Court was fostering elaborate exhibitions (see MASQUE) and encouraging DRAMA with spectacular features, and it is from them rather than from the PUBLIC THEATRES that the elaborate playhouses of the RESTORATION and later times are directly descended. See PUBLIC THEATRES.

**Problem Novel:** A name given to that type of PROSE FICTION which derives its chief interest from working out, through characters and incidents, some central problem. In a loose sense almost every NOVEL or PLOT presents a problem since the opposition of forces which make for PLOT and CONFLICT also should arouse some interest in the reader as to "how this is to turn out." However, the term is usually more restricted than this. It is sometimes carelessly applied to those novels which are written for deliberate purpose, a thesis, which are better called PROPAGANDA NOVELS, since they present a brief for or against one class of people, one type of living, one activity of civilization. Since human character is the subject matter surest to interest readers and since humankind is constantly confronted by the problems of life and conduct, it follows that the *problem novel*—when it is thought of as a story *with* a purpose rather than *for* a purpose—is fairly common. The realistic novel, centered as it is in social setting, has often employed social issues as the cruxes of its PLOTS. It is this matter of illustrating a problem by showing people confronted by it which is at the core of the *problem novel*. See PROPAGANDA NOVEL.

**Problem of Belief:** See BELIEF, PROBLEM OF.

**Problem Play:** Like its ANALOGUE in non-dramatic FICTION, the PROBLEM NOVEL, this term is used both in a broad sense to cover all serious drama in which problems of human life are presented as such, e.g., Shakespeare's *King Lear*, and in a more specialized sense to designate the modern "drama of ideas," as exemplified in the plays of Ibsen, Shaw, Galsworthy, and many others. Its most common usage is in the latter sense, and here it means the representation in dramatic form of a general social problem or issue, shown as it is confronted by or must be solved by the PROTAGONIST. See PROBLEM NOVEL.

**Proem:** A brief introduction, a PREFACE or PREAMBLE.

**Progress:** The belief that in many significant ways human history shows a pattern of improvement over the past is often called "the idea of *progress*." In some cases, this idea is almost made into a system under which *progress*—that is, improvement of the human and social condition—is inevitable with the passage of time. In its naive statements, a childishly optimistic doctrine—as in Coué's "Day by day, in every way, I am getting better and better"—when held by serious and thoughtful men, as it often has been, the idea of *progress* is a strong antidote to the doctrine of CHRONOLOGICAL

PRIMITIVISM. It has often been said that American ROMANTICISM in the nineteenth century rested upon the doctrine of natural goodness (CULTURAL PRIMITIVISM) and the idea of *progress*. See PRIMITIVISM.

**Prolegomenon:** A foreword or PREFACE. The heading *prolegomena* (the plural form) may be given to the introductory section of a book containing observations on the subject of the book itself.

**Prolepsis:** An anticipating; the type of ANACHRONISM in which an event is pictured as taking place before it could have done so, the treating of a future event as if past. Rhetorically, the word may be applied to a preliminary statement or summary which is to be followed by a detailed treatment. In ARGUMENTATION *prolepsis* may mean the device of anticipating and answering an opponent's argument before the opponent has an opportunity to introduce it, thus detracting from its effectiveness if later employed.

**Prologue:** A PREFACE or INTRODUCTION most frequently associated with DRAMA and especially common in England in the plays of the RESTORATION and the eighteenth century. In the plays of ancient Greece a speaker announced, before the beginning of the play proper, such salient facts as were necessary for the audience to know to understand the play itself. In Latin DRAMA the same custom prevailed, Plautus having left some of the most mature *prologues* in dramatic literature. European dramatists in both France and England followed the classical tradition, from the time of the MIRACLE and MYSTERY PLAYS (which may be said to have used *prologues* of a "moral" nature) well into modern times. *Prologues* were frequently written by the author of a play and delivered by one of the chief actors; it was, however, in the eighteenth century, common practice for writers of established reputations, such as Pope, Doctor Johnson, and Garrick, to write *prologues* for the plays of their friends and acquaintances. Sometimes, as in the play within the play in *Hamlet,* the actor who spoke the *prologue* was himself called "the prologue." The first part of Shakespeare's *King Henry IV* opens with an explanatory speech, not formally a *prologue,* which serves the function of a real *prologue*. Part two of the same play opens with a *prologue* called an INDUCTION. See INDUCTION and EPILOGUE.

**Propaganda Novel:** A NOVEL dealing with a special social, political, economic, or moral issue or problem and strongly advocating a doctrinaire solution. See PROBLEM NOVEL.

**Proscenium:** Properly used, the term now designates that part of the stage in a modern theatre which lies between the orchestra and the curtain. In the ancient theatre the *proscenium* extended from the orchestra to the background, and the term is not infrequently used, even nowadays, merely as a synonym for the stage itself.

**Prose:** In its broadest sense, the term is applied to all forms of written or spoken expression which do not have a regular rhythmic pattern (see METER). Such a definition, however, needs some elaboration, for a collection of words thrown together, a mere setting down of haphazard conversation, for instance, is not usually considered *prose*. *Prose* is most often meant to designate a conscious, cultivated writing, not merely a bringing together of vocabularies, a listing of ideas, a catalogue of objects. And, while *prose* is like VERSE in that good *prose* has a RHYTHM, it is unlike VERSE in that this RHYTHM is not to be scanned by any of the normal metrical schemes. But a clear line between *prose* and POETRY is difficult to draw. Is bad VERSE *prose?* Is rhythmical *prose* VERSE? Is Miss Lowell's POLYPHONIC PROSE a *prose* form, a VERSE form, or something between the two? It is easier, perhaps, to list some of the qualities of *prose:* (1) it is without sustained rhythmic regularity; (2) it has some logical, grammatical order and its ideas are connectedly stated rather than merely listed; (3) it is characterized by the virtues of STYLE, though the STYLE will vary, naturally, from writer to writer; (4) it will secure variety of expression through DICTION and through sentence structure.

*Prose,* interestingly enough, has in all literatures developed more slowly than VERSE. English *prose* is usually said to find its beginnings in the work of Alfred, whose *Handbook* (887) is sometimes cited as the earliest specimen of finished English *prose*. Other names significant in the development of English *prose* are Thomas Usk, John Wycliffe, Malory, Caxton, Roger Ascham, Holinshed, Lyly, Raleigh, Donne, Jeremy Taylor, Milton, Dryden, Addison, and Hemingway. For many centuries English *prose* had to compete with Latin for recognition, and for many more years Latin forms and syntax modeled its STYLE. The single book which did most to mold present English *prose* STYLE was the King James version of the BIBLE.

**Prose Poetry:** A form of PROSE with marked (although preferably not too regular) CADENCE and frequently with extensive use of FIGURATIVE LANGUAGE and IMAGERY. If *prose poetry* is to be distinguished from POLYPHONIC PROSE, the distinction is that POLYPHONIC PROSE is usually reserved for a kind of writing which has marked VERSE characteristics in PROSE form, whereas *prose poetry* is predominantly PROSE but borrows enriching characteristics from the RHYTHMS and IMAGERY of POETRY. See POLYPHONIC PROSE, PROSE RHYTHM.

**Prose Rhythm:** The recurrence of ACCENT and EMPHASIS at regular or, much more usually, irregular intervals which gives to some PROSE a pleasurable rise and fall of movement. *Prose rhythm* is distinguished from the RHYTHM of VERSE in that it never for long falls into a recognizable pattern, for if it does, of course, it becomes VERSE rather than PROSE. RHYTHM in PROSE is essentially a quality of STYLE, the superior stylist using a more rhythmical expression than the jerky staccato of a beginner, avoiding, as he does, the sing-song monotony of regularity and making every effort to secure a constant *flow* of ACCENT, always changing yet always harmonizing with the thought and sense he is expressing. In emotional passages the author may trust RHYTHM more deliberately than in his more pedestrian moments since RHYTHM is itself so definitely and naturally one aspect of the voice of passion.

The greater freedom of *prose rhythm,* as compared with the RHYTHM of VERSE, springs from its wider choice in the placing of ACCENTS. There is no necessity to force a line to a certain rhythmic pattern. The normal ACCENT of words, of course, first determines the rhythmic emphasis. But this is augmented by the secondary AC-CENTS (in such words as ob″-ser-va′-tion and el″-e-men′-ta-ry) and increased again by the tendency of the reader to emphasize certain words importantly placed or rendered significant because of their meaning. (RHETORICAL ACCENT, see ACCENT.) A brief passage from the writing of Walter Pater, an author whose work is among the most rhythmic writings in English, is selected at random and accented according to the ear of at least one reader:

To such a tremulous wisp constantly reforming itself on the stream, to a single sharp impression, with a sense in it, a relic more or less fleeting, of such moments gone by, what is real in our life fines itself down.

# Prosody

A rhythmic analysis of the sentence shows an almost consistent use of ANAPESTS and IAMBS—a preponderant tendency toward the use of one or two (or sometimes three) unaccented syllables followed by an accented one. But, granting that Pater is exceptional, that the accents indicated are perhaps arbitrary, and that some other reader will record the emphasis differently, the fact will remain that the passage is definitely rhythmical. Attempts have been made from time to time to evolve a system of SCANSION for PROSE, but none of them has proved satisfactory to any sizeable group of critics.

**Prosody:** The theory and principles of VERSIFICATION, particularly as they refer to RHYTHM, ACCENT, and STANZA. See METER, SCANSION, VERSIFICATION.

**Prosopopoeia:** A term sometimes used for PERSONIFICATION.

**Protagonist:** The chief character in a play or story. When the PLOT involves CONFLICT, the chief opponent or rival of the *protagonist* is called an ANTAGONIST. If the main PLOT centers about the career of a HERO who overcomes a VILLAIN who tries to thwart his efforts, the hero would be called the *protagonist*, the villain the ANTAGONIST. If, however, the main interest lies in the career of a VILLAIN, whose plans are defeated by the appearance of a successful HERO, the villain would be called the *protagonist* and the HERO the ANTAGONIST. In Shakespeare's *Hamlet,* Hamlet is himself the *protagonist*, as his fortunes are the chief interest in the play. King Claudius and Laertes are his ANTAGONISTS. The sentence "The protagonists of Christopher Marlowe's tragedies are usually of the super-personality type" illustrates a usual use of the word. In a looser sense *protagonist* is sometimes used in the sense of champion or chief advocate of a cause or movement, as when Bryan is referred to as the *protagonist* of the free-silver movement in 1896. The word *protagonist* was originally applied to the first actor added to CHORUS and leader in the early Greek DRAMA; hence its continuing sense of "first" or chief player in the DRAMA.

**Protasis:** The term applied by the classical critics to the introductory ACT or the EXPOSITION of a DRAMA. See DRAMATIC STRUCTURE.

**Prototype:** A first form or original instance of a thing, or model or pattern for later forms or examples. Thus the PERIODICAL ESSAY of the eighteenth century as written by Addison or Steele may be referred to as the *prototype* of the modern FAMILIAR ESSAY as written by Lamb or Stevenson, the later form being developed from the earlier. Or the "Vice" of the MORALITY PLAYS may be regarded as the *prototype* of the clown of ELIZABETHAN DRAMA.

**Proverb:** A sentence or phrase which briefly and strikingly expresses some recognized truth or shrewd observation about practical life and which has been preserved by oral tradition, though it may be preserved and transmitted in written literature as well. It commonly originates with the folk. So far as form goes, *proverbs* may owe their appeal to the use of a METAPHOR ("Still waters run deep"); ANTITHESIS ("Man proposes, God disposes"), a play on words ("Forewarned, forearmed"); RIME ("A friend in need is a friend indeed"); or such devices as ALLITERATION or parallel structure. Some are epigrammatic. Since the true *proverb* is old, its language is sometimes archaic. Words or meanings or idioms or grammatical constructions not now common may be used. A misunderstanding of the original meaning may result. Thus in "Time and tide wait for no man" *tide* is probably the old word for "season." "Feed a cold, starve a fever," which seems to be medical advice of questionable value, becomes sensible if it means "If you feed a cold, you'll have a fever to starve." The range of interest of the *proverb* is, of course, wide: the weather, remedies for illness, legal shifts, superstitions, agriculture, efficiency in practical life, SATIRE on other races or on rival countries or localities, etc. *Proverbs* pass freely from language to language. Those with a long "literary" history, though popular in origin, are sometimes called "learned proverbs."

**Provincialism:** See COLLOQUIALISM.

**Psalm:** A lyrical composition of praise. Most frequently, of course, the term is applied to the sacred and devout LYRICS in the Book of Psalms ascribed to David.

**Pseudonym:** A fictitious name sometimes assumed by writers and others. See NOM DE PLUME, PUTATIVE AUTHOR.

**Pseudo-Shakespearean Plays:** The list of plays attributed to Shakespeare at one time or another but not accepted as his by the best authorities. There are about as many plays in this list as in the "true" list. Because of Shakespeare's reputation, some non-Shakespearean plays, such as *Locraine,* were printed during Shakespeare's lifetime with his initials or name on the title page; others, such as *The Birth of Merlin,* were so printed after Shakespeare's death. Another group, including *Mucedorus,* consists of plays labeled as Shakespeare's in the copies of them found in the library of Charles II. Many others, including *Sir Thomas More* (the manuscript copy of which is thought by some experts to be partly in Shakespeare's handwriting) and *Arden of Feversham,* have been assigned to Shakespeare by editors, booksellers, or critics chiefly on the basis of their literary or technical qualities. The First Folio (1623) contains plays assembled by Shakespeare's fellow actors, Heming and Condell, who, it would seem, were in position to know the facts. But they may have been forced to omit some genuine plays because of ownership difficulties (they omit, for example, *Pericles,* now regarded as largely Shakespeare's). Further, they included some plays, such as *Henry VIII, Titus Andronicus,* and the *Henry VI* plays, which there are grounds for regarding as partly non-Shakespearean. The custom of collaboration—the writing of a single play by two or more playwrights—may have left the 1623 editors in doubt as to the inclusion of plays of which Shakespeare was a reviser or part author. A collection of *pseudo-Shakespearean plays* has been printed by Tucker Brooke in his *Shakespeare Apocrypha.* Some of the plays dubiously assigned to Shakespeare, such as *Cardenio,* have not survived.

**Psychological Novel:** PROSE FICTION which places more than the usual amount of emphasis on interior CHARACTERIZATION, and on the motives, circumstances, and internal action which springs from, and develops, external action. The *psychological novel* is not content to state what happens but goes on to explain the *why* and the *wherefore* of this action. In this type of writing character and CHARACTERIZATION are more than usually important. Of course in one sense the psychological story is as old as the first DRAMA or TALE or BALLAD which accounted for external action by recounting the qualities of the character of the PROTAGONIST. Chaucer's *Troilus and Criseyde* is a *psychological novel* in VERSE. *Hamlet* is a psychological DRAMA; but, in somewhat lesser degree, so are most of Shakespeare's better plays. The *psychological novel* is, as one critic has said, an interpretation of "the invisible life." The term was first importantly applied to a group of novelists in the middle of the nineteenth century, a group of which Mrs. Gaskell, George Eliot, and George Meredith were the chief writers. Mrs. Gaskell, writing about the middle of the nineteenth century, stated that "all deeds however hidden and long passed by have their external consequences"—thus giving expression to an attitude long realized and felt if not always deliberately expressed. Thackeray and Dickens, too, were interested enough in motives and details to be classified, in a looser sense, with the forerunners of the *psychological novel*. Hardy and Conrad were also interested in the picturing of interior motive and psychological effect. Henry James, with his intense concern for the psychological life of his characters and with his development of a novelistic technique that centered itself in the representation of the effect produced in the inner self by external events, may be said to have created the modern *psychological novel*. In the twentieth century, with the advance of psychology as a science, the term has come into popular use. Freudianism particularly gave impetus to the type. The modern *psychological novel* may at one extreme record the inner experience of characters as reported by an author, as James tends to do, or at the other extreme utilize the INTERIOR MONOLOGUE to recount the non-verbalized and subconscious life of a character, as in some of the work of James Joyce and William Faulkner. See NOVEL, STREAM-OF-CONSCIOUSNESS NOVEL, INTERIOR MONOLOGUE.

**Public Theatres:** The English playhouse developed in Elizabethan times as a natural accompaniment of the increased interest in the DRAMA. In earlier times plays had been produced on PAGEANTS and in indoor rooms such as guild halls and the halls of great houses, schools, and INNS OF COURT. The demand for larger places resulted in the use of inn-yards, which were square or rectangular courts enclosed by the inner porches or balconies of the inn building. In one end would be erected a temporary stage connected with rooms of the inn. The spectators might stand in the open court ("groundlings") or get seats on the surrounding balconies. Meantime the need for a place for bear- or bull-baiting spectacles and acrobatic performances had been met in the development of a sort of ring or amphitheatre. Out of the physical features of the inn-yard (surrounding galleries or boxes, open central space or pit, stage extending into pit) and the bear garden (circular form of building) the plan of the first *public theatre* was evolved. The front stage was open to the sky, the rear stage covered by a ceiling. Above this ceiling was a room for the machinery needed in lowering persons and objects to the stage below, or raising them from it. There was an "inner" stage at the rear, provided with a curtain and connected with a balcony above, also curtained. The rear stage was used chiefly for special settings such as a forest or bedroom, while the bare outer stage was used for street scenes, battles, and the like. The scenery and the costumes of the actors were largely conventional and symbolic, though certainly very realistic at times.

The first *public theatre* in London was the Theatre, built in 1576 by James Burbage in Shoreditch. It was followed in 1577 by the Curtain in the same neighborhood. About ten years later Henslowe built the Rose on the Bankside, and in this locality appeared also the Swan (1594). In 1599 the Theatre was torn down and re-erected on the Bankside as the Globe, the most important one of the *public theatres*. The Globe was used and controlled by the company to which Shakespeare belonged. Henslowe built the Fortune in 1600, the Red Bull appeared soon after in St. John's Street, and the Hope in 1614 near the Rose and the new Globe. For distinction between "public" and "private" theatres see PRIVATE THEATRES.

**Pun:** A play on words based on the similarity of sound between two words with different meanings. An example is Thomas Hood's: "They went and told the sexton and the sexton tolled the bell." See EQUIVOQUE.

**Pure Poetry:** A term applied to POETRY which is free from conceptualized statement, instructive content, or moral preachment; or those portions of a poem which remain after such materials as can be paraphrased adequately in PROSE are removed. The term was first used by Baudelaire in an essay on Edgar Allan Poe. For many critics Poe's theory and practice of POETRY are archetypally pure; as George Moore said of Poe's poems when including them in an anthology of *pure poetry*, they "are almost free from thought." Wallace Stevens is often cited as a contemporary poet who practices an art close to that of *pure poetry*.

**Purist:** One who habitually stresses, or overstresses, correctness or "purity" in language, particularly in minor or "fine" points of grammar, DICTION, pronunciation, and rhetorical style. The term is commonly used in a spirit of deprecation or mild reproach, because the extreme *purist* is felt not only to have lost his sense of proportion in his zeal for preserving fine distinctions but also frequently to exhibit ignorance of the actual laws of language, since he is prone to regard language as a static thing instead of a developing instrument of communication. An example is perhaps the insistence upon certain subjunctive forms of the English verb in constructions where the subjunctive mood would be demanded by formal grammar based upon the rules of Latin grammar but where actual English usage has substituted the indicative for the subjunctive, as in the sentence "if it *be* a good thing, let us approve it" where "if it *is* a good thing, let us approve it" has become established as more common and equally good English. The *purist*, too, is likely to ignore the existence of different levels of speech and to insist upon the use of "bookish" English on all occasions, ignoring the fact that an English style which would be eminently appropriate at a White House audience might be highly injudicious and inappropriate in a lumber camp or on the sporting pages of a newspaper. It must be remembered, however, that it is difficult to draw the line between the *purist* and the person who takes a commendable interest in achieving that accuracy and precision in language which are regarded as an important social grace and which lend dignity to his personality. The distinction is often one of degree only or of manner, and after all the *purist* has a more wholesome attitude toward the problem than does the careless person who is satisfied in his use of slovenly English.

A related though quite different use of the word is seen in its application to a person who feels that the "purity" of a language can be preserved only by the exclusion of foreign words and of words not used by the best stylists. Thus the so-called CICERONIANS of the RENAISSANCE, a group of Latin stylists who would not use any Latin word that could not be found in Cicero's writings, have been called *purists*, as have the English scholars of the sixteenth century and later who insisted upon a "pure" English diction "unmixed and unmangled with borrowing of other tongues." The famous schoolmasters Sir John Cheke and Roger Ascham and the rhetorician Thomas Wilson were leaders in this movement. In the main they were not absolute *purists*, however, since they recognized that English might legitimately be enriched by the use of some foreign words; but they opposed strongly the pedantic tendency of the time which threatened to make literary English a mere Latin *patois*. The struggle between these *purists* and their INKHORNIST opponents is sometimes referred to as the "purist-improver" controversy.

Later movements toward purism included: the unsuccessful effort in the seventeenth century to establish (on the model of the French Academy) a British Academy to regulate language; eighteenth-century efforts at standardization through the establishment of some definite linguistic authority (opposed by Doctor Johnson); Wordsworth's attempt to employ in his poems only simple words drawn from actual speech; and later efforts to stress the Anglo-Saxon elements in the vocabulary and to check the importation of foreign words (noteworthy is Edna St. Vincent Millay's attempt to write a long poem, *The King's Henchman*, employing only words of Anglo-Saxon derivation). Some good doubtless has resulted from efforts to preserve the strong and picturesque elements of native English speech and to check foolish or unnecessary adoption of foreign words; yet it seems clear that the English language will continue to enrich its resources in the future as it has done in the past by appropriating needed words wherever it finds them.

**Puritanism:** A religious-political movement which developed in England about the middle of the sixteenth century and later spread its influence most importantly into the New England colonies in America. While politically it died with the return of Charles the Second to London in 1660, *Puritanism* left its impress and many of its attitudes on the habits and thought of the people, especially of America today. As a term, *Puritan* was, in Elizabeth's reign, applied to those who wished to "purify" the Church of England. The name was at first one of derision. The spirit which prompted the reforms of *Puritanism* was an outgrowth of CALVINISM which had spread from Geneva to England.

In principle the Puritans objected to certain forms of the established Church. They objected, for instance, to the wearing of the surplice, and to government by the prelates, and they demanded the right to partake of the communion in a sitting posture. The Millenary Petitions (1603) of the Puritans requested a reform of the church courts, a doing away with "superstitious" customs, a discarding of the use of APOCRYPHAL books of the BIBLE, a serious observance of Sunday, and various ecclesiastical reforms. While at first *Puritanism* in England was not directly affiliated with Presbyterianism, it later on allied itself, largely for political reasons, very definitely with the Presbyterian movement. Thomas Cartwright, the first important spokesman of *Puritanism,* hated most emphatically the Church of England; "his bigotry," writes John Richard Green, "was that of a medieval inquisitor. The relics of the old ritual, the cross in baptism, the surplice, the giving of a ring in marriage, were to him not merely distasteful, as they were to the Puritans at large, they were idolatrous and the mark of the beast."

The conception of the Puritans popularly held today, however, is very unfair to the general tone and temper of the early sponsors of the movement. These early English Puritans were not long-faced reformers, not teetotalers, not haters of art and music. They were often, later on, patrons of art and lovers of music, fencing, and dancing. They were intelligent, self-controlled, plainly dressed citizens who held to simplicity and to democratic principles. But it is true that under the persecution of Charles and the double-dealing of Laud they were harried into bitterness. To quote Green again,

Humour, the faculty which above all corrects exaggerations and extravagance, died away before the new stress and strain of existence. The absolute devotion of the Puritan to a Supreme Will tended more and more to rob him of all sense of measure and proportion in common matters. Little things became great things in the glare of religious zeal; and the godly man learnt to shrink from a surplice, or a mince-pie at Christmas, as he shrank from impurity or a lie. Life became hard, rigid, colourless, as it became intense. The play, the geniality, the delight of the Elizabethan age were exchanged for a measured sobriety, seriousness, and self-restraint. But the self-restraint and sobriety which marked the Calvinist limited itself wholly to his outer life. In his inner soul sense, reason, judgment, were too often overborne by the terrible reality of invisible things.

The history of the rise and fall of *Puritanism* in England is too much involved with religious, political, and social attitudes for even a simple presentation here. All that can be said is that, as we look back from this period of time, *Puritanism* seems a natural enough aftermath of the RENAISSANCE, the REFORMATION, the establishment of the Church of England, and the growth of Presbyterianism. Through all of these great movements one somehow sees steadily emerging the right of the individual to political and religious independence. The reading of the BIBLE had become general. The Catholic Church had lost its pristine power in England, but there were still thousands of Catholics who wanted their old power restored. The people were always suspicious that their rulers, a James I or a Charles I, might swing back to the faith of Spain and Italy. Political power for the commoners lay with Presbyterianism, a religious movement based on the political control of presbyters drawn from the people. Catholicism and even the Church of England were far too reminiscent of autocracy and of divine right to rule. Whitgift and Laud wished to stamp out *Puritanism;* James I had promised that if necessary he would "harry the Puritans out of the land." Charles I and Laud fought popular rights and suppressed Parliament. The Church of England took little note of the handwriting on the wall. Milton at this time wrote his famous digression in *Lycidas* to condemn the Church and the clergy: "Blind mouths! that scarce themselves know how to hold a sheephook." From 1642 to 1646 civil war was waged in England, a civil war from which rose to power a new Puritan leader, Oliver Cromwell. In 1649 Charles was beheaded. The Puritan Commonwealth was established. And then, on May 25, 1660, Charles II landed at Dover.

So far we have noted the trend of *Puritanism* only in England. But to America *Puritanism* was almost of more moment, since to the dissatisfaction with political life in England and the consequent emigration to the colonies, American life, and thought, and literature may be said to owe a sizeable portion of their origins. Some of the "Brownists," a group of Puritans who had left England for seclusion in Holland, came to America in the *Mayflower.* They wished to set up a new theocracy in which the Puritan ideas of religion and government were to go hand in hand. "I shall call that my country where I may most glorify God and enjoy the presence of my dearest friends," said young Winthrop. In one year as many as three thousand rebels left England for the Colonies; in ten years there were twenty thousand English in America. And many of these newcomers were men of education, of intelligence, of family position and culture. And those at least who settled in and around Massachusetts were bent on forming a new government, a theocracy, with God and Christ at the head, and with their own chosen rulers to interpret God's will for them. What now seems, as we look back at it all, a gesture toward conservatism, a threat against freedom of speech, and art, and individualism, was, it should be remembered, at that time essentially a radical movement. If in the twentieth century the Puritan attitude seems pretty strait-laced, we should recall that its exponents were rebels against religious and governmental intolerance at home.

No great change, no political and religious upheaval such as the development of *Puritanism,* can be isolated from the literature of the time. From the writers of this mood in England two great names emerge to tower over all others of the century, John Bunyan and John Milton.

In America, a dozen or two writers have attained a sort of immortality in American literature largely because they happened to stand at the source of the stream. Such theologians as John Cotton, Thomas Hooker, John Eliot, Cotton Mather; such historians as William Bradford, John Winthrop, Thomas Hutchinson, and Samuel Sewall; and such poets as Nathaniel Ward, Anne Bradstreet, Michael Wigglesworth, and Edward Taylor derive importance from their historical position. But whatever their importance to literature may be, the early divines left clear-cut their imprint on American life. *The Bay Psalm Book* (1640) became almost the book of a people. In America the difficulties of settlement, the sordidness of life during the early years in a new land, the religious fervor of most of the settlers—these gave a dim color to Colonial life which is not yet erased and which still gives tone to our literature and criticism.

With the Scotch-Irish settlements of the Middle Atlantic and Southern colonies came another and a strong strain of *Puritanism,* that of the Scotch Presbyterians. And as the restless and the discontented, North and South, moved westward into the beckoning frontier they carried with them the BIBLE, a simple and fundamentally Puritan faith, and the stern impulse to independence and freedom. Across the pages of American literature *Puritanism* is written large. It may almost be considered the ethical mode of American thought. See CALVINISM.

**"Purple Patch":** A piece of "fine writing." Now and then authors in a strongly emotional passage will give free play to most of the stylistic tricks in their bag. They will write PROSE which is intensely colorful, more than usually rhythmic, marked by an involved PARALLELISM, full of IMAGERY and FIGURES OF SPEECH, characterized by a POETIC DICTION, etc. When there is an unusual piling up of these devices in such a way as to evidence a self-conscious literary effort, the section is spoken of as a *purple patch*—a colorful passage standing out from the writing around it. Although frequently used in this non-evaluative, descriptive sense, the term is more often employed in a derogatory sense, to suggest overstraining.

**Putative Author:** The fictional author of a work, supposedly written by someone other than its actual author. Lemuel Gulliver is the *putative author* of his *Travels,* not Jonathan Swift; Tristram Shandy is the *putative author* of his *Life and Opinions,* not Laurence Sterne. When an author uses a NOM DE PLUME, he merely hides his identity behind an assumed name, but when he uses a *putative author,* he creates a character who writes the book. Washington Irving merely hid his name when he signed the *Sketch Book* as "Geoffrey Crayon," but he created a *putative author* who wrote and signed Diedrich Knickerbocker's *History of New York.* See POINT OF VIEW, NARRATOR.

**Pyrrhic:** A FOOT of two unaccented syllables ($\smile \smile$); the opposite of SPONDEE (\_\_ \_\_). Common in classical poetry, the *pyrrhic* is unusual in English VERSIFICATION and is not accepted as a FOOT at all by some prosodists since it contains no accented syllable. Fowler states that the English *pyrrhic* is represented chiefly by double ANACRUSIS, as *O my* in

$$\breve{O} \, \breve{my} \mid \overline{Ma}\breve{ri} \mid \overline{on}\text{'s } \breve{a} \mid \overline{bonny} \mid \overline{lass}.$$

**Quadrivium:** In the medieval university curriculum, the four subjects leading to the M. A. degree: arithmetic, music, geometry, and astronomy. See THE SEVEN ARTS.

**Quantitative Verse:** VERSE whose basic RHYTHM is determined by QUANTITY, that is, duration of sound in utterance. Classical poetry was quantitative, as English poetry has been accentual-syllabic. However, a number of English poets have experimented with *quantitative verse* forms, among them Campion, Sidney, Spenser, Coleridge, Tennyson, Longfellow, and Lanier. A few of the classical quantitative forms occasionally are used in English, among them ALCAICS, CHORIAMBICS, ELEGIACS, HENDECASYLLABICS, SAPPHICS. See METER.

**Quantity:** In classical PROSODY, the fundamental rhythmic unit, *quantity* is the relative length of time required to utter a syllable. In Greek and Latin VERSIFICATION a syllable was considered long if it contained a long vowel or a short vowel followed by two consonants; otherwise, it was considered short, except for a few vowels and syllables which varied in duration between these limits and were called common. A long syllable was roughly the equivalent of two short syllables in duration; or a long syllable may be thought of as equivalent to a quarter note in music and a short syllable to an eighth. While duration is unquestionably a quality in English VERSIFICATION, the distinguishing and determining rhythmic pattern of English appears to be accentual-syllabic, so that the RHYTHMS which a skillful poet gains from the control of *quantity* or duration are merely subsidiary or complementary to the fundamental RHYTHMS of regularly recurring ACCENT. See METER, ACCENT, STRESS.

*Quarterly Review, The:* A British Tory critical JOURNAL founded in 1809. See EDINBURGH REVIEW.

**Quarto:** A BOOK SIZE designating a book whose SIGNATURES result from sheets folded to four leaves or eight pages. See BOOK SIZES.

**Quatorzain:** A STANZA or POEM of fourteen lines. The term, however is not now specifically applied to the SONNET (though of course the SONNET is a fourteen-line form) but is usually reserved for poems which do not otherwise conform to one or another of the SONNET patterns.

**Quatrain:** A STANZA consisting of four VERSES. In its narrow meaning, the term is restricted to a complete poem consisting of four lines only, but in its broader sense it signifies any one of many four-VERSE STANZA forms. The possible RIME-SCHEMES within the STANZA vary from an unrimed *quatrain* to almost any arrangement of one-RIME, two-RIME, or three-RIME lines. Perhaps the most common form is the *abab* sequence; other popular RIME-patterns are *aabb; abba; aaba; abcb.* A *quatrain* of this last pattern is quoted from Robert Burns:

> Ye flowery banks o' bonnie Doon
> How can ye blume sae fair?
> How can ye chant, ye little birds,
> And I sae fu' o' care?

**Quibble:** A PUN or play upon words, or especially a verbal device for evading the point at issue, as when debaters engage in *quibbles* over the interpretation of a question or term.

**Quip:** A retort or sarcastic jest; hence any witty saying, especially a PUN or QUIBBLE.

**Ratiocination:** A systematic process of reasoning which proceeds from the examination of data to the formulation of conclusions. The term was given literary significance by Poe, who wrote several tales which he called "ratiocinative," among them "The Murders in the Rue Morgue," "The Gold Bug," "The Purloined Letter," "The Mystery of Marie Rogêt," and "Thou Art the Man." The introductory paragraphs of "The Murders in the Rue Morgue" manifest Poe's high respect for the type of mind which works in this way. In general, then, *ratiocination*, as a literary or critical term, signifies a type of writing which solves, through the application of logical processes, some sort of enigma. It was once commonly applied to the DETECTIVE STORY.

**Rationalism:** This term embraces related "systems" of thought (philosophical, scientific, religious) which rest upon the authority of reason rather than sense-perceptions, revelation, or traditional authority. In England the rationalist attitude, especially in the eighteenth century, profoundly affected religion and literature. The early humanists (see OXFORD REFORMERS) had insisted upon the control of reason, but their teachings had little effect upon prevailing religious thought until reinforced by the scientific thinking of the seventeenth century (Newton), although as early as 1624 Lord Herbert of Cherbury had drawn up certain general principles which he thought all existing religious factions could accept. By the end of the century the theologians were generally agreed that the most vital religious doctrines were deducible from reason or NATURE. The more conservative ones ("supernatural rationalists") insisted also upon the importance of revelation in addition, while the more radical "deists" (see DEISM) rejected revelation. The former group included Newton himself and the great philosopher John Locke. The "natural religion" arising from *rationalism* stressed reason as a guide and good conduct as an effect. Its three propositions were: (1) there is an omnipotent God, (2) he demands virtuous living in obedience to his will, (3) there is a future life where the good will be rewarded and the wicked punished. This creed was accepted both by radicals and conservatives. The stressing of reason made *rationalism* an ally of NEO-CLASSICISM, while the stressing of the potential power and good in human nature, as by Shaftesbury, led toward ROMANTICISM. For notices of some of the effects of *rationalism* upon literature, see DEISM, PRIMITIVISM, ROMANTICISM, SENTIMENTALISM, NEO-CLAS-

SICISM, HUMANISM. See also CALVINISM, PURITANISM, and MYSTI-
CISM for opposing attitudes.

**Rationalize:** A verb used to indicate a rather specious form of
*ex parte* reasoning. An author is said "to *rationalize*" when, once
having accepted a position, a belief, through some intuitive process
or through some prejudice, he tries to justify his stand by some
process of the mind. That is, writing is said to *rationalize* when the
author reasons insincerely and with intellectual sophistry to justify
a position prompted by his emotions rather than by his reason.

**Realism:** *Realism* is, in the broadest sense, simply fidelity to
actuality in its representation in literature; a term loosely synonymous with VERISIMILITUDE; and in this sense it has been a significant element in almost every school of writing in human
history. In order to give it more precise definition, however, one
needs to limit it to the movement which arose in the nineteenth
century, at least partially in reaction against ROMANTICISM, which
was centered in the NOVEL, and which was dominant in France,
England, and America from roughly mid-century to the closing
decade, when it was replaced by NATURALISM. In this latter sense,
*realism* defines a literary method, a philosophical and political
attitude, and a particular kind of subject matter.

*Realism* has been defined as "the truthful treatment of material"
by one of its most vigorous advocates, William Dean Howells, but
the statement means little until the realist's concept of truth and
his selection of materials are designated. Generally, the realist is
a believer in PRAGMATISM, and the truth he seeks to find and express
is a relativistic truth, associated with discernible consequences and
verifiable by experience. Generally, too, the realist is a believer in
democracy, and the materials he elects to describe are the common,
the average, the everyday. Furthermore, *realism* can be thought
of as the ultimate of middle-class art, and it finds its subjects in
bourgeois life and manners. Where the romanticist transcends
the immediate to find the ideal, and the naturalist plumbs the
actual to find the scientific laws which control its actions, the
realist centers his attention to a remarkable degree on the immediate, the here and now, the specific action, and the verifiable
consequence. (See NATURALISM for a further discussion of the
distinctions among these three terms.)

The realist espouses what is essentially a MIMETIC THEORY OF

ART, centering his attention in the thing imitated and asking for something close to a one-to-one correspondence between the representation and the subject. He usually has, however, a powerful interest in the audience to whom his work is addressed, feeling it to be his obligation to deal with it with absolute truthfulness. Furthermore, the realist is unusually interested in the effect his work has on the audience and its life (in this respect he tends toward a PRAGMATIC THEORY OF ART); George Eliot, in Chapter XVII of *Adam Bede* (a classic statement of the intention of the realist), expresses her desire that her pictures of common life and average experience should knit more tightly the bonds of human sympathy among her readers. Howells, concerned with his audience of young ladies, felt so strongly the obligation not to do them moral injury that he shut the doors of his own works to most of the aspects of life connected with passion and sex.

The realist eschews the traditional patterns of the NOVEL. In part the rise of *realism* came as a protest against the falseness and sentimentality which the realist thought he saw in romantic FICTION. Life, he felt, lacked symmetry and PLOT; FICTION which truthfully reflected life should, therefore, avoid symmetry and PLOT. Simple, clear, direct prose was the desirable vehicle, and objectivity on the part of the novelist the proper attitude. The central issues of life tend to be ethical—that is, issues of conduct—FICTION should, therefore, concern itself with such issues, and—since selection is a necessary part of any art—select with a view to presenting these issues accurately as they affect men and women in actual situations. Furthermore, the democratic attitudes of the realist tended to make him value the individual very highly and to praise CHARACTERIZATION as the center of the NOVEL. Hence, he had a great concern for the effect of action upon character, and a tendency to explore the psychology of the actors in his stories. In Henry James, perhaps the greatest of the realists, this tendency to explore the inner selves of characters confronted with complex ethical choices earned for him not only the title of "father of the psychological novel" but also "biographer of fine consciences."

The surface details, the common actions, and the minor catastrophes of a middle-class society constituted the chief subject matter of the movement. Most of the realists avoided situations with tragic or cataclysmic implications. Their tone was often comic, frequently satiric, seldom grim or somber. Their general attitude was broadly optimistic, although James is a great exception.

Although aspects of *realism* appeared almost with the beginnings of the English NOVEL, for they are certainly present in Defoe, Richardson, Fielding, Smollett, Jane Austen, Trollope, Thackeray, and Dickens, the realistic movement found its effective origins in France with Balzac, in England with George Eliot, and in America with Howells and Mark Twain. Writers like Arnold Bennett, John Galsworthy, and H. G. Wells in England; and Henry James, Edith Wharton, Ellen Glasgow, Sinclair Lewis, John O'Hara, and John P. Marquand in America kept and are keeping the realistic tradition alive in the contemporary NOVEL.

It should be emphasized, however, that no single realistic NOVEL exemplifies all the characteristics that are listed in this article. In general, though, the realistic NOVEL tends toward the directions here indicated. See NATURALISM, ROMANTICISM.

**Realistic Comedy:** Any COMEDY employing the methods of REALISM, but particularly the COMEDY developed by Jonson, Chapman, Middleton, and other Elizabethan and Jacobean dramatists. It is opposed to the ROMANTIC COMEDY; in fact it appeared more or less as a protest against the ROMANTIC COMEDY of the Elizabethans. It reflects the general reaction in the late 1590's against Elizabethan ROMANTICISM and extravagance as well as an effort to produce an English COMEDY after the manner of classical COMEDY. This *realistic comedy* deals with London life, is strongly satirical and sometimes cynical in tone, is interested in both individuals and types of character, and rests upon an observation of contemporary life. The appeal is intellectual and the tone coarse. This COMEDY is sometimes treated as COMEDY OF MANNERS, various subclasses being distinguishable in Jacobean plays (see F. E. Schelling, *Elizabethan Drama*). It became especially popular in the reign of James I. The COMEDY OF HUMOURS was a special form representing the first stage of the development of important *realistic comedy*. Jonson's *The Alchemist* and Middleton's *A Trick to Catch the Old One* are typical Jacobean *realistic comedies*. Though in the main Shakespeare represents the tradition of ROMANTIC COMEDY, it is to be noted that the comic SUBPLOT of the *King Henry IV* plays and some others is realistic in technique. The RESTORATION COMEDY OF MANNERS, though chiefly a new growth, owes something to this earlier form, and one RESTORATION dramatist (Shadwell) actually wrote COMEDY of the Jonsonian type.

**Realistic Novel:** See NOVEL, REALISM.

**Realistic Period in American Literature, 1865–1900:** In the period between the end of the Civil War in 1865 and the dawn of the twentieth century, modern America was born and grew to a lusty although not always happy or attractive adolescence. The Civil War had been, at least in part, a struggle between the concept of agrarian democracy and that of industrial and capitalistic democracy, and the result of the Northern victory was the triumphant emergence of industrialism. This industrialism was to bring great mechanical and material advances for the nation but it was also to bring great difficulties in the form of severe labor disputes, economic depression, and strikes that erupted in violence; its capitalistic aspect was to produce a group of powerful and ruthless moneyed men who have gone down in history as "The Robber Barons"; its application to politics, particularly in the rapidly developing great cities, was to produce "bossism" and a form of political corruption known by Lincoln Steffens' phrase, "the shame of cities." The impact of invention and industrial development was tremendous. The greatest advances were made in communications; the Atlantic cable was laid in 1866, the transcontinental railroad completed in 1869, the telephone invented in 1876, the automobile with the internal-combustion engine being manufactured by the 1890's. By the last two decades of the century many thoughtful men had begun to march under various banners declaring that somewhere and somehow the promise of the American dream had been lost—they often said "betrayed"—and that drastic changes needed to be made in order to recapture it. The Populist Party, the Grange, Henry George's "single tax," and the socialism of the American intellectual were all reflections of a disillusionment with American life never before widespread in the nation.

Intellectually, too, the average American was living in a new world, although he did not always realize it. The impact of Darwin, Marx, Comte, Spencer, and others advancing a scientific view of man sharply at variance with the older religious view was cutting from beneath the thoughtful American—even while he vehemently denied it—his old certainty about his perfectibility and about the inevitability of progress. The passing by 1890 of the physical frontier removed from his society a natural safety valve that had acted to protect him against the malcontents and the restless in his world; now he must absorb them and adjust to the fact of their presence; no longer could they seek virgin land on which to build their notions of a world. The rapid growth of education and the rise of the mass-circulation MAGAZINE, paying its way by advertising, created a mass audience for his authors, and the passage in 1891 of the International Copyright Act protected foreign authors from piracy in America and by the same token protected the native literary product from being undercut by PIRATED EDITIONS of foreign works.

In poetry the field appeared to be held by a group of sweetly singing but sentimental imitators of the English Romantics—Stedman, Stoddard, Hovey, Aldridge—but, in fact, three new and authentic poetic voices were raised in the period: Walt Whitman's in his democratic chant cast in experimental rhythmic poetry; Sidney Lanier's in his moral statements couched in experimental musical poetry; and Emily Dickinson's in her gnomic utterances cast in witty variations on traditional forms. Toward the close of the century Stephen Crane raised a haunting but strident voice in sparse experimental VERSE that was close to that of the IMAGISTS of the twentieth century and Edwin Arlington Robinson published his first volume.

On the stage the older melodramatic habits held and the "star system" subordinating play and players to a "name" actor continued to fill the American theatre with spectacle but little meaning. American DRAMA saw little that was new and felt only slight impacts of the new European "problem plays" before the end of the century. James A. Herne's *Margaret Fleming* demonstrated a realistic promise that was largely unrealized. *Uncle Tom's Cabin* and *Rip Van Winkle* continued to dominate the American boards.

In FICTION, however, the new turbulence, the growing skepticism and disillusionment found an effective voice. The developing mass audience was served by LOCAL-COLOR WRITING, which filled the popular MAGAZINES, and by the HISTORICAL NOVEL, which had a great upsurge of popularity as the century drew toward a close. But in the work of Mark Twain, of William Dean Howells, and of Henry James the greatest contributions of the age were made. In the works of these men and of lesser writers—largely from the Middle West—REALISM was formulated as a literary doctrine and practiced as an art form which came to dominate the American literary scene. William James's PRAGMATISM not only expressed the mood of the *Realistic Period*, it also shaped its literary expression, an expression that became increasingly critical of American life as the century drew toward its end.

By the 1890's a cynical application of Darwinism to social

structures, together with an acceptance of Nietzsche's doctrine of the superman and of Emile Zola's concept of the experimental NOVEL, resulted in a NATURALISM markedly different from anything America had previously known. The publication of Theodore Dreiser's *Sister Carrie* in 1900 told, perhaps more clearly than any historical document could have, that a new America had grown from the travail of the post-Civil War period. See REALISM, *Outline of Literary History.*

**Realistic Period in English Literature, 1870–1914:** In the latter portion of the reign of Queen Victoria and during the reign of Edward, the reaction to ROMANTICISM, which had had its beginnings fairly early in Victoria's reign, reached its peak in full-fledged REALISM and by the beginning of the first World War had itself begun to come under attack. This fact brings into question the customary division of the literature of England in the nineteenth century, a division in which ROMANTICISM is considered to dominate until 1832, after which time VICTORIAN literature holds sway until the end of the century. The early portion of Victoria's reign saw a continuance and a gradual weakening of ROMANTICISM (see EARLY VICTORIAN AGE); whereas the LATE VICTORIAN AGE witnessed the arrival of a literary movement that was to reach its fruition and pass into the early years of its decline in the EDWARDIAN AGE.

The last three decades of the nineteenth century saw the great parliamentary contests between Gladstone and Disraeli, the rise of the concept of British imperialism, and a growth in British sophistication and cosmopolitanism. Intellectually, the serious Englishman began to feel the impact of the scientific revolution which distinguished nineteenth-century thought. Newton's mechanics, Darwin's evolution, Marx's view of history, Comte's view of society, Taine's view of literature—each in its way chipped away at the complacency and the optimism that had characterized the early years of the Victorian rule. Foreign writers began to be widely read—Zola, Balzac, Flaubert, Maupassant, Sudermann, Ibsen, Tolstoi, Chekhov, Turgenev. By the turn of the century a reaction to Victorian life and to complacent earnestness was being expressed, notably in the work of DECADENTS like Oscar Wilde, Ernest Dowson, and Aubrey Beardsley. A full-fledged revolt against the mores and standards of the Victorian world marked the early years of the twentieth century. Politically, the protest of writers like Carlyle and Ruskin gave way to a full embracing of Fabian socialism in writers like William Morris and the young George Bernard Shaw. The imperial adventure of the Boer War (1899–1902) was hailed by many as a proper extension of the empire and at the same time it raised grave doubts.

In POETRY, the voices of the great Victorians, Tennyson and Browning, were still heard, but a new poetry, interested in French forms and lacking in "moral earnestness," was present in Swinburne and the DECADENTS. Hardy, Kipling, Yeats, and Bridges were to do distinguished work before the beginning of the first World War, but of the group only Kipling would have felt at home in the England of Victoria's early reign.

In the DRAMA, the French stage and Ibsen combined to offer examples of REALISM. The LITTLE THEATRE MOVEMENT got under way in England in the 1890's, about the same time that the CELTIC RENAISSANCE was enlivening the Irish stage. The PROBLEM PLAY established itself as a serious and respectable form in the works of A. W. Pinero, H. A. Jones, and John Galsworthy. In the last decades of the century Wilde's wit and the LIGHT OPERAS of Gilbert and Sullivan brightened the English theatre, while the witty wisdom of G. B. Shaw's plays enlightened most of the period. Under the impact of REALISM the British stage abandoned Shakespeare for a life of its own.

In the serious ESSAY Arnold, Huxley, Spencer, and Pater explored a variety of topics with earnestness and force, but it was the NOVEL in which the age found its fullest expression. A few writers like Kipling and Stevenson continued a romantic vein, but George Eliot, Thomas Hardy, George Meredith, George Gissing, Joseph Conrad, John Galsworthy, Arnold Bennett, H. G. Wells, and Samuel Butler established a realistic mode for the NOVEL strong enough to make it the point against which the SYMBOLISTS of the next age launched their attacks. See REALISM, EDWARDIAN AGE, LATE VICTORIAN AGE, and *Outline of Literary History.*

**Rebuttal:** A term borrowed from debating procedure and signifying a rejoinder or reply to an argument; particularly it is a final summing up of answers to the arguments of the opposition.

**Recognition Plot** (or **Scene**): A *recognition plot* is one in which the principal REVERSAL or PERIPETY results from the acquisition by one of the characters of knowledge which was previously withheld (either by the characters in the play or story or by the author in constructing the PLOT) and which now known results in a decisive change of course for the character. In *Oedipus Rex*, considered by Aristotle the finest example of a *recognition plot*, the King, seeking the one whose crime has brought on the national calamity in order to banish him, at last discovers that he has killed his father and married his mother. In James's *The Ambassadors* Lambert Strether discovers the true nature of the liaison between Chad and Madame de Vionnet, with the result that his whole course of action is changed. A *recognition plot* may result in either TRAGEDY or COMEDY. A DETECTIVE STORY, for instance, is sometimes said to have a *recognition plot* used as an end in itself, in that the entire purpose of the PLOT is to have the PROTAGONIST (the detective) come into knowledge ("whodunit") which he did not possess at the beginning of the story. The SCENE in a DRAMA, a NOVEL, or a SHORT STORY in which the recognition occurs is called a *recognition scene*. See DRAMATIC STRUCTURE.

**Redaction:** A revision or editing of a MANUSCRIPT. The purpose of *redaction* is to express appropriately writing inappropriately phrased or stated in a wrong form. Sometimes, too, the term implies simply a digest of a longer piece of work, or a new version or edition of an older piece of writing. Malory's *Le Morte Darthur* is a *redaction* of many of the Arthurian stories.

**Reductio ad absurdum:** A "reducing to absurdity" to show the falsity of an ARGUMENT or position. As a method of ARGUMENT or PERSUASION this is a process which carries to its extreme, but logical, conclusion some general statement. One might say, for instance, that the more sleep one takes the more healthy one is, and then, by the logical *reductio ad absurdum* process someone would be sure to point out that, on such a premise, he who has sleeping sickness and sleeps for months on end is really in the best of health.

**Redundant:** Writing which is characterized by the use of superfluous words. As a critical term *redundant* is applied to a literary STYLE marked by verbiage, an excess of repetition, pleonastic expression. (See PLEONASM, TAUTOLOGY.) The use of REPETITION and PLEONASM may, on occasion, be justified by a desire to secure EMPHASIS, but redundancy differs from these rhetorical devices in

that it is usually applied to the superfluous, the unjustified REPETI-
TION which springs from carelessness or ignorance. Old Polonius is
made the doddering old man he is largely through the redundancies
of his expression:

> Madam, I swear I use no art at all.
> That he is made, 'tis true; 'tis true 'tis pity;
> And pity 'tis 'tis true; a foolish figure;
> But farewell it, for I will use no art.
> Mad let us grant him, then; and now remains
> That we find out the cause of this effect,
> Or rather say, the cause of this defect,
> For this effect defective comes by cause;
> Thus it remains, and the remainder thus.

**Reform Bill of 1832:** Much of the interest in problems of democracy
and social justice which has been shown in increasing degree by
English and American writers of the last hundred and fifty years
is traceable to the agitation which preceded and followed this
important liberal enactment of the English Parliament. It was
proposed in 1830 and passed in 1832 with the support of King
William IV and the Whig Party under Earl Grey over the strong
opposition of Wellington. The measure denied Parliamentary
representation to 56 "rotten" boroughs, provided representation for
156 new communities, and extended the voting power so as to
include large numbers of the middle classes hitherto denied the
ballot; it did not, however, give the franchise to the laborers. It
was but the beginning of a series of reform measures which followed during the next decade, including the suppression of slavery
in the British colonies (1833); the curbing of commercial monopoly;
a lessening of pauperism; a liberalization of the marriage laws;
and great expansion and extension of public educational facilities.
These events stimulated the idealism of many of the great authors
of the time, some of whom were active agitators for reform, and
consequently affected profoundly the spirit and body of literature
in the Victorian period. Carlyle and Ruskin in their lectures and
essays, Dickens, Disraeli, Mrs. Gaskell, Kingsley, and George Eliot
in their novels, and Hood, Tennyson, and Mrs. Browning in their
poems reflect the new aspirations aroused by these humanitarian
movements and the subsequent efforts for further reforms in
social, political, and educational realism. The Reform Bill of
1867, passed by the Conservatives under pressures from the
Liberals, further extended the franchise. Democratic representation

was carried still further by the Franchise Act of 1884, extending
suffrage to nearly all men. In 1918 suffrage was extended to all
men and to women over thirty, and in 1928 to all persons over
twenty-one. See CHARTISM, INDUSTRIAL REVOLUTION.

**Refrain:** A group of words forming a phrase or sentence and
consisting of one or more lines repeated at intervals in a poem,
usually at the end of a STANZA.

*Refrains* are of various types. First and most regular is the use
of the same line at the close of each STANZA (as is common in the
BALLAD). Another, less regular form, is that in which the *refrain*
line (or lines) recurs somewhat erratically throughout the STANZA
—sometimes in one place, sometimes in another. Again a *refrain*
may be used with a slight variation in wording at each recurrence,
though here it approaches the REPETEND. Still another variety of
the *refrain* is the use of some rather meaningless phrase which,
by its mere repetition at the close of STANZAS presenting different
ideas and different moods, seems to take on a different significance
upon each appearance—as in Poe's "Nevermore" and William
Morris's "Two red roses across the moon." Poets have made so much
of the *refrain,* have wrought so many variations in form and manner,
as to have greatly enriched English verse.

**Regionalism:** A quality in literature which is the product of its
fidelity to a particular geographical section, accurately representing
its habits, speech, manners, history, folklore, or beliefs. In one
sense, the test of *regionalism* is that the action and personages of a
NOVEL, a SHORT STORY, or a DRAMA that is called regional cannot
be moved, without major loss or distortion, to any other geographical setting. Thomas Hardy in his portrayal of life in Wessex
wrote regional NOVELS. The LOCAL-COLOR WRITING in America in
the last third of the nineteenth century was a form of *regionalism.*
Arnold Bennett's novels of the Five Towns are markedly regional.
The literature of the recent American South has been regional in
large part. In this century a concept of *regionalism* much more
complex and philosophically deeper than that of nineteenth-
century *regionalism,* has developed, partly as the result of the
work of cultural anthropologists and sociologists (notably Howard
W. Odum), and has expressed itself in literature through the
conscious seeking out in the local and the particular of those
aspects of the human character and of the human dilemma com-

mon to all men in all ages and places. In this respect the work of Willa Cather, Ellen Glasgow, William Faulkner, and Robert Penn Warren has gained great distinction. See LOCAL-COLOR WRITING.

**Relief Scene:** A SCENE in a TRAGEDY, usually as a part of the FALLING ACTION, whose purpose is to provide emotional relaxation for the audience. See DRAMATIC STRUCTURE.

**Religious Drama:** See MEDIEVAL DRAMA, MYSTERY PLAY, MIRACLE PLAY, MORALITY PLAY.

**Relique:** An old spelling for "relic," something which survives. The famous use of the term in literature is in the title of Bishop Percy's printed collection of old ballads: *Reliques of Ancient Poetry* (1765).

**Renaissance:** This word, meaning "rebirth," is commonly applied to the movement or period which marks the transition from the medieval to the modern world in Western Europe. Although special students of the movement may be inclined to trace the impulse back to the earlier renaissance of the twelfth and thirteenth centuries and to date the full realization or effects of *Renaissance* forces as late as the eighteenth century, in the usual sense of the word *Renaissance* suggests especially the fourteenth, fifteenth, sixteenth, and early seventeenth centuries, the dates differing for different countries (the English *Renaissance*, for example, being a full century behind the Italian *Renaissance* in its flowering). The break from medievalism was gradual, some "Renaissance" attitudes going back into the heart of the medieval period and some "medieval" traits persisting well into or even through the *Renaissance*. Yet the fact that a break *was* effected is the essential thing about the *Renaissance*, and the change when completed was so radical a one that "medieval" on the one hand and "Renaissance" or "modern" on the other imply a sharp contrast.

It is perhaps best to regard the *Renaissance* as the result of a new emphasis upon and a new combination of tendencies and attitudes already existing, stimulated by a series of historical events. Regarding the central feature as "an outgrowing, a freeing from ties that have proved to be bonds," Professor Randall notes that "we have to do with new forces arising within an old order, with stresses and strains, with unstable attempts to effect some kind of adjustment between traditional allegiances and modern appeal."[1] So it was an age of compromise, a chief aspect of which was a noble but difficult and confusing endeavor to harmonize a newly interpreted Christian tradition with an ardently admired and in part a newly discovered tradition of pagan classical culture.

The new humanistic learning (see HUMANISM) which resulted from the rediscovery of classical literature is not infrequently taken as the beginning and the heart of the *Renaissance* on its conscious, intellectual side, since it was to the treasures of classical culture and to the authority of classical writers that the man of the *Renaissance* turned for inspiration. Here the break with medievalism was unescapable. In medieval society, man's interests as an individual were subordinated to his function as an element in a social unit (see FEUDALISM); in medieval theology man's relation to the world about him was largely reduced to a problem of adapting or avoiding the circumstances of earthly life in an effort to prepare his soul for a future life. But the *Renaissance* man had caught from his glimpses of classical culture a vision of human life quite at odds with these attitudes. The hellenistic spirit (see HEBRAISM) had taught him that man, far from being a groveling worm, was a glorious creature, capable of infinite individual development in the direction of perfection, and set in a world it was his not to despise but to interrogate and explore and enjoy. And the full realization of his capacities as an individual rested upon a balanced development of mind and body.

The individualism implied in this view of life exerted a strong influence upon English *Renaissance* life and literature, as did many other facts and forces; such as: the Protestant Reformation, itself in part an aspect of the *Renaissance* in Germany; the introduction of printing (see PRINTING, INTRODUCTION INTO ENGLAND), leading to a commercial market for literature; the great economic and political changes leading to the rise of democracy, the spirit of nationalism, an ambitious commercialism, opportunities for individuals to rise above their birth economically and politically; the revitalized university life; the courtly encouragement of literature; the new geography (discovery of America); the new astronomy (Copernicus, Galileo); and the growing "new science" which made

---

[1] J. H. Randall, *The Making of the Modern Mind*, Houghton Mifflin Company, 1926, p. 111. Reprinted by permission of and by arrangement with the publishers.

man and nature the results of natural and demonstrable law rather than a mysterious group of entities subject to magic and occult powers.

The period in English literature generally called the *Renaissance* is usually considered to have begun a little before 1500 and to have lasted until the COMMONWEALTH INTERREGNUM. It consisted of the EARLY TUDOR AGE (*ca.*1500–1557), the ELIZABETHAN AGE (1558–1603), the JACOBEAN AGE (1603–1625), the CAROLINE AGE (1625–1642). In the early period, English authors felt the impact of classical learning and of foreign literatures, together with the sudden, although painful, release from the authority of the church. The new world lying to the west was transforming England into a trading nation no longer at the periphery of the world but at its very crossroads. During the reign of Elizabeth England reached status as a world power; its DRAMA and its POETRY attained great heights in the work of men like Spenser, Sidney, and Shakespeare. By the time that James came to the throne, a reaction was beginning to set in, expressed through a growing cynicism, a classical dissatisfaction with the extravagance and unbounded enthusiasm of the sixteenth century, a tendency toward melancholy and DECADENCE. As the conflict of PURITAN and CAVALIER grew in intensity, these elements grew also. And by the time Charles lost his head, the PURITANISM which was itself a major outgrowth of the intense individualism of the *Renaissance* had spelled an end to most of its literary greatness. Yet Cromwell had as Latin Secretary the last of the great English *Renaissance* men, John Milton, who was to produce his greatest work in the hostile world of the neo-classical RESTORATION. For details about the *Renaissance* in England, see EARLY TUDOR AGE, ELIZABETHAN AGE, JACOBEAN AGE, CAROLINE AGE, HUMANISM, ELIZABETHAN DRAMA, and the *Outline of Literary History.*

**Repartee:** A quick, ingenious response or rejoinder; a retort aptly twisted; conversation made up of brilliant witticisms, or, more loosely, any clever reply; also anyone's facility and aptness in such ready wit. The term is borrowed from fencing terminology. Sydney Smith, Charles Lamb, and Oscar Wilde are figures important in literature famous for their command of *repartee.* An instance of *repartee* may be cited from an Oxford account of the meeting of "Beau" Nash and John Wesley. According to this tradition the two met on a narrow pavement. Nash was brusque. "I never make way for a fool," he said insolently. "Don't you? I always do," responded Wesley, stepping to one side.

**Repetend:** A poetical device marked by a REPETITION or partial REPETITION of a word, phrase, or clause more or less frequently throughout a STANZA or poem. *Repetend* differs from REFRAIN in that the REFRAIN usually appears at predetermined places within the poem whereas the chief poetic merit of the *repetend* is the element of pleasant surprise it is supposed to bring to the reader through its irregular appearance. A further difference from the REFRAIN lies in the fact that the *repetend* only partially repeats whereas the REFRAIN usually repeats in its entirety a whole line or combination of lines. Both Coleridge and Poe make frequent use of the *repetend*. An example from Poe's *Ulalume* is quoted, with some of the *repetends* italicized:

> The skies *they were* ashen *and* sober:
> *The leaves they were* crisped *and sere*—
> *The leaves they were* withering *and sere;*
> *It was* night in the lonesome October
> Of my most immemorial year;
> *It was* hard *by the* dim lake *of Auber,*
> *In the* misty mid region *of Weir*—
> *It was* down *by the* dank tarn *of Auber,*
> *In the* ghoul-haunted woodland *of Weir.*

**Repetition:** A rhetorical device reiterating a word or phrase, or rewording the same idea, to secure EMPHASIS. *Repetition* used carelessly (see TAUTOLOGY, PLEONASM) is unpleasantly noticeable. Employed by deliberate design, it adds force and clarity to a statement. Particularly effective in PERSUASION, *repetition* is a favorite form with orators. The use of the REPETEND or REFRAIN in verse, use essentially based on *repetition*, makes this rhetorical method more obvious than is usual in prose. One of the most notable examples is, of course, Poe's *The Bells. Repetition* as a stylistic and poetic device gives pleasure by arousing, by satisfying, or by producing surprise by failing to satisfy a sense of expectancy. In the broadest sense, *repetition* is present in RIME of all kinds, in METER, and in STANZA forms. It appears to be an inescapable element of POETRY. Whitman, for example, who eschews *repetition* in the form of RIME, METER, or STANZA, employs it widely in his elaborate verbal and grammatical PARALLELISMS. See REFRAIN, REPETEND, ANAPHORA, PLEONASM.

**Requiem:** A CHANT embodying a prayer for the repose of the dead; a DIRGE; a solemn mass beginning as in *Requiem aeternam dona eis, Domine* ("Give eternal rest to them, O Lord"). The following lines are an example from Matthew Arnold's *Requiescat:*

> Strew on her roses, roses
> And never a spray of yew!
> In quiet she reposes;
> Ah, would that I did too!

**Resolution:** See PLOT, FALLING ACTION, DRAMATIC STRUCTURE.

**Restoration Age:** The restoration of the Stuarts in the person of Charles II in 1660 has given a name to the period of literary history embracing the latter part of the seventeenth century. The fashionable literature of the time reflects the reaction against PURITANISM, the receptiveness to French influence, and the dominance of the "classical" point of view in criticism and original compositions. The revival of the DRAMA, under new influences and theories, is an especially interesting feature of the *Restoration Age.* The COMEDY OF MANNERS was developed by such writers as Etherege, Wycherly, and Congreve; the HEROIC DRAMA by such writers as Dryden, Howard, and Otway. Dryden was the greatest poet of the period, although no one equaled Milton, whose greatest works came in the 1660's and 1670's. John Locke, Sir William Temple, and Samuel Pepys were, in their differing ways, the major prose writers after John Bunyan. See NEO-CLASSIC PERIOD, and *Outline of Literary History.*

**Restraint:** A critical term applied to writing which holds in decent check the emotional elements of a given situation. Great literature, FICTION and POETRY especially, makes frequent use of emotion, but distinguishes itself from tawdry writing in that the emotional qualities of the situation are held in reserve. Psychologically it is true that mankind attributes greater strength and force of character to the person who gives the impression of holding something back than to the person who pours forth all his feelings and sensibilities. In fact, it is largely this very matter of *restraint* in emotional situations which marks off the work of great artists from that of mere scribes. It is *restraint* which so often surcharges a Shakespeare line with feeling. In the last scene of *King Lear,* for instance, when the old king comes to the end of his tether, deserted by his courtiers and his daughters, with the dead Cordelia in his arms, everything, even life itself, falling away from him, he says to Kent, "Pray you, undo this button," and somehow the reader is more moved by the crowding emotions of Lear than he could possibly be had Shakespeare given a thousand words of detailed effects.

**Revenge Tragedy:** A form of TRAGEDY made popular on the Elizabethan stage by Thomas Kyd, whose *Spanish Tragedy* is an early example of the type. It is largely SENECAN in its inspiration and technique. The theme is the revenge of a father for a son or *vice versa,* the revenge being directed by the ghost of the murdered man, as in *Hamlet.* Other traits often found in the *revenge tragedies* include the hesitation of the hero, the use of either real or pretended insanity, suicide, intrigue, an able scheming villian, philosophic soliloquies, and the sensational use of horrors (murders on the stage, exhibition of dead bodies, etc.) Examples of the type are Shakespeare's *Titus Andronicus,* Marston's *Antonio's Revenge,* Shakespeare's *Hamlet, Hoffman* (author not known), and Tourneur's *Atheist's Tragedy.* See SENECAN TRAGEDY, TRAGEDY OF BLOOD.

**Reversal:** The change in fortune for the PROTAGONIST in a dramatic or fictional PLOT; the PERIPETY. See PERIPETY, DRAMATIC STRUCTURE.

**Review:** A notice of a current book or play, published in a PERIODICAL. It is important to distinguish between a *review* and a piece of serious CRITICISM. The *review* announces a work, describes its subject, discusses its method and its technical qualities, and examines its merit when it is compared with other similar works; its function is to give its reader an accurate idea of the book under consideration, in order that he may decide whether he wishes to read it or not. The CRITIC, on the other hand, usually writes about works which have some standing and which are not brand new, judging them by critical standards which are either consciously formulated or implied in the critical article. The boundary line between the two forms is very uncertain in actual practice, however. For example, Poe's *review* of Hawthorne's *Twice-Told Tales* fits almost perfectly the description here given and yet it is one of the major critical documents in American literary history. On the other hand, the critical quarterlies often carry pieces that are ostentatiously CRITICISM and yet remain at the core merely journalistic *reviews*.

*Review* is also used in the titles of PERIODICALS to indicate the presence in the journal both of critical articles and of articles on current affairs; for example, the *North American Review*, the *Saturday Review*, the *Review of Reviews*, the *Kenyon Review*. See CRITICISM, TYPES OF.

**Revolutionary Age in American Literature, 1765–1790:** In the period between the Stamp Act in 1765 and the formation of the Federal Government in 1789, American writers were, by and large, engaged in non-belletristic pursuits. Poetry was largely NEO-CLASSICAL, with the influence of Pope dominating, although strains of early ROMANTICISM, notably those associated with the GRAVEYARD SCHOOL and with a renewed appreciation of wild NATURE, were felt. Trumbull, Freneau, Hopkinson, Dwight, and Barlow sang a patriotic strain in varied forms, often burlesque and satiric. The first play written by an American and acted in America, Godfrey's *The Prince of Parthia*, was performed in 1767, and the stage grew to be an increasing influence on American art outside of New England. In Philadelphia and New York it was particularly important and, after 1773, it was a significant aspect of Southern life through the theatre at Charleston. Much of the prose writing of the age was polemical, like that of Thomas Paine, Samuel Adams, and Hamilton and Madison (*The Federalist* papers). The first American novel, *The Power of Sympathy*, by William Hill Brown, was published in 1789. But the two major prose writers of the period were Franklin, with his *Autobiography*, and Thomas Jefferson, whose *Declaration of Independence* has certainly proved to be one of the most influential pieces of writing in human history. See REVOLUTIONARY AND EARLY NATIONAL PERIOD IN AMERICAN LITERATURE and *Outline of Literary History*.

**Revolutionary and Early National Period in American Literature, 1765–1830:** The period in American history between the Stamp Act and the triumph of the "second revolution" represented by the ascendancy of Jacksonian democracy was the time of the establishment of the new nation. A time of beginnings, it saw the first strong reaction to British rule in the response to the Stamp Act in 1765, the First Continental Congress in 1774, the beginnings of armed rebellion in 1775, the *Declaration of Independence* in 1776, the surrender of Cornwallis in 1781, the Constitutional Convention in 1787, the establishment of a Federal government in 1789, the founding of the Library of Congress in 1800, and in 1812–1814 a second successful war with England. In 1820 the Missouri Compromise, following by twelve years the abolition of the importing of slaves, established a pattern of political compromise over the issue of slavery; in 1823 America asserted its dominance in the New World through the Monroe Doctrine. In 1829 Andrew Jackson, as seventh president of the nation, brought backwoods egalitarianism into triumph over the conservative Federalism which for a while had dominated the early life of the young land.

It was a time of literary beginnings as well. It fell into two relatively distinct ages, that of the Revolution, 1765–1790, and that of the Federalists, 1790–1830. During this time the faint and imitative voices of the Revolutionary poets—Brackenridge, Freneau, and Hopkinson—and the HARTFORD WITS gave way before the calm strength of Bryant's verses. By 1827, Poe had published *Tamerlane*. In 1767 Thomas Godfrey's *Prince of Parthia*, the first American play to be acted, was performed, and American playwrighting was established, although it was to be highly imitative of English DRAMA and largely lacking in literary value throughout the period. In 1789 the first American novel, *The Power of Sympathy*, by William Hill Brown, was published. Charles Brockden Brown, the first American novelist of marked ability, flourished briefly between 1798 and 1801; his *Wieland* (1798) was a distinguished piece of American GOTHIC. Before 1830 the career of James Fenimore Cooper, America's first major novelist, was well launched; his first significant novel, *The Spy*, appeared in 1821, and the first of the "Leatherstocking Tales" in 1823. Washington Irving, writing with urbane wit and Addisonian grace, became the first truly successful American prose writer, gaining international fame, particularly for his *Knickerbocker's History* (1809) and his *Sketch Book* (1820). The first major American magazine that was to have a long history was established in 1815, *The North American Review*.

In 1830 America was a young nation, fully established, rawboned and robust and self-confident, but possessed of a great internal problem, slavery, which was just beginning to put the Federal

Union to a serious test. Those who were to produce the important literary works of the nation's first major artistic period had already been born and many were already at work. See FEDERALIST AGE IN AMERICAN LITERATURE, REVOLUTIONARY AGE IN AMERICAN LITERATURE, and *Outline of Literary History.*

**Revue:** A light musical entertainment without connected PLOT and consisting of a variety of songs, dances, choruses, and skits. Satiric comment on contemporary personalities and events forms a characteristic element as does the effort to impress by a spectacular display of magnificence in setting and scenery.

**Rhetoric:** The body of principles and theory having to do with the presentation of facts and ideas in clear, convincing, and attractive language. *Rhetoric* as an art has had a long and honorable career in the curricula of ancient and modern schools. Along with grammar and logic it made up the basic TRIVIUM of medieval academic study. Before this, such ancients as Aristotle, who wrote a *rhetoric* about 320 B.C.; Quintilian, whose *De Institutione Oratoria* (about A.D. 90) long served as the background for study even in the more modern days of Oxford and Cambridge; Longinus, who wrote an *Art of Rhetoric* (about A.D. 260), and Aphthonius (about A.D. 380) gave the subject a code and organization which have persisted throughout the centuries. The actual founder of *rhetoric* is said to be Corax of Syracuse, who in the fifth century B.C. stipulated certain fundamental principles for public argument and laid down five divisions for a speech: proem, narrative, argument, remarks, and peroration or conclusion. For a period the sophists emphasized the importance of *rhetoric* for its own sake—deftness, skill, and cleverness in performance being rated above soundness and truth of argument.

In general it may be pointed out that to the ancients the aim of *rhetoric* was to give effectiveness to public speech, to ORATORY. According to the Aristotelian conception *rhetoric* was a manner of effectively organizing material for the presentation of truth, for an appeal to the intellect through speech, and was distinct from POETICS, a manner of composition presenting ideas emotionally and imaginatively. At one time the sophists and others so exalted *rhetoric* that it threatened to become little more than a system of public discussion whereby, rightly or wrongly, by fair means or foul, a point was carried. It was, as Isocrates once noted, "the art of making great matters small, and small things great." This tendency has given to modern ears the suggestion of oratorical emptiness which we so often associate with the word "rhetorical."

In England the RENAISSANCE brought little that was new to *rhetoric* though such books as Sir Thomas Wilson's *The Arte of Rhetorique* (1553) did much to popularize the best practice of the early classical writers on the subject. In modern education *rhetoric* as a subject by itself has largely disappeared though, of course, it still is respected as a phase of study in "English" courses and persists in debating and oratorical contests. The great number of rhetorical terms included in this Handbook shows, perhaps as clearly as any other testimony, the basic importance of rhetorical principles in their relation to literature.

**Rhetorical Accent:** The ACCENT resulting from the placement of stress as determined by the meaning or intention of the sentence; used in METRICS in opposition to METRICAL ACCENT, in which the prosodic pattern of the line determines the placement of stress. See ACCENT.

**Rhetorical Question:** A question propounded for its rhetorical effect and not requiring a reply or intended to induce a reply. The *rhetorical question* is most used in PERSUASION and in ORATORY, the principle supporting the use of the *rhetorical question* being that since its answer is obvious and usually the only one possible, a deeper impression will be made on the hearer by raising the question than by the speaker's making a direct statement. The too frequent use of this device imparts a tone of artificiality and insincerity to discourse.

> Was it for this you took such constant care
> The bodkin, comb, and essence to prepare?
> For this your locks in paper durance bound?
> For this with tort'ring iron wreath'd around?
> For this with fillets strain'd your tender head,
> And bravely bore the double loads of lead!
> Gods! shall the ravisher display your hair,
> While the fops envy, and the ladies stare?
> —Pope

**Rhythm:** The passage of regular or approximately equivalent time intervals between definite events or the recurrence of specific sounds or kinds of sounds is called *rhythm*. Man has a seemingly basic need for such regularity of recurrence, or for the effect produced by it, as laboratory experiments in psychology have demonstrated and as one can see for himself by watching a crew of men digging a deep ditch or hammering a long stake or by listening to CHANTEYS and work songs.

In both PROSE and POETRY the presence of rhythmic patterns lends both pleasure and heightened emotional response to the listener or reader, for it establishes for him a pattern of expectations and rewards him with the pleasure of a series of fulfillments or gratifications of expectation. In POETRY three different elements may function in a pattern of seemingly regular temporal occurrence: QUANTITY, ACCENT, and number of syllables (see METER). In English poetry, the rhythmic pattern is most often established by a combination of ACCENT and number of syllables. This pattern of a fairly regular number of syllables with a relatively fixed sequence of stressed and unstressed syllables lends itself to certain kinds of basic rhythmic analysis in English VERSIFICATION. The *rhythm* may be "marching" or double—that is, involve one stressed and one unstressed syllable, as in IAMBS and TROCHEES. Or it may be "dancing" or triple—that is, involve one stressed and two unstressed syllables, as in DACTYLS and ANAPESTS. It may be "rising"— that is, beginning with unstressed and ending with stressed syllables, as in IAMBS and ANAPESTS. Or it may be "falling"—that is, beginning with stressed and ending with unstressed syllables, as in TROCHEES and DACTYLS. Other kinds of *rhythm* than these are, of course, possible (and even common) in English verse, as witness SPRUNG RHYTHM and FREE VERSE, as well as the *rhythm* used in OLD ENGLISH VERSIFICATION or that used by Walt Whitman.

In PROSE, despite the absence of the formal regularity of pattern here described for VERSE, CADENCE is usually present and in impassioned PROSE it often establishes definite patterns of rhythmic recurrence. See PROSE RHYTHMS, QUANTITY, ACCENT, METER, SCANSION.

**Riddle:** The modern *riddle* has its more dignified ancestor in the *riddles* of medieval literature. Based on Latin prototypes, *riddles* became an important "type" of the vernacular literatures of Western Europe, including Anglo-Saxon. The *riddles* of Aldhelm (seventh century), though written in Latin, are English in tone, and the Exeter Book (eleventh century) contains an interesting collection of nearly a hundred *riddles* in Old English. They are of unknown authorship (formerly ascribed to Cynewulf). The interpretation of the *riddles* is sometimes obvious, sometimes obscure; but the descriptive power of the POETRY is often high, and the IMAGERY is fresh and picturesque. The new moon is a young viking sailing the skies; the falcon wears the bloom of trees upon her breast; the swan is a wandering spirit wearing a "noiseless robe." The swan, the falcon, the helmet, the horn, the hen, the onion, beer, the Bible manuscript, the storm-spirit, and many other objects connected with war, seamanship, nature, religion, and everyday life, describe themselves by descriptive EPITHET, characteristic act, apt METAPHOR, and end with a "Tell me what I'm called." These *riddles* contain some of the best existing evidence of the use of external nature in the period and have been termed the most secular of all existing Old English literature.

**Rime:** Similarity or identity of sound existing between accented syllables occupying corresponding positions within two or more lines of verse. The correspondence of sound is based on the *vowels and succeeding consonants* of the accented syllables, which must, for a perfect *rime*, be preceded by different consonants. That is, "fan" and "ran" constitute perfect *rimes* because the vowel and succeeding consonant sounds are identical and the preceding consonants ("f" and "r") are different. *Rime,* in that it is based on this correspondence of sounds, is related to ASSONANCE and ALLITERATION, but is unlike these two forms both in construction and in the fact that it is commonly used at stipulated intervals, whereas ASSONANCE and ALLITERATION are pretty likely to range freely through various positions.

*Rime* is more than a mere ornament or device of VERSIFICATION. It performs certain valuable functions. To begin with, it affords pleasure through the sense impression it makes. The ear of the reader recognizes a sound already echoing in his consciousness and the accord the two similar sounds set up is likely, if the poet has deftly rimed, to bring the reader a real, sensuous gratification. Again, the recurrence of *rime* at regular intervals serves to establish the form of the STANZA. *Rime* serves to unify and distinguish divisions of the poem since it is likely that the *rime* sounds followed in one STANZA—the Spenserian for instance—will be changed when the next STANZA is started. This principle at once gives UNITY to the one STANZA and marks it off as separate from the next, affording a sense of movement and progress to the poem as a whole.

The fact that these qualities as well as others reside in *rime* will be immediately granted when we recall how commonly folklore and the play of children—to take only two instances—resort to *rime* to make memorizing easy.

The types of *rime* are classified according to two schemes: (1) as to the position of the rimed syllables in the line, and (2) as to the number of syllables in which the identity of sound occurs.

On the basis of the position of the rime, we have:

1. END RIME, much the most common type, which occurs at the end of the verse.

2. INTERNAL RIME (sometimes called LEONINE RIME), which occurs at some place after the beginning and before the closing syllables.

3. BEGINNING RIME, which occurs in the first syllable (or syllables) of the verse.

On the basis of the number of syllables presenting similarity of sound, we have:

1. MASCULINE RIME, where the correspondence of sound is restricted to the final accented syllable as "fan" and "ran." This type of *rime* is generally more forceful, more vigorous than those below.

2. FEMININE RIME, where the correspondence of sound lies in *two* consecutive syllables, as in "lighting" and "fighting." This is sometimes called *double rime*. FEMININE RIME is used for lightness and delicacy in movement.

3. TRIPLE RIME, where the correspondence of sound lies in *three* consecutive syllables, as in "glorious" and "victorious." Triple rime has been used for serious work—such as Thomas Hood's *Bridge of Sighs*—but much more frequently it is reserved for humorous, satirical verse, for the sort of use Byron makes of it in his satiric poems, and Ogden Nash in his comic ones.

While at one time or another most poets have been responsible for poor *rimes,* have violated consciously one or another of the riming customs, still these conventions persist. Some of them may be mentioned here:

1. Syllables which are spelled differently but which have the same pronunciation (such as "rite" and "right") do not make acceptable *rimes*.

2. A true *rime* is based on the correspondence of sound in *accented* syllables as opposed to unaccented syllables. "Stating" and "mating" thus make a good *rime,* and for the same reason, "rating" and "forming" make a bad *rime* since the correspondence is between unaccented syllables.

3. For a true *rime* all syllables *following* the accented syllable must *rime,* as is the case, for instance, with "fascinate" and "deracinate." According to this rule "fascinate" and "deracinating" would not be true *rime* because of the difference between the last syllables.

4. It is well to avoid repetition of the same vowel sounds in different *rimes* which occur near each other. For instance "stone" and "bone" are good rimes as are also "home" and "tome" but a QUATRAIN composed of those four *rimes* would usually be condemned as weak because of the repetition of the long *o* throughout. Of course, like all rules, this may be violated when there is a special reason for doing so.

5. Conversely to 4 above, it should be noted that there should not be too great a separation between *rime*-sounds since such separation will result in a loss of effect. A *rime* occurring in the first line and the sixth line, for instance, is rather a strain on the reader's attention.

6. It is permissible, when not done too frequently, to allow a *rime* to fall on an unaccented syllable. There is a certain variety coming from the riming of "free" and "prosperity," for instance, which justifies its use occasionally.

*Rime* and the importance it enjoys in modern VERSIFICATION are comparatively modern developments. The ancient Greek and Latin poetry was not rimed; our earliest English verse (*Beowulf* is an example) was not based on *rime*. Historians of the subject generally credit the development of *rime* to ceremonials within the Catholic Church and suggest that the priests made use of *rime* as a device to aid the worshipers in their singing and memorizing of the ritualistic procedure. *Dies Irae* is an example of one of the earliest rimed songs of the Church.

Among contemporary poets a tendency to use imperfect *rimes,* substituting ASSONANCE, CONSONANCE, and DISSONANCE for true *rimes,* is widespread; and most present-day poets take interesting liberties with the traditional "rules" for *rime* cited in this article. See ASSONANCE, DISSONANCE, CONSONANCE, SLANT RIME.

**Rime Royal:** A seven-line IAMBIC PENTAMETER STANZA riming *ababbcc.* The name has been said to derive from its employment by the Scottish king James I; but since Chaucer and other predecessors of James had used *rime royal* extensively it must be attributed to James, if at all, as an honor in recognition of the fact that a king wrote VERSE at all rather than that he originated the pattern. Chaucer used *rime royal* in the *Parlement of Foules,* the *Man of Law's Tale,* the *Clerk's Tale,* and in *Troilus and Criseyde,* and found the form adapted to his best descriptive, narrative, and reflective manners. Some other poets who have written in *rime royal* are Lydgate, Hoccleve, Dunbar, Skelton, Wyatt, Shakespeare, and Morris. In recent times the poet who has used it with most success has perhaps been John Masefield, who wrote both *The Widow in the Bye*

*Street* and *Dauber* in *rime royal*. As an example, the last stanza of Shakespeare's *Rape of Lucrece* is quoted:

> When they had sworn to this advised doom,
> They did conclude to bear dead Lucrece thence;
> To show her bleeding body thorough Rome,
> And so to publish Tarquin's foul offence:
> Which being done with speedy diligence,
>     The Romans plausibly did give consent
>     To Tarquin's everlasting banishment.

**Rime-scheme:** The pattern, or sequence, in which the RIME sounds occur in a STANZA or POEM. *Rime-schemes*, for the purpose of analysis, are usually presented by the assignment to each similar sound in a STANZA of the same letter of the alphabet. Thus, the pattern of the SPENSERIAN STANZA is *ababbcbcc*. An example of another rime pattern follows:

| | |
|---|---|
| The time I've lost in wooing, | *a* |
| In watching and pursuing | *a* |
| The light that lies | *b* |
| In woman's eyes, | *b* |
| Has been my heart's undoing. | *a* |
| Tho' wisdom oft has sought me, | *c* |
| I scorned the lore she brought me, | *c* |
| My only books | *d* |
| Were woman's looks, | *d* |
| And folly's all they've taught me. | *c* |
|  —Thomas Moore | |

Here *wooing, pursuing, undoing* all have the same RIME and are arbitrarily marked with the symbol *a; lies, eyes* are alike and assigned the symbol *b; sought me, brought me, taught me* are all alike and given the symbol *c; books* and *looks* are alike and are set down as symbol *d*. Thus finally the *rime-scheme* of the stanza is *aabbaccddc*.

**Rising Action:** The part of a dramatic PLOT which has to do with the COMPLICATION of the action. It begins with the EXCITING FORCE, gains in interest and power as the opposing groups come into CONFLICT (the HERO usually being in the ascendancy), and proceeds to the CLIMAX or turning point. See DRAMATIC STRUCTURE.

**Rococo:** In the history of European architecture the *rococo* period follows the BAROQUE and precedes the NEO-CLASSIC, embracing in time most of the eighteenth century. The style arose in France, flourished on the Continent, but made little headway in England. It was marked by a wealth of decorative detail suggestive of grace, intimacy, playfulness. The fashion spread to furniture. It avoided the grandiose, the serious, the "logical" effects. As the style was often regarded in England as a decadent phase of the RENAISSANCE or BAROQUE styles, the term *rococo* has been frequently employed in a derogatory sense to suggest the overdecorative or "impudently audacious," and is not infrequently confused with the BAROQUE (also unfavorably interpreted). An example of the older use of the term in English is found in Swinburne's use of it as the title of one of his love lyrics—one in which the lover implores his three-day mistress not to forget their ardent but brief love. An example of the more discriminating use of the term is found in Professor Friedrich Brie's phrase the *rococo* EPIC, as applied to such pieces as Pope's *Rape of the Lock* and Gay's *Fan,* in which the small luxuries of life, particularly of fashionable women, are prominent sources of interest. See BAROQUE.

**Rodomontade:** Ostentatious bragging or blustering. Falstaff's famous description of his bold fight with the highwaymen is an example of *rodomontade,* as is his boastful, "There live not three good men unhanged in England, and one of them is fat and grows old. . . ." So called after the braggart Moorish king Rodomonte in Ariosto's *Orlando Furioso.*

**Roman à Clef:** A NOVEL in which actual persons and events are presented under the guise of FICTION. Notorious examples of the GENRE have been Aldous Huxley's *Point Counter-Point* and Ernest Hemingway's *The Sun Also Rises.* See FICTION.

**Romance:** This word was first used for Old French as a language *derived* from Latin or "Roman" to distinguish it from Latin itself (this meaning has now been extended so that any of the languages derived from Latin, such as Spanish or Italian, is called a Romance language). Later *romance* was applied to any work written in French, and as stories of knights and their deeds were the dominant form of Old French literature, the word *romance* was narrowed to mean such stories. It has also been noted that the first Old French *romances* were translated from Latin and this fact may have helped to fix the name *romance* upon them. For a further account of these early *romances,* see MEDIEVAL ROMANCE. Special

modern uses of the word *romance* may be noted from the account
in the *New English Dictionary:* "romantic fiction"; "an extravagant
fiction"; "a fictitious narrative in prose of which the scene and incidents are very remote from those of ordinary life, especially of the
class prevalent in the sixteenth and seventeenth centuries, in which
the story is overlaid with digressions." In RENAISSANCE criticism the
ROMANTIC EPIC was called simply *romance*. See NOVEL, ROMANTIC
NOVEL, ROMANTICISM, MEDIEVAL ROMANCE, METRICAL ROMANCE,
ARTHURIAN LEGEND.

**Romances of Chivalry:** See CHIVALRIC ROMANCE.

**Romanesque:** A term sometimes used to characterize writing which
is fanciful or fabulous. It is more rarely used simply to denote the
presence of a ROMANCE quality in a work.

**Romantic Comedy:** A COMEDY in which serious love is the chief concern and source of interest, especially the type of COMEDY developed on the early Elizabethan stage by such writers as Robert
Greene and Shakespeare. Greene's *James the Fourth* represents the
*romantic comedy* as Shakespeare found it and is supposed to have
influenced Shakespeare in his *Two Gentlemen of Verona*. A few
years later Shakespeare perfected and glorified the type in such
plays as *The Merchant of Venice* and *As You Like It*. Characteristics commonly found include: love as chief motive; much out-of-
door action; an idealized heroine (who usually masks as a man);
love subjected to great difficulties; POETIC JUSTICE often violated;
balancing of characters; easy reconciliations; happy ending. Italian
stories were often employed for the plots. Shakespeare's last group
of plays, the TRAGI-COMEDIES or "serene romances" (such as *Winter's
Tale* and *Cymbeline*), are in some sense a modification of the earlier
*romantic comedy*.

**Romantic Criticism:** A term sometimes used for the body of critical
ideas which developed late in the eighteenth and early in the nineteenth century as a part of the triumph of ROMANTICISM over NEO-
CLASSICISM. It accompanied and to some extent guided and justified
the revolt against the "classical" attitudes of the eighteenth century, and was inspired in part by the necessity of "answering" such
conservative critics as Francis Jeffrey, Sydney Smith, and William
Gifford. The "artificial" character of Pope's poetic IMAGERY was at-

tacked by W. L. Bowles, who in turn was "answered" by Lord Byron and others. New theories about the genius of Shakespeare were espoused by Coleridge and others: instead of being regarded as a "wild, irregular genius," who succeeded in spite of his violation of the "laws" of dramatic composition, his art was studied on the assumption that it succeeded because it followed the laws of its own organism, which were more authentic than man-made "formal" rules. This view harmonized with the new critical ideas as to the nature of the poetic imagination (see IMAGINATION AND FANCY). The *romantic criticism* of Shakespeare thus led to the view that Shakespeare, like Nature, was infallible. "If we do not understand him, it is our fault or the fault of copyists or typographers" (Coleridge). Much extravagant Shakespeare "idolatry" followed in the wake of this attitude. Another aspect of *romantic criticism* may be mentioned—Wordsworth's famous theory of poetry as calling for simple themes drawn from humble life expressed in the language of ordinary life—a sharp reaction from the conventions of neo-classic poetry. In general the romantic critic saw art as an expression of the artist (the EXPRESSIVE THEORY OF ART), valued it as a living organism, sought its highest expressions among simple people, primitive cultures, and aspects of the world unsullied by artifice or by commerce with human society. See PRIMITIVISM; CULTURAL PRIMITIVISM; ROMANTICISM; CRITICISM, TYPES OF.

**Romantic Epic:** A type of long narrative POEM developed by Italian RENAISSANCE poets (late fifteenth and sixteenth centuries) by combining the materials and something of the method of the MEDIEVAL ROMANCE with the manner and technique of the classical epic (see EPIC). Such poets as Pulci, Boiardo, and Ariosto produced *romantic epics* which were like MEDIEVAL ROMANCES in their stressing of the love element, in their complicated and loose structure, in the multiplicity of characters and episodes, and in freedom of verse form. Yet they were like the Virgilian epic in their use of a formal INVOCATION, statement of theme, set speeches, formal descriptions, use of EPIC SIMILES, supernatural machinery, division into books, etc. Later, Tasso (*Jerusalem Delivered*, 1581) infused a strong tone of moral instruction and religious propaganda into the type. The method of ALLEGORY was also employed in the Italian *romantic epics*. The literary critics of the time were divided in their attitudes toward the new type of EPIC, the conservatives strongly opposing it because of its departure from classical standards. The form proved generally popular with readers, however, and when Edmund Spenser came to write his ambitious English EPIC, he actually modeled his poem largely upon the *romantic epics* of Ariosto (*Orlando Furioso*, 1516) and Tasso. Thus *The Faerie Queene*, EPIC in its high patriotic purpose and in much of its technique, romantic in its chivalric atmosphere and Arthurian setting, became, by following the general method of Ariosto and Tasso, the great example in English literature of a *romantic epic*.

**Romantic Novel:** A type of NOVEL marked by strong interest in action and presenting EPISODES often based on love, adventure, and combat. The term ROMANTIC owes its origin to the early type of story embraced by the ROMANCE of medieval times, but with the march of time other elements have been added. The FABLIAU and the NOVELLA particularly have contributed qualities. A ROMANCE, in its modern meaning, signifies that type of NOVEL which is more concerned with action than with character, which is more properly fictional than legendary since it is woven so largely from the imagination of the author, which is read more as a means of escape from existence than of familiarity with the actualities of life. The writers of modern ROMANCE are too numerous to mention: Sir Walter Scott's name may be allowed to represent the long list of romancers in English and American literature. See NOVEL.

**Romantic Period in American Literature, 1830–1865:** The period between the "second revolution" of the Jacksonian Era and the close of the Civil War in America saw the testing of the American nation and its development by ordeal. It was an age of great westward expansion, of the increasing gravity of the slavery question, of an intensification of the spirit of embattled sectionalism in the South, of a powerful impulse to reform in the North. Its culminating act was the trial by arms of the opposing views of the two sections in a Civil War, whose conclusion certified the fact of a united nation dedicated to the concepts of industry and capitalism and philosophically committed to the doctrine of absolute egalitarianism. In a sense it may be said that the three decades following the inauguration of Andrew Jackson as president in 1829 put to the test his views of democracy and saw emerge from the test a secure union committed to essentially Jacksonian principles.

In literature it was America's first great creative period, a full flowering of the romantic impulse on American soil. Surviving from the FEDERALIST AGE were its three major literary figures: Bryant, Irving, and Cooper. Emerging as new writers of strength and creative power were the novelists Hawthorne, Simms, Melville, and Mrs. Stowe; the poets Poe, Whittier, Longfellow, Lowell, and Whitman; the essayists and poets, Thoreau, Emerson, Holmes; the critics, Poe, Lowell, and Simms. The South, moving toward a concept of Southern independence, advanced three distinguished PERIODICALS, the *Southern Review*, the *Southern Literary Messenger*, and the *Southern Quarterly Review*. In the North *Knickerbocker's Magazine* and the *Democratic Review* joined the continuing arbiter of Northern taste, the *North American Review*, and then were followed by *Harper's Magazine* (1850) and the *Atlantic Monthly* (1857). Between 1830 and 1855 the GIFT BOOKS and ANNUALS proved to be remunerative markets for ESSAYS and TALES.

The POETRY of the period was predominantly romantic in spirit and form. Moral qualities were significantly present in the VERSE of Emerson, Bryant, Longfellow, Whittier, Lowell, and Thoreau. The sectional issues were debated in POETRY by Whittier and Lowell speaking for abolition, and Timrod, Hayne, and Simms speaking for the South. Poe formulated his Aristotelian theory of POETRY and in some fifty LYRICS practiced a symbolist VERSE that was to be, despite the charge of triviality by his contemporaries like Emerson, the strongest single poetic influence emerging from pre-Civil War America, particularly in its impact on European POETRY. Lowell wrote satiric VERSE in DIALECT. Whitman, beginning with the 1855 edition of *Leaves of Grass* was the ultimate expression in America of a POETRY organic in form and romantic in spirit, united to a concept of democracy that was pervasively egalitarian.

In the ESSAY and on the lecture platform the New England transcendentalists—Emerson, Thoreau, Margaret Fuller, and Alcott—carried the literary expression of philosophic and religious ideas to a high level. In critical ESSAYS, Lowell wrote with distinction, Simms with skill, and Poe with genius. Until 1850 the NOVEL continued to follow the path of Scott, with Cooper and Simms as its major producers. In the 1850's, however, emerged the powerful symbolic NOVELS of Hawthorne and Melville, and the effective PROPAGANDA NOVEL of Mrs. Stowe. Poe, Hawthorne, and Simms practiced the writing of SHORT STORIES throughout the period, taking up where Iriving had left off in the development of the form. Humorous writing by A. B. Longstreet, George W. Harris, Artemus

Ward, Josh Billings, and the early Mark Twain was establishing a basis for a realistic literature in the language of the common man, but it failed in this period to receive the critical attention it was later to have.

In the DRAMA the "star" system, the imitation of English "spectacle" DRAMA, and ROMANTIC TRAGEDY modeled on Shakespeare were dominant. Although N. P. Willis and R. M. Byrd were successful dramatists, only George Henry Boker, with his *Francesca da Rimini,* displayed any distinctive literary talent in the theatre. *Uncle Tom's Cabin* and *Rip Van Winkle* began stage careers that were to be phenomenally successful.

At the end of the Civil War a new nation had been born in the ordeal of war, and it was to demand and receive a new literature less idealistic and more practical, less exalted and more earthy, less consciously artistic and more direct than that produced in the age when the American dream had glowed with greatest intensity and American writers had made a great literary period by capturing on their pages the enthusiasm and the optimism of that dream. See *Outline of Literary History.*

**Romantic Period in English Literature, 1798–1870:** In the period between the publication of *Lyrical Ballads* (1798) and the death of Dickens, English literature was dominated by the spirit of ROMANTICISM. One commonly used way for designating literary periods in English history is to call the AGE OF THE ROMANTIC TRIUMPH (1798–1832) the *Romantic Period* and to lump together the time between the death of Scott in 1832 and the end of the century as the VICTORIAN AGE, since Queen Victoria reigned through much of it. However, the romantic impulse which flowered with such spectacular force in 1798 remained the dominant literary impulse well into the 1860's; hence the divisions employed in this Handbook. (See REALISTIC PERIOD IN ENGLISH LITERATURE.)

The *Romantic Period* came into being during the Napoleonic Wars, and flourished during the painful economic dislocations which were their aftermath. It saw union with Ireland; it witnessed the suffering which was attendant upon the INDUSTRIAL REVOLUTION; it was torn by CHARTISM and the great debates centering around the REFORM BILL; it developed a sensitive humanitarianism out of witnessing the suffering of the masses; it both espoused and despised the doctrine of UTILITARIANISM. An industrial England was being born in pain and suffering. The throes of developing democracy, the ugliness of the sudden growth of cities, the prevalence of human pain, the blatant presence of the "profit motive"—all helped to characterize what was in many respects "the best of times . . . the worst of times."

In the first half of the period, during the AGE OF THE ROMANTIC TRIUMPH, a philosophical ROMANTICISM based on value in the individual, on the romantic view of NATURE, and on an organic concept of art dominated the English literary mind. Optimism was the spirit of the times, although it was often an optimism closely associated with the impulse to revolt and with radical political reform. In the second half of the period, the EARLY VICTORIAN AGE, the impact of the INDUSTRIAL REVOLUTION was more immediately felt and the implications of the new science upon philosophy and religious belief began to be obvious. The romantic philosophy still held, and the spirit of ROMANTICISM permeated literature and much of life, but it found itself seriously in conflict with much of the world it saw around it, and out of that conflict came a literature of doubt and questioning. If, for example, the attitudes of Coleridge and Shelley are compared with those of Carlyle—all three clearly romantics—the extent to which the ROMANTICISM of the earlier period was being qualified by the conditions of industrial England and was being used to test those conditions becomes obvious.

In POETRY the *Romantic Period* was a "golden age," rich with the sonorous voices of Wordsworth, Coleridge, Shelley, Keats, Byron, Tennyson, Arnold, and the Pre-Raphaelites, and enlivened by the harsher tones of Browning. It was a great age for the NOVEL, producing Godwin, Scott, Austen, the Brontës, Thackeray, Dickens, Trollope, and the early George Eliot. A period of serious critical and social debate in the ESSAY, it produced Carlyle, Ruskin, Macaulay, Arnold, and Newman. In the INFORMAL ESSAY, it produced Lamb, Hazlitt, Hunt, and DeQuincey. Only in the DRAMA, bound by the PATENT THEATRES and a blind idolatry of Shakespeare and hampered by the "star" system, did the *Romantic Period* fail to produce work of true distinction; it was the weakest period in the English stage since Elizabeth I ascended the throne.

For the literary history of the period, see AGE OF THE ROMANTIC TRIUMPH, EARLY VICTORIAN AGE, and *Outline of Literary History*. See, also, ROMANTICISM.

**Romantic Tragedy:** Non-classical TRAGEDY. The term is used for such modern TRAGEDY as does not conform to the traditions or aims

of "classical" TRAGEDY. It differs from the latter in its greater freedom of technique, its wider scope of theme and treatment, its
greater emphasis on character (as compared with emphasis on
PLOT), its looser structure, its freer employment of IMAGINATION,
its greater variety of STYLE, and its easy readiness to admit humorous and even grotesque elements. ELIZBETHAN TRAGEDY is largely
romantic, e.g., Shakespeare's. See CLASSICAL TRAGEDY; TRAGEDY;
and CRITICISM, HISTORICAL SKETCH.

**Romanticism:** A movement of the eighteenth and nineteenth centuries which marked the reaction in literature, philosophy, art, religion, and politics from the NEO-CLASSICISM and formal orthodoxy
of the preceding period. *Romanticism* arose so gradually and exhibited so many phases that a satisfactory definition is hardly possible. The aspect most stressed in France is reflected in Victor
Hugo's phrase "liberalism in literature," meaning especially the
freeing of the artist and writer from the restraints and rules of the
classicists and suggesting that phase of individualism marked by the
encouragement of revolutionary political ideas. The poet Heine
noted the chief aspect of German *romanticism* in calling it the
revival of medievalism in art, letters, and life. A late nineteenth-
century English critic, Walter Pater, thought the addition of
strangeness to beauty (the neo-classicists having insisted upon
order in beauty) constituted the romantic temper. An American
transcendentalist, Dr. F. H. Hedge, thought the essence of *romanticism* was aspiration, having its origin in wonder and mystery. An
interesting schematic explanation calls *romanticism* the predomi-
nance of IMAGINATION over reason and formal rules (CLASSICISM)
and over the sense of fact or the actual (REALISM), a formula which
recalls Hazlitt's statement (1816) that the "classic" beauty of a
Greek temple resided chiefly in its actual form and its obvious connotations, while the "romantic" beauty of a Gothic building or ruin
arose from associated ideas which the IMAGINATION was stimulated
to conjure up. The term is used in many senses, a favorite recent
one being that which sees in the romantic mood a psychological desire to escape from unpleasant realities.

Perhaps more useful to the student than definitions will be a list
of romantic characteristics or "earmarks," though *romanticism* was
not a clearly conceived system. Among the aspects of the "romantic"
movement in England may be listed: SENSIBILITY; PRIMITIVISM;
love of NATURE; sympathetic interest in the past, especially the

medieval (see GOTHIC); MYSTICISM; individualism; ROMANTIC
CRITICISM; and a reaction against whatever characterized NEO-
CLASSICISM. Among the specific characteristics embraced by these
general attitudes are: the abandonment of the HEROIC COUPLET and
the ODE in favor of BLANK VERSE, the SONNET, the SPENSERIAN
STANZA, and many experimental verse forms; the dropping of the
conventional POETIC DICTION in favor of fresher language and
bolder figures; the idealization of rural life (Goldsmith); enthusiasm for the wild, irregular, or grotesque in NATURE and art; unrestrained IMAGINATION; enthusiasm for the uncivilized or "natural";
interest in human rights (Burns, Byron); sympathy with animal life
(Cowper); sentimental melancholy (Gray); emotional psychology
in fiction (Richardson); collection and imitation of popular BAL-
LADS (Percy, Scott); interest in ancient Celtic and Scandinavian
mythology and literature (see CELTIC REVIVAL); renewed interest
in Spenser, Shakespeare, and Milton. Typical literary forms of the
romantic writers include the LYRIC, especially the love LYRIC, the
reflective LYRIC, the nature LYRIC (see NATURE), and the LYRIC of
morbid melancholy (see GRAVEYARD SCHOOL); the SENTIMENTAL
NOVEL; the METRICAL ROMANCE; SENTIMENTAL COMEDY; the BAL-
LAD; the PROBLEM NOVEL; the HISTORICAL NOVEL; the GOTHIC
ROMANCE; the SONNET; and the CRITICAL ESSAY (see ROMANTIC
CRITICISM).

Although the romantic movement in English literature had its
beginnings or anticipations in the earlier eighteenth century
(Shaftesbury, Thomson, Dyer, Lady Winchilsea), it was not till
the middle of the century that its characteristics became prominent
and self-conscious (Blair, Akenside, Joseph and Thomas Warton,
Gray, Richardson, Sterne, Walpole, Goldsmith, and somewhat later
Cowper, Burns, and Blake), while its complete triumph was reserved for the early years of the nineteenth century (Wordsworth,
Coleridge, Scott, Southey, Byron, Shelley, Keats). A little later in
the nineteenth century came the great romantic period in American
literature (Bryant, Emerson, Lowell, Thoreau, Whittier, Hawthorne, Melville). (For additional details of the movement see
*Outline of Literary History* and the ROMANTIC PERIOD IN ENGLISH
LITERATURE.)

The last third of the nineteenth century witnessed the substitution of a soberer mood than prevailed earlier in the century, and
although the late nineteenth century and the early twentieth century, both in England and America, have been marked by a sharp

reaction against the romantic, especially the sentimental, spirit in literature, it is to be remembered that much late VICTORIAN literature was romantic and that the vitality of *romanticism* is evidenced by the great volume of romantic writing being produced in the twentieth century.

By way of caution it may be said that such descriptions of *romanticism* as this one probably overstress the distinction between *romanticism* and CLASSICISM or NEO-CLASSICISM, and cannot hope to resolve that confusion over what "romantic" means which Professor A. O. Lovejoy asserts has "for a century been the scandal" of literary history and criticism. As early as 1824 an effort to discover what the authorities meant by the term proved disappointing, and the succeeding century has increased the number of divergent, often contradictory, senses in which the term is employed. Some writers, like Professor Walter Raleigh and Sir Arthur Quiller-Couch, have even urged the desirability of abandoning the terms "romantic" and "classic," pointing out that their use adds to the critical confusion and tends to distort the facts of literary history and divert attention away from the natural processes of literary composition. Several have noted that Homer's *Odyssey*, for example, is cited by some as the very essence of the romantic, by others as a true exemplar of CLASSICISM. Professor Lovejoy, noting that the "romantic" movement has meant different things in different countries and that even in a single country "romantic" is often used in conflicting senses, proposes that the term be employed in the plural only, as a recognition of the various *romanticisms*. Even if the term "romantic" were always employed in the same sense and its characteristics could be safely and comprehensively enumerated, it would still be true that one could not use a single characteristic, like the love of wild scenery or the use of BLANK VERSE, as a "key" for classifying as romantic any single poem or poet.

Yet, viewed in philosophical terms, *romanticism* does have a fairly definite meaning for the student of literature. The term designates a literary and philosophical theory which tends to see the individual at the very center of all life and all experience, and it places him, therefore, at the center of art, making literature most valuable as an expression of his unique feelings and particular attitudes (the EXPRESSIVE THEORY OF ART) and valuing its accuracy in portraying his experiences, however fragmentary and incomplete, more than it values its adherence to completeness, UNITY, or the demands of GENRE. It places a high premium upon the creative function of the IMAGINATION, seeing art as a formulation of intuitive imaginative perceptions that tend to speak a nobler truth than that of fact, logic, or the here and now. It sees in NATURE a revelation of Truth, the "living garment of God," and often, pantheistically, a sensate portion of deity itself, and certainly a more suitable subject for true art than those aspects of the world sullied by man's artifice (CULTURAL PRIMITIVISM). It differs significantly from the literary movements which were to follow it, REALISM and NATURAL-ISM, in where it finds its values. Employing the commonplace, the natural, the simple as its materials, it seeks always to find the Absolute, the Ideal, by transcending the actual, whereas REALISM finds its values in the actual, and NATURALISM in the scientific laws which undergird the actual (see NATURALISM).

Ultimately, it must be admitted that the conflict of ideas and attitudes which occurred in the eighteenth century and which saw the triumph of *romanticism* over CLASSICISM, however much exaggerated in standard literary histories, did go a very long way toward the establishment of our modern democratic world, and where REALISM and NATURALISM are significantly different from *romanticism*, they are closer to it than they are to the CLASSICISM with which it broke. Wherever faith in the individual and in his freedom from rules, systems, or even from RATIONALISM appear, there one aspect of *romanticism* speaks. Contradictory as its attributes are and however true Professor Lovejoy's assertion that it should be spoken of always in the plural, *romanticisms* shape the controlling attitudes of the democratic world. See NATURALISM, REALISM, NEO-CLASSICISM, CLASSICISM, PRIMITIVISM, GOTHIC, ROMANTIC CRITICISM, ROMANTIC PERIOD IN ENGLISH LITERATURE, ROMANTIC PERIOD IN AMERICAN LITERATURE.

**Romany:** The language of the gypsies. It is a DIALECT form of the Indian branch of the Indo-Iranian languages, blended with many words and phrases from various European languages and spoken in many DIALECTS. A gypsy; or a descriptive way of designating anything pertaining to the gypsies. *Romany* ways and manners have been much written about by George Borrow.

**Rondeau:** A set French verse pattern, artificial but very popular with many English poets. Generally used for light and fanciful expression. The *rondeau* pattern consists characteristically of fifteen lines, the ninth and fifteenth being short lines—a REFRAIN. Only two RIMES (exclusive of the REFRAIN) are allowed, the RIME-SCHEME running *aabba aabc aabbac*. The *c*-rime here represents the REFRAIN, a group of words, usually the first half of the line, selected from the opening VERSE. The form divides itself into three STANZAS with the REFRAIN at the end of the second and third STANZAS. The VERSES most frequently consist of eight syllables. There is also a form of the *rondeau* which consists of twelve lines, ten using two RIMES plus REFRAINS, riming *abba abc abbac*. Another, known as the *rondeau redoublé*, consists of six QUATRAINS riming *abab*, with the first four lines forming in succession the last lines of the second, third, fourth, and fifth QUATRAINS.

**Rondel:** A French verse form, a variant of the RONDEAU, to which it is related historically. It consists of fourteen or thirteen lines (depending on whether the two-line REFRAIN is kept at the close or simply one line). The RIME-SCHEME most usual is *ab*baabab-abba*ab* (the italicized RIMES here representing verses used as a REFRAIN and repeated in their entirety). As in the other French forms repetition of rime-words is not allowed. The *rondel* differs from the RONDEAU in two chief respects: the number of lines, and the use of complete (rather than partial) lines for the REFRAIN.

**Roundel:** A variation of the French RONDEAU pattern, generally attributed to Swinburne who wrote "A Century of Roundels" and gave the form its popularity. The *roundel* is characterized by its eleven-line form and the presence, in the fourth and eleventh lines, of a REFRAIN taken, as in the RONDEAU, from the first part of the first line. The RIME-SCHEME (using *c* to indicate the refrain) is *abacbababac*. *Roundel* is also the Chaucerian spelling for RONDEL.

**Roundelay:** A modification of the RONDEL, a French lyric verse form. The *roundelay* is a simple poem or song of about fourteen lines in which part of one line frequently recurs as a REFRAIN. The term may also mean the musical setting of a RONDEAU so that it may be sung or chanted as an accompaniment for a folk-dance.

**Roundheads:** During the English Civil War, the members of the Puritan or Parliamentarian party. See CAVALIER LYRICISTS.

**Rune:** A character in a sort of alphabet developed about the second or third century by the Germanic tribes in Europe. A *boc* (modern "book") was a runic tablet of "beech" wood. Later, *runes* were carved upon stones, drinking horns, weapons, and ornaments. In very early times *rune* developed the special meaning of a character or sign or written formula which had magical power. *Runes* were used for charms, healing formulas, incantations, etc. The Norse god Odin is said to have been driven to insanity by the power of a *rune* sent to him by a certain maiden who was declining his love. Likewise, a *rune* came to mean any secret means of communication. Thus the Anglo-Saxon poet Cynewulf signed some of his poems by placing in runic characters in these poems a sequence of words the first letters of which spelled his name. Runic writing was very common in Anglo-Saxon England until gradually crowded out by the Latin alphabet used by the Christian missionaries. *Rune* may also mean a Finnish poem and (less accurately) an old Scandinavian poem. Emerson even used the word in the sense of "any song, poem, or verse."

**Run-on Lines:** The carrying over of sense and grammatic structure from one verse to a succeeding one for completion. The opposite of END-STOPPED LINES. See ENJAMBEMENT.

**Saga:** In its strictest sense, applied to Icelandic or other Scandinavian stories of the medieval period recording the legendary and historical accounts of heroic adventure, especially of members of certain important families. The earlier Icelandic *sagas,* like the early Irish EPICS and ROMANCES, were in PROSE. There were also "mythological" *sagas.* Less strictly, the term came to be used for an historical legend developed by oral tradition till it was popularly accepted as true—a form lying between authentic history and intentional fiction. This meaning is not confined to Scandinavian pieces, and indeed the commonest meaning nowadays for *saga* is a narrative having the characteristics of the Icelandic *sagas;* hence any traditional tale of heroic achievement or extraordinary or marvelous adventure. Perhaps the best example of the true *saga* is that of Grettir the Strong, suggestive of the story of Beowulf. Others are included in the famous *Heimskringla,* from which Longfellow drew material for his *Saga of King Olaf.* John Galsworthy has used the term happily in the title of his story of the Forsytes, a series of novels called *The Forsyte Saga.*

**Saints' Lives:** Highly eulogistic accounts of the miraculous experiences of the Saints; a kind of religious ROMANCE extremely popular in the medieval world. Chaucer's "Man of Law's Tale" in *The Canterbury Tales* is typical in everything except its literary excellence. See BIOGRAPHY.

**Saint's Play:** See MIRACLE PLAY.

**Sapphic:** A stanzaic pattern deriving its name from the Greek poetess, Sappho, who wrote love LYRICS of great beauty about 600 B.C. The pattern consists of three VERSES of eleven syllables each ($—\cup | —— | —\cup\cup | —\cup | —\cup$) called HENDECASYLLABICS and a fourth VERSE of five syllables ($—\cup\cup | —\cup$). The pattern has been frequently tried in English, but the demand for three SPONDEES in each STANZA results too often in distortion. Swinburne and Ezra Pound are generally conceded to have been the most successful modern writers of *sapphics*. A stanza from Swinburne is quoted:

Then to | me so | lying a | wake a | vision
Came with | out sleep | over the | seas and | touched me,
Softly | touched mine | eyelids and | lips; and | I too,
    Full of the | vision, (etc.)

**Sarcasm:** A form of verbal IRONY, in which, under the guise of praise a caustic and bitter expression of strong and personal disapproval is given. *Sarcasm* is personal, jeering, intended to hurt, and is intended as a sneering taunt. See IRONY.

**Satanic School:** A phrase used by Southey in the "Preface" to his *Vision of Judgment* (1821) to designate the members of the literary group made up of Byron, Shelley, Hunt, and their associates, whose irregular lives and radical ideas—defiantly flaunted in their writings—suggested the term. They were not infrequently contrasted with the "pious" group of the LAKE SCHOOL—Wordsworth, Coleridge, and Southey. By a natural extension in the use of the term writers of more recent times who have attacked conventional moral standards sometimes have been spoken of as belonging to the *Satanic School* of literature.

**Satire:** A literary manner which blends a critical attitude with HUMOR and WIT to the end that human institutions or humanity may be improved. The true satirist is conscious of the frailty of institutions of man's devising and attempts through laughter not so much to tear them down as to inspire a remodeling. If the critic simply abuses he is writing INVECTIVE; if he is personal and splenetic he is writing SARCASM; if he is sad and morose over the state of society he is writing IRONY or mere gloom. As a rule modern *satire* spares the individual and follows Addison's self-imposed rule: to "pass over a single foe to charge whole armies."

*Satire* existed in early classical literature of Greece and Rome. It is only necessary to name Aristophanes, Juvenal, Horace, Martial, and Petronius to recall the rich vein which ran at that time. Through the Middle Ages the manner persisted in the FABLIAU and BEAST-EPIC. In Spain the PICARESQUE NOVEL developed a strong element of *satire* to lend it interest; in France Molière and Le Sage proved themselves capable of handling the manner deftly, and somewhat later Voltaire established himself as the arch-satirist of literature. In England, from the time of Gascoigne (*Steel Glass*—1576) and Lodge (*Fig for Momus*—1595) writers condemned the vices and follies of the age in verse and prose (Hall, Nash, Donne, Jonson). By the time of Charles I, however, interest in *satire* had declined, only to revive with the struggle between Cavaliers and Puritans. At the hands of Dryden the HEROIC COUPLET, already the favorite form with most English satirists, developed into the finest satiric verse form. The eighteenth century in England became a period of *satire;* POETRY, DRAMA, ESSAYS, CRITICISM, all took on the satirical manner at the hands of such men as Dryden, Swift, Addison, Steele, Pope and Fielding,—a golden age of *satire*, which, great as are such later satirists as Byron and Thackeray, marks off the period as that in English literature most definitely satirical.

Early American *satire* naturally followed English in style. Before the Revolution, American *satire* dealt chiefly with the political struggle. Of the HARTFORD WITS Trumbull produced *M'Fingal*, a Hudibrastic *satire* on Tories. Freneau (*The British Prison Ship*) wrote the strongest and most original Revolutionary *satire*. Shortly after the Revolution, the *Anarchiad* (verse), by Trumbull, Barlow, Humphreys, and Hopkinson, and *Modern Chivalry* (fiction) by Breckenridge, attacked domestic political difficulties and the crudities of our frontier. Irving's good-humored *satire* in *The Sketch Book* and *Knickerbocker's History*, Holmes' society verse, Lowell's DIALECT poems (*Biglow Papers*), and Mark Twain's prose represent the general trend of American *satire* up to the twentieth century.

In the twentieth century English writers like G. B. Shaw, Noel Coward, Evelyn Waugh, and Aldous Huxley have maintained the satiric spirit in the face of the gravity of NATURALISM and the earnestness of SYMBOLISM. In America, Eugene O'Neill (on occasion), Edith Wharton, Sinclair Lewis, Kaufman and Hart, and John P. Marquand have commented critically upon man and his institutions.

*Satire* is fundamentally of two types, named for their most distinguished classical practitioners: *Horatian satire* is gentle, urbane, smiling; it aims to correct by gentle and broadly sympathetic laughter; *Juvenalian satire* is biting, bitter, angry; it points with contempt and moral indignation to the corruption and evil of men and institutions. Addison is a *Horatian* satirist, Swift a *Juvenalian* one.

For centuries the word *satire*, which literally means "a dish filled with mixed fruits," was reserved for long poems, such as the pseudo-Homeric *Battle of the Frogs and Mice,* the poems of Juvenal and Horace, *The Vision of Piers Plowman,* Chaucer's "Nun's Priest's Tale," Butler's *Hudibras,* Pope's *The Rape of the Lock,* Lowell's *A Fable for Critics.* Almost from its origins, however, the DRAMA has been suited to the satiric spirit, and from Aristophanes to Shaw and Noel Coward, it has commented with penetrating IRONY on human foibles. There was a notable concentration of its attention on Horatian *satire* in the COMEDY OF MANNERS of the RESTORATION AGE. But it has been in the fictional narrative, particularly the NOVEL, that *satire* has found its chief vehicle in the modern world. Cervantes, Rabelais, Voltaire, Swift, Fielding, Jane Austen, Thackeray, H. H. Brackenridge (*Modern Chivalry*), Mark Twain, Sinclair Lewis, Aldous Huxley, Evelyn Waugh, John P. Marquand—all have made extended fictional narratives the vehicles for a wide-ranging and powerfully effective satiric treatment of man and his institutions.

In England since 1841 *Punch* has maintained a high level of comic *satire.* In America, the *New Yorker* has demonstrated since 1925 the continuing appeal of sophisticated Horatian *satire.* The motion pictures, the plastic and graphic arts, and the newspaper comic strip and political cartoon have all been instruments of telling, satiric comment on human affairs.

For satiric methods, see IRONY, BURLESQUE, PARODY, SARCASM, INVECTIVE, INNUENDO.

**Satiric Poetry:** Verse treating its subject with IRONY or ridicule. (See SATIRE above.) The term is a loose one, since it characterizes method of treatment rather than content or form. Thus we may have a satiric EPIC (Pope's *Dunciad*) or a satiric LYRIC (Stephen Crane's *War Is Kind*). Perhaps the greatest masters of SATIRE in English poetry are Dryden, Pope, and Byron. In America, Lowell with his *Biglow Papers* and *Fable for Critics* holds first place although both Emily Dickinson and Stephen Crane have written fine ironic verses.

**Saturday Club:** A club of literary and scientific people in and around Cambridge and Boston in the mid-nineteenth century, the members of which came together chiefly for social intercourse and good conversation, at irregular intervals. There were no by-laws. Some of the more famous members were: Emerson, Longfellow, Agassiz, Pierce, and Holmes; among the frequent visitors were Hawthorne, Motley, and Sumner. Holmes paid tribute to the organization in verse (*At the Saturday Club*) and Dr. E. W. Emerson wrote an official history of the Club.

**Scald:** See SKALD.

**Scansion:** The dividing of VERSE into FEET by indicating ACCENTS and counting syllables to determine the METER of a poem. *Scansion* is a means of studying the mechanical elements by which the poet has established his rhythmical effects. The METER, once the scanning has been performed, is named according to the type and number of FEET employed in a VERSE. The major types of METER, explained elsewhere, are IAMBUS ($\smile$ ___), TROCHEE (___ $\smile$), ANAPEST ($\smile\smile$ ___), DACTYL (___ $\smile\smile$), SPONDEE (___ ___), and PYRRHIC ($\smile\smile$). A verse of one foot (of any type) is called MONOMETER; of two feet, DIMETER; of three feet, TRIMETER; of four feet, TETRAMETER; of five feet, PENTAMETER; of six feet, HEXAMETER; of seven feet, HEPTAMETER; of eight feet, OCTAMETER. Thus a verse consisting of two trochaic feet is called TROCHAIC DIMETER; of five iambic feet, IAMBIC PENTAMETER; of six dactylic feet, DACTYLIC HEXAMETER, and so on.

Applied to a single STANZA of *The Eve of St. Agnes,* a scanning would show (if we are pretty mechanical and are content to resort to singsong for the sake of emphasis and clearness) the following ACCENTS and divisions into FEET:

> And still | she slept | an az | ure-lid | ded sleep |
> In blanch | éd lin | en, smooth | and lav | endered, |
> While he | from forth | the clos | et brought | a heap |
> Of can | died ap | ple, quince, | and plum, | and gourd; |
> With jel | lies sooth | er than | the cream | y curd, |
> And lu | cent syr | ops, tinct | with cin | namon; |
> Manna | and dates, | in ar | gosy | transferred |
> From Fez; | and spic | éd dain | ties, ev | ery one |
> From silk | en Sam | ar cand | to ce | dared Leb | a non. |

Such a mechanical marking of ACCENTS and dividing into FEET discloses that the METER of the STANZA is predominantly composed of one unaccented syllable followed by an accented syllable, and this we have called above the IAMBIC FOOT. We next discover that characteristically there are five of these FEET to the line, and a five-foot line we have called PENTAMETER. We are now, as the result of our scanning, prepared to state that the METER of *The Eve of St. Agnes* is IAMBIC PENTAMETER. As the STANZA is scanned above, there are only two obvious exceptions to this pattern: (1) the first FOOT of the seventh VERSE consists of an accented syllable preceding an unaccented (and is thus a TROCHEE) and, (2) the ninth VERSE consists of six IAMBIC FEET instead of five (and is thus an HEXAMETER or an ALEXANDRINE). So, finally, we have found that our STANZA consists of eight IAMBIC PENTAMETER VERSES with a ninth VERSE which is an ALEXANDRINE—a pattern called the SPENSERIAN STANZA. *Scansion* is often considered to include the RIME-SCHEME as well as the VERSE analysis. In that case we would say of the above STANZA that it rimes *ababbcbcc*.

It should be noted that this mechanical system of *scansion*, which is almost universally employed in the analysis of English poetry, was borrowed entire from classical QUANTITATIVE VERSE, and does not always fit readily on the English accentual-syllabic rhythmic pattern. It obviously cannot be applied to SPRUNG RHYTHM or to FREE VERSE. An additional caveat is in order: the failure of a

# Scenario

VERSE or a STANZA of English poetry to fit readily into a regular *scansion* pattern does not necessarily indicate ineptness on the part of the poet; it may indicate that he is constructing his poem upon rhythmic patterns that do not readily lend themselves to such mechanical analysis. See METER, ACCENT, RHYTHM.

**Scenario:** A skeleton outline of a DRAMA, which gives the sequence of actions that make up the PLOT and the successive appearances of the principal characters. The PLOT of a DRAMA is itself sometimes called the *scenario*. A play written in a form ready for filming as a motion picture DRAMA is also called a *scenario*.

**Scenes** (in a **Novel**): In the NOVEL which is dramatic, that is, presents its actions as they are imagined to occur rather than summarizes them in narrative EXPOSITION, there is a tendency of the author to construct his story in a sequence of self-explanatory *scenes*, similar in many respects to those of the DRAMA. This tendency in NOVELS using the SELF-EFFACING AUTHOR is sufficiently marked to result in the dramatic technique of the NOVEL being called the "scenic method." The construction of a typical chapter of a Henry James novel illustrates the "scenic method": such a chapter (it may be selected almost at random from *The Portrait of a Lady*) will usually open with a detailed description of setting and of the interior state of the character through whom the action is being presented (Isabel Archer, in *The Portrait*); then, when everything has been well prepared for, the action and conversation are presented directly and in great detail, the action rising to a CLIMAX upon which the curtain figuratively falls, such a curtain being represented by the abrupt ending of the chapter. See SCENES (of a DRAMA).

**Scenes** (of a **Drama**): The division of the ACT of a DRAMA into *scenes* is less logical or scientifically systematic even than the division of the play itself into ACTS. This is partly due to the lack of agreement as to what should constitute a *scene*. Sometimes the entrances and exits of important personages determine the beginning and ending of *scenes*, as in French DRAMA. In some plays a *scene* is a logical unit in the development of the action. Many English dramatists regard the clearing of the stage as the sign of a change of *scene*. Some authorities, however, think that not all stage-clearness or entrances and exits really indicate a new *scene*. Thus Sir Edmund Chambers (*Elizabethan Stage*) uses *scene* as "a continuous section of action in an unchanged locality." Theoretically, a well-managed *scene* should have a structure comparable with that of a play itself, with the five logical parts (see DRAMATIC STRUCTURE). The plays of Shakespeare, of course, do not conform to this requirement, though some of the *scenes* can be analyzed successfully on this basis. The most important principle in scene-construction, perhaps, is that of climactic arrangement. *Scenes* have been loosely classified on such varying principles as length, structural function, internal technique, external background. Thus there may be long *scenes* and short *scenes;* transitional *scenes,* expository *scenes,* development *scenes,* climactic *scenes,* relief *scenes,* and the like; messenger *scenes,* MONOLOGUE *scenes,* DIALOGUE *scenes, ensemble scenes;* forest *scenes,* battle *scenes,* balcony *scenes,* street *scenes,* garden or orchard *scenes,* court *scenes,* banquet-hall *scenes,* and chamber *scenes.*

**Scholasticism:** The name is said to have come from the title *doctor scholasticus* applied to a teacher in the religious "schools" established in the ninth and tenth centuries. Although such doctors were supposed to teach the SEVEN ARTS, they became chiefly professors of logic. As developed a century or so later, *scholasticism* became a complicated system which relied upon logical methods in an effort to reconcile the tenets of Christianity with the demands of reason, "an application of reason to theology, not in order to revise the creed or to explore for new truth, but to systematize and prove existing traditional beliefs."[1] The logical method of Aristotle was employed. It has been said that no problem was so difficult that the Schoolmen would not confidently attempt to solve it by syllogistic reasoning. "The ordinary method of discussion . . . was to state general subjects, which are then resolved into subordinate topics, and the ramification is carried forward until it is considered complete. Under each head, questions are proposed, each question being pluralized by analysis, and its branches separately handled. First, the grounds negative of the thesis are set down in order, including pasages from Augustine, Aristotle, and other authors. Then follow the grounds in the affirmative, and, in

[1]George P. Fisher, *History of Christian Doctrine,* Charles Scribner's Sons, 1908, p. 213. Reprinted by permission of the publishers.

the last place, the writer sums up, answering the objections and reconciling seeming contradictions."[2] Such speculative problems as the relations to one another of the persons of the Holy Trinity, the nature and attributes of God, and the relation of the finite to the infinite were so treated.

Scholastic reasoning as applied by different men led to diverging views. The "first era" of *scholasticism* (twelfth century) marked the break from the freer reasoning of the earlier ("patristic") theologians, and includes Abelard, Bernard of Clairvaux, and Anselm, "father of scholasticism." The second era (thirteenth century) was the flourishing period, marked by the dominance of Aristotelian influence, and includes the two great Schoolmen Thomas Aquinas and Duns Scotus, heads of opposing groups known as "Thomists" and "Scotists." The third era (especially fifteenth century) marked the decline of *scholasticism,* when, though its methods were perfected, it became largely occupied with trivialities. This lost vitality made it an easy victim to the fresh and vigorous intellectualism of the RENAISSANCE, and *scholasticism* had lost its dominance by the early sixteenth century. Indeed, the great Erasmus, typical of Renaissance HUMANISM, at first an adherent of scholastic method, is said to have been persuaded to forsake it by the English scholar, John Colet. *Scholasticism* employed the deductive method of reasoning, and its overthrow prepared the way for the inductive method, advocated by Francis Bacon, which has led to the achievements of modern science. The positive effect of scholastic thinking upon all medieval literature and thinking was incalculable in extent, and its insistence upon rigid, accurate reasoning has had a wholesome effect upon succeeding thought and writing, while the indirect influence upon philosophy and literature of its overthrow has been even more pronounced.

**Scholiast:** One who wrote *scholia* or marginal comments explaining the grammar or meaning of passages in medieval MANUSCRIPTS, particularly copies of Greek and Latin texts.

**School Plays:** One of the most important traditions contributing to the development of ELIZABETHAN DRAMA was the practice of writing and performing plays at schools. Little is known of the history, extent, or character of dramatic activities in universities

²*Ibid.,* p. 215.

before the RENAISSANCE, though there is some evidence that student plays existed throughout the late Middle Ages. Records of *school plays* from the fifteenth century possibly refer to such medieval forms as DISGUISINGS (see MASQUE). The interest in Latin DRAMA aroused by the Italian RENAISSANCE (Petrarch wrote a Terentian comedy about 1331) led to translations and imitations of Plautus and Terence in other countries, such as Germany and Holland (where *school plays* of the "Prodigal Son" formula flourished), and eventually England (early sixteenth century). Boys in grammar schools (St. Paul's, Eton) acted both classical and original plays in the 1520's. By 1560 both Latin and English plays were produced at Eton, and in Spenser's time (1560's) Richard Mulcaster's boys at the Merchant Taylors School performed plays annually before the queen. Nicholas Udall's *Ralph Roister Doister*, probably written before 1553 for performance by the boys of Westminster School, is regarded as the first regular English COMEDY.

However important the production of plays in the grammar schools may have been, of still greater significance in the development of the DRAMA was the practice, common in the sixteenth century, of writing and performing plays at the universities. Plays of Terence were acted by undergraduates in Cambridge as early as 1510. In 1546 at Trinity College, Cambridge, refusal of a student to take part in a play was punishable by expulsion. Though the primary purpose of the plays was educational, entertainment for its own sake was more and more recognized, and the use of English became more and more common. When Queen Elizabeth visited Cambridge in 1564 and Oxford in 1566 she was entertained with series of plays of various types, foreshadowing later forms on the Elizabethan stage. The earliest extant university play in English is *Gammar Gurton's Needle* (written *ca.*1560). Some university pieces were connected with later Elizabethan plays, such as Thomas Legge's SENECAN TRAGEDY on Richard III, which may have contributed features to Shakespeare's play.

The full influence of academic DRAMA upon the professional stage can only be estimated, but it is to be remembered that the UNIVERSITY WITS left the universities at a time when academic plays were flourishing and went to London to play important rôles during the formative period of ELIZABETHAN DRAMA. In the main the academic DRAMA transmitted to the professional DRAMA the classical forms and techniques represented by Seneca in TRAGEDY and by Plautus and Terence in COMEDY, though Italian sources were also employed. One interesting group of UNIVERSITY PLAYS had to do with problems of student life, such as town *vs.* college quarrels, an important instance being the trilogy of "Parnassus" plays at Cambridge about 1600, which incidentally reflect also the close connection then existing between dramatic interests in London and the universities. The plays were most commonly performed at night in the college hall before a restricted audience. The actors were costumed.

**School of Sensibility:** See SENSIBILITY.

**School of Spenser:** A name given to a group of seventeenth-century poets who showed the influence of Edmund Spenser. The chief poets of the school were Giles and Phineas Fletcher, William Browne, George Wither, William Drummond of Hawthornden, Sir John Davies, and the Scottish Sir William Alexander. The school is marked by such characteristics as sensuousness, melody, PERSONIFICATIONS, pictorial quality, interest in narrative, medievalism (especially in use of ALLEGORY), ARCHAISMS, modified or genuine SPENSERIAN STANZA, pastoralism, moral earnestness. The art and outlook of the school led in the direction of Milton, whom they influenced. They thus form a link between Spenser and Milton, the two great Puritan poets of the English RENAISSANCE.

**Schoolmen:** Medieval philosophers who followed the method of SCHOLASTICISM in their "disputations." Called "hair-splitters" by Francis Bacon. See SCHOLASTICISM.

**Science Fiction:** A form of FANTASY in which scientific facts, assumptions, or hypotheses form the basis, by logical extrapolation, of adventures in the future, on other planets, in other dimensions in time, or under new variants of scientific law. See FANTASY.

**Scop:** A sort of Anglo-Saxon court poet. Though the *scop* perhaps traveled about from court to court like the GLEEMAN, he occupied a position of importance and permanence in the king's retinue comparable to that of the Welsh BARD (see WELSH LITERATURE) and the Irish FILIDH (see IRISH LITERATURE). He was a composer as well as a reciter, and his themes were drawn chiefly from the heroic traditions of the early Germanic peoples, though later he employed Biblical themes, and he no doubt was expected in general to eulogize the family which employed him. He has been called a precursor of the modern POET LAUREATE.

**Scottish Chaucerians:** See SCOTTISH LITERATURE.

**Scottish Literature:** Though the main stream of the literature of Scotland is rightly regarded as a part of English literary history, the fact of political independence in early times and the use of the Scots language or Scottish DIALECT of English by many writers warrants some special notice of *Scottish literature*. John Barbour's *Bruce* (1375), a sort of Scottish national EPIC (in twenty books), is often taken as the beginning of *Scottish literature*. In the fifteenth and sixteenth centuries there flourished a school of SCOTTISH CHAUCERIANS, Robert Henryson (*Testament of Cresseid*), William Dunbar (*Thrissil and the Rois, Golden Targe*), Gavin Douglas (trans. of *Aeneid*), and James I (*The King's Quair*). Somewhat later appeared Sir David Lyndsay (*Satire of the Three Estates,* an ambitious MORALITY play said to have been acted in 1540). Early Scotland is noted, too, for her popular BALLADS, some of which probably belong to the fifteenth and sixteenth centuries, though most of the existing ones seem to have been composed a century or more later. The controversial prose, on religious and historical or political topics, of the famous John Knox (sixteenth century) aided a tendency toward the use of English by Scottish writers. Among the poets Alexander Montgomerie (ca.1545–ca.1610) is sometimes called the last of the native Scottish "makers." By the seventeenth century the Scots DIALECT as a literary vehicle was rare.

A migration of Scottish professional and business men to London in the early eighteenth century makes increasingly difficult a separation of Scottish and English literature. In poetry the works of James Thomson (*The Seasons*) and Robert Blair (*The Grave*) are noteworthy monuments in English literary history, as are such prose pieces as Adam Smith's *Wealth of Nations* and David Hume's *Inquiry Concerning the Human Understanding.* At the very end of the century appeared the immortal Robert Burns, whose use of native DIALECT (following a tradition set by Allan Ramsay and others) found an immediate response among the romantically inclined literary circles of Edinburgh.

Though much conscious feeling for native tradition appears in some nineteenth-century Scottish writers (like Sir Walter

Scott) and though the native DIALECTS have been employed by such writers of regional literature as J. M. Barrie (see KAILYARD SCHOOL), in general literary men of Scottish birth (e.g., Carlyle, Stevenson) have been regarded, since 1800, as "English." One notable achievement in English literary history was the establishment in Scotland in the early nineteenth century of literary and critical MAGAZINES, e.g., *The Edinburgh Review* (1802).

**Scriblerus Club:** A club of writers organized in London in 1714 by Jonathan Swift with the object of satirizing literary incompetence. Among its members were Pope, Arbuthnot, Bolingbroke, Gay, and Congreve. It expressed its opinions of the false taste of the age, particularly in learning, through the satiric fragment, *The Memoirs of the Extraordinary Life, Works, and Discoveries of Martinus Scriblerus*, written in large part by Dr. Arbuthnot.

**Scriptural Drama:** See MYSTERY PLAY.

**Self-Effacing Author:** When, in the NOVEL or the SHORT STORY, OBJECTIVITY is so used in the narrative POINT OF VIEW that the author ostensibly ceases to exist and becomes merely an impersonal and non-evaluating medium through which the actions and actors of the story are seen, he is said to be *self-effacing*. The *self-effacing author* is a typical device in the "scenic method." See SCENE (IN A NOVEL), NARRATOR, POINT OF VIEW, OBJECTIVITY.

**Senecan Tragedy:** The Latin TRAGEDIES attributed to the Stoic philosopher Seneca (first century). They were modeled largely upon the Greek TRAGEDIES of Euripides (but written to be recited rather than acted) and exerted a great influence upon RENAISSANCE playwrights, who thought them intended for actual performance. In general the nine plays are marked by: (1) conventional five-ACT division; (2) the use of a CHORUS (for comment rather than participation in the action) and such stock characters as a ghost, a cruel tyrant, the faithful male servant, and the female CONFIDANTE; (3) the presentation of much of the action (especially the horrors) through long narrative reports recited by messengers as a substitute for stage-action; (4) the employment of sensational themes drawn from Greek mythology, involving much use of "blood and lust" material connected with unnatural crimes (adultery, incest, infanticide, etc.) and often motivated by revenge and leading to retribution; (5) a highly rhetorical style marked by hyperbolic expressions, detailed descriptions, exaggerated comparisons, APHO-RISMS, EPIGRAMS, and the sharp line-for-line DIALOGUE known as STICHOMYTHIA; (6) lack of careful character delineation but much use of introspection and SOLILOQUY.

Renaissance HUMANISM stimulated interest in the *Senecan tragedies* and they were translated and imitated in early academic and court DRAMA in Italy, France, and England. The "first" English TRAGEDY, Sackville and Norton's *Gorboduc* (acted 1562), was an imitation of Seneca as were such later Inns-of-Court plays as *Jocasta* (acted 1566), *Tancred and Gismunda* (acted 1568), and *The Misfortunes of Arthur* (1588), some of which were influenced by Italian Senecan plays rather than by the Latin plays themselves. After 1588 two groups of English *Senecan tragedies* are to be distinguished. The Countess of Pembroke and playwrights under her influence produced "true" Senecan plays modeled upon the French *Senecan tragedies* of Robert Garnier. In this group are Kyd's translation of Garnier's *Cornélie*, Daniel's *The Tragedy of Cleopatra* and his *Philotas* (1603), and Fulke Greville's original plays based on Senecan models, e.g., *Mustapha*.

The second and far more important group begins with the plays produced by Marlowe and Kyd for the popular stage. These plays combined native English tragic tradition with a modi-fied Senecan technique and led directly toward the typical ELIZA-BETHAN TRAGEDY. Kyd's *Spanish Tragedy*, for example, though re-flecting such Senecan traits as sensationalism, bombastic rhetoric, the use of the CHORUS and the ghost, departed from the Senecan method in that it placed the murders and horrors upon the stage, in response to popular Elizabethan taste and in defiance of Horace's dictum that good taste demanded leaving such matters for off-stage action. The fashion so inaugurated led to a long line of ELIZA-BETHAN TRAGEDIES, the greatest of which is perhaps Shakespeare's *Hamlet*. The importance of the Latin Senecan plays in the evolu-tion of English TRAGEDY is very great. In Professor A. H. Thorn-dike's words, they called attention to DRAMA "not as an exposition of events or as an allegory of life, but as a field for the study of human emotion. Their brilliant if bombastic rhetoric aroused en-thusiasm for the drama as literature and poetry; and their reflective and aphoristic style encouraged an effort to elevate tragedy above its too familiar converse with comedy into the realm of austere phi-losophy." See REVENGE TRAGEDY, TRAGEDY OF BLOOD.

**Sensibility:** A term used to indicate emotionalism as opposed to RATIONALISM; a reliance upon the feelings as guides to truth and conduct as opposed to reason and law as regulations both in human and metaphysical relations. It is connected with such eighteenth-century attitudes as PRIMITIVISM, SENTIMENTALISM, the nature movement (see NATURE), and other aspects of ROMANTICISM. Joseph Warton in *The Enthusiast* (1744) reflects many of the attitudes of the "School of Sensibility": "on the one hand, he expressed the contempt for cities, formal gardens, conventional society, business, law-courts, and Augustan style; on the other, the love of the simple life, solitude, mountains, stormy oceans, instinctively noble savages, untutored poets who 'warbled wildly,' and tragedies of terror" (Bernbaum). The high value that the eighteenth century put upon *sensibility* was a reaction against the Stoicism of the seventeenth century and the theories advanced by Hobbes and others that man was motivated primarily by self-interest. Benevolence, resting upon the ability to sympathize to a marked degree with the joys and the sorrows of one's fellows, was asserted by many, notably the Earl of Shaftesbury, as an innate human characteristic. From this position to the idea of the virtue of the sympathetic tear was a short distance soon traveled. This extreme *sensibility* expressed itself in the DRAMA in SENTIMENTAL COMEDY, in FICTION in the SENTIMENTAL NOVEL.

In the twentieth century, the term *sensibility* is used in a radically different sense, to designate the innate sensitivity of the poet (and his reader) to sensory experience, out of which he fashions his art. It is most common in T. S. Eliot's phrase "dissociation of *sensibility,*" by which he means the disunion of feeling and thought which, he thinks, occurred in English poetry with Dryden and Milton. Only when thought and feeling have been re-united can English poetry again establish its true mode, he thinks. See METAPHYSICAL POETRY, SENTIMENTALISM, SENTIMENTAL COMEDY, SENTIMENTAL NOVEL.

**Sensual and Sensuous:** *Sensuous* is a critical term characterizing writing which plays fully upon the various *senses* of the reader. The term is not to be confused with *sensual* which is now generally used in an unfavorable sense and implies writing which is fleshly or carnal, in which the author displays the voluptuous and abandons his work to the presentation of a single sense impression. *Sensuous,* then, denotes writing that makes a restrained use of the various senses; *sensual* denotes writing that approaches unrestrained abandonment to one sense—the passion of physical love. Through the careful use of pictures and IMAGES which appeal to the senses, such a use as Keats makes in *The Eve of St. Agnes,* writing may be said to be made *sensuous,* a quality which Milton stipulated as characterizing good poetry in his famous estimate of poetry as "simple, sensuous, and passionate." The writing of Ernest Hemingway, with its use of physical IMAGES and its attempt to "rub the fact on the exposed nerve end," is markedly *sensuous,* although it is only occasionally *sensual.* In a quite different style, Thomas Wolfe's writing, evoking sharp sensory response, is also *sensuous.*

**Sentence:** A rhetorical term formerly in use in the sense of APOTHEGM or MAXIM (Lat. *sententia*), usually applied to quoted "wise sayings." In old writings, too, the student may come upon the use of *sentence* for *sense, gist,* or *theme,* as when Chanticleer in Chaucer's *Nun's Priest's Tale* tells Pertelot (trickily) that the *sentence* of the Latin phrase is such and such. In modern grammatical usage, of course, *sentence* is restricted to a group of words having a subject and predicate and expressing a complete thought.

**Sentimental Comedy:** Just as the COMEDY OF MANNERS reflected in its immorality the reaction of the RESTORATION from the severity of the Puritan code of the Commonwealth period, so the COMEDY which displaced it, known as *sentimental comedy,* or "reformed comedy," sprang up in the early years of the eighteenth century in response to a growing reaction against the tone of RESTORATION plays. Signs of this reaction appeared soon after the dethronement of James II (1688) and found influential expression in Jeremy Collier's famous *Short View of the Immorality and Profaneness of the English Stage* (1698), which charged that plays as a whole "rewarded debauchery," "ridiculed virtue and learning," and were "disserviceable to probity and religion." Although Colley Cibber's *Love's Last Shift* (1696) shows transitional anticipations of the new reformed COMEDY, Richard Steele is generally regarded as the founder of the type. His *The Funeral* (1701), *The Lying Lover* (1703), and *The Tender Husband* (1705) reflect the development of the form, while his *The Conscious Lovers* (1722) is the classic example of the fully developed type.

Through the violence of its reaction *sentimental comedy* became a very weak thing dramatically, lacking humor, reality, spice, and lightness of touch. The characters were either so good or so bad that they became mere CARICATURES, and PLOTS were violently handled so that virtue should triumph. The dramatists resorted shamelessly to sentimental emotion in their effort to interest and move the spectators. The hero in *The Conscious Lovers* ("conscious" in the sense of "conscientious") is perfectly moral; he has no bad habits; he is indifferent to "sordid lucre"; he is good to inferiors from principle, even thanking servants for paid services; he is guided by a sense of honor and is superior to all ordinary passions. His conversations with the heroine Indiana, whom he loves but who agrees with him that he must marry Lucinda to please his parents, are veritable TRAVESTIES upon the art of love-making. Where the COMEDY OF MANNERS of the preceding age had sacrificed moral tone in its effort to amuse, the *sentimental comedy* sacrificed dramatic reality in its effort to instruct through an appeal to the heart. The domestic trials of middle-class couples are usually portrayed: their "private woes" are exhibited with much emotional stress intended to arouse the spectator's pity and suspense in advance of the approaching melodramatic happy ending.

This COMEDY held the boards on the English stage for more than a half century. Hugh Kelley's *False Delicacy* (1768), first acted shortly before the appearance of Goldsmith's *Good Natured Man* (brought out in protest against *sentimental comedies*), and Richard Cumberland's *The West Indian* (1771) illustrate the complete development of the type. Though weakened by the attacks and dramatic performances of Goldsmith and Sheridan, who revived in a somewhat chastened form the old COMEDY OF MANNERS, plays of the sentimental type lived on till after the middle of the nineteenth century, though no longer dominant. The DOMESTIC TRAGEDY of a sentimental sort developed by Nicholas Rowe (1674–1718) and George Lillo (1693–1739) shows much the same characteristics as the COMEDY with which it coëxisted. Both forms are based upon the same fundamentals as those of MELODRAMA.

**Sentimental Novel:** The SENTIMENTALISM of the eighteenth century was reflected not only in the SENTIMENTAL COMEDY and in the DOMESTIC TRAGEDY, but in the early NOVELS as well. Richardson's *Pamela, or Virtue Rewarded* (1740) was the beginning of the vogue, and although the rival REALISTIC NOVEL sprang up in protest (e.g., Fielding's *Tom Jones*) the *sentimental novel* (also called NOVEL OF SENSIBILITY) continued popular for many years. One of the best of the type is Goldsmith's *The Vicar of Wakefield* (1766) and one of the most extravagant is Henry Mackenzie's *Man of Feeling* (1771). Laurence Sterne's *Tristram Shandy* (1760–1767) is another example of the type. See NOVEL, SENTIMENTALISM.

**Sentimentalism:** The term is used in two senses important in the study of literature: (1) an overindulgence in emotion, especially the conscious effort to induce emotion in order to analyze or enjoy it; also the failure to restrain or evaluate emotion through the exercise of the judgment; (2) an optimistic overemphasis of the goodness of humanity (SENSIBILITY), representing in part a reaction against orthodox Calvinistic theology, which regarded human nature as depraved. It is connected with the development of PRIMITIVISM. In the first sense given above *sentimentalism* is found in MELODRAMA, in the fainting heroines of sentimental fiction, in the melancholic verse of the GRAVEYARD SCHOOL, in humanitarian literature, and in such modern phenomena as moving pictures and legal and political oratory. In the second sense it appears in SENTIMENTAL COMEDY, sentimental fiction, and primitivistic poetry. Both types of sentimentality figured largely in the literature of the romantic movement. Writers reflecting eighteenth-century *sentimentalism* include Richard Steele (*The Conscious Lovers*); Joseph Warton (*The Enthusiast*); the poems of William Collins and Thomas Gray; Laurence Sterne (*A Sentimental Journey*); Oliver Goldsmith (*The Deserted Village*); Henry Mackenzie (*The Man of Feeling*). The neo-classicists themselves, though opposed fundamentally to *sentimentalism,* sometimes exhibit it, as when Addison avers that he resorts to Westminster Abbey for the purpose of enjoying the emotions called up by the sombre surroundings. In its broadest sense *sentimentalism* may be said to result whenever a reader or an audience is asked to experience an emotional response in excess of that merited by the occasion or one that has not been adequately prepared for. See SENSIBILITY.

**Sentimentality:** See SENTIMENTALISM.

**Septenary:** A seven-stress VERSE often employed in medieval and RENAISSANCE poetry. See FOURTEENERS.

**Septuagint:** A Greek version of the Old Testament begun in the third century before Christ. It is still in use in the Greek Church and is the version from which New Testament writers quote. It takes its name from an old but discredited story that it was prepared by seventy-two Jewish scholars at the request of Ptolemy Philadelphus (284–247 B.C.).

**Serenade:** A sentimental composition, written as though intended to be sung out of doors at night under a lady's window and in praise of a loved one. Bayard Taylor's "Bedouin Song," the last stanza of which is quoted, is a *serenade* which once was very popular:

> My steps are nightly driven,
>    By the fever in my breast
> To hear from thy lattice breathed
>    The word that shall give me rest.
> Open the door of thy heart,
>    And open thy chamber door,
> And my kisses shall teach thy lips
>    The love that shall fade no more
>       *Till the sun grows cold,*
>       *And the stars are old,*
>    *And the leaves of the Judgment Book unfold!*

**Sestet:** The second, six-VERSE division of a SONNET. Following the eight-VERSE division (see OCTAVE) the *sestet* usually makes specific a general statement which has been presented in the OCTAVE or indicates the personal emotion of the author in a situation which the OCTAVE has developed. The most authentic RIME-SCHEME is the *cdecde* (following the *abbaabba* of the OCTAVE), but sonneteers have tried so many rearrangements of the SONNET rime pattern as to make almost any sequence now acceptable.

**Sestina:** One of the most difficult and complex of the various French lyrical forms. The *sestina* is a poem consisting of six six-line STANZAS and a three-line ENVOY. It makes no use of the REFRAIN. This form is usually unrimed, the effect of RIME being taken over by a fixed pattern of end-words which demands that these end-words in each STANZA be the same, though arranged in a different sequence each time. If we take 1–2–3–4–5–6 to represent the end-words of the first STANZA, then the first line of the second STANZA must end with 6 (the last end-word used in the preceding STANZA), the second with 1, the third with 5, the fourth with 2, the fifth with 4, the sixth with 3—and so to the next STANZA. The order of the first three STANZAS, for instance, would be: 1–2–3–4–5–6; 6–1–5–2–4–3; 3–6–

4–1–2–5. The conclusion, or ENVOY, of three lines must use as end-words 5–3–1, these being the final end-words, in the same sequence, of the sixth STANZA. But the poet must exercise even greater ingenuity than all this since buried in each line of the ENVOY must appear the other three end-words, 2–4–6. Thus so highly artificial a pattern affords a form which, for most poets, can never prove anything more than a poetic exercise. Yet it has been practiced with success in English by Swinburne, Kipling, and Auden.

**Setting:** The physical, and sometimes spiritual, background against which the action of a narrative (NOVEL, DRAMA, SHORT STORY, etc.) takes place. The elements which go to make up a *setting* are: (1) the actual geographical location, its topography, scenery, and such physical arrangements as the location of the windows and doors in a room; (2) the occupations and daily manner of living of the characters; (3) the time or period in which the action takes place, e.g., epoch in history, season of the year, etc.; (4) the general environment of the characters, e.g., religious, mental, moral, social, and emotional conditions through which the people in the narrative move. From one point of view most fiction can be broken up into four elements: *setting*, INCIDENT (or PLOT), CHARACTERIZATION, and—added at Poe's insistence—EFFECT. When *setting* dominates, or when a piece of fiction is written largely to present the manners and customs of a locality, the writing is often called a piece of LOCAL COLOR WRITING or of REGIONALISM. The term is also often applied to the stage *setting* of a play. See MISE EN SCÈNE.

**Seven Arts, The:** The seven subjects studied in the medieval university. The three studies pursued during the four-year course leading to the A.B. degree were known as the TRIVIUM. They were grammar (Latin), logic, and RHETORIC (especially public speaking). The four branches followed in the three-year course leading to the M.A. degree were arithmetic, music, geometry, astronomy. These were called the QUADRIVIUM.

**Seven Deadly Sins, The:** The seven cardinal sins which, according to medieval theology, entailed spiritual death and could be atoned for only by perfect penitence: pride, envy, wrath, sloth, avarice, gluttony, and lust. Dante treats all seven as arising from imperfect love—pride, envy, and wrath resulting from perverted love; sloth from defective love; avarice, gluttony, and lust from excessive love.

Pride was the most heinous of the sins, because it led to treachery and disloyalty, as in the case of Satan. Innumerable didactic and theological works on the *seven deadly sins* appeared in the Middle Ages and thousands of sermons were based upon them. The conception of the *seven deadly sins* was so widespread that it permeated the literature of medieval and RENAISSANCE times, its influence appearing not only in the ideas implicit in many literary works but often controlling the very structure, as in the "visions" built around a framework of the seven sins. A few examples of the idea in English literature are: Chaucer's "Parson's Tale" in the *Canterbury Tales; The Vision of Piers the Plowman,* Gower's *Confessio Amantis,* and Spenser's *The Fairie Queene* (Book 1, Canto iv).

The seven sins were matched by seven cardinal virtues: faith, hope, and love (theological and Biblical); and prudence, justice, fortitude, and temperance (adapted from the four cardinal virtues of the Greeks). Seven was, of course, a mystic number, and there were also THE SEVEN ARTS, "the seven ages of the world," "the seven blessings of heaven," "the seven gifts of the Holy Spirit," "the seven joys of Mary in Heaven," "the seven sacraments," "the seven heresies," "the seven points to be asked a dying man," etc.

**Shakespeare, Editors and Editions of:** About half of Shakespeare's plays were printed separately during his lifetime in QUARTO editions, presumably without the author's consent in most cases. Shakespeare was a shareholder in the company which acted his plays, and companies owning acting rights often objected to efforts to sell their plays to the public in printed form while the plays were in their current repertoire. Though there may have been an imperfect effort in 1619, three years after the dramatist's death, to get together a collection of Shakespeare's plays (involving the false dating of certain QUARTOS), the first edition is the famous First Folio (1623) prepared by Shakespeare's friends, the actors John Heminge and Henry Condell. For several reasons the texts of the plays in the First Folio vary greatly in accuracy. Some of them follow QUARTO texts closely, others vary both in length and readings, and there are a good many mistakes—e.g., the printing of one word for another word similar in sound or spelling—so that in many passages we cannot be sure what Shakespeare wrote. There is also reason for thinking that the FOLIO both omits plays which Shakespeare wrote, at least in part (as *Pericles*), and includes some which he possibly had little to do with (see PSEUDO-SHAKESPEAREAN PLAYS). This situation has created a series of problems which have greatly concerned later editors and critics eager to find out as nearly as possible just what Shakespeare wrote. The Second Folio appeared in 1632 and a third in 1663, the third being reissued in 1664 with *Pericles* and six "spurious" plays added. The fourth FOLIO was printed in 1684. These late FOLIOS were only slightly edited.

The first real editor of Shakespeare was Nicholas Rowe, POET LAUREATE. In his editions (1709 and 1714) Rowe made some corrections in the text, modernized the punctuation and spelling, supplied lists of characters and made ACT- and SCENE-divisions for most of the plays (this had been partly done in the FOLIOS), and added stage directions. In 1725 Alexander Pope undertook to make an "authoritative" edition. In fact, however, he did much mischievous tampering with Rowe's text. He "corrected" the METER, emended (by guess largely) difficult passages, placed "degrading" passages at the foot of the page, and placed marks of approval on what he thought to be fine passages. He omitted the seven plays not in the First Folio. Pope's work was followed by a careful edition by Lewis Theobald (1733), who had before exposed some of Pope's pretences and mistakes and made some ingenious emendations. In retaliation Pope made him the chief dunce in the revised edition of his *Dunciad*. In 1744 Sir Thomas Hanmer printed an elegant edition, which followed Pope. William Warburton's edition (1747) was of little value, but in 1765 appeared the famous edition of Samuel Johnson, whose "Preface" and notes have high critical value.

Edward Capell (1768) made the first serious effort to prepare a scientific text based on all the early editions, including QUARTOS. In 1773 appeared the Johnson-Steevens VARIORUM EDITION; this reappeared in 1785 with revisions by Isaac Reed. In 1790 was printed an edition by the important scholar Edward Malone, whose still more extensive "third variorum" edition, published after Malone's death by James Boswell (the younger), came in 1820. Many editions appeared after 1800, only a few of which can be mentioned here. Charles Knight's editions (1838–1844) relied entirely on the First Folio for the texts. John Payne Collier's edition (1844) used the QUARTOS rather slavishly. Collier's desire to provide authority for some of his guesses led him later to forge corrections in an old FOLIO copy. An edition by the German scholar Delius appeared in 1854, and in 1865 was completed the handsome edition of J. O. Halliwell-Phillipps, a scholar whose knowledge of Elizabethan life and literature proved valuable. In 1857 came an excellent edition by Alexander Dyce. The first important American edition, by Richard Grant White, was completed in 1860. The widely used "Cambridge Shakespeare" appeared first from 1863 to 1866 edited by W. G. Clark, J. Glover, and W. A. Wright, and in a revised edition in 1891–1893. This Cambridge edition, done with great care and good judgment, is the "standard" modern text, though the excellent one-volume editions of W. J. Craig (Oxford Shakespeare) and of W. A. Neilson (Students' Cambridge) are widely used, as is that of George Lyman Kittredge (1935). In 1955 the Yale University Press published a facsimile edition of the First Folio, which, although attacked by some critics, has been widely used. Most of the plays have been edited separately in the *New Variorum Shakespeare* (beginning in 1871), by Henry Howard Furness (father and son), which undertakes to give a complete abstract of all earlier efforts to establish a text and of all important Shakespearean criticism.

**Shakespearean Plays, Pseudo-:** See PSEUDO-SHAKESPEAREAN PLAYS.

**Short Measure** (or **Meter**): A STANZA widely used for HYMNS, consisting of four VERSES, riming either *abab* or *abcb*. It usually has the first and third lines in IAMBIC TETRAMETER and the second and fourth in IAMBIC TRIMETER; although occasionally the first, second, and fourth lines are IAMBIC TRIMETER and the third is IAMBIC TETRAMETER. When *short measure* is $a_4b_3c_4b_3$ it is, in fact, a COUPLET in POULTER'S MEASURE.

**Short Story, The:** Stories, in one form or another, have existed throughout all history. Egyptian papyri, dating from 3000 to 4000 B.C., reveal how the sons of Cheops regaled their father with narrative. Some three hundred years before the birth of Christ, we had such Old Testament stories as those of Jonah and of Ruth. Christ spoke in PARABLES. The Greeks and Romans left us EPISODES and INCIDENTS in their early classics. In the Middle Ages the impulse to story-telling manifested itself in FABLES and EPICS about beasts, and in the MEDIEVAL ROMANCE. In England, about 1250, some two hundred well-known TALES were collected in the *Gesta Romanorum*. In the middle of the fourteenth century, Boccaccio assembled a hundred TALES in a book called *The Decameron*. In the same century Chaucer wrote his frame-work collection, *The Canter-*

*bury Tales.* In the fifteenth century Malory, in *Le Morte Darthur,* gathered a series of long narratives recounting the exploits of ancient knighthood. In the eighteenth century came the NOVEL, growing out of the PICARESQUE NOVEL of the sixteenth and seventeenth centuries, both continuing tributes to man's love of narrative and both factors in the development of a formal kind of story-telling. The eighteenth century also saw the development of the INFORMAL ESSAY, which frequently derived some of its interest from such EPISODES and SKETCHES as Addison uses in the "Sir Roger de Coverley papers" or in "The Vision of Mirzah." In the nineteenth century came Sir Walter Scott, Washington Irving, Nathaniel Hawthorne, Edgar Allan Poe, Mérimée and Balzac, Gautier and Musset, Maupassant, Chekhov, and E. T. A. Hoffman. With these writers the *short story* as a distinct literary GENRE came into being.

In view of this long development it seems foolish to name one man as the founder of the *short story* or to credit one nation with its development. A form which comes to us from the ancient past and was known in both the Orient and the Occident, which drew its first breath from oral tradition, and which has existed as a portion of much of man's literary expression in all ages can ultimately be said to have no origin more specific than the inherent creative spirit of man satisfying his desire to tell and to hear stories. Yet in the nineteenth century a group of writers did consciously formulate the *short story* as an art form, notable among them being Hawthorne and Poe in America, Mérimée and Balzac in France, and E. T. A. Hoffman in Germany. This development flowered with such speed and force in America that the modern *short story* is often called an American art form, with only minor exaggeration.

In the early nineteenth century, under the impulse of Poe's persuasive statement in his 1842 review of Hawthorne's *Twice-Told Tales,* critics formulated a definite structure and technique for the *short story*. To this was added around the end of the century the tightly constructed "surprise-ending story" of O. Henry, and the *short story* came to be thought of as corresponding to a "formula," a pattern which is still repeated in endless retellings of its limited variations in the popular *short story* today. Around the turn of the century, however, the impact of REALISM and the advent of NATURALISM joined with the example of Chekhov's "slice of life" stories to force the "formula" open for the serious writer, and such masters of the form as Somerset Maugham and Katherine Mansfield in England and Sherwood Anderson and Ernest Hemingway in America began producing *short stories* of great integrity which reflected the complex formlessness of life itself.

A practical definition of the *short story*, must be broad enough to include the "surprise-ending" story of Maupassant and O. Henry, the tale of unified effect of Poe, the "slice of life" story of Chekhov, Katherine Mansfield, and Sherwood Anderson, and the symbolic and mythic stories that are extremely popular in the LITTLE MAGAZINES today. At the same time, within the breadth which such a statement must have, there should be distinguishing characteristics that set the *short story* off from other PROSE FICTION forms.

A *short story* is a relatively brief fictional narrative in PROSE. It may range in length from the "short-short story" of 500 words up to the "long-short story" of 15,000 to 20,000 words. It may be distinguished from the SKETCH and the TALE in that it has a definite formal development, a freedom from looseness in construction; however, it finds its UNITY in many things other than PLOT, although it often finds it there—in effect, in theme, in character, in TONE, in MOOD, even, on occasion, in STYLE. It may be distinguished from the NOVEL in that it tends to reveal character through a series of actions or under stress, the purpose of the story being accomplished when the reader comes to know what the true nature of a character (or sometimes a SITUATION) is (James Joyce called a *short story* an "epiphany," because of this quality of "revelation"); whereas, the NOVEL tends to show character developing as a result of actions and under the impact of events. This generalization, like every generalization about the *short story* and the NOVEL, grossly overstates its case; yet in a broad sense, it does define a basic difference between the two GENRES.

However natural and formless the *short story* may sometimes give the impression of being, however much it may appear to be the simple setting down of an overheard oral narration, as in Ring Lardner's or Somerset Maugham's stories, or the unadorned report of an action, as in Hemingway's or John O'Hara's, a distinguishing characteristic of the GENRE is that it is consciously *made*, that it reveals itself, upon careful analysis, to be the result of conscious craftsmanship and artistic skill. Furthermore, however slight the *short story* may appear, it consists of more than a mere record of an INCIDENT or an ANECDOTE. It has, or tends to have, a beginning, a middle, and an end; it possesses the rudiments of PLOT, with the conscious STRUCTURE that the possession of PLOT implies.

To be more specific as to form about so protean a GENRE would be to invite error. Although it differs from DRAMA, even from the ONE-ACT PLAY, in not being prepared for dramatic presentation but for reading and from the NOVEL in the attitude it takes toward CHARACTERIZATION, the comments on the nature of DRAMATIC STRUCTURE, of TRAGEDY, of the NOVEL, of CHARACTERIZATION, and of PLOT made elsewhere in this Handbook, apply to the *short story.*

**Sibilants (Sigmatism):** The letters *s, z, j* and such related combinations of letters as *sh, zh,* and *ch* are called *sibilants.* They are mentioned here because of their relation to ASSONANCE and because a too great profusion of *sibilant* sounds constitutes a fault which good writers avoid. On the other hand, for certain effects they have been much used in poetry. Poe, in the "Valley of Unrest," has twenty-seven lines each with its *sibilants,* the whole somehow planned to give an effect of unease:

> Now each visitor shall confess
> The sad valley's restlessness.
> Nothing there is motionless—
> Nothing save the airs that brood
> Over the magic solitude.

Tennyson tried to avoid the too frequent use of *sibilants* and is credited with calling his efforts to rid his verse of them "kicking the geese out of the boat."

**Sigmatism:** See SIBILANTS.

**Signature (in printing):** A letter or figure placed at the foot of the first page of each gathering or section of a book, such a gathering consisting of the pages resulting from a sheet folded to page size and cut; hence the term *signature* is also applied to the gathering itself, or to the sheet after it is folded and ready to be gathered. In early printing the *signature* was often placed on the first, third, fifth, and seventh pages of an OCTAVO gathering (sixteen pages). See BOOK SIZE.

**Silver-Fork School, The:** A name applied in derision to a group of nineteenth-century English novelists who placed a great emphasis upon gentility and matters of etiquette. Among the members of the *Silver-Fork School* were Frances Trollope, Theodore Hook, Lady Blessington, Lady Caroline Lamb, and Benjamin Disraeli.

**Simile:** A figure of speech in which a similarity between two objects is directly expressed, as in Milton's

> *A dungeon horrible,* on all sides round,
> *As one great furnace flamed;*

Here the comparison between the dungeon (Hell) and the great furnace is directly expressed in the *as* which labels the comparison a *simile.* Most *similes* are introduced by *as* or *like.* In the illustration above, the similarity between Hell (the dungeon) and the furnace is based on the great heat of the two. So it is generally with this figure of speech: the comparison of two things essentially unlike, on the basis of a resemblance in one aspect, forms a *simile.* It is, however, no *simile* to say, "My house is like your house," although, of course, comparison does exist. Another way of expressing it is to say that in a *simile* both TENOR and VEHICLE are clearly expressed and are joined by an indicator of resemblance, "like" or "as." See METAPHOR, EPIC SIMILE.

**Sincerity:** A term used in criticism in two distinct senses. In one it reflects the correspondence of the work produced by an author to the ideas and beliefs of the author and thus examines the work in the light of biographical data (see BELIEF, PROBLEM OF). In the other sense, it refers to the integrity with which the work adheres to its own demands, assumptions, and attitudes; if a work has *sincerity,* it restricts the emotions it calls for to those demanded by its actions and actors (see SENTIMENTALITY); it avoids the use of unmotivated actions (see MELODRAMA); it avoids the use of POETIC JUSTICE when the universe it depicts does not contain an order which justifies such a concept. An author may construct the micro-cosmic universe of his story or poem according to any principle he chooses, but, if his work is to meet the test of *sincerity,* having chosen, he must act consistently with that choice.

**Situation:** A term used in the discussion of PLOT to denote (1) a given group of circumstances in which a character finds himself, or (2) the given conditions under which a story opens before the action of the PLOT proper actually begins. Thus, to use *Hamlet* for illustration, the question might be asked, in the first sense, what the proper line of action was for Hamlet when he found himself in the *situation* brought about by the fact that Laertes had challenged him to a duel. In the second, and more technical sense, the *situation* consists of those events which had taken place before the play opens: the murder of Hamlet's father, the incestuous acts of his mother, the general down-at-the-heel condition of the state. In its primary relation to PLOT, then, the *situation* is the group of circumstances in which the character or characters find themselves at the beginning of the dramatic action.

**Skald (Scald):** An ancient Scandinavian poet, especially of the Viking period, corresponding roughly with the Anglo-Saxon SCOP.

**Skeltonic Verse ("Skeltonics" or "Skeltoniads"):** A rollicking form of VERSE employed by the English poet John Skelton (*ca.*1460–1529) consisting of short lines rimed in groups of varying length, intentionally designed to give the effects of unconventionality and lack of dignity which Skelton felt to be a fitting vehicle for his "poetry of revolt." *Skeltonic verse* is felt, especially by a modern reader, to be closely akin to DOGGEREL. Something of its spirit and characteristics, though not its full variety, may be found in the following brief passage from *The Tunnynge of Elynoure Rummynge:*

> But to make up my tale,
> She brueth noppy ale,
> And maketh thereof sale
> To travellers, to tinkers,
> To sweaters, to swinkers,
> And all good ale-drinkers,
> That will nothing spare
> But dryncke till they stare
> And bring themselves bare,
> With now away the mare
> And let us slay Care,
> As wise as an hare.

Much of Skelton's poetry is satirical, and Skelton himself was at outs with the humanists of his day. In his desire to shock, to be novel, and to write in a VERSE form as defiant as was his SATIRE, he plays with this peculiar VERSE form in a fashion that was apparently intentionally irritating to his more formal and orthodox contemporaries. No doubt the conditions attending upon an age of transition had much to do with Skelton's experimentation, but Professor Berdan has pointed out that *Skeltonic verse* has its analogues in French (the *fratrasie*) and in Italian (the *frottola*) and that it derives from a form of medieval Latin VERSE which was associated with the unruly side of university life and which was particularly distasteful to Skelton's humanistic, learned contemporaries. That Skelton deliberately chose the form and developed it for his own particular purposes is evident from the fact that he sometimes, as in his autobiographical and apologetic *Garland of Laurel,* used the conventional RIME ROYAL. *Skeltonic verse* is also called TUMBLING VERSE.

**Sketch:** A brief composition simply constructed and usually most unified in that it presents a single scene, a single character, a single incident. Its simplicity means that it lacks developed PLOT or any very great CHARACTERIZATION. Originally used in the sense of an artist's *sketch* as preliminary groundwork for more developed work, it is now often employed for a finished product of simple proportions, as a *character sketch,* a *vaudeville sketch,* a *descriptive sketch,* etc. See SHORT STORY.

**Slang:** A vernacular speech, not accepted as suitable for formal usage, though much used in conversation and colloquial expression. The purpose behind the origin of all *slang* is that of stating an idea vividly and freshly, though sometimes the expressions themselves are not obvious enough to reveal how this purpose is accomplished. The aptness of *slang* is usually based on its humor, its exaggeration, its onomatopoeic effect, or on a combination of these qualities. Frequently, too, *slang* develops as a short cut, an abbreviated form of expression. And there are, as well, the special terms developing in professions or trades, in sports, in localities, among groups possessing any common interest, and in the underworld.

Collections of *slang* date from the sixteenth century, but there are plenty of instances to show that *slang* expressions developed much earlier than this. François Villon, for instance, introduced much rogue's *argot* in his VERSES of the fifteenth century. *Slang* terms ultimately pass in one of three directions: (1) they die out and are lost unless their vividness is such that (2) they continue as *slang* over a long period and (3) they frequently become accepted good usage. "Skidoo" in the sense of "go away" is an instance of the first; "cove" meaning "a man" is an instance of the second; and "banter" in the sense of "ridicule" is an example of the third. See JARGON.

**Slant Rime:** Approximate or near RIME; usually the substitution of ASSONANCE or CONSONANCE for true RIME. Although *slant rime* is a common device in contemporary poetry, the reader should always be certain that he is dealing with something intended to be an imperfect RIME rather than a mere change in pronunciation with the passage of time or change from one region to another before he assigns the term *slant rime* to what seems to him to be an imperfect RIME.

**Society Verse:** See VERS DE SOCIÉTÉ and OCCASIONAL VERSE.

**Sociological Novel:** A form of the PROBLEM NOVEL which centers its principal attention on the nature, function, and effect of the society in which the characters live and on the social forces playing upon them. Usually the *sociological novel* presents a thesis and argues for it as a resolution to a social problem, but it is by no means always a PROPAGANDA NOVEL. The serious examination of social issues became an important element of FICTION with the INDUSTRIAL REVOLUTION, which centered attention on the condition of the laborer and his family and resulted in such NOVELS as Dickens' *Hard Times,* Kingsley's *Yeast,* and Mrs. Gaskell's *Mary Barton.* George Eliot in *Middlemarch* subjected an entire provincial town to sociological examination. American novelists have always had a serious interest in social issues. Mrs. Stowe's *Uncle Tom's Cabin* explored the conditions and the social status of the Negro, a theme that was to prove of enduring interest as a social problem through such works as G. W. Cable's *The Grandissimes,* and the NOVELS of Richard Wright and Ralph Ellison. The MUCKRAKERS at the turn of the century produced a number of *sociological novels,* the most successful being Upton Sinclair's *The Jungle.* John Steinbeck, John Dos Passos, Erskine Caldwell, and James T. Farrell have all written NOVELS whose central issues were sociological in implication. See PROBLEM NOVEL.

**Sock:** The low-heeled slipper conventionally worn by the comic actor on the ancient stage, hence (figuratively) COMEDY itself. See BUSKIN.

**Socratic:** The "*Socratic* method" in argument or explanation is the use of the question-and-answer formula employed by Socrates in Plato's *Dialogues.* Socrates would feign ignorance of the subject under discussion and then proceed to develop his point by the question-and-answer device. The method of assuming ignorance for the sake of taking advantage of an opponent in debate is known as "*Socratic* irony." This pretense of ignorance on the part of Socrates, who was really regarded as the most intellectual of the group, was referred to as his IRONY by his companions.

**Solecism:** A violation of grammatical structure or IDIOM in speech or writing. "He don't" and "between you and I" are *solecisms*. Loosely any error in DICTION or grammar or propriety is called a *solecism*. Strictly interpreted, however, the term *solescism* is reserved for errors in grammar and idiom and is distinguished from "impropriety," which is employed to indicate the false use of one part of speech for another (as "to suicide" for "to commit suicide"), and from BARBARISM, which is used to indicate words coined from analogies falsely made with other words in good standing (as "preventative" for "preventive").

**Soliloquy:** A speech of a character in a play or other composition delivered while the speaker is alone (*solus*) and calculated to inform the audience or reader of what is passing in the character's mind or to give information concerning other participants in the action which it is essential for the reader to know. Hamlet's famous *soliloquy*, "To be, or not to be," is an obvious example.

**Solution:** A term sometimes employed in place of CATASTROPHE or DÉNOUMENT to indicate the outcome of a piece of FICTION. It is used in the sense that a *solution* is presented for the COMPLICATION which was developed in the PLOT.

**Song:** A LYRIC poem adapted to musical expression. *Song* LYRICS are usually short, simple, sensuous, emotional—perhaps the most spontaneous LYRIC form. Since civilized and barbaric man has always sought emotional outlet through *songs,* either communal or individual, the record of the form extends back into the dim past. *Songs* have been of every type and subject; no satisfactory classification for the various types can be devised. There have been, for instance, a variety of working-songs, dance-songs, love-songs, war-songs, play-songs, drinking-songs, and songs for festivals, church gatherings, and political meetings, as well as a host of others. Perhaps the period in English literature richest in *songs* was the ELIZABETHAN, when Shakespeare gave us such *song* poems as "Who is Sylvia?" and Jonson the famous "Drink to Me Only with Thine Eyes."

**Sonnet:** A LYRIC poem of fourteen lines, highly arbitrary in form, and following one or another of several set RIME conventions. Critics of the *sonnet* have recognized varying classifications, but to all essential purposes two types only need be discussed if the student will understand that each of these two, in turn, has undergone various modifications by experimenters. The two characteristic *sonnet* types are the Italian (Petrarchan) and the English (Shakespearean). The first, the Italian form, is distinguished by its bipartite division into the OCTAVE and the SESTET: the OCTAVE consisting of a first division of eight lines riming *abba abba* and the SESTET, or second division, consisting of six lines riming *cde cde, cdc cdc,* or *cde dce.* On this twofold division of the Italian sonnet Gayley notes: "The octave bears the burden; a doubt, a problem, a reflection, a query, an historical statement, a cry of indignation or desire, a vision of the ideal. The sestet eases the load, resolves the problem or doubt, answers the query, solaces the yearning, realizes the vision." Again it might be said that the OCTAVE presents the narrative, states the proposition or raises a question; the SESTET drives home the narrative by making an abstract comment, applies the proposition, or solves the problem. So much for the strict interpretation of the Italian form; as a matter of fact English poets have varied these items greatly. The OCTAVE and SESTET division is not always kept; the RIME-SCHEME is often varied, but within limits —no Italian *sonnet* properly allowing more than five RIMES. IAMBIC PENTAMETER is essentially the METER, but here again certain poets have experimented with HEXAMETER and other METERS.

The English (Shakespearean) *sonnet,* on the other hand, is so different from the Italian (though it grew from that form) as to permit of a separate classification. Instead of the OCTAVE and SESTET divisions, this *sonnet* type characteristically embodies four divisions: three QUATRAINS (each with a RIME pattern of its own) and a rimed COUPLET. Thus the typical RIME-SCHEME for the English sonnet is *abab cdcd efef gg.* The COUPLET at the end is usually a commentary on the foregoing, an epigrammatic close. The Spenserian *sonnet* combines the Italian and the Shakespearean forms, using three QUATRAINS and a COUPLET but employing linking RIMES between the QUATRAINS, thus *abab bcbc cdcd ee.*

Certain qualities common to the *sonnet* as a type should be noted. Its definite restrictions as to form make it a challenge to the artistry of the poet and call for all the technical skill at the poet's command. The more or less set RIME patterns occurring regularly within the short space of fourteen lines afford a pleasant piquancy to the ear of the reader, and create truly musical effects. The rigidity of the form precludes a too great economy or too great prodigality of words. Emphasis is placed on exactness and perfection of expression. The brevity of the form favors concentrated expression of idea or passion.

The *sonnet* as a form developed in Italy probably in the thirteenth century. Petrarch, in the fourteenth century, raised the *sonnet* to its greatest Italian perfection and so gave it, for English readers, his own name. The form was introduced into England by Thomas Wyatt, who translated Petrarchan *sonnets* and left over thirty examples of his own in English. Surrey, an associate with Wyatt the credit for introducing the form to England and is important as an early modifier of the Italian form. Gradually the Italian *sonnet* pattern (which had proved somewhat too rigid for English poets) was modified and since Shakespeare attained greatest fame for poems of this modified type his name has often been given to the English form. Among the most famous sonneteers in England have been Shakespeare, Milton, Wordsworth, and D. G. Rossetti. Longfellow, Jones Very, G. H. Boker, and E. A. Robinson are generally credited with writing some of the best *sonnets* in America. With the interest in this poetic form, certain poets following the example of Petrarch have written a series of *sonnets* linked one to the other and dealing with some unified subject. Such series are called SONNET SEQUENCES. Some of the most famous SONNET SEQUENCES in English literature are those by Shakespeare (154 in the group), Sidney's *Astrophel and Stella,* Spenser's *Amoretti,* Rossetti's *House of Life,* and Mrs. Browning's *Sonnets from the Portuguese.* William Ellery Leonard, Elinor Wylie, Edna St. Vincent Millay, and W. H. Auden have done distinguished work in the *sonnet* and the SONNET SEQUENCE in this century.

**Sonnet Sequence:** See SONNET.

**Source:** The person, manuscript, or book from which information is derived. If such a person, manuscript or book represents a direct and immediate acquaintance with the information—a person with firsthand experience, a book which is itself the subject of the discussion, a manuscript written at the time or on the scene—the *source* is called a "primary" *source.* If the person, book, or manuscript represents an indirect acquaintance with the information—

the person recounting experience at second- or third-hand, the book being about the book under discussion, the manuscript being a copy or a summary of primary material—the *source* is called a "secondary" *source*. The term *source* is also used to designate the origin of literary works, philosophical ideas, or artistic forms. In this sense, Lodge's *Rosalynde* is a *source* for Shakespeare's *As You Like It,* since the dramatist took his PLOT in part from the prose IDYL.

**Spasmodic School:** A phrase applied by W. E. Aytoun in 1854 to a group of English poets who wrote in the 1840's and 1850's. The spirit of the VERSE (influenced by Shelley and Byron) reflected discontent and unrest, while its style was marked by jerkiness and forced or strained EMPHASIS. In his poem "America" (1855) Sydney Dobell in addressing "Columbia" alludes to the typical early English progenitor of Americans as "thy satchelled ancestor." Belonging to the group, besides Dobell, were Alexander Smith, P. J. Bailey, George Gilfillan, and other minor writers. The general *spasmodic* tendency is said also to appear in the early verse of Robert Browning and Elizabeth Barrett Browning, and in Tennyson's *Maud.*

**Specific Words:** See GENERAL TERMS.

**Spenserian Stanza:** A stanzaic pattern consisting of nine VERSES, the first eight being IAMBIC PENTAMETER, the ninth an IAMBIC HEXAMETER. The RIME-SCHEME is *ababbcbcc.* (See SCANSION.) The form derives its name from Edmund Spenser, who created the pattern for *The Faerie Queene,* from which the first stanza of Canto I is cited as an example:

> A Gentle Knight was pricking on the plaine,
> Y-cladd in mightie armes and silver shielde,
> Wherein old dints of deepe wounds did remaine,
> The cruell markes of many' a bloudy fielde;
> Yet armes till that time did he never wield:
> His angry steede did chide his foming bitt,
> As much disdayning to the curbe to yield:
> Full jolly knight he seemd, and faire did sitt,
> As one for knightly giusts and fierce encounters fitt.

This stanzaic form is notable for two qualities: the method of "tying-in" the three RIMES promotes unity of effect and tightness of thought; the ALEXANDRINE at the close adds dignity to the sweep of the form and, at the same time, affords an opportunity for summary and epigrammatic expression which permits the line to knit up the thought of the whole STANZA. Other poets than Spenser have made notable use of the form. Burns used the *Spenserian stanza* in *The Cotter's Saturday Night*, Shelley in *The Revolt of Islam* and in *Adonais;* Keats used it in *The Eve of St. Agnes*, and Byron in *Childe Harold*.

**Spondee:** A FOOT composed of two accented syllables (——— ———). The form is rare in English VERSE, since most of our polysyllabic words carry a primary ACCENT. *Spondees* in our poetry are usually composed of two monosyllabic words as *all joy!* Poe in writing of the subject found only three or four instances (one of which was *football*) in English where real *spondees* occurred in a single word. Untermeyer finds a longer list (really compounds composed of monosyllabic words) and cites *heartbreak, childhood, bright-eyed, bookcase, wineglass*, and *Mayday*. In Milton's line:

> Silence, ye troubled waves, and thou deep, peace!

"deep, peace" presents a perfect spondaic FOOT.

**Spoonerism:** An accidental interchange of sounds, usually the initial ones, in two or more words, such as *bl*ushing *cr*ow for *cr*ushing *bl*ow or well-*b*oiled icicle for well-oiled *b*icycle. The term owes its name to Dr. W. A. Spooner, of New College, Oxford, who was inordinately guilty of such transpositions.

**Sprung Rhythm:** A term coined by Gerard Manley Hopkins to designate the METER of poetry whose RHYTHM is based on the number of stressed syllables in a VERSE without regard to the number of unstressed syllables. Put another way, *sprung rhythm* may be said to designate the METER of a VERSE which contains feet of varying numbers of syllables, with the first syllable accented in each case. The feet possible are the monosyllabic (a single stressed syllable), the TROCHEE, the DACTYL, and the first PÆON: ——— | ——— ∪ | ——— ∪ ∪ | ——— ∪ ∪ ∪. The obvious result of a line composed of combinations of such varying feet is extreme metrical irregularity. The SCANSION of such poetry is, as W. B. Yeats noted, difficult because "it may not be certain at first glance where the stress falls." The following lines from Hopkins' "The Starlight Night" indicate both the effect of *sprung rhythm* and the difficulty of scanning it:

> Look at the ʲstars! ǀlook,ʲ look up at theʲskies!
> Oˇ look at all theʲfire-folkʲsitting in theʲair!
> Theʲbrightʲborough, theʲcircle-citadelsʲthere!
> Down inʲdim woods theʲdiamondʲdelves! theʲelves'-eyes!

(Note that a FOOT may continue to the beginning of the next line.) This passage, the opening lines of a SONNET, is clearly PENTAMETER, but of an indeterminable type of FOOT.

Hopkins said that he used *sprung rhythm* because "it is nearest to the rhythm of prose, that is the native and natural rhythm of speech," and he cited as earlier users the author of *Piers Plowman,* the CHORUS in Milton's *Samson Agonistes,* and old nursery rimes. See PROSE RHYTHM, ACCENT, METER, OLD ENGLISH VERSIFICATION.

**Stanza:** A recurrent grouping of two or more lines of a poem in terms of length, metrical form, and, often, RIME-SCHEME. However, the division into *stanzas* is sometimes made according to *thought* as well as form, in which case the *stanza* is a unit not unlike a paragraph of prose. STROPHE is another term used for *stanza,* but one should avoid VERSE in this sense, since VERSE is properly reserved to indicate a single line of poetry. Some of the more common stanzaic forms are COUPLET, TERCET, QUATRAIN, RIME ROYAL, OTTAVA RIMA, and the SPENSERIAN STANZA, all of which are discussed in their proper places.

**Static Character:** A character in the NOVEL, the SHORT STORY, or the DRAMA who changes little if at all in the progress of the action. Things happen to *static characters* without modifying their interior selves; the pattern of action reveals characters as they are without showing them in the process of development. See CHARACTERIZATION.

**Stave:** A STANZA, particularly of a poem intended to be sung.

**-stich:** A stem word meaning "line," as in HEMISTICH, a half line, or DISTICH, a couplet.

**Stichomythia:** A form of REPARTEE developed in classical DRAMA and often employed by Elizabethan writers, especially in plays which imitated the SENECAN TRAGEDIES. It is a sort of line-for-line "verbal fencing match" in which the principals in the DIALOGUE retort sharply to each other in lines which echo the opponent's words and FIGURES OF SPEECH. ANTITHESIS is freely used. The thought is often sententious. A few lines quoted from Hamlet's interview with his mother in the scene where Polonius is killed will serve as an instance of *stichomythia:*

> *Hamlet:* Now, mother, what's the matter?
> *Queen:* Hamlet, thou hast thy father much offended.
> *Hamlet:* Mother, you have my father much offended.
> *Queen:* Come, come, you answer with an idle tongue.
> *Hamlet:* Go, go, you question with a wicked tongue.

A more sustained example is found in the interview between King Richard and Queen Elizabeth in *King Richard III* (IV, iv, 343 ff.).

**Stock Characters:** Conventional character types belonging by custom to given forms of literature. Thus a boisterous character known as the Vice came to be expected in a MORALITY play. The Elizabethan REVENGE TRAGEDY commonly employed, among other *stock characters,* a high-thinking vengeance-seeking HERO (Hamlet), the ghost of a murdered father or son, and a scheming murderer-villain (Claudius). In Elizabethan dramatic tradition in general one may expect such stock figures as a disguised romantic heroine (Portia), a melancholy man (Jacques), a loquacious old counsellor (Polonius), a female servant-confidante (Nerissa), a court fool (Feste), a witty clownish servant (Launcelot Gobbo). In fairy tales the cruel stepmother and prince charming are examples. In the SENTIMENTAL NOVEL one expects a fainting heroine. So every type of fictional literature—NOVELS, ROMANCES, DETECTIVE TALES, moving pictures, the various kinds of COMEDIES and TRAGEDIES, METRICAL ROMANCES—tends to develop *stock characters* whose conventional nature a reader does well to recognize so that he can distinguish between the individual, personal characteristics of a given character and the conventional traits drawn from the tradition of the *stock character* represented. See further under various types of literature, such as COMEDY OF HUMOURS, PICA-RESQUE NOVEL.

**Stock Response:** The traditional, conventional response to literature or art; poor artists and writers, like the preparers of advertising copy, call for *stock responses* by the use of STOCK CHARACTERS, STOCK SITUATIONS, and traditional symbols and standardized attitudes, such as the flag, mother love, etc. Such materials have a "built-in" response for the unsophisticated reader. The serious artists and writers, however, attempt to provide sound grounds for the desired responses within the work itself. See SINCERITY.

**Stock Situation:** A SITUATION recurring frequently in a literary form, whether it be a general PLOT SITUATION, such as boy-meets-girl or rags-to-riches, or a recurrent detail, such as mixed identity or birthmarks that betray kinship. Note, however, that certain fundamental SITUATIONS, such as the search for a father, death and rebirth, the Oedipus attachment, and the loss of Paradise are more nearly archetypal patterns than *stock situations*, since they seem to echo recurrent human views of our life and its meaning. See ARCHETYPE.

**Storm and Stress:** See STURM UND DRANG.

**Stream-of-Consciousness Novel, The:** The type of PSYCHOLOGICAL NOVEL which takes as its subject matter the uninterrupted, uneven, and endless flow of consciousness of one or more of its characters. By consciousness in this context is meant the total range of awareness and emotive-mental response of an individual, from the lowest pre-speech level to the highest fully articulated level of rational thought. The assumption is that in the mind of an individual at a given moment his *stream of consciousness* (the phrase originated in this sense with William James) is a mixture of all the levels of awareness, an unending flow of sensations, thoughts, memories, associations, and reflections; if the exact content of the mind ("consciousness") is to be described at any moment, then these varied, disjointed, and illogical elements must find expression in a flow of words, images, and ideas similar to the unorganized flow of the mind. The *stream-of-consciousness novel* uses varied techniques to represent this consciousness adequately. In general, most PSYCHOLOGICAL NOVELS report the flow of conscious and ordered intelligence, as in Henry James, or the flow of memory recalled by association, as in Marcel Proust; but the *stream-of-consciousness novel* tends to concentrate its attention chiefly on the pre-speech, non-verbalized level, where the IMAGE must express the unarticulated response and where the logic of grammar belongs to another world. However differing the techniques employed, the writers of the *stream-of-consciousness novel* seem to share certain common assumptions: (1) that the significant existence of man is to be found in his mental-emotional processes and not in the outside world, (2) that this mental-emotional life is disjointed, illogical, and (3) that a pattern of free psychological association rather than of logical relationship determines the shifting sequence of thought and feeling.

Attempts to concentrate the subject matter of FICTION on the inner consciousness are not new by any means. The earliest impressive example seems to be Laurence Sterne's *Tristram Shandy* (1759–1767), with its motto from Epictetus: "It is not actions, but opinions about actions, which disturb men," and with its application of Locke's psychological theories of association and duration to the functioning of the human mind. Yet Sterne, although he freed the sequence of thought from the rigors of logical organization, did not get beneath the speech level in his portrait of Tristram's consciousness. Henry James, in his PSYCHOLOGICAL NOVELS, too, remained on a consciously articulated level. In a major sense, the present-day *stream-of-consciousness novel* is a product of Freudian psychology with its structure of psychological levels, although it first appeared in *Les lauriers sont coupés,* by Edouard Dujardin, in 1887, where the INTERIOR MONOLOGUE was used for the first time in the modern sense. Other important users of the INTERIOR MONOLOGUE to create reports on the *stream-of-consciousness* have been Dorothy Richardson, Virginia Woolf, James Joyce, William Faulkner. The tendency today is to see the *stream-of-consciousness* subject matter and the INTERIOR MONOLOGUE technique as tools to be used in the presentation of character in depth, but not as the exclusive subjects or methods of whole NOVELS. See PSYCHOLOGICAL NOVEL, INTERIOR MONOLOGUE.

**Stress:** The EMPHASIS given a syllable or word in rhythmic writing. See ACCENT, ARSIS, ICTUS, SCANSION, METER.

**Strophe:** A STANZA. In the PINDARIC ODE (see ODE) the *strophe* signifies particularly the first STANZA, and every subsequent third STANZA—i.e., the fourth, seventh, etc.

**Structure:** The planned framework of a piece of literature. Though such external matters as kind of language used (French or English, PROSE or VERSE, or kind of VERSE, or type of sentence) are sometimes referred to as "structural" features, the term usually is applied to the general plan or outline. Thus the scheme of topics (as revealed in a topical outline) determines the *structure* of a FORMAL ESSAY. The logical division of the action of a DRAMA (see DRAMATIC STRUCTURE) and also the mechanical division into ACTS and SCENES are matters of *structure*. In a narrative the PLOT itself is the structural element. Groups of stories may be set in a larger structural plan (see FRAME STORY) such as the pilgrimage in Chaucer's *Canterbury Tales*. The *structure* of an Italian SONNET suggests first its division into OCTAVE and SESTET, and more minutely the internal plan of each of these two parts. A PINDARIC ODE follows a special structural plan which determines not only the development of the theme but the sequence of stanzaic forms. Often the author advertises his *structure* as a means of securing clearness (as in some college textbooks), while at other times the artistic purpose of the author leads him to conceal his *structure* (as in narratives) or subordinate it altogether (as in some INFORMAL ESSAYS). In the NOVEL, the SHORT STORY, and the DRAMA, the *structure* is generally regarded today as the most reliable as well as the most revealing key to the meaning of the work. In the contemporary criticism of poetry, too, *structure* is used to define not only VERSE form and formal arrangement but also the sequence of IMAGES and ideas which unite to convey the meaning of the poem.

**Sturm und Drang** (**Storm and Stress**): The name given a literary movement important in Germany during the last quarter of the eighteenth century. The movement derives its name from the title of a drama, *Sturm und Drang* (1776) by Klinger, although Goethe's *Götz von Berlichingen* was probably the most significant single literary production of the group. Goethe's *Werthers Leiden* (a novel) reflects the *Strum und Drang* attitude as does Schiller's *Die Räuber* (1781). The real founder and pioneer of the movement was Herder (1744–1803). Other leaders were Lenz, Wagner, and Müller. The DRAMA was much used as a medium of expression and the dramatists themselves were greatly influenced by the power of Shakespeare and the freedom of the English playwright from classical standards. In essence the *Sturm und Drang* movement was a revolt from classical conventions and, particularly, an expression of dissatisfaction with the tenets of French CLASSICISM. The writing was imbued with a strong nationalistic and folk element, was characterized by fervor and enthusiasm, a restless turbulency of spirit, the portrayal of great passion, a reliance upon emotional experiences and spiritual struggles and was intensely personal. The writers were more interested in character than in PLOT or in literary form.

Style: The arrangement of words in a manner which at once best expresses the individuality of the author and the idea and intent in his mind. The best *style*, for any given purpose, is that which most nearly approximates a perfect adaptation of one's language to one's ideas. In a perfect world, it is perhaps true that each speaker or writer would find expression in words which would exactly present the idea in his mind and would carry with them the exact personality of the author; but this side of paradise all that authors can do is to labor to achieve that end as closely as human limitations will permit.

*Style*, then, is a combination of two elements: the idea to be expressed, and the individuality of the author. It is, as Lowell said, "the establishment of a perfect mutual understanding between the worker and his material." From this point of view it is impossible to change the DICTION or to alter the phrasing of a statement and thus to say exactly the same thing; for what the reader receives from a statement is not alone what is said, but also certain connotations which affect his consciousness from the manner in which the statement is made. And from this it follows that, just as no two personalities are alike, no two *styles* are actually alike.

There are, in fact, many *styles*. The critic is fond of categories and fixes a label to a Milton, a Lyly, a Pope; gives a name to a *style* and calls it ornamental, forceful, poetic, or what-not, in the conviction perhaps that he has described the *style* of a writer when all he has done has been to place him in a group with many others who have written ornate or forceful or poetic prose. A mere recital of some of these categories may, however, be suggestive of the infinite range of manners the one word *style* covers. We speak, for instance, of journalistic, scientific, or literary *styles;* we call the manners of other writers ABSTRACT or CONCRETE, rhythmic or pedestrian, sincere or artificial, dignified or comic, original or imitative, dull or vivid, as though each of these was somehow a final category of its own. But, if we are actually to estimate a *style*, we need more delicate tests than these; we need terms which will be so final in their sensitiveness as ultimately to distinguish the work of each writer from that of all other writers, since, as has been said, in the last analysis no two *styles* are exactly comparable.

A study of *styles* for the purpose of analysis will include, in addition to the infinity of personal detail suggested above, such general qualities as: DICTION, sentence structure and variety, IMAGERY, RHYTHM, COHERENCE, EMPHASIS, and *arrangement of ideas*.

**Subject Bibliography:** A list of books, articles, manuscripts or other forms of writing, either complete or selected on any of various principles, on one specific subject. See BIBLIOGRAPHY.

**Subjective:** A term frequently used in criticism to denote writing which is expressive in an intensely personal manner of the inner convictions, beliefs, dreams, or ideals of the author. *Subjective* writing is, of course, opposed to objective writing, which is impersonal, CONCRETE, and concerned largely with narrative, analysis, or the description of externalities. One might, for instance, speak of the *subjective* element in Shakespeare's SONNETS and of the objective qualities of *The Rape of Lucrece;* the first tells of Shakespeare's reflective spirit; the second retells an old Roman story.

Another way of seeing the distinction between *subjective* and objective is to associate *subjective* with the seer of an object or the reporter of it and objective with the object seen or reported. If the emphasis is upon the response of the reporter, the work is *subjective;* if it is upon the object reported, the work is objective. It should be noted that *subjective* may be used in two distinct senses, just as the reporter has two possible distinct relationships with the author. *Subjective,* in one sense, may refer to the presence in the work of events and emotions that are autobiographical (the reporter speaks the author's personal responses, as the character Eugene Gant speaks Thomas Wolfe's). In the other sense, *subjective* may refer to the recounting of an emotional response by a reporter who is a dramatically realized character, assumed to be feeling emotions peculiar to the dramatic situation and not necessarily those of the author, as the NARRATOR Ishmael speaks dramatically rather than autobiographically in Melville's *Moby-Dick*. By present-day critical standards the first kind of subjectivity is suspect, the second admirable. See OBJECTIVITY, NEGATIVE CAPABILITY, OBJECTIVE CORRELATIVE, AESTHETIC DISTANCE.

**Subplot:** A subordinate or minor COMPLICATION running through a piece of FICTION. This secondary PLOT interest, if skillfully handled, has a direct relationship to the main PLOT, contributing to it in interest and in COMPLICATION and struggle. (See PLOT.) Some writers—particularly English and American authors—have carried the intricacies and surprises of PLOT relationships so far as to create not only one, but sometimes three or four—or more—*subplots*. The characteristic difference, it has been observed, between the FICTION of France, Italy—the romance countries in general—and the FICTION of the Anglo-Saxons is that the romance authors are generally satisfied with simple, unified PLOT relationships, whereas northern writers are more given to an intricate series of *subplots* supporting and complicating the major PLOT. There are said to be seventy-five characters in Dickens' *Our Mutual Friend* and sixty in Thackeray's *Vanity Fair*. (Bliss Perry.) When so many people are introduced into a work of FICTION it is obvious that their relationship to the chief characters of the main PLOT must shade off into very subordinate *subplots*. As instances of *subplots* in Shakespeare may be cited from *Hamlet* the Laertes-Hamlet struggle (as subordinate to the Claudius-Hamlet major PLOT), and from *The Merchant of Venice* the love interest of the Jessica-Lorenzo story (as subordinate to the Portia-Bassanio PLOT). It may be observed that writers use *subplots* of at least two different degrees: first, those which are directly related to, and which give impetus and action to, the main PLOT; and second, those which are more or less extraneous to the chief PLOT interest and which are introduced frankly as a secondary story to give zest and EMPHASIS, or relief, to the main PLOT.

**Substitution:** In PROSODY, a term used to describe the use of one kind of FOOT in place of the one normally demanded by the METER of a VERSE, as a TROCHEE for an IAMB or a DACTYL or ANAPEST for a TROCHEE or IAMB. See COMPENSATION.

**Surrealism:** A movement in art and literature emphasizing the expression of the imagination as realized in dreams and presented without conscious control. It developed in France under the leadership of André Breton, whose *Manifeste du surréalisme* appeared in 1924. *Surrealism* is often regarded as an outgrowth of DADA, although it has discernible roots reaching back to Baudelaire and Rimbaud, and it demonstrates the marked influence of Freud. As a literary movement it has been confined almost entirely to France, but as a movement in modern art it has had many followers, among them Dali, Miró, Duchamp, and Max Ernst. See DADA.

**Suspense:** The poised anticipation of the reader or audience as to the outcome of the events of a SHORT STORY, a NOVEL, or a DRAMA, particularly as these events affect a character in the work for whom the reader or audience has formed a sympathetic attachment. *Suspense* is a major device for the securing and maintaining of interest in all forms of FICTION. It may be either of two major types: in one, the outcome is uncertain and the *suspense* resides in the question of who or what or how; in the other, the outcome is inevitable from the events which have gone before (see DRAMATIC IRONY) and the *suspense* resides in the audience's frightened anticipation, in the question of when.

**"Sweetness and Light":** A phrase given great popularity by Matthew Arnold, who used it as the title for the first chapter of *Culture and Anarchy* (1869). Arnold did not create the term but borrowed it from Swift's *The Battle of the Books*, where Swift, in recounting the APOLOGUE of the Spider and the Bee, summarized the argument relating to the superiority of ancient over modern authors (see ANCIENTS AND MODERNS, QUARREL OF) in these words: "Instead of dirt and poison we have rather chose to fill our hives with honey and wax, thus furnishing mankind with the two noblest of things, which are sweetness and light." These two "noblest of things," as Arnold uses the term, are *beauty* and *intelligence*—and it is to these two qualities that "sweetness and light" refers.

**Syllabus:** An outline or abstract containing the major heads of a book, a course of lectures, an ARGUMENT, program of study. A digest of the chief "points" of a larger work.

**Syllepsis:** See ZEUGMA.

**Syllogism:** A formula for presenting an argument logically. The *syllogism* affords a method of demonstrating the logic of an argument through analysis. It consists of three divisions, a major premise, a minor premise, and a conclusion.

> *Major premise:* All public libraries should serve the people.
> *Minor premise:* This is a public library.
> *Conclusion:* Therefore this library should serve the people.

There are, it is to be noticed, three terms as well as three divisions to the *syllogism*. In the major premise "should serve the people" is the "major term"; in the minor premise "this (library)" is the "minor term"; and the term appearing in both the major and the minor premise, "public library," is called the "middle term."

**Symbol:** On the most literal level, a *symbol* is something which is itself and yet stands for or suggests or means something else; as the letters *a p p l e* form a word which stands for a particular objective reality; or as a flag is a piece of colored cloth which stands for a nation. All language is symbolic in this sense, and many of the objects which we commonly use in daily life are.

In a literary sense, a *symbol* is a TROPE which combines a literal and sensuous quality with an abstract or suggestive aspect, a definition which also applies to the function of the flag as *symbol*. However, in criticism it is necessary to distinguish *symbol* from IMAGE, ALLEGORY, and METAPHOR. If we consider an IMAGE to have a concrete referent in the objective world and to function as IMAGE when it powerfully evokes that referent, then a *symbol* is like an IMAGE in doing the same thing but different from it in going beyond the evoking of the objective referent by making that referent suggest to the reader or audience a meaning beyond itself; in other words, a *symbol* is an IMAGE which evokes an objective, concrete reality and has that reality suggest another level of meaning. However, the *symbol* does not "stand for" the meaning; it evokes an object which suggests the meaning. As Coleridge said, "It partakes of the reality which it renders intelligible." *Symbol* differs from ALLEGORY in that in ALLEGORY the objective referent evoked is without value until it is translated into the fixed meaning that it has in its own particular structure of ideas (see ALLEGORY), whereas a *symbol* has permanent objective value, independent of the meanings which it may suggest. It differs from METAPHOR in that a METAPHOR evokes an object in order to illustrate an idea or demonstrate a quality, whereas a *symbol* embodies the idea or the quality. As W. M. Urban said, "The metaphor becomes a symbol when by means of it we embody an ideal content not otherwise expressible"

Literary *symbols* are of two broad types: one includes those which embody within themselves universal suggestions of meaning, as the ocean and land suggest time and eternity, the voyage suggests life, and phallic *symbols* are universally recognized. Such *symbols* are used widely (and sometimes unconsciously) in the world's literature. The other type of *symbol* secures its suggestiveness not from qualities inherent in itself but from the way in which it is used in a given work. Thus in *Moby-Dick* the voyage, the land, the ocean—these objects are pregnant with meanings that seem almost independent of Melville's use of them in his story; on the other hand, the white whale is invested with meaning—and differing meanings for different crew members—through the handling of materials in the novel. Similarly, in Hemingway's *A Farewell to Arms*, rain, which is merely a physical fact in the opening chapter, is converted into a *symbol* of death through the uses to which it is put in the book. See ALLEGORY, IMAGE, IMAGERY, METAPHOR, SIMILE, TROPE.

**Symbolism:** In its broad sense, *symbolism* is the use of one object to represent or suggest another; or, in literature, the use of SYMBOLS in writing, particularly the serious and extensive use of such SYMBOLS.

*Symbolism* is also the name given to a literary movement which originated in France in the last half of the nineteenth century, strongly influenced Irish and British writing around the turn of the century, and has been a dominant force in much British and American poetry in the twentieth century. This *symbolism* represents one of the romantic reactions to REALISM. It sees the immediate, unique, and personal emotional response as the proper subject of art, and its full expression as the ultimate aim of art. Since the emotions experienced by a poet in a given moment are unique to that person and that moment and are finally both fleeting and incommunicable, the poet is reduced to the use of a complex and highly private kind of symbolization in an effort to give expression to his ineffable feeling. The result is a kind of writing consisting of what Edmund Wilson has called "a medley of metaphor" in which SYMBOLS lacking apparent logical relation are put together in a pattern, one of whose characteristics is an indefiniteness as great as the indefiniteness of the experience itself and another of whose characteristics is the conscious effort to use words for their musical effect, without very much attention to precise meaning. As Baudelaire, one of the principal forerunners of the movement, said, man lives in a "forest of symbols" which results from the fact that the materiality and individuality of the physical world dissolves into the "dark and confused unity" of the unseen world. In this process SYNAESTHESIA takes place. Baudelaire and the later symbolists, particularly Mallarmé and Valéry, were greatly influenced by the theory and poetic practice of Edgar Allan Poe. Other important French writers in the movement were Rimbaud, Verlaine, Leforgue, Rémy de Gourmont, and Claudel, and Maeterlinck in the DRAMA and Huysman in the NOVEL. The Irish writers of this century, particularly Yeats in POETRY, Synge in the DRAMA, and Joyce in the NOVEL, have been notably responsive to the movement. In Germany Rilke and Stefan George have functioned as symbolist poets. In America the IMAGIST poets reflected the movement, as did Eugene O'Neill in the DRAMA. Through its pervasive influence on T. S. Eliot, *symbolism* has affected much of the best British and American poetry in our time.

**Symposium:** A Greek word meaning "a drinking together" or banquet. As such convivial meetings were characterized by free conversation, the word later came to mean discussion by different persons of a single topic, or a collection of speeches or ESSAYS on a given subject. One of Plato's best known DIALOGUES is *The Symposium* and later literary uses of the word are much under its influence, as is G. Lowes Dickinson's *A Modern Symposium*.

**Symposium Club:** See TRANSCENDENTAL CLUB, TRANSCENDENTALISM.

**Synaesthesia:** The concurrent response of two or more of the senses to the stimulation of one. The term is applied in literature to the description of one kind of sensation in terms of another—that is, the description of sounds in terms of colors, as a "blue note," of colors in terms of temperature, as a "cool green," etc. Poe employed *synaesthesia* often; Baudelaire gave it wide currency through his practice and particularly his sonnet, "Correspondances," and it is one of the most distinctive characteristics of the poetry of the SYMBOLISM movement. Dame Edith Sitwell employs it as a major poetic device.

**Syncopation:** A term used in music to describe the effect produced by a temporary displacing or shifting of the regular metrical accent. In PROSODY it is used to describe the effect produced by SUBSTITUTION and also the effect produced when the METRICAL ACCENT and the RHETORICAL ACCENT differ sufficiently in a VERSE to create the effect of two different metrical patterns existing concurrently in the line.

**Syncope:** A cutting short of words through the omission of a letter or a syllable. *Syncope* is distinguished from ELISION in that it is usually confined to omissions of letters (usually vowels) within the word, whereas ELISION usually runs two words together by the omission of a final or initial letter. *Ev'ry* for *every* is an example of *syncope*. Naturally the greatest use for this omission of sounds is in VERSE where a desired metrical effect is sought. However, *syncope* has taken place frequently in English simply to shorten words, as *pacificist* has become *pacifist*.

**Synecdoche:** A form of METAPHOR which in mentioning a part signifies the whole or the whole signifies the part. In order to be clear, a good *synecdoche* must be based on an *important* part of the whole and not a minor part and, usually, the part selected to stand for the whole must be the part most directly associated with the subject under discussion. Thus under the first restriction we say *motor* for automobile (rather than *tire*), and under the second we speak of infantry on the march as *foot* rather than as *hands* just as we use *hands* rather than *foot* for men who are at work at manual labor.

**Synonyms:** Words in the same language with the same or similar meanings. Rarely in English are two words exact *synonyms* although it may happen that in a single sentence any one of two or three words may serve the desired purpose. Conventional usage has given most of our words certain associations and CONNOTATIONS, certain idiomatic connections, which make impossible a free substituting of one for another. As one commentator has pointed out *humble* and *lowly* may appear synonymous, but no one yet has signed a letter "your *lowly* servant." The presence of so many romance words in English has enriched the language by offering choice between Old English and romance forms—*help* and *assist* for example.

**Synopsis:** A summary, a résumé of the main points of a composition or argument so made as to show the relationship of each part to the whole. An abstract. A *synopsis* is usually more connected than an outline since it is likely to be given in complete sentences.

**Syzygy:** In classical PROSODY, a term used to designate two coupled feet serving as a unit. As used by Sidney Lanier and later prosodists, it refers to the use of consonant sounds at the end of one word and at the beginning of another that can be spoken together easily and harmoniously. Both Poe and Lanier were greatly concerned with *syzygy*.

**Tail-rime Romance:** A term applied to METRICAL ROMANCES employing the TAIL-RIME STANZA, especially the large group, including *Amis and Amiloun, Athelston, Horn Child* (and some twenty others), which employed a TAIL-RIME STANZA of twelve lines made up of four groups or parts, each with a short "tail" line, such as aa*b* aa*b* cc*b* dd*b*. There existed a "school" of minstrels writing *tail-rime romances* in East Anglia in the fourteenth century.

**Tail-rime Stanza:** A STANZA of VERSE containing among longer lines two or more short lines which RIME with each other and serve as "tails" to the divisions or parts of the STANZA. The form developed in medieval times and is known in French as *rime couée*. Chaucer's "Rime of Sir Thopas" in the *Canterbury Tales* is written in *tail-rime stanza*.

**Tale:** A simple narrative in PROSE or VERSE without complicated PLOT. Formerly no very real distinction was made between the *tale* and the SHORT STORY; the two terms were used interchangeably. *Tale*, however, has always been a more general term than SHORT STORY since the latter has been reserved for narrative following a fairly technical routine and the former has been loosely used to denote any short narrative, either true or fictitious.

**Tall-tale:** A kind of humorous TALE common on the American frontier, which uses realistic detail, a literal manner, and common speech to recount extravagantly impossible happenings, usually resulting from the superhuman abilities of a character. The TALES about Paul Bunyan, Mike Fink, and Davy Crockett are typical frontier *tall-tales*. The German *Adventures of Baron Munchausen* is, perhaps, the best known literary use of the *tall-tale*.

**Tanka:** A type of Japanese poetry similar to the HAIKU. It consists of thirty-one syllables, arranged in five lines, each of seven syllables, except the first and third, which are each of five. See HAIKU.

**Taste:** A term used in criticism to designate the basis for the personal acceptance or rejection of a work of art as producing pleasure or pain in its reader, hearer, or viewer. Perhaps no critical term remains, despite all efforts at analysis, more purely subjective than does *taste*. However, as it is commonly used, it does have two distinct meanings: it may refer to the mere condition of liking or disliking an object, in which case it may be deplored but not debated ("There is no accounting for taste." "Each to his own taste." *"De gustibus non est disputandum."*); on the other hand, it may refer to the ability to discern the beautiful and to appreciate it, in which case *taste* is capable of being educated and is subject to examination in terms of its operating principles. T. S. Eliot has such a view of *taste* when he sees one of the functions of criticism to be "the correction of taste," and so had Addison when he said that *taste* "discerns the Beauties of an Author with Pleasure, and the Imperfections with Dislike." *Taste* in the first sense is used to describe a purely impressionistic response, as in the criticism of Croce; in the second sense it designates a kind of aesthetic judgment, as it does with Eliot. In the latter case, *taste* becomes a sense of what is harmonious, appropriate, or beautiful, a kind of critical tact, and as such it designates a quality essential to the artist, the critic, and the serious student.

**Tautology:** The use of superfluous, repetitious words. "He wrote an autobiography of his life" might much better be stated "He wrote an autobiography." *Tautology* differs from the kinds of REPETITION used for clarity, EMPHASIS, or effect, in that it repeats the idea without the addition of forcefulness or clearness to the expression.

**Telestich:** See ACROSTIC.

**Tenor** and **Vehicle:** Terms used by I. A. Richards for the two essential elements of a METAPHOR. The *tenor* is the discourse or subject which the *vehicle* illustrates or illuminates; or, stated another way, the *vehicle* is the figure that carries the weight of the comparison, while the *tenor* is the subject to which the *vehicle* refers. According to Richards' definition, a METAPHOR always involves two ideas—*tenor* and *vehicle*. If it is impossible to distinguish them, we are dealing with a literal statement; if we can distinguish them, even slightly, we are dealing with a metaphoric expression. Hamlet's question, "What should such fellows as I do crawling between earth and heaven?" is metaphoric. While Hamlet may literally crawl, there is, as Richards points out, "an unmistakable reference to other

things that crawl . . . and this reference is the *vehicle* as Hamlet
. . . is the *tenor*." See METAPHOR.

**Tension:** A term introduced into contemporary criticism by Allen
Tate, by which he means the integral UNITY of a poem, a UNITY
which results from the successful resolution in the work of the conflicts of abstraction and concreteness, of general and particular, of
DENOTATION and CONNOTATION. The term results from removing
the prefixes from two terms in logic: *intension*, which refers to the
abstract attributes of objects which can properly be named by a
word; and *extension*, which refers to the specific object named by
the word. Good poetry, Tate asserts, is the "full, organized body of
all the extension and intension that we can find in it." This concept
has been widely used by the New Critics, particularly in their examination of poetry as a pattern of PARADOX or as a form of IRONY. See
CONCRETE UNIVERSAL.

**Tercet:** A stanza of three lines, a TRIPLET, in which each line ends
with the same RIME. The term is also used to denote either one
of the two three-line groups forming the SESTET of the Italian SON-
NET. A *tercet* of the type first mentioned is quoted from Herrick:

> Whenas in silks my Julia goes,
> Then, then, methinks, how sweetly flows
> That liquefaction of her clothes.

The term is also applied to the TERZA RIMA stanza.

*Terza rima:* A three-line STANZA form borrowed from the Italian
poets. The RIME-SCHEME is *aba, bcb, cdc, ded*, etc. In other words,
one RIME-sound is used for the first and third line of each STANZA
and a new RIME introduced for the second line, this new RIME, in
turn, being used for the first and third lines of the subsequent
STANZA. Usually the METER is IAMBIC PENTAMETER, but in the illustration quoted (from Browning's *The Statue and the Bust*) the
meter is IAMBIC TETRAMETER:

> There's a palace in Florence, the world knows well,   *a*
> And a statue watches it from the square,   *b*
> And this story of both do our townsmen tell.   *a*
>
> Ages ago, a lady there,   *b*
> At the farthest window facing the East   *c*
> Asked, "Who rides by with the royal air?"   *b*

The *terza rima* has been popular with English poets, being used by
Milton, Shelley, and Byron, among many others. With variations
in METER and the use of imperfect RIMES, it has been widely used
by contemporary poets, particularly MacLeish, Auden, and Eliot.

**Testament:** As a literary form the term has two rather distinct
meanings. It may be a literary "last will and testament" or it may
be a piece of literature which "bears witness to" or "makes a covenant with" in the Biblical sense. The former sort of *testament* originated with the Romans of the decadent period and was developed
by the French in the late medieval and early RENAISSANCE periods.
It was especially popular in the fifteenth century and was often
characterized by HUMOR, ribaldry, and SATIRE, as in the half-serious,
half-ribald *Grand Testament* and *Petit Testament* of François Villon,
perhaps the greatest examples of this type. In the popular literature
of the first half of the sixteenth century in England there were
many wills and *testaments* of the humorous and satiric sort, such as
*Jyl of Breyntford's Testament, Colin Blowbol's Testament,* and Humphrey Powell's popular *Wyll of the Devil* (*ca.*1550). Some literary
*testaments,* however, were more serious; for example, the *Testament
of Cresseid* by the Scotch poet Robert Henryson (1430–1506), a
continuation of Chaucer's *Troilus and Criseyde* in which Cressida
is pictured as thoroughly degraded in character and suffering from
leprosy. In her poverty-stricken last days she bequeaths her scant
belongings to her fellow-sufferers. Another serious *testament* is the
love COMPLAINT, "The Testament of the Hawthorne" in *Tottel's
Miscellany* (1557).

The second type of *testament,* that which "bears witness to," was
also developed in the late medieval period. Its best representative
in English is perhaps *The Testament of Love* by Thomas Usk (?),
written about 1384. This is a long prose treatise in which Divine
Love appears in a role similar to that of Philosophy in Boëthius'
*Consolation of Philosophy,* to which it is somewhat akin. A notable
modern representative of this type is Robert Bridges' *The Testament
of Beauty* (1929).

**Tetrameter:** A line of VERSE consisting of four FEET. See SCANSION.

**Textual Criticism:** A scholarly activity which attempts by all available means to reconstruct the original manuscript or the authoritative text of a work. See CRITICISM, TYPES OF.

# Texture

486

**Texture:** A term applied to the elements which remain in a work of literary art after a PARAPHRASE of its ARGUMENT has been made. Among such elements are details of SITUATION, METAPHOR, METER, IMAGERY, TONE COLOR, RIME—in fact, all elements that are not considered to be a part of the STRUCTURE of the work. The separation of TEXTURE and STRUCTURE is a strategy often employed by the NEW CRITICS.

**Theatres, English:** See PUBLIC THEATRES, PRIVATE THEATRES, PATENT THEATRES.

**Theme:** The central or dominating idea in a literary work. In non-FICTION PROSE it may be thought of as the general topic of discussion, the subject of the discourse, the THESIS. In POETRY, FICTION, and DRAMA it is the abstract concept which is made concrete through its representation in person, action, and IMAGE in the work.

**Theoretical Criticism:** A kind of criticism that attempts to arrive at the general principles of art and to formulate inclusive and enduring aesthetic and critical tenets. See CRITICISM, TYPES OF.

**Thesis:** An attitude or position on a problem taken by a writer or speaker with the purpose of proving or supporting it. The term is also used for the paper which is written to support the *thesis*. That is, *thesis* is used both for the problem to be established and for the ESSAY which, presumably, establishes it. In college and university circles the word has the special connotation of a paper expounding some special problem and written as a requirement for a bachelor's or master's degree. See DISSERTATION. For *thesis* as a term in PROSODY, see ICTUS, ACCENT.

**Threnody:** A SONG of death, a DIRGE, a lamentation.

**Title:** The distinguishing name attached to any written production, a book, a section of a book, a chapter, a short story, a poem, etc. Although modern *titles* are usually brief, an older practice produced *titles* that sometimes filled a closely printed page. For bibliographical purposes, the entire *title* page, including the author's name and the publication facts, is considered the *title*, and when it is copied, the actual typography and lineation are usually indicated.

**Tone (Tone Color):** *Tone* is used in contemporary criticism, following I. A. Richards' example, as a term designating the attitudes toward the subject and toward the audience implied in a literary work. In such a usage, a work may have a *tone* that is formal, informal, intimate, solemn, sombre, playful, serious, ironic, condescending, or any of many other possible attitudes. Clearly, *tone* in this sense contributes in a major way to the effect and the effectiveness of a literary work.

In another sense, *tone* is used to designate the mood of the work itself and the various devices that are used to create that mood. In this sense, *tone* results from combinations and variations of such things as METER, RIME, ALLITERATION, ASSONANCE, CONSONANCE, DICTION, SENTENCE STRUCTURE, REPETITION, IMAGERY, SYMBOLISM, etc.

*Tone* or *tone color* is sometimes used to designate a musical quality in language which Sidney Lanier discussed in *The Science of English Verse,* where he asserts that the sounds of words have qualities equivalent to timbre in music. "When the ear exactly coordinates a series of sounds with primary reference to their tone-color, the result is a conception of (in music, flute-tone as distinct from violin-tone, and the like; in verse, rhyme as opposed to rhyme, vowel varied with vowel, phonetic syzygy, and the like), in general . . . *tone-color.*"

**Tract:** A pamphlet, usually an argumentative document on some religious or political topic, often distributed free for propaganda purposes. For a classic example of the use of the term, see OXFORD MOVEMENT.

**Tractarian Movement:** See OXFORD MOVEMENT.

**Tradition:** A body of beliefs, customs, sayings, or skills handed down from age to age or from generation to generation. Thus BALLADS and folk literature in general as well as superstitions and popular proverbs are passed on by oral *tradition.* A set idea may be called a *tradition,* like the idea which prevailed throughout the Middle Ages that Homer's account of the Trojan War was to be discredited in favor of certain forged accounts claiming to be written by participants in the war. The *tradition* of PASTORAL literature means the underlying conceptions and technique of PASTORAL literature carried down, with modifications, from Theocritus (third century B.C.) to Pope. A *traditional* element in literature suggests something which the author has inherited from the past rather than something of his own invention. In another sense, *tradition* may be thought of as the inheritance from the past of a body of literary CONVENTIONS that are still alive in the present, as opposed to CONVENTIONS of the past which died with their peculiar age and circumstance.

**Tragedy:** A DRAMA, in PROSE or VERSE, which recounts an important and causally related series of events in the life of a person of significance, such events culminating in an unhappy CATASTROPHE, the whole treated with great dignity and seriousness. According to Aristotle, whose definition in the *Poetics* is an inductive description of the Greek *tragedies,* the purpose of a *tragedy* is to arouse the emotions of pity and fear and thus to produce in the audience a CATHARSIS of these emotions. Such a definition as this is broad enough to admit almost any DRAMA that is serious and that ends with an unhappy CATASTROPHE, although its various formulations have been interpreted from time to time in terms of the attitudes and conventions of the age in which the formulations have been made. The question of the nature of the significance of the tragic HERO is answered in each age by the concept of significance that is held by that age. In a period of monarchy, Shakespeare's PROTAGONISTS were kings and rulers; in other ages they have been and will be other kinds of men. In a democratic nation, founded on an egalitarian concept of man, a tragic HERO can be the archetypal common man—a shoe salesman, a policeman, a gangster, a New England farmer, a Negro servant. From time to time the basis of UNITY has been debated. With the classical writers of the RENAISSANCE and in the NEO-CLASSIC PERIOD, the UNITIES were observed with rigor. Yet ages which find UNITY in other aspects of DRAMA than its technique, may wed the serious and the comic, may take liberties with time and place, may use multiple PLOTS, and still achieve a unified effect as the non-classic RENAISSANCE writers did. What constitutes dignity and seriousness in presentation is also subject to the interpretation of the age in which the play is produced. In its own way Arthur Miller's *The Death of a Salesman* is fully as serious and as dignified for our world as *Hamlet* was for Elizabethan England, although it is a lesser play. CLASSICAL TRAGEDY and ROMANTIC TRAGEDY both emphasize the significance of a choice made by the PROTAGONIST but dictated by his "flaw," his HAMARTIA;

yet to insist that *tragedy* be confined to this particular view of man and life is to limit it in indefensible ways. Clearly *tragedy* defies specific definition, each age producing works that speak in the conventions and beliefs of that age the enduring sense that man seems to have of the tragic nature of his existence and of the grandeur of the human spirit in facing it.

In the Middle Ages the term *tragedy* did not refer to a DRAMA but to any narrative which recounted how a person of high rank, through ill fortune or his own vice or error, fell from high estate to low. The *tragedies* recounted in Chaucer's "Monk's Tale," in Lydgate's *Fall of Princes,* and in the RENAISSANCE collection, *The Mirror for Magistrates,* are of this sort. In the sixteenth century the influence of CLASSICAL TRAGEDY, particularly of SENECAN TRAGEDY, combined with notable elements of the MEDIEVAL DRAMA to produce English *tragedy.* In 1559 came the first translation of a SENECAN TRAGEDY, and in 1562 was acted Sackville and Norton's *Gorboduc,* "the first regular English *tragedy.*" The genius for the stage which characterized the ELIZABETHAN AGE worked upon this form to produce the greatest flowering in the DRAMA that England has known. Yet the *tragedy* which emerged was not the CLASSICAL TRAGEDY of Aristotle's definition, despite the efforts of men like Ben Jonson to school it into being so, but plays of a heterogeneous character known as ROMANTIC TRAGEDY—plays which tended to ignore the UNITIES, which followed medieval tradition in mixing sadness and mirth, and which strove at any cost—including SUB-PLOTS and comic RELIEF SCENES—to satisfy the spectators with vigorous action and gripping spectacle. Shakespeare worked in the forms of the REVENGE TRAGEDY, the DOMESTIC TRAGEDY, and the CHRONICLE PLAY.

The seventeenth century saw the ELIZABETHAN TRAGEDY continued with a growing emphasis on violence and shock during its first half, to be replaced with the HEROIC DRAMA, with its stylized conflict of love and honor, during its second half. The eighteenth century saw the development of a DRAMA around middle-class figures, known as DOMESTIC TRAGEDY, which was serious in intent but superficial in importance. With the emergence of Ibsen in the late nineteenth century came the concept of middle-class *tragedy* growing out of social problems and issues. In the twentieth century, middle-class and laboring-class characters are often portrayed in their circumstances as the victims of social, hereditary, and environmental forces. When, as often happens, they receive their fate with a self-pitying whimper, they can hardly be said to have tragic dimensions. But when, as also happens in much modern serious DRAMA, they face their destiny, however evil and unmerited, with courage and dignity, they are probably as truly tragic, *mutatis mutandis*, as Oedipus was to Sophocles' Athenians or Hamlet was to Shakespeare's Englishmen. See DRAMATIC STRUCTURE, CATHARSIS, DRAMA.

**Tragedy of Blood:** An intensified form of the REVENGE TRAGEDY popular on the Elizabethan stage. It works out the theme of revenge and retribution (borrowed from Seneca) through murder, assassination, mutilation, and downright carnage. The horrors which in the Latin Senecan plays had been merely described were placed upon the stage to satisfy the craving for morbid excitement displayed by an Elizabethan audience brought up on bear-baiting spectacles and public executions (hangings, mutilations, burnings). Besides including such revenge plays as Kyd's *Spanish Tragedy*, Shakespeare's *Titus Andronicus*, and *Hamlet*, the *tragedy of blood* led to such later "horror" TRAGEDIES as Webster's *The Duchess of Malfi* and *The White Devil*. See REVENGE TRAGEDY, SENECAN TRAGEDY.

**Tragic Force:** The event or force which starts the FALLING ACTION in a TRAGEDY. It is either a separate event following closely upon the CLIMAX or is identified with the CLIMAX itself. The escape of Fleance is the *tragic force* in *Macbeth*, marking as it does the beginning of Macbeth's misfortunes and leading to the overthrow of the HERO in the resulting CATASTROPHE. See DRAMATIC STRUCTURE.

**Tragic Irony:** That form of DRAMATIC IRONY in which a character in a TRAGEDY uses words which mean one thing to him and another to those better acquainted with his real situation, especially when he is about to become a victim of Fate. Othello's allusion to the VILLAIN who is about to deceive him as "honest Iago" is an example.

**Tragi-comedy:** A play which employs a PLOT suitable to TRAGEDY but which ends happily like a COMEDY. The action, serious in THEME and subject matter and sometimes in TONE also, seems to be leading to a tragic CATASTROPHE until an unexpected turn in events, often in the form of a DEUS EX MACHINA, brings about the happy DÉNOUEMENT. In this sense Shakespeare's *The Merchant of Venice* is a *tragi-comedy*, though it is also a ROMANTIC COMEDY. If the "trick" about the shedding of blood were omitted and Shylock allowed to "have his bond," the play might easily be made into a TRAGEDY; conversely Shakespeare's *King Lear*, a pure TRAGEDY, was made into a COMEDY by Nahum Tate for the RESTORATION stage. In English dramatic history the term *tragi-comedy* is usually employed to designate the particular kind of play developed by Beaumont and Fletcher about 1610, a type of which *Philaster* is perhaps most typical. Fletcher's own definition may be quoted: "A tragi-comedy is not so called in respect of mirth and killing, but in respect it wants deaths, which is enough to make it no tragedy, yet brings some near it, which is enough to make it no comedy, which must be a representation of familiar people, with such kind of trouble as no life be question'd; so that a god is as lawful in this [tragi-comedy] as in a tragedy, and mean people as in a comedy" (from "To the Reader," *The Faithful Shepherdess*). Some of the characteristics are: improbable PLOT; unnatural SITUATIONS; actors of high social class, usually of the nobility; love as the central interest, pure love and gross love often being contrasted; highly complicated PLOT; rapid action; contrast of deep villainy and exalted virtue; saving of HERO and HEROINE in the nick of time; penitent VILLAIN (as Iachimo in *Cymbeline*); disguises; surprises; jealousy; treachery; intrigue; enveloping action of war or rebellion. Shakespeare's *Cymbeline* and *The Winter's Tale* are examples of the GENRE. Fletcher's *The Faithful Shepherdess* is a PASTORAL *tragi-comedy*. Later seventeenth-century *tragi-comedies* are Massinger's *The Prisoner*, Davenant's *Fair Favorite*, Shadwell's *Royal Shepherdess*, and Dryden's *Secret Love* and *Love Triumphant*. Such plays as these tended to approach the HEROIC DRAMA. The type practically disappeared in the early eighteenth century, though the name is still sometimes employed, Henry Arthur Jones having called his *Galilean's Victory* (1907) a "tragi-comedy of religious life in England."

**Transcendental Club:** An informal organization of leading transcendentalists living in or near Boston. The group came together for their first meeting, September 19, 1836, at the home of George Ripley. Thereafter, they met occasionally at Emerson's home in Concord and elsewhere for seven or eight years, calling themselves "The Symposium" and "The Hedge Club." Their chief interests were the new developments in theology, philosophy, and literature,

# Transcendentalism

and the purpose of their coming together was simply to discuss the "new thought" of the day. The movement was closely associated with the growth of the Unitarian spirit in New England. The leading members of the Club were such figures as Ralph Waldo Emerson, Convers Francis, Frederick Henry Hedge, Amos Bronson Alcott, George Ripley, Margaret Fuller, Nathaniel Hawthorne, Henry D. Thoreau, and William Ellery Channing. See TRANSCENDENTALISM.

**Transcendentalism:** A reliance on the intuition and the conscience, a form of idealism; a philosophical ROMANTICISM reaching America a generation or two after it developed in Europe. *Transcendentalism*, though based on doctrines of ancient and modern European philosophers (particularly Kant) and sponsored in America chiefly by Emerson after he had absorbed it from Carlyle, Coleridge, Goethe, and others, took on especial significance in the United States, where it so largely dominated the New England authors as to become a literary movement as well as a philosophic conception. The movement gained its impetus in America in part from meetings of a small group which came together to discuss the "new thought" of the time. While holding different opinions about many things, the group seemed in general harmony in their conviction that within the nature of man there was a something which transcended human experience—an intuitive and personal revelation. Variously called the SYMPOSIUM CLUB and the HEDGE CLUB, the group was soon known as the TRANSCENDENTAL CLUB because of the ideas advanced by its members.

As the "movement" developed, it sponsored two important activities: the publication of THE DIAL from 1840–1844 and BROOK FARM. Some of the various doctrines which one or another of the American transcendentalists promulgated and which have somehow been accepted as "transcendental" may be restated here. They believed in living close to nature (Thoreau) and taught the dignity of manual labor (Thoreau). They strongly felt the need of intellectual companionships and interests (Brook Farm) and placed great emphasis on the importance of spiritual living. Man's relationship to God was a personal matter and was to be established directly by the individual himself (UNITARIANISM) rather than through the intermediation of the ritualistic church. They held firmly that man was divine in his own right, an opinion opposed to the doctrines held by the Puritan Calvinists in New England, and they urged strongly the essential divinity of man and one great brotherhood. Self-trust and self-reliance were to be practised at all times and on all occasions, since to trust self was really to trust the voice of God speaking intuitively within us (Emerson). The transcendentalists felt called upon to resist the "vulgar prosperity of the barbarian"; believed firmly in democracy, and insisted on an intense individualism. Some of the extremists in their number went so far as to evolve a system of dietetics and to rule out coffee, wine, and tobacco—all on the basis that the body was the temple of the soul and that for the tenant's sake it was well to keep the dwelling undefiled. And most of the transcendentalists were by nature reformers, though Emerson—the most vocal interpreter of the group —refused to go so far in this direction as, for instance, Bronson Alcott. Emerson's position here is that it is man's responsibility to be "a brave and upright man, who must find or cut a straight path to everything excellent in the earth, and not only go honorably himself, but make it easier for all who follow him to go in honor and with benefit." In this way most of the reforms were attempts to awaken and regenerate the human spirit rather than to prescribe particular and concrete movements which were to be fostered. The transcendentalists were, for instance, among the early advocates of the enfranchisement of women.

Ultimately, despite these practical manifestations, *transcendentalism* was an epistemology, a way of knowing, and the ultimate characteristics which tied together the frequently contradictory beliefs of the loosely formed group called "The Transcendentalists" was the belief that man can intuitively transcend the limits of the senses and of logic and receive directly higher truths and greater knowledge denied to these mundane methods of knowing.

Among the most famous of the transcendental leaders, in addition to Emerson, Thoreau, and Alcott already mentioned, were Margaret Fuller, George Ripley, F. H. Hedge, James Freeman Clark, Elizabeth Peabody, Theodore Parker, Jones Very, and W. H. Channing. But the arch-advocates in literature of most that the transcendentalists stood for were Emerson and Thoreau; and the two documents which most definitely give literary expression to their views were Emerson's *Nature* (1836) and Thoreau's *Walden* (1854).

**Transferred Epithet:** An adjective used to limit a noun which it cannot logically modify. See EPITHET.

**Translation:** The rendering of a literary work, originally produced in one language, into another. At one extreme of *translation* stands the literal rendering of the work into the other language, word for word, without concern for the primary differences in IDIOM and IMAGERY between the two languages. At the other extreme is the ADAPTATION of the work into the other language, an attempt to comprehend and communicate the spirit and meaning of the work by adapting it to the conventions and idioms of the language into which it is being rendered. Each translator must strike some kind of balance between these extremes—which Croce called "faithful ugliness or faithless beauty." Some *translations* have great literary merit in themselves; notably, the King James Version of the Holy BIBLE, Amyot's Plutarch, Schlegel's Shakespeare, Baudelaire's and Mallarmé's Poe, Putnam's Cervantes.

**Travesty:** Writing which by its incongruity of STYLE or treatment ridicules a subject inherently noble or dignified. The derivation of the word, from *trans* (over or across) and *vestire* (to clothe or dress) clearly suggests the meaning of presenting a subject in a dress intended for another type of subject. *Travesty* may be thought of as the opposite of the MOCK EPIC since the latter treats a frivolous subject seriously and the *travesty* usually presents a serious subject frivolously. *Don Quixote* is, in a very real sense, a *travesty* on the MEDIEVAL ROMANCE. See BURLESQUE.

**"Tribe of Ben":** A contemporary nickname for the young poets and dramatists of the seventeenth century who acknowledged "rare Ben Jonson" as their master. The boasted chief of the "tribe" was Robert Herrick, and the group included the CAVALIER LYRISTS and other of the younger poets and dramatists of Jacobean times. Jonson's influence upon his followers was in the direction of classical polish and sense of FORM, study and imitation of classical writers and literary types (as the ODE, the EPIGRAM, SATIRE), and classical ideals of criticism. The attitude represented a revolt from the PURITANISM and Italian ROMANTICISM represented in Spenser. The poets strove to make the LYRIC graceful and in general the group followed the creed: "Live merrily and write good verses."

**Trilogy:** A literary composition, more usually a NOVEL or a play, written in three parts, each of which is in itself a complete unit. Shakespeare's *King Henry VI* is an example. The *trilogy* usually is written against a large background which may be historical, philosophical, or social in its interests.

**Trimeter:** A line of VERSE consisting of three FEET. See SCANSION.

**Triolet:** One of the simpler French VERSE forms. It consists of eight lines, the first two being repeated as the last two lines and the first recurring also as the fourth line. There are only two RIMES, and their arrangement is: *ab*aa*ab*ab. (Italics indicate repetition of whole lines.) Certain skillful poets, notably Austin Dobson, have contrived to add piquancy to the form by giving a different meaning to the REFRAIN lines from that which they carried at the opening of the poem. Example:

A KISS[1]

Rose kissed me today,
  Will she kiss me tomorrow?
Let it be as it may,
Rose kissed me today.
But the pleasure gives way
  To a savor of sorrow;—
Rose kissed me today,—
*Will* she kiss me tomorrow?
      —Austin Dobson

**Triple Rime:** RIME in which the correspondence of sounds lies in three consecutive syllables. See RIME.

**Triplet:** A sequence of three riming VERSES, often introduced as a variation in the HEROIC COUPLET. See TERCET.

**Trite Expression:** A CLICHÉ.

**Trivium:** The three studies leading to the bachelor's degree in the medieval universities: grammar, logic, and RHETORIC. See SEVEN ARTS.

**Trochee:** A two-syllabled poetic FOOT consisting of an accented

and an unaccented syllable, as in the word $\overline{hap}\breve{py}$. Trochaics are generally unpopular with poets for sustained writing since they so soon degenerate into hobby-horse RHYTHM, a fact which makes

[1]Printed with the courteous permission of Mr. Alban Dobson, representing the executors, and of the Oxford University Press.

them, perversely, popular with children and undeveloped minds. The ease and frequency with which Longfellow's *Hiawatha* has been parodied ("Sweet trochaic milk and water") bears evidence to this quality of the trochaic measure. On the other hand, for short songs and lyrics the *trochee* has been very popular. It is often used as the meter of the supernatural as in Shakespeare's

> Double, double, toil and trouble,
> Fire burn and cauldron bubble.

**Trope:** In RHETORIC a *trope* is a FIGURE OF SPEECH involving a "turn" or change of sense—the use of a word in a sense other than its proper or literal one; in this sense figures of comparison (see METAPHOR, SIMILE) as well as ironical expressions are *tropes* or FIGURES OF SPEECH.

Another use of the word is important to students of the origin of MEDIEVAL DRAMA. As early as the eighth or ninth centuries, certain musical additions to the Gregorian antiphons in the liturgy of the Catholic Church were permitted as pleasurable elaborations of the service. At first they were merely prolongations of the melody on a vowel sound, giving rise to *jubila,* the manuscript notation for a *jubilum* being known as a *neuma,* which looked somewhat like shorthand notes. Later, words were added to old *jubila* and new compositions of both words and music added, the texts of which were called *tropes.* These *tropes,* or "amplifications of the liturgical texts," were sometimes in PROSE, sometimes in VERSE; sometimes purely musical, sometimes requiring DIALOGUE, presented antiphonally by the two parts of the choir. From this DIALOGUE form of the *trope* developed the LITURGICAL DRAMA. See MEDIEVAL DRAMA.

**Troubadour:** A name given to the aristocratic LYRIC poets of Provence (Southern France) in the twelfth and thirteenth centuries. The name is derived from a word meaning "to find," suggesting that the *troubadour* was regarded as an inventor and experimenter in poetic technique. *Troubadours* were essentially LYRIC poets, occupied with themes of love and chivalry. The conventional themes arose from the social conditions, the *troubadour* usually addressing his VERSE to a married lady, whose patronage he courted. *Troubadour* poetry figured importantly in the development of COURTLY LOVE, and influenced the TROUVÈRE of Northern France. The earliest *troubadour* of record is William, Count of Poitiers (1071–1127), other famous *troubadours* being Bernard de Ventadour, Arnaut de Mareuil, Bertran de Born, and Arnaut Daniel. Some of the forms invented by the *troubadours* are: the CANSO (love song), *ballata* (dance song), *tenso* (dialogue), *pastorela* (pastoral wooing song), and the ALBA (dawn song). Much use was made of RIME, and varied stanzaic forms were developed, including the SESTINA used later by Dante and others. The SONNET form itself probably developed from *troubadour* stanzaic inventions. The poetry was intended to be sung, sometimes by the *troubadour* himself, sometimes by an assistant or apprentice or professional entertainer, as the JONGLEUR.

**Trouvère:** A term applied to a group or school of poets who flourished in Northern France in the twelfth and thirteenth centuries. The *trouvères* were much influenced by the art of the TROUBADOURS of Southern France, and concerned themselves largely with LYRICS of love, though they produced also CHANSONS DE GESTE and CHIVALRIC ROMANCES. Indeed, to the activity of one of them, the famous Chrétien de Troyes (twelfth century), we owe some of the earliest and best of the Arthurian romances. See ARTHURIAN LEGEND.

**Truncation:** See CATALEXIS.

**Tudor:** The royal house that ruled England from 1485 to 1602. The rulers were Henry VII (1485–1509), Henry VIII (1509–1547), Edward VI (1547–1553), Mary (1553–1558), and Elizabeth (1558–1603).

**Tumbling Verse:** See SKELTONIC VERSE, for which it is another name.

***Ubi sunt* Formula:** A convention much used in VERSE, especially in the French forms, which asks "where are" (*ubi sunt*) these things, and these, and these, the poetic impression on the reader being largely effected by the emphasis the formula places on the transitory qualities of life. The most famous example in English is probably Dante Gabriel Rossetti's "The Ballade of Dead Ladies," a poetic TRANSLATION of François Villon's famous BALLADE:

> But where are the snows of yester-year?

In Justin McCarthy's poem, "I Wonder in What Isle of Bliss," successive STANZAS close with "Where are the Gods of Yesterday?"

"Where are the Dreams of Yesterday?" "Where are the Girls of Yesterday?" "Where are the Snows of Yesterday?" In Edmund Gosse's "The Ballad of Dead Cities," the three STANZAS begin with "Where are the Cities of the plain?" "Where now is Karnak, that great fane . . . ?" "And where is white Shushan, again . . . ?" Each of the STANZAS in this poem closes with "Where are the cities of old time?" These examples illustrate the tendency to place the *ubi sunt* query in the opening line of a STANZA or to use it as a REFRAIN or REPETEND.

*Ultima Thule:* The farthest possible place. Used often in the sense of a remote goal, an ideal and mysterious country. To the ancients *Thule* was one of the northern lands of Europe, most likely one of the Shetland Islands, although Iceland and Norway have been suggested. From the Latin reference to the region as the *ultima* (farthest) *Thule,* the expression has taken on the literary significance given it above.

**Understatement:** A form of IRONY in which something is intentionally represented as less than in fact it is. See MEIOSIS.

**Unitarianism:** The creed of a sect coming into importance in America about 1820, a sect which discarded the earlier faith in the existence of a Trinity and held for the unity of God, accepting Christ as divine in the same sense that man is, but not as a member of a divine Trinity. In its more evolved form this new *Unitarianism* stood for "the fatherhood of God, the brotherhood of man, the leadership of Jesus, salvation by character, and the progress of mankind onward and upward forever."

**Unities:** The principles of DRAMATIC STRUCTURE involving *action, time,* and *place.* The most important *unity* and the only one enjoined by Aristotle is that of action. He called a TRAGEDY "an imitation of an action that is complete, and whole, and of a certain magnitude"; a whole should have beginning, middle, and end, with a causal relationship in the different parts of the play. Inevitability and concentration result from adherence to the *unity of action.* This *unity,* Aristotle warned, was not necessarily obtained simply by making one man the subject. Later critics declared that a SUBPLOT tends to destroy the *unity* of any serious play and that tragic and comic elements should not be mixed. Thus the legitimacy of TRAGI-COMEDY was for a long time a matter of dispute; Sidney opposed it and Doctor Johnson vindicated it.

The *unity of time* was developed from Aristotle's simple and undogmatic statement concerning tragic usage: "Tragedy endeavors, as far as possible, to confine itself to a single revolution of the sun, or but slightly to exceed this limit." The Italian critics of the sixteenth century formulated the doctrine that the action should be limited to one day; many French and English critics of the seventeenth and eighteenth centuries accepted this *unity,* and many dramatists used it. There were different interpretations of the *unity of time*—some favored the natural day of twenty-four hours, others the artificial day of twelve hours, and others the several hours that correspond to the actual time of theatrical representation.

The *unity of place,* limiting the action to one place, was the last to emerge and was not mentioned by Aristotle. It followed, quite naturally, the requirement of limiting the action to a particular time; as the RENAISSANCE critics of Italy developed their theories of VERISIMILITUDE, of making the action of a play approximate that of stage representation, the *unity of place* completed the trilogy. Some critics were content to have the action confined merely to the same town or city. The *unity of place* was closely allied to that of time in the theory and practice of neo-classic writers.

The dramatic *unities* have had a long and extremely complicated history. For more than two centuries in England the three *unities* were denounced and defended and (as in Dryden's *Essay of Dramatic Poesy*) debated. When NEO-CLASSICISM gave way to ROMANTICISM, they lost their importance.

Many great English plays violate all three *unities. Unity of action,* however, is commonly recognized as an important requirement in serious DRAMA, and Shakespeare's greatest TRAGEDIES, such as *Hamlet* and *Othello,* show the effects of such *unity.* In two plays, the *Comedy of Errors* and *The Tempest,* Shakespeare observed all three of the *unities.* The theory of the *unities* has been, in truth, a matter of more concern to critics than to dramatists. Yet the concentration and strength that result from efforts at attaining *unity of action, time, and place* may be regarded as dramatic virtues.

Modern dramatists are less interested in traditional formulae than in the *unity of impression,* the singleness of emotional EFFECT, which is related to the *unity of action.* Moreover, in recent years effective experiments with the minor *unities of time and place* have been made in stage and screen plays. See CRITICISM, HISTORICAL SKETCH.

**Unity:** The concept that a literary work shall have in it some organizing principle to which all its parts are related so that, viewed in the light of that principle, the work is an organic whole. A work which has *unity* is cohesive in its parts, complete, self-contained, and integrated; it possesses one-ness. The concept of *unity* in the DRAMA has often been mechanically applied (see UNITIES). In other literary forms, it is often considered to reside in a unified action or PLOT or in CHARACTERIZATION. A work may, however, be unified by FORM, by intent, by THEME, by SYMBOLISM—in fact, by any means which can so integrate and organize its elements that they have a necessary relationship to each other and an essential relationship to the whole of which they are parts.

**Universality:** A critical term frequently employed to indicate the presence in a piece of writing of an appeal to all readers of all time. When writing presents the great human emotions common to all peoples of all civilizations—jealousy, love, pride, courage, etc.—in literary form and through characters and actions that remain meaningful to other ages, it may be said to have *universality*. Of all qualities which make for *universality* in literature, the successful portrayal of human character is the most important. See CONCRETE UNIVERSAL.

**University Plays:** See SCHOOL PLAYS.

**University Wits:** A name used for certain young University men who came to London in the late 1580's and undertook careers as professional men of letters. They played an extremely important part in the development of the great literature, especially the DRAMA, that characterized the latter part of Elizabeth's reign. The most important one was Christopher Marlowe. Others included are Robert Greene, George Peele, Thomas Lodge, Thomas Nash, and Thomas Kyd. Some authorities include John Lyly, though Lyly was an older man and perhaps not personally associated with the others. They lived irregular lives, Greene and Marlowe being particularly known as Bohemians. Their literary work, while uneven in quality, much of it being hack work, was varied and influential, especially in the field of DRAMA. They were largely instrumental in freeing TRAGEDY from the artificial restrictions imposed by classical authority, and their cultivation of BLANK VERSE, especially the "mighty line" of Marlowe, paved the way for Shakespeare's masterful use of this form. They devised or developed types of plays later perfected by Shakespeare: the REVENGE TRAGEDY or TRAGEDY OF BLOOD (Kyd), the TRAGEDY built around a great personality (Marlowe), ROMANTIC COMEDY (Greene and Peele), CHRONICLE PLAY (Marlowe and others), and the COURT COMEDY (Lyly). Lodge and Greene cultivated the PASTORAL ROMANCE and Nash wrote the first PICARESQUE NOVEL in English. The group was especially active between 1585 and 1595. The personal and literary interests of these "wits" sometimes made them rivals or enemies of one another.

**Usage:** The standard which sets the speech of a people. Good *usage* is established by the forms of language used by educated people and by intelligent writers, but this does not mean at all that *usage* is *fixed*. It is, in fact, constantly shifting, old forms becoming obsolescent and obsolete, new forms entering by way of SLANG, passing through the colloquial stage, and sometimes finally arriving at recognition as "good *usage*." Dictionaries and grammars properly *follow usage* rather than *set* it, though, of course, both do much toward standardization and stabilization.

**Utilitarianism:** A theory of ethics formulated in England in the eighteenth century by Jeremy Bentham, who believed that the test of ethical concerns was their usefulness to society and who defined utility as "the greatest happiness for the greatest number." The theory was advanced and modified in the nineteenth century by James Mill and his son John Stuart Mill, both of whom wanted to define "happiness" in qualitative rather than quantitative terms, whereas Bentham had equated it with pleasure. It is a significant movement in nineteenth-century thought not only because of the excellence with which John Stuart Mill expounded it but also because it was a central issue for a number of writers, among them Thomas Carlyle and Charles Dickens, both of whom attacked the system. It is also sometimes called "Benthamism" after its originator.

**Utopia:** A word meaning "nowhere" coined by Thomas More to represent the seat of his ideal republic as pictured in his *Utopia* (1516). The idea of presenting plans for ideal commonwealths has interested many philosophers and writers. Plato's *Republic,* of course, is the best known. Some others are Campanella's *Civitas Solis* (1623), Bacon's *New Atlantis* (1627), Harrington's *Oceana* (1656), Samuel Butler's *Erewhon* (1872), Bellamy's *Looking Backward* (1888), William Morris' *News from Nowhere* (1890), H. G. Wells' *A Modern Utopia* (1905), and Aldous Huxley's satiric *Brave New World* (1932).

**Vade mecum:** An article which one keeps constantly with him. By association the term has come to mean any book much used, as a *handbook,* a *thesaurus.*

**Vapours:** A word commonly used in eighteenth-century literature to account for the eccentric action of people. *Vapours* were exhalations which were presumably given off by the stomach or other organs of the body and rose to the head causing depression, melancholy, hysteria, etc. As early as 1541 Sir Thomas Elyot wrote that "of humours some are more grosse and cold, some are subtyl and hot and are called vapours." Heroines of eighteenth-century fiction were particularly subject to attacks of this malady. Young, in 1728, gave us these lines:

> Sometimes, thro' pride the sexes change their airs;
> My lord has vapours, and my lady swears.

See HUMOURS.

**Variorum Edition:** An edition of an author's work presenting complete variant readings of the possible texts and full notes of critical comments and interpretation passed upon the text by major writers. The term is an abbreviation of the Latin phrase *cum notis variorum* ("with notes of various persons"). In the field of English literature, the most conspicuous successes in this type of editing are the "New Variorum Shakespeare" edited by Furness, and the "Variorum Spenser," edited by Edwin Greenlaw.

**Vaudeville:** An entertainment consisting of successive performances of unrelated SONGS, dances, dramatic SKETCHES, acrobatic feats, juggling, PANTOMIME, puppet-shows, and varied "stunts."

The word is derived from *Vau-de-Vire*, a village in Normandy, where a famous composer of lively, satirical SONGS lived in the eighteenth century. From these SONGS, modified later by PANTO-MIME, developed the "variety" shows now known as *vaudeville*. The elements of *vaudeville* are, of course, old (see LOW COMEDY, BURLESQUE, FARCE), but the modern *vaudeville* type of variety show developed in the eighteenth and nineteenth centuries. Under the direction of John Rich these shows became very popular in eighteenth-century England and continued so through the nineteenth century. The name *vaudeville* seems to have become finally attached to the variety show as a result of its development in America, especially in the early years of the twentieth century, when *vaudeville* actors were organized into "circuits" by B. F. Keith and others and when elaborate theatres were devoted to their use. The popularity of *vaudeville* decreased after the advent of the talking moving pictures.

**Vehicle:** See TENOR AND VEHICLE.

**Verisimilitude:** The appearance or semblance of truth and actuality. The term has been used in criticism to indicate the degree to which a writer faithfully creates the semblance of the truth. In his *Life of Swift*, Scott writes: "Swift possessed the art of verisimilitude." The word was a favorite one with Poe who used it in the sense of presenting details, howsoever far-fetched, in such a way as to give them the *semblance* of truth. In *The Facts in the Case of M. Valdemar*, for instance, Poe gives way to the wildest kind of romancing, but the items are so marshalled as to sweep the reader into at least a momentary acceptance of them, and the story may, therefore, be said to respect Poe's own demands for *verisimilitude*.

**Vers de société:** Brief lyrical verse written in genial, sportive mood and sophisticated both in subject and treatment. Sometimes called LIGHT VERSE. Its characteristics are polish, *savoir faire*, grace, and ease of expression. It usually presents aspects of conventional social relationships. Locker-Lampson in a much-quoted introduction to his collection of *vers de société*, *Lyra Elegantiarum*, states: "Occasional Verse should be short, graceful, refined, and fanciful, not seldom distinguished by chastened sentiment, and often playful. The tone should not be pitched high; it should be terse and idiomatic, and rather in the conversational key. The rhythm should be crisp and sparkling, the rhyme frequent and never forced, while the entire poem should be marked by tasteful moderation, high finish and completeness." Though perhaps gaining in favor in recent centuries, LIGHT VERSE was popular in Greek and Latin classical literature. The seventeenth and eighteenth centuries in England, too, saw a high development of the type. See LIGHT VERSE, OCCASIONAL VERSE.

**Verse:** Is used in two senses: (1) as a unit of POETRY, in which case it has the same significance as *line;* and (2) as a name given generally to metrical composition. In the second sense, *verse* is simply a generic term applied to rhythmical and, most frequently, metrical and rimed composition, in which case it implies little as to the merit of the composition, the term POETRY or POEM being reserved especially to indicate *verse* of high merit. An inherent suggestion that *verse* is of a lower order than POETRY lies in the fact that *verse* is used in association with such terms as *society verse, occasional verse,* etc., which, it is generally conceded, are rarely applied to great POETRY. The use of *verse* to indicate a STANZA, while common, is hardly justified.

**Versification:** The art and practice of writing VERSE. Like PROSODY the term is an inclusive one, being generally used to connote all the mechanical elements going to make up poetic composition: ACCENT, RHYTHM, the FOOT, METER, RIME, STANZA FORM, DICTION, and such aids as ASSONANCE, ONOMATOPOEIA, and ALLITERATION. In a narrower sense *versification* signifies simply the *structural* form of a VERSE or STANZA such as is revealed by careful SCANSION.

*Vers libre:* See FREE VERSE.

**Victorian:** A term used (1) to designate broadly the literature written during the reign of Queen Victoria (1837–1901) or its characteristic qualities and attitudes; and (2) more narrowly, to suggest a certain complacency or hypocrisy or squeamishness more or less justly assumed to be traceable to or similar to prevailing Victorian attitudes. Pride in the growing power of England, optimism born of the new science, the dominance of Puritan ideals tenaciously held by the rising middle class, and the example of a royal court scrupulous in its adherence to high standards of "decency" and respectability combined to produce a spirit of moral earnestness linked with self-satisfaction which was protested against at the time and in the generations immediately to follow as hypocritical, false, complacent, and narrow. The cautious manner in which "mid-Victorian" writers in particular were prone to treat such matters as profanity and sex has been especially responsible for the common use of the term *Victorian* or "mid-Victorian," to indicate false modesty, empty respectability, or callous complacency. Though justified in part, this use of *Victorian* rests in some degree upon exaggeration, and at best fails to take into consideration the fact that even in the heart of the *Victorian* period a very large part of the literature either did not exhibit such traits or set itself flatly in protest against them. As a matter of fact, *Victorian* literature is many-sided and complex, and reflects both romantically and realistically the great changes that were going on in life and thought. The religious and philosophical doubts and hopes raised by the new science, the social problems arising from the new industrial conditions, the conscious resort of literary men to foreign sources of inspiration, the rise of a new middle-class audience and new media of publication (the MAGAZINES) are among the forces which colored literature during Victoria's reign. Since there are marked differences between the literature written in the early years of Victoria's reign and that written in the later years, this Handbook treats the early years as a part of the ROMANTIC PERIOD and the later years as a part of the REALISTIC PERIOD. See EARLY VICTORIAN AGE, LATE VICTORIAN AGE, ROMANTIC PERIOD IN ENGLISH LITERATURE, REALISTIC PERIOD IN ENGLISH LITERATURE, and the *Outline of Literary History*.

**Villanelle:** A French VERSE form calculated, through its complexity and artificiality, to give an impression of simplicity and spontaneity. The *villanelle* was perhaps originally chiefly PASTORAL and an element of formal lightness is still uppermost since it is most frequently used for poetic expression which is idyllic, delicate, simple, and slight. In form the *villanelle* is characterized by nineteen lines divided into five TERCETS and a final four-line STANZA, and the presence of only two RIMES. The division of VERSES is, then: *aba aba aba aba aba abaa*. Line 1 is repeated entirely to form lines 6, 12, and 18, and line 3 is repeated entirely to form lines 9, 15, and 19: thus eight of the nineteen lines are REFRAIN.

**Virelay:** A French VERSE form (related to LAI) of which the number of STANZAS and the number of lines to the STANZA are unlimited. Each STANZA is made up of an indefinite number of TERCETS riming *aab* for the first STANZA, *bbc* for the second, *ccd* for the third, etc. The *virelay* has never become popular among English poets, probably because of the monotony of the riming.

**Virgin Play:** See MIRACLE PLAY.

**Vulgate:** The word comes from Lat. *vulgus*, "crowd" and means "common" or commonly used. Note two chief uses: (1) the *Vulgate* BIBLE is the Latin version made by Saint Jerome in the fourth century and is the authorized BIBLE of the Catholic Church; (2) the "*Vulgate* ROMANCES" are the versions of various CYCLES of Arthurian ROMANCE which were written in Old French prose (common or colloquial speech) in the thirteenth century and were the most widely used forms of these stories, forming the basis of Malory's *Le Morte Darthur* and other later treatments. See ARTHURIAN ROMANCE.

**Wardour-Street English:** A style strongly marked by ARCHAISMS; an insincere, artificial expression. Wardour Street, in London, is a street housing many antique dealers selling genuine and imitation antiques. *Wardour-Street English* is a term coined on the ANALOGY of imitation ARCHAISMS in writing and imitation antiques in furniture, etc. It was, for instance, applied to William Morris's translation of the *Odyssey*.

**War of the Theatres:** A complicated series of quarrels among certain Elizabethan dramatists in the years 1598–1602. Ben Jonson and John Marston were the chief opponents, though many other dramatists, including Dekker certainly and Shakespeare possibly, were concerned. Among the causes of the quarrel may be mentioned the personal and professional jealousies among some of the playwrights and the keen competition among the rival theatres and their associated companies of actors. Particularly important was the struggle for supremacy between the stock companies of professionals (see PUBLIC THEATRES) and the companies of boy actors, the "Children of the Chapel"—acting at the Blackfriars—and the "Children of Paul's." The child actors were becoming very popular and were threatening to supersede the "common stages," as Shakespeare himself termed his fellows and himself in his allusion to the situation in *Hamlet* (Act II, Scene ii). The details of the affair have not been very completely recovered by modern students. Some of the plays concerned are: Jonson's *Everyman in his Humour* (1598), Marston's *Histriomastix* (1599) and *Jack Drum's Entertainment* (1600), Dekker and others' *Patient Grissel* (1600), Jonson's *Cynthia's Revels* (1601), Dekker's *Satiromastix* (1601). Shakespeare's connection with the quarrel is inferred from the statement in the university play *The Return from Parnasus* (1601–1602) that Shakespeare had bested Jonson, and from the theory that *Troilus and Cressida* reflects the "war." There is a clear allusion to the rivalry of the boy actors and the "common stages" in *Hamlet* (Act II, Scene ii). See SCHOOL PLAYS.

**Welsh Literature:** Though records are scanty it is probable that there was much literary activity in Wales in the early Middle Ages (sixth to ninth centuries). In eastern and central Wales there developed the *englyn,* a form of epigrammatic VERSE possibly derived from Latin literature. The northern district produced the most famous of early Welsh poets, Taleissin and Aneiren (sixth century?), who sang of early Welsh warriors, including heroes traditionally associated with King Arthur. This literature is probably related to the Irish. The western CYCLE deals with very early material, such as myths of the gods. Chiefly from this Western literature come the best known stories of early Welsh authorship, those now collected in the famous MABINOGION. These tales were probably collected and written down in the eleventh and twelfth centuries, though the manuscripts of the MABINOGION date from a few centuries later. The stories in the MABINOGION fall into five classes. The first is the MABINOGION proper, or the "four branches." It includes four stories which are the written versions of spoken TALES belonging to the repertory of the lower orders of Welsh BARDS, and which preserve primitive tradition. The titles are *Pwyll Prince of Dyved, Branwen daughter of Llir, Manawyddan son of Llir,* and *Math son of Mathonwy.* The second group includes two TALES based on legendary British historical tradition: *Dream of Maxen Wledig, Llud and Llwellys.* The third class, old Arthurian folk-tales current in southwest Wales retold by eleventh- or twelfth-century writers with some admixture of other matter, partly Irish, is represented by *Kulwch and Olwen.* This story is of great interest to students of Arthurian ROMANCE as it may reflect a very early stage of the development of Arthurian stories, when magic and grotesqueness had not been displaced by chivalric manners. The fourth class consists of Arthurian stories paralleled in courtly French versions of the twelfth century (some and perhaps all based partly at least upon the French versions): *Peredur, Geraint, The Lady of the Fountain* (or *Owein*). The fifth class (imaginary, sophisticated literary TALES) is represented by *The Dream of Rhonabwry*.

Under Griffith son of Cynan (1054–1137) there was a renaissance of Welsh poetry with courtly patronage—the bardic system was now flourishing. These court poets followed a traditional poetic technique, employing ancient conventions and archaic words to such an extent that a contemporary could hardly understand the verse. With the English conquest (1282) the old poetry declined, and in the fourteenth and fifteenth centuries, known as a "golden age," under the leadership of the poet David ap Gwilynn, a contemporary of Chaucer, the basis of modern Welsh poetry was laid. The language actually spoken was employed, and love and nature were exploited as poetic themes. Under the TUDORS the aggressive English influence depressed native Welsh poetry, though the bards remained active till mid-seventeenth century. In the seventeenth century a new school of poets who utilized native folk materials arose and in the eighteenth century came the classical revival under the influence of the English AUGUSTANS. Poetry in the nineteenth century was largely religious.

The development of PROSE in Wales, as in England, in the sixteenth and seventeenth centuries was fostered by the availability of the printing press and by the vogue of controversial writings, especially those connected with the religious movements of early Protestant times. In the late eighteenth and early nineteenth centuries the liberal movement in politics stimulated further activity in PROSE, and thereafter Welsh literature, both PROSE and POETRY, has been inclined to follow general European movements, as has criticism. Coincident with other phases of the CELTIC RENAISSANCE there was a distinct revival of literary activity in the late nineteenth and early twentieth centuries.

**Whimsical:** A critical term characterizing writing which is fanciful, odd, eccentric. Whimsy, in a sense now obsolete, was used as "a whimsy in the head, or in the blood," implying a sort of vertigo.

*Whimsical* writing, then, is writing inspired by a fantastic or fanciful mood. Lamb's ESSAYS are often *whimsical* in this sense.

**Wit and Humor:** Although neither of these words originally was concerned with the laughable, both now find their chief uses in this connection. At present the distinction between the two terms, though generally recognized to exist, is difficult to draw, although there have been numerous attempts at definition. One great "wit" in fact made a witticism out of his observation that any person who attempted to distinguish between *wit* and *humor* thereby demonstrated that he himself possessed neither *wit* (in the sense of superior mental powers) nor *humor* (which implies a sense of proportion and self-evaluation that would show him the difficulty of attempting a cold analysis of so fugitive a thing as *humor*).

*Humor* is the American spelling of HUMOUR, originally a physiological term which because of its psychological implications came to carry the meaning of "eccentric": from this meaning developed the modern implications of the term. *Wit,* meaning originally knowledge, came in the late Middle Ages to signify "intellect," "the seat of consciousness," the "inner" senses as contrasted with the five "outer" senses. In RENAISSANCE times, though used in various senses, *wit* usually meant "wisdom" or "mental activity." An important critical use developed in the seventeenth century when the term, as applied for example to the metaphysical poets (see METAPHYSICAL VERSE), meant "fancy," in the sense of inspiration, ORIGINALITY, or creative IMAGINATION—this being the literary virtue particularly prized at the time. With the coming of NEO-CLASSICISM, however, the term took on new meanings to reflect new critical attitudes, and for a hundred years many philosophers (including Hobbes, Locke, and Hume) and critics (including Dryden, Addison, Pope, and Johnson) wrestled with efforts to define *wit*. Hobbes asserted that fancy without judgment or reason could not constitute *wit,* though judgment without fancy could. Pope used the word in both of the contrasting senses of fancy and judgment. Dryden had called *wit* "propriety of thought and words," and Locke thought of it as an agreeable and prompt assemblage of ideas, ability to see comparisons. Hume stressed the idea that *wit* is that which pleases ("good TASTE" being the criterion). Amid the confusing variety of eighteenth-century uses of the word, this notion of *wit* as a social grace which gave pleasure led to its comparison with *humor*, and before 1800 both words came to be associated with the laughable, though the older, serious meaning of *wit* did not die out, as the earlier meanings of *humor* (both the medical meaning of one of the four liquids of the human body and the derived meaning of "individual disposition" or "eccentricity") had done. Modern definitions of *wit* reflect both the original and the late eighteenth-century conceptions: "that quality of speech or writing which consists in the apt association of thought and expression, calculated to surprise and delight by its unexpectedness; later always with reference to the utterance of brilliant or sparkling things in an amusing way" (*New English Dictionary*).

It is for the most part agreed that *wit* is primarily intellectual, the perception of similarities in seemingly dissimilar things—the "swift play and flash of mind,"—and is expressed in skillful phraseology, plays upon words, surprising contrasts, PARADOXES, EPIGRAMS, comparisons, etc., while *humor* implies a sympathetic recognition of human values and deals with the foibles and incongruities of human nature, good-naturedly exhibited. A few quotations from writers who have made serious attempts to distinguish between the two terms may help further to clarify the conceptions. *Humor* "deals with incongruities of character and circumstance, as *Wit* does in those of arbitrary ideas" (Hunt). "*Wit* is intensive or incisive, while *humor* is expansive. *Wit* is rapid, *humor* is slow. *Wit* is sharp, *humor* is gentle. . . . *Wit* is subjective while *humor* is objective. . . . *Wit* is art, *humor* is nature."[1] "Wit apart from *Humor*, generally speaking, is but an element for professors to sport with. In combination with *Humor* it runs into the richest utility, and helps to humanize the world" (Hunt). "*Humor* always laughs, however earnestly it feels, and sometimes chuckles; but it never sniggers" (Saintsbury).

Falstaff in Shakespeare's *Henry IV*, Part I, is an example of a subtle interweaving of *wit* and *humor*. The verbal fencing, the punning, and particularly the sophistical maneuvering whereby Falstaff invariably extricates himself from difficult situations with an apparent saving of his face, rest upon his *wit*. On the other hand, the easy recognition on the part of the reader not only that Falstaff is bluffing and is cutting a highly ludicrous figure but also that the old rascal is inwardly laughing at himself, that he sees clearly the

[1]Carolyn Wells, *An Outline of Humor*, G. P. Putnam's Sons, 1923, p. 17. Reprinted by permission of the publishers.

incongruities of his situation and behavior and realizes that his lies will be recognized as such by the Prince, is an element of *humor*. See HUMOURS, COMEDY, SATIRE.

**Women as Actors:** Although they appeared on the Italian and French stages during the RENAISSANCE, women were not countenanced on the professional stage in England, where boys were specially trained to act women's parts. There were sporadic cases of the appearance of women on the stage in England, as in the case of the French actresses in London in 1629, but they were unfavorably received. The part of Ianthe in Davenant's *Siege of Rhodes* (1656) was played by Mrs. Coleman, and the tradition of English actresses is usually dated from this event. However, this piece was more musical and spectacular than dramatic, and Mrs. Coleman's appearance may have been regarded as justified by the custom of having women (not professional actresses) take parts in MASQUES. The lady may have been employed in this entertainment because of her powers as a singer. With the sudden revival of dramatic activity in 1660, actresses became a permanent feature of the English stage. The influence of the French theatre and the lack of a supply of trained boy-actors were perhaps chiefly responsible. Boy-actors were by no means unknown in feminine roles on the RESTORATION stage, however. Some women who early gained fame as actresses were: Mrs. Barry, Mrs. Betterton, Mrs. Bracegirdle (seventeenth century); and Mrs. Susannah Cibber, Mrs. Prichard, and Mrs. Siddons (eighteenth century).

**Word Accent:** The normal or accepted placement of STRESS on the syllables of a word. See ACCENT.

**Wrenched Accent:** An alteration in the customary pronunciation of a word—that is, a shift in WORD ACCENT—to accommodate the demands of METRICAL ACCENT in a line of VERSE. See ACCENT.

**Zeugma:** A term usually applied in America to any construction in which one word is placed in the same grammatical relationship to two other words with which it can be yoked only in different senses, as *stain* is linked in different senses with *honour* and *brocade* in Pope's line, "Or stain her honour, or her new brocade." Strictly speaking, if the linkage is grammatically correct, as the above example is, the yoking is called SYLLEPSIS rather than *zeugma,* with *zeugma* restricted to yokings that are grammatically incorrect, as in "With *weeping* eyes and hearts" or "The orange *was* eaten but the grapes neglected." The distinction, however, is rarely made and *zeugma* is commonly used to include both *zeugma* and SYLLEPSIS.

# SOME STANDARD WORKS ON
# English and American
# Literature

ALTHOUGH an attempt is made in this Handbook to give the salient information about most of the topics with which the serious student of English and American literature is likely to be concerned, the very fact that he is a serious student means that he will frequently be unsatisfied with merely the facts given. It is with the idea of suggesting some of the places where he may look for additional information that this brief essay is prepared. It makes no claim to being definitive, and it is obviously an extremely brief and selective listing. Many other works than those cited may be consulted with equal propriety and profit; the only brief that can be made for this listing is that it cites works which will give authoritative answers to the questions commonly raised or will send the seeker to sources which contain such authoritative answers. Studies of specific authors and limited movements and periods are not listed, although ample information on where to go to learn about such authors and movements is given in the more general works that are cited.

The student seeking information on particular points about English or American literature probably should be urged not to overlook such obvious but often forgotten works as the *Encyclopaedia Britannica* and the *Encyclopedia Americana* and to consult the indexes to these compendiums in instances when the specific thing he seeks does not appear in the normal alphabetic listing. He can often profitably consult *The Oxford Companion to English Literature,* edited by Sir Paul Harvey, and *The Oxford Companion to American Literature,* edited by J. D. Hart. A wealth of data also reposes in *The New Century Handbook of English Literature,* edited by C. L. Barnhart.

Three bibliographical guides are widely used: *A Bibliographical Guide to English Studies,* by T. P. Cross; *A Concise Bibliography for Students of English,* by A. G. Kennedy; and *A Bibliographical*

*Manual for Students of the Language and Literature of England and the United States,* by J. W. Spargo. Each of these guides will direct the student to the basic works in the area in which he is seeking information. Especially useful for students of American literature is *Bibliographical Guide to the Study of the Literature of the U. S. A.,* by Clarence Gohdes. If none of these help, the student may consult I. G. Mudge's *Guide to Reference Books.*

For materials dealing with English literature, the standard bibliographical work is *The Cambridge Bibliography of English Literature,* edited by F. W. Bateson, in four volumes, with a supplementary fifth volume. George Watson has edited a very useful *Concise Cambridge Bibliography of English Literature,* which will often answer quickly questions whose answers it would require more time to seek out in the complete *Bibliography;* the *Concise CBEL* has the advantage of running to 1950, where the parent volume stops at 1900. Students seeking answers to questions about American literature will find in the third volume of *The Literary History of the United States* (described below) an invaluable guide to studies in all significant areas of American literature and on all important American writers. A supplement by Richard Ludwig covers the period 1948–1958.

The "Annual Bibliography" published in the *Publications of the Modern Language Association of America* lists books and articles appearing the preceding year on most of the modern languages and literatures. Prior to 1957 it restricted itself to materials published in America; since 1957 it has been international in its scope. *The Year's Work in English Studies,* a publication of the English Association, in essays by various hands summarizes scholarly publications in the many fields of English literature. Since 1955 it has included an essay on materials about American literature. *The Year's Work* has been appearing since 1919, usually being published about two years after the period being summarized. *Articles on American Literature 1900–1950,* edited by Lewis Leary, is an indispensable listing for workers in American literature. It can be supplemented for materials since 1950 by the quarterly listings appearing in the journal *American Literature. Contemporary Literary Scholarship: a Critical Review,* edited by Lewis Leary, is a detailed survey of recent work on all areas of English and American literary study. In it the student will find an evaluative summary of most of the scholarly work done in the last quarter of a century.

Other important guides to periodical publication are *The Interna-*

*tional Index to Periodicals,* an annual publication which began in 1907 and which includes foreign-language periodicals and scholarly journals; *Poole's Index to Periodical Literature,* an annual running from 1802 to 1881, with supplements from 1882 to 1907, which is an incomplete but still priceless guide to nineteenth century periodicals; and *The Readers' Guide to Periodical Literature,* an annual since 1900, which is especially useful for materials published in nonprofessional magazines.

For detailed technical information on bibliographical problems and methods, the student should consult *An Introduction to Bibliography for Literary Students,* by R. B. McKerrow, and *The Principles of Bibliographical Description,* by Fredson Bowers.

The major work on English literary history is still *The Cambridge History of English Literature,* published in fourteen volumes between 1907 and 1916 under the editorship of A. W. Ward and A. W. Waller. It contains a great many excellent articles on the many topics and facets of English literary history by a variety of authorities. An index in a fifteenth volume increases the ready usefulness of the work. The five-volume series of *Introductions to English Literature,* edited by Bonamy Dobrée, and written by various authors, constitute a group of brief introductions covering the beginnings to 1509, 1510 to 1688, 1689 to 1830, 1831 to 1914, and 1915 to the present. *The Oxford History of English Literature,* edited by F. P. Wilson and Bonamy Dobrée, in a projected fourteen volumes, consists of authoritative treatments of the periods by noted scholars. The following volumes have so far appeared: *Chaucer and the Fifteenth Century,* by H. S. Bennett; *English Literature in the Earlier Seventeenth Century, 1600–1660,* by Douglas Bush; *English Literature at the Close of the Middle Ages,* by E. K. Chambers; and *English Literature in the Sixteenth Century Excluding Drama,* by C. S. Lewis. Two one-volume histories of English literature are noteworthy: *A Literary History of England,* edited by A. C. Baugh, contains long sections by five American scholars and is particularly valuable for its detailed bibliographical data; *The Concise Cambridge History of English Literature,* by George Sampson, is a graceful rendering of the essential substance of the 14-volume work.

*The Cambridge History of American Literature,* published between 1917 and 1921 under the editorship of W. P. Trent, John Erskine, S. P. Sherman, and Carl Van Doren, in four volumes, is a compilation of essays by experts, which, although dated, is still of considerable value. *The Literary History of the United States,* edited by R. E. Spiller, Willard Thorp, H. S. Canby, and T. H. Johnson, presents essays by 55 experts on American literature. Originally in three volumes (the third is the bibliography), this useful work has been reprinted in a one-volume edition without the bibliography. V. L. Parrington's *Main Currents in American Thought* traces social, economic, and philosophical thought as it is reflected in American literature. The first two volumes represented a detailed history, although one biased by Parrington's "Jeffersonian" liberalism, of American thought to 1860; the third, posthumously published and incomplete, carries the record down to 1920. Van Wyck Brooks' *Makers and Finders* is a "history of the writer in America, 1800–1915"; it consists of *The World of Washington Irving; The Flowering of New England; The Times of Melville and Whitman; New England: Indian Summer;* and *The Confident Years: 1885–1915. The Literature of the American People,* edited by A. H. Quinn, is a detailed and thorough one-volume history of American literature by four authorities; it has very valuable selective bibliographies. Notable treatments of periods of American literature are M. C. Tyler's *A History of American Literature During the Colonial Period, 1607–1765,* and *The Literary History of the American Revolution, 1765–1783,* and F. O. Matthiessen's *American Renaissance: Thought and Expression in the Age of Emerson and Whitman.*

Significant special studies of American literature include *The South in American Literature, 1607–1900,* by Jay B. Hubbell; *The Literature of the Middle Western Frontier,* by R. L. Rusk; *Virgin Land: The American West as Symbol and Myth,* by H. N. Smith; *Native American Humor (1800–1900),* by Walter Blair; and *American Humor: A Study of the National Character,* by Constance Rourke.

Of special interest to students of the periodical are Walter Graham, *English Literary Periodicals;* F. L. Mott, *A History of American Magazines,* in four volumes, from the beginnings to 1905; and K. K. Weed and R. P. Bond, *Studies of British Newspapers and Periodicals from Their Beginnings to 1800* (a bibliography).

The history of criticism is covered in George Saintsbury's *A History of Criticism and Literary Taste in Europe* (in three volumes), an early work (1900–1904) but still useful. W. K. Wimsatt, Jr., and Cleanth Brooks, *Literary Criticism: A Short History* is an excellent treatment. René Wellek, *A History of Modern Criticism,*

*1750–1950,* in a projected four volumes of which two have appeared, is detailed and thorough. The history of American criticism is recorded in a cooperative volume by five members of the American Literature Group of the Modern Language Association, *The Development of Literary Criticism in America,* edited by Floyd Stovall; and in *Criticism in America,* by J. P. Pritchard. On the problems of the application of critical principles to literature René Wellek and Austin Warren, in *Theory of Literature,* are informative and helpful. M. H. Abrams' *The Mirror and the Lamp: Romantic Theory and the Critical Tradition* is a brilliant explication of the Romantic aesthetic. I. A. Richards' *Practical Criticism: A Study of Literary Judgment* is an indispensable introduction to the chief attitudes of contemporary criticism; Northrop Frye's *Anatomy of Criticism* is a highly sophisticated exploration of basic critical assumptions, while Wayne Shumaker's *Elements of Critical Theory* is a more elementary and briefer approach to many of the same issues.

For the history of English poetry, the student should consult H. J. C. Grierson and J. C. Smith, *A Critical History of English Poetry.* The following works are useful on problems of technique, form, and interpretation: R. M. Alden, *English Verse;* T. S. Omond, *A Study of Metre;* C. T. Jacobs, *The Foundation and Nature of Verse;* Babette Deutsch, *Poetry Handbook;* P. F. Baum, *The Principles of English Versification;* Cleanth Brooks and R. P. Warren, *Understanding Poetry;* and P. F. Baum, *The Other Harmony of Prose,* a study of prose rhythm.

The standard history of British drama is Allardyce Nicoll, *History of English Drama,* in five volumes, and *British Drama,* in one. For American drama, the standard history is A. H. Quinn, *A History of American Drama: From the Beginning to the Civil War* and *From the Civil War to the Present.* Alan S. Downer, *The British Drama,* is valuable for its analyses of typical plays. Special studies that merit attention include Karl Young, *The Drama of the Mediaeval Church* (two volumes); E. K. Chambers, *The Medieval Stage* (two volumes); E. K. Chambers, *The Elizabethan Stage* (four volumes); and G. E. Bentley, *The Jacobean and Caroline Stage* (five volumes). The basic work on the nature of drama is, of course, Aristotle's *Poetics.* Other studies that are worthy of study include Francis Fergusson, *The Idea of a Theater;* M. E. Pryor, *The Language of Tragedy;* James Feibleman, *In Praise of Comedy;* and R. B. Sharpe, *Irony in the Drama.*

The authoritative work on the English novel is E. A. Baker's ten-volume *History of the English Novel*. Important one-volume histories are R. M. Lovett and Helen S. Hughes, *The History of the Novel in England;* Edward Wagenknecht, *Cavalcade of the English Novel*, with valuable bibliographies; and Walter Allen, *The English Novel*. The best studies of the American novel are Alexander Cowie, *The Rise of the American Novel*, a thorough and scholarly study to 1880; A. H. Quinn, *American Fiction: An Historical Survey*, a work valuable because it treats the short story as well as longer fiction and because it contains many plot summaries; and Edward Wagenknecht, *The Cavalcade of the American Novel*, with valuable bibliographies. On the novel as a form, the following works can be studied with profit: J. W. Beach, *The Twentieth Century Novel: Studies in Technique;* Percy Lubbock, *The Craft of Fiction;* E. M. Forster, *Aspects of the Novel;* Edwin Muir, *The Structure of the Novel;* and Henry James's prefaces, collected as *The Art of the Novel*.

On biography, the following books are useful: Harold Nicolson, *The Development of English Biography;* D. A. Stauffer, *English Biography Before 1700* and *The Art of Biography in Eighteenth Century England;* Edward H. O'Neill, *A History of American Biography, 1800–1935;* and J. A. Garraty, *The Nature of Biography*.

Valuable and even essential though the information that he can get from these and other scholarly works is, the student should be reminded that in the final analysis there is no substitute for the work itself, and the ultimate authority to which every serious student of literature must bow is the living poem, play, or novel reproducing in his imagination the eternal miracle of its indefinable vitality.

# OUTLINE OF
# Literary History
# English and American

EXPLANATORY NOTE. The authors have prepared this outline in the belief that a tabular display of the chief external facts in the history of English and American literature, arranged by periods, will be of definite assistance to students of the literature itself, especially those who find it difficult to acquire from running accounts of literary history the "backbone" of chronology necessary to an understanding of men and movements. Beginning with the year 1607 American items appear in a separate column which runs parallel with the English. The dated items are intended to be suggestive, not comprehensive. A few "non-literary" items are included for their value either as chronological guide-posts or as indications of prevailing cultural conditions.

Both English and American literary history have been divided into relatively arbitrary *periods*, and historical subdivisions within these periods are designated as *ages*. Although this outline gives a few historical facts and general statements about the characteristics of *periods* and *ages*, the fuller treatment of such historical units is reserved for the Handbook, where brief essays on the *periods* and shorter comments on the *ages* are given at the proper places in the alphabetic listings.

*Titles* are often abbreviated or modernized to forms commonly encountered by the student. Translated titles appear in quotation marks in the early periods.

*Dates* for titles of printed books are ordinarily the dates of first publication. Dates for works written before the era of printing are dates of composition, often approximate.

*Abbreviations and Symbols*
    ?   —questionable date or statement of fact.
    °   —non-English item.
    *w*   —written.
    *a*   —acted.
    *ca.*  —about: dating is approximate.
    *fl*  —flourishing, or flourished.
    Lat.—Latin.
    A.S.—Anglo-Saxon.

## ? B.C.–A.D. 428 CELTIC AND ROMAN BRITAIN

| | |
|---|---|
| ? B.C.–A.D. 82 | Celtic Britain. |
| 55, 54 B.C. | Julius Caesar invades Britain. |
| 31 B.C.–A.D. 180 | *Flourishing period of Roman Empire. |
| 43–410 | Roman-Celtic period in Britain: government Roman, population largely Celtic. No literature extant. |
| 43 | Invasion of Claudius. |
| 82 | Roman power established in Britain. |
| 98 | *Tacitus, *Germania* (Lat.): early account of Teutonic ancestors of English. |
| 180–476 | *Decline of Roman Empire. |
| 313 | *Christianity established at Rome by Constantine. |
| 410 | *Rome sacked by Alaric. Roman legions leave Britain. |

## 428–1100 OLD ENGLISH (ANGLO-SAXON) PERIOD

| | |
|---|---|
| 428 | Germanic tribes begin invasion of Britain. |
| 449 | Traditional date (from Gildas and Bede) for Germanic invasion of Britain under Hengist and Horsa. |
| ca.450–ca.700 | Probable period of composition of Old English poems reflecting Continental life: *Beowulf,* epic; *Waldhere,* fragmentary epic of Theodoric saga; *Finnsburg,* fragmentary, related to *Beowulf* background; *Widsith,* lyric, adventures of a wandering poet; *Deor's Lament,* lyric account of poet's troubles; *The Wanderer,* reflective poem on cruelty of fate; *The Seafarer,* reflective, descriptive lyric on sailor's lot in life; *The Wife's Complaint, The Husband's Message:* love poems notable for romantic treatment of nature; *Charms,* miscellaneous incantations reflecting early superstitions, ceremonies, and remedies; formulistic. |
| ca.500–ca.700 | *Christian culture flourishes in Ireland after being almost obliterated on Continent by Teutonic invasion; activity of Irish missionaries in Scotland, Iceland, France, Germany, Switzerland, and Italy aids in rechristianizing Western Europe. |
| 509 | *Closing of Athenian philosophical schools (founded by Plato). |
| ca.524 | *Boëthius, "Consolation of Philosophy" (Lat.): one of greatest books of early Middle Ages; translated into |

English, successively, by King Alfred, Chaucer, and Queen Elizabeth.

563      St. Columba (Irish monk) establishes monastery at Iona, thus preparing for spread of Celtic Christianity in Scotland and Northern England.

570–632      °Mohammed.

590–604      °Pope Gregory the Great: temporal power of papacy, Gregorian Calendar, Gregorian music.

597      Saint Augustine (the missionary) places Roman Christianity on firm basis in Southern England.

600–700      Establishment of powerful Anglo-Saxon kingdoms.

ca.600–ca.800      °Irish saga literature assumes written form.

ca.633      °The Koran.

650?–709      Aldhelm: famous scholar of Canterbury school—Latin works survive; English poems (probably ballads) lost.

664      Synod of Whitby: triumph of Roman over Celtic Christianity in Britain.

ca.670      Caedmon, *Hymns,* etc.: first English poet known by name.

ca.690      Adamnan, *Life of St. Columba* (Lat.): "first authentic manifestation of the biographical impulse in Britain."

ca.700      "School of Caedmon" *fl.*: Genesis, Exodus, Daniel—Biblical paraphrases; Judith, apocryphal.

     *Beowulf* composed in present form: great Anglo-Saxon epic.

731      Bede (Bæda), The Venerable, "Ecclesiastical History" (Lat.): important source-book; first history of English people.

## 750

ca.750–ca.800      Flourishing period of Christian poetry in Northumbria (preserved in later West Saxon versions).

     Cynewulf and his "school": *Crist,* narrative; *Elene,* saint's legend; *Juliana,* saint's legend (dialogue form); *Fates of the Apostles,* saints' legends; *Andreas,* saint's legend (voyage tale); *The Phoenix,* myth interpreted as Christian allegory, notable for conscious poetic art, esp. nature descriptions.

787      First Danish invasion.

     °Charlemagne orders schools established in abbeys.

| | |
|---|---|
| *ca.*800 | Nennius (a Welshman), "History of the Britons" (Lat.): first mention of Arthur. |
| 800–814 | *Reign of Charlemagne: renaissance of learning and literature. |
| 827–1017 | Anglo-Saxon kings (Egbert to Edmund Ironside). |

## 850

| | |
|---|---|
| *ca.*850 | Danish conquest of England. |
| 871–901 | Reign of Alfred the Great: Danes repulsed; Wessex leadership in literature; Alfred both author and patron of literature, esp. prose translations; Alfred's translations of Pope Gregory's *Pastoral Care,* Boëthius, Orosius, Bede; *Anglo-Saxon Chronicle* revised and continued to 892; West Saxon *Martyrology;* sermons; saints' lives. |
| *ca.*875–900 | *Probable beginnings of medieval drama. Dramatization of liturgy. First known text an Easter trope, *Quem Quaeritis,* from Swiss monastery of St. Gall. |
| 878 | Peace of Wedmore; partial Danish evacuation. |
| 893 | Asser, *Life of Alfred the Great:* "first life-record of a layman." |
| 901–1066 | Later Old English Period. *Chronicle* continued; poetry, sermons, Biblical translations and paraphrases, saints' lives, lyrics. |
| *ca.*937 | *Battle of Brunanburh:* heroic poem. |
| 950–1000 | Monastic revival under Dunstan, Aethelwold, and Aelfric. |
| *ca.*950 | *Junius* MS written: contains Caedmon poems. |
| 971 | *Blickling Homilies:* colloquial tendencies. |
| *ca.*975 | St. Ethelwold's *Concordia Regularis,* directions for acting a trope at Winchester: earliest evidence of dramatic activity in England. |
| 979–1016 | Second period of Danish invasions. |
| *ca.*991 | *Battle of Maldon:* heroic poem. |

## 1000

| | |
|---|---|
| 1000–1200 | Transition period, English to Norman French. Decline of A.S. heroic verse; reduced literary activity in English; medieval English lyrics possibly developing; germs of English romances possibly existing in tales and ballads. |
| *ca.*1000 | A.S. *Gospels* written. |

Aelfric, *Sermons:* Aelfric comparable to Bede and Alfred in influence upon Old English culture.

*Beowulf* MS written.

| | |
|---|---|
| 1000–1025 | The *Exeter Book:* A.S. MS containing Cynewulf poems. |
| *ca.*1000–1100 | *Vercelli Book:* A.S. MS containing *Andreas,* etc. |
| | °Probable period of full development of Christmas and Easter cycles of plays in Western Europe. |
| 1017–1042 | Danish kings (Canute to Hardicanute). |
| 1042–1066 | Saxon kings restored (Edward the Confessor to Harold II). |
| 1066 | Battle of Senlac (Hastings). Norman conquest. |
| 1066–1154 | Norman kings (William I to Stephen). |
| 1079 | °Abélard born. Died 1142. French ecclesiastical philosopher. Lover of Héloïse. |
| 1086 | *Domesday Book:* important English census. |
| 1087–1100 | William II: centralization of kingdom. |
| 1096–1099 | The First Crusade: the crusades exerted some influence upon Western European literature by stimulating the imagination, widening mental horizons, and by making Oriental culture available. |

## 1100–1350 ANGLO-NORMAN PERIOD

### 1100

| | |
|---|---|
| 1100–1200 | °French literature dominating Western Europe. |
| 1100–1135 | Reign of Henry I ("Beauclerc"). |
| *ca.*1100–1250 | °Icelandic sagas written: *Grettirsaga, Volsungsaga,* etc. |
| *ca.*1100 | "Play of St. Catherine" (*a.* at Dunstable): first recorded "miracle" or saint's play in England. |
| | °Earlier tales in Welsh *Mabinogion* (*w*). |
| | °"The Book of the Dun Cow": earliest existing MS containing early Irish romantic literature. |
| | °Great period of French poetry begins, lyric in South (Provence), narrative in North. *Chanson de Roland:* French epic. Count William of Poitiers (Provençal lyricist), "the first modern poet." |
| *ca.*1125–1300 | Latin chronicles *fl.* |

| | |
|---|---|
| *ca.*1125 | Henry of Huntingdon and William of Malmesbury: chronicles. |
| 1135–1154 | Reign of Stephen. |
| *ca.*1136 | Geoffrey of Monmouth, "History of the Kings of Britain" (Lat. chronicle). Stresses Arthur as national hero and monarch: first elaborate, romantic account of Arthurian court; a source for many later writers. |
| *ca.*1140 | Eadmer, *Life of Anselm:* human element in biography. |

### 1150

| | |
|---|---|
| 1150–1200 | *Influential French poets flourishing: Wace, Chrétien de Troyes, Marie de France, Thomas, Benoît de Ste. More, etc. Romance themes, courtly ideals. |
| *ca.*1150 | *The *Nibelungenlied:* great epic poem treating early Germanic history. |
| 1154–1399 | Plantagenet kings (Henry II to Richard II). |
| 1154–1189 | Reign of Henry II: his court a center of literature and learning—historians, philosophers, theologians, poets. French and Latin chiefly employed. |
| 1154 | End of entries in *A.S. Chronicle* (Peterborough). |
| *ca.*1155 | *Wace, *Brut* (French). |
| *ca.*1160 | *Benoît de Ste. More, *Roman de Troie.* |
| *ca.*1170 | *Poema Morale.* |
| 1172 | First English effort to conquer Ireland. |
| *ca.*1185–1190 | *Giraldus Cambrensis, "Itinerary": description of Wales. |
| 1187 | *Saracens capture Jerusalem. |
| 1189–1199 | Reign of Richard I ("The Lion-hearted"). |
| *ca.*1190 | Nigel Wireker, *Speculum stultorum* (Lat.), "The Fool's Looking-glass." |
| 1199–1216 | Reign of John. |

### 1200

| | |
|---|---|
| 1200–1300 | *Gothic architecture *fl.* |
| *ca.*1200–1250 | *King Horn, Beves of Hampton* (earliest form): English metrical romances using English themes. |
| *ca.*1200–1225 | *The Vulgate Romances (expansion of Arthurian romance material in French prose). |
| | *Walther von der Vogelweide *fl.* (German lyric poet). |

| | |
|---|---|
| *ca.*1200 | Walter Map *fl.*: court satirist, reputed author of Arthurian prose romances. |
| | Orm, *Ormulum:* Scriptural poem; early, though detached, effort to spell English words systematically. |
| | * Robert de Boron: trilogy of Arthurian poems (French): connects Grail story with Christian legend. |
| *ca.*1205 | Layamon, *Brut.* |
| 1215 | *Magna Charta.* |
| 1216–1272 | Reign of Henry III. |
| *ca.*1225 | *St. Thomas Aquinas born. Died 1274. One of the greatest of medieval "scholastic" teachers and writers. Founder of "Thomists." |
| *ca.*1230, *ca.*1270 | *Roman de la Rose* by Guillaume de Lorris and Jean de Meun. |

### 1250

| | |
|---|---|
| *ca.*1250–1300 | Satiric spirit prominent in literature. *Sir Tristrem, Floris and Blanchefleur* (romances). |
| *ca.*1250 | Nicholas of Guilford, *The Owl and the Nightingale.* The "Cuckoo Song" (*Sumer is Icumen in*). *Gesta Romanorum.* |
| 1258 | Henry III uses English as well as French in proclamation. |
| 1265 | *Dante born. Died 1321. |
| 1272–1307 | Reign of Edward I. |
| 1287 | *Guido delle Colonna, "History of Troy" (Lat.): widely read medieval version of Trojan war. |
| *ca.*1294 | *Dante, *Vita Nuova.* |

### 1300

| | |
|---|---|
| 1300–1400 | Leveling of inflections. Growth of English language in subtlety and power, as it is increasingly used for learned works. Decay of dialectal forms in English progressing. East Midland dialect (descended from Mercian) becomes standard literary English. English displaces French in speech of upper classes, and in schools and law pleadings. Mystery plays now in hands of guilds: more actors, more spectators, outdoor stages, comic elements, "cyclic" development (York plays probably oldest existing cycle). |
| *ca.*1300–1321 | *Dante's later works: *Il Convito* (begun *ca.*1300), *De Vulgari Eloquentia* (*ca.*1305, criticism), *Divina Commedia* (*ca.*1307–1321). |

| | |
|---|---|
| *ca.*1300–1350 | *Guy of Warwick, Havelok the Dane, Richard Lionheart, Amis and Amiloun:* romances. |
| *ca.*1300 | °Marco Polo, "Travels." <br> *Cursor Mundi.* |
| 1304 | °Petrarch born. Died 1374. Great influence upon English poetry of Renaissance, esp. sonnet sequences. |
| 1306 | °Bruce crowned in Scotland. |
| 1307–1327 | Reign of Edward II. |
| 1311 | Feast of Corpus Christi established, leading to popularization of cyclic plays at this summer festival and perhaps to use of movable stages or "pageants." |
| 1313 | °Boccaccio born. Died 1375: important source-influence on Chaucer and many Renaissance authors; author of world-famous tales. |
| 1314 | Battle of Bannockburn. |
| *ca.*1325 | °Giotto (Ital. painter) and Jan van Eyck (Flemish painter) *fl.* |
| 1327–1377 | Reign of Edward III. |
| 1328? | Chester cycle of plays composed. |
| 1337–1453 | The Hundred Years' War. |
| *ca.*1340 | Geoffrey Chaucer born. Died 1400. <br> Rolle, *The Prick of Conscience.* |
| 1342 | °Boccaccio, *Ameto:* "first pastoral romance." |
| 1346 | Battle of Crécy. |
| 1348–1350 | The Black Death. |
| 1349 | Order of the Garter established. |

## *1350–1500 MIDDLE ENGLISH PERIOD*

| | |
|---|---|
| 1350–1400 | *Sir Eglamour, Morte Arthure, Sir Gawayne and the Green Knight, Athelstan, William of Palerne, Sir Ferumbras, Sir Isumbras,* and other romances. |
| *ca.*1350 | °Petrarch, eclogues (Lat.), printed 1504. "Sonnets to Laura" partly written. <br> °Boccaccio, *Decameron.* |
| 1356 (?) | "Sir John Mandeville," *Voyage and Travels.* |
| *ca.*1360 | *The Pearl.* |
| 1362 | English language used in court pleadings and in opening Parliament. |

| | |
|---|---|
| *ca.*1362 *et. seq.* | *Piers Plowman.* |
| *ca.*1370 | Chaucer, *The Book of the Duchess.* |
| *ca.*1375 | Barbour, *Bruce.* |
| | "Paternoster" and "Creed" plays (*a*): forerunners of morality plays. |
| 1377–1399 | Richard II. |
| *ca.*1379 | Chaucer, *House of Fame.* |
| *ca.*1380 | Wycliffe and others, translation of Bible into English. |
| 1381 | Wat Tyler's rebellion. |
| *ca.*1383 | Chaucer, *Troilus and Criseyde.* |
| | Usk (?) *The Testament of Love.* |
| *ca.*1385 | English replaces French as language of the schools. |
| | Chaucer *Legend of Good Women.* |
| *ca.*1387 | Chaucer, "Prologue" to *Canterbury Tales* (tales themselves written some earlier, some later). |
| 1390–1392 | Gower, *Confessio Amantis.* |
| 1399–1461 | House of Lancaster (Henry IV to Henry VI). |
| 1399–1413 | Reign of Henry IV. |
| 1400 | Death of Chaucer. |

## 1400

| | |
|---|---|
| 1400–1450 | Later romances in prose and verse: *Lancelot of the Lake, Four Sons of Aymon, Squire of Low Degree, Huon of Bordeaux, Sir Triamour, Godfrey of Boulogne,* etc. |
| | °Brunelleschi (Ital. architect) and Vittorino de Feltre (Ital. educator) *fl.* |
| 1400–1425 | Wakefield cycle of plays (MS, *ca.*1450). |
| | *The Pride of Life* (fragmentary): earliest extant morality play. |
| 1400 | °Froissart, *Chronicles.* |
| *ca.*1412 | Hoccleve, *The Regiment of Princes* (*w*). |
| 1413–1422 | Reign of Henry V: further progress of English in replacing French among guilds and in other similar everyday business. |
| 1415 | Battle of Agincourt. |
| *ca.*1415 | Lydgate, *Troy Book.* |
| 1422–1507 | The *Paston Letters:* family correspondence reflecting social conditions. |

| | |
|---|---|
| 1422–1461 | Reign of Henry VI. |
| *ca.*1425 | Humanists active under patronage of Humphrey, Duke of Gloucester: Lydgate, Pecock, etc. English students attend Italian universities. Manuscripts collected. Translations made. |
| | *Castle of Perseverance:* first complete morality play. |
| 1440 | Galfridus Grammaticus, *Promptorium Parvulorum:* English-Latin word-list, beginning of English lexicography. |

## *1450*

| | |
|---|---|
| 1450 | Jack Cade's rebellion. |
| *ca.*1450 | "Tiptoft" School of humanists active. |
| | °Gutenberg press: beginning of modern printing. |
| | Beginning of Lowland Scotch as northern literary dialect. |
| *ca.*1450–1525 | Scottish poets of Chaucerian school: Henryson, Dunbar, Douglas, and probably King James I of Scotland. |
| | °Italian Renaissance at its height: scholars, theologians, teachers, philosophers, painters, poets. |
| *ca.*1450–1490 | °Platonic Academy at Florence flourishing under Lorenzo the Magnificent: Ficino, Poliziano, Pico della Mirandola, etc. |
| 1453 | °Fall of Constantinople: end of Eastern Empire. |
| 1455–1485 | Wars of the Roses: depressing effect on literary activity. |
| 1456 | °The Gutenberg Bible. |
| 1458–1464 | °Pope Pius II (Æneas Sylvius Piccolomini): great humanist. |
| *ca.*1460 | John Skelton born. Died 1529. |
| 1461–1485 | House of York (Edward IV to Richard III). |
| 1461–1483 | Reign of Edward IV. |
| 1469 | Sir Thomas Malory completes composition of *Le Morte Darthur* (pub. 1485). |
| 1474 | °Ariosto born. Died 1532. |
| *ca.*1474 | Caxton prints (at Bruges) the *Recuyell of the Histories of Troy:* first book printed in English. |
| 1475–1500 | Renewal of French influence. Italian influence continues. Transition to Renaissance. Printing of books begins in England. Humanistic activity renewed. °Romantic epics written in Italy. |
| *ca.*1477 | Caxton's press set up at Westminster: first printing press |

|  |  |
|---|---|
| | in England. *Dictes and Sayings of the Philosophers,* the first dated book (1477) printed in England. |
| 1478 | Sir Thomas More born. Died 1535. |
| 1483 | Reign of Edward V. |
| 1483–1485 | Reign of Richard III. |
| 1485–1603 | House of Tudor (Henry VII to Elizabeth). |
| 1485–1509 | Reign of Henry VII. |
| 1485 | Caxton publishes Malory's *Le Morte Darthur:* great prose compilation of Arthurian lore; important source-book for later English poets. |
| *ca.*1490 | °Sanazzaro, *Arcadia.* |
| | °Rabelais born. Died 1553. |
| 1490–1520 | "Oxford Reformers" (Linacre, Grocyn, Colet, Erasmus, More) active: classical scholarship, Biblical and literary criticism, humanistic education. |
| 1491 | Greek taught at Oxford. |
| 1492 | °Discovery of America by Columbus. |
| *ca.*1497 | Medwall, *Fulgens and Lucres* (*a*). |
| 1498 | °Savonarola executed. |
| 1499 | Erasmus in England. |

## *1500–1660 THE RENAISSANCE*

### *1500–1557 EARLY TUDOR AGE*

|  |  |
|---|---|
| 1500–1550 | °Artists flourishing: Dürer, Holbein (German), Leonardo da Vinci, Michelangelo, Raphael, Titian, Correggio (Italian). |
| | Romances.—*Valentine and Orson,* Lord Berners' *Arthur of Little Britain, Huon of Bordeaux,* etc. |
| *ca.*1500 | *Everyman.* |
| 1503 (?) | Sir Thomas Wyatt born. Died 1542. |
| *ca.*1508 | Skelton, *Philip Sparrow.* |
| 1509–1547 | Reign of Henry VIII. |
| 1509 | Barclay, *Ship of Fools.* <br> Hawes, *Pastime of Pleasure.* |
| 1510 | Acting of Terence's comedies an established practice at at Oxford and Cambridge. |
| *ca.*1511 | °Erasmus, "The Praise of Folly" (Lat.), social satire. |

| 1515 | Roger Ascham born. Died 1568. |
|------|-------------------------------|
| 1516 | More, *Utopia* (Lat.). |
| 1516 (?) | *Ariosto, *Orlando Furioso*. |
| | Skelton, *Magnificence*. |
| | Henry Howard, Earl of Surrey born. Died 1547. |
| 1517 | *Luther posts his theses in Wittenberg; leads to Protestant Revolution, 1520 *et seq.* |
| 1518 | Linacre founds Royal College of Physicians. |
| 1519 | Rastell, *The Four Elements* (*w. ca.*1512): first published interlude. Advocates adequacy of English for literary purposes. |
| | *Cortez conquers Mexico. |
| 1520–1530 | Latin plays (both original and translated from classics) acted in grammar schools. |
| *ca.*1520 | Skelton's poetical satires, personal, political, ecclesiastical (*Colin Clout, Why Come Ye Not to Court,* etc.). |
| 1523 | Lord Berners' trans. of Froissart's *Chronicles*. |
| 1523 | *Ronsard born. Died 1585. |

*1525*

| 1525 | Tyndale, *New Testament:* printed at Worms; first printed English translation of any part of Bible; influenced phraseology of later versions. |
|------|-------------------------------|
| 1528 | *Castiglione, *The Courtier*. |
| 1529 | Simon Fish, *Supplication for Beggars*. |
| | Fall of Wolsey. |
| 1530–1535 | *Marot (French poet) *fl.:* influenced Spenser. |
| *ca.*1530–1540 | Heywood's "Interludes": realistic farce; approach to comedy. |
| *ca.*1530 | The "New Poetry" movement under way; Italian influence. |
| 1531 | Elyot, *The Book of the Governour*. |
| 1532 | *Machiavelli, *The Prince* (*w.* 1513). |
| 1533 | Separation of English church from Rome. |
| | John Leland made "King's Antiquary." |
| | *Rabelais, *Pantagruel*. |
| 1534 | Act of Supremacy: Henry VIII head of Church of England. |

°Loyola founds Society of Jesus ("Jesuits").

1535    Suppression of monasteries under way: loss of precious manuscripts; redistribution of land; changed social conditions.

Execution of More.

Coverdale's first complete English Bible.

°Rabelais, *Gargantua.*

1536    Execution of Tyndale.

°Calvin, *Institutes of Christian Religion* (Lat.).

1538    Sir Thomas Elyot, *Dictionarie.*

1540    English Bible (the "Great Bible") set up in churches.

1542    Death of Wyatt.

Hall's *Chronicle.*

1542 (?)    George Gascoigne born. Died 1577.

1543    °Death of Copernicus.

1545    Ascham, *Toxophilus.*

°Council of Trent.

1547–1553    Reign of Edward VI.

1547    Execution of Surrey.

1548–1552    *Book of Common Prayer.*

1549    °Du Bellay, *Defense et Illustration de la Langue Française:* poetic platform of the *Pléiade.*

### 1550

1550–1575    °The *Pléiade* group of French poets *fl.* (Du Bellay, Ronsard, etc.).

1552    Lyndsay, *Satyre of the Three Estaits.*

°Ronsard, *Amours:* French sonnets.

ca.1552    Edmund Spenser born. Died 1599.

Sir Walter Raleigh born. Died 1618.

Udall, *Ralph Roister Doister* (*w*): first "regular" English comedy.

1553–1558    Reign of Mary.

1553    Wilson, *Arte of Rhetorique.*

1554    Sir Philip Sidney born. Died 1586.

°Bandello, *Novelle* (Ital. tales).

ca.1554    °*La Vida de Lazarillo de Tormes:* Spanish picaresque tale.

| *ca*.1555 | Roper, *Life of Sir Thomas More* (*w*). |
| | Cavendish, *Life of Cardinal Wolsey* (*w*). |
| 1557 | *Songs and Sonnets* ("Tottel's Miscellany"). |
| | Surrey's trans. of two books of the *Aeneid* in blank verse. |
| | North's trans. of Guevara's *Dial of Princes*. |
| | Stationers' Company incorporated. |

### 1558–1603   ELIZABETHAN AGE

### 1558

| 1558–1603 | Reign of Elizabeth. |
| 1558–1575 | Period of experiment and preparation. Age of Gascoigne. Translations numerous, classics often translated into English through French versions. Much interest in lyrics. |
| 1558 | John Knox, *First Blast of the Trumpet against the Monstrous Regiment of Women.* |
| 1559 | Elizabethan Prayer-book. |
| | *The Mirror for Magistrates.* |
| | *Amyot, Plutarch's *Lives* translated into French: basis of North's English version of Plutarch. |
| | *Minturno, *De Poeta:* Italian critical work. |
| 1559 (?) | George Chapman born. Died 1634. |
| *ca*.1560 | *Gammer Gurton's Needle* (*w*). |
| 1561 | Hoby's translation of Castiglione's *The Courtier.* |
| | Francis Bacon born. Died 1626. |
| | *Scaliger, *Poetics:* Italian critical work. |
| 1562 | Sackville and Norton, *Gorboduc* (*a*): first English tragedy. |
| | Samuel Daniel born. Died 1618. |
| 1563 | Foxe, *Book of Martyrs:* (Lat. original, 1559). |
| | Sackville's "Induction" (to portion of *Mirror for Magistrates*). |
| | Michael Drayton born. Died 1631. |
| *ca*.1563 | Sir Humphrey Gilbert, *Queen Elizabeth's Academy.* |
| 1564 | Preston, *Cambises* (*a*). |
| | Christopher Marlowe born. Died 1593. |
| | William Shakespeare born. Died 1616. |
| | *Galileo born. Died 1642. |
| 1565–1567 | Golding's translation of Ovid's *Metamorphoses.* |

| | |
|---|---|
| 1566 | Gascoigne's *Supposes* (*a*) and *Jocasta* (*a*). |
| 1566–1567 | Painter, *Palace of Pleasure.* |
| 1567 | Turberville, *Epitaphs, Epigrams, Songes, and Sonets.* |
| 1570 | Ascham, *Schoolmaster.* |
| 1572 | *Massacre of St. Bartholomew. <br> Founding of Society of Antiquaries. |
| 1573 | John Donne born. Died 1631. <br> Ben Jonson born. Died 1637. |

## 1575

| | |
|---|---|
| 1575–1590 | Activity of Shakespeare's predecessors and early contemporaries—Kyd, Lyly, Marlowe, Peele, Greene, Nash. Court comedies, melodramatic tragedies, chronicle history plays popular. Interest in literary criticism. Puritan attack on poetry. Patriotic poems. Translations. Spenser's early work. Early pastoral and euphuistic romances. |
| 1575 | Gascoigne, *The Posies:* Poems with first English treatise on versification appended. <br> Mystery plays still being acted at Chester. |
| 1576–1580 | Spenser's early poetry (*w*). |
| 1576 | *Paradise of Dainty Devices.* <br> The Theatre (first London playhouse) built. <br> Gascoigne, *The Steel Glass.* <br> George Pettie, *A Petite Palace of Pettie his Pleasure.* |
| 1578 | Holinshed, *Chronicles:* important source for patriotic chronicle plays on London stage. <br> Drake circumnavigates globe. <br> *A Gorgeous Gallery of Gallant Inventions:* poetical miscellany. |
| 1579 | Lyly, *Euphues, the Anatomy of Wit.* <br> Spenser, *The Shepheardes Calender* (pub. anonymously). <br> Gosson, *School of Abuse:* attack on poetry and the stage. <br> North, trans. of Plutarch's *Lives.* <br> John Fletcher born. Died 1625. |
| 1580–1600 | Elizabethan "novels" popular: Lyly, Greene, Lodge, Sidney, Nash, Deloney. Pastoral poetry popular. |
| 1580 | *Montaigne, *Essays:* beginning of modern "personal" essay. |
| *ca.*1580 | Lyly, *Alexander and Campaspe* (*a*). |

| 1581 | °Tasso, *Jerusalem Delivered:* Ital. romantic epic. |
| *ca.*1581 | Peele, *Arraignment of Paris* (*a*). |
| | Sidney, *Defence of Poesie* (*w*) (pub. 1595): first great critical essay in English. |
| 1582–1600 | Hakluyt publishes various collections of "voyages"— Renaissance and medieval, notably *Principal Navigations* (1st ed. 1589). |
| 1582 | Camden, *Britannia* (Lat.). |
| | Stanyhurst, trans. of Virgil's *Æneid* (i–iv) in quantitative verse. |
| 1583 | P. Stubbs, *Anatomie of Abuses.* |
| 1584 | Scot, *Discovery of Witchcraft.* |
| | *Handful of Pleasant Delights:* ballad miscellany. |
| 1585 | Raleigh fails in effort to colonize Virginia. |
| | °Guarini, *Pastor Fido* (*a*): Italian pastoral drama. |
| 1586 | Kyd, *The Spanish Tragedy* (*a*). |
| | Warner, *Albion's England.* |
| | Death of Sidney. |
| 1586 (?) | Shakespeare comes to London. |
| 1587 | Marlowe, *Tamburlaine* (*a*). |
| | Execution of Mary Queen of Scots. |
| 1588–1589 | "Martin Marprelate" papers. |
| 1588 | Defeat of Spanish Armada. |
| *ea.*1588 | Marlowe, *Doctor Faustus* (*a*). |
| 1589 | Greene, *Menaphon.* |
| | Puttenham (?), *The Arte of English Poesie.* |

## 1590

| 1590–1600 | Greatly increased literary activity, richest decade of Elizabethan literature; great activity in poetry, flourishing of lyrics, pastorals, sonnets, dramatic poetry, serious verse (historical, didactic, patriotic), classical verse-satire; rapid development of drama of all types; realistic tendencies beginning to challenge romantic; classical spirit rising. Prose fiction continues: pastoral romance, picaresque novel. |
| 1590 | Lodge, *Rosalynde.* |
| | Sidney, *Arcadia* (*w. ca.*1581). |
| | Spenser, *Faerie Queene,* Books I–III. |

| | |
|---|---|
| *ca.*1590 | Greene, *James IV* (*a*). |
| | Shakespeare begins career as playwright. |
| 1591–1596 | Flourishing period of sonnet cycles: Sidney, Daniel, Drayton, Lodge, Spenser, and others. |
| 1591 | Spenser, *Complaints:* includes *Mother Hubberds Tale* (satirical beast fable in heroic couplets), and other poems. |
| | Harrington, trans. of Ariosto's *Orlando Furioso.* |
| | Sidney, *Astrophel and Stella.* |
| | Robert Herrick born. Died 1674. |
| 1593 | Shakespeare, *Venus and Adonis.* |
| | *Phoenix Nest:* poetical miscellany. |
| | Death of Marlowe. |
| | Izaak Walton born. Died 1683. |
| | George Herbert born. Died 1633. |
| 1594 | Hooker, *Ecclesiastical Polity*, Books I–IV. |
| | Shakespeare, *Rape of Lucrece.* |
| | Nash, *The Unfortunate Traveler:* picaresque romance. |
| 1595 | Shakespeare, *Richard III* (*a*). |
| | Spenser, *Amoretti; Epithalamion.* |
| | Sidney, *Defence of Poesie* (*w. ca.*1581). |
| | Daniel, *Civil Wars.* |
| | Lodge, *A Fig for Momus.* |
| | Donne's poetry of revolt and classical satires circulating in manuscript. |
| 1596 | Raleigh, *Discovery of Guiana* (*w*) (pub. 1606). |
| | Shakespeare, *Romeo and Juliet* (*a*), *Midsummer Night's Dream* (*a*). |
| | Spenser, *Faerie Queene*, Books IV–VI. |
| 1597–1599 | Shakespeare's Falstaff plays (*a*): *Henry IV*, 1, 2; *Henry V; Merry Wives of Windsor.* |
| 1597 | Shakespeare, *Merchant of Venice* (*a*). |
| | Drayton, *Heroical Epistles.* |
| | Bacon, *Essays* (1st ed.). |
| | Hall, *Virgidemiarum.* |
| | King James (of Scotland), *Demonology:* answers Scot (see p. 534), defends reality of witchcraft. |
| 1598 | Shakespeare, *Julius Caesar* (*a*). |
| | Meres, *Palladis Tamia,* "Wit's Treasury." |
| | Ben Jonson begins career as playwright—*Everyman in His Humour* (*a*). |

Marston, *The Scourge of Villainy.*

Chapman, translation of *Iliad* (seven books in "four-teeners").

Globe theatre built: used by Shakespeare's company.

*ca.*1598    Deloney, *The Gentle Craft.*

1599    Shakespeare's "joyous comedies": *Much Ado about Nothing; As You Like It; Twelfth Night.*

*The Passionate Pilgrim:* miscellany containing some of Shakespeare's poems.

Death of Spenser.

### 1600

1600–1625    Artists flourishing: Inigo Jones (Eng. architect); °Rubens, Van Dyck (Flemish painters).

1600    *England's Helicon:* poetical miscellany.

°Peri, *Euridice* (Ital.): beginning of Italian opera.

1601    Failure of Essex rebelllion.

1602–1603    Shakespeare, the "bitter comedies": *Troilus and Cressida, All's Well That Ends Well, Measure for Measure* (*a*).

1602    Shakespeare, *Hamlet* (*a*).

Campion, *Observations in the Art of English Poesie.*

Founding of the Bodleian Library (Oxford).

*ca.*1602    Daniel, *Defence of Ryme.*

### 1603–1625   JACOBEAN AGE

---

1603–1649    The Stuarts.

1603–1625    Reign of James I—union of English and Scottish crowns.

1603    T. Heywood, *A Woman Killed with Kindness* (*a*).

Jonson, *Sejanus* (*a*).

Florio, translation of Montaigne.

1604    Shakespeare, *Othello* (*a*).

1605    Bacon, *Advancement of Learning.*

Gunpowder Plot.

°Cervantes, *Don Quixote,* Part I.

Sir Thomas Browne born. Died 1682.

1606    Shakespeare, *Macbeth* (*a*), *King Lear.*

Jonson, *Volpone* (*a*).

Sir William Davenant born. Died 1668.

°Corneille born. Died 1684.

**ENGLISH**

1607 Bacon made Solicitor-General.

Shakespeare, *Antony and Cleopatra* (*a*).

Beaumont and Fletcher, *Knight of the Burning Pestle* (*a*).

1608 John Milton born. Died 1674.

Joseph Hall, *Characters of Virtues and Vices.*

1609 Shakespeare, *Sonnets* (*w.* earlier).

Beaumont and Fletcher, *Philaster* (*a*).

Dekker, *Gull's Hornbook.*

*Life of Sir Thomas Bodley* (*w*) (pub. 1647): "oldest prose autobiography in English."

*Galileo active with telescope.

1607 Settlement at Jamestown, Va.

1608 *Champlain founds Quebec.

Capt. John Smith, *True Relation:* early experiences in Virginia.

1609 Champlain discovers Lake Champlain.

Henry Hudson explores Hudson River.

*1610*

1610 Jonson, *Alchemist* (*a*).

1610–1611 Shakespeare, the "serene romances" or tragi-comedies: *Cymbeline, Winter's Tale, Tempest* (*a*).

1611 King James or "authorized" translation of the Bible.

*ca.*1611 Shakespeare returns to Stratford.

1612 Bacon, *Essays* (2nd ed.).

1610 Lord Delaware becomes governor of Virginia.

Strachey, *True Repertory.*

1612 Capt. John Smith, *A Map of Virginia.*

Donne, First and Second *Anniversaries.*

Samuel Butler born. Died 1680.

1613 *Purchas His Pilgrimage:* travel literature.

Wither, *Abuses Stript and Whipt.*

1614 Overbury, *Characters.*

Raleigh, *History of the World.*

Webster, *Duchess of Malfi* (*a*).

°Lope de Vega *fl.*

1615 Harrington, *Epigrams.*

1616 Death of Shakespeare and of °Cervantes.

1616 Capt. John Smith, *A Description of New England.*

Chapman, *Odyssey* translated in heroic couplets.

1618–1648 °The Thirty Years' War, Protestants against Catholics.

1618 Raleigh executed.

Bacon made Lord Chancellor.

Harvey discovers circulation of the blood.

Abraham Cowley born. Died 1667.

1619 Drayton, *Collected Poems.*

1619 First American legislative assembly, at Jamestown.

Negro slavery introduced into Virginia.

*1620*

1620 Bacon, *Novum Organum* (Lat.).

1620 Pilgrims land at Plymouth.

*Mayflower Compact* (*w*).

1621 Burton, *Anatomy of Melancholy.*

1622 °Molière (French dramatist) born. Died 1673.

Donne, *Sermon on Judges xx. 15* (other sermons published in 1623, 1624, 1625, 1626, 1627, and later).

1623 First Folio edition of Shakespeare's *Plays.*

1622 George Sandys completes poetical translation of Ovid's *Metamorphoses* (English author writing in America).

Mourts' *Relation* by Bradford and others: journal.

1624 Capt. John Smith, *General History of Virginia.*

Edward Winslow, *Good News out of New England.*

---

## 1625–1649   CAROLINE AGE

---

### 1625

1625–1649 Reign of Charles I.

1625 Bacon, *Essays,* final edition.

1626 Death of Bacon.

1627 Bacon, *New Atlantis* (Lat.): fragmentary "utopia."

Drayton, *Ballad of Agincourt.*

1628 John Bunyan born. Died 1688.

1629 Ford, *The Broken Heart* (*a*).

Milton, *Ode on the Morning of Christ's Nativity* (*w*).

Unsuccessful appearance of French actresses on English stage.

1625 Morrell, *Nova Anglia.*

1626 Minuit founds New Amsterdam.

1627 Thomas Morton sets up Maypole at Merrymount: reflects opposition to Puritans.

### 1630

1630–1649 Winthrop, *History of New England* (*w*).

1630–1647 Bradford, *History of the Plymouth Plantation* (*w*).

1630 Milton, *On Shakespeare* (*w*).

°Malherbe (1555–1628), *Works:* Renaissance French forerunner of classicism.

1631 Deaths of Drayton and Donne.

John Dryden born. Died 1700.

1632 Second Folio edition of Shakespeare.

1633 Herbert, *The Temple.*

Donne, *Poems* (first collected edition).

Phineas Fletcher, *The Purple Island.*

1633(?) Milton's *L'Allegro* and *Il Penseroso* written.

Samuel Pepys born. Died 1703.

1634 Milton, *Comus* (*a*).

Davenant, *The Temple of Love:* French Platonic love.

1635 Quarles, *Emblems.*

°French Academy incorporated.

1636 °Corneille, *The Cid.*

1637 Death of Jonson.

°Descartes, *Discours sur la Méthode.*

1638 Milton, *Lycidas.*

1639 °Racine (French dramatist) born. Died 1699.

---

1630 Massachusetts Bay colony established at Salem by non-Separatist dissenters.

1632 Thomas Hooker, *The Soul's Preparation.*

1634 Maryland settled by English.

Connecticut Valley settled.

1635 Roger Williams decides Massachusetts belongs to Indians and is banished.

1636 Roger Williams founds Providence; all sects tolerated.

Harvard College founded.

1637 Pequot War.

Thomas Morton, *New English Canaan.*

1639 Baptist Church in America founded by Williams.

First printing press in America set up at Cambridge.

Increase Mather born. Died 1723.

## 1640

| ENGLISH | AMERICAN |
|---|---|

1640 Jonson, *Timber, or Discoveries Made upon Men and Matter.*

Izaak Walton, *Life of Donne.*

1640 *Bay Psalm Book:* first book printed in America.

1641 Shepard, *The Sincere Convert.*

1642 Fuller, *Holy State.*

Denham, *Cooper's Hill.*

Sir Thomas Browne, *Religio Medici.*

Sir Isaac Newton born. Died 1727.

Theatres closed. Civil War.

1643–1715 °Louis XIV King of France.

1643–1647 Height of religious toleration controversy between John Cotton and Roger Williams.

1644 Milton, *Areopagitica.*

Milton, *Tractate on Education* and divorce pamphlets.

1644 Roger Williams, *Bloody Tenent of Persecution.*

Roger Williams visits Milton; teaches him Dutch.

1645 Howell, *Familiar Letters.*

Waller, *Poems.*

Founding of Philosophical Society.

ca. 1645 Edward Taylor born. Died 1729. *Poems,* posthumously pub. 1939.

1646 Vaughan, *Poems.*

1647 Nathaniel Ward, *Simple Cobbler of Aggawam.*

1648 Herrick, *Hesperides* (including "Noble Numbers").

*1649–1660 COMMONWEALTH INTERREGNUM*

1649 Epidemic of "witch-finding."

Execution of Charles I.

Lovelace, *Lucasta.*

## 1650

1650–1728 Flourishing of the "Mather Dynasty."

1650 Davenant, *Gondibert.*

Taylor, *Holy Living.*

1650 Anne Bradstreet, *The Tenth Muse, Lately Sprung up in America.*

*ca.*1650 Many French romances and novels translated into English.

1651 Milton, *Defence of the English People* (Lat.).

Hobbes, *Leviathan.*

1651 *Cambridge Platform* passed by General Court; reflects prevailing intolerance in Massachusetts under Endicott and Norton.

1652 "Quaker" Movement culminating.

Milton becomes blind.

1652 "Half-Way Covenant": lowers requirements for church membership in Massachusetts.

1653 Walton, *The Compleat Angler.*

1654 Boyle, *Parthenissa.*

1654 Capt. Edward Johnson, *Wonder-Working Providence.*

1656 Cowley, *Poems, Davideis, Pindaric Odes.*

Davenant, *Siege of Rhodes* (*a*).

1656 Hammond, *Leah and Rachel, or The Two Fruitful Sisters, Virginia and Maryland.*

Quakers arrive in Massachusetts (four executed by 1661).

1658 Dryden, *Stanzas on the Death of Cromwell.*

1659 \*Molière, *Les Précieuses ridicules.*

1659 John Eliot, *The Christian Commonwealth.*

*1660–1798 NEO-CLASSICAL
PERIOD*

*1660–1700  RESTORATION
AGE*

---

1660–1714 Stuarts restored
(Charles II to Anne).

1660–1685 Reign of Charles II.

1660–1688 Many books on both
sides of witchcraft controversy.

1660–1669 Pepys's *Diary* (*w*) (pub.
1825).

1660 Dryden, *Astraea Redux:* wel-
comes Charles II.

*ca.*1660 Daniel Defoe born. Died
1731.

1662 Fuller, *Worthies of England.*

The Royal Society founded as
reorganization of the Philosophical Society.

1663 Butler, *Hudibras,* Part I.

Drury Lane Theatre (first
called Theatre Royal) built.

1664 Dryden and Howard, *The Indian Queen* (*a*).

1665 Dryden, *The Indian Emperor.*

Head, *The English Rogue.*

1666 Bunyan, *Grace Abounding.*


°Molière, *Le Misanthrope:*
satiric play.

1667 Jonathan Swift born. Died
1745.

Sprat, *History of the Royal
Society.*

Milton, *Paradise Lost.*

1660–1700 Verse elegies popular.

1662 Wigglesworth, *Day of Doom.*

1663 Eliot translates Bible into
Indian language.

Cotton Mather born. Died
1728.

1665 Baptist Church established in
Boston.

1666 George Alsop, *A Character of
the Province of Maryland.*

ENGLISH

AMERICAN

*Molière, *Tartuffe*.

*Racine, *Andromaque:* classical tragedy.

1668 Sprat, *Life of Cowley:* starts tradition of "discreet" biography.

*La Fontaïne, *Fables*.

Dryden, *Essay of Dramatic Poesy*.

### 1670

1670 Dryden, *Conquest of Granada* (*a*).

*Pascal, *Thoughts*.

Dryden made Poet Laureate.

1671 Milton, *Paradise Regained* and *Samson Agonistes*.

Villiers (Buckingham) and others, *The Rehearsal* (*a*): burlesque satire on Dryden and heroic plays.

1672 Joseph Addison born. Died 1719.

Sir Richard Steele born. Died 1729.

1673 *Death of Molière.

1674 Wycherley, *The Plain-Dealer* (*a*).

*Boileau, *L'Art Poétique*.

Death of Milton.

1676 Etherege, *The Man of Mode*.

1670 Denton, *Brief Description of New York*.

Mason, *Pequot War* (*w*) (pub. 1736).

1671 Eliot, *Progress of the Gospel Among the Indians in New England*.

1672 Eliot, *The Logick Primer:* "for the use of praying Indians."

1673 Increase Mather, *Woe to Drunkards*.

1674–1729 Samuel Sewall, *Diary* (*w*).

1677 Urian Oakes, *Elegy on Thomas Shepard*.

Peter Folger, *Looking-Glass for the Times*.

# Outline of Literary History

**1678** Bunyan, *Pilgrim's Progress,* Part I.

Dryden, *All for Love.*

Popish Plot.

**1679** Cessation of censorship of press. Rise of Whig and Tory parties.

## 1680

**1681** Dryden, *Absalom and Achitophel.*

**1682** Otway, *Venice Preserved.*

Dryden, *MacFlecknoe.*

**1685–1688** Reign of James II.

**1685–1688** Catholic-Protestant conflict.

**1687** Sir Isaac Newton, *Principia* (Lat.).

Dryden, *The Hind and the Panther.*

**1688** The "Bloodless Revolution": Parliament regains power.

Death of Bunyan.

Alexander Pope born. Died 1744.

Mrs. Behn, *Oroonoko.*

*La Bruyère, *Characters.*

**1680–1700** The Mathers at height of power in New England.

**1680** *The Burwell Papers* (*w*).

**1682** Penn settles Pennsylvania.

La Salle explores Mississippi.

Mary Rowlandson, *Narrative of the Captivity* (*w*): life among the Indians.

**1683** Increase Mather, *Discourse Concerning Comets.*

**1684** Increase Mather, *Illustrious Providences.*

**1685** Cotton Mather, *Memorable Providences.*

**1687** Church of England worship established in Boston.

1689–1702 Reign of William and Mary.

1689 The Toleration Act: establishing freedom of worship.

Samuel Richardson born. Died 1761.

### 1690

1690–1699 "Ancient and Modern" controversy ("Battle of the Books").

1690 Locke, *Essay Concerning the Human Understanding.*

1691 Dunton, *Athenian Gazette.*

1691 (or earlier) *New England Primer.*

1692 Sir William Temple, *Essays.*

Increased power of Parliament.

1692 Salem Witchcraft executions.

1692–1702 Reaction from Salem Witchcraft breaks power of conservative clergy. Harvard somewhat liberalized.

1693 William and Mary College founded.

Cotton Mather, *Wonders of the Invisible World.*

1694 Wotton, *Reflections upon Ancient and Modern Learning.*

°Voltaire (French philosopher and man of letters) born. Died 1778.

1696 Toland, *Christianity not Mysterious.*

1697 Dryden, *Alexander's Feast.*

1698 Congreve, *Love for Love.*

Jeremy Collier, *Short View of the Immorality and Profaneness of the English stage.*

1699 Jonathan Dickinson, *God's Protecting Providence.*

## 1700

### 1700–1750    AUGUSTAN AGE

| ENGLISH | AMERICAN |
|---|---|
| | 1700–1720 Decline of influence of the Mathers in New England church. |
| 1700 Death of Dryden. | 1700 Samuel Sewall, *The Selling of Joseph.* |
| 1701 Steele, *The Christian Hero; The Funeral.* | 1701 Cotton Mather, *Death Made Easy and Happy.* |
| | Yale University founded as conservative center. |
| 1702 *The Daily Courant:* first daily newspaper. | 1702 Cotton Mather, *Magnalia Christi Americani:* encyclopedic history of Puritan movement in New England. |
| Defoe, *The Shortest Way with the Dissenters.* | Increase Mather, *Ichabod.* |
| 1702–1714 Reign of Anne. | |
| 1703 John Wesley (founder of Methodist Church) born. Died 1791. | 1703 Jonathan Edwards born. Died 1758. |
| Rowe. *The Fair Penitent.* | |
| 1704–1711 Defoe, *Weekly Review:* periodical with tendencies toward style of the essay. | |
| 1704 Swift, *Battle of the Books* (*w. ca.*1697); *Tale of a Tub.* | 1704 First American newspaper established, *Boston News Letter.* |
| Marlborough's victory at Blenheim (War of Spanish Succession). | Sarah K. Knight, *Journal of a Journey* (*w*). |
| 1705 Steele, *The Tender Husband.* | 1705 Anon., *Questions and Proposals:* scheme for strengthening power of clergy. |
| | 1706 Benjamin Franklin born. Died 1790. |
| 1707 Henry Fielding born. Died 1754. | |
| | 1708 Ebenezer Cook, *Sot-Weed Factor.* |

ENGLISH

AMERICAN

Cotton Mather, *Consequences of the Prevailing Abuse of Rum.*

1709–1711 Steele (and Addison), *The Tatler:* beginning of the periodical essay.

1709 Pope, *Pastorals.*

Rowe's edition of Shakespeare: Shakespeare "edited" for the first time.

Samuel Johnson born. Died 1784.

## 1710

1710–1713 Swift, *Journal to Stella* (*w*).

1710 Berkeley, *Principles of Human Knowledge.*

First complete performance of Italian opera in England (*Almahide*).

Handel comes to England.

1710 Cotton Mather, *Essays to Do Good.*

John Wise, *The Churches' Quarrel Espoused.*

1711–1712 Addison, Steele, etc. *The Spectator:* perfection of periodical essay.

1711 Pope, *Essay on Criticism.*

Shaftesbury, *Characteristics of Men.*

1712, 1714 Pope, *Rape of the Lock.*

1712 *Rousseau born. Died 1778.

1713 Pope, *Windsor Forest.*

Addison, *Cato.*

Lady Winchilsea, *A Nocturnal Reverie.*

1713 Increase Mather, *A Plain Discourse Showing Who Shall and Who Shall not Enter Heaven.*

1714–1901 House of Hanover (George I to Victoria).

1714–1727 George I.

1714 Mandeville, *Fable of the Bees.*

*Spectator* revived.

| ENGLISH | AMERICAN |
|---|---|
| 1715 Pope, trans. *Iliad,* i–iv. | |
| Jacobite Revolt. | |
| *Death of Louis XIV. | |
| 1716 Thomas Gray born. Died 1771. | |
| 1717 Last witchcraft trial in England. | 1717 William Penn, *Religion Professed by the Quakers.* |
| Horace Walpole born. Died 1797. | William Southeby, *An Anti-Slavery Tract.* |
| David Garrick born. Died 1779. | |
| 1719 Watts, *Psalms and Hymns.* | 1719 Establishment of *Boston Gazette* and the *American Weekly Mercury* (Phila.). |
| Defoe, *Robinson Crusoe.* | |
| Death of Addison. | |

### 1720

|  |  |
|---|---|
| | 1720–1750 Flourishing of religious revivals. |
| 1720 "South Sea Bubble." | 1720 Wadsworth, *The Lord's Day Proved to be the Christian Sabbath.* |
| | 1721 James Franklin establishes the *New England Courant.* |
| 1722 Defoe, *Journal of the Plague Year; Moll Flanders.* | 1722 Benjamin Franklin, *Silence Dogood* papers. |
| Steele, *The Conscious Lovers* (*a*). | |
| Parnell, *Night-Piece on Death.* | 1723 Death of Increase Mather. |
| | Franklin arrives in Philadelphia. |
| 1724 Swift, *Drapier's Letters.* | |
| Ramsay, *The Evergreen:* collection of old Scotch poetry. | |
| *Kant born. Died 1804. | |
| | 1725–1775 Nathaniel Ames, *Astronomical Diary and Almanac.* |
| 1725 Pope's edition of Shakespeare. | 1725 Josiah Dwight, *Essay to Silence the Outcry . . . against Regular Singing.* |

*New York Gazette* estab.

| ENGLISH | AMERICAN |
|---|---|
| 1726 Thomson, *Winter.*<br>Swift, *Gulliver's Travels.*<br>Dyer, *Grongar Hill.* | 1726 Anon., *Hoop Petticoats Arraigned and Condemned by the Light of Nature and the Law of God.* |
| 1727–1760 George II. | 1727 Byles, *Poem on Death of King George I.* |
| 1728 Pope, *Dunciad.*<br>Gay, *Beggar's Opera.*<br>Oliver Goldsmith born. Died 1774. | 1728 First newspaper in Maryland estab.<br>Death of Cotton Mather. |
| 1729 Swift, *A Modest Proposal.*<br>Death of Steele.<br>Edmund Burke born. Died 1797. | 1729 Byrd, *History of the Dividing Line* (*w*).<br>Death of Edward Taylor. |

## 1730

| ENGLISH | AMERICAN |
|---|---|
| 1730 Methodist Society at Oxford.<br>Tindal, *Christianity as Old as the Creation.* | 1730 Seccomb, *Father Abbey's Will.*<br>Printing press set up in Charleston, S. C. |
| 1731 *Gentleman's Magazine* estab.<br>Lillo, *The London Merchant:* bourgeois tragedy.<br>Death of Defoe.<br>William Cowper born. Died 1800. | |
| | 1732–1757 Franklin, *Poor Richard's Almanac.* |
| 1732 Covent Garden Theatre built. | 1732 Byles, *Sermon on the Vileness of the Body.*<br>Franklin opens first public library in America (Philadelphia). First newspapers in South Carolina and Rhode Island established.<br>First issue of Franklin's *Poor Richard's Almanac.* |

George Washington born. Died 1799.

1733 Pope, *Essay on Man.*

     Theobald's edition of Shakespeare: advances scientific method of editing Shakespearean text.

1733 William Byrd, *Journal of Journey to the Land of Eden* (North Carolina) (*w*).

     Georgia settled by Oglethorpe.

     J. P. Zenger begins publication of *New York Weekly Journal.*

1734 Edwards conducts his first great revival meetings at Northampton.

     Important victory for freedom of press won by Zenger.

1735 Pope, *Epistle to Dr. Arbuthnot.*

1735 John and Charles Wesley visit America.

1736 Joseph Butler, *The Analogy of Religion.*

1736 First newspaper in Virginia.

1737 Shenstone, *Schoolmistress.*

     Edward Gibbon born. Died 1794.

     Theatre Licensing Act: confirms monopoly of patent theatres.

1738 Johnson, *London.*

     Wesley, *Psalms and Hymns.*

     Bolingbroke, *Letters on the Study of History.*

1738 Whitefield's first preaching tour in America.

1739 Beginnings of Methodist preaching in America.

## 1740

1740–1786 °Reign of Frederick the Great of Prussia.

1740 Cibber, *Apology for the Life of Colley Cibber.*

     Richardson, *Pamela.*

1741 Fielding, *Joseph Andrews.*

1740–1745 The "Great Awakening" (religious revival).

1741 Edwards, *Sinners in the Hands of An Angry God.*

# Outline of Literary History

1742 Young, *Night Thoughts.*

1742–44 Roger North, *Lives of the Norths.*

1743 Blair, *The Grave.*

1744 Joseph Warton, *The Enthusiast.*

Dr. Johnson, *Life of Richard Savage.*

Death of Pope.

1745 Death of Swift.

Jacobite Rebellion.

1747 Collins, *Odes.*

1748 Thomson, *Castle of Indolence.*

Richardson, *Clarissa Harlowe.*

Smollett, *Roderick Random.*

Hume, *Inquiry Concerning Human Understanding.*

°Montesquieu, *L'Esprit des Lois.*

1749 Fielding, *Tom Jones.*

Johnson, *The Vanity of Human Wishes.*

°Goethe born. Died 1832.

°Swedenborg, *Arcana Celesta.*

1743 Thomas Jefferson born. Died 1826.

1744–1745 Pamphlets against Whitefield issued from Harvard and Yale.

1747 Stith, *First Discovery and Settlement of Virginia.*

1749 University of Pennsylvania founded.

## 1750–1798    AGE OF JOHNSON

### 1750

1750–1798 Artists flourishing: Gainsborough and Reynolds (painters), Blake (painter and engraver), °Haydn, °Mozart (German musicians).

| ENGLISH | AMERICAN |
|---|---|

**1750–1752** Johnson, *The Rambler:* periodical essays.

**1750** Edwards dismissed from Northampton pastorate.

**1751** Gray, *Elegy Written in a Country Churchyard.*

°Vol. I of French *Encyclopédie.*

**1751** Bartram, *Observations on American Plants.*

Franklin, *Experiments and Observations in Electricity.*

**1752** Gregorian Calendar adopted.

**1752** Franklin's discovery that lightning is electrical.

Philip Freneau born. Died 1832.

**1753** British Museum founded.

**1754** T. Warton, *Observations on the Fairy Queen of Spenser.*

**1754** Franklin's plan for union of colonies.

Edwards, *Freedom of the Will.*

**1755–1756** °Mallet's French history of Denmark: helped introduce Norse mythology into romantic poetry.

**1755–1772** Woolman, *Journal* (*w*) pub. 1774.

**1755** Johnson, *Dictionary.*

**1756** J. Warton, *Essay on Pope.*

Home, *Douglas.*

**1757** Gray, *The Bard* and *The Progress of Poesy.*

William Blake born. Died 1827.

**1757** Edwards made President of Princeton.

Witherspoon, *Serious Inquiry into the Nature and Effects of the Stage.*

**1758–1760** Johnson, The "Idler" papers: periodical essays.

**1758** Edwards, *The Great Christian Doctrine of Original Sin Defended.*

Death of Edwards.

**1759** Johnson, *Rasselas.*

**1759** Winthrop, *Lectures on the Comets.*

*Annual Register* established: annual review of "history, politics, and literature."

Robert Burns born. Died 1796.

°Voltaire, *Candide.*

*1760*

**ENGLISH**

1760–1820 George III.

1760–1767 Sterne, *Tristram Shandy.*

1760–1761 Goldsmith, *Letters from a Citizen of the World.*

1760 °Rousseau, *Nouvelle Héloïse.*

MacPherson publishes his Ossianic *Fragments of Ancient Poetry Collected in the Highlands of Scotland.*

1761 Churchill, *The Rosciad.*

1762 MacPherson, *Fingal.*

Leland, *Longsword.*

°Rousseau, *Contrat Social.*

1764–1770 The Chatterton poems (*w*) (pub. 1777).

1764 Walpole, *Castle of Otranto:* first important Gothic novel.

Literary Club established in London (Doctor Samuel Johnson and others).

°Winckelmann, *History of the Art of Antiquity.*

1765 Percy, *Reliques of Ancient English Poetry.*

Invention of steam engine by Watt.

1766–1770 Brooke, *The Fool of Quality.*

1766 Goldsmith, *The Vicar of Wakefield.*

**AMERICAN**

1761 Otis, Speeches.

1762 Printing press set up in Georgia.

1764 Otis, *Rights of British Colonies.*

*1765–1830 REVOLUTIONARY AND EARLY NATIONAL PERIOD*

*1765–1790    REVOLUTIONARY AGE*

1765 The Stamp Act.

1766 Franklin, *Examination before the House of Commons.*

| ENGLISH | AMERICAN |
|---|---|

*Lessing, *Laokoön:* criticism (art and literature).

Colman and Garrick, *The Clandestine Marriage.*

                                          1767–1768 Dickinson, *Letters of a Farmer in Pennsylvania.*

                                          1767 Godfrey, *Prince of Parthia* (*a*): tragedy, first American play to be acted.

1768 Kelly, *False Delicacy* (*a*).

Goldsmith, *Good-Natured Man* (*a*).

Gray, *Poems.*

Sterne, *Sentimental Journey.*

Spinning machine invented.

1769–1772 *Letters of Junius.*

                                          1769 Samuel Adams (and others), *Appeal to the World.*

## 1770

1770 Goldsmith, *Deserted Village.*

Burke, *Thoughts on the Present Discontent.*

Lord North becomes Prime Minister.

William Wordsworth born. Died 1850.

                                          1771, 1784, and later, Franklin, *Autobiography* (*w*).

1771 Beattie, *The Minstrel.* Bk. I.

Smollett, *Expedition of Humphrey Clinker.*

Mackenzie, *The Man of Feeling.*

Sir Walter Scott born. Died 1832.

                                          1771 Charles Brockden Brown born. Died 1810.

1772 Samuel Taylor Coleridge born. Died 1834.                              1772 Trumbull, *Progress of Dullness,* Part I.

Freneau, *Rising Glories of America.*

**1773** Goldsmith, *She Stoops to Conquer.*

Steevens' edition of Shakespeare.

Lord Monboddo, *Origin and Progress of Language.*

Kenrich's *Dictionary:* first in which vowel sounds are marked.

**1773** Phillis Wheatley (Peters), *Poems:* poetry written by a young slave girl.

First theatre in Charleston, S. C.

**1774** T. Warton, *History of English Poetry,* Vol. I.

Chesterfield, *Letters to His Son.*

*Goethe, *Sorrows of Werther.*

Death of Goldsmith.

Robert Southey born. Died 1843.

**1775–1783** War with American colonies.

**1774** Jefferson, *Summary of View of Rights of British America.*

Rush, *Natural History of Medicine Among Indians of North America.*

Boston Port Bill.

First Continental Congress.

**1775–1788** Patrick Henry's Speeches.

**1775–1783** Revolutionary War.

**1775** Sheridan, *The Rivals.*

Burke, *Speech on Conciliation.*

Mason, *Memoirs of the Life and Writings of Thomas Gray.*

Charles Lamb born. Died 1834.

Walter Savage Landor born. Died 1864.

Jane Austen born. Died 1817.

**1775** Trumbull, *M'Fingal,* Canto I.

Mrs. Warren, *The Group.*

Battles of Lexington and Bunker Hill.

**1776–1783** Thomas Paine, *The Crisis.*

**1776** Paine, *Common Sense.*

**1776** Gibbon, *Decline and Fall of the Roman Empire.*

Adam Smith, *Wealth of Nations.*

Brackenridge, *Battle of Bunker Hill.*

Jefferson, *Declaration of Independence.*

| ENGLISH | AMERICAN |
|---|---|
| 1777 Sheridan, *School for Scandal* (*a*). | 1777 *Articles of Confederation.* |
| Burke, *Letter to the Sheriffs of Bristol.* | Surrender of Burgoyne. |
| Capt. Cook, *A Voyage toward the South Pole and Round the World.* | |
| 1778 Frances Burney, *Evelina.* | 1778 Franklin, *Ephemera.* |
| William Hazlitt born. Died 1830. | Freneau, *American Independence.* |
| °Death of Rousseau and Voltaire. | Carver, *Travels.* |
| | Treaty with France. |
| | 1779–1785 Franklin in France. |
| 1779 Cumberland, *Wheel of Fortune.* | 1779 Odell, *The Conflagration.* |
| Johnson, *Lives of the Poets.* | Hopkinson, *Battle of the Kegs.* |
| Rev. John Newton and William Cowper, *Olney Hymns.* | Ethan Allen, *Narrative of the Captivity.* |
| Lord Monboddo, *Ancient Metaphysics.* | Paul Jones' naval victories. |
| Hume, *Natural History of Religion.* | |
| Death of Garrick. | |

## 1780

| | |
|---|---|
| 1781 Macklin, *Man of the World.* | 1781 Surrender of Cornwallis at Yorktown. |
| °Kant, *Critique of Pure Reason.* | *Articles of Confederation* ratified. |
| °Schiller, *Die Räuber* (*a*). | State constitutions framed. |
| 1782 Cowper, *Table Talk.* | 1782 Crèvecoeur, *Letters from an American Farmer.* |
| | Paine, *Letter to the Abbé Raynal.* |
| | 1783–1785 Noah Webster, *Grammatical Institute of the English Language* (speller, grammar, reader). |

**1783** Crabbe, *The Village.*

Blair, *Rhetoric.*

Ritson, *Collection of English Songs.*

**1784** Death of Samuel Johnson.

Pitt (the younger), Prime Minister.

Leigh Hunt born. Died 1859.

**1785** Cowper, *The Task.*

Thomas De Quincey born. Died 1859.

**1786** Burns, *Poems.*

Beckford, *Vathek.*

**1787** John Wesley, *Sermons.*

**1788** George Gordon, Lord Byron, born. Died 1824.

**1789** Blake, *Songs of Innocence.*

Bowles, *Fourteen Sonnets.*

°French Revolution begins.

**1783** Washington Irving born. Died 1859.

England acknowledges American independence.

**1784** Franklin, *Information for Those Who Would Remove to America.*

**1785** Dwight, *Conquest of Canaan:* epic.

**1786–1787** Trumbull and others, *The Anarchiad.*

**1786** Freneau, *Poems.*

**1787–1788** Hamilton (and others), *The Federalist.*

**1787** Barlow, *Vision of Columbus:* American epic.

Tyler, *The Contrast* (*a*): first American comedy acted by professionals.

Constitutional Convention.

**1788** Markoe, *The Times.*

Constitution ratified by eleven states.

**1789** William Hill Brown, *The Power of Sympathy:* first American novel.

Washington, *First Inaugural.*

James Fenimore Cooper born. Died 1851.

Federal government established.

## 1790

*ca.*1790 German influence strong, esp. on romantic literature.

1790 Burke, *Reflections on the Revolution in France.*

Malone's edition of Shakespeare.

*Goethe, Faust, A Fragment.*

1791 Boswell, *Life of Johnson.*

Erasmus Darwin, *The Botanic Garden.*

Paine, *Rights of Man.*

Wordsworth visits France.

1792 Paine, *Age of Reason.*

Wollstonecraft, *Rights of Woman.*

Percy Bysshe Shelley born. Died 1822.

1793 Wordsworth, *Descriptive Sketches.*

Godwin, *Political Justice.*

*Louis XVI executed.

War with France.

1794 Blake, *Songs of Experience.*

Radcliffe, *Mysteries of Udolpho.*

Godwin, *Caleb Williams.*

*Fall of Robespierre.

1795 Lewis, *The Monk.*

Ritson, *Robin Hood Poems.*

John Keats born. Died 1821.

Thomas Carlyle born. Died 1881.

1795–1796 *Goethe, *Wilhelm Meister.*

1790 Death of Franklin.

1791 William Bartram, *Travels through North and South Carolina.*

1792–1806 Brackenridge, *Modern Chivalry.*

1793 Barlow, *Hasty Pudding.*

Imlay, *Emigrants.*

1794 Dwight, *Greenfield Hill.*

Mrs. Susanna Rowson, *Charlotte Temple.*

Dunlap, *Leicester: "The Fatal Legacy"* (a).

William Cullen Bryant born. Died 1878.

1795 Murray, *English Grammar.*

| ENGLISH | AMERICAN |
|---|---|
| 1796 Coleridge, *The Watchman.*<br><br>Southey, *Joan of Arc.*<br><br>Colman, *Iron Chest* (*a*).<br><br>Scott, *William and Helen:* trans. of Bürger's *Lenore.*<br><br>Death of Burns. | 1796 Washington, *Farewell Address.*<br><br>Dennie, *Lay Preacher.* |
| 1797–1798 *The Anti-Jacobin.* | |
| 1797 Wordsworth, *The Borderers* (*w*) (pub. 1842). | 1797 C. B. Brown, *Alcuin: a Dialogue on The Rights of Women.* |

## 1798–1870 ROMANTIC PERIOD

### 1798–1832 AGE OF THE TRIUMPH OF ROMANTICISM

| | |
|---|---|
| 1798 Wordsworth and Coleridge, *Lyrical Ballads.*<br><br>Landor, *Gebir.*<br><br>Malthus, *Essay on Population.* | 1798 Brown, *Wieland.* |
| 1799 *Memoirs of the Life and Writings of Edward Gibbon.* | 1799 Death of Washington.<br><br>Tyler, *Algerian Captive.*<br><br>Brown, *Ormond; Arthur Mervyn,* Part I. |

## 1800

| | |
|---|---|
| 1800 Coleridge, trans. of Schiller's *Wallenstein.*<br><br>Maria Edgeworth, *Castle Rackrent.*<br><br>Wordsworth and Coleridge, *Lyrical Ballads,* 2d ed., with famous *Preface.*<br><br>Thomas Babington Macaulay born. Died 1859. | 1800 Weems, *Life of Washington.*<br><br>Library of Congress founded. |
| 1801 Southey, *Thalaba.* | 1801 Brown, *Edgar Huntly, Clara Howard, Jane Talbot.* |

*A. W. and F. Schlegel, *Characteristics*: romantic criticism.

John Henry Newman born. Died 1890.

1802 Scott, *Minstrelsy of the Scottish Border*.

*Edinburgh Review* founded.

*Victor Hugo born. Died 1885.

1803 Jane Porter, *Thaddeus of Warsaw*.

Campbell, *Poems*.

Bulwer-Lytton born. Died 1873.

1803 Wirt, *Letters of a British Spy*.

Louisiana Purchase.

Ralph Waldo Emerson born. Died 1882.

1804 *Schiller, *Wilhelm Tell*.

Benjamin Disraeli, Earl of Beaconsfield born. Died 1881.

1804 J. Q. Adams, *Letters*.

Marshall, *Life of Washington*.

Nathaniel Hawthorne born. Died 1864.

1805 Wordsworth, *Prelude* (*w*) (pub. 1850).

Scott, *Lay of the Last Minstrel*.

1806 Elizabeth Barrett (Browning) born. Died 1861.

John Stuart Mill born. Died 1873.

1806 Noah Webster, *Compendious Dictionary of the English Language*.

William Gilmore Simms born. Died 1870.

1807 Byron, *Hours of Idleness*.

C. and M. Lamb, *Tales from Shakespeare*.

Abolition of slave trade.

*Hegel, *Phenomenology*.

1807 Barlow, *Columbiad*.

Irving and Paulding, *Salmagundi Papers*.

John Greenleaf Whittier born. Died 1892.

Henry Wadsworth Longfellow born. Died 1882.

1808 Hunt, *The Examiner*.

Scott, *Marmion*.

1808 Bryant, *The Embargo*.

Congress stops importation of slaves.

Lamb, *Specimens of English Dramatic Poets.*

\*Goethe, *Faust,* Part I.

1809 Byron, *English Bards and Scotch Reviewers.*

Charles Darwin born. Died 1882.

Alfred, Lord Tennyson born. Died 1892.

William E. Gladstone born. Died 1898.

First issue of *Quarterly Review.*

1809 Irving, *Knickerbocker's History.*

Edgar Allan Poe born. Died 1849.

Oliver Wendell Holmes born. Died 1894.

Abraham Lincoln born. Died 1865.

## *1810*

1810 Scott, *Lady of the Lake.*

Porter, *Scottish Chiefs.*

Crabbe, *The Borough.*

Southey, *Curse of Kehama.*

1811 Austen, *Sense and Sensibility.*

William Makepeace Thackeray born. Died 1863.

1812–1814 War with England.

1812 American Academy of Natural Science founded.

1812 Byron, *Childe Harold,* Cantos I, II.

\*The Grimm brothers: *Fairy Tales.*

Charles Dickens born. Died 1870.

Robert Browning born. Died 1889.

1813 Byron, *Bride of Abydos.*

Shelley, *Queen Mab.*

Austen, *Pride and Prejudice.*

Southey made Poet Laureate.

Southey, *Life of Nelson.*

1813 Allston, *Sylphs of the Seasons.*

Massachusetts Temperance Society founded.

*Madame de Staël, *De l'Alle-magne:* "romantic" interpretation of the new German literature.

1814 Scott, *Waverley:* begins vogue of historical novel.

Wordsworth, *Excursion.*

1815 Scott, *Guy Mannering.*

Battle of Waterloo.

Anthony Trollope born. Died 1882.

1816 Coleridge, *Christabel.*

Byron, *Prisoner of Chillon.*

Shelley, *Alastor.*

Peacock, *Headlong Hall.*

1817 Mary Shelley, *Frankenstein.*

Moore, *Lalla Rookh.*

Byron, *Manfred:* dramatic poem.

Coleridge, *Biographia Literaria.*

Keats, *Poems.*

*Blackwood's Magazine* established.

1818 Keats, *Endymion.*

Scott, *Heart of Midlothian.*

Shelley, *Revolt of Islam.*

Austen, *Northanger Abbey* (*w. ca.*1800).

1819 Byron, *Don Juan,* I, II.

Shelley, *The Cenci:* tragedy.

Mary Ann Evans ("George Eliot") born. Died 1880.

John Ruskin born. Died 1900.

Charles Kingsley born. Died 1875.

*Schopenhauer, *The World as Will and Idea.*

1815 Freneau, *Poems on American Affairs.*

*North American Review* established.

1816 Pickering, *Vocabulary of Americanisms.*

1817 Bryant, *Thanatopsis* (*w.* 1811).

Henry David Thoreau born. Died 1862.

1818 Payne, *Brutus* (*a.* London).

1819 Halleck, *Fanny.*

Drake, *The Culprit Fay.*

James Russell Lowell born. Died 1891.

Herman Melville born. Died 1891.

Walt Whitman born. Died 1892.

## *1820*

1820–1830 George IV.

1820–1823 Lamb, *Essays of Elia.*

*ca.*1820–1846 °Balzac's tales and novels.

| | |
|---|---|
| 1820 Scott, *Ivanhoe.* | 1820 Missouri Compromise. |
| Shelley, *Prometheus Unbound.* | Irving, *Sketch Book.* |
| Keats, *Lamia . . . and other Poems.* | |
| Maturin, *Melmoth the Wanderer.* | |
| *London Magazine* established. | |
| Herbert Spencer born. Died 1903. | |
| 1821 Scott, *Kenilworth.* | 1821 Bryant, *Poems.* |
| Southey, *Vision of Judgment.* | Cooper, *The Spy.* |
| Shelley, *Adonais.* | |
| De Quincy, *Confessions of an English Opium-Eater.* | |
| Byron, *Cain.* | |
| Death of Keats. | |
| 1822 Byron, *Vision of Judgment.* | 1822 Irving, *Bracebridge Hall.* |
| Matthew Arnold born. Died 1888. | |
| Death of Shelley. | |
| 1823 Scott, *Quentin Durward.* | 1823 Cooper, *Pioneers:* first of Leatherstocking series. |
| Carlyle, *Life of Schiller.* | The Monroe Doctrine. |
| | Francis Parkman born. Died 1893. |
| 1824 Landor, *Imaginary Conversations,* Vol. I. | 1824 Irving, *Tales of a Traveler.* |
| Death of Byron. | E. Everett, *Progress of Literature in America.* |
| 1825 Macaulay, *Essay on Milton.* | 1825 Halleck, *Marco Bozzaris.* |

| ENGLISH | AMERICAN |
|---|---|
| Hazlitt, *Spirit of the Age.* | Italian opera introduced into America. |
| Thomas Henry Huxley born. Died 1895. | |
| 1826 Scott, *Woodstock.* | 1826 Cooper, *Last of the Mohicans.* |
| Disraeli, *Vivian Gray.* | Payne, *Richelieu* (*a*). |
| | Clay's speeches in Congress. |
| | *The Atlantic Souvenir:* annual "gift book." |
| 1827 °Heine, *Songs.* | 1827 Cooper, *The Prairie.* |
| | Dana, *Poems.* |
| | Poe, *Tamerlane.* |
| | Simms, *Lyrical and Other Poems.* |
| | Mrs. Sigourney, *Poems.* |
| | Willis, *Sketches:* poems. |
| 1828–1830 Taylor, *Historic Survey of German Poetry.* | |
| 1828 Catholic Emancipation Act. | 1828 Hawthorne, *Fanshaw.* |
| Dante Gabriel Rossetti born. Died 1882. | Irving, *Columbus.* |
| George Meredith born. Died 1909. | Webster, *An American Dictionary.* |
| | Hall, *The Western Souvenir.* |
| 1829 Jerrold, *Black-ey'd Susan.* | 1829 Irving, *Conquest of Granada.* |
| | Henry B. Timrod born. Died 1867. |

## 1830–1865 ROMANTIC PERIOD

### 1830

| | |
|---|---|
| 1830–1837 William IV. | 1830–1838 Audubon, *Birds of America.* |
| 1830–1833 Lyell, *Principles of Geology.* | |
| 1830 Tennyson, *Poems Chiefly Lyrical.* | 1830 Webster, *Speeches.* |

Moore, *Letters and Journals of Lord Byron.*

Scott, *Letters on Demonology and Witchcraft.*

*Heine, *The Romantic School.*

1831 Scott, *Castle Dangerous.*

Disraeli, *The Young Duke.*

Worcester, *Dictionary.*

Holmes, *Old Ironsides.*

*Godey's Lady's Book* founded.

Emily Dickinson born. Died 1886.

1831 Poe, *Poems.*

Whittier, *Legends of New England.*

Garrison founds the *Liberator.*

American Anti-Slavery Society founded.

*1832*

## 1832–1870 EARLY VICTORIAN AGE

1832–1840 Important scientific developments; appearance of new literary figures; increasing optimism follows postwar depression.

1832 Reform Bill.

"Lewis Carroll" (C. L. Dodgson) born. Died 1898.

Death of Scott and *Goethe.

1832 Poe: five tales appear in *Philadelphia Saturday Courier.*

Bryant, *Poems* (2d ed.).

Simms, *Atalantis.*

Whittier, *Moll Pitcher.*

Irving, *The Alhambra.*

Dunlap, *History of the American Theatre.*

1833–1841 The Oxford Movement (Tractarians)

1833–1834 Carlyle, *Sartor Resartus.*

1833 Lamb, *Last Essays of Elia.*

Browning, *Pauline.*

Newman, *Tracts for the Times* (begun).

1833 Longfellow, *Outre-Mer* (first numbers).

Poe, *Manuscript Found in a Bottle.*

| ENGLISH | AMERICAN |
|---|---|

Surtees, *Jorrock's Jaunts and Jollities.*

1834 Bulwer-Lytton, *Last Days of Pompeii.*

William Morris born. Died 1896.

Death of Coleridge and Lamb.

1835 Browning, *Paracelsus.*

Samuel Butler born. Died 1902.

Alfred Austin born. Died 1913.

1836 Dickens, *Pickwick Papers.*

Marryat, *Mr. Midshipman Easy.*

1837–1901 Victoria.

1837 Dickens, *Oliver Twist.*

Browning, *Strafford.*

Carlyle, *French Revolution.*

Lockhart, *Life of Scott.*

Algernon Charles Swinburne born. Died 1909.

1838–1849 The Chartist Movement for extending the franchise.

1838 First railway train enters London.

Ocean steamships connect England and United States.

1834 Bancroft, *History of the United States,* Vol. I.

Crockett, *Autobiography.*

*Southern Literary Messenger* established.

1835 Simms, *The Partisan; The Yemassee.*

Frances A. Kemble, *Journal.*

Longstreet, *Georgia Scenes.*

"Mark Twain" born. Died 1910.

1836 Emerson, *Nature.*

Holmes, *Poems.*

Irving, *Astoria.*

Morse's invention of telegraph instrument.

Bret Harte born. Died 1902.

1837 Hawthorne, *Twice-Told Tales.*

Whittier, *Poems.*

Emerson, *The American Scholar.*

Prescott, *Ferdinand and Isabella.*

John Burroughs born. Died 1921.

William Dean Howells born. Died 1920.

1838 Morse demonstrates telegraph apparatus before President Van Buren.

| ENGLISH | AMERICAN |
|---|---|
| 1839 Bulwer-Lytton, *Cardinal Richelieu*. | 1839 Longfellow, *Hyperion; Voices of the Night*. |
| Carlyle, *Chartism*. | |
| Ainsworth, *Jack Sheppard*. | |
| Walter Pater born. Died 1894. | |

## 1840

| | |
|---|---|
| 1840–1841 Hood, *Miss Kilmansagg and her Golden Leg*. | |
| 1840 Browning, *Sordello*. | 1840 Cooper, *Pathfinder*. |
| Dickens, *Old Curiosity Shop*. | Dana, *Two Years before the Mast*. |
| Thomas Hardy born. Died 1928. | Poe, *Tales of the Grotesque and Arabesque*. |
| | Brook Farm established. |
| | *The Dial* established (discontinued 1844). |
| 1841 Browning, *Pippa Passes*. | 1841 Cooper, *The Deerslayer*. |
| Carlyle, *Heroes and Hero-Worship*. | Emerson, *Essays*. |
| Macaulay, *Warren Hastings*. | Longfellow, *Ballads and Other Poems*. |
| Boucicault, *London Assurance* (a). | |
| 1842 Browning, *Dramatic Lyrics*. | 1842 Longfellow, *Poems on Slavery*. |
| Tennyson, *Poems*. | |
| Dickens, *American Notes*. | Griswold, *Poets and Poetry of America*. |
| Macaulay, *Lays of Ancient Rome*. | Sidney Lanier born. Died 1881. |
| Newman, *Essay on Miracles*. | |
| 1843 Carlyle, *Past and Present*. | 1843 Prescott, *Conquest of Mexico*. |
| Dickens, *Christmas Carol*. | Whittier, *Lays of My Home and Other Poems*. |
| Ruskin, *Modern Painters*, Vol. I. | Henry James born. Died 1916. |
| Hood, *Song of the Shirt*. | |
| Wordsworth made Poet Laureate. | |

**ENGLISH**

**AMERICAN**

Repeal of Licensing Act of 1737: end of monopoly of the "patent" theatres in London.

1844 Thackeray, *Barry Lyndon.*

Elizabeth Barrett (Browning), *Poems.*

Disraeli, *Coningsby.*

\*Dumas, *The Three Musketeers.*

Robert Bridges born. Died 1930.

1844 Emerson, *Essays* (2d ser.).

Margaret Fuller (Ossoli), *Woman in the Nineteenth Century.*

First private telegraph company organized by Morse and others.

1845 Dickens, *Cricket on the Hearth.*

Repeal of Corn Laws.

\*Wagner, *Tannhäuser.*

1845 Poe, *The Raven.*

1846 Brontë sisters, *Poems.*

Thackeray, *Vanity Fair.*

1846 Hawthorne, *Mosses from an Old Manse.*

Holmes, *Poems.*

Melville, *Typee.*

1847 E. Brontë, *Wuthering Heights.*

C. Brontë, *Jane Eyre.*

Tennyson, *The Princess.*

Hunt, *Men, Women, and Books.*

1847 Emerson, *Poems.*

Longfellow, *Evangeline.*

Prescott, *Conquest of Peru.*

Agassiz, *Introduction to Natural History.*

Melville, *Omoo.*

1848 Mill, *Political Economy.*

Macaulay, *History of England,* Vols. I, II.

Pre-Raphaelite Brotherhood founded by Rossetti.

1848 Lowell, *A Fable for Critics. Bigelow Papers.*

Bartlett, *Dictionary of Americanisms.*

1849 Dickens, *David Copperfield.*

Thackeray, *Pendennis.*

Ruskin, *Seven Lamps of Architecture.*

Bulwer-Lytton, *The Caxtons.*

1849 Irving, *Life of Goldsmith.*

Whittier, *Voices of Freedom.*

Parkman, *Oregon Trail.*

Thoreau, *Week on the Concord and Merrimac Rivers.*

Melville, *Mardi.*

Death of Poe.

ENGLISH                        AMERICAN

## 1850

*ca.*1850–*ca.*1875 \*Dumas *fils fl.:*
important realistic drama.

1850 Mrs. Browning, *Sonnets from
the Portuguese.*

Tennyson, *In Memoriam.*

Hunt, *Autobiography; Table
Talk.*

Kingsley, *Alton Locke.*

Death of Wordsworth.

Tennyson made Poet Laureate.

Robert Louis Stevenson born.
Died 1894.

1851 Ruskin, *Stones of Venice.*

Borrow, *Lavengro.*

1852 Dickens, *Bleak House.*

Thackeray, *Henry Esmond.*

Reade, *Peg Wolffington.*

Newman, *The Idea of a University.*

Tennyson, *Ode on the Death
of the Duke of Wellington.*

1853 Thackeray, *English Humorists.*

Mrs. Gaskell, *Cranford.*

Kingsley, *Hypatia.*

Arnold, *Poems.*

C. Brontë, *Villette.*

George Moore born.

1854 Dickens, *Hard Times.*

The Crimean War.

1855–1876 \*Turgenev's novels of
character and Russian life.

1850 Emerson, *Representative
Men.*

Hawthorne, *Scarlet Letter.*

Irving, *Mahomet.*

Whittier, *Songs of Labor.*

Poe, *Poetic Principle.*

*Harper's Magazine* established.

1851 Hawthorne, *House of Seven
Gables.*

Melville, *Moby Dick.*

1852 Hawthorne, *Blithedale Romance.*

Mrs. Stowe, *Uncle Tom's
Cabin.*

1854 Thoreau, *Walden.*

1855 Browning, *Men and Women.*

Tennyson, *Maud.*

Thackeray, *The Newcomes.*

Dickens, *Little Dorrit.*

Trollope, *The Warden.*

Kingsley, *Westward Ho.*

Gaskell, *North and South.*

Spencer, *Principles of Psychology,* Vol. I.

Lewes, *Life of Goethe.*

1856 Mrs. Browning, *Aurora Leigh.*

James Anthony Froude, *History of England,* Vols. I, II.

Oscar Wilde born. Died 1900.

George Bernard Shaw born. Died 1950.

*Death of Heine.

1857 Thackeray, *The Virginians.*

Trollope, *Barchester Towers.*

Borrow, *The Romany Rye.*

*Flaubert, *Madame Bovary.*

Joseph Conrad born. Died 1924.

1858–1888 *Daudet, French novels and tales, psychological, realistic.

1858 "George Eliot," *Scenes of Clerical Life.*

Carlyle, *Frederick II,* Vols. I, II.

Morris, *Defence of Guinevere.*

1859 Tennyson, *Idylls of the King.*

Dickens, *Tale of Two Cities.*

1855 Whitman, *Leaves of Grass.*

Longfellow, *Hiawatha.*

Irving, *Life of Washington* (begun).

Hayne, *Poems.*

Boker, *Francesca da Rimini.*

Duyckinck, *Cyclopedia of American Literature.*

1856 Emerson, *English Traits.*

Motley, *Rise of the Dutch Republic.*

Woodrow Wilson born. Died 1924.

1857 Child, ed., *English and Scottish Ballads.*

*Atlantic Monthly* established.

Dred Scott decision.

1858 Holmes, *Autocrat of the Breakfast Table.*

Longfellow, *Courtship of Miles Standish.*

Theodore Roosevelt born. Died 1919.

1859 Marsh, *Lectures on the English Language.*

Eliot, *Adam Bede.*

Meredith, *Ordeal of Richard Feverel.*

Fitzgerald, trans. *Rubaiyat of Omar Khayyam.*

Darwin, *Origin of Species.*

John Stuart Mill, *On Liberty.*

Deaths of Macaulay, Hunt, DeQuincey.

Alfred E. Housman born. Died 1936.

Arthur Conan Doyle born. Died 1930.

Francis Thompson born. Died 1907.

Margaret Fuller (Ossoli), *Life Without and Life Within.*

Joseph Jefferson, *Rip Van Winkle* (*a*).

## 1860

1860–1863 Thackeray, *Roundabout Papers.*

1860 Eliot, *Mill on the Floss.*

"Owen Meredith," *Lucille.*

Collins, *Woman in White.*

James Barrie born. Died 1937.

1860 Emerson, *Conduct of Life.*

Hawthorne, *Marble Faun.*

Timrod, *Poems.*

Harte, *The Work on Red Mountain.*

South Carolina secedes from Union.

1861 Eliot, *Silas Marner.*

Reade, *The Cloister and the Hearth.*

Arnold, *On Translating Homer.*

Imprisonment for debt abolished.

1861 Holmes, *Elsie Venner.*

Lincoln becomes President.

Outbreak of Civil War.

1862 Ruskin, *Unto This Last.*

Spencer, *First Principles.*

Meredith, *Poems and Ballads.*

*Turgenev, *Fathers and Sons.*

*Ibsen, *Love's Comedy.*

1862 Browne, *Artemus Ward: His Book.*

Battle of Shiloh; *Monitor* and *Merrimac.*

1863 Eliot, *Romola.*

Huxley, *Man's Place in Nature.*

Kingsley, *Water Babies.*

Death of Thackeray.

1864–1866 *Tolstoi, *War and Peace:* realistic historical novel.

1864 Browning, *Dramatis Personae.*

Tennyson, *Enoch Arden.*

Swinburne, *Atalanta in Calydon.*

Newman, *Apologia pro Vita Sua.*

Dickens, *Our Mutual Friend.*

*Taine, *History of English Literature.*

*ca.*1865–*ca.*1900 *Zola's "naturalistic" novels.

1865 Arnold, *Essays in Criticism.*

Ruskin, *Sesame and Lilies.*

"Lewis Carroll," *Alice's Adventures in Wonderland.*

Robertson, *Caste.*

Rudyard Kipling born. Died 1936.

William Butler Yeats born. Died 1939.

1866 Arnold, *Thyrsis.*

Swinburne, *Poems and Ballads.*

1863 Bryant, *Thirty Poems.*

Longfellow, *Tales of a Wayside Inn.*

Louisa M. Alcott, *Hospital Sketches.*

Whittier, *In War Time.*

Emancipation Proclamation.

Lincoln, *Gettysburg Address.*

1864 Thoreau, *The Maine Woods.*

Lowell, *Fireside Travels.*

1865 Thoreau, *Cape Cod.*

Lowell, *Commemoration Ode.*

Whitman, *Drum Taps.*

Whittier, *National Lyrics.*

End of Civil War.

Assassination of Lincoln.

## 1865–1900 REALISTIC PERIOD

1866 Shaw, *Josh Billings: His Sayings.*

Whittier, *Snow-Bound.*

Ruskin, *Crown of Wild Olive.*

Kingsley, *Hereward the Wake.*

*Dostoyevski, *Crime and Punishment:* powerful realistic novel.

H. G. Wells born. Died 1946.

1867 Bagehot, *English Constitution.*

Darwin, *Plants and Animals under Domestication.*

*Karl Marx, *Das Kapital:* socialistic.

Arnold Bennett born. Died 1931.

John Galsworthy born. Died 1933.

1868 Browning, *The Ring and the Book.*

Collins, *The Moonstone.*

Morris, *Earthly Paradise,* Vols. I, II.

*Müller, *Chips from a German Workshop.*

1869 Trollope, *Phineas Finn.*

Blackmore, *Lorna Doone.*

Ruskin, *Queen of the Air.*

Arnold, *Culture and Anarchy.*

Suez Canal opened.

Howells, *Venetian Life.*

Atlantic cable completed.

1867 Mark Twain, *The Celebrated Jumping Frog of Calaveras County.*

Holmes, *Guardian Angel.*

Lanier, *Tiger Lilies.*

Longfellow, translation of Dante.

Lowell, *Biglow Papers* (2d ser.).

Whittier, *Tent on the Beach.*

1868 Alcott, *Little Women.*

Hawthorne, *American Notebooks.*

Whittier, *Among the Hills.*

1869 Mark Twain, *The Innocents Abroad.*

Transcontinental railroad completed.

Edwin Arlington Robinson born. Died 1935.

William Vaughn Moody born. Died 1910.

*1870–1914 REALISTIC
PERIOD*

*1870–1901   LATE VICTORIAN
AGE*

---

*ca.*1870–1922 °"Anatole France"
*fl.:* French novelist, satirist,
and critic.

1870 Rossetti, *Poems.*

Huxley, *Lay Sermons.*

Death of Dickens.

1871 Darwin, *Descent of Man.*

John Millington Synge born.
Died 1909.

1872 Butler, *Erewhon.*

Hardy, *Under the Green-
wood Tree.*

Eliot, *Middlemarch.*

1873 Arnold, *Literature and
Dogma.*

Pater, *Studies in the Renaissance.*

1874 Hardy, *Far from the Mad-
ding Crowd.*

L. Stephen, *Hours in a Library.*

John Stuart Mill, *Autobiography.*

1870 Lowell, *Among My Books*
(1st ser.): essays.

Whitman, *Democratic Vistas:*
prose.

Harte, *Luck of Roaring
Camp.*

Bryant, blank verse translation of the *Odyssey.*

1871 Burroughs, *Wake-Robin.*

Eggleston, *Hoosier School-
master.*

Hay, *Pike County Ballads.*

Howells, *Their Wedding
Journey.*

Joaquin Miller, *Songs of the
Sierras.*

Lowell, *My Study Windows.*

1872 Mark Twain, *Roughing It.*

1873 Aldrich, *Marjorie Daw.*

1874 Amy Lowell born. Died
1925.

Disraeli, Prime Minister.

1875–1877 *Tolstoi, *Anna Karenina:* realistic novel.

1875 Arnold, *God and the Bible.*

1875 Henry James, *Roderick Hudson.*

Howells, *A Foregone Conclusion.*

1876 Eliot, *Daniel Deronda.*

Morris, *Sigurd the Volsung.*

Tennyson, *Queen Mary* (*a*).

Trevelyan, *Life of Macaulay.*

1876 Mark Twain, *Tom Sawyer.*

Lanier, *Poems.*

Lowell, *Among My Books* (2d ser.).

Invention of telephone.

1877 James, *The American.*

1878 Stevenson, *An Inland Voyage.*

Hardy, *Return of the Native.*

Bagehot, *Literary Studies.*

*Zola, *L'Assommoir:* naturalistic fiction.

1878 James, *Daisy Miller.*

1879 Meredith, *The Egoist.*

Spencer, *Data of Ethics.*

Browning, *Dramatic Idylls* (1st ser.).

*Ibsen, *The Doll's House.*

1879 Howells, *The Lady of the Aroostook.*

Cable, *Old Creole Days.*

Fiske, *Darwinism.*

Burroughs, *Locusts and Wild Honey.*

Henry George, *Progress and Poverty.*

### 1880

1880–1892 *De Maupassant: novels and influential short stories.

1880 Gissing. *Workers in the Dawn.*

Gladstone Prime Minister.

1880 Longfellow, *Ultima Thule.*

Harris, *Uncle Remus.*

Cable, *The Grandissimes.*

Wallace, *Ben Hur.*

Lanier, *Science of English Verse.*

|

1881 Stevenson, *Virginibus Puerisque.*

Rossetti, *Ballads and Sonnets.*

Swinburne, *Mary Stuart.*

Death of Carlyle.

*Ibsen, *Ghosts.*

*"Anatole France," *The Crime of Sylvestre Bonnard.*

1882 Swinburne, *Tristram of Lyonesse.*

Stevenson, *Familiar Studies, New Arabian Nights, Treasure Island.*

Froude, *Life of Carlyle.*

Deaths of Darwin, Rossetti, Trollope.

1883 Schreiner, *The Story of an African Farm.*

1884 Tennyson, *Becket.*

Jones, *Saints and Sinners* (a).

*Daudet, *Sapho.*

1885 Hudson, *The Purple Land.*

Gilbert and Sullivan, *The Mikado* (a).

Meredith, *Diana of the Crossways.*

Ruskin, *Praeterita.*

Stevenson, *Child's Garden of Verses.*

*Dictionary of National Biography,* Vol. I.

1881 James, *Portrait of a Lady.*

Cable, *Madame Delphine.*

*Century Magazine* established (ceased publication, 1930).

1882 Mark Twain, *The Prince and the Pauper.*

Howells, *A Modern Instance.*

Whitman, *Specimen Days.*

1883 Mark Twain, *Life on the Mississippi.*

Riley, *The Ole Swimmin' Hole.*

Howe, *Story of a Country Town.*

1884 Mark Twain, *Huckleberry Finn.*

Jewett, *A Country Doctor.*

"Charles Egbert Craddock," *In the Tennessee Mountains.*

1885 Howells, *Rise of Silas Lapham.*

| ENGLISH | AMERICAN |
|---|---|
| 1886 Hardy, *Mayor of Casterbridge*. | 1886 Lowell, *Democracy*. |
| Stevenson, *Doctor Jekyll and Mr. Hyde; Kidnapped*. | Howells, *Indian Summer*. |
| Tennyson, *Locksley Hall Sixty Years After*. | James, *The Bostonians*. |
| Kipling, *Departmental Ditties*. | *Scribner's Magazine* established. |
| 1887 Lang, *Myth, Ritual, and Religion*. | 1887 Page, *In Ole Virginia*. |
| *Strindberg, *The Fathers:* Swedish influence on realistic novel and drama. | Freeman, *A Humble Romance*. |
| 1888 Kipling, *Plain Tales from the Hills*. | 1888 James, *Partial Portraits*. |
| Ward, *Robert Elsmere*. | Lowell, *Political Essays*. |
| Doughty, *Travels in Arabia Deserta*. | Bellamy, *Looking Backward*. |
| Death of Arnold. | |
| 1889 Browning, *Asolando*. | 1889 Mark Twain, *A Connecticut Yankee at King Arthur's Court*. |
| Stevenson, *Master of Ballantrae*. | Fiske, *Beginnings of New England*. |
| Pater, *Appreciations*. | |
| Barrie, *A Window in Thrums*. | Howard, *Shenandoah* (*a*). |
| Death of Browning. | |

## 1890

| | |
|---|---|
| 1890 Watson, *Wordsworth's Grave*. | 1890 Dickinson, *Poems*. |
| Bridges, *Shorter Poems*. | William James, *Principles of Psychology*. |
| 1891 Hardy, *Tess of the D'Urbervilles*. | 1891 Garland, *Main Travelled Roads*. |
| Doyle, *Adventures of Sherlock Holmes*. | Bierce, *In the Midst of Life*. |
| Kipling, *The Light that Failed*. | Freeman, *A New England Nun*. |
| Barrie, *The Little Minister*. | Howells, *Criticism and Fiction*. |

**ENGLISH**

Gissing, *The New Grub Street.*

Independent Theatre opened: beginning of "Little Theatre" movement in England.

1892 Kipling, *Barrack Room Ballads.*

Zangwill, *Children of the Ghetto.*

Wilde, *Lady Windermere's Fan* (*a*).

Death of Tennyson.

1893 W. H. Hudson, *Idle Days in Patagonia.*

Thompson, *Poems.*

Shaw, *Mrs. Warren's Profession* (*w.* acted 1902).

Pinero, *The Second Mrs. Tanqueray* (*a*).

1894 Yeats, *Land of Heart's Desire.*

Moore, *Esther Waters.*

Kipling, *Jungle Book.*

"Anthony Hope," *Prisoner of Zenda.*

"Ian Maclaren," *Beside the Bonny Briar Bush.*

Death of Stevenson.

1895 Wilde, *The Importance of Being Earnest* (*a*).

Wells, *The Time Machine.*

Conrad, *Almayer's Folly.*

Kipling, *The Brushwood Boy.*

1896 Housman, *A Shropshire Lad.*

Barrie, *Sentimental Tommy.*

Hardy, *Jude the Obscure.*

Alfred Austin made Poet Laureate.

**AMERICAN**

International Copyright Act: protecting rights of foreign authors and publishers.

1892 Page, *The Old South.*

Howard, *Aristocracy* (*a*).

*Yale Review* established.

1893 James, *The Real Thing and Other Tales.*

1894 Howells, *A Traveler from Altruria.*

Hearn, *Glimpses of Unfamiliar Japan.*

1895 Crane, *The Red Badge of Courage.*

1896 Crane, *Maggie: A Girl of the Streets.*

Robinson, *The Torrent and the Night Before.*

| ENGLISH | AMERICAN |
|---|---|
| 1897 Conrad, *The Nigger of the Narcissus*. | 1897 Allen, *The Choir Invisible*. |
| Kipling, *Captains Courageous*. | |
| 1898 Hardy, *Wessex Poems*. | 1898 Page, *Red Rock*. |
| Shaw, *Plays Pleasant and Unpleasant*. | |
| Wilde, *Ballad of Reading Gaol*. | |
| Moore, *Evelyn Innes*. | |
| Wells, *The War of the Worlds:* romance. | |
| 1899 Irish Literary Theatre founded in Dublin. | 1899 Churchill, *Richard Carvel*. |
| | Crane, *War is Kind*. |
| | Dunne, *Mr. Dooley in Peace and War*. |
| | Tarkington, *Gentleman from Indiana*. |
| | Markham, *The Man with the Hoe*. |

### 1900–1930 NATURALISTIC AND SYMBOLISTIC PERIOD

| ENGLISH | AMERICAN |
|---|---|
| 1900 Binyon, *Odes*. | 1900 Ade, *Fables in Slang*. |
| Conrad, *Lord Jim*. | Bacheller, *Eben Holden*. |
| Hudson, *Nature in Downland*. | Crane, *Wounds in the Rain*. |
| *Edmond Rostand, *L'Aiglon*. | Dreiser, *Sister Carrie*. |
| Death of Ruskin. | Dunne, *Mr. Dooley's Philosophy*. |
| | London, *The Son of the Wolf*. |
| | Tarkington, *Monsieur Beaucaire*. |
| 1901 Barrie, *Quality Street*. | 1901 Churchill, *The Crisis*. |
| Kipling, *Kim*. | Moody, *Poems*. |
| Death of Victoria. | Norris, *The Octopus*. |
| | Washington, *Up From Slavery*. |

## 1901–1914   EDWARDIAN AGE

1901–1910 Reign of Edward VII.

1902 Bennett, *Anna of the Five Towns.*

Conrad, *Youth.*

Lady Gregory, *Cuchulain of Muirthemne.*

Masefield, *Saltwater Ballads.*

Yeats, *Cathleen ni Hoolihan.*

Death of Samuel Butler.

1903 Conrad, *Typhoon and Other Stories.*

Hudson, *Hampshire Days.*

Kipling, *The Five Nations.*

Shaw, *Man and Superman.*

Butler, *The Way of All Flesh.*

1904 Barrie, *Peter Pan.*

Hardy, *The Dynasts* (first part).

Conrad, *Nostromo.*

Hudson, *Green Mansions.*

Kipling, *Traffics and Discoveries.*

\*Anton Chekhov, *The Cherry Orchard.*

\*Romain Rolland, *Jean Christophe:* "an epic of French life," publication begun 1904, finished 1912.

1905 Jones, *Mrs. Dane's Defence.*

Masefield, *A Mainsail Haul.*

Synge, *Riders to the Sea.*

1906 Conrad, *Mirror of the Sea.*

Kipling, *Puck of Pook's Hill.*

Watson, *Collected Poems.*

1902 Glasgow, *The Battle-Ground.*

Wister, *The Virginian.*

Death of Bret Harte.

1903 London, *The Call of the Wild.*

Norris, *The Pit.*

1904 Churchill, *The Crossing.*

O. Henry, *Cabbages and Kings.*

Herrick, *The Common Lot.*

Huneker, *Overtones.*

London, *The Sea-Wolf.*

Moody, *The Fire-Bringer.*

1905 Wharton, *The House of Mirth.*

1906 Adams, *The Education of Henry Adams* (privately printed).

O. Henry, *The Four Million.*

Sinclair, *The Jungle.*

Beginning of "Little Theatre" movement in America.

1907 Beerbohm, *A Book of Carica-tures.*

1907 Fitch, *The Truth.*

Russell (A. E.), *Deirdre.*

Synge, *Playboy of the Western World.*

Yeats, *Deirdre.*

*Maxim Gorki, *Mother:* the proletarian in fiction.

1908 Bennett, *The Old Wives' Tale.*

1908 O. Henry, *The Voice of the City.*

Chesterton, *The Man Who Was Thursday.*

Herrick, *Together.*

Wells, *New Worlds for Old; Tono-Bungay.*

Barrie, *What Every Woman Knows.*

*Anatole France, *Penguin Island.*

1909 Granville-Barker, *Three Plays.*

1909 Reese, *A Wayside Lute.*

Galsworthy, *Plays.*

Garland, *Cavanagh, Forest Ranger.*

Gregory, *Seven Short Plays.*

Kipling, *Actions and Reactions.*

Huneker, *Promenades of an Impressionist.*

Wells, *Ann Veronica.*

Moody, *The Great Divide.*

Death of Meredith.

Stein, *Three Lives.*

Masefield, *The Tragedy of Nan.*

## 1910

1910 Aldington, *Images.*

1910 Robinson, *The Town Down the River.*

Granville-Barker, *The Madras House.*

Sheldon, *The Nigger.*

Bennett, *Clayhanger.*

Death of William Vaughn Moody.

Lord Dunsany, *A Dreamer's Tales.*

Death of Mark Twain.

Galsworthy, *Justice.*

Hudson, *A Shepherd's Life.*
Kipling, *Rewards and Fairies.*
Newbolt, *Collected Poems.*
Noyes, *Collected Poems.*
Death of Edward VII.

1910–1936 Reign of George V.

1911 Beerbohm, *Zuleika Dobson.*
Bennett, *Hilda Lessways.*

Galsworthy, *The Patrician.*
Gosse, *Collected Poems.*
Masefield, *The Everlasting Mercy.*
Moore, *Hail and Farewell.*
Pinero, *Mid-Channel.*

1912 Bridges, *Poetical Works.*
Galsworthy, *The Pigeon.*
Monro (ed.), *Georgian Poetry.*
Stephens, *The Crock of Gold.*
Tomlinson, *The Sea and the Jungle.*

1913 Gosse, *Collected Essays.*
Lawrence, *Sons and Lovers.*
Masefield, *Dauber.*
Death of Alfred Austin.
Robert Bridges made Poet Laureate.
*Marcel Proust, *A la recherche du temps perdu:* publication begun 1913 and finished 1925.

*1914—*        *CONTEMPORARY PERIOD*

1914 Barrie, *Admirable Crichton.*
Barrie, *Half Hours:* plays.
Graham, *Scottish Stories.*
Sinclair, *The Three Sisters.*

1911 Belasco, *The Return of Peter Grimm.*

Dreiser, *Jennie Gerhardt.*
Van Dyke, *Collected Poems.*
Wharton, *Ethan Frome.*

1912 Carman, *Echoes from Vagabondia.*

*Poetry: A Magazine of Verse:* edited by Harriet Monroe, founded in Chicago.

1913 Cather, *O Pioneers!*

Eastman, *The Enjoyment of Poetry.*

Lindsay, *General William Booth Enters into Heaven.*

1914 Frost, *North of Boston.*

Lindsay, *The Congo.*

Amy Lowell, *Sword Blades and Poppy Seeds.*

Gertrude Stein, *Tender Buttons.*

| ENGLISH | AMERICAN |
|---|---|

**1915** Conrad, *Victory.*

Galsworthy, *The Freelands.*

Maugham, *Of Human Bondage.*

Richardson, *Pointed Roofs.*

Shaw, *Fanny's First Play.*

Wells, *The Research Magnificent.*

**1916** Davies, *Collected Poems.*

Lord Dunsany, *Tales of Wonder.*

Joyce, *Portrait of the Artist as a Young Man.*

Moore, *The Brook Kerith.*

Shaw, *Androcles and the Lion; Pygmalion.*

Walpole, *The Dark Forest.*

*Henri Barbusse, *Le Feu:* brutally realistic chronicle of the World War.

Wells, *Mr. Britling Sees It Through.*

**1917** Douglas, *South Wind.*

Hodgson, *Poems.*

Swinnerton, *Nocturne.*

**1918** Barrie, *Echoes of the War.*

Brooke, *Collected Poems.*

D. H. Lawrence, *New Poems.*

**1915** Brooks, *America's Coming of Age.*

Cabell, *The Rivet in Grandfather's Neck.*

Frost, *A Boy's Will.*

Huneker, *Ivory Apes and Peacocks.*

Masters, *Spoon River Anthology.*

Neihardt, *The Song of Hugh Glass.*

Poole, *The Harbor.*

**1916** Frost, *Mountain Interval.*

Lowell, *Men, Women and Ghosts.*

Repplier, *Counter-Currents.*

Robinson, *The Man Against the Sky.*

Sandburg, *Chicago Poems.*

Seeger, *Poems.*

Tarkington, *Seventeen.*

Mark Twain, *The Mysterious Stranger.*

*Some Imagist Poets:* a collection of the work of several poets.

Death of Henry James.

Death of Jack London.

**1917** Garland, *A Son of the Middle Border.*

Hergesheimer, *The Three Black Pennys.*

Mencken, *A Book of Prefaces.*

Millay, *Renascence.*

**1918** Cather, *My Antonia.*

Amy Lowell, *Can Grande's Castle.*

| ENGLISH | AMERICAN |
|---|---|
| Hopkins, *Poems* (first published). | Sandburg, *Cornhuskers.* |
| Strachey, *Eminent Victorians.* | Theatre Guild established. |
| *Spengler, *The Decline of the West.* | |
| 1919 Conrad, *The Arrow of Gold.* | 1919 Anderson, *Winesburg, Ohio.* |
| Maugham, *The Moon and Sixpence.* | Babbitt, *Rousseau and Romanticism.* |
| Shaw, *Heartbreak House.* | Cabell, *Jurgen.* |
| Hardy, *Collected Poems.* | Hergesheimer, *Java Head.* |
| | Amy Lowell, *Pictures of the Floating World.* |
| | Mencken, *The American Language.* |
| | O'Neill, *The Moon of the Caribbees.* |
| | Sinclair, *The Brass Check.* |
| | Pound, first *Cantos* (magazine publication). |

## 1920

| | |
|---|---|
| 1920 Barrie, *A Kiss for Cinderella.* | 1920 Anderson, *Poor White.* |
| De la Mare, *Collected Poems.* | Dell, *Moon-Calf.* |
| Mansfield, *Bliss.* | Eliot, *Poems.* |
| Wells, *The Outline of History.* | Fitzgerald, *This Side of Paradise.* |
| *Maxim Gorki, *Recollections.* | Lewis, *Main Street.* |
| | Millay, *A Few Figs from Thistles.* |
| | O'Neill, *Beyond the Horizon.* |
| | Robinson, *Lancelot.* |
| | Sandburg, *Smoke and Steel.* |
| | Wharton, *The Age of Innocence.* |

Death of William Dean Howells.

1921 De la Mare, *Memoirs of a Midget.*

Kipling, *Verse* (Inclusive Edition).

Strachey, *Queen Victoria.*

Lawrence, *Women in Love.*

Huxley, *Crome Yellow.*

Moore, *Héloise and Abelard.*

1922 Galsworthy, *The Forsyte Saga* (1906–1922).

Garnett, *Lady into Fox.*

Housman, *Last Poems.*

Joyce, *Ulysses.*

Mansfield, *The Garden Party.*

Walpole, *The Cathedral.*

Woolf, *Jacob's Room.*

Yeats, *Later Poems.*

1923 Coppard, *The Black Dog.*

Drinkwater, *Collected Poems.*

Ellis, *The Dance of Life.*

Hardy, *Collected Poems.*

Huxley, *Antic Hay.*

Macaulay, *Told by an Idiot.*

Mansfield, *Poems.*

Milne, *Three Plays.*

Meynell, *Poems.*

Lawrence, *Classic Studies in American Literature.*

1924 Ford, *Some Do Not.*

Forster, *A Passage to India.*

Masefield, *Sard Harker.*

Richards, *Principles of Literary Criticism.*

1921 Anderson, *The Triumph of the Egg.*

Dos Passos, *Three Soldiers.*

O'Neill, *The Emperor Jones.*

Robinson, *Collected Poems.*

Tarkington, *Alice Adams.*

Wylie, *Nets to Catch the Wind.*

1922 Cummings, *The Enormous Room.*

Eliot, *The Waste Land.*

Lewis, *Babbitt.*

O'Neill, *The Hairy Ape* and *Anna Christie.*

Stribling, *Birthright.*

Thomas, *The Copperhead.*

1923 Cabell, *The High Place.*

Cather, *A Lost Lady.*

Frost, *New Hampshire.*

Lindsay, *Collected Poems.*

Rice, *The Adding Machine.*

Santayana, *Poems.*

Stevens, *Harmonium.*

Teasdale, *Poems.*

Vechten, *The Blind Bow-Boy.*

Wylie, *Jennifer Lorn.*

1924 Ade, *The County Chairman.*

Maxwell Anderson (with L. Stalling), *What Price Glory.*

S. Anderson, *A Story-Teller's Story.*

Shaw, *Saint Joan.*

Death of Joseph Conrad.

*Kafka, *The Trial.*

*Mann, *The Magic Mountain.*

Bromfield, *The Green Bay Tree.*

Hemingway, *In Our Time.*

Jeffers, *Tamar and Other Poems.*

Melville, *Billy Budd* (first published).

Ransom, *Chills and Fever.*

1925 Galsworthy, *Caravan* (collected stories).

Huxley, *Selected Poems.*

Woolf, *Mrs. Dalloway.*

*Gide, *The Counterfeiters.*

1925 S. Anderson, *Dark Laughter.*

Cather, *The Professor's House.*

Cummings, *XLI Poems.*

Fitzgerald, *The Great Gatsby.*

H.D. (Hilda Doolittle), *Collected Poems.*

Lewis, *Arrowsmith.*

Pound, *A Draft of XVI Cantos.*

Dos Passos, *Manhattan Transfer.*

Dreiser, *An American Tragedy.*

Glasgow, *Barren Ground.*

Heyward, *Porgy.*

O'Neill, *Desire Under the Elms.*

Death of Amy Lowell.

*New Yorker* magazine founded.

1926 Gibson, *Collected Poems.*

L. Housman, *Ironical Tales.*

Kipling, *Debits and Credits.*

D. H. Lawrence, *The Plumed Serpent.*

T. E. Lawrence, *The Seven Pillars of Wisdom.*

1926 Faulkner, *Soldier's Pay.*

Glasgow, *The Romantic Comedians.*

Hemingway, *The Sun Also Rises.*

O'Neill, *The Great God Brown.*

ENGLISH

Stephens, *Collected Poems.*

1927 Chesterton, *Collected Poems.*
T. E. Lawrence, *Revolt in the Desert.*
Tomlinson, *Gallions Reach.*
Woolf, *To the Lighthouse.*
*Kafka, *Amerika.*

1928 Davies, *Collected Poems.*
Huxley, *Point Counter Point.*
Lawrence, *Lady Chatterley's Lover.*
*Arnold Zweig, *The Case of Sergeant Grischa.*
Death of Thomas Hardy.

1929 Aldington, *Death of a Hero.*
Bridges, *The Testament of Beauty.*
Graves, *Goodbye to All That.*
G. Greene, *The Man Within.*
Priestley, *The Good Companions.*
Woolf, *A Room of One's Own.*

AMERICAN

E. M. Roberts, *The Time of Man.*
Sandburg, *Selected Poems.*
Wilder, *The Cabala.*
Young, *Heaven Trees.*

1927 Cather, *Death Comes for the Archbishop.*
Green, *In Abraham's Bosom.*
Jeffers, *The Women at Point Sur.*
Millay, *The King's Henchman.*
Parrington, *Main Currents in American Thought.*
O'Neill, *Marco Millions.*
Robinson, *Tristram.*
Wilder, *The Bridge of San Luis Rey.*

1928 Benét, *John Brown's Body.*
Frost, *West-Running Brook.*
Amy Lowell, *Selected Poems.*
MacLeish, *The Hamlet of A. MacLeish.*
Pound, *Selected Poems.*
Tate, *Mr. Pope and Other Poems.*
*Dictionary of American Biography* begins with publication of first volume.

1929 Connelly, *Green Pastures.*
Faulkner, *The Sound and the Fury.*
Glasgow, *They Stooped to Folly.*
Hemingway, *A Farewell to Arms.*
Lewis, *Dodsworth.*
Rice, *Street Scene.*

Galsworthy, *The Modern Comedy.*

*Remarque, *All Quiet on the Western Front.*

Scott, *The Wave.*

Wolfe, *Look Homeward, Angel.*

### 1930

### 1930— PERIOD OF CONFORMITY AND CRITICISM

1930 Masefield, *Collected Poems.*

Maugham, *Cakes and Ale.*

Coward, *Private Lives.*

Priestley, *Angel Pavement.*

Edith Sitwell, *Collected Poems.*

Tomlinson, *All Our Yesterdays.*

Waugh, *Vile Bodies.*

Death of Bridges.

Masefield made Poet Laureate.

1931 Binyon, *Collected Poems.*

Galsworthy, *Maid in Waiting.*

D. H. Lawrence, *The Man Who Died.*

Maugham, *First Person Singular.*

Woolf, *The Waves.*

1932 Auden, *The Orators.*

Coward, *Cavalcade.*

Huxley, *Brave New World.*

Masefield, *Tale of Troy.*

Shaw, *Pen Portraits.*

1930 Eliot, *Ash Wednesday.*

M. Anderson, *Elizabeth the Queen.*

H. Crane, *The Bridge.*

Dos Passos, *The 42nd Parallel.*

Frost, *Collected Poems.*

Porter, *Flowering Judas.*

"Twelve Southerners," *I'll Take My Stand.*

Roberts, *The Great Meadow.*

Sinclair Lewis awarded the Nobel Prize.

1931 Buck, *The Good Earth.*

Cather, *Shadows on the Rock.*

Cozzens, S. S. *San Pedro.*

Faulkner, *Sanctuary.*

Millay, *Fatal Interview.*

O'Neill, *Mourning Becomes Electra.*

Steffens, *Autobiography.*

Wilson, *Axel's Castle.*

1932 Caldwell, *Tobacco Road.*

Farrell, *Young Lonigan.*

Faulkner, *Light in August.*

Dos Passos, *1919.*

Eliot, *Selected Essays.*

Glasgow, *The Sheltered Life.*

Jeffers, *Thurso's Landing.*

MacLeish, *Conquistador.*

Wylie, *Collected Poems.*

1933 Caldwell, *God's Little Acre.*

Cozzens, *The Last Adam.*

Hemingway, *Winner Take Nothing.*

Lewis, *Anne Vickers.*

MacLeish, *Frescoes for Mr. Rockefeller's City.*

Robinson, *Talifer.*

Stein, *The Autobiography of Alice B. Toklas.*

1933 Auden, *Dance of Death.*

Coward, *Play Parade.*

Spender, *Poems.*

Osbert Sitwell, *Miracle on Sinai.*

Woolf, *Flush, a Biography.*

Yeats, *Collected Poems.*

*Malraux, *Man's Fate.*

*Mann, *Joseph and His Brothers.*

1934 Coward, *Play Parade.*

Graves, *I, Claudius.*

Swinnerton, *Elizabeth.*

Waugh, *A Handful of Dust.*

*Rilke, *Poems.*

1934 Cowley, *Exile's Return.*

Farrell, *The Young Manhood of Studs Lonigan.*

Fitzgerald, *Tender Is the Night.*

Millay, *Wine from These Grapes.*

O'Hara, *Appointment in Samarra.*

Saroyan, *The Daring Young Man on the Flying Trapeze.*

W. C. Williams, *Collected Poems.*

1935 Lewis, *A Time to Dance.*

MacNeice, *Poems.*

Spender, *Destructive Element.*

1935 M. Anderson, *Winterset.*

Eliot, *Murder in the Cathedral.*

Farrell, *Judgment Day* (final novel in the Studs Lonigan trilogy).

Odets, *Waiting for Lefty.*

Santayana, *The Last Puritan.*

Steinbeck, *Tortilla Flat.*

Wolfe, *Of Time and the River.*

**ENGLISH**

1936 Benson, *Collected Short Stories.*

Auden, *Look, Stranger.*

Coward, *Tonight at Eight-Thirty.*

Housman, *More Poems.*

Huxley, *Eyeless in Gaza.*

Thomas, *25 Poems.*

West, *The Thinking Reed.*

*Malraux, *Days of Wrath.*

*Sartre, *Imagination.*

1937 Housman, *Poems, Letters, and Memories.*

Masefield, *The Square Peg.*

Maugham, *Theatre.*

Woolf, *The Years.*

1938 Graves, *Collected Poems.*

Hughes, *In Hazard.*

Maugham, *The Summing Up.*

Richardson, *Pilgrimage.*

*Malraux, *Man's Hope.*

**AMERICAN**

1936 Edmonds, *Drums along the Mohawk.*

Eliot, *Collected Poems.*

Frost, *A Further Range.*

Faulkner, *Absalom, Absalom!*

Cozzens, *Men and Brethren.*

Dos Passos, *The Big Money* (final novel in the *U.S.A.* trilogy).

Mitchell, *Gone with the Wind.*

Sandburg, *The People, Yes.*

Tate, *Reactionary Essays.*

Eugene O'Neill awarded the Nobel Prize.

1937 M. Anderson, *High Tor.*

Hemingway, *To Have and Have Not.*

Jeffers, *Such Councils You Gave Me.*

Marquand, *The Late George Apley.*

Millay, *Conversations at Midnight.*

Steinbeck, *Of Mice and Men* and *The Red Pony.*

Stevens, *The Man with the Blue Guitar.*

1938 Cummings, *Collected Poems.*

Hemingway, *The Fifth Column and the First Forty-Nine Stories.*

Faulkner, *The Unvanquished.*

Rawlings, *The Yearling.*

Sherwood, *Abe Lincoln in Illinois.*

Wilder, *Our Town.*

ENGLISH            AMERICAN

W. C. Williams, *Complete Collected Poems.*

Pearl Buck awarded the Nobel Prize.

1939 Housman, *Collected Poems.*

Joyce, *Finnegans Wake.*

Lewis, *A Hope for Poetry.*

Thomas, *The World I Breathe.*

Death of W. B. Yeats.

1939 Coffin, *Collected Poems.*

Frost, *Collected Poems.*

Taylor, *Poetical Works* (first published).

Marquand, *Wickford Point.*

Porter, *Pale Horse, Pale Rider.*

Steinbeck, *The Grapes of Wrath.*

Wolfe, *The Web and the Rock.*

## 1940

1940 Auden, *Selected Poems.*

G. Greene, *The Power and the Glory.*

Meynell, *Poems.*

Edith Sitwell, *Poems New and Old.*

Wells, *Babes in the Darkling Wood.*

Yeats, *Last Poems and Plays.*

1940 Cather, *Sapphira and the Slave Girl.*

Cozzens, *Ask Me Tomorrow.*

Eliot, *The Idea of a Christian Society.*

Faulkner, *The Hamlet.*

Hemingway, *For Whom the Bell Tolls.*

Pound, *Cantos.*

Wolfe, *You Can't Go Home Again.*

Wright, *Native Son.*

1941 Barker, *Selected Poems.*

*Cambridge Bibliography of English Literature.*

Cary, *Herself Surprised.*

De la Mare, *Bells and Grass.*

Huxley, *Grey Eminence.*

Spender, *Ruins and Visions.*

1941 Fitzgerald, *The Last Tycoon.*

Glasgow, *In This Our Life.*

Jeffers, *Be Angry at the Sun.*

Marquand, *H. M. Pulham, Esq.*

Welty, *A Curtain of Green.*

| ENGLISH | AMERICAN |
|---|---|
| Woolf, *The Death of the Moth.* | |
| Deaths of Joyce, Virginia Woolf, Walpole. | |
| 1942 Bowen, *Seven Winters.* | 1942 Aiken, *Eclogues.* |
| Cary, *To Be a Pilgrim.* | M. Anderson, *Eve of St. Mark.* |
| Coward, *Blithe Spirit.* | |
| C. S. Lewis, *The Screwtape Letters.* | Cozzens, *The Just and the Unjust.* |
| Waugh, *Put Out More Flags.* | Faulkner, *Go Down, Moses.* |
| | Jarrell, *Blood for a Stranger.* |
| | Steinbeck, *The Moon Is Down.* |
| | Warren, *Eleven Poems on the Same Theme.* |
| | Wilder, *Skin of Our Teeth.* |
| 1943 Coward, *This Happy Breed.* | 1943 Benét, *Western Star.* |
| H. Green, *Caught.* | Dos Passos, *Number One.* |
| | Eliot, *Four Quartets.* |
| | Glasgow, *A Certain Measure.* |
| | Warren, *At Heaven's Gate* and *Selected Poems.* |
| 1944 Barker, *Eros in Dogma.* | 1944 Hersey, *A Bell for Adano.* |
| Cary, *The Horse's Mouth.* | R. Lowell, *Land of Unlikeness.* |
| Connolly, *The Unquiet Grave.* | |
| | Porter, *The Leaning Tower.* |
| Huxley, *Time Must Have a Stop.* | Shapiro, *V-Letter.* |
| | Smith, *Strange Fruit.* |
| 1945 Connolly, *The Condemned Playground.* | 1945 Frost, *A Masque of Reason.* |
| De la Mare, *The Burning-Glass.* | Jarrell, *Little Friend, Little Friend.* |
| H. Green, *Loving.* | Ransom, *Selected Poems.* |
| Isherwood, *Prater Violet.* | Shapiro, *Essay on Rime.* |
| C. D. Lewis, *Collected Poems.* | T. Williams, *The Glass Menagerie.* |
| | Wright, *Black Boy.* |

1946 Cary, *The Moonlight.*

Fry, *A Phoenix Too Frequent.*

H. Green, *Back.*

Masefield, *Thanks Before Going.*

Orwell, *Animal Farm.*

Spender, *European Witness.*

Thomas, *Deaths and Entrances.*

Waugh, *Brideshead Revisited.*

1947 Auden, *The Age of Anxiety.*

Barker, *Love Poems.*

Spender, *Poems of Dedication.*

1948 Beckett, *Murphy.*

Betjeman, *Selected Poems.*

Fry, *The Lady's Not for Burning.*

Graves, *Collected Poems.*

H. Green, *Concluding.*

G. Greene, *The Heart of the Matter.*

Huxley, *Ape and Essence.*

1946 E. Bishop, *North and South.*

Dreiser, *The Bulwark.*

Farrell, *Bernard Clare.*

Jeffers, *Medea.*

O'Neill, *The Iceman Cometh.*

Warren, *All the King's Men.*

Welty, *Delta Wedding.*

W. C. Williams, *Patterson, I.*

1947 M. Anderson, *Joan of Lorraine.*

Dreiser, *The Stoic.*

Frost, *A Masque of Mercy.*

H. James, *Notebooks.*

Steinbeck, *The Wayward Bus.*

Stevens, *Transport to Summer.*

T. Williams, *A Streetcar Named Desire.*

1948 Cozzens, *Guard of Honor.*

Faulkner, *Intruder in the Dust.*

Jarrell, *Losses.*

Jeffers, *The Double Axe.*

Kinsey, *Sexual Behavior in the Human Male.*

Mailer, *The Naked and the Dead.*

Pound, *Pisan Cantos.*

Shaw, *The Young Lions.*

Tate, *On the Limits of Poetry.*

Viereck, *Terror and Decorum.*

| ENGLISH | AMERICAN |
|---|---|

**1949** Barker, *News of the World.*
Cary, *A Fearful Joy.*
Orwell, *Nineteen Eighty-Four.*
Spender, *The Edge of Being.*
Waugh, *The Loved One.*

**1949** Dos Passos, *The Grand Design.*
Eliot, *Notes Toward the Definition of a Society.*
Faulkner, *Knight's Gambit.*
Frost, *Complete Poems.*
Marquand, *Point of No Return.*
Miller, *Death of a Salesman.*
Welty, *The Golden Apples.*

*1950*

**1950** Auden, *The Enchafèd Flood.*
Barker, *The Dead Seagull.*
De la Mare, *Inward Companion.*
H. Green, *Nothing.*
Thomas, *Twenty-Six Poems.*

**1950** Cummings, *XAIPE: seventy-one poems.*
Eliot, *The Cocktail Party.*
Farrell, *The Road Between.*
Faulkner, *Collected Short Stories.*
Hemingway, *Across the River and Into the Trees.*
Hersey, *The Wall.*
R. Lowell, *Poems, 1938–1949.*
Stevens, *Auroras of Autumn.*
Warren, *World Enough and Time.*
W. C. Williams, *Collected Poems* and *Patterson.*
Faulkner awarded the Nobel Prize for 1949.

**1951** Auden, *Nones.*
De la Mare, *Winged Chariot.*
Fry, *A Sleep of Prisoners.*
G. Greene, *The End of the Affair.*
Spender, *World Within View.*

**1951** Dos Passos, *District of Columbia* (trilogy).
Faulkner, *Requiem for a Nun.*
Jarrell, *Seven-League Crutches.*
Jones, *From Here to Eternity.*

| ENGLISH | AMERICAN |
|---|---|
| | R. Lowell, *Mills of the Cava-naughs.* |
| | McCullers, *Member of the Wedding.* |
| | Moore, *Collected Poems.* |
| | Salinger, *Catcher in the Rye.* |
| | T. Williams, *The Rose Tattoo.* |
| 1952 Betjeman, *First and Last Loves.* | 1952 Davis, *Wings of Morning.* |
| Cary, *Prisoner of Grace.* | Eliot, *Complete Poems and Plays.* |
| Fry, *The Firstborn.* | Farrell, *Yet Other Waters.* |
| H. Green, *Doting.* | Hemingway, *The Old Man and the Sea.* |
| Thomas, *In Country Sleep.* | |
| Waugh, *Men at Arms.* | O'Neill, *A Moon for the Mis-begotten.* |
| | Steinbeck, *East of Eden.* |
| 1953 Cary, *Except the Lord.* | 1953 Farrell, *The Face of Time.* |
| De la Mare, *O Lovely Eng-land.* | MacLeish, *Collected Poems, 1917–1952.* |
| Thomas, *Collected Poems.* | Roethke, *The Waking.* |
| Waugh, *Love Among the Ruins.* | Shapiro, *Poems, 1940–1953.* |
| | Warren, *Brother to Dragons.* |
| Churchill awarded the Nobel Prize. | T. Williams, *Camino Real.* |
| | Death of O'Neill. |
| 1954 Barker, *A Vision of Beasts and Gods.* | 1954 Cummings, *Poems, 1923–1954.* |
| Beckett, *Waiting for Godot.* | Eliot, *The Confidential Clerk.* |
| Betjeman, *A Few Late Chrysanthemums.* | Faulkner, *A Fable.* |
| | Glasgow, *The Woman Within.* |
| C. D. Lewis, *Collected Poems.* | Jarrell, *Pictures from an In-stitution.* |
| MacNeice, *Autumn Sequel.* | Jeffers, *Hungerfield and Other Poems.* |
| Thomas, *Under Milk Wood.* | |
| Woolf, *A Writer's Diary.* | MacLeish, *Songs for Eve.* |
| | Steinbeck, *Sweet Thursday.* |
| | Stevens, *Collected Poems.* |
| | Welty, *The Ponder Heart.* |

Hemingway awarded the Nobel Prize.

1955 Auden, *The Shield of Achilles.*

Beckett, *Molloy.*

Bowen, *A World of Love.*

Cary, *Not Honour More.*

Compton-Burnett, *Mother and Son.*

Empson, *Collected Poems.*

Fry, *The Dark is Light Enough.*

Huxley, *The Genius and the Goddess.*

Spender, *Collected Poems, 1928–1953.*

Thomas, *Adventures in the Skin Trade.*

1956 Amis, *Lucky Jim.*

Beckett, *Malone Dies.*

G. Greene, *The Quiet American.*

Cotterell, *The Strange Enchantment.*

O'Casey, *Mirror in My House.*

Osborne, *Look Back in Anger.*

West, *The Fountain Overflows.*

Wilson, *Anglo-Saxon Attitudes.*

1957 Barker, *Collected Poems, 1930–1955.*

Compton-Burnett, *A Father and His Fate.*

Edith Sitwell, *Collected Poems.*

Joyce, *Letters.*

1955 E. Bishop, *Poems.*

Faulkner, *The Big Woods.*

Jarrell, *Selected Poems.*

Marquand, *Sincerely, Willis Wayde.*

Warren, *Band of Angels.*

T. Williams, *Cat on a Hot Tin Roof.*

O'Hara, *Ten North Frederick.*

1956 Moore, *Like a Bulwark.*

Morris, *The Field of Vision.*

O'Neill, *A Long Day's Journey into Night.*

Levin, *Compulsion.*

Millay, *Collected Poems.*

Pound, *Section: Rock Drill.*

Wolfe, *Letters.*

Wilbur, *Things of This World.*

1957 Agee, *A Death in the Family.*

Cheever, *The Wapshot Chronicle.*

Cozzens, *By Love Possessed.*

Eliot, *Of Poetry and Poets.*

Faulkner, *The Town.*

## ENGLISH

Ustinov, *Romanoff and Juliet.*

Waugh, *The Ordeal of Gilbert Pinford.*

West, *The Court and the Castle.*

1958 Amis, *I Like It Here.*

Beckett, *Endgame.*

Cary, *Art and Reality.*

Hartley, *The Hireling.*

Huxley, *Collected Short Stories.*

D. H. Lawrence, *Selected Letters.*

C. D. Lewis, *Pegasus and Other Poems.*

Osborne, *The Entertainer.*

Wain, *The Contenders.*

White, *The Once and Future King.*

1959 Cary, *The Captive and the Free.*

Compton-Burnett, *A Heritage and Its History.*

Golding, *Free Fall.*

Sacheverell Sitwell, *Journey to the Ends of Time,* Volume I.

Wain, *A Travelling Woman.*

## AMERICAN

O'Neill, *A Touch of the Poet.*

Steinbeck, *The Short Reign of Pippin IV.*

Warren, *Promises.*

W. C. Williams, *Selected Letters.*

1958 Cummings, *95 Poems.*

Dos Passos, *The Great Days.*

Jones, *Some Came Running.*

Kunitz, *Selected Poems, 1928–1958.*

MacLeish, *J. B.*

Marquand, *Women and Thomas Harrow.*

O'Hara, *From the Terrace.*

Pound, *Pavannes and Divagations.*

Scott, *The Dark Sister.*

Warren, *Selected Essays.*

1959 Eliot, *The Elder Statesman.*

Faulkner, *The Mansion.*

Hersey, *The War Lover.*

O'Neill, *Hughie.*

Warren, *The Cave.*

T. Williams, *Sweet Bird of Youth.*

# GUIDE TO PRONUNCIATION

The system of respelling for pronunciation is used by permission of the publishers of *Webst*
*New International Dictionary*, G. & C. Merriam Co.

## A

**Acatalectic** (ă·kăt′à·lĕk′tĭk)
**Adonic** (á·dŏn′ĭk)
**Alcaics** (ăl·kā′ĭks)
**Alexandrine** (ăl′ĕg·zăn′drĭn)
**Amerind** (ăm′ĕr·ĭnd′)
**Amphibrach** (ăm′fĭ·brăk)
**Amphigory** (ăm′fĭ·gō′rĭ)
**Amphimacher** (ăm·fĭm′à·sĕr)
**Ana** (ā′ná)
**Anachronism** (á·năk′rŏ·nĭz′m)
**Anacoluthon** (ăn′á·kŏ·lū′thŏn)
**Anacreontic** (á·năk′rē·ŏn′tĭk)
**Anacrusis** (ăn′á·krōō′sĭs)
**Anagnorisis** (ăn′ăg·nŏr′ĭ·sĭs)
**Anagoge** (ăn′á·gō′jē)
**Analecta** (ăn′á·lĕk′tá)
**Anapest** (ăn′á·pĕst)
**Anaphora** (á·năf′ŏ·rá)
**Anastrophe** (á·năs′trŏ·fē)
**Antimasque** (ăn′tĭ·màsk′)
**Antiphrasis** (ăn·tĭf′rá·sĭs)
**Antistrophe** (ăn·tĭs′trŏ·fē)
**Antithesis** (ăn·tĭth′ē·sĭs)
**Aphorism** (ăf′ŏ·rĭz′m)
**Apocryphal** (á·pŏk′rĭ·fál)
**Apophasis** (á·pŏf′á·sĭs)
**Aposiopesis** (ăp′ŏ·sĭ′ŏ·pē′sĭs)
**Apothegm** (ăp′ŏ·thĕm)
**Archaism** (är′kā·ĭz′m)
**Architectonics** (är′kĭ·tĕk·tŏn′ĭks)
**Areopagus** (ăr′ē·ŏp′á·gŭs)
**Arminianism** (är·mĭn′ĭ·ăn·ĭz′m)
**Arsis** (är′sĭs)
**Assonance** (ăs′ŏ·năns)
**Asyndeton** (á·sĭn′dĕ·tŏn)
**Aubade** (ō′bàd′)
**Autotelic** (ô′tŏ·tĕl′ĭk)

## B

**Bacchius** (bă·kī′ŭs)
**Ballade** (bă·läd′)
**Baroque** (bá·rōk′)
**Bathos** (bā′thŏs)
**Belles-Lettres** (bĕl′lĕt′r′)
**Bestiary** (bĕs′tĭ·ĕr′ĭ)
**Billingsgate** (bĭl′ĭngz·gāt′)
**Bon mot** (bôn′ mō′)
**Bourgeois** (bŏŏr·zhwä′)
**Bowdlerize** (boud′lĕr·īz)
**Bucolic** (bū·kŏl′ĭk)
**Burlesque** (bûr·lĕsk′)
**Burletta** (bûr·lĕt′á)

## C

**Cacophony** (ká·kŏf′ŏ·nĭ)
**Caesura** (sē·zū′rá)
**Calligraphy** (ká·lĭg′rá·fĭ)

---

**Canzone** (kän·tsō′nä)
**Carpe diem** (kär′pĕ dī′ĕm)
**Catalexis** (kăt′á·lĕk′sĭs)
**Catastasis** (ká·tăs′tá·sĭs)
**Catastrophe** (ká·tăs′trŏ·fē)
**Catharsis** (ká·thär′sĭs)
**Celtic** (sĕl′tĭk)
**Cento** (sĕn′tō)
**Chanson de geste** (shäN′sôN′ dĕ zhĕst′)
**Chant royal** (shäN′ rwä′yàl′)
**Chantey** (shăn′tĭ)
**Chiasmus** (kī·ăz′mŭs)
**Choriambus** (kō′rĭ·ăm′bŭs)
**Chronique scandaleuse** (krŏ′nēk′ skäN′dà′lūz′)
**Clerihew** (klĕr′ĭ·hū)
**Cliché** (klē·shā′)
**Colloquy** (kŏl′lŏ·kwĭ)
**Colophon** (kŏl′ŏ·fŏn)
**Commedia dell' arte** (kŏm·mā′dyä dĕl·lär′tä)
**Coronach** (kŏr′ŏ·năk)
**Corpus Christi** (kôr′pŭs krĭs′tĭ)
**Coup de théâtre** (kōō′ dĕ tā′ä′tr′)

## D

**Dactyl** (dăk′tĭl)
**Dadaism** (dä′dä·ĭz′m)
**Débat** (dā′bà′)
**Dénouement** (dā·nōō′mäN)
**Deus ex machina** (dē′ŭs ĕks măk′ĭ·nä)
**Dieresis** (dī·ĕr′ē·sĭs)
**Dilettante** (dĭl·ĕ′tăn′tĭ)
**Dimeter** (dĭm′ē·tĕr)
**Distich** (dĭs′tĭk)
**Dithyramb** (dĭth′ĭ·rămb)
**Divine Afflatus** (dĭ·vīn′ ă·flā′tŭs)
**Drame** (dràm)

## E

**Eclogue** (ĕk′lŏg)
**Elegiac** (ĕl′ē·jī′ăk)
**Elision** (ē·lĭzh′ŭn)
**Ellipsis** (ē·lĭp′sĭs)
**Empathy** (ĕm′pá·thĭ)
**Empiricism** (ĕm·pĭr′ĭ·sĭz′m)
**Encomium** (ĕn·kō′mĭ·ŭm)
**Enjambement** (äN′zhäNb′mäN′)
**Enthymeme** (ĕn′thĭ·mēm)
**Envoy—envoi** (ĕn′voi·äN′vwà′)
**Epicurean** (ĕp′ĭ·kū·rē′ăn)
**Epistolary** (ē·pĭs′tŏ·lĕr′ĭ)
**Epithalamium** (ĕp′ĭ·thà·lā′mĭ·ŭm)
**Epitome** (ē·pĭt′ŏ·mē)
**Epode** (ĕp′ōd)
**Eponym** (ĕp′ŏ·nĭm)
**Equivoque** (ĕk′wĭ·vōk)
**Esperanto** (ĕs′pĕ·rän′tō)

---

**Euphemism** (ū′fē·mĭz′m)
**Euphony** (ū′fŏ·nĭ)
**Euphuism** (ū′fū·ĭz′m)
**Exemplum** (ĕg·zĕm′plŭm)
**Explication de texte** (ĕks′plĭ·kä·sĭ
dĕ tĕkst′)

## F

**Fabliau** (făb′lĭ·ō)
**Filidh** (fĭl′ĭ)
**Fin de siècle** (făn′ dĕ syâ′kl′)

## G

**Gallicism** (găl′ĭ·sĭz′m)
**Gasconade** (găs′kŏn·ād′)
**Genre** (zhäN′r′)
**Gest** (jĕst)
**Gnomic** (nō′mĭk)
**Goliardic** (gōl′yĕr·dĭk)
**Gongorism** (gŏng′gŏ·rĭz′m)

## H

**Hagiography** (hăg′ĭ·ŏg′rá·fĭ)
**Harlequinade** (här′lē·kwĭn·ād′)
**Hemistich** (hĕm′ĭ·stĭk)
**Hendecasyllabic** (hĕn′dĕk·á·sĭ·lăb′ĭk
**Heptameter** (hĕp·tăm′ē·tĕr)
**Hexameter** (hĕks·ăm′ē·tĕr)
**Hiatus** (hī·ā′tŭs)
**Hudibrastic** (hū′dĭ·brăs′tĭk)
**Hypallage** (hī·păl′á·jē)
**Hyperbole** (hī·pûr′bŏ·lē)

## I

**Iambus** (ī·ăm′bŭs)
**Ictus** (ĭk′tŭs)
**Incremental** (ĭn′krē·mĕn′tăl)
**Incunabulum** (ĭn′kū·năb′ū·lŭm)
**Innuendo** (ĭn′ū·ĕn′dō)
**Ipse dixit** (ĭp′sē dĭk′sĭt)

## J

**Jacobean** (jăk′ŏ·bē′ăn)
**Jeu d'esprit** (zhû dĕs′prē′)
**Jongleur** (zhôN′glûr′)

## K

**Kailyard** (kāl′yärd′)
**Katharsis** (ká·thär′sĭs)

## L

**Lai** (lā)
**Lexicography** (lĕk′sĭ·kŏg′rá·fĭ)
**Litotes** (lī′tŏ·tēz)
**Litterateur** (lĭt′ĕr·á·tûr′)

## M

**Mabinogion** (măb′ĭ·nō′gĭ·ŏn)